Herbert Samuel:
A Political Life

Herbert Samuel, 1912

Herbert Samuel
A Political Life

Bernard Wasserstein

CLARENDON PRESS · OXFORD
1992

Oxford University Press, Walton Street, Oxford OX2 6DP
Oxford New York Toronto
Delhi Bombay Calcutta Madras Karachi
Petaling Jaya Singapore Hong Kong Tokyo
Nairobi Dar es Salaam Cape Town
Melbourne Auckland
and associated companies in
Berlin Ibadan

Oxford is a trade mark of Oxford University Press

Published in the United States
by Oxford University Press, New York

British Library Cataloguing in Publication Data
Data available

Library of Congress Cataloging in Publication Data
Wasserstein, Bernard.
Herbert Samuel: a political life / Bernard Wasserstein.
Includes bibliographical references (p.   ) and index.
1. Samuel, Herbert Louis Samuel, Viscount, 1870–1963. 2. Great
Britain—Politics and government—20th century. 3. Liberalism—
Great Britain—History—20th century. 4. Statesmen—Great Britain—
Biography. 5. Liberal Party (Great Britain). 6. Zionism—History.
I. Title.
DA566.9.S36W37 1991
941.08'092—dc20
[B]   91–23884
ISBN 0–19–822648–9

Typeset by Hope Services (Abingdon) Ltd
Printed and bound in
Great Britain by Bookcraft Ltd.
Midsomer Norton, Bath

for Charlotte

'The body is more than the raiment', and the political life is the raiment not the body.

(Gladstone)

Preface

I NEVER met Herbert Samuel, but for three years, as an undergraduate at Oxford, I used to eat breakfast every morning under his portrait in Balliol College hall. Since then I have spent so many years, in the interstices between other projects, collecting and reading his papers, talking to people who knew him, and dissecting various aspects of his life, that I may perhaps be forgiven for thinking, in odd moments of professional vanity, that I know him almost better than he knew himself. Samuel was not a particularly introspective person—on the contrary, contemporaries complained that he seemed to suffer from the *atrofia del cuore* allegedly induced by a Balliol education.[1] Reviewers of his *Memoirs*[2] praised their charm but complained that they were overdiscreet. 'He never speaks out. They reflect a kind of Roman austerity and aloofness, almost of coldness', wrote one reviewer who knew Samuel well.[3]

Herbert Samuel's extraordinarily long political life coincided with the long-drawn-out sunset of Liberalism as a dominant force in the world. A witness of the slow descent from the Bulgarian horrors to Auschwitz and Hiroshima, he was an 18-year-old tourist in the USA when he observed the election of Benjamin Harrison as American president in 1888 and a 92-year-old elder statesman when he contemplated the Cuban missile crisis in 1962. His career in the Liberal Party began in the age of Gladstone and ended in the era of Grimond—thus spanning the period of its greatest triumphs and of its collapse as a major contender in British politics.

Samuel played a vital role in the formulation of the 'New Liberalism' of the turn of the century—the crucial moment at which the centre of gravity of British liberal ideology moved from individualism towards collectivism. As a member of the great reforming administrations of Campbell-Bannerman and Asquith after 1905 he helped translate this doctrine into legislation that laid the foundations for the welfare state. As a Cabinet minister in early August 1914 he devised the compromise formula which preserved the unity of the Cabinet and the Liberal Party on the eve of Britain's entry to the most destructive war in its history. During the war he

[1] Leonard Stein, *The Balfour Declaration* (London, 1961), 105.
[2] Viscount Samuel, *Memoirs* (London, 1945).
[3] Sir Andrew MacFadyean in *International Affairs*, 22/1 (Jan. 1946).

was the first minister to promote the idea of a Jewish State in Palestine. As High Commissioner there between 1920 and 1925 he inaugurated the British mandate over the country and laid the basis for the Jewish National Home. In the General Strike of 1926 he negotiated the terms for the ending of the largest industrial stoppage in British history. In the crisis of 1931 he was at the centre of the discussions that led to the creation of the National Government. Thereafter he served as Liberal leader in succession to Lloyd George. To Samuel, more perhaps than to any other leader, the Liberal Party owed its survival as a distinctive, albeit attenuated, element in the British political spectrum. He remained politically active into old age, at the same time forging a new role for himself as a philosopher, writer, and broadcaster who commanded a national audience and international reputation.

Samuel's buttoned-up public persona was of a piece with his well-ordered, apparently unemotional private life. Yet behind the calm front lay areas of deep feeling. While at Oxford in the early 1890s he passed through a spiritual crisis that marked his relationship to his family and his attitudes to religion and politics for the rest of his life. His commitment to social reform grew out of a personal disgust at the horrors of late Victorian industrial society. But his early radicalism waned over the years as he appeared to develop into an efficient administrative workhorse rather than a tribune of the downtrodden. Then, in middle age, he astonished his contemporaries by donning the mantle of a prophet. His romantic embrace of the cause of Zionism revealed something of the inner emotional motor that drove his political career. It gave the lie to the accusation that he was merely an unimaginative careerist on the greasy pole.

When he returned to British politics in the late 1920s, after his sojourn in Palestine, he did so *à contre-cœur*. He had intended to spend the rest of his days writing philosophy. At the head of a fractious, disintegrating Liberal Party between 1931 and 1935 he seemed to lack the ambitiousness of which his detractors had earlier complained. But he displayed qualities of patience and forbearance, above all towards Lloyd George who treated him abominably. Samuel despised Lloyd George's corruption, demagogy, and lack of scruple. Lloyd George felt utter contempt for Samuel's integrity and old-fashioned decorum. To many Lloyd George represented Liberalism's most vigorous hope for survival in a democratic polity. Yet, as Keynes noted, 'One catches in his company that flavour of final purposelessness, inner irresponsibility, existence outside or away from our Saxon good and evil, mixed with cunning, remorselessness, love of power.'[4] No such criticism could ever be applied to Samuel. For better

---

[4] John Maynard Keynes, *Essays in Biography* (New York, 1951), 36–7.

or worse he embodied, in his personality no less than his policies, the
survival of the Gladstonian tradition of high seriousness in politics.

Samuel was clearly a major figure whose achievement demands serious
critical assessment. The only biography, by John Bowle, was published in
1957 when Samuel was still alive: a readable narrative account, this is
inevitably now somewhat outdated both in its approach and in its
sources.[5] Bowle enjoyed access to much, but not all, of the great mass of
Samuel's private papers, one of the largest and most fascinating of such
collections in modern British history. During the intervening thirty years
the documentary sources for Samuel's service in government have become
available as a result of the release of official records in London and
Jerusalem. The private papers of nearly all of Samuel's major contemporaries in British politics have similarly been opened. And substantial
further private papers of Samuel himself have surfaced: these include his
lifelong correspondence with his sons Edwin (2nd Viscount Samuel) and
Godfrey. They also include the contents of his desk, as it was left on the
day of his death, which turned up out of the blue in Connecticut recently.
When I arrived at the home of his grandson Dan to witness the opening of
this virtual Tutankhamun's tomb we found a complete list of books read
by Samuel between 1889 and 1962, an invaluable source for charting his
intellectual progression. We also discovered Lady (Beatrice) Samuel's
'Dinner Books' for the period 1904 to 1933, useful for reconstructing
the Samuels' social world, and Samuel's alpaca writing jacket—a little
crumpled but quite serviceable after a trip to the dry-cleaner's.

The object of this biography is to draw together these sources, to
analyse them in the light of the great volume of secondary literature now
in print, and to attempt a new appreciation both of the role of Herbert
Samuel in politics and of some of the larger historical issues in which he
was engaged. Two caveats are in order. First, two chapters dealing with
Samuel's attitude to Zionism and his experience in Palestine between
1920 and 1925 discuss matters on which I have already written more fully
in an earlier book.[6] Here I have tried to refine the earlier argument on the
basis of new evidence and also to focus on Samuel's personal impact on
the history of Palestine. Secondly, this book does not attempt a full-scale
assessment of Samuel's philosophical writings. Such a task would in any
case be beyond my capacities. Whatever their intrinsic merits, Samuel's
later philosophical works have had little impact on professional philosophy
and are largely unread today. Moreover, with the exception of his first
book, *Liberalism*, published in 1902, their subject-matter is not germane

[5] John Bowle, *Viscount Samuel: A Biography* (London, 1957).
[6] Bernard Wasserstein, *The British in Palestine: The Mandatory Government and the
Arab–Jewish Conflict 1917–1929* (London, 1978; 2nd edn. Oxford, 1991).

to the main political themes of this biography. I have therefore restricted myself to discussing Samuel's philosophy in the context of his biography rather than embarking on an elaborate analysis of his place in the history of thought.

The epigraphs at the heads of chapters are all quotations selected by Samuel himself for inclusion in his *Book of Quotations*.[7] He collected them on small slips of paper over a period of sixty-four years. They may give something of the flavour of his intellectual outlook as well as affording innocent amusement to his shade.

After several years of cohabiting with a historical figure, the biographer must guard against the dangers of unwittingly adopting his subject's angle of vision, of exaggerating his importance, or of executing a mere celebration. I have sought to discount for all this. Yet in the end the evidence persuades me that Herbert Samuel was a more human personality as well as a more substantial political figure than he has hitherto been reckoned.

Brandeis University
October 1990

[7] 2nd, enlarged edn., London, 1954.

Acknowledgements

THE SAMUEL family have been helpful to me in many ways; I particularly wish to thank Lady (Brunel) Cohen, the Hon. Nancy Salaman, Dr William Salaman, the Hon. Dan Samuel, Professor David Samuel (3rd Viscount Samuel), Mr Dennis Samuel, Mr Donald Samuel, the late Edwin Samuel (2nd Viscount Samuel), the late Godfrey Samuel, the Hon. Philip Samuel, and Mrs Gillian Sinclair-Hogg.

The stimulation of my colleagues, the efficiency of library staff, and the provision of technical facilities by Sheffield and Brandeis Universities have sustained me in the course of my work on this book. The American Council of Learned Societies and Brandeis University awarded me research grants which I happily acknowledge. Much of the research for this book was conducted during a year's leave of absence from teaching which I spent at the Institute for Advanced Studies at the Hebrew University of Jerusalem in 1984–5. I am grateful to my friends there and also to the Institute for Historical Research at London University which has made its facilities available to me on several occasions. I also wish to thank the many archives, libraries, and private individuals who have answered my enquiries over many years. A list of institutions which provided me with unpublished material is given in the list of sources at the end of the book. I have been fortunate in enjoying the research assistance at various times of Dr Elazar Barkan, Miss Sandra Gereau, Miss Maura Hametz, Dr Paul Salstrom, Mr David Soule, and Dr Daniel Szechi.

I acknowledge the gracious permission of Her Majesty the Queen Elizabeth II to use material in the Royal Archives. Crown-copyright material in the Public Record Office is reproduced by permission of the Controller of Her Majesty's Stationery Office. I also want to express my appreciation to the following for permission to use copyright materials and for assistance in divers other ways: Professor Chimen Abramsky, Sir Richard Acland, Mrs G. N. Adam, the Baha'i World Centre, Dr Michael Bentley, Mr Alex Berlyne, Professor Eugene C. Black, Mr Vernon Bogdanor, the Trustees of the Bowood Manuscript Collection, Dr M. G. Brock, Miss Penelope Bulloch, Mr Geremy Butler, Mr Stanley Clement-Davies, Professor Frank Eyck, Dr Celia Fassberg, the Rt. Hon. Michael Foot MP, Dr Michael Freeden, Professor Isaiah Friedman, Mrs J. Geddes, Professor B. B. Gilbert, Mr Martin Gilbert, Mr Tibor Gold, Mr Walter D'Arcy

Hart, Mrs Machiko Hollifield, Mr D. F. Hubback, Mr Michael Hurst, Mr Tristan Jones, Dr A. Kadish, Mr John Lavagnino, Mrs T. Levi, the Liverpool Athenaeum, Dr K. J. Lunn, Lady (Compton) Mackenzie, Mr Scott Magoon, Professor J. M. McEwen, Mrs Mary McManus, Mr Philip Mallett, Lady Mander, Mr N. Masterman, Merseyside Jewish Welfare Council, the late Hon. Ewen Montagu, Dr Moshe Mossek, Mr Joseph Munk, Professor Aubrey Newman, the Oxford Centre for Hebrew Studies, the Oxford Union Society, Mr Geoffrey Paul, Rabbi Chaim Pearl, Mr E. V. Quinn, Professor Benjamin Ravid, the Reform Club, Professor Jehuda Reinharz, Mr P. J. Riden, Messrs Samuel Montagu & Co., Professor S. A. Schuker, Mrs H. Schwab, Mr John H. MacCallum Scott, the Society of Authors, Messrs Sotheby & Co., Professor Sefton Temkin, Mr A. F. Thompson, Toynbee Hall, the Trevelyan family, the Board of Trinity College, Dublin, Mrs J. Vinogradoff, Professor Robert Vogel, the Revd Dr Carl Voss, Mr J. Wolfman, Mr Adolf Wood, the late Mr Ralph Yablon, and Mr A. Zvielli. I owe a special debt of gratitude to Dr Ivon Asquith, Ms Anne Gelling, and Dr Anthony Morris of Oxford University Press.

Throughout the long process of gestation of this book I have received the encouragement, help, and forbearance of my wife and other members of my family. In the cases of my father and brother this has extended to a quite unusual degree and I therefore thank them most of all.

Contents

List of Illustrations

Figures

Abbreviations Used in the Notes

BL	British Library, London
BLPES	British Library of Political and Economic Science, London
BS	Beatrice Samuel
CPT	C. P. Trevelyan papers, Newcastle University Library
CS	Clara Samuel
CUL	Cambridge University Library
CZA	Central Zionist Archives, Jerusalem
ES	Edwin Samuel (2nd Viscount Samuel)
HC Deb. 5 s.	*Parliamentary Debates: House of Commons*, 5th Series
HL Deb. 5 s.	*Parliamentary Debates: House of Lords*, 5th Series
HLRO	House of Lords Record Office, London
HS	Herbert Samuel
ISA	Israel State Archives, Jerusalem
Parl. Deb. 4 s.	*Parliamentary Debates*, 4th Series
PRO	Public Record Office, Kew
SRO	Scottish Record Office, Edinburgh
WA	Weizmann Archives, Rehovot
WR	Walter Runciman papers, Newcastle University Library

I

The Making of a Meliorist

===

The proper time to influence the character of a child is about a
hundred years before he is born.

(Dean Inge)

HERBERT SAMUEL described himself most happily as a 'meliorist'. He
borrowed the term from George Eliot and defined it as 'one who
believes that the present is on the whole better than the past, and that the
future may be better still, but that effort is needed to make it so'.[1] This was
the credo of a man deeply secure in his roots and confident in his ability to
influence the world around him. The social and intellectual self-assurance
which marked Samuel's outlook throughout his life grew naturally from
his family origins, his solid bourgeois background, and his educational
formation.

The Samuels were middle-class Jews of Ashkenazi (German) origin.
They were much intermarried with three other families of a similar social
type: the Franklins, the Spielmanns, and another Samuel family one
branch of which adopted the name Yates. Together these families formed
part of the Victorian Jewish élite—the 'cousinhood'.[2] Concerned to
document their English vintage they drew up formidable genealogical
treatises which they printed 'for private circulation'.[3] One line of Samuel's
ancestry may have settled in England in the late seventeenth century;
Herbert Samuel himself took great interest in this possibility, although the
evidence for it is inconclusive.[4] On his mother's side he was descended
from Ralph Samuel, a 'slop-seller' who was born in Germany in 1738,
married in London in 1769, and settled in Liverpool before 1780.[5]

[1] *Memoirs*, 251.
[2] See Chaim Bermant, *The Cousinhood: The Anglo-Jewish Gentry* (London, 1971).
[3] Lucien Wolf (ed.), *The History and Genealogy of the Jewish Families of Yates and
Samuel of Liverpool* (London, 1901); Arthur Franklin (ed.), *Records of the Franklin
Family* (London, 1935); Percy Spielmann, *The Early History of the Spielmann Family*
(Reading, 1951); Ronald D'Arcy Hart, *The Samuel Family of Liverpool and London from
1755 Onwards* (London, 1958).
[4] See correspondence between HS and Cecil Roth, Feb. 1935 (Family papers in
possession of 3rd Viscount Samuel).
[5] Wolf, *History and Genealogy*, 39.

Herbert's great-grandfather in the direct male line, Menachem Samuel, immigrated to England in about 1775 from Kempen in the province of Posen, and died at 3 Frying Pan Alley, off Aldgate, some time before 1805. His eldest son Nathan moved to Liverpool where he set up as a pawn-broker, and it was on this humble basis that the foundations of the family's fortunes were laid.[6]

Louis (1794–1859), the second son of Menachem Samuel, was Herbert Samuel's paternal grandfather. According to a family history he was taunted by his mother with laziness and as a result left the family home and walked to Liverpool to join his brother's business. His mother, a superstitious woman, waited for some time and then fasted for three days until she received news of his safe arrival in Liverpool. Every year thereafter she forwent food for three days in commemoration of the incident—ultimately dying as a consequence of her abstinence.[7]

A third son, Moses Samuel (1795–1860), also settled in Liverpool and achieved minor literary distinction. Allegedly the master of twelve languages including Chinese, he wrote anti-missionary tracts, campaigned for the emancipation of the Jews, and translated into English the works of Moses Mendelssohn, the leader of the German-Jewish enlightenment. From the unlikely perch of his watchmaker's shop in Paradise Street, Liverpool, he also edited a Hebrew journal entitled *Kos Yeshuot* (Cup of Salvation). In the prospectus issued to potential subscribers in 1845, the editors declared it a 'monthly Jewish orthodox magazine'. But it was clearly open to broader influences than would have been acceptable to the strictly orthodox of eastern Europe, for among the authorities quoted were not only Moses Mendelssohn (himself orthodox although his doctrines were suspect to the precisians) but Francis Bacon's essay 'Of the Vicissitude of Things'.[8]

Meanwhile, Louis Samuel established his own business as a silversmith and watchmaker and made enough money to retire in 1846 and return to live in London. At his death in 1859 he left his family something under £12,000—a sum which moved them definitively into the upper middle class.[9]

In the next generation, that of Herbert Samuel's father, the Samuels advanced from affluence to great wealth. The central figure in this progression, and an important influence on Herbert Samuel's early life,

[6] Arthur Franklin to HS, 24 Aug. 1931 (Family papers in possession of 3rd Viscount Samuel); Franklin, *Records*, 140.
[7] Hart, *Samuel Family*, 82.
[8] Prospectus bound with issues 1–9 of *Kos Yeshuot* in the Mocatta Library, University College, London.
[9] Will and probate of Louis Samuel, Principal Probate Registry, Somerset House, London.

was Montagu, youngest son of Louis Samuel. At some stage in his early life he turned his name round and was known henceforth as Samuel Montagu. The story of his foundation of the merchant bank which still bears his name was one of the fables of nineteenth-century finance. After leaving school in Liverpool at the age of 13, he went to London and started work as a money-changer with his brother-in-law, Adam Spielmann. Later he decided to set up his own bank and asked his father for some initial capital. Montagu was still under 21 and his father viewed the enterprise with some misgivings, but he eventually agreed to lend him £5,000 on condition that he went into partnership with his elder brother Edwin who was already established in business in Liverpool.

'Samuel & Montagu', as the London bank was originally known, opened in 1853 at 142 Leadenhall Street. An advertisement announced 'Highest Prices allowed for every description of Gold and Silver in Coin, Bars, Plate, Lace [apparently a reference to gold braid], etc. Platinum and Palladium bought. Foreign Bank Notes and Coupons of every Country Exchanged at the most favourable rates.'[10] In the early years Montagu lived above the premises together with his sister and an associate, Ellis Franklin, who later became a partner in the bank. Samuel & Montagu soon achieved enormous success, specializing in foreign exchange transactions. Samuel Montagu's own reputation, and that of the bank, were registered as early as 1859 when the Bank of England for the first time purchased bills from Montagu to the value of £6,897. 1s. 4d. Drawers were to be found in St Petersburg, Paris, Singapore, Bordeaux, Epernay, Paris, Havana, and Rio de Janeiro, and among the drawees were Justerini and Brooks, Rothschilds, Barings, and Hambros.[11] During the following decade Samuel & Montagu developed into a major force in the City of London.

Montagu's elder brother, Edwin, though a partner in the London bank, took little active role in its affairs in the early years. When he was aged 14 an indenture had been drawn up for his apprenticeship to a watchmaker, James Rigby. But the indenture was not receipted and never took effect. Edwin's first avocation seems to have been literature rather than finance. He contributed two sets of 'stanzas' to the magazine edited by his uncle Moses. These bemoaned attacks on Judaism and deplored the lack of communal and national feeling of some of his co-religionists:

> 'Tis sad to see our hallowed creed
> By ignorance decried;
> The faith for which our hearts would bleed,
> Fell prejudice deride.

[10] Records of Samuel Montagu & Co.   [11] Ibid.

But sadder far 'tis to behold
The men who should protect
The members of the Jewish fold
Conspiring against their sect.

Whose hearts—to Pity's promptings dead—
No patriot flame can feel;
The germs of dire dissension spread,
Regardless of our weal.[12]

Edwin remained in his home town where his business developed from the traditional family interest in precious metals into a more specialized banking concern: in *Gore's Liverpool Directory* for 1849 he is listed as conducting business at 9 Castle Street as 'optician, watchmaker & bullion office'. Later the optometric and chronometric sides of the business appear to have lapsed, since directories after 1851 drop the first two words of the description.[13]

These were years of tremendous economic growth in Liverpool whose port was by 1857 handling 45 per cent of the entire export trade of the United Kingdom.[14] Edwin Samuel participated in the general prosperity, building up an expertise in the financing of foreign trade. The only surviving letter-book of the bank, that for 1867, records transactions with correspondents in Danzig, Antwerp, Amsterdam, Hamburg (M. M. Warburg), Brussels, Paris, and Berlin.[15]

By the end of the 1860s both brothers were wealthy men, had married and had children. Samuel Montagu married into the Cohen family, part of the upper crust of English Ashkenazim. Edwin's wife was drawn from one of the leading Jewish families in Liverpool. Clara Yates, Herbert Samuel's mother, had been born in 1837 and married Edwin Samuel in 1855. She was a descendant of Ralph Samuel (the 'slop-seller'), but earlier in the century her family had taken the name Yates. She bore her husband four sons and one daughter. The eldest, Stuart, was born in 1856. Dennis followed in 1858 and Gilbert in 1859. The daughter Mabel, known as May, was born in 1862. Herbert Louis Samuel, the youngest child, was born in Liverpool on 6 November 1870.

By the time of Herbert's birth the Samuel family had followed others of the rising Liverpool middle class, mainly Unitarians, Presbyterians, and Jews, out of the congested central area near the docks to the new

[12] *Kos Yeshuot*, 1/1, Mar. 5606 (1846).
[13] See also manuscript notes by Stuart M. Samuel opp. p. 34 in his personal copy of Wolf (ed.), *History and Genealogy*, in the possession of Mrs Gillian Sinclair-Hogg.
[14] Francis Hyde, *Liverpool and the Mersey: An Economic History of a Port 1700–1970* (Newton Abbot, 1971), 97.
[15] Letter-book in possession of Mr Donald Samuel.

suburban districts around Sefton and Princes Parks. Their home was 'Claremont', a comfortable, medium-sized house in Belvedere Road. The family's rise in status was also reflected in an increased domestic staff: in 1841 Louis Samuel's household had boasted only one resident servant; in 1861 Edwin Samuel employed three; and by 1871 the staff consisted of a butler, nurse, lady's maid, cook, housemaid and kitchen-maid— the normal complement of an upper-middle-class household at the time although conditions 'below stairs' at 'Claremont' must have been crowded.[16]

Reflecting the sentiment of his juvenile verses, Edwin Samuel played a leading part in the activities of the Liverpool Jewish community, which by this period numbered some 3,000—second in size only to London. He served as Senior Warden of the Old Hebrew Congregation in 1863 and again in 1870; in 1853 he was elected President of the Hebrew Philanthropic Society and in 1869 became President of the Hebrew Educational Institution and Endowed Schools. Clara Samuel undertook good works 'for the relief of poor married women during sickness and confinement' under the auspices of the Liverpool Jewish Ladies' Benevolent Institution.[17]

Herbert Samuel retained no childhood memories of residence in Liverpool, for in December 1871, when he was 1 year old, Edwin Samuel moved to London and activated his partnership in Samuel & Montagu. Foreign trade through Liverpool at this time was going through a temporary recession as a result of the Franco-Prussian war, and it may have been this that persuaded him that the London bank presented much greater opportunities. He installed his family in a large and opulent house (later the Yugoslav embassy) that he had commissioned in Kensington Gore. The family bank had moved to Old Broad Street, where it remained until 1986, and Edwin went to work there with his brother and Ellis Franklin, by now a brother-in-law as well as a business associate, since he had married a sister of Edwin and Montagu in 1856. Although they lived on a more elegant plane than in Liverpool, the Samuels continued to pursue a similar style of existence, adhering to orthodox Jewish practice, and mixing mainly with other members of the 'cousinhood'. They retained their links with relatives in Liverpool: one of Herbert Samuel's earliest recollections was of a visit to the home of his maternal grandmother in Huskisson Street where he recalled the large pictures and horsehair furniture.[18]

[16] Census returns for 1841, 1861, and 1871, PRO.
[17] Liverpool Jewish records at Liverpool Central Library; David Hudaly, *Liverpool Old Hebrew Congregation 1780–1974* (Liverpool, 1974); information from Mr J. Wolfman.
[18] HS to CS, 17 Feb. 1907, HLRO HS A/156/259.

The scale of business of Samuel & Montagu had by now grown immense, and the firm had attained international recognition. In the year 1871 alone, they took a participation of $587,500 in a $75,000,000 United States funded loan syndicate; they underwrote $875,000 of a $45,000,000 US loan, as well as participating in Peruvian, Spanish, Hungarian, and Japanese loans, a Turkish Government advance, Egyptian bills, and an Imperial Mexican Railway Debenture.[19] Edwin Samuel, in consequence, became a very wealthy man, and had he survived would no doubt have ranked with his brother as a latter-day Croesus.

But in March 1877 he died suddenly at the age of fifty-one, the cause of death being registered as a 'malignant abdominal growth'.[20] He left his family an estate which was proved at 'under £200,000', but this understated his true worth since it did not include his leaseholds nor his interest in Samuel & Montagu. Apart from charitable and other legacies the bulk of his fortune was left as a trust, part of the income from which was to be paid to his widow and the remainder in allowances to his children upon their reaching the age of 25. Clara Samuel moved with her children and six servants to a house in Kensington Palace Gardens a few doors away from the Montagus.

Herbert Samuel was 6 years old when his father died, and therefore had next to no memory of him. His response when told of his father's death was a nonchalant question to one of his Montagu cousins: 'May says I oughtn' t to play as Father is dead. What do you think?'—which was of a piece with his matter-of-fact attitude towards death, including the prospect of his own, throughout his life.[21] This, his earliest recorded utterance, exhibits a characteristic that puzzled and frequently irritated Samuel's contemporaries throughout his life: a strange inability to display emotion, perhaps even to feel it deeply.

His mother was now left to bring him up on her own, with his uncle Montagu appointed guardian. Samuel Montagu and Clara Samuel were therefore the dominant influences in his early life. Clara Samuel, a plain but sweet-tempered and commonsensical woman of old-fashioned views, retired to a life of reading The Times, playing bezique, holidaying by the seaside, and contentedly contemplating the activities of her extended family. Her son-in-law, Marion Spielmann, called her 'clever and charming with humour of her own'.[22] She doted on her youngest son, employed a French nurse and then a Swiss governess to look after him. She took him

[19] Records of Samuel Montagu & Co.
[20] Death certificate, 25 Mar. 1877, General Register Office, London.
[21] Henrietta (Netta) Franklin to HS, 20 Feb. 1944, HLRO HS B/12/126.
[22] Marion Spielmann to Frank Singleton (Samuel's projected biographer), 14 May 1939, HLRO HS A/160/1.

on trips to Brighton, where he grew to savour the 'dear old sweet smell [that] greets one at the station', and to Harrogate, where he was allowed to ride a white pony at Burgess's riding school.[23]

In politics Clara Samuel was a Conservative and a member of the Primrose League. Spielmann wrote: 'She was always very strong in her political views and always considered the importance, almost the first importance, of controlling the lower classes and keeping them happy. The first and most important and fundamental of her rules was "Never interfere with the working-man's beer!" '—a precept that her son was subsequently to disregard when he helped to draft Liberal temperance legislation. There were some early indications, however, of political divergence between mother and son. In later years the probably apocryphal story was often told that she had hung a portrait of Disraeli above the 8-year-old Herbert's bed, only to find that he refused on political grounds to keep it there and tore it down.[24] Among his earliest surviving writings are doggerel verses, composed at the age of 13, which poke playful fun at 'my anti-Liberal mother'.[25]

Samuel suggests in his autobiography that his father had been a Conservative, and may even have been invited to stand for Parliament in the Tory interest.[26] But at least in his younger days Edwin Samuel had been a Liberal. A poll-book for the Liverpool by-election of 1853 records Edwin Samuel as having 'plumped' for the sole Liberal candidate in this two-member constituency. In doing so he appears to have been following a family tradition since both his father, Louis and his uncle Moses voted Liberal in the election of 1841 and in all other elections for which it has been possible to trace their votes.[27] His mother's Conservatism notwithstanding, the dominant political influence in the Samuel family therefore appears to have been Liberal.

This was reinforced by the Liberalism of Herbert's guardian, Samuel Montagu, who entered the House of Commons in 1885 as Liberal MP for the heavily Jewish working-class immigrant constituency of Whitechapel in the East End of London. Montagu was a major contributor to Liberal party funds and an admirer, almost a worshipper, of W. E. Gladstone. His daughter Lily recalled his 'sentimental joy over the cards and letters which

[23] HS to BS, 28 Jan. 1906, HLRO HS A/157/322; HS to CS, 25 Jan. 1914, HLRO HS A/156/454.
[24] Text of speech by Marion Spielmann, c.1906, HLRO HS B/1. Samuel wrote 'not correct' in the margin next to one version of this tale as recounted in Spielmann's letter to Frank Singleton, 14 May 1939, HLRO HS A/160/1.
[25] HS to Dennis Samuel, 22 June 1884, HLRO HS B/4/8.
[26] Memoirs, 3.
[27] See Liverpool poll-books for elections of 1820, 1832, 1835, 1837, 1841, 1853, and 1857 at the Institute for Historical Research, London University.

the Grand Old Man addressed to him'.[28] Although by this time a
millionaire, he sympathized with many of the radical concerns of his
constituents: he advocated manhood (and womanhood) suffrage, and
lent his support to efforts for trade union organization.

Samuel Montagu was second only to the Rothschilds as a major figure
in the Anglo-Jewish community. He was the founder and patron of the
Federation of Synagogues—a body established to draw Jewish immigrants
out of allegedly unhealthy *shtiblech*, or back-room conventicles, into what
were supposedly more salubrious places of worship built with Montagu
largesse. He practised strict orthodoxy in his bank, where no business was
transacted on the sabbath, and in his personal life, enjoining similar
scrupulousness on his children and his wards. Another daughter recalled:

We were allowed to play tennis on the Sabbath, but not allowed to play croquet! My
father said that we chipped the mallets when we played croquet, and according to the
strictest rabbinical interpretation of the Mosaic law, breaking or damaging things is a
form of work. There was an even subtler distinction to be observed when we went to
Brighton. There we could hire a bath-chair on the Sabbath, pushed by a man, but we
might not drive in an open victoria. The man was a rational being and could observe
his day of rest next day, if he chose. But the horse was a member of the 'brute' creation
and would be given no choice in the matter.[29]

Edwin and Montagu had been among the initiators of the New West End
Synagogue in St Petersburg Place, Bayswater, which opened in 1879. This
elegant and dignified edifice became virtually the house chapel of the
'cousinhood'. As a child Herbert Samuel walked to sabbath morning
service there each week and he was to remain a member all his life. The
synagogue's minister, the Revd Simeon Singer, compiler of what is still the
standard prayer book of the mainstream orthodox communities in Britain,
was his religious teacher.

No doubt some of his uncle's Liberalism rubbed off on Herbert Samuel,
but with him as with other members of the family, notably his cousin
Edwin Montagu, his uncle's strict religiosity seems to have jarred. One of
his earliest surviving letters to his mother, written at about the age of 11,
refers in uncomplimentary terms to his uncle's rendition of the *benching*
or grace after meals.[30] The relations of Montagu with his nephew, as with
his own children, seem to have been formal and distant. When Herbert
came to deliver his first public speech, on the occasion of his bar mitzvah
(confirmation), at the age of 13, he paid dutiful tribute to the Delegate (i.e.

[28] Lily Montagu, *Samuel Montagu, First Baron Swaythling: A Character Sketch*
(London, 'for private circulation', n.d.; a copy is in the Mocatta Library, University
College, London).
[29] Monk Gibbon, *Netta* (London, 1960), 11.
[30] HS to CS, 27 Nov. [1881?], HLRO HS A/156/528.

acting) Chief Rabbi, Dr Hermann Adler, who was in attendance, to the Revd Singer, and to his mother, but scored out a passage of thanks to his uncle which had been present in an early draft.[31]

Herbert Samuel seems to have concentrated his childhood emotions on his mother. He read widely and maintained into adulthood an interest in conjuring tricks and a penchant for practical jokes. His playmates were not his own much older siblings, but the younger Montagu cousins as well as some of his Liverpool cousins whom he was allowed to visit during holidays. Whenever separated from his mother he would send her affectionate letters, fretting if her reply was delayed. He continued to write to her once a week with metronomic regularity until her death in 1920.

The Samuels, like many Jewish families of their type, did not send their children away to public schools, since these were almost invariably institutions in which it would be impossible for pupils to eat kosher food or practise Judaism. In the case of Herbert his mother may well not have wished to send him away from home in any case. At first he attended a nearby preparatory school where he edited the school magazine.[32] During the general election of 1880, when he was aged 9, he campaigned at school on behalf of Gladstone—his first public political action.[33]

In the summer of 1884, during a stay with his relatives in Liverpool, he visited an International Health Exhibition where he was measured in an 'anthropometric laboratory arranged by Francis Galton FRS'. This recorded that he had good eyesight and hearing, and a strength of 30 lb. 'of pull' and 44 lb. 'of squeeze'.[34] A robust child who enjoyed outdoor activities such as tennis, fishing, bicycling, and tricycling, he remained in excellent health most of his life and seldom needed to see a doctor.

In the same year he was entered as a day-pupil at University College School in Gower Street. UCS had been founded as an offshoot of University College in 1830 by Henry Hallam, Lord Brougham, Isaac Lyon Goldsmid, James Mill, and other opponents of the religious tests which still excluded non-Anglicans from the ancient universities. From the outset the school boasted of being 'free from any doctrinal restriction'. There was no school assembly nor were prayers said. UCS naturally attracted Nonconformists such as the Unitarian Joseph Chamberlain and the offspring of Jewish families such as the Mocattas, the Montefiores, and the Spielmanns. All three of Herbert Samuel's elder brothers had studied at UCS, as had Rabbi Hermann Adler, and Rufus Isaacs, later a

[31] See drafts, HLRO HS B/4/1.
[32] See copy in HLRO HS B/2/1; unfortunately the ink has faded.
[33] Speech by Samuel at memorial meeting for Asquith, *Yorkshire Observer*, 13 Oct. 1952.
[34] Card dated 11 June 1884, HLRO HS B/4/7.

colleague of Samuel in the Cabinet. UCS was almost unique among major boys' schools in England at the time in eschewing corporal punishment. Discipline was maintained by a body of 'monitors', largely a self-perpetuating élite who wore silver lapel-badges and took responsibility for maintaining order in the corridors.[35]

The school's managers were inspired by Jeremy Bentham's ideal of a 'chrestomathic school', one where all useful knowledge would be taught. Such subjects as chemistry and modern languages, absent from the curricula of many schools in this period, were taught intensively at UCS. The headmaster from 1876 (when he had been chosen over the famous Oscar Browning, who had been dismissed as a housemaster at Eton on suspicion of homosexuality) was H. Weston Eve, described by one of his pupils as a 'tall and impressive figure, arrayed always in a frock-coat and gown. His drawl and his habit of playing with his watch-chain while speaking were occasions of derisive imitation among our smaller fry.'[36] Eve was an imaginative teacher whose method of demonstrating the course of ocean currents was to twirl a globe and pour ink over it.

Herbert Samuel seems to have enjoyed his schooldays, performing well in class and participating in a variety of extracurricular activities which UCS specially encouraged. He won prizes in the third form for his performance in chemistry and in the fourth for English.[37] He joined the school Scientific Society, to which he lectured in November 1885 on 'Balloons'. In the 1886–7 session he was appointed Photographic Officer of the Society—in which capacity he presented it with a portable cistern. In 1887 he took the examination for the University of London matriculation certificate and was placed in the first division. After a summer holiday with his mother in Switzerland, he returned to his final session at UCS, during which he won two prizes, was appointed a monitor, and served as editor of the school magazine. In a school debate that session he opposed the motion 'that total abstinence from alcoholic beverages is desirable': the motion was lost by seven votes to six.[38]

In the summer of 1888, although only 17, he left school early. His brother Stuart, now aged 32 and a partner in the family bank specializing in American business, suggested they travel together on a two-month visit to the United States and Canada, and it was agreed that Herbert's education should be interrupted to take advantage of this opportunity. The brothers sailed across the Atlantic in September 1888 on the Cunard

[35] See C. G. H. Page (ed.), An Angel Without Wings: The History of University College School 1830–1980 (London, 1981); and University College School Register for 1860–1931 with a Short History of the School (London, 1931).
[36] H. C. Barnard, Were Those the Days? A Victorian Education (Oxford, 1970), 102.
[37] HS to ES, 3 July 1960, ISA 100/73A.
[38] University College School Magazine, July 1888.

steamship *Etruria* in a record-breaking time of six days, one hour, and fifty minutes. They journeyed by steamer up Lake George, marvelled at Niagara, inspected the Plains of Abraham above Quebec, at that time still a bare stretch of wasteland, bathed in the Great Salt Lake, were disgusted by the stench of Armour's pig-slaughtering yards in Chicago, and met some distant Samuel cousins in New York. Herbert celebrated his eighteenth birthday in New York on 6 November 1888 as Benjamin Harrison defeated Grover Cleveland in the presidential election. The trip was an exhilarating experience for him, although he confessed, like Oscar Wilde of the Atlantic Ocean, that he found New York 'disappointing'.[39]

On his return to England he faced the question of what he was to do with his life. He could not enter the family bank, even had he wished to do so, since his brothers Stuart and Dennis were already there and it was held that they filled the Samuel family's quota. None of Herbert's brothers had been to university and his uncle, a self-made man whose own education had terminated at the Liverpool Mechanics' Institute, thought he should train for a profession. Clara Samuel, however, supported her son's wish to apply to university. After a tussle Montagu agreed that he might try for the Oxford entrance examinations while at the same time being formally registered at one of the Inns of Court, the Inner Temple, where his only obligation for the time being would be to eat the prescribed number of dinners.[40] He therefore settled down to prepare for the Oxford examinations.

During this interval between school and university Samuel experienced a social awakening that determined the future course of his life. The immediate catalyst was the first election to the newly established London County Council in January 1889. The Unionists and Liberals did not contest this election under their familiar labels. Instead, candidates concentrated in two main groups called 'Moderates' (mainly Conservatives) and 'Progressives' (mainly Liberals with socialist and maverick Conservative support). The Progressives were led by Lord Rosebery, and one of the highlights of the campaign in east London was a descent on the district by Gladstone to a welcome by vast cheering crowds and delegations of notables headed by the MP for Whitechapel, Samuel Montagu.[41]

With the encouragement of Montagu, who increasingly regarded himself as the feudal baron of the East End, Stuart Samuel stood in the election as a Progressive candidate in Whitechapel. The influx of Russian Jews to the East End since 1881 had heightened the Jewish character of the area. But many Jews were disqualified from voting either as aliens or

---

[39] Herbert Samuel, 'A Trip to America', *University College School Magazine*, Oct. 1889, 215–18.
[40] *Memoirs*, 8.   [41] *East London Advertiser*, 22 Dec. 1888.

by the provisions of the LCC franchise which was slightly more restrictive than that for parliamentary elections. The electorate was therefore estimated to be no more than one-third Jewish.[42] The contest in Whitechapel was reported to be the keenest in the entire LCC area.[43] The Montagu and Samuel families supported Stuart Samuel's candidacy strongly. Clara Samuel even compromised her Conservative principles in the cause of maternal pride by lending her son a carriage to carry voters to the poll on election day. Herbert Samuel worked hard canvassing for his brother. On the eve of the poll he delivered a lecture on his visit to America at the Jewish Lads' Institute in the East End. He was on his feet for twenty hours on election day helping to gather in the votes—'altogether it was by far the hardest day's work I have ever done', he wrote to his mother.[44] The result was a victory for the Progressives who won a majority on the LCC, and a personal triumph for Stuart Samuel who came top of the poll in Whitechapel.

Herbert Samuel's encounter with extreme poverty, overcrowding, poor sanitation, and the general wretchedness of working-class existence in the slums of Whitechapel engendered a shock of social and political awareness which found adolescent expression in a scrawled memorandum condemning the indifference of the rich to the sufferings of the poor:

And yet every one of them has a brain, an intelligence, above all a stomach, and 'if you prick him he will bleed'. . . . The masses, oh how my heart burns and my hands clench to hear that word, epitome of endless generations of oppression. . . . May it be well led our English revolution—antimonarchical? No. Nor yet anti-privileges. No, nor anti-wealth. But anti-unsympathy it will be. A rising of hopelessness against cold don't care.

The document reveals the emotional intensity which lay at the root of his ideological formation. In his later life Samuel was to be accused, as Bevan subsequently accused Attlee,[45] of behaving like a desiccated calculating machine. As a description of his characteristic public demeanour the charge has some merit; but the origin of his 'meliorist' social philosophy lay not in abstract ratiocination but in this first confrontation with raw poverty. This was what made him decide to follow his uncle and eldest brother and embark on a political career.

The more immediate challenge, however, was the Oxford entrance exam, which he took in June 1889. Special arrangements had to be made to enable him to sit the exam on a day other than Saturday in order not to

[42] Paul Thompson, *Socialists, Liberals and Labour: The Struggle for London 1885–1914* (London, 1967), 29, 80; Geoffrey Alderman, *The Jewish Community in British Politics* (Oxford, 1983), 44–5, 183, 187.

[43] *East London Advertiser*, 19 Jan. 1889.

[44] HS to CS, 18 Jan. 1889, HLRO HS A/156/13.   [45] *Not Gaitskell*.

violate the sabbath by writing. His mother gave him a supply of kosher meat which he took with him to Oxford and handed over for cooking to the chef of the Mitre Hotel. Thereby sustained, he succeeded in gaining admission to Oxford University, and the following October returned as a freshman to Balliol College.

These were the great days of Balliol as a progressive educational force which overshadowed all the other Oxford colleges. Benjamin Jowett, Master of Balliol since 1870, dominated both the college and the university. By the time Samuel came up, Jowett was an old man who 'looked and spoke something like a eunuch'.[46] One of Samuel's contemporaries recalled the Master irreverently as 'looking like an old pink and white parrot'.[47] But neither age nor infirmity diminished the halo with which he was invested by his students. 'This Balliol of mine was Jowett's Balliol. Every one of us was inordinately proud of being *e tribu Benjamin*', wrote one of them.[48] Jowett's conversation tended to consist of long pauses leading up to high-pitched apophthegms. He took a particular interest in advising his students on their future careers and was celebrated for his confession that 'he had a general prejudice against all persons who do not succeed in the world'.[49] Jowett had been the creator of the modern system of tutorial teaching at Oxford and under his leadership all the efforts of Balliol tutors were strained towards the overriding objective of securing from their pupils the largest number of first-class degrees of any college in the university. As a result most of the dons were known less for their published works than for their pedagogic skills—but this did not upset Jowett, whose idea of the university had no room in it for creative scholarship: 'Research!' he scoffed, 'Research! A mere excuse for idleness; it has never achieved, and will never achieve any results of the slightest value!'[50]

The most intellectually respectable subject in Oxford in that period was still classics, but Samuel, following the 'modern' emphasis of his secondary education, read modern history. The core of the history syllabus consisted of the study of the development of constitutional law as set forth most authoritatively in Stubbs's *Constitutional History of England*.[51] The history tutor at Balliol, A. L. Smith, was a gifted teacher who conceived the study of history in broad social terms and 'had a stout and eager

[46] Geoffrey Faber, *Jowett: A Portrait with Background* (Cambridge, Mass., 1957), 36.
[47] Logan Pearsall Smith, *Unforgotten Years* (London, 1938), 156.
[48] R. R. Marett, *A Jerseyman at Oxford* (London, 1941), 72.
[49] H. W. C. Davis *et al.*, *A History of Balliol College* (Oxford, 1963), 202, 206.
[50] Pearsall Smith, *Unforgotten Years*, 169.
[51] See Reba Sofer, 'Nation, Duty, Character and Confidence: History at Oxford, 1850–1914', *Historical Journal*, 30 (1987), 77–104.

interest in men and causes'.[52] But he could not escape from the general contemporary notion of history as a form of applied ethics. As one of his successors at Balliol put it: 'For A. L. the significance of the past lay in great moral truths. . . . In his history A. L. was, like everyone else, a disciple of Stubbs, who traced the Divine purpose in the long evolutionary process which has ended in making England top nation.'[53]

In spite of the limitations of the official syllabus, teaching at Balliol was broad-minded and not altogether constricted by the narrow university curriculum. In his first term Samuel had to write essays on such subjects as 'The Legend of King Arthur' and 'The Authorship of the Letters of Junius'. The Master, to whom he presented these, told him they were 'nicely written', but Samuel ruefully noted that he seemed to refer to the calligraphy rather than the contents.[54] Both Jowett and Smith took an interest in Samuel. Smith remained a friend throughout his life. Jowett was a more remote figure. On one occasion Samuel tried to draw him out of his notorious taciturnity, 'but he refused to be drawn and made me talk for half an hour'.[55]

College life, then as now, was a strange union of the elegant and the squalid, the scholarly and the philistine. These combinations were embodied in the recently perpetrated architecture of Balliol's Broad Street frontage, a monument of Victorian bad taste and inconvenience, allegedly in the 'Scottish baronial' style. Balliol had under two hundred students out of about three thousand in the university as a whole. This was a small society—and an exclusively masculine one, since the girls at the three recently founded women's colleges were not only precluded from taking degrees but also strictly chaperoned. None of this, however, troubled Samuel. The relatively open-minded, tolerant tradition of high seriousness at Balliol suited his temperament exactly and he soon adjusted to this first extended period of life away from home. He corresponded faithfully with his mother who visited him soon after his installation in college and was shocked at his spartan living conditions. 'There's not much luxury here!' was her reaction.[56]

On a typical day Samuel would be woken by the peal of the chapel bell and hurry to take an uncomfortable sponge bath—'a cold tub tempered with a kettle-full of boiling water'.[57] This would be followed by 8.00 a.m. roll-call (8.45 a.m. on Sundays). The morning might be occupied with

[52] Sir Stephen Tallents, *Man and Boy* (London, 1943), 124.
[53] V. H. Galbraith in Davis *et al.*, *History*, 241.
[54] HS to CS, 12 Nov. 1889, HLRO HS A/156/45.
[55] HS to CS, 28 May 1893, HLRO HS A/156/57.
[56] HS to CS, 5 Mar. 1916, HLRO HS A/156/503.
[57] HS to CS, 20 Oct. 1889, HLRO HS A/156/27; see also HS to BS, 5 Mar. 1916, ibid. A/157/813.

preparation of an essay and perhaps a tutorial, for which, as for all formal occasions, a gown would be worn. Although lectures were given under the aegis of the university, Balliol men at this period seem to have made it a point of honour to attend lectures rarely if at all. The story was told of E. A. Freeman, who had succeeded Stubbs in the Chichele chair of modern history, that just before a scheduled lecture he would send his parlour-maid over to the lecture-hall to check whether anybody had turned up, in which case, as he put it, he would feel compelled to attend himself: but the answer generally came back that the hall was empty. In the afternoons Samuel played tennis or hockey, took fencing lessons, and went for long walks in the countryside around Oxford, at that time not yet sullied by the expansion and suburban sprawl set in motion by the arrival of the motor industry. Following formal dinner in hall, the evening would be occupied either with reading or with college or university club meetings.

Complex arrangements concerning Jewish observance had to be made from the moment of Samuel's arrival at Balliol. Since he lived in the college and ate in hall, a supply of kosher meat had to be provided, and Jowett gave permission for it to be cooked and sent to the hall for consumption. Samuel at first continued his previous practice of attending synagogue services regularly on the sabbath and holidays—apparently the only Jewish student in Oxford at the time to do so. A problem arose on the first Saturday, when the new students were presented to the Vice-Chancellor to be matriculated and each was summoned to sign his name: in the event, a fellow of Balliol signed on Samuel's behalf. The frequent Jewish festivals in the early autumn led to further difficulties: 'The holidays [he wrote to his mother] have been a most frightful nuisance, as I had to go to lectures but could not take any notes and so have to spend an immense time copying out another man's.'[58]

He continued to read widely and in his first term at Oxford he began a list, which he was to maintain without interruption until his death, of all the books he read. The only works not listed were what he called 'work books'—such as set texts for Oxford exams, government blue books, and pamphlets. The list is remarkable for its length and catholicity of taste. In the first year it included Lamb, Bunyan, Buckle, Hawthorne, Tolstoy, Tennyson, Browning, Chaucer, Wilkie Collins, Thackeray, Austen, Matthew Arnold, Motley, Byron, Hugo, Goldsmith, Macaulay, and Carlyle. Of particular interest in the light of Samuel's evolving social and political interests is the inclusion of Herbert Spencer's *Sociology*, essays by Mazzini, and 'A Symposium on the Land Question'.

Samuel never spoke at the Oxford Union while an undergraduate, but

[58] HS to CS, 20 Oct. 1889, HLRO HS A/156/27.

from the outset he took part in Liberal politics in the university. He joined the Liberal and Radical Association, but went further than many of its members in flirting with the new and dangerous doctrines of socialist collectivism. Here the chief influences came from outside the college— from dons such as Sidney Ball of St John's and L. T. Hobhouse at Merton. They were sponsors of the Social Science Club at which undergraduates and young dons of 'advanced' views gathered to hear visiting speakers. Among those Samuel met at these meetings was Graham Wallas whose ideas and personality were to have an enduring influence on him. At that time in his early 30s, Wallas was an empiricist strongly critical of the idealist philosophical tradition bequeathed to Balliol by T. H. Green and still strong there in the 1890s. An early member of the Fabian Society, Wallas had contributed to the first volume of *Fabian Essays*, published in 1889.[59] His favoured slogan at this period was 'Postulate! Permeate! Perorate!'[60] He had an earnestness and quiet moral power which led one unkind critic to complain that he 'always represented his chance thoughts as direct communications from the Holy Ghost'.[61] A little more generously, H. G. Wells described Wallas as 'rather slovenly, slightly pedantic, noble-spirited, disinterested'.[62] Although favouring the extension of the area of state action for social purposes, Wallas was far from being a Marxist and adopted a detached, sympathetic, but critical approach to socialism which attracted Samuel and exactly matched his own developing tendencies.

Another speaker was the London dockers' leader, Tom Mann. Samuel Montagu had been a supporter of Mann in his efforts to unionize the dockers, and had played a part in the great dockers' strike of 1889, led by Mann, Ben Tillett, and John Burns. This was the first manifestation of mass strength by a trade union representing unskilled workers. Montagu's motives for supporting the dockers' union seem to have been a prudential mixture of political calculation (since many dockers lived in his constituency) and concern to guide the union away from dangerous socialist influences. His nephew, on the other hand, seems at this period to have been under the spell of exactly such influences. Mann told Samuel of his plans to extend the membership of his Dock, Wharf, Riverside, and General Labourers' Union to agricultural workers, and, in company with

[59] In his reply in 1936 to a biographical questionnaire sent to him by the History of Parliament Trust, Samuel mentioned the *Fabian Essays* among the books that had particularly influenced him: the others were the works of Mill and Carlyle, and 'General' William Booth's *In Darkest England and the Way Out*. See HS to Josiah Wedgwood, 2 Sept. 1936, HLRO HS A/100/3.
[60] Peter Clarke, *Liberals and Social Democrats* (Cambridge, 1981), 43.
[61] H. W. Nevinson quoted ibid. 9.
[62] H. G. Wells, *Experiment in Autobiography* (London, 1969), ii 598–9.

a few other radical undergraduates and dons, Samuel helped recruit members to the union. By the spring of his second year at Balliol he was devoting almost every weekend to forays to hamlets in the rural hinterland of Oxford in search of union members. In April 1891 he wrote to his mother:

We had a couple of fine meetings on Sunday and yesterday. At Great Milton there were five hundred people on the village green who, many of them, had come in from miles around to hear Tillett. He is a splendid orator and had his audience well in hand. I spoke for a quarter of an hour and got on well, though the size of the crowd together with the fact that I had drunk a little water before beginning made me rather hoarse. Yesterday there were quite seven hundred people in the large space in front of the town-hall at Thame—a little country town. I got on much better and was a good deal cheered. The people were very hearty in the cause and enthusiastic. At the end of the meeting I jumped on to the big packing-case that had been our platform and led three cheers for 'Tillett and the Union', which must have been heard over half the country.[63]

Week after week Samuel accompanied Hobhouse, other university men, London visitors such as George Bernard Shaw, and a radical college window-cleaner, William Hines, to meetings at Abingdon, Sutton Courtenay, Ickford, Great Haseley, Cuddesdon, Tetsworth, Wheatley, Stanton St John, and dozens of other towns and villages of the countryside around Oxford.

Meanwhile the connection with Tom Mann had involved Samuel deeply in another great contemporary cause of sympathizers with the labour movement—the working conditions of women workers in match factories. The strike of the 'matchgirls' at Bryant and May's factory in London in July 1888, protesting against conditions that gave rise to the industrial disease known as 'phossy jaw' (necrosis), had been another harbinger of the 'new unionism' of the unskilled workers. Early in 1891 Samuel wrote to Lady Dilke, second wife of the radical Liberal politician Sir Charles Dilke, offering help in her work on behalf of the matchgirls. One of the arguments used by the match manufacturers to justify their refusal to improve conditions was the danger of being undercut by foreign competition. Samuel therefore offered to travel to Sweden to investigate conditions in rival factories there. The offer was accepted and in the summer of 1891 he set off, accompanied by his cousin Louis Montagu. He began his investigations in Gothenburg where he discovered that Swedish matchbox-manufacturers were selling their products direct to Bryant and May. On his return he presented Lady Dilke with a report giving details of wages and conditions in the Swedish match industry and showing that Swedish workers were in fact treated better than their

[63] HS to CS, 21 Apr. 1891, HLRO HS A/156/85.

English counterparts. Samuel's findings were published in the *Women's Trades Union Review* with the comment:

We hear so much now-a-days of foreign labour dragging British labour down because of its low standard of living, that the particulars about the Swedish match-makers are a pleasant surprise. We know at any rate that when we buy foreign matches or foreign boxes containing home-made matches . . . we are not helping to drag down our workers here to a still lower position. But surely there is no occasion for British workers to starve on a bloater or a crust whilst their Swedish sisters are eating meat for their dinner and stinting neither themselves nor their children. . . . I think most people will say that where a plain issue of humanity is at stake there can be no doubt as to the right course.[64]

While thus drawn into the larger world of radical activity, Samuel stamped his mark on Liberal politics within the university. He was elected to the Russell Club, a Liberal essay society with a limited membership. He also joined the newly formed Society for the Study of Social Ethics, which, he wrote, 'contains what Oxford can produce in the way of social reformers and will help, I think, to give direction to a good deal of promiscuous philanthropy that is in the air'.[65] In November 1891 Samuel read the society a paper on 'The Eight Hours Day'. He dwelt particularly on the means of implementing the reform:

The courses that are generally suggested are three—trade union action, a universal compulsory act, and the compromise as it may be called, an act embodying the principle of trade option. The difficulties and want of permanence of the first method, and the dislocation of industry that would be caused by the adoption of the second were dwelt upon at some length, as were the objections to the employment of the third. But it was urged that these objections are not very hard to meet, and that a bill embodying the principle of trade option would be the best course to adopt.[66]

The cautious, pragmatic approach to state intervention characterized Samuel's evolving conception of liberal collectivism.

The crystallization of Samuel's social and political beliefs at Oxford was accompanied by a jettisoning of religious faith. The drama followed a characteristic late-Victorian pattern and, as in the case of his mentor, Wallas, Samuel's rejection of God was also in some sense a repudiation of family.[67] The first sign of approaching storm may be detected in a series of seemingly trivial incidents in 1891. During his first two years at Oxford Samuel continued, in accordance with orthodox precepts, to eat only kosher food. But in May 1891 the *shochet* (ritual slaughterer) who

[64] *Women's Trades Union Review*, 15 Oct. 1892.
[65] HS to Oscar Browning, 23 Aug. 1891, Eastbourne Central Library.
[66] *Journal of the Society for the Study of Social Ethics*, 1/2 (1892), 220–3.
[67] Clarke, *Liberals*, 18.

supplied his meat went off to Russia for some weeks and there was a hiatus before a replacement could be found. Samuel wrote to his mother to ask for an emergency supply of 'two chickens, a small brisket, sausages and a couple of chops'. Telegrams followed arranging for the supply of mutton and tongue.[68] The immediate difficulty eased with the arrival of a replacement *shochet*, but the problem arose again in a different form that summer during Samuel's visit to Scandinavia with Louis Montagu. About three weeks after leaving England he wrote to his brother Dennis complaining bitterly of his mother's failings as a correspondent: 'I was much disgusted, I might say exceedingly angry at receiving one scrappy and uninteresting letter two and a half pages long, written four days after we left, when she had ten days to write in. . . . and considering she has nothing else to do all day long, you will understand my indignation at her want of consideration.' In a postscript he added: 'I write under protest, to oblige Louis, to ask you if you know or can get to know of any kosher restaurant in Christiania [Oslo], Stockholm or Gothenborg.'[69] A few days later he complained to his mother of the paucity of letters from her, adding that he was eating tinned meat.[70] The question of *kashrut* and of religion in general seems to have been bound up in Samuel's mind with that of his relations with his mother.

Matters came to a head in the following spring. In his memoirs Samuel discusses this 'period of acute tension', recalling an 'upheaval' that followed his reading of John Morley's *On Compromise* in February 1892—the work which, he wrote, 'affected my life more than any other'.[71] In a chapter entitled 'Religious Conformity', Morley, a sceptic in religion, discusses the question of avowal of lack of faith, arguing that under modern conditions it is possible to dissent openly from generally held religious beliefs without inflicting upon those who retain them 'any intolerable kind or degree of mental pain'. On this basis he concludes that it is 'all the plainer, as well as easier, a duty not to conceal such dissent'. Morley adds, however, the reservation that

one relationship in life, and one only, justifies us in being silent where otherwise it would be right to speak. The relationship is that between child and parents. . . . Where it would give them sincere and deep pain to hear a son or daughter avow disbelief in the inspiration of the Bible, it seems that the younger person is warranted in refraining from saying that he or she does not accept such and such doctrines. This, of course, only where the son or daughter feels a tender and genuine attachment to the parent. Where the parent has not earned this attachment, has been selfish, indifferent, or cruel,

---

[68] HS to CS, 13 and 17 May 1891, HLRO HS A/156/89, 91.
[69] HS to Dennis Samuel, 12 July 1891, HLRO HS B/4/50.
[70] HS to CS, 16 July 1891, HLRO HS A/156/108.   [71] *Memoirs*, 18.

the title to the special kind of forbearance of which we are speaking, can hardly exist.[72]

Whether Samuel consciously felt that his mother had been sufficiently 'selfish, indifferent, or cruel' to warrant his dispensing with the 'special kind of forbearance', or whether he was persuaded by Morley's argument that in the late nineteenth century it was possible to disavow faith without inflicting pain on believers, he now took the radical step of informing his mother that he no longer believed in Judaism. Indeed, he went even further and announced that he was no longer prepared to adhere to the outward practice of religion. The latter declaration undoubtedly inflicted the greater shock on his family who, in the general spirit of Victorian Anglo-Jewish latitudinarianism, probably cared less about inward belief than outward conduct.[73]

Greatly distressed by his declaration, Clara Samuel wrote asking him to talk the matter over with his uncle and 'in the meantime to continue the usual practises [sic]'.[74] Although he agreed to meet Montagu, he warned that there was 'no likelihood of such a discussion having the least effect on me'. With uncharacteristic arrogance, a symptom, no doubt, of his inward turmoil, he added: 'My opinion of Uncle Montagu's theology and of his philosophic qualities is not such as to lead me to bow to his wishes in this matter.' In slightly softer tone he continued the letter to his mother:

As to the comparatively unimportant details of the observance of kosher [sic] and of the Sabbath, I have never given them up and, as general rules, probably never shall—though not regarding them as questions of principle never to be infringed, but as, so far as I know, good hygienic regulations. It is a different matter in the case of attending synagogue. When one has become as thoroughly convinced as I have of the non-interference of God with the working of his own laws and of the absurdity of prayer and the insincerity of a ritual worship, it would be the grossest hypocrisy for him to conform to the observances of a religion such as the Jewish and to allow others to think that he is a believer. . . . Consequently, not being an unprincipled person, or one who will not take the trouble to act up to his beliefs, it is impossible for me to continue to profess the Jewish religion. Do not think that I underestimate the importance of the step I am taking. I feel it very strongly; and I feel very keenly the possibility of any estrangement from the family. But I would feel far more keenly the loss of my own self-respect. I have been a sham in my own eyes long enough.[75]

Later in the same letter he referred to his 'renouncing the Jewish religion'. At about this time he also informed his mother that he was sending

[72] John Morley, On Compromise (London, 1874), ch. 4.
[73] See Todd M. Endelman, 'Communal Solidarity among the Jewish Elite of Victorian London', Victorian Studies, 28/3 (Spring 1985), 491–526.
[74] CS to HS, 8 May 1892, HLRO HS B/4/53.
[75] HS to CS, 9 May 1892 (copy), HLRO HS A/156/127.

cheques as contributions to the Salvation Army. Although he was probably attracted more by its social activism than its evangelical mission, his mother was plainly agonized by what may have seemed her son's incipient apostasy. She wrote back expressing her grief and pleading with him to relent: 'Let me beseech you, if you have any particle of love for me, & respect for your late dear father, not to persevere ... I was watching your career with such joy & pride, & now all my hopes of your future happiness and distinction are crushed.'[76]

In the end, in what was perhaps the truer spirit of Morley's doctrine, the wayward sheep returned, if not to the faith, at any rate to the fold. A compromise was patched up whereby, while he would not be required to attend synagogue, he would nevertheless remain a member of the Jewish community. His mother was much relieved: 'I am sure you will never regret deferring to my wishes in this matter—it will be a satisfaction to you when I am no longer with you.'[77] Relations between mother and son quickly returned to an even keel and the episode left little outward residue. But his emphatic self-assertion constituted a declaration of independence from his family, most daringly from his uncle Montagu. There was, however, no definitive breach. Herbert worked for his uncle's re-election as MP for Whitechapel in the general election in the summer of 1892, and Montagu reciprocated by taking a benevolent interest in his nephew's political career.

Samuel's political activity in and around Oxford meanwhile gathered pace. His evolving social ideas were strongly influenced by Sidney Webb whom he first met in November 1891. Eleven years older than Samuel, Webb was at this time in the process of adoption as Progressive candidate for an LCC seat at Deptford in south-east London and of engagement to Beatrice Potter—the beginning of their celebrated 'partnership'. A close friend of Wallas, and a fellow-member of the Fabian Society executive, Webb lectured on 'A Practical Programme of State Action' to the Society for the Study of Social Ethics. Samuel took along his brother Stuart who happened to be visiting Oxford, and the next morning gave a breakfast party in honour of the two of them.[78] Webb's rigorous approach to social questions evoked an immediate response in Samuel. He reviewed Webb's *London Programme* for the society's journal, suggesting that though its proposals for municipal socialism might 'to an ignorant eye' appear 'extreme and Utopian, the signs of the times certainly point the same way as Mr Webb'.[79]

[76] CS to HS, 12 May 1892, HLRO HS B/4/54.
[77] CS to HS, 23 May 1892, HLRO HS B/4/55.
[78] HS to CS, 8 Nov. 1891, HLRO HS A/156/119; Society for the Study of Social Ethics programme for Michaelmas term 1891, HLRO HS A/3/7.
[79] *Journal of the Society for the Study of Social Ethics*, 1/2 (1892), 164.

Webb's stress on the importance of empirical social research struck a sympathetic chord in Samuel who resolved to apply to the rural proletariat of Oxfordshire the sociological method which had previously yielded fruitful results in London. Immediately after his encounter with Webb he wrote to Beatrice Potter's cousin Charles Booth, whose *Life and Labour of the People*, the pioneering social survey of working-class poverty in east London, had appeared two years previously. Samuel asked for guidance in his proposed rural enquiry. Booth's advice was encouraging although hardly precise: 'The facts to be tried for', he replied, 'are in brief "all you can get"—nothing which indicated the conditions under which the people live and work would come amiss, & the principles of classification will depend on the nature and completeness of the information obtained.'[80] Samuel took the project very seriously, devoting much of his time over the following two years to a study of social and economic conditions in the village of Great Milton, not far from Oxford.[81] Although he never published the results, the exercise influenced his thinking on such subjects as rural depopulation, the land question, and property rights. This close and direct contact with rural poverty affected Samuel almost as deeply as his earlier encounter with its urban counterpart in Whitechapel.

Another new acquaintance in this period opened doors for Samuel in the higher reaches of Liberalism. Oscar Browning had been the unsuccessful candidate for headmaster of University College School in 1876. Historian, snob, pederast, and fellow of King's College, Cambridge, a man who with all his faults had a genius for friendship, he took pride in guiding the careers of young men in both of the ancient universities.[82] Soon after their first meeting at Balliol in 1890, Samuel asked Browning to propose him for membership of the Eighty Club, a Liberal organization named in celebration of Gladstone's election victory of 1880.[83] 'O. B.', as he was known, willingly obliged, and henceforth public notices of Liberal meetings in Oxfordshire and elsewhere announced the appearance of Herbert L. Samuel, Esq. 'of the Eighty Club'. Subsequently Samuel corresponded with Browning and invited him to lecture to the Russell Club and to dine at Toynbee Hall, the Balliol-sponsored 'settlement' in the East End. The Warden, Canon Samuel Barnett, a leading advocate of social reform, was another friend of Samuel's. Samuel became an 'associate' of Toynbee Hall in February 1893 and remained in close touch with its work for several years thereafter.

In spite of the energy that he injected into his political activities at

[80] Booth to HS, 10 Nov. 1891, HLRO HS A/155/I/10.
[81] See notebook, HLRO HS A/4.
[82] See Ian Anstruther, *Oscar Browning: A Biography* (London, 1983).
[83] HS to Browning, 7 Dec. 1890, Eastbourne Public Library.

Oxford, Samuel organized his time effectively so as not to fall behind with his academic work. In his fourth and final year at Balliol, 1892–3, he moved out of college to rooms in New Inn Hall Street. He worked a steady seven hours a day and entered for the Stanhope Historical Essay Prize, writing a lengthy paper on the thought of the *philosophe* the marquis d'Argenson, one of the first writers to speak of a 'science of politics'.[84] As his education approached its end the question of his future career came to the fore once again. Although he had continued to pay his subscription to the Inner Temple, he had no intention of taking up law seriously. He turned for advice to Graham Wallas who wrote to him, 'I agree absolutely and without the faintest doubt with your suggestion that you ought to go straight for the main purpose of your life and not waste two or three years in a pretence of going to the bar.'[85]

An unexpected offer effectively decided the matter. Samuel had by now won a considerable reputation in Oxford Liberal circles. In the Michaelmas (autumn) term of 1892 he was elected President of the Russell Club and in this capacity acted as host to prominent visiting Liberals. In February 1893 he wrote to his mother with surprising news:

The secretary of the South Oxfordshire Liberal Association came to see me yesterday and asked me to offer myself as candidate at the next election for that constituency. I am at present ruminating. My first impulse was to refuse on account of my age. But I asked for time to consider it, and now feel more inclined to accept. It is very improbable that I should have the offer of a suitable constituency again for a long time. The Tory majority is 412, and they tell me there has been a Liberal gain on this last register of 390. Sir Walter Phillimore, the Liberal candidate, was not a good candidate, and I feel fairly confident that if I stood with a good radical programme I should get in. Especially as I am very well known in the northern part of the division— scene of most of my speechifying for the last three years. . . . Some time ago I made up my mind not to devote my life to accumulating more money. . . . And as my life is clearly going to be devoted to politics, it would be a pity to let an opportunity such as this, which seldom comes to a young man, go by out of any excess of modesty.

Turning to the practical aspect, he broached the question of how his candidacy was to be financed during the period of nearly three years remaining before he came into his inheritance at the age of 25: 'About £150 to £200 a year would be needed, I suppose, in addition to my personal income, and £500 for the election; the rest can be got out of headquarters. Perhaps some kind relative could lend me that for a couple of years.'[86]

---

[84] See Peter Gay, *The Englightenment: An Interpretation*, ii, *The Science of Freedom* (London, 1973), 448.
[85] Wallas to HS, 20 Feb. 1893, HLRO HS A/155/I/17.
[86] HS to CS, 26 Feb. 1893, HLRO HS A/156/54.

While Samuel and the South Oxfordshire Liberal Association were 'ruminating', the Colonial Secretary and prominent Christian Socialist, Lord Ripon, visited Oxford under the auspices of the Russell Club. Samuel organized a dinner in his honour, attended by leading local Liberals. The climax of the minister's visit was a public meeting addressed by Ripon at the Randolph Hotel. Samuel took the chair and delivered a speech which, he reported to his brother Dennis, 'went off with great éclat'.[87] The success of the dinner emboldened Samuel to say that he would be prepared to accept the nomination, though he added that in his own opinion he was 'rather young to stand for Parliament'.[88] The decision was made easier by the agreement of his father's executors to a financial arrangement which would provide for the interim period before his twenty-fifth birthday.

The South Oxfordshire Liberals had been compelled to select a candidate in mid-Parliament because their previous candidate, Sir Walter Phillimore, QC, had been taken ill with typhoid. Some thought appears to have been given to running a local alderman as candidate, but this proposal gave an opening for contemptuous scoffing by the local Conservative press and was not pursued.[89] No doubt Samuel's friends among university Liberals and his assiduous 'speechifying' over the previous three years helped his cause. By coincidence his uncle accepted an invitation to dine with Gladstone on 23 March, just as the constituency association was making up its mind, and it is possible that a quiet word was dropped from on high on Samuel's behalf.[90] On 11 April a meeting of the association at the Oxford Reform Club unanimously approved Samuel's adoption as prospective parliamentary candidate.[91]

The following few weeks afforded him little opportunity to savour the sweetness of this early political success. More than any other college in the university, Jowett's Balliol placed an emphasis on securing first-class degrees in 'Schools', the final university examinations. Samuel increased his work-load to nine or ten hours a day, yet still managed to find time during the term to participate in some public meetings and to speak at the Arnold Society, a Balliol debating club, in opposition to the motion that 'the Liberal party is carrying the principle of State-interference to a dangerous degree'.[92] In the examinations he took papers in political economy, English history, foreign history, English political history, English

[87] HS to Dennis Samuel, 4 Mar. 1893, HLRO HS B/4/63; see also Oxford Chronicle, 4 Mar. 1893.
[88] HS to CS, 5 Mar. 1893, HLRO HS A/156/55.
[89] Henley and South Oxfordshire Standard, 10 Mar. 1893.
[90] Montagu to Gladstone, 20 Mar. 1893, BL Add MS 44789 fo. 130.
[91] Henley Advertiser, 15 Apr. 1893.
[92] Arnold Society minute book, Balliol College archives.

constitutional history (he discussed 'the history of Thegnhood' and the composition of the Witenagemot), political science (he 'accounted for the omissions' of Aristotle and criticized the view that Hobbes's conjectural account of the origin of society and government was 'worthless'), and two papers on the French Revolution (where he analysed the views of Robespierre and the proposition that the Girondins were ruined by their own moderation).[93]

The results came a few weeks later. He was disappointed to learn that his essay on d'Argenson had earned him only a *proxime accessit*; the defeat by a fellow Balliol man rankled in his mind long after. But this was more than compensated for by an outstanding performance in Schools where he secured the required 'first'—an achievement in its own right, but the more considerable given the extent of his non-academic activities during his undergraduate career. Graham Wallas wrote to congratulate him: 'You must have worked steadily and hard under the most distracting conditions. No one can limit the amount of good that you may do if you will take up politics with the same sort of persistence.'[94] With this success behind him, the 22-year-old 'meliorist' now set out to shape definitively his political ideas and to realize these by 'adding a little to the stock of happiness in the world'.[95]

---

[93] Examination papers with questions answered marked by Samuel, HLRO HS B/5/49.
[94] Wallas to HS, 26 [?] July 1893, HLRO HS B/5/1.
[95] HS to Wallas, 28 July 1893, BLPES Wallas papers 1/13.

2

The New Liberalism

===

The man, at any given moment, is the result of the action of his experience on his nature.

(Graham Wallas)

SAMUEL'S GRADUATION from Oxford in 1893 in a sense marked his coming of age. Four years earlier he had entered Balliol as an emotional schoolboy, overdependent on his mother, the product of a protective upbringing in a sheltered environment. He left university a self-confident junior politician, able to hold his own in any setting. If anything he gave the impression of a middle-aged head on a young body. Physically he seemed even younger than his age, although he was a little over average height and had taken to wearing a moustache. But the characteristic features of his adult personality were already fixed: his equanimity of temper, slowness to anger or to take offence, his fairness to enemies—all these often infuriating to supporters and antagonists alike. He was more prudish than his brother Stuart, and less sophisticated, subtle, or quick-witted than his cousin Edwin Montagu: but his brain was exceptionally well-organized and his capacity for systematic thought and ability to separate complex problems into their component parts were already apparent. While hardly an original thinker, he was not a prisoner of intellectual fashions or fads; he stocked his retentive memory with data and ideas drawn from broad reading of literature, the social sciences, and government blue books. In personal encounters he would be courteous but not effusive, businesslike rather than expansive, rarely opening out into intimacy. His sense of humour was of the sort that delights in puns and practical jokes rather than malicious wit; he despised gossip and had a limited capacity for small talk. He smoked cigarettes but drank little. A believer in vigorous exercise, he played tennis, swam, and took long walking and bicycling holidays in Britain, France, and Italy—these generally alone or with male companions. Women, apart from his mother and female cousins, played little part in his life at this period. He enjoyed travel abroad, spoke French fluently, and admired the treasures of European art and architecture, but his artistic sensibility was conventional and his intellectual outlook was fundamentally English rather than cosmopolitan. Above all, he possessed an immense energy and capacity for work, and he now threw himself into the political fray with zeal and optimism.

On one score he soon discovered that he had deluded himself: South Oxfordshire was by no means a likely Liberal prospect. Since its creation in 1885, the seat had returned a Conservative at each of the three general elections, and the sitting member, Frank Parker, was a local man, well liked and secure in a comfortable majority. Stretching along the north bank of the Thames, from just south of Oxford to just north of Reading, the constituency was a large one, covering more than 400 square miles. In this predominantly rural area the influence of Conservative landowners was still strong. The largest town, Henley, was generally Conservative, but Caversham, an expanding suburb of Reading, had a Liberal middle-class vote as well as working-class Liberals who worked on the Great Western Railway or in the biscuit factories in Reading.[1] Samuel's chances of election would turn, however, primarily on his success in mobilizing the agricultural labourers enfranchised since 1884. His village tub-thumping over the previous three years had helped raise political consciousness in the Oxfordshire countryside, and the slow growth of trade union membership was an encouraging sign. But Samuel was over-sanguine in believing that 'a good radical programme' and boundless enthusiasm would of themselves suffice to enable him to reap a Liberal harvest from this alien soil.

The immediate reaction of the local Conservative press to his candidacy was one of disdainful unconcern. The local Conservative newspaper declared confidently: 'Although the Radicals are gleefully murmuring "Welcome little stranger", we have no fear that this carpet-bag politician will supplant a gentleman who by residence and associations has a strong hold upon the constituency.' And it sneered that 'the advent into the field of the verdant and youthful Mr Samuel was looked upon as a good joke'.[2] In his inaugural speech at Henley in July 1893, he tried to answer these personal objections and to present his programme to the electors. Echoing contemporary radical concerns he pronounced the 'condition of the poor' to be the 'supremely great question'; he laid stress on the benefits for the rural poor of the Liberal Government's recent measures; he denounced the 'curse and crime of drunkenness' and called for a new licensing system for public houses; he avowed himself 'an out-and-out Home Ruler' on the Irish question; he promised to vote for the abolition of the hereditary basis of membership of the House of Lords, for payment of MPs, and for

---

[1] Henry Pelling, *Social Geography of British Elections 1885–1910* (London, 1967), 118.

[2] *Henley and South Oxfordshire Standard*, 21 and 28 Apr. 1893.

disestablishment of the church in Wales and Scotland.[3] It was a rousing initiation, but the local Tory paper noted that the hall had been 'barely three-parts full' and denounced him as 'a down-right, red-hot Radical'.[4]

The following autumn Samuel embarked in earnest on a campaign to build a Liberal following in South Oxfordshire. Between 21 September and 15 November he spoke at thirty-nine meetings in small towns and villages throughout the constituency.[5] The culmination was a large meeting at Henley where Samuel was accompanied on the platform by the Irish nationalist John Dillon. The House of Lords had recently thrown out Gladstone's second Home Rule Bill and the Irish controversy was, as a result, at a height. Fighting broke out during Dillon's speech. As for Samuel, he earned a barbed accolade from the local Tory paper: 'Mr Samuel delivered an excellent address from an oratorical point of view. He will reform the world in twelve months if only the constituents of South Oxon. will give him a chance.'[6] Over the next year Samuel spent much of his time in the constituency, reinvigorating the Liberal organization and trying to drum up public support. By February 1894 the local Liberal press was claiming 'a great Liberal revival'.[7]

Samuel's uncle continued to help him politically, the differences over religion no longer disturbing their relations. At a reception at Montagu's house in June 1893 the newly adopted candidate was introduced to Gladstone, whose fourth administration was drawing to a close. When Gladstone was succeeded by Rosebery the following spring, a similar festivity was held in honour of the new Prime Minister, and once again Samuel was present. A few days later it became known that Montagu was to be made a baronet in the Queen's birthday honours. Herbert Samuel wrote to his mother to congratulate her 'on the title in the family', adding 'though personally I should have preferred it non-hereditary'.[8] That summer he visited his uncle's country estate, South Stoneham, near Southampton, and Montagu proposed that Herbert join his brother Stuart in the representation of Whitechapel (a two-member district) on the LCC. Montagu offered to provide the necessary campaign expenses, pointing out that there was 'no other Liberal Jew who would command success' and suggesting that Herbert's association with Toynbee Hall would be a further asset to his candidacy.[9] Samuel eventually decided to focus his efforts on South Oxfordshire but the family connection was a

[3] Leaflet containing speech delivered on 12 July 1893, HLRO HS A/5/3.
[4] *Henley and South Oxfordshire Standard*, 14 July 1893.
[5] List of Meetings, HLRO HS A/6.
[6] *Henley and South Oxfordshire Standard*, 17 Nov. 1893.
[7] *South Oxfordshire News and Thame and Watlington Herald*, 24 Feb. 1894.
[8] HS to CS, 27 May 1894, HLRO HS A/156/75.
[9] Montagu to HS, 29 Aug. 1894, HLRO HS A/155/I/33.

boon in other ways. The introduction to Rosebery led in February 1895 to an invitation to dinner at 10 Downing Street, an unusual honour for an obscure young prospective candidate. At this occasion Rosebery took Samuel aside for a long private talk.[10]

Samuel's slowly growing reputation was enhanced about this time in other ways. He joined the British Economic Association and the Royal Agricultural Society and accepted office as treasurer of the English Land Colonisation Society which sought to establish a 'test farm for the unemployed'.[11] In September 1893 he published a small pamphlet drawing attention to the democratizing tendency of the Liberal Government's proposed legislation on parish councils.[12] In May 1894 he was invited, at the suggestion of Graham Wallas, to review thirteen books on rural politics for the Daily Chronicle. Later that year he published five unsigned Fabian Society tracts on local government issues, particularly the workings of the Parish Councils Act of 1894 and its provisions for the encouragement of allotments.[13] Samuel did not become an active member of the Fabian Society,[14] but he was sympathetic to its aims and friendly with several of its leading members, including the secretary, Edward Pease. The following April he published a further pamphlet, The Agricultural Depression, in which he developed a more general programme for rural reform. The tone of some of these publications, particularly the Fabian tracts, was patronizing and didactic, but Samuel explained to Pease that 'the agricultural labourer's vocabulary for everyday use is extremely limited, and it requires a great deal of political energy on his part to take him past a difficult word. In writing the pamphlet I have often preferred to be crude for fear of being obscure.'[15] Pease was delighted with Samuel's booklets, acclaiming the first as 'a sensation (of a sort)' and

---

[10] Invitation for 21 Feb. 1894, HLRO HS A/155/I/40; Rosebery to HS, 7 Nov. 1902, ibid., A/19/158.

[11] Minutes of conference of society, 19 Oct. 1893, HLRO HS A/155/I/22.

[12] What is the Parish Councils Bill? (London, 1893). A copy is in HLRO HS A/9/1.

[13] The Parish Councils Act: What it is and How to Work it (Fabian Tract 53, London, 1894); Questions for Parish Council Candidates (Fabian Tract 56, London, 1894); Questions for Candidates for Rural District Councils (Fabian Tract 57, London, 1894); Allotments and How to Get Them (Fabian Tract 58, London, 1894); Questions for Candidates for Urban District Councils (Fabian Tract 59, London, 1894). Samuel's authorship of these pamphlets has been established on the basis of his correspondence with Edward Pease and from a handwritten list, made by Pease, of authors of all the Fabian tracts published up to 1913; I am grateful to Professor Chimen Abramsky for showing me this list which is in his possession.

[14] In his Memoirs, Samuel states, 'I did not join the Society' (p. 13). But the Society's records at Nuffield College, Oxford, record the dropping of his name from the membership roll in Sept. 1905 (Fabian Society Records, Nuffield College, Oxford, C7).

[15] HS to E. R. Pease, 21 May 1894, Fabian Society Papers, Nuffield College, Oxford.

ordering a reprint.[16] More than half a century later it was still in print: in February 1946, Pease wrote to Samuel: 'the latest edition now in the press has been prepared by my son.'[17]

These writings reveal the radical thrust of Samuel's political thought but also its limitations. The movement from countryside to town, which reached its peak in the 1890s, greatly alarmed contemporary social observers. The depopulation of rural areas, rather than being regarded as an inevitable product of industrial capitalism, was held to be a danger to the national weal. Hence the emphasis on allotments and smallholdings which might stimulate the rebirth of a sturdy class of English yeomen. Similar social attitudes led those concerned with the problem of urban unemployment to see a solution at least partly in terms of a return to the land—hence the 'test farm' proposal.[18] For Samuel there was the added concern of trying to break the power of large landowners (generally Conservatives) in agricultural constituencies such as South Oxfordshire. One means would be the provision of capital to landless labourers to enable them to set up on their own:

I do not suppose for a moment that there is likely to be a sudden change in England from the system of agriculture on a large scale to the foreign system of small culture. Nor is it at all desirable. . . . And there is no ground for any rosy expectation of the small holder living in luxury. . . . But at least experience shows that his condition will be far above that of the hired labourer, both financially and morally. . . . The difficulty of finding sufficient capital to stock and work the land is more formidable, but experience shows that it may generally be overcome by the small holding developing itself gradually out of the allotment. With the profits of the first acre the labourer is able to stock another. Later he adds perhaps some pasture land and a cow. . . . At the end of a few years he finds himself an independent small farmer with enough land to yield him a decent livelihood.[19]

The prognosis of bucolic efficiency, reminiscent of the 'three acres and a cow' of Joseph Chamberlain's 'unauthorized programme' of 1885, was painted, like its predecessor, with an eye on the farm labourer enfranchised by the third Reform Act. Of course, Samuel's analysis, with its stress on the alleged virtues of an independent peasantry, underestimated the dynamic forces that were driving surplus labour off the land. There was nothing specially original about Samuel's views on this subject. The

[16] E. R. Pease to HS, 24 Aug. 1894, HLRO HS A/155/I/32. It was rewritten and republished as Parish and District Councils: What they are and what they can do (Fabian Tract 62, London, 1895).

[17] E. R. Pease to HS, 11 Feb. 1946, HLRO HS A/124/48.

[18] See Michael Freeden, The New Liberalism: An Ideology of Social Reform (Oxford, 1978), 207; José Harris, Unemployment and Politics: A Study in English Social Policy 1886–1914 (Oxford, 1972), 117, 135–44.

[19] The Agricultural Depression (Thame, 1895), 8–9.

nostalgic but flawed vision of a revitalized, prosperous (and, incidentally, Liberal) class of smallholders remained part of the common stock of Liberal thinking on rural problems—an obsessive intellectual leftover that maintained what has been called its 'digressionary if not pernicious hold' on Liberal minds until as late as the 1920s.[20]

Samuel's hopes of weaning the rural poor from their continued deference to the Conservative gentry were soon to meet an electoral test. In late 1894 an upheaval within the local Conservative association led the sitting MP, Frank Parker, to decide not to contest the seat. He was replaced as prospective candidate by Robert Hermon-Hodge, a local gentleman farmer, huntsman, and former MP for Accrington. Samuel told an interviewer from the *Sunday Times* in January 1895 that he considered his chances of victory over the newcomer 'very bright'. 'The villages have never been known to be so excited before.' When asked to define his 'specialities in political views' he replied: 'At present all politics hinge on the Labour question. I am one of the Labour Radicals. . . . I am very much more interested in social reform than in points of constitutional reform, though it is true that the latter are often necessary preliminaries to the former, as we realize now in the question of the House of Lords.' He specified, however, that he was not a socialist: 'I do not accept the Collectivist ideas of the State ownership of all the means of production; at least I don't think a case has been sufficiently made out for the practicability of widely extended State action in this direction in the present moral condition of the people.'[21] In the face of Samuel's successful local evangelization and growing national prominence, his local opponents began to betray a certain unease. The Conservative *Oxford Times* descended to straightforward abuse, terming his speeches 'hopeless twaddle' and 'Gladstonian flapdoodle for babes'. The paper continued: 'We are assured that Mr Hermon-Hodge has at most a mere fox-hunting acquaintance with his poorer constituents. Well, we shall have some fine fox-hunting soon of a different kind and on a larger scale, and we pity the fox that has been poaching in the Conservative preserves.'[22]

The call of the political hunting-horn sounded sooner than had been expected. In June 1895 Rosebery's ministry was defeated in the House of Commons and he resigned after only fifteen months in power. Salisbury took office at the head of a ministry that included both Conservatives and Chamberlain's Liberal Unionists, and a general election was called for the following month. The Liberals were in a demoralized condition under an

---

[20] Michael Freeden, *Liberalism Divided: A Study in British Political Thought 1914–1939* (Oxford, 1986), 102; see also R. E. Ellins, 'Aspects of the New Liberalism 1895–1914', Ph.D. thesis (Sheffield, 1980), 166.

[21] *Sunday Times*, 13 Jan. 1895.   [22] *Oxford Times*, 23 Mar. 1895.

irresolute leader. 'I can't help feeling that defeat may be good for us', wrote Herbert Gladstone, son of the former Prime Minister.[23] Although the national position was unpromising for the Liberals, Samuel entered the local contest in a confident mood. His election address laid particular stress on social questions. He advocated a national scheme for 'giving all who are in need of it, and who are not clearly undeserving, an Old Age Pension in place of Poor-Law Relief'. He urged the establishment of 'a national system of secondary and technical education'. He repeated his proposals for agricultural reforms, reiterated his support for Irish Home Rule, demanded franchise reform on the basis of 'one man, one vote', and declared that 'the hereditary peerage is unfitted to possess a control over the legislation of the country'. Finally he avowed himself 'an upholder of the greatness of the British Empire and of the unity of the mother country with her colonies and dependencies'.[24]

Among the problems Samuel faced was the hostility and partisan reporting of the local press, most of which was Conservative. The *Oxford Times* poured scorn on what it termed his 'crazy schemes for the re-generation of the rustic', and another Conservative paper ridiculed his 'most dangerous and revolutionary policy'.[25] By way of a counterblast, Samuel launched, at his own expense, a free propaganda-sheet of his own, the *South Oxfordshire Elector*, which was issued twice weekly in editions of five to six thousand copies throughout the election period. He conducted a strenuous campaign on which he spent more than £1,000. But he never-theless found difficulty in arousing public interest. His first public meeting, in the Liberal stronghold of Caversham, was inauspicious. Although he was supported on the platform by R. B. Haldane, with whose radical views he was at this period in close harmony, only seventy-two people attended.[26] He was unlucky in the timing of the election campaign which coincided with the week of the Henley Regatta. Inevitably the sporting festivity tended to overshadow all political issues. Half-way through the campaign he wrote to his mother complaining that 'the religious question' was 'being quietly made use of' by his opponents, and warning her 'not to build up any strong hopes'.[27] In an effort to counter the Conservative accusation of carpet-bagging, he had posters printed announcing 'Herbert Samuel, if elected, will live *here*'. His opponents turned these to humorous account by removing them to pigsties and other such unprepossessing locations.

[23] Quoted in D. A. Hamer, *Liberal Politics in the Age of Gladstone and Rosebery: A Study in Leadership and Policy* (Oxford, 1972), 207.
[24] Election address, 5 July 1895, HLRO HS A/5/18.
[25] *Oxford Times*, 6 July 1895; *Henley and South Oxfordshire Standard*, 19 July 1895.
[26] *Henley Advertiser*, 29 June 1895.
[27] HS to CS, undated letter, mid-July 1895, HLRO HS A/156/95.

The second half of the campaign proved more successful. The *Daily Chronicle* published a complimentary article under the headline 'An Agrarian Reformer', approving his propaganda sheet as 'bright and snappy' and opining that 'even in sleepy Oxfordshire' a Liberal victory seemed to be in the making.[28] The Liberal *Reading Observer* declared, 'If ability, combined with indomitable pluck and self-sacrificing labour, ever deserved success, then Mr Herbert Samuel should now be the Member for South Oxon.'[29] Even the Conservative press acknowledged the vigour of his campaign: 'Never has South Oxfordshire been so tenaciously fought by the radicals. They had considerable assistance from headquarters. . . . On Monday a number of members of the Eighty Club came swarming into the division like locusts, no fewer than twenty-four simultaneous meetings being held in different villages.'[30] Another Conservative paper reported: 'Mr Samuel's undoubted activity was obtruded upon the attention of all who walked in the streets. In square acreage of paper he carried the election by an overwhelming majority. His name in red letters several feet long was strung across every street. . . . Whole houses were papered from ground to roof-tree with his poster.'[31] At an eve-of-poll rally at the town hall in Thame, Herbert Gladstone spoke on his behalf and the candidate read out a postcard of support from the Grand Old Man himself. All the resources of the Samuel and Montagu clan were thrown into the fray. Sir Samuel Montagu himself came up to speak for his nephew, although whether his voice was heard with the same respect in rural Oxfordshire as in Whitechapel is open to doubt.

On election day Samuel drove sixty miles around the constituency in a carriage lent by his brother Stuart, with cyclist outriders and red streamers flying (red was the Liberal colour in the district). But even with the loan of family carriages, the Liberals had far fewer vehicles to carry voters to the polls than their opponents. By the time South Oxfordshire electors voted it was already clear from the results in districts which had polled earlier that the Liberal Party nationally had suffered a major defeat. This news dimmed some of the hopes generated by Samuel's energetic campaigning. The votes were counted on the day following the poll, and the result was announced by the High Sheriff to a large crowd gathered at County Hall in Oxford:

HERMON-HODGE (Unionist)	3,830
SAMUEL (Liberal)	3,471
Majority	359

[28] Repr. in *Jewish Chronicle*, 19 July 1895.
[29] *Reading Observer*, 27 July 1895.
[30] *Henley and South Oxfordshire Standard*, 26 July 1895.
[31] *Reading Mercury*, 27 July 1895.

Given the enormous effort and expense of the Liberal campaign, this was a disappointment, although some crumbs of comfort might be drawn from the reduction of the previous Conservative majority of 419. Moreover, as Samuel pointed out in a letter to W. E. Gladstone, the South Oxfordshire result ran counter to the pro-Conservative trend in all the neighbouring counties.[32] The *Oxford Times* commented that he was 'welcome to the tepid joys of the Consolation Stakes, though they provide rather innutritious diet', and rubbed salt into the wound by commenting that while he had 'made a good fight' he had spoilt it by 'a callow innocence and crude fatuousness that would be hard to beat'.[33] Samuel himself took the defeat cheerfully, telling one of his supporters that he was not altogether sorry and would now devote some time to reading philosophy and history.[34] His reading list for the next few months included works by Morley, Mill, Bentham, Hume, Rousseau, Arnold, T. H. Green, and Sidney Webb.

After the setback Samuel did not retire into his tent. His commitment to politics in no way diminished and he was fortified by encouragement from friends and supporters. The Liberal Chief Whip, Thomas Ellis, told him he was anxious to bring him into Parliament at a by-election. And Rosebery wrote to commiserate, mentioning that he had taken a personal interest in Samuel's candidature and inviting him to call if he should pass through Edinburgh.[35] Shortly before the election, Samuel had been appointed Secretary of the Home Counties Liberal Federation. He held the post until 1903 and during the early part of that period he made it the focus of his political activity. The position was not grand but it brought him into the centre of the party organization and into touch with many of its leaders. He enjoyed the work and his exceptional administrative capacity now found a productive outlet.

In November 1895 Samuel reached the age of 25 upon which he entered into an income from his father's estate of about £2,000 a year, equivalent to about £75,000 in 1991 value. This handsome private income, later to be supplemented from other family sources, gave him complete financial independence and was the bedrock on which he was able to construct a political career without being beholden to any patron. He ploughed a large part of his income into politics: 'I always calculated [he later wrote] that my political activities cost me about £1,000 a year, of

---

[32] HS to W. E. Gladstone, 27 July 1895, BL Add. MS 44520.
[33] *Oxford Times*, 3 Aug. 1895.
[34] Maurice Jacobs to CS, n.d. [July 1895], HLRO HS A/5/22a.
[35] Rosebery to HS, 25 Aug. 1895, HLRO HS A/5/23a.

which perhaps £250 represented the provision necessary to meet the cost of successive elections.'[36]

Over the next few years Samuel's closest political affinities remained with the Fabians and their associates on the left-wing fringes of the Liberal Party. In October 1895 Beatrice Webb wrote in her diary: 'Now we collectivists have to assert ourselves as a distinct school of thought. . . . Our special mission seems to be to undertake the difficult problems ourselves and to gather round us young men and women who will more or less study under inspiration. At present we have a certain set of young people all more or less devoted to the Fabian Junta.'[37] Samuel's was the first name mentioned as a member of this 'certain set'. In April 1895 he had spent an enjoyable holiday with the Webbs, Graham Wallas, Bernard Shaw and others at Beachy Head. Beatrice Webb, in her self-conscious way, recalled it as 'a "jolly" time'.[38] One afternoon several of the party learned how to ride the new 'safety bicycle'; forty-four years later Samuel recollected the strange spectacle of the Fabians at play with this novel machine:

I had tried once or twice and soon grasped the principle. Beatrice, too, soon had the idea. Shaw, characteristically, would accept no help from anybody, and with his long spindly legs he would hop on to the bracket at the back, hop, hop, wobble, wobble, hop, hop, hop off again. . . . I can see Sidney Webb now, this tiny little man, who, as you must have seen, runs forward on his toes. His hat was blown off and he jumped off to pursue it, but didn't know what to do with his new bicycle, so he ran forward across the fields leading it, reluctant to abandon it by the roadside, running with his little steps on his toes. Every time he got the hat it bowled away again, right away to the top of the downs. I can still see him running for it. . . .[39]

Several of the Fabians progressed from these wobbly beginnings into enthusiastic cyclists, and Samuel in particular rejoiced for years in the strenuous pleasure of long bicycling holidays.

Shaw was again among the guests when Samuel went to stay with the Webbs at Saxmundham in September 1896. On this occasion Samuel described to his mother the regime of the Webb household:

We do absolutely nothing but work, talk, eat, bicycle and sleep. . . . We all write in separate rooms all morning. Chat all afternoon. Bicycle twenty miles or so between tea

[36] HS to Josiah Wedgwood, 2 Sept. 1936 (Samuel's response to a biographical questionnaire issued by the History of Parliament Trust), HLRO HS A/100/3.
[37] Entry dated 18 Oct. 1895, BLPES Beatrice Webb diary, 1417.
[38] Retrospective entry for 25 Apr. 1895, BLPES Beatrice Webb diary, 1390.
[39] Record by Frank Singleton of talk with HS, 6 Feb. 1939, HLRO HS A/161/2. For further descriptions of this afternoon see Norman and Jeanne MacKenzie, The Fabians (New York, 1977), 220, and Michael Holroyd, Bernard Shaw, i (New York, 1988), 267.

and dinner. Talk as a rule after dinner till ten, when we go to bed. Last night Shaw read an extremely brilliant one act comedietta in which Napoleon is the chief figure.[40]

A little later Webb invited Samuel to join the managing committee of the newly established London School of Economics.[41] Unlike several of his Fabian friends, notably Graham Wallas, Samuel did not become deeply involved in the affairs of the LSE, but its ethos of positivistic social research and its ethic of social reform rubbed off and influenced his thinking over the next decade.

Another member of the Webbs' circle was Charles Trevelyan whom Samuel first met in about 1893 and who soon became his closest friend. Great-nephew of Macaulay, son of a member of Gladstone's last Cabinet, and elder brother of the future historian G. M. Trevelyan (also a friend of Samuel), Trevelyan was almost exactly the same age as Samuel and his friendship therefore fulfilled for Samuel a different function from that of the older Wallas who remained his political mentor. During the next ten years Samuel and Trevelyan became confidants and political allies. Samuel often visited the Trevelyans' family home in Northumberland; the two went on walking and bicycling holidays together, conducted a regular correspondence, and when in London met frequently—at some periods almost every day. Trevelyan was one of the few political associates with whom Samuel was on first-name terms, and although, as will be seen, their paths subsequently diverged their personal relations remained un-clouded. It was Samuel who introduced Trevelyan to the Rainbow Circle, a radical discussion group which played an important role in the re-formulation of Liberalism in the late 1890s. The Circle began meeting in 1894 and Samuel was active in it from an early stage. Among the other members were the wealthy City merchant Richard Stapley, the journalist and economist J. A. Hobson, and the future Labour Prime Minister James Ramsay MacDonald. On 6 November 1895, his twenty-fifth birthday, Samuel read a paper to the Rainbow Circle entitled 'The New Liberalism'. He argued that classical Liberalism, as based on Bentham's philosophy and Adam Smith's economics, was 'sapped and riddled'. Its most effective opponents had been the socialists, but the Social Democratic Federation, the small Marxist group led by the cricketing stockbroker H. M. Hynd-man, could command only a 'limited amount of intelligent support'. As for the Fabians they had 'no complete and self-sufficing theory of govern-

---

[40] HS to CS, 3 Sept. 1896, HLRO HS A/156/106. 'In an idle moment in 1895 [wrote Shaw] I began the little scene called *The Man of Destiny*, which is hardly more than a bravura piece to display the virtuosity of the two principal performers' (*Plays Pleasant* (Harmondsworth, 1962), 10).

[41] Webb to HS, 5 Nov. 1896, HLRO HS A/155/II/11. See also note by Lady Beveridge on talk with Samuel, 26 Feb. 1959, HLRO HS A/155/XIII/374.

ment'. Samuel propounded 'a third social philosophy' whose root idea must be 'the unity of society'. He urged 'a very positive view of the State as "a partnership in every virtue and all perfection" '. The minutes recorded that the subsequent discussion 'turned upon whether there was a sufficiently strong grasp of sociological principle in the paper to bear a comprehensive political construction' and on 'whether apart from some wing of the Socialist party any party would be likely to adopt Mr Samuel's view; & whether the Liberal Party would'.[42] After the meeting Trevelyan wrote to congratulate Samuel on the paper and suggested that he expand it into 'a series of essays, offshoots of this original tree'.[43] Samuel took the advice to heart and devoted much time and effort over the next six years to the writing of such a book which would reformulate Liberal ideas in the light of the radicals' new emphasis on social reform and state intervention.

Samuel also played a central role in the founding and management of the *Progressive Review*, a new journal designed to be the chief organ of the Rainbow Circle's ideas. Together with Stapley and Hobson he provided the initial capital for the venture. Samuel himself was a director, and his brother Gilbert acted as solicitor. Planning meetings for the review took place over dinner at Samuel's mother's house. He told her that he could have been editor if he had wished, but had decided to refuse the position because of pressure of work.[44] The post went instead to Ramsay MacDonald and the first number appeared in October 1896. Among the contributors were Haldane, Dilke, and the Webbs.

Samuel himself contributed to the third issue in which the leader of the Independent Labour Party, Keir Hardie, published an article firmly rejecting 'proposals for some sort of alliance or fusion between what they are pleased to call "the forces of progress" '. Samuel followed with a rejoinder in which he argued that the Liberals were no longer divided from the ILP by 'a disinclination on principle to use the powers of the State to effect economic change'. That summer Samuel had attended the rowdy sessions of the Congress of the Second International in London.[45] This closer acquaintance with socialism did not persuade him to make a leap of faith in the direction of Marx, whose *Capital* he appears not to have read until 1937. In his reply to Hardie he explicitly rejected nationalization of the means of production, distribution, and exchange as a panacea for society's ills. At the same time he pointed out that 'the newer Liberal school' favoured

[42] Rainbow Circle minutes, 6 Nov. 1895, BLPES Coll. Misc. 575/1.
[43] Trevelyan to HS, 11 Nov. 1895, CPT 4.
[44] HS to CS, 13 Feb. 1896, HLRO HS A/156/99.
[45] See HS to E. R. Pease, 20 and 23 July 1896, Fabian Society Archive, Nuffield College, Oxford A9/1/70, 72.

a large use of the powers of the State: to enforce, whenever possible, such conditions of employment as the public conscience approves as just, to improve the surroundings of working-class life, to render the resources of education equally available for the poor and the rich, to alleviate the miseries of unemployment and the destitution of the old, to reform the system of land tenure, to take under public control any industry which it is found can be managed in that way with greater advantage to the community, and to provide a fair standard of comfort for all who are in State employ.

Urging that Labour efforts would be best expended on trying to strengthen progressive currents within the Liberal Party, Samuel urged that the 'luxury of independence' should be sacrificed 'to the humbler quality of usefulness'.[46]

At a public meeting shortly after the publication of this exchange Samuel was shouted down by supporters of the ILP. No doubt in order to dispel the impression that he was opposed to direct Labour representation in Parliament, Samuel played an important role, early in 1897, in helping the candidacy of the working-class Sam Woods as 'Liberal and Labour' candidate in a by-election at Walthamstow. Woods was not a member of the ILP. His election literature, largely written by Samuel, specified that 'the tactics of Mr Keir Hardie did not, and do not now, command his sympathy'.[47] Walthamstow had one of the largest electorates in England and had been held by the Conservatives at the previous three elections. Samuel acted, in effect, as unpaid election agent for Woods, seeing the election as an opportunity to prove his good faith in urging a fusion of Labour and Liberal causes. The result was a famous victory for Woods and for the idea of direct working-class representation. Cock-a-hoop over the triumph, Samuel wrote to his mother: 'the event will be of much use in the practical side of my career. The reputation of an electioneer is not one, however, that I am very ambitious for, and I propose to push on with my writing in order to set the balance right.'[48]

He resumed work on his book on Liberalism and published pamphlets on reform of the land laws.[49] At the same time he continued his work for the Liberal organization and his heavy programme of speaking engagements: 34 in 1898, 57 in 1899—a total between 1893 and 1902 of 502 meetings, of which 250 were in South Oxfordshire.[50] 'What a wonder you are for work', Lord Carrington, Liberal grandee, cousin of Rosebery,

[46] 'The Independent Labour Party', Progressive Review, 1/3 (Dec. 1896), 247–59.
[47] Walthamstow by-election leaflet, HLRO HS A/155/II/16.
[48] HS to CS, 7 Feb. 1897, HLRO HS A/156/112.
[49] The Ratepayer and the Landowner: A Statement of the Case for the Rating of Ground Values in Towns (London, 1898); Village Reform: Cottages and the Land (London, n.d. [1899 ?]).
[50] List of meetings (with Samuel's computation of numbers), HLRO HS A/7.

and Samuel's chief in the party organization, wrote to him in April 1898.[51]

In spite of Samuel's labours on behalf of progressive causes, his connections with some of his fellow-radicals came under some strain in the late 1890s. The *Progressive Review*, founded with such high hopes in 1896, began to dissolve in acrimony the following summer. Samuel did his best to compose the quarrels which erupted between the editor, Ramsay MacDonald, who complained bitterly that he was being treated like a 'menial', and other partners in the scheme.[52] These squabbles ostensibly related to business and administrative disputes, but deeper political conflicts within the Rainbow Circle and within the larger body of radical opinion were already becoming apparent.[53] One such difference was over the question of an independent labour party. Samuel, Trevelyan, and the other Liberals remained firmly committed to the idea of one great 'party of progress' in which Liberalism would, as it were, take Labour by the hand and lead it into the political arena. Others such as Ramsay MacDonald and the Webbs were moving closer towards Keir Hardie's doctrine of a separate Labour movement, not tied to the Liberals' apron-strings, looking to the trade unions rather than the Liberal organization for financial support, and to Marx as well as to Mill for ideological inspiration. This stream of thought flowed into the Labour Representation Committee, formed in 1900, and thence into the twentieth-century Labour Party.

The outbreak of the Boer War in October 1899 brought to a head a second source of strain within the radical group: the question of empire. The war and the larger problems of empire quickly became 'the test issue for this generation' as Hobson termed it.[54] Some members of the Rainbow Circle, most notably Hobson, were out-and-out opponents of the war, and by extension of imperialism as a doctrine. Others, among them Samuel, declared themselves supporters of empire, and, while criticizing the Conservative Government's handling of the pre-war crisis, refrained from attacks on the war itself. The issue was bound up with the acute conflicts within the leadership of the Liberal Party following its electoral defeat in 1895, the resignation of Rosebery from the party leadership in 1896, and the death of Gladstone in 1898. 'What a disgusting condition of things in the party!' wrote Trevelyan to Samuel on his return from a world tour in December 1898.[55]

[51] Carrington to HS, 15 Apr. 1898, HLRO HS A/155/II/39.
[52] MacDonald to HS, 3 July 1897, HLRO HS A/10/6.
[53] See Bernard Porter, *Critics of Empire: British Radical Attitudes to Colonialism in Africa 1895–1914* (London, 1968), 165–6.
[54] Quoted in Clarke, *Liberals*, 68.   [55] Trevelyan to HS, 19 Dec. 1898, CPT 4.

The emergence of Sir Henry Campbell-Bannerman as party leader at the end of the year did not excite Samuel's enthusiasm. Rosebery's supporters, who now began to be called Liberal Imperialists, joined issue with the so-called 'pro-Boers', particularly after Campbell-Bannerman's famous 'methods of barbarism' speech of June 1901 in which he denounced British concentration camps in South Africa. Samuel sympathized with Asquith's public challenge shortly afterwards to Campbell-Bannerman's leadership. Asquith's aim was not party schism but assertion of the right to express imperialist views within the party, the better to prevent a secession.[56] But that was not how others saw it. Samuel was one of many who feared a descent into factionalism that might lead to the disintegration of the party. For that reason he declined to participate in a banquet in Asquith's honour convened in July 1901 by way of public demonstration of support. He explained his refusal in a letter to Charles Trevelyan:

I welcomed Asquith's speech of ten days ago—although not wholly agreeing with what he said—because it was necessary to make it clear that the Pro-Boers were not entitled to speak with the voice of the whole Liberal Party. That has now been sufficiently made clear. To go further and hold a banquet in recognition of the speech is an act of provocation against the other sections, and will drive in further the wedge which we should wish to remove at the earliest possible opportunity. There are hundreds of thousands of working-men who are opposed to the war. A split would have more serious results at the bottom of the party than at the top.[57]

Rosebery's supporters were later organized by Haldane into the Liberal League. Although Samuel did not join the League at its inception in early 1902, his position throughout this period remained close to that of Haldane and Asquith. Inevitably this harmed his standing with the opposing faction of the party.

Samuel's zest for empire had been outspoken since the outset of his political career. 'He was an imperialist', he told one of his constituency meetings in 1894. 'He was not a "Little Englander". He believed that the Liberal Party, headed by Lord Rosebery, had quite as great an interest in the empire as the other party, bluster about it as they might.'[58] In early 1897 he became a member of the council of the British Empire League. When the Boer War broke out he complained that it was 'lamentable and unnecessary'.[59] In a talk to the Rainbow Circle in May 1899 he maintained that 'the progressive party must not close its doors upon the man who believes in the high calling of this country amongst the nations & who,

---

[56] H. C. G. Matthew, *The Liberal Imperialists: The Ideas and Politics of a post-Gladstonian Élite* (Oxford, 1973), 64–5.
[57] HS to Trevelyan, 30 June 1901, HLRO HS A/14/2.
[58] *South Oxfordshire News and Thame and Watlington Herald*, 5 May 1894.
[59] HS to CS, 29 July 1898, HLRO HS A/156/145.

nevertheless, is not a Jingo. The party must, therefore, have a policy of rational patriotism.'[60] The following January he returned to the theme in a paper on 'Imperialism and Social Reform'. Denying that the two causes were in any way contradictory, he argued the Empire created the wealth that made domestic social reform possible while at the same time uplifting the indigenous populations in the colonies. But in discussion afterwards 'it was pointed out that Empire produced pride & contempt; materialised the Imperial people; increased the volume of trade without increasing the organisation of industry; that the test of the advantages of Empire was how far the subject populations were educated up; that further expansion ought to be avoided & the responsibilities of Empire studied.'[61]

The war was the foremost issue in the 'khaki' election of 1900 in which Samuel, in spite of blandishments from more promising seats, again contested South Oxfordshire. He set out his position explicitly in a speech at Henley in August 1900:

Once the war had begun, whatever be their view as to its inauguration, there should be no doubt that the end of it must be the annexation of the two [Boer] republics. To his mind it was a sad and regrettable thing that this should be the outcome of a war of this character, and that England, whose boast had always been that she was the guardian of freedom everywhere, the friend of national independence, should be the country to suppress the independence of two small republics. But however much they might regret the fact it was inevitable; there could be no peace if the Boer republics were to be re-established.[62]

During the previous five years Samuel had nursed the constituency assiduously, spending so much time calling on villagers that, as one local paper put it, he 'took upon himself the role of District Visitor'.[63] But the circumstances of the election were not auspicious for the Liberals nationally, and Samuel warned his mother not to expect him to win.[64] Continuing anxiety about the influence of Conservative landowners over the votes of agricultural labourers was indicated by Samuel's repeated stress on the secrecy of the ballot and his offer of £100 'to anyone who could prove that it was possible to find out how a man had voted at the ballot box'.[65]

The Conservatives fielded the sitting member, Hermon-Hodge, whose lack-lustre parliamentary record proved an inviting target for the barbs of the *South Oxfordshire Elector*, resuscitated by Samuel for the election. Even the Tories, leaping to Hermon-Hodge's defence, had to scrape the

[60] Minutes of meeting, 3 May 1899, BLPES Coll. Misc. 575/1.
[61] Minutes of meeting, 17 Jan. 1900, ibid.
[62] *Reading Standard*, 11 Aug. 1900.
[63] *Henley and South Oxfordshire Standard*, 12 Oct. 1900.
[64] HS to CS, 22 Sept. 1900, HLRO HS A/156/170.
[65] *Oxfordshire Telegraph*, 22 Sept. 1900.

barrel for proof of their candidate's worthiness. One Conservative orator uttered the strange boast that Hermon-Hodge 'had the biggest moustache he ever saw in his life' and declared, apparently in all seriousness, that 'he went so much to the House of Commons that he had even seen him sleep there'.[66] The leading local Conservative newspaper could say little more in favour of their candidate than that 'he is diligent in his attendances at the House and gives the Conservative whip no trouble'.[67] Samuel orchestrated a vigorous campaign in which he was assisted by speakers from the Eighty Club and local supporters, among them the writer Jerome K. Jerome.

The Conservatives responded to the onslaught by exploiting the issue of the war. Denouncing Samuel's 'slippery' views on the subject, Hermon-Hodge complained of his 'sneering at the members of the aristocracy who have gone to the front and perilled their health and lives to serve their country'. In an obvious reference to Samuel's Jewish origins he added that 'he did not know of what breed Mr Samuel was, but he did know that sneer was an unworthy one and a deliberate attempt to stir up the feeling of the working-men against the nobility of England, who deserved well at their hands'.[68] Samuel repulsed the attack, protesting against 'the attempt made by the Tory party to take the common patriotism which was the heritage of all English people and to use it for the purpose of party. . . . War was a curse and not a blessing.'[69] But in the emotional atmosphere of the time Samuel's middle position alienated some erstwhile supporters without winning new adherents. 'The war will probably defeat us', he wrote gloomily.[70]

On election day the family carriages were again mobilized to ferry voters to the polls. But the register was old, the day was wet and stormy, and the sixteen polling stations in the far-flung division were distant from many villagers' homes. Moreover, the Conservatives could count on four or five times as many carriages as the Liberals. As the polls closed Samuel wrote, 'It was sad to see the labourers being driven up in blue traps and waggons like calves to the market.'[71] The result, while creditable to Samuel, was predictable:

HERMON-HODGE Unionist)	3,622
SAMUEL (Liberal)	3,450
Majority	172

The Liberal *Reading Observer* comforted itself with the observation that 'illiterate voters' had been ' "got at" by the squire, the parson and the

---

[66] *Oxford Times*, 29 Sept. 1900.   [67] Ibid., 22 Sept. 1900.
[68] Ibid., 29 Sept. 1900.   [69] *Reading Observer*, 29 Sept. 1900.
[70] HS to BS, 29 Sept. 1900, HLRO HS A/157/61.
[71] HS to BS, 5 Oct. 1900, HLRO HS A/157/65.

farmer'.[72] Samuel was philosophical about this poor return on seven years of exhaustive campaigning in the constituency. But he decided that he had now done his duty by South Oxfordshire. A few weeks later he announced that he would look for a more promising seat. Meanwhile, as he awaited the opportunity to play an active part in the realization of the new liberalism, he set the final touches to its theoretical formulation in his first book, completed in the course of the following year.

Liberalism, published in February 1902, was Samuel's most ambitious work of political thought and the fullest expression of his ideological outlook. Historians have called the book 'the Koran of the advanced Liberals'.[73] Its historical significance is more than biographical for the book was one of the major statements to emerge from the coterie of young left-liberal thinkers in and around the Rainbow Circle. Nor was its importance limited to the realm of political theory for, as will be seen, it foreshadowed many of the social reforms enacted after 1905 by Liberal governments. As early as 1896, in a speech to the National Liberal Federation, Samuel had called on Liberals to restate their doctrine to show that 'they regarded as the main purpose and object of Liberalism in this day to carry out such wise legislative proposals as would enable the powers of the State to be used to improve the conditions of the masses of the population, to assist in raising the standards of living of the people'.[74] Having detected this lacuna, Samuel himself now sought to fill it.

The book's influence arose in part from its author's muting of his own voice, as he explained in the preface: 'My aim has not been to express my personal views as to the character of the reforms that are needed; but to state only those opinions ... held by the main body of Liberals.'[75] Hence the work's subtitle: *An Attempt to State the Principles and Proposals of Contemporary Liberalism in England*. Samuel's motives in adopting this self-denying ordinance were of a piece with his consistent reluctance throughout his political career to identify himself too closely with any group within the Liberal Party. While such a view might be regarded as to some extent self-serving (he was, after all, seeking a winnable parliamentary seat at this time), the genuineness of his horror of factionalism is not open to doubt—witness his refusal to join the Liberal League in spite of his sympathy with its aims and support for its leaders. In the hope that the book might win acceptance as a statement of the creed acceptable to all progressive Liberals, Samuel consciously dulled some of the sharp edges

---

[72] *Reading Observer*, 13 Oct. 1900.

[73] H. C. G. Matthew, R. I. McKibbin, and J. A. Kay, 'The Franchise Factor in the Rise of the Labour Party', *English Historical Review*, 91 (1976), 723–52.

[74] Speech to NLF annual meeting, Huddersfield, 25–8 Mar. 1896, quoted in Ellins, 'Aspects', 255.

[75] Herbert Samuel, *Liberalism* (London, 1902), pp. xv–xvi.

of his radicalism. As he explained to his mother, 'My own opinions appear throughout the book in many subordinate ways, but had I set out to draw up a programme for Liberalism on my own responsibility the book would have been of little value and would have had no sale.' His aim was to explain what Liberalism was, not what he himself thought it should be.[76]

This was one of the book's strengths. It also helps explain some of its limitations considered both as a work of political philosophy and as propaganda. *Liberalism*'s lack of a sense of passion, odd in a quasi-manifesto, no doubt derived in part from his desire to avoid intra-party controversy; also perhaps from a singularly unemotional temperament, for the style presaged the peculiar bloodlessness of much of Samuel's mature writing. Nor was *Liberalism* strikingly original. The attempt to formulate a generally acceptable doctrine inevitably militated against that. Samuel drew on the ideas of Wallas, Hobson, and the Webbs, and he owed much to the empirical investigations of Booth and Rowntree— debts he freely acknowledged. He would probably have accepted that the book belonged to what has been called the 'middle range of ideological activity', 'an intervening stage between the moulding of a socio-political *Weltanschauung* . . . and the drawing-up of detailed suggestions for legislative and administrative measures'.[77] Yet in spite of, and to a great extent because of, its author's self-effacement, *Liberalism* found broad acceptance as an articulation and justification of the programme of advanced Liberals at a crucial moment in the history of the party.

Liberalism was, in fact, a broadly conceived, well-researched, and ably argued tract for the times. The opening chapter, 'The Root of Liberalism', demonstrated how far the centre of gravity of the Liberal idea had travelled since the era of Mill. Boldly attempting a single-sentence definition of Liberalism, Samuel did so in terms that might have brought a shudder to the ghost of his former hero, Gladstone: 'That it is the duty of the State to secure to all its members, and all others whom it can influence, the fullest possible opportunity to lead the best life.'[78] After a cursory discussion of basic political theory, the main body of the book was divided into three parts, the first, entitled 'State Action', reflecting the emphasis Samuel, in company with his fellow 'new liberals', placed on an enhanced interventionist role for government in social reform. While there is some ground for the criticism that Samuel failed to offer theoretical guidelines as to how the role of the state was to be delimited, the general tendency of the book was clear in its espousal of a greatly expanded state

[76] HS to CS, 12 Jan. 1902, HLRO HS A/156/190.
[77] Freeden, *New Liberalism*, 117.
[78] Samuel, *Liberalism*, 4.

responsibility.[79] This responsibility, according to Samuel, again voicing a characteristic 'new liberal' concept, found its source in the social ethic according to which the state was 'the agent of the community'.[80]

The greater part of the book, however, dealt less with first principles than with practical proposals for legislation. Some of these involved old Liberal shibboleths such as free trade, religious disestablishment, education, and temperance. The last two themes were viewed less through the old Nonconformist prism than through the concept of 'national efficiency' fashioned by the Webbs and popular among the liberal imperialists. Unable to jettison the abiding Liberal preoccupation with land questions, Samuel, by now an acknowledged authority on the subject, enlarged on his earlier arguments without surmounting their limitations. Discussing the problem of rural depopulation, he noted: 'The English nation is becoming more and more a people of dwellers in cities. And this change is widely recognized to be full of danger to the national future.' His answer to this alleged threat remained little changed: 'reformers fix their chief hopes in a gradual growth in the system of small holdings.'[81] And as before, the problems of rural and urban distress met in the proposal for the establishment by the state of 'farm colonies' that might temporarily absorb some of the industrial unemployed.

In his consideration of unemployment Samuel revealed some of the unresolved contradictions in his social philosophy, echoing a basic conflict among social reformers. Opposing complete abolition of the Poor Law, Samuel opened on a moralistic note: people who refused to work, he argued, should be regarded as 'deserters from the ranks of the industrial army' who deserved 'punishment that is suited to their case'. This was akin to the approach based on distinction between 'deserving' and 'undeserving' poor drawn by the Charity Organization Society, whose secretary, C. S. Loch, portrayed the unemployed as an insatiable, relief-consuming giant sea anemone that could not survive in the 'thin smooth unsalted water' of social independence.[82] On the other hand, a little later in his discussion, Samuel leant more towards the newer view that unemployment had nothing to do with morality: 'the theory that the unemployed are the unemployable, bad characters and bad workmen whom no master will engage' was demonstrably false, he asserted, pointing out that the alleged unemployables at the bottom of the economic cycle turned out to be eminently employable when good times returned.[83]

---

[79] Freeden, New Liberalism, 65.   [80] Samuel, Liberalism, 23.   [81] Ibid. 103.
[82] Loch's diary for 13 Sept. 1888, quoted in Harris, Unemployment, 105.
[83] Samuel, Liberalism, 121, 125. For a discussion of the two views see A. M. McBriar, An Edwardian Mixed Doubles: The Bosanquets versus the Webbs: A Study in British Social Policy 1890–1929 (Oxford, 1987). See also Harris, Unemployment, esp. 42–3.

In response to this central problem of industrial capitalism Samuel had little to offer. Charity, he insisted, was not the answer since it was 'universally held, and soundly held, to be degrading to able-bodied men'. The Poor Law might cope with the unemployables but not with those whose distress arose from chronic economic causes. 'To offer the workhouse is to offer to men of good character a system which has been elaborately framed for the punishment of the idle and the vicious.'[84] National insurance against unemployment, which was to enter the Liberals' legislative programme in dramatic fashion only eight years later, Samuel relegated to a footnote. Such schemes had been tried in Germany and Switzerland, he noted, but they did 'not seem to be very successful'. He put forward the standard objection that workers' contributions would impose an intolerable burden on the poor. 'Besides,' he added, 'the deserving and the undeserving must be equally helped, and a share of the State subsidy goes to the man whose dismissal was due to idleness or incompetence as well as to the man who has been displaced by movements of trade.'[85]

Samuel proposed four partial solutions: state-run 'farm colonies', state-employment in forestry works, public improvements under the aegis of local authorities, and labour registries (exchanges). But these amounted to little more than palliatives, and Samuel was bound to admit that none of these formed 'part of the adopted programme of the Liberal party'.[86] Since unemployment, in his view, was generally a temporary phenomenon, save in the case of chronic work-shirkers or unemployables, 'the unemployed need work of only a temporary kind, to enable them to tide over the time until they can be again absorbed into the trade to which they belong'.[87] Samuel had been exposed to the 'under-consumptionist' theory through the Rainbow Circle, and had read Hobson's *The Evolution of Modern Capitalism* (1894) and *The Problem of the Unemployed* (1896) shortly after publication, but if he had absorbed them he had not accepted their fundamental propositions. Samuel's proposals for limited public works included no hint of the idea that these might be a demand-expanding economic good in themselves, although in his general proposals for government finance he maintained that taxation for expenditure on social reform 'should not be regarded as an evil' but as productive investment.[88] This, however, seems to have been more a rhetorical than a genuinely economic argument.

The next part of the book, 'The Constitution', tackled more traditional liberal concerns from a moderately radical position. Calling for universal and equal manhood suffrage, Samuel excepted not only peers, aliens,

---

[84] Samuel, *Liberalism*, 126.   [85] Ibid. 127.
[86] Ibid. 135.   [87] Ibid. 128.   [88] Ibid. 180–1.

and convicts but also 'paupers who receive regular or frequent relief'. He devoted special attention to the arguments in favour of payment of Members of Parliament, in particular the desirability of increasing working-class representation. He urged the abolition of plural voting, including university seats—a standard radical bogey since they increased the voting strength of the propertied classes. He advocated reduction of the length of Parliaments to four or five years, redistribution to create equal electoral districts, abolition of the hereditary and ecclesiastical elements in the House of Lords, and limitation of the powers of the second chamber. Most of this had been the stuff of conventional radicalism since at least the time of the Chartists. On two constitutional issues, however, Samuel trod cautiously.

The first was Ireland on which a fissure had developed in 1901 between Rosebery, who had moved close to Unionism, and the proponents of Home Rule. Samuel had long been a passionate upholder of Irish self-government and he had kept up his early connection with John Dillon. While he shared the view that a Liberal government's entire programme should not be held hostage to the Home Rule issue (all Liberals in this period were haunted by the memory of the travails of Gladstone's last two administrations), Samuel had not wavered in his view of the objective: 'The more I think about the Irish problem,' he wrote to his mother in March 1901, 'the more convinced I am that Home Rule is necessary and inevitable.'[89] Nevertheless, in *Liberalism* he tamed his enthusiasm in order to present a view that might find general acceptance among Liberals. Avoiding the phrase 'Home Rule' as if it were a taboo, he remarked that 'a party is not necessarily tied to the details of former proposals' and talked vaguely of 'the broad policy of Irish local self-government'.[90] Samuel's approach, similar to the 'step-by-step' policy of Asquith, Grey, and Haldane, was designed less to clarify the party position than to fudge the issues of timing and extent of any Irish devolutionary measure.

Samuel lodged himself even more firmly on the fence on the issue of women's suffrage. His personal view, not revealed clearly in the book, was unsympathetic to women's suffrage, although he did not object to women being elected Members of Parliament. He had argued on the subject both with members of the Rainbow Circle and with Hilda Runciman, wife of his friend Walter Runciman and herself a future Liberal MP.[91] Samuel rejected women's suffrage less as a matter of

[89] HS to CS, 17 Mar. 1901, HLRO HS A/156/180.
[90] Samuel, *Liberalism*, 293.
[91] Rainbow Circle minutes, 7 Oct. 1896, BLPES Coll. Misc. 575/1; HS to BS, 29 Mar. 1901, HLRO HS A/157/68.

principle than as one of political tactics. Later, as an MP, his policy was
not to vote either way on suffragist resolutions. Privately he argued that
there was no evidence that women's suffrage would strengthen the Liberal
cause, pointing out that there were more women members of the Primrose
League than of Women's Liberal Associations. He denied the existence of
an absolute right to vote, citing minors and native races in the colonies as
examples of other groups that were unenfranchised.[92] He did not exclude
the possibility of female suffrage altogether, approving it at the local
government level, and arguing only that the Liberal Party should not
introduce it at the parliamentary level until the existing electorate was
clearly in favour of such a change.[93] This was a common, although not
universal, approach to the problem among radical Liberals until much
later. In *Liberalism* he simply laid out the arguments for and against,
concluding that, as the Liberal Party was divided on the issue, women's
suffrage could 'neither be denied discussion in its counsels nor find a place
in its immediate programme'.[94]

The difficulty of expounding with clarity the programme of a party that
was disunited on so many issues was most obvious in the final section of
the book, devoted to imperial and foreign policy. Here Samuel was again
reduced to presenting alternatives. One chapter was devoted to 'disadvantages of empire', another, obviously written with greater inner
conviction, to its advantages. A further chapter then attempted to marry
the two views by developing a 'middle position', allegedly held by 'the
main body of Liberals', that avoided the Scylla of jingoism and the
Charybdis of Little Englandism. This afforded Samuel the opportunity to
set out his own imperial views in detail. He laid stress on the civilizing role
of empire, on the duties and obligations of colonizers towards colonized,
proposing a policy of imperial federation in the white colonies, and native
protection and reform in the others. He did not oppose further imperial
acquisitions, arguing only against 'constant and indiscriminate expansion'.
As for the burning imperial controversy of the moment, South Africa,
Samuel was virtually silent. But he apparently felt compelled to address
the issue somehow. He therefore appended a note admitting the 'profound . . . division' among Liberals over the war, then suggesting 'that the

[92] HS to BS, 9 Nov. 1901, HLRO HS A/157/82. See also Brian Harrison, *Separate
Spheres: The Opposition to Women's Suffrage in Britain* (New York, 1978), 47.
[93] From 1902 onwards Samuel was a subscriber to the Women's Local Government
Society which defined its object as 'promoting the eligibility of women to elect to and serve
on all Local Governing Bodies'. Some women had acquired the vote in municipal elections
in 1869, but their right to serve on local government bodies was not fully established in law
until 1907. See Women's Local Government Society *Annual Reports*, 1902–12; see also
Martin Pugh, *Women's Suffrage in Great Britain* (London, 1980), 13; and Harrison,
Separate Spheres, 134.
[94] Samuel, *Liberalism*, 253.

division was not on questions of principle but on questions of fact'. He concluded that a party that was neither composed of jingoists nor of Little Englanders 'would inevitably be divided in conscientious opinion; for the points of fact were complicated and uncertain . . .'.[95] Here Samuel's consensual approach collapsed into patent absurdity and he might have done better simply to present his own moderately imperialist position on the war. But with the war drawing to a close there was little point, particularly given Samuel's overall aim, in fanning the flame of controversy. Platitude in this case doubtless seemed the better part of political valour.

In spite of its defects *Liberalism* was a considerable achievement as a work of synthesis and exposition. Remarkably, in spite of Samuel's elaborate disclaimers at the outset, it also serves as an invaluable vademecum to Samuel's fundamental political ideas, which changed little over the remainder of his long political career. His affirmation of the responsibility of the state, conceived as an organic community, to care for children might have been uttered in the same form at the time of his Children Act of 1908. The marriage of imperialism and social reform lay at the back of his later thinking on Zionism. His stout defence of free trade found its echo in his speeches during the crisis of 1931–2. His rejection of socialist policies of nationalization was recapitulated in similar terms into the 1950s.

A similar continuity emerges in his puritanical attitude to certain moral issues. One historian notes that Samuel was 'curiously insensible to the problems of the idle, drunk, and incapable for whom moral opprobrium was still predominant', though the same critic acknowledges that Samuel 'realized that low surroundings bred low character'.[96] All this was part of the received wisdom of the period, but in Samuel's case it went a little further. Charles Trevelyan, who saw eye to eye with most of Samuel's exposition of Liberal doctrine, took issue with his declaration that 'the publication of books and pictures, and the performance of plays which incite to sexual immorality are properly forbidden'.[97] Trevelyan drew Samuel's attention to Shaw's critique of the Lord Chamberlain's powers of theatrical censorship.[98] Samuel himself was to engage Shaw directly on this issue a few years later. But even a bout of Shavian intellectual pugilistics did not change Samuel's settled opinion on the subject. Although an exponent of freedom of thought and expression in most spheres, he remained conservative in sexual matters. One of his last major speeches, half a century later, was a stirring denunciation of homosexuality. In all these ways *Liberalism* unlocks the door to a personal credo that remained virtually static until the end of Samuel's life.

[95] Ibid. 327–45.
[96] Freeden, *New Liberalism*, 173.
[97] Samuel, *Liberalism*, 208.
[98] Trevelyan to HS, 27 Dec. 1902, CPT 4.

Judged in its political rather than its biographical context the book was more significant than influential. Its success as a work of prophecy may be gauged from the extent to which it prefigured the legislative programme of the Liberal governments after 1906. Here Samuel's method may be said retrospectively to have served him well. With the end of hostilities in South Africa the moment was ripe for the Liberal Party to put aside its differences and unite round a programme of social reform, such as that formulated by Samuel, on which Campbell-Bannerman and Asquith, Lloyd George and Haldane could all, by and large, agree. His book thus appeared at a happy moment. It helped thrust to the forefront of Liberal aims the enactment of such measures as old age pensions, workmen's compensation, licensing reform, labour exchanges, and a more steeply graduated income tax, all of which were introduced into Parliament by the Liberal governments in which Samuel served. Asquith's readiness to write an introduction enhanced the book's standing. Yet by the end of the year it had sold only 1,183 copies and its total sale was only 2,250. Even in a period when the political class remained small this was not impressive.

The influence of the book was broader than might be indicated by these figures. It received wide and generally favourable reviews. The *Manchester Guardian* praised Samuel's 'moderate and judicious' tone and his 'restrained and cautious' conclusions, adding that 'if not a profound thinker, neither is he ever superficial'.[99] Other Liberal papers such as the *Westminster Gazette* and the *Daily Chronicle* echoed these judgements, although the *New Liberal Review* complained: 'For a modern Liberal he is curiously liberal-minded. So large is his tolerance that it would not be easy to discover from his book to which of the conflicting schools of Liberal thought he belongs.'[100] Conservative reactions were more captious. The *Glasgow Herald* affirmed that the book 'fails to prove that Liberalism is a living force now or has a future as Conservatism on the one hand and Socialism on the other have futures'.[101] And the *Scotsman* asserted: 'It will be found by a perusal of Mr Samuel's book that the whole system of Liberalism he expounds is permeated and vitiated by the principle of State compulsion.'[102] On the other hand the *Daily Express* published a favourable review, as did the *Daily Telegraph* which pronounced the book a 'painstaking and well-ordered exposition' and concluded that 'in the main, the most Conservative reader will admit that the author has done his best to lay the pros and cons impartially before him'.[103]

A little surprisingly, the most telling criticisms of the book came from the left. Sidney Webb, apparently put out by Samuel's concessions to

[99] *Manchester Guardian*, 27 Feb. 1902.
[100] *New Liberal Review*, May 1902.
[101] *Glasgow Herald*, 24 Feb. 1902.
[102] *Scotsman*, 24 Feb. 1902.
[103] *Daily Telegraph*, 25 Feb. 1902.

consensus, sent him a letter that began with conventional compliments but continued:

Now for the criticism; of course, my main one is that you are weak and vague in the *connection* between your fundamental principle of liberalism and some of your particular projects—you need more accepted 'axiomata media'. Thus, without such, Factory Acts & Housing Acts are apt to be *merely* empirical.

The sort of middle axioms you need, I think, are such as to raise compulsorily the Standard of Life, to Enforce a National Minimum on each important point, Collective Regulation of all matters of common concern, and so on. These are the instruments by which your fundamental principle can be applied—the lathes in which particular reforms are but the cutting tools to be changed from time to time as the task requires.[104]

Although couched in friendly terms the letter cannot have pleased Samuel. At least this was a private communication. Other critics were less cordial and more public.

In one of the few signed reviews, H. W. Massingham, writing in the *Speaker*, fiercely attacked Samuel's imperialism and labelled him an 'opportunist' for his apparent lack of commitment on many issues.[105] Further criticism of Samuel's imperialist views was voiced in the *Daily News* and in a review in the *New Age* by J. M. Robertson, a fellow-member of the Rainbow Circle.[106] The most hostile review of all appeared in the socialist *Labour Leader*, again attacking Samuel's imperialism. This provoked Samuel to make the common mistake of responding to a negative review. He wrote a letter to the editor pointing out that his argument had not been that the material advantages of empire to Britain outweighed harm done to natives, but rather that empire brought with it boons to 'the coloured peoples'. The reviewer returned to the charge in the next issue, anathematizing the book as 'an irritating product' and making the obvious rejoinder: 'His defence of imperialism, in which he makes England the sole judge of what is or is not good for other nations who are supposed to be weak, is of the most blatant and irresponsible kind.'[107] In this riposte the reviewer ripped off the mask of anonymity and signed himself 'Keir'—thus personalizing and heightening the difference between Hardie and Samuel that dated back to their exchange over the issue of independent labour representation in the *Progressive Review* in 1896. On that occasion, Samuel had had the last word in a journal that he controlled. No doubt Hardie relished the opportunity to

[104] Webb to HS, 20 Mar. 1902, HLRO HS A/15/3; see also H. V. Emy, *Liberals, Radicals and Social Politics 1892–1914* (Cambridge, 1973), 129–30.
[105] *Speaker*, 15 Mar. 1902.
[106] *Daily News*, 28 Feb. 1902; *New Age*, 20 Mar. 1902.
[107] *Labour Leader*, 28 May, 5 June, 26 July 1902.

repay Samuel in kind. For Samuel, who saw himself as an exponent of Lib–Lab co-operation in a progressive movement, this must have been a stinging attack. But events soon conspired to enable Samuel to avenge this literary snub in a different arena.

3

Darkest England and Darkest Africa

===

When we learn to say that Britons never will be masters we shall make an end of slavery.

(George Bernard Shaw)

IN THE summer of 1897 Samuel's life, hitherto filled with political activity, speaking engagements, work on his book, and socializing either with the Webbs and their entourage or with members of the Anglo-Jewish 'cousinhood', took on a new aspect when he became engaged to his first cousin Beatrice Franklin. His previous interest in women seems to have been slight. As a teenager he had carried on an affectionate correspondence with one of his cousins in Liverpool, but this terminated when he went to America in 1888. At Oxford his sole contacts with women consisted of occasional visits from other cousins and from the two unmarried daughters of the Chief Rabbi, Dr Hermann Adler. At one stage Samuel seems to have been interested in Henrietta, the elder of the rabbi's daughters. She shared Samuel's enthusiasm for social reform and her activity as a social worker in the East End and a lobbyist for reformist legislation earned her the approval of Beatrice Webb—though whether that inveterate matchmaker commended her also as a suitable bride is not recorded. Samuel's mother seems to have been an active promoter of this scheme for he wrote to her in February 1896 to announce that he was 'dining at Dr Adler's—with an open mind'.[1] A few days later, however, he reported: 'You probably have such family news as there may be from the daughters-in-law, and you know that I am not able to contribute to that column.'[2]

Samuel's eventual fiancée, Beatrice Franklin, was the daughter of Samuel Montagu's banking partner Ellis Franklin and of Montagu's sister Adelaide. Seven months younger than Herbert Samuel, she had known her cousin all her life: the two had been childhood playmates. The Franklins, like the Samuels, regarded themselves as ornaments of the Anglo-Jewish patriciate. They too were amateur genealogists and indeed

[1] HS to CS, 10 Feb. 1896, HLRO HS A/156/98.
[2] HS to CS, 13 Feb. 1896, HLRO HS A/156/99.

claimed illustrious ancestry. Family records traced their ancestry back to the distinguished Chief Rabbi of Prague, Judah Löw ben Bezalel (*c.*1520–1609), alleged creator of the *Golem* (a robot-like clay monster). Löw himself claimed descent from Hai Gaon (died 1038), head of the celebrated Talmudic academy of Pumbedita in Babylonia. Since the Gaon was reputedly of the Davidic line, the Franklin pedigree might bear comparison with that of the oldest Anglo-Norman families and they might even claim royal lineage.[3] A tall young woman, handsome rather than beautiful, Beatrice was intelligent but not an intellectual, strongminded and wilful. In religious practice she was conventionally orthodox.

Samuel proposed to his cousin in August 1897 while they were both guests at their uncle Montagu's country residence. She seems to have accepted quickly, but the match encountered some family opposition. This may have arisen from concern about the dangers of inbreeding—a real problem since the 'cousinhood' lived up to its name in this respect. Another difficulty may have arisen from strained personal relations between Herbert Samuel and the Franklins. In a letter to his mother in 1894 he had complained, 'The Franklins have been very attentive—too much so in fact, for I find it difficult to refuse Aunt Adelaide's numerous invitations—and Uncle Ellis's conversation is not edifying.'[4] Perhaps the difference was political since Ellis Franklin appears to have been a Liberal Unionist. The matter of religion too may have given rise to anxiety on the part of the Franklins who were anxious that their daughter should marry in a synagogue, should keep a kosher home, and should continue all the traditional observances.

In the event, family opposition soon dissipated. Clara Samuel, who had initially evinced great distress at the proposed match, eventually gave her blessing. The wedding took place in the New West End Synagogue on 18 November 1897—the date coincided with the anniversary of the wedding in 1819 of their common grandparents, Louis and Henrietta Samuel.[5] Samuel's former teacher the Revd Simeon Singer officiated, and Charles Trevelyan acted as best man. It was a grand affair, and there were 314 gifts, among them eighty books. Immediately after the ceremony the newly-weds set off for a honeymoon in Italy. The marriage was overall a happy one, although an early difference over religious matters momentarily clouded the relationship. Shortly after their return from Italy, Beatrice seems to have raised the issue with her mother who urged her to 'go hand in hand' with her husband, complying with his wishes. But she added:

---

[3] See Franklin, *Records*, 1–3.
[4] HS to CS, 29 Sept. 1894, HLRO HS A/156/82.
[5] See HS to ES, 6 Feb. 1941, ISA 100/65A.

To you my dear son Herbert, I will also take upon myself to say a few words of advice. Your upbringing has unfortunately been faulty, you are a man of rare intelligence & laws without reason cannot appeal to you. You have been goaded to declare that you would not enter a synagogue, well circumstances compelled you to go twice, & you have entered a new life with the prospect of grave responsibilities, therefore my dear boy, brave everything, I do not suggest belief, but occasionally accompany your good wife, as you would to any other building. She I am sure will not urge it—but I can see perhaps further than you can, & it will be easier now, that you have passed the threshold, than later. . . . You will, I am sure, forgive me if I have said too much, but this is unstudied & just as my heart dictates.[6]

The letter seems to have achieved its intended effect. Although he accompanied his wife to services only rarely, Samuel remained a member of the New West End Synagogue. He followed the practice for the rest of his life of doing no work on the sabbath, instead devoting it to reading, recreation, and family pursuits. His wife, who remained more punctilious on such points, refused to write or travel on the sabbath or holy days.

Upon their return from the honeymoon the couple settled temporarily at the Franklins' family home at 35 Porchester Terrace while Samuel's parents-in-law discreetly withdrew for a holiday in Cannes. In August 1898 they moved into a leasehold house at 88 Gloucester Terrace which was to be their home for the next decade. At the same time Clara Samuel decided to give up the house in Kensington Palace Gardens which was now too large for her. For the remainder of her life she lived in an apartment, furnished in satinwood, at the nearby Royal Palace Hotel, generally spending the winter season in the south of France. Until her death in 1920 she remained an uncompromisingly old-fashioned figure, wearing a cap with lace on top, and a tight-fitting bodice with jet down the front.[7] Still faithful to her Conservative convictions, she nevertheless took a keen maternal interest and pride in the political careers of Herbert and of Stuart, who succeeded Sir Samuel Montagu as MP for Whitechapel at the general election of 1900.

Beatrice Samuel brought a large income of her own into the marriage, derived like her husband's from the profits of the family bank. As a result, Samuel's already comfortable income more than doubled. In spite of the increased expenses of married life, therefore, he remained financially independent and under no compulsion to earn a living. In the period before payment of MPs this was of critical importance to his continued resolve to seek a seat in Parliament.

---

[6] Adelaide Franklin to BS, 27 Jan. 1898, HLRO HS B/6/39.
[7] Conversation of the author with Lady (Vera) Cohen, daughter of Sir Stuart Samuel, granddaughter of Clara Samuel, 22 June 1984.

Beatrice was a moderate suffragist but she took little active part in politics. In the early years of the marriage much of her time was devoted to child-bearing and rearing. Their first son, Edwin, was born in September 1898, and four other children followed in rapid succession.[8] After Edwin's birth Beatrice sometimes accompanied her husband to South Oxfordshire, but she was unable to participate in his election campaign in 1900 as she was in an advanced stage of her second pregnancy.

In some ways the tastes of the couple were different. Beatrice did not share her husband's liking for vigorous exercise. A lifelong hypochondriac, she preferred to take quiet rests in the country while her husband set off alone on cycling tours fully equipped with cycling suit, cap, canvas shirt, and special stockings and shoes. Socially too they tended to lead separate lives. Samuel spent a great deal of time away from home on political speaking trips; apart from visits to his constituency, his wife seldom accompanied him. During the early years of his marriage he continued to attend the Rainbow Circle assiduously as well as meetings of Liberal bodies such as the Eighty Club. Beatrice's social circle was circumscribed by the restricted world of the Anglo-Jewish upper crust. Her closest friend was Lucy Gaster, wife of Moses Gaster, the *Haham* (Chief Rabbi) of the Sephardic community. Samuel and Gaster were on cordial terms and discussed Zionism, of which Gaster was an early supporter, at their occasional meetings; but otherwise they had little in common. Samuel often entertained political acquaintances to lunch or dinner at the National Liberal Club or the Reform Club. Sometimes there were small dinner parties at home for political acquaintances. But Samuel seems to have been more comfortable entertaining male colleagues to dinner at a private hotel in St James's. Even on these occasions, it seems, he found it difficult to unbutton. At a dinner at the House of Commons in May 1904 to discuss agricultural policy his guests found in their places a printed card:

Menu
of suggested subjects of conversation
Potage
Compensation for Tenants' Improvements
Freedom of Cultivation

Poisson
Desirability of Rent Courts

[8] Edwin, 2nd Viscount Samuel (1898–1978), a civil servant in Palestine from 1921 to 1948; Philip (born 1900), interned in Hong Kong during the Second World War; Godfrey (1904–82), an architect, served as secretary of the Royal Fine Art Commission from 1948 to 1969; Nancy (born 1906), married Dr Arthur Salaman; another daughter, born in Aug. 1902, died after one day.

Entrée
Free Trade in Land

Rôtis
Desirability of an English Land Purchase Act

Volaille
Small Holdings

Entremets
Building and Sanitation of Cottages

Dessert
Railway Rates
Agricultural Co-operation[9]

Was this a joke? His guests probably could not be quite sure. With the exception of Sidney and Beatrice Webb there can have been few among his acquaintances who would relish such a table d'hôte. But the Webbs were not present. The guests included Edwin Montagu and Philip Morrell (a contemporary of Samuel at Balliol and Samuel's successor as Liberal candidate for South Oxfordshire, which he won at the 1906 election), and five other young Liberal politicians, two of them Balliol men. Samuel recorded that they kept to the allotted subjects throughout the dinner and at the end drew up a manifesto to be presented to Campbell-Bannerman and Lord Spencer.[10]

A glimpse of Samuel's daily life at this period is provided by his diary for 1904—the only period, apart from some overseas journeys, during which he kept such a record.[11] For the most part the journal is a bare enumeration of activities with next to nothing in the way of introspection or general reflections. It shows Samuel playing tennis at the Montagus, dining frequently with his mother, reading aloud to his wife, playing backgammon and verbal parlour games, dining frequently with friends such as Charles Trevelyan and Russell Rea, mixing socially with the Montagus, the Montefiores, and Rufus Isaacs, and above all reading and working systematically on politics or on such bodies as the committee of the London School of Economics. In spite of Samuel's sympathy with the Liberal Imperialists, he and his wife did not gain entrée into the upper reaches of Liberal society inhabited by such figures as Asquith and his second wife Margot Tennant. Unlike Samuel's cousin Edwin they were rarely to be found at country-house weekends—unless at Sir Samuel Montagu's rural retreat of Swaythling. Or perhaps it would be more correct to say that Samuel, unlike his cousin, did not particularly care to

[9] Menu card dated 16 May 1904, HLRO HS A/155/III.
[10] HS diary entry, 16 May 1904, HLRO HS A/22.
[11] HS diary for 1904, ibid.

belong to the country-house world. He preferred earnest conversation to small talk, committee meetings to dinner parties—ideally, as we have seen, dinner parties would be transformed into committee meetings. This was largely a bachelor's world that he preserved in aspic for several years after his marriage.

Samuel's social relationships nevertheless gradually changed in character, in part as a result of the loosening of his radical connections around the turn of the century. He slowly drifted away from the Webbs, at whose court he had hitherto paid frequent homage. The turning-point seems to have come immediately after Samuel's marriage. In early 1898 the Webbs set off on a round-the-world tour accompanied by Charles Trevelyan. Samuel too had originally contemplated the trip but abandoned the idea after his engagement. When the Webbs returned a year later their relations with Samuel, while still friendly, somehow lost their former easy intimacy. They still met from time to time but the carefree atmosphere of jolly holidays at Beachy Head now receded into memory. In after years Beatrice Webb would complain and wonder how they had lost touch with their 'old comrades'.[12] But in the case of Samuel the fault was probably more the Webbs'. Sidney's criticism of Samuel's book cannot have helped—though Samuel was not one to take such comments amiss. Beatrice Webb, indeed, acknowledged years later that Samuel 'had the valuable quality of being able to differ from people without disliking them'.[13] But the incident was symptomatic of an imbalance in the relationship. Samuel always admired and respected the Webbs; whereas Sidney, as Beatrice Webb confided to her diary shortly before her death, had 'rather a contempt for him'.[14]

Neither Webb's critical letter nor the other reactions to *Liberalism* reached Samuel immediately, for shortly before the book appeared he had taken the sudden and surprising decision to pay a lengthy visit to Uganda. He had not hitherto betrayed special interest in the affairs of the dark continent and his motives for this expedition remain obscure. Possibly he wanted to equip himself better to deal with the objections that his espousal of imperialism had aroused.[15] The explanation he gave his family was that after his political and literary exertions of the previous six years he felt out of sorts and in need of a long sea voyage. In a letter to his mother he added, 'I should like, if possible, to go somewhere where

[12] Entry dated 2 May [1904], BLPES Beatrice Webb diary, typed transcript, 2290.

[13] Note by Frank Singleton, 6 Feb. 1939, of talk with the Webbs about Samuel, HLRO HS A/161.

[14] Entry dated 5 Mar. 1943, BLPES Beatrice Webb diary, 7487–9.

[15] There is no evidence of interest by Samuel, prior to his journey, in the scheme for Jewish settlement in East Africa that was advanced a year later by Joseph Chamberlain: see below, p. 203.

one could get knowledge that would be useful politically and perhaps journalistically.'[16] Samuel's father-in-law was aghast when he heard of Samuel's plans and wrote to express his 'unspeakable distress of mind'. Urging him to reconsider, Ellis Franklin reminded him of his duties at home: 'Is it not universally understood that when a man chooses a wife, a life's companion, he is supposed to settle down and devote himself to watching over his home ties? I'm sure no one would call you selfish, yet is it not thinking of your own whim or caprice regardless of those you leave behind—the choice of such an outlandish country to spend your time in—to gather information that can be obtained by books of travel such as abound?'[17] Samuel, however, persisted, writing to his mother that 'the problems of that region are certain to play a large part in future Imperial politics, and it is essential for me to be known not only as a social reform politician but also as one who has some first-hand knowledge of some, at all events, of the chief questions of Imperial statesmanship'.[18] His family soon relented, and, the decision taken, Samuel wasted no further time. He left England on 20 February 1902, a few days before the publication of his book, and remained abroad for nearly three months.

Although it had been under British protection only since 1894, Uganda at the time of Samuel's visit was not quite as 'outlandish' as Ellis Franklin imagined. The country had just been opened to easy access by the Uganda railway, begun in 1896, which ran 584 miles across the neighbouring British East Africa Protectorate from the port of Mombasa via Nairobi to Port Florence (Kisumu) on the eastern shore of Lake Victoria Nyanza. Samuel travelled along the railway marvelling at 'the antithesis between civilization and barbarism'.[19] The East African landscape made a deep impression on him. Half a century later he recalled:

The train stopped for some hours at a spot in the midst of a vast plain, then totally uninhabited. I was travelling by myself and went for a walk for a few miles away from the railway, and over a hill. The whole country was treeless and apparently featureless, except for a faint glimpse of Mount Kilimanjaro on the far horizon. I have never forgotten the feeling of desolation.[20]

Samuel crossed the Victoria Nyanza to Entebbe aboard the recently launched steamship *Sir William McKinnon*. He then traversed the eighteen miles to Kampala on muleback, accompanied by a servant, a cook, and seven porters. In Kampala he visited the Kabaka of Buganda, Daudi Chwa, and presented the boy-king, aged 5, with a toy steamer. He

[16] HS to CS, 10 Feb. 1902, HLRO HS A/156/193.
[17] Ellis Franklin to HS, 10 Feb. 1902, HLRO HS B/6/68.
[18] HS to CS, 11 Feb. 1902, HLRO HS A/156/194.
[19] Samuel's Uganda diary, 13 Mar. 1902, HLRO HS A/16.
[20] Herbert Samuel, 'Some Walks I Remember', *The Countryman*, 39/1 (Spring 1949).

struck up an unconventional friendship with the Katikiro (Regent) of Buganda, Apolo Kagwa, who subsequently visited him in England. The two conducted a quaint correspondence for several years.[21] From Kampala he continued by mule and canoe, rowed by twenty-two singing oarsmen, to Jinja at the source of the White Nile. After camping on an uninhabited island in Lake Victoria he returned by rail to Mombasa and from there via Suez to England.

While his six-week stay in East Africa hardly qualified him as an expert, he took the opportunity to question senior British administrators about the political and social problems of the region, and he continued to read widely on Africa after his return to England. In November 1902 the *Westminster Gazette* published five articles by Samuel, entitled 'A Tourist in Uganda', in which he discussed prospects for European colonization and maintained: 'If the annexation of Uganda results in nothing more than the elevation of the morals and the development of the intelligence of its remarkable people through the work of the missions and in their greater security and material comfort through the watchful care of British administrators, the English people would be well repaid for the lives and the money they have spent in this region.'[22] Later Samuel delivered several public lectures on Uganda including one at the Society of Arts in which he discussed possibilities for European and Indian settlement in East Africa. The meeting was attended by his precursors in that region, Sir H. M. Stanley and Sir Harry Johnston, both of whom commented approvingly on his speech.[23] Though of little importance in itself, Samuel's Ugandan expedition helped equip him for the leading role he was to play in two major African controversies within the next three years.

Back in England and reinvigorated by his journey, Samuel set about the task of looking for a safe Liberal seat in Parliament. After his defeat in South Oxfordshire in 1900 he had refused a safe seat on the London County Council on the ground that this would divert him from the parliamentary road.[24] He had been approached by several constituencies, but most were unappealing prospects. He turned down an invitation to be a sacrificial lamb for the Liberals in Oxford City which had returned a Tory in the previous eight elections.[25] York, where the Liberal Rowntree

[21] Samuel's Uganda Diary, HLRO HS A/16; Ham Mukasa, *Uganda's Katikiro in England* (London, 1904).

[22] *Westminster Gazette*, 4 Dec. 1902; the other articles appeared on 11, 14, 20, and 24 Nov.

[23] Report of meeting on 3 Mar. 1903, *Journal of the Society of Arts*, 20 Mar. 1903, 390–400.

[24] HS to CS, 2 Feb. 1901, HLRO HS A/156/175.

[25] Exchange of letters between HS and Arthur Sidgwick, Nov. 1900, HLRO HS A/12/4–6.

influence was strong, made an overture but this too seemed a hopeless seat for the Liberals.[26] Charles Trevelyan, who had entered the House of Commons at a by-election in 1899, put his name forward in August 1901 for North-East Lanarkshire where a by-election was pending. This was a Liberal-held seat with a strong miners' vote, but the ILP put up its own candidate and the constituency Liberal association adopted Cecil Harmsworth. The split radical vote led to a Liberal Unionist victory. Samuel was in any case reluctant to stand, explaining to Trevelyan:

Even if they had asked me I should have been very loth to stand against any-one holding the office of President of the Scottish Miners' Federation. Had he been a socialist of a very outrageous type I should not mind opposing him. Anyone who had no other claim on the labour vote than that he was a member of the I.L.P. might be opposed. But I am so eager for more Labour representation of the right type that I should be the last man to try to keep out of Parliament the leader of one of the chief trade unions in the country.[27]

After his return from Africa Samuel turned down an offer from Reading, where he had some personal following as the seat abutted on to his old stamping ground of South Oxfordshire.[28] Samuel did not want to have to wait until the next general election when the sitting member would retire (in the event, he withdrew in 1904 and Rufus Isaacs held the seat for the Liberals). By mid-1902 it began to seem doubtful whether Samuel's mixture of realism, ambition, and scruple would ever allow him to find a suitable seat. But in August 1902 word came of an imminent vacancy in Cleveland where the sitting Liberal, Alfred Pease, was on the verge of bankruptcy and therefore compelled to vacate the seat.

Cleveland was a large county constituency in the North Riding of Yorkshire. Stretching inland from the coast south of the River Tees over the rolling Cleveland Hills, the division presented striking contrasts of landscape and ideological allegiance. In the mainly agricultural western portion, the inhabitants of the hamlets and old-fashioned towns generally voted Conservative. The Liberal strongholds were in the east amidst the raw grandeur of 'Darkest England'. The great ironworks and foundries of Eston and other former villages had grown within the previous two generations into monuments of Victorian industrialism. The ironstone miners were the single largest block of voters, estimated to number about 3,000 out of a total electorate of 12,357. Heavily Nonconformist in religion, the miners had always voted overwhelmingly Liberal. But the Conservatives could count on some support in Redcar, the largest town in

[26] J. W. Procter [?] to HS, 18 Apr. 1901, HLRO HS A/12/7.
[27] HS to Trevelyan, 2 Sept. 1901, HLRO HS A/14/3.
[28] James Cooper to HS, 21 and 28 June 1902, HLRO HS A/12/14–15.

the constituency with a population in 1901 of 7,695, as well as in the seaside 'villa-dom' of Saltburn. Moreover, the borough freehold franchise, comprising 1,835 voters, could also be expected to lean against a radical candidate.[29]

The Pease family, members of the so-called 'Quakerocracy' that dominated the economy and society of much of the north-east, owned many of the collieries and forges as well as a bank, railway lines, and railway construction and repair works in and around the constituency.[30] Cleveland had been represented by a Pease continuously since the formation of the seat in 1885. When news of the impending vacancy reached the Liberal Chief Whip, Herbert Gladstone, in July 1902, he tried to arrange for Augustine Birrell, who had sat in Parliament from 1889 to 1900 but had been defeated in the 1900 election, to stand. One problem, however, was money.[31] The Peases had customarily paid their own election expenses and Gladstone was not anxious to add Cleveland to the list of constituencies in receipt of subventions from central party funds under his control. Birrell earned a steady income from his Chancery practice and from writing, but he preferred to spend his money on expanding his private library.[32] Moreover, Birrell was already bespoken to Bristol North, which he won in 1906.

Samuel's work as Secretary of the Home Counties Liberal Federation had brought him into close contact with the Liberal Chief Whip who was much impressed by him. Gladstone therefore suggested his name to the Cleveland Liberals. Samuel had to consider the proposal at a difficult time for his family. Beatrice Samuel had suffered a double blow in the loss of a daughter in childbirth and the death of her mother, Adelaide Franklin. His initial reaction to the offer was not favourable since it seemed at first

---

[29] Pelling, Social Geography, 317, 329, 338–9; North-Eastern Daily Gazette, 15 Sept. 1902, 26 and 29 June 1909; Yorkshire Post, 1 and 6 Nov. 1902 Most of the borough freehold voters were from Middlesbrough; about 300 were from Thornaby in the borough of Stockton. These boroughs were outside the constituency boundary, but freeholders in most English boroughs could exercise a second vote in a neighbouring division.

[30] See M. W. Kirby, Men of Business and Politics: The Rise and Fall of the Quaker Pease Dynasty of North-East England, 1700–1943 (London, 1984).

[31] Gladstone diary, 30 July 1902, BL Add. MS 46484.

[32] In the famous essay in which he made the shocking public confession of his addiction, Birrell wrote: 'Until you have ten thousand volumes the less you say about your library the better. Then you may begin to speak.' ('Book-Buying', Obiter Dicta: Second Series (New York, 1888), 289.) In his lifetime, Birrell's book-purchasing mania was probably excelled only by that of another Liberal MP, Sir Isaac Foot, described by his son Michael as a 'bibliophilial drunkard'. Rumour had it that Foot's house collapsed under the weight of his purchases. By Birrell's exacting standard Samuel's several-thousand-volume library, of which he was (quietly) proud, hardly merited the name. Unlike his friends Birrell and Foot, Samuel did not collect first editions of rare books. He valued books primarily for their content.

as if Pease would, in spite of his faltering finances, hold the seat until the next general election which might be five years distant. Moreover, Joseph ('Jack') Pease, brother of the sitting member and himself a Liberal MP and whip, gave Samuel the impression that the agricultural nature of the constituency rendered it less safe for the Liberals than might appear from the large Liberal majorities at successive elections and from the Conservatives' failure even to field a candidate in 1900. Samuel therefore wrote to Charles Trevelyan, whose family home in Northumberland was not too far away, seeking advice.[33] After soundings, Trevelyan reported: 'If you ran, without a Labour candidate, you would be bound to win.'[34] It soon emerged that Pease's troubles were so severe that the seat would be vacated immediately and Samuel decided to put his name forward. The reservation in Trevelyan's letter, however, was a warning of trouble ahead in the shape of a further joust between Samuel and his old literary sparring partner, Keir Hardie.

The decision whether to run an Independent Labour candidate lay effectively in the hands of the ironstone miners' union, the Cleveland Miners' and Quarrymen's Association, which boasted a bank account containing £7,000 that might be used to support a candidacy. The union was affiliated to the Labour Representation Committee, formed in 1900 to promote direct labour representation in Parliament. The miners' decision partly depended on economic conditions in the iron industry. Miners' average wages had declined by 29.5 per cent in 1901 and many had lost their jobs. The industry had barely recovered in 1902, with average wages in Cleveland rising 4.5 per cent. The year 1902 was still one of the least productive in the recent history of the industry (it was not at the time generally realized that the Cleveland iron mines, once thought almost inexhaustible, were, in fact entering a long secular decline).[35] The resulting distress might be expected to increase labour militancy—but it might also lead the union to be sparing in the expenditure of funds on political objectives. Immediately the vacancy was announced the union came under strong pressure to support an Independent Labour candidate. J. Bruce Glasier, Chairman of the ILP, visited the constituency and was followed by Keir Hardie who threatened that if the local trade unionists did not do 'what appeared to him to be their obvious duty', the ILP would consider putting up its own candidate.[36] The hectoring tone was perhaps

[33] HS to Trevelyan, 20 Aug. 1902, CPT 9.
[34] Trevelyan to HS, 1 Sept. 1902, CPT 4; see also Trevelyan to HS, 29 Aug. 1902, ibid.
[35] Iron and Steel Trade Review for 1902 in North-Eastern Daily Gazette, 2 Jan. 1903.
[36] North-Eastern Daily Gazette, 24 Sept. 1902; see also reports in issues dated 15, 18, and 20 Sept. 1902; George Hobbs (for Cleveland Miners' and Quarrymen's Association) to Labour Representation Committee, 24 Sept. 1902, Labour Party Archives, LRC 5/78.

ill-judged since the ironstone miners, like their coal-mining brethren, were of a stubbornly independent breed that did not brook dictation from outsiders and did not take kindly to being instructed where their duty lay or how best to spend their hard-earned funds.

A conference of all trade union and labour organizations in the constituency was called for 11 October and in the meantime the Liberals held off selecting a candidate in the hope that no Labour man would stand. Samuel made it clear that he would withdraw his name in the event of an Independent Labour candidacy. In the hope of demonstrating that he could be a worthy representative of Labour interests, he persuaded Sam Woods to write to Joseph Toyn, the Cleveland miners' leader, recalling that Samuel had 'worked like a "Trojan"' for him at the Walthamstow by-election and declaring that he knew 'no man more sound on the Labour programme than Mr Samuel'.[37] The Labour conference at Guisborough was attended by Keir Hardie on behalf of the ILP. The Labour Representation Committee was represented by Samuel's old Fabian friend Edward Pease (Ramsay MacDonald, Secretary and moving spirit of the LRC, was on a visit to South Africa at the time).[38] Hardie presided and sought to steer the meeting towards the adoption of a Labour candidate. But discussion bogged down in an argument over finance and it soon became clear that neither the miners' association nor the LRC was prepared to put up the necessary cash. Hardie nevertheless called for the nomination of candidates. Toyn was immediately nominated to general acclamation, but he said he was not prepared to stand. A second nominee declined on ground of age. Thereupon a delegate from the floor enquired 'whether the opinion of the meeting could be tested as to Mr Herbert Samuel'. Hardie responded that Samuel was a supporter of Lord Rosebery and 'that was of no advantage to them'. A voice from the hall called out, 'Has he done nothing for Labour?' To which Hardie retorted, 'Well, he has written some books.' When an attempt was made to propose Samuel's name formally, Hardie high-handedly ruled this out of order, adding that 'it was evident that some sections of the meeting were in favour of a rich man rather than one of their own class'. Then, sensing that the proceedings were developing in altogether the wrong direction, he abruptly declared the meeting closed.[39]

The affair was a disheartening setback for the nascent cause of Labour representation. A feeling that the matter had somehow been bungled produced a spate of recriminations. Hardie, furious at the outcome of his descent on Cleveland, vented his rage to an audience of ILP faithful at

[37] Woods to Toyn, 28 [?] Sept. 1902, HLRO HS A/18/1.
[38] Edward Pease was only very distantly related to the Pease family of Cleveland.
[39] North-Eastern Daily Gazette, 13 Oct. 1902.

Darlington that evening. What evidently stung him most keenly was that working men should seem to prefer 'a young rich gentleman to represent them'. Glasier fumed at the 'imperialism and pseudo-labour pretensions of Samuel'.[40] Another LRC activist wrote to the head office complaining that the whole affair had been 'farcical'.[41]

Samuel was not yet assured of the Liberal nomination, although a major barrier had been cleared away. Of the several rival contenders for the candidacy the most formidable was Philip Stanhope, who had served in Parliament for thirteen years until his defeat at Burnley in 1900. Stanhope's political record was soundly radical and unlike Samuel he was not tainted with the stain (in the eyes of some) of imperialism; indeed, he was regarded as a 'pro-Boer'. He was also a younger son of an earl and a nephew of Rosebery's wife and could thus wield discreet influence in high Liberal circles. At first, Samuel despaired, writing to Trevelyan, 'Various strings are being pulled in connection with the Cleveland Election, but from what I hear it is very possible that Philip Stanhope may be adopted.' A fortuitous intervention aided Samuel:

The position here [Samuel wrote to his wife from Nunthorpe Hall, the country seat of Sir Joseph Pease, patriarch of the dynasty] is in some ways amusing. Joseph Walton, MP for the neighbouring Barnsley Division, is an out-and-out Imperialist and has got into trouble with some of his own constituents in consequence. He lives in the Cleveland Division and is Treasurer of its Liberal Association. Solely in order to display his impartiality in the eyes of the Barnsley people he is strongly supporting Philip Stanhope. . . . and he tried to suppress my name when H. Gladstone suggested it. The Peases, however, strongly object to Walton's manœuvrings in their territory, and on that account, and because they object to Stanhope on general grounds, they are energetically supporting me.

This Trollopean circumstance helped ensure Samuel's triumph. In spite of the collapse of the Pease family bank, and the personal ruin of Alfred Pease, other branches of the Pease empire remained intact and the prestige of the family in the constituency was hardly dented by Alfred's misfortunes.

With a view to bolstering his position with the other great influence in the constituency, Samuel turned to another old Labour acquaintance, John Burns, who had sent him a letter of support in the 1895 election.[42] At that time Samuel had assured Burns that his views were 'practically the same as your own on almost every question. I put social reform first and would take up an attitude in the House identical with that of Haldane

[40] Glasier to Hardie, 21 Oct. 1902, quoted in Kenneth O. Morgan, Keir Hardie: Radical and Socialist (London, 1975), 131.
[41] W. Pickles to John McNeil, 25 Oct. 1902, Labour Party Archives, LRC 5/110.
[42] Burns to HS, 12 July 1895, HLRO HS A/5/19.

whose collectivist view of Society I share.'[43] Since then, however, the controversy over imperialism and the Boer War had moved to the fore and Burns replied to Samuel's renewed request for support with a non-committal note.[44] Samuel's failure to secure letters of support from Labour leaders was noted adversely by the major Liberal newspaper of the area, the *North-Eastern Daily Gazette*, which seemed to lean to Stanhope. Eventually a letter reached Samuel from Ben Tillett, warmly recalling their joint efforts to unionize agricultural workers in Oxfordshire in the early 1890s.[45] But this arrived after the adoption meeting on 18 October at which Walton was able to announce that Stanhope enjoyed the support of Burns 'and even of Mr Keir Hardie when there was no longer a chance of a direct Labour representative'. When Walton was asked why the ILP was so opposed to Samuel, he replied that 'Mr Keir Hardie did not enter into a statement of the why and the wherefore of their opposition, but said merely that they would offer no opposition to Mr Philip Stanhope, but would oppose Mr Samuel for all they were worth because he was not of their school'. Alfred Pease, who was received with great warmth, said that 'he did not wish to use his influence unduly' and that he hardly knew Samuel, but that 'if the question was put straight to him . . . he should give his vote for Mr Herbert Samuel'. The loud cheers which greeted this announcement indicated that the Pease imprimatur together with Samuel's personal courting of the miners' support during the previous few weeks had won the day. When a vote of the Liberal delegates was taken, the result was five to one in Samuel's favour. It was a popular decision and after the meeting a miners' band accompanied the candidate from the hall to the station.[46]

After the decision, the Stanhope supporters rallied round and promised their support to Samuel—all, that is, except the ILP and Burns who, in response to yet another plea from Samuel, wrote: 'Frankly at this juncture I deplore your selection, because it will stimulate a bastard Imperialism that just now is cursing England and playing havoc with the forces of progress everywhere.'[47] And Samuel's announcement that he would stand as a 'Liberal and Labour' candidate was denounced by Glasier who called it 'a vulgar piece of electioneering, that ought to be strongly resented by all self-respecting working men'.[48] But the hostility of Labour

[43]   HS to Burns, 7 July 1895, BL Add. MS 46295.
[44]   Burns to HS, 13 Oct. 1902, HLRO HS A/18/2, replying to HS to Burns, 13 Oct. 1902, BL Add. MS 46298.
[45]   Tillett to HS, 19 Oct. 1902, HLRO HS A/18/4.
[46]   *North-Eastern Daily Gazette*, 20 Oct. 1902; HS to BS, 19 Oct. 1902, HLRO HS A/157/115.
[47]   Burns to HS, 24 Oct. 1902, HLRO HS A/18/11.
[48]   *North-Eastern Daily Gazette*, 30 Oct. 1902.

politicians in London had little effect on Samuel's standing in Cleveland. Toyn worked hard to bring the miners into line behind Samuel, pointing out that it was not, after all, Samuel's fault that the 'farce at Guisborough' had not produced a Labour candidate.

With Toyn's valuable backing, Samuel set about building up support among the Cleveland miners, whose interests, particularly the demand for a miners' eight-hour-day bill, he undertook to promote in Parliament. Despite his formality and restrained manner he eventually succeeded, as he had in South Oxfordshire, in winning a personal following among working-class voters. The Conservative candidate, Geoffrey Drage, an Old Etonian who had served as secretary of the Royal Commission on Labour between 1891 and 1894, could also claim to be seriously concerned about social issues, but he could make little headway among the miners or blast-furnace-men. The hottest campaign issue was the Education Bill, then proceeding through Parliament, which had aroused fierce Non-conformist opposition. Samuel adopted the standard Liberal position against the bill. Mistakenly glimpsing an opening here, Drage, like Samuel's previous opponent in South Oxfordshire, made a thinly veiled allusion to Samuel's Jewish origin by referring to 'atheists and others' who opposed the bill. But this merely offended the Nonconformists. Anti-Semitic feeling was in any case almost unknown in this area in which there was only a tiny Jewish community and no 'aliens question'.

Otherwise the by-election campaign took a standard course. In spite of Samuel's Liberal Imperialist connections he secured the usual letter of support from Campbell-Bannerman. Samuel addressed fifty-one meetings in the course of a fortnight. Nine MPs came to Cleveland to speak on his behalf, among them his friends Walter Runciman and Charles Trevelyan. As usual the family's financial, oratorical, and vehicular resources were mobilized. Clara Samuel seems to have paid her son's entire election expenses which, in the hard-fought race, amounted to £1,500.[49] Stuart Samuel came up to speak for his brother and Edwin Montagu also joined in the campaign. Beatrice Samuel put in an obligatory appearance evoking the only complimentary comment in an otherwise hostile report in the arch-conservative *Yorkshire Post*. But this Leeds organ had few readers in Cleveland. By contrast, the *North-Eastern Daily Gazette* gave Samuel's campaign massive coverage and editorial support. On election day, 5 November, the Conservatives were able to deploy over a hundred carriages. The Liberals had far fewer though Samuel had brought his own barouche up from London.[50]

[49] HS to CS, 16 Nov 1902, HLRO HS A/156/206.
[50] *North-Eastern Daily Gazette* and *Yorkshire Post*, Oct.–Nov. 1902.

The result, announced on the day after the poll, Samuel's thirty-second birthday, was a resounding Liberal victory:

SAMUEL (Liberal)	5,834
DRAGE (Unionist)	3,798
Majority	2,036

Samuel thus reaped the reward of his decade-long labours on behalf of the 'New Liberal' idea. Among the several hundred letters and messages of congratulation that he received was one from Rosebery, saying 'I have not forgotten our long talk in Downing Street'.[51] Oscar Browning wrote recalling that he had recognized Samuel's qualities at their first encounter when Samuel had still been an undergraduate. 'I was very enthusiastic about you, and was a good deal laughed at for it by some of your contemporaries', he added indiscreetly, but now, he said, his judgement had been vindicated.[52]

In an interview with the *Westminster Gazette* Samuel attributed the triumph to two causes: 'the unpopularity of the Education Bill and the cordiality of the alliance between Liberalism and Labour.'[53] The second alleged cause was open to question, but Samuel undoubtedly succeeded in winning the hearts of many working-class electors. A writer in the *Methodist Times* commented perceptively on this aspect of Samuel's character:

He has a clear, cold mind, absolutely destitute of prejudice, the sort of reasoning machine that Huxley craved but did not possess. His mental impartiality is wonderful. His chief fault, the absence of passion, except it be for the cause of Labour, a remarkable enthusiasm in one so rich, and socially so distant from the manual toiler. Mentally he most resembles Mr Asquith of all living political leaders.[54]

The comparison would have pleased Samuel and even perhaps the reference to his lack of fire, for Samuel, while admiring and striving for effective oratory, always despised crowd-pleasing demagogues.[55] His ideal auditorium, given this temperament and these prejudices, was, indeed, the one to which he had at last gained admission—the Edwardian House of Commons.

After a rapid post-declaration victory circuit of the mining villages by motor car, at that time still a novelty, Samuel rushed off to London in

[51] Rosebery to HS, 7 Nov. 1902, HLRO HS A/19/158.
[52] Browning to HS, 7 Nov. 1902, ibid., A/19/179.
[53] *Westminster Gazette*, 7 Nov. 1902.
[54] Article repr. in the *North-Eastern Daily Gazette*, 17 Sept. 1902.
[55] In 1918 Samuel wrote of Asquith: 'His style of speaking never evokes much enthusiasm in his audience or stimulates applause, but he always impresses them by his thoughtfulness and good judgement. He is lacking (like me!) in the lighter touch.' (HS to BS, 27 Sept. 1918, HLRO HS A/157/941.)

order to fulfil a campaign promise to be present in Parliament the following day to vote against one of the clauses of the Education Bill. In a public message to his constituents a few days later (the first of a series of regular 'Letters from St Stephen's' that Samuel published in the *North-Eastern Daily Gazette* between 1902 and 1905), he reported that his 'first duty' after being sworn in as an MP 'was to seek those of the Labour members who were in the House, and to assure them of my wish to co-operate with them when Labour questions came under discussion'.[56]

His first two questions in the House concerned Uganda and the Education Bill. When John Burns and Keir Hardie asked questions a few days later about 'scarcity of employment', Samuel rose to support them with a supplementary, enquiring whether the Government would agree to the appointment of a committee or Royal Commission to deal with the issue. The Prime Minister, Balfour, replied that he thought the time was 'hardly ripe'.[57] This was a question to which Samuel was to return. Samuel's maiden speech on 2 December was a competent 23-minute exposition of the Nonconformists' objections to the Education Bill.[58] It was neither a resounding success like Churchill's the previous year, nor a calamitous failure like Parnell's, but at least Samuel was audible unlike Gladstone, and was not laughed down like Disraeli. He attracted more attention the following day when he issued a challenge to the senior member for Oxford University, a Conservative, who had accused him of issuing an election leaflet in Cleveland saying falsely that if the Education Bill were passed 'universal payment of school fees would be enforced for every child'.[59] Samuel demanded a copy of the alleged leaflet and when that was not forthcoming elicited an apology from his accuser.[60] A few days later Samuel was granted permission by the Speaker to make a gracefully worded 'personal explanation' (an unusual parliamentary procedure, especially from a member of barely three weeks' standing) in which he acknowledged and accepted the withdrawal of the charge.[61] On 10 December he again supported Hardie on unemployment, but the following day he had an altercation with Burns over the Uganda railway grant. Burns had said he would rather spend £10 million on a railway in Essex than £1,000 on a railway in Uganda. Samuel made an effective speech in which, speaking as 'the only Member of this House who had visited the Kingdom of Uganda and had travelled throughout its length', he defended the expenditure on the railway. In response to an interjection

[56] *North-Eastern Daily Gazette*, 15 Nov. 1902.
[57] *Parl. Deb.* 4 s., vol. 115 (27 Nov. 1902), col. 623.
[58] Ibid. (2 Dec. 1902), cols. 973–80.
[59] Ibid. (3 Dec. 1902), cols. 1133–4, 1138.
[60] John G. Talbot to HS, 6 Dec. 1902, HLRO HS A/155/III.
[61] *Parl. Deb.* 4 s., vol. 116 (8 Dec. 1902), col. 244.

by Burns he said: 'It appeared to him [Samuel] to be a monstrous doctrine that the duties of this country were limited solely to the people of this country, and that because a man's skin was black you should not help him.... The principles of progress could not be limited merely to our own shores.'[62] This speech earned the accolade, unknown to Samuel, of a mention in the Home Secretary's daily parliamentary report to the King.[63] Thus within a month of his entrance to the House, Samuel had begun to make his mark as a persistent critic of the Government's failure to deal adequately with the unemployment problem and as an expert on African affairs. These subjects became the dominant themes of his speeches as a back-bench MP over the next three years.

That Samuel's expression of concern for the welfare of black people was not merely, as in the case of some of his fellow-imperialists, a debating point or a rationalization is demonstrated by his central role in the great humanitarian *cause célèbre* of these years—the controversy over treatment of natives in the Congo. The genocidal personal autocracy of Leopold of the Belgians over the Etat indépendant du Congo (sometimes translated as Congo Free State—but it was neither free nor independent; indeed, it was hardly, properly speaking, a state, since more than half of it was the *domaine privé* of Leopold himself) had been sanctioned by the powers in the Berlin Act of 1885. Allegations of cruelty by the king's agents were first broadcast in the early 1890s. In 1896 the Aborigines' Protection Society took up the issue, and in the following year Sir Charles Dilke raised it in the House of Commons. But it was not until 1900 that it attained the dimensions of an international scandal. Two men were primarily responsible for promoting the campaign against the atrocities in the Congo: E. D. Morel, a young Liverpool shipping clerk until 1901, thereafter a journalist, political organizer, and agitator; and Roger Casement, a former missionary who was serving at this time as British Consul in the Congo.[64] Morel had begun his ferocious series of attacks on 'a secret society of murderers with a king for a crony' in 1900.[65] Samuel, who was a member of the Aborigines' Protection Society, had followed the affair but did not become involved until the spring of 1903. His

[62] *Parl. Deb.* 4 s., vol. 116 (11 Dec. 1902), cols. 937 ff.

[63] Aretas Akers-Douglas to King Edward VII, 11 Dec. 1902, Royal Archives, R 31/50.

[64] See S. J. S. Cookey, *Britain and the Congo Question 1885–1913* (New York, 1968); William Roger Louis and Jean Stengers (eds.), *E. D. Morel's History of the Congo Reform Movement* (Oxford, 1968); E. D. Morel, *Great Britain and the Congo* (London, 1909); Porter, *Critics of Empire*, ch. 8; Ruth Slade, *King Leopold's Congo* (London, 1962); Jean Stengers and Jan Vansina, 'King Leopold's Congo, 1886–1908', in Roland Oliver and G. N. Sanderson (eds.), *The Cambridge History of Africa*, vi (Cambridge, 1985), 315–58.

[65] Quoted in Catherine Ann Cline, *E. D. Morel 1873–1924: The Strategies of Protest* (Belfast, 1980), 21. Morel used this phrase some years later.

intervention was not only a brilliant personal success. It also helped change the course of African history.

In late April 1903 Samuel learned that he had been successful in the ballot among back-benchers for putting forward a resolution on a 'private members' evening'. He decided to seize the opportunity to propose a motion on the Congo and concerted his preparations with Dilke and Morel whom he had not previously met.[66] Samuel's motion declared: 'That the Government of the Congo Free State having, at its inception, guaranteed to the Powers that its native subjects should be governed with humanity, and that no trading monopoly or privilege should be permitted within its dominions, and both these guarantees having been constantly violated, This House requests His Majesty's Government to confer with the other powers, signatory of the Berlin General Act, by virtue of which the Congo Free State exists, in order that measures may be adopted to abate the evils prevalent in that state.'[67] The debate was opened by Samuel, seconded by Dilke, at the evening sitting of 20 May 1902.

Addressing a thin House, Samuel spoke forcefully and effectively. He argued that British interests were involved, among other reasons because the Congo bordered on four British possessions. He claimed that Britain had both a responsibility and a *locus standi* in the Congo arising from her signature to the Berlin Act. And he cited voluminous evidence from impeccable witnesses, including missionaries and consuls, of legally imposed forced labour, forced military service, 'never-ending tyranny and constant atrocities'. The Hansard record continued:

He [Samuel] was not one of those short-sighted philanthropists who thought that the natives must be treated in all respects on equal terms with white men. In the speeches he had made on behalf of the negro population of Africa he had never put forward such excessive claims. But there were certain rights which must be common to humanity. The rights of liberty and of just treatment should be common to all humanity. . . . If the administration of the Congo State was civilization, then he asked, what was barbarism?

Succeeding speakers echoed Samuel's outrage and the Foreign Secretary, Lansdowne, later termed 'feeling in the House . . . so strong and widespread' that 'any attempt to obtain withdrawal or rejection of the resolution would undoubtedly have resulted in the defeat of the Government'.[68] Replying for the Government, Lord Cranborne, Under-Secretary

---

[66] Louis and Stengers (eds.), *E. D. Morel's History*, 102; HS to Morel, 28 Apr., 17 [?] May 1903, BLPES Morel papers F8/125.

[67] *Parl. Deb.* 4 s., vol. 122 (20 May 1903), cols. 1289 ff.

[68] Lansdowne to Phipps (Minister in Brussels), 21 May 1903, quoted in Cookey, *Congo Question*, 83.

for Foreign Affairs, acknowledged that 'he was in a peculiar position, because no general attack had been delivered against His Majesty's Government'. While admitting that the system of government in the Congo 'was not altogether in accordance' with the Berlin Act, he dwelt on the question of Britain's right to intervene in the matter. Other governments too had signed the Berlin Act and therefore Britain could not take action alone. The Government could not assent to the motion in its present form, but he announced that they would be prepared to communicate with the other signatories to the Act. At the end of the debate the Prime Minister, Balfour, who had left the chamber, returned and said that he agreed with the purpose of the motion but urged that as a matter of 'Parliamentary decorum', the phrase alluding to the violation of guarantees should be deleted. On that basis the Government would not vote against the motion. Samuel agreed to the amendment whereupon the resolution carried *nemine contradicente*.

'The unanimous adoption of this resolution [writes one recent historian], although it was not realized at the time, was a turning point in the history of the Congo. It set in motion a chain of actions and reactions which inevitably forced Leopold II to surrender his African empire.'[69] Morel called it 'the first nail in the coffin of the Congo Free State'.[70] The Government had hoped before the debate that Leopold would agree to the establishment of a commission to investigate the charges, but the failure to secure his assent left them in an exposed position. Passage of the resolution aroused patriotic indignation in Belgium where the Liberal leader, Paul Janson, declared to the Chamber of Deputies in July: 'I cannot admit that the Congo State should be particularly suspect. Above all I cannot associate myself with a campaign whose last words seem to be "Ôte-toi de là que je m'y mette." '[71] British critics of the Congolese regime, particularly Morel, were vilified in the Belgian press and accused of ulterior motives.

Perhaps for this reason, Samuel, for many years afterwards, showed special solicitude for Belgian interests: as President of the Local Government Board during the First World War, he was responsible for care of Belgian refugees. Together with Alfred Emmott, a fellow-critic of Leopold's Congo in 1903–4, he helped form the Anglo-Belgian Union in 1917 and he served as its first president. In 1919 he was sent to Belgium by the British Government as Special Commissioner. Samuel's attitude towards the question of British support for Belgium at a moment of destiny, 2 August 1914, should perhaps be understood partly in this context.

[69] Lansdowne to Phipps (Minister in Brussels), 21 May 1903, quoted in Cookey, *Congo Question*, 84.
[70] Louis and Stengers (eds.), *E. D. Morel's History*, 130.
[71] Quoted in Stengers and Vansina, 'Leopold's Congo', 324.

Samuel continued to be actively involved in Morel's campaign until the end of 1905. In parliamentary questions during the summer of 1903 he nagged the Government to dispatch its 'communication' to the other powers in accordance with the terms of the parliamentary resolution.[72] The British note was eventually dispatched to the powers on 8 August but was couched in such vague terms that not a single foreign government responded. The Foreign Office thereupon instructed the British Consul in the Congo, Roger Casement, to furnish a report on the allegations of atrocities.[73] Casement conducted an investigation lasting two and a half months and then returned to England to draft his report which was presented to Parliament in February 1904. It was a savage indictment that bore out many of Morel's charges against Leopold's regime. Samuel supported Morel's Congo Reform Association formed, at Casement's suggestion, in early 1904 and circularized Morel's propaganda leaflets to fellow MPs.[74] One of the recipients, Winston Churchill, replied that he had not had time to study the subject but wished the cause '(privately) all success'.[75] Others, both in Parliament and outside, were persuaded by the whirlwind of publicity to give support in public as well as private. Sir Edward Grey later said, 'No question has so stirred the country for thirty years.'[76]

In a second debate on the Congo question, on 9 June 1904, Samuel spoke again. He described Casement as 'a gentleman of the highest standing and reliability', an encomium that he must have regretted twelve years later when, as Home Secretary, he was responsible for sending Casement to the gallows. Samuel described in horrifying detail evidence of atrocities including amputations, decapitations, crucifixions, and a 'horrible cannibal orgy' committed by Congolese troops 'under the eyes of two white officers'. Grey, speaking from the Opposition front bench, made it clear that his objective was to secure transfer of the Congo from Leopold himself to the Belgian State.[77] In response to the international agitation Leopold established an allegedly independent commission of inquiry composed of distinguished Belgian, Italian, and Swiss jurists. The commissioners took evidence in the Congo from October 1904 to February 1905. Their report, published in November 1905, came as something of a blow to Leopold's supporters. The commissioners' moderately expressed, but all the more damning, critique of his system of rule in the Congo

---

[72] *Parl. Deb.* 4 s., vol. 124 (29 June 1903), col. 795; vol. 127 (6 Aug. 1903), col. 135.
[73] Cookey, *Congo Question*, 85–9.
[74] HS to Morel, 6 May 1904, BLPES Morel papers F8/125.
[75] Churchill to HS, 9 May 1904, HLRO HS A/23/1.
[76] Quoted in A. J. P. Taylor, *The Trouble Makers: Dissent over Foreign Policy 1792–1939* (Harmondsworth, 1985), 119.
[77] *Parl. Deb.* 4 s., vol. 135 (9 June 1904), cols. 1236–90.

substantiated many of the most serious charges that the campaigners had laid against him.[78]

This vindication of the Congo Reform Association's position brought the controversy to a head. Samuel, who had co-operated closely with Morel over the previous year in broadening the base of the campaign, published a response to the commission's report in the December 1905 number of the *Contemporary Review*. Samuel had repeatedly warned Morel not to place too much faith in the impartiality of the commission and he was critical of several of their recommendations for reform. But the fact that such a commission had endorsed the reports of atrocities and slavery evidently afforded him a grim satisfaction. During the previous three years he had often urged Morel not to reply to the venomous personal attacks by the Belgian press and by journalists in other countries who were paid by Leopold to discredit the campaigners. Now that the 'anomaly and scandal in the modern world, an avowed Slave State' had been exposed for what it was, Samuel seized the opportunity to pay generous tribute to the disinterestedness of his colleagues, most notably Morel. The transfer of the Congo from the personal rule of Leopold to the Belgian State was now merely a matter of time, and, with the help of the Liberal Government that took power in Britain in December 1905, was accomplished within three years.

It was characteristic of Samuel's calmly reasoned approach to the most passionate controversies that throughout this three-year agitation he did not indulge in the wild charges and conspiracy-mongering that disfigured the rhetoric of Morel and Casement. Morel confessed a little later that he was 'Congo possessed'.[79] For Samuel, by contrast, keeping his temper was an aid to clear thinking and also a tactical principle. One of his objectives was to seek broad cross-party support and therefore to steer the campaign away from any partisan taint. After Sir Albert Rollit, the Belgophile Liberal MP for Islington South, had called the atrocity reports a 'calumny', Samuel bearded him in his den, denouncing his attitude to the Congo at a Liberal meeting in Rollit's own constituency.[80] Unlike Dilke and Morel, Samuel avoided attacks on the British Government, reserving his strongest epithets for the agents of the Congolese autocrat. Indeed, he wrote privately to Trevelyan acknowledging that 'the Government have acted very fairly well in the matter and have written some strong despatches'.[81]

By contrast, in the other great African issue of these years Samuel emerged as a powerful critic of Balfour's Government and contributed

[78] See Cookey, *Congo Question*, 140–9.   [79] Quoted in Cline, *Morel*, 54.
[80] HS to Morel, 27 Nov. 1905, BLPES Morel papers F8/125.
[81] HS to Charles Trevelyan, 16 Oct. 1905, HLRO HS A/14/17.

significantly to its downfall. This was the dispute over importation of indentured Chinese labour to work in the gold-mines in the Transvaal—the arrangement that acquired the indelible historic label of 'Chinese slavery'. Samuel's involvement in the South African labour question antedated the clash over the Chinese and arose out of his settled views on imperial and labour questions. There was at this time a direct connection between the Congolese and South African labour issues since recruitment gangs for mine labourers were reported by Casement in 1902 to be ranging as far north as the Congo.[82] In March 1903 Samuel participated in a deputation to the Foreign Secretary, Lansdowne, to protest against proposals for fiscal legislation in South Africa designed to stimulate movement of African labour out of agriculture into the gold-mines of the Rand which were suffering from an acute shortage of unskilled manpower. The shortage arose in part from the atrocious conditions in the mines where the mortality rate in 1903 was 79.3 per thousand per annum.[83] The day after the meeting with Lansdowne, Samuel denounced the 'monstrous proposal' in the House of Commons. He argued that there was no need to force the natives into the mines by taxation, 'to whip them to work with an economic sjambok'. White labour, he suggested, could meet the shortfall. Objecting, in his reply to the debate, to use of the term 'forced labour', the Colonial Secretary, Joseph Chamberlain, resorted to euphemistic circumlocution: 'Do not call forced labour what is after all at the worst only labour which has been induced by legislation which indirectly effects that result.' As for the question of employing Asiatics, referred to by some opposition speakers, Chamberlain remarked that this was premature.[84]

Only a few days later, however, Milner, the High Commissioner for South Africa, wrote in a 'private and confidential' letter: 'Certain as I am that African labour, with every improvement we can make, will not be sufficient to supply our wants in the early future, I think we must call in the aid of the Asiatics. I look upon this as a temporary expedient, but for the time being essential.'[85] Milner did not believe that white men should perform unskilled labour in the mines. Moreover, the wages commanded by white miners were so much higher than those of blacks that most mine-owning companies did not believe it made economic sense to try to solve

[82] D. J. N. Denoon, 'The Transvaal Labour Crisis, 1901–6', *Journal of African History*, 7 (1967), 3, 482.

[83] Denoon, 'Transvaal Labour Crisis', 482. See also Shula Marks, 'Southern and Central Africa, 1886–1910' in Oliver and Sanderson, *Cambridge History of Africa*, vi. 469.

[84] *Parl. Deb.* 4 s., vol. 120 (24 Mar. 1903), cols. 78 ff.

[85] Milner to Dr J. E. Moffat, 1 Apr. 1903, in Cecil Headlam (ed.), *The Milner Papers*, ii (London, 1933), 460.

the labour shortage by recruiting whites. Over the previous few years the gold-mining industry had gradually moved towards 'low-grade' operation as the richest reefs had been exhausted. This trend dictated a low-wage labour policy which appeared to preclude white labour.[86] In November 1903 a commission reported that there was a shortage of 129,364 unskilled labourers in the gold-mining industry.[87] Under pressure from the Chamber of Mines, the Government approved a Labour Importation Ordinance in February 1904 that provided for the importation of labourers from China on short-term contracts. The 'indenture' of these workmen specified that they could be employed only in the Witwatersrand mines and were to be housed in mine company compounds with restrictions on their movement. They were paid lower wages than Africans and were to be compulsorily repatriated at the end of three years. These strict conditions of employment, which bulked large in Liberal opposition to the scheme in England, were introduced primarily in order to meet objections by whites in South Africa who feared that the Chinese, like the Indians who had been imported to Natal after 1860, would remain in the country and compete with whites in the labour market and as traders.[88] Between May 1904 and November 1906, when recruiting in China was halted, 63,695 Chinese workers were imported into South Africa.[89]

On 27 January 1904 Samuel attended a meeting at the Park Lane rooms of F. H. P. Cresswell, former manager of the Village Main Reef Mine and a prominent advocate of white labour.[90] At Samuel's suggestion an organizing committee was established, among whom the most active figures over the next few months were Samuel himself, Charles Trevelyan, Cresswell, who remained in touch with Samuel after his return to South Africa later that year, and the Conservative J. E. B. Seely, who crossed the floor to the Liberals in March 1904 mainly over this issue. They decided, since the Government would not submit the ordinance to Parliament for approval, to appeal to the public with a mass meeting in London. On 10 February Samuel noted in his diary: 'The meeting at the Queen's Hall which I had organized was attended by about 2,000 brightly enthusiastic people—not bad considering that we had only four days in which to arrange it and that the night was very wet. Carrington presided, and there

---

[86] See Peter Richardson, *Chinese Mine Labour in the Transvaal* (London, 1982), 18–21.

[87] L. M. Thompson, *The Unification of South Africa 1902–1910* (Oxford, 1960), 13.

[88] Denoon, 'Transvaal Labour Crisis', 489–90.

[89] Richardson, *Chinese Mine Labour*, 166.

[90] Samuel diary, 27 Jan. 1904, HLRO HS A/22. Cresswell's success with white labour at the Village Main Reef Mine was often cited by opponents of Chinese labour. But others disputed the results of this 'experiment'. Moreover, the geological peculiarities of the mine rendered it untypical of the Rand as a whole.

were about half a dozen M.P.s there.' At the meeting a letter from Sir William Harcourt, a former leader of the Liberal Party, was read out, in which he inveighed against the 'yellow peril' and warned that under the scheme 'the gold mines are to be manned, not by men, but by animals in human form who are to be treated as if they were pariahs not fit to be at large, as lepers infected with some foul disease compelled to cry "Unclean, unclean" '.[91] This inflammatory document set the tone for much of the ensuing controversy. In spite of his moderation of temperament Samuel too was drawn into immoderate utterances.

After peppering the Government daily with question after question on the issue, Samuel's repeated demands for parliamentary consideration of the issue were eventually met when he was given the opportunity to open a debate (technically on an amendment to the King's Speech) on 16 February 1904. He prepared the speech with special care, writing full notes on seventeen long envelopes, but in the event he hardly looked at them. Addressing a good House at the start of the day's proceedings, he delivered one of the great speeches of his life and established his parliamentary reputation.

Samuel began by complaining of the Government's refusal to allow a free vote which thus transformed the subject into a party issue. Like Harcourt and many other enemies of the measure, he lapsed into racialist rhetoric that seemed less concerned with the plight of the Chinese workers than with their evil influence on those who might come into contact with them: 'He had no wish to use hard words concerning the Chinese nation as a whole. . . . But the class of Chinamen who were accustomed to emigrate were in the main a degraded people. They were vicious, immoral and unclean. Their only amusements were gambling and opium smoking. Wherever they went they carried with them those qualities, and wherever they settled in white communities they were hated.' In his condemnation of the proposed compounds Samuel, like other critics, laid bare a mixture of racial and sexual preoccupations: 'They could not keep 300,000 men in a ring fence. . . . They must mix with the neighbouring white population, and with the native black population. He did not wish to dwell on a distasteful subject, but he asked the House to imagine what would be the effect of that vast body of men living together, and belonging to a race admittedly immoral. . . . If the Ordinance was passed in its present form they would be inoculating Africa with the worst vices of Asia.'

Perhaps more effective than such moralizing was Samuel's analysis of the detailed provisions of the ordinance. He pointed out that a labourer could be transferred without his consent from one employer to another.

[91] *The Times*, 11 Feb. 1904.

Once he had signed a contract he could not terminate it. If he went on strike he could be arrested and imprisoned. He could not leave the mine compound without permission, and not for more than forty-eight hours even with permission. If he escaped he could be tracked down and imprisoned without a warrant. Anybody harbouring an escaper could also be arrested. Furthermore, he drew attention to the obvious point that Englishmen who complained about Russian pogroms, or Turkish massacres, or about atrocities in the Congo would lay themselves open to justified criticism from other powers if they countenanced this scheme.

Apart from ethical objections, he said, there were political ones. It was urgent to increase the British population of South Africa to balance the Boers. Now they had a 'natural economic attraction for the British population', they were 'slamming the door' in their faces. Samuel admitted the shortage of mine labour; his solution was white labour. 'It was true', he conceded, 'that white men would not work side by side with Kaffirs; whites and blacks would no more mix than oil and water. But white men could be employed in one part of a mine and black men in another part at the same class of work.' Samuel produced evidence to counter the argument that white labour was too expensive: white men, he said, could use machinery. 'The secret of the matter', he claimed, 'was that white labour was not desired. It was not that white labour was impossible. . . . It was not so much coloured labour or cheap labour that they [the mine-owners] desired. They needed above all labour which would be voteless and subservient.' Milner himself had said 'We do not want a white proletariate in this country.'

Who could doubt [Samuel continued] that South Africa would have been a cleaner and happier place if the Kaffirs had never been there. But the Kaffirs were there; and they must naturally take their place in the economic system; and he was not, of course, going on the assumption that the blacks could be removed. But the helot system was always an evil system, and they wished as far as they could to work away from it, and to make Transvaal as far as possible a homogeneous white country.

Samuel insisted that he had spoken without party feeling. He concluded by telling the House that 'it had to decide whether it would lightly permit a new community of serfs to be established under its flag. It had to decide whether the waste places of the earth should be peopled by Mongolians or should be the homes of the white peoples.'[92]

The speech lasted eighty-five minutes and evoked wide admiration. The Speaker told Samuel privately that it had been 'admirable'.[93] The Colonial Secretary, Alfred Lyttelton, who was genuinely impressed by

---

[92] *Parl. Deb.* 4 s., vol. 129 (16 Feb. 1904), cols. 1501 ff.
[93] HS to BS, 16 Feb. 1904, HLRO HS A/157/182.

Samuel's speech, paid his opponent more than conventional compliments in his reply.[94] Samuel felt elated after the speech:

For the first time in the House [he wrote to his wife afterwards] I felt thoroughly at home, knew exactly what I was going to say and let myself go. There are moments in speaking, if the occasion is an important one and if one has one's audience thoroughly in hand, when the spirit seems to get free, and the body to disappear, and one soars away in a kind of transcendental release from all sub-lunary things. It is, to the mind, what flying would be to the body. I have had two such moments—the first when I was speaking to that great meeting at Bradford,[95] the second yesterday.[96]

Samuel had scrupulously avoided the dread word 'slavery' in his speech, but others were less fine in their distinctions. Later in the debate the radical MP Henry Labouchère demanded to know, 'If this scheme was not slavery, what was slavery?' At the end of the two-day debate the Government's majority was reduced to 51, half its normal size. A little to his surprise, Samuel found that he had hit on an issue that evoked a tremendous public response and that helped to reunite the radical and imperialist wings of the Liberal Party. Churchill remarked to Samuel in the lobby of the House a few days later, 'You have started a very good hare to run in this business.' The apparent cynicism did not impress Samuel: 'A very characteristic remark', he wrote to his wife, 'and a good many others look at the matter in the same light unfortunately.'[97]

In spite of the depth of feeling aroused by the policy, the Government dug in its heels. Transportation of 'coolies', mainly desperate peasants from the far north of China who had been economically dislocated by the Russo-Japanese War, began in May 1904 under an Anglo-Chinese Labour Convention signed that month. Even the opponents of the policy were compelled to admit that from one point of view Milner's policy was a startling success: it speedily eradicated the labour shortage. On the other hand some of the pessimistic forecasts of the opponents also proved correct. Under the draconian regime of the mining compounds, many of the Chinese rebelled. There were 11,754 offences against the ordinance in

[94] See also Edith Lyttelton, *Alfred Lyttelton: An Account of His Life* (London, 1917), 316.
[95] On 10 Dec. 1903 Samuel addressed an audience of 4,500 people at Bradford; the main speaker at the meeting was Asquith.
[96] HS to BS, 17 Feb. 1904, HLRO HS A/157/183.
[97] HS to BS, 24 Feb. 1904, HLRO HS.A/157/189. Samuel's attitude towards Churchill at this period was admiring but wary: 'On Friday went to the Speaker's levée [Samuel wrote to his mother in Mar. 1905]—very dull as usual. Winston Churchill was there in a cavalry uniform with a long row of medals. He is a most astounding person. His speeches in the House this session have been very fine. Unfortunately he takes oxygen as a stimulant and, it is said, drugs himself in other ways, so that it is not improbable that he may collapse physically like his father. However, one may hope for better things.' (HS to CS, 11 Mar. 1905, HLRO HS A/156/238.)

the year 1905–6.[98] Riots broke out in some areas. In order to restore order Milner authorized the mining companies to resort to the illegal flogging of miscreants. When this was revealed in Britain in December 1905 it provoked further indignation and fanned the protest into a wildfire that helped destroy the Unionist Government.[99]

Recognized after February 1904 as the Liberals' leading expert on the question, Samuel gradually moved to a more extreme position as it became apparent that the Government would not withdraw the ordinance. In an article in the *Contemporary Review* in April 1904, Samuel pressed home the attack. Alluding to the 'peculiarly degrading vices' of 'celibate communities' of Chinese labourers, Samuel, with his lifelong horror of homosexuality, again sounded fiercely hostile to, rather than a champion of, the victims of the scheme. He declared that it represented a 'grave injustice to the English working-classes'. And he broached the sensitive issue of 'slavery': 'Technically, no doubt, these conditions do not constitute slavery. . . . But the terms of their service approximate too closely to servile terms to be palatable.'

Until December 1905 Samuel was one of the main orchestrators of the Liberals' opposition to Chinese labour both in Parliament and in the country, although in order to show the breadth of the opposition to the Government's policy he deliberately avoided thrusting himself too much into the foreground. In July he engaged in a bitter contretemps with Lyttelton over the question of wage rates on the Rand, after which he wrote to his wife: 'Lyttelton's reply to my speech had a poor effect. He was evidently angry at my points and made an entirely unprovoked personal attack upon me which was much resented on our side of the House and not approved on his.'[100] Throughout the year, primed by letters from Cresswell in Johannesburg, he tormented Lyttelton with well-informed parliamentary questions which often left Lyttelton wriggling on the hook of what was becoming ever more clearly an untenable and unpopular policy.

In the autumn Samuel, Trevelyan, and Seely organized a collective letter of protest to Balfour. Efforts to give this a non-partisan flavour proved, not surprisingly, unsuccessful. Balfour, it appears, interpreted it as a partisan onslaught, for he immediately sent back a lengthy and harshly worded reply in which he castigated the 'foolish, but persistent, delusion which assumes the readiness of the white working man to fill the gaps which may occur in the ranks of the black working man' adding that

[98] Richardson, *Chinese Mine Labour*, 174.
[99] See A. M. Gollin, *Proconsul in Politics: A Study of Lord Milner in Opposition and in Power* (New York, 1964), 68–74.
[100] HS to BS, 28 July 1905, HLRO HS A/157/266.

'those (if such there be) who preach the doctrine that in the South African mines is to be found an opening for the unskilled labour now asking for employment in this country, are, knowingly or unknowingly, acting no better part than that of the demagogue'. Samuel no doubt winced as he read this barb. The final paragraph of the letter, however, was more welcome, containing a broad hint of an impending dramatic change in the entire political situation:·

The system of indentured labour, whether coolie or native, must therefore be treated as a whole: and if, indeed, those critics be right who identify it with slavery, it must ruthlessly be extirpated from every colony where it has insidiously taken its root. This, however, is not the view of His Majesty's present Government: and I trust that, on the acceptance of official responsibility, it will cease to be the view of any who may hereafter succeed them.[101]

Twelve days later, Balfour, whose ministry had been visibly tottering for several months, assailed not only by the Liberals from without but also by Chamberlain's tariff reform campaign from within, resigned. Balfour appears to have withdrawn as a tactical manœuvre, hoping that the dissensions of his Liberal successors would prove even more un-manageable than those of his own party. In this he woefully miscalculated. In the general election of January 1906 the Liberals exploited the Chinese labour issue to great effect, in the process offending some of the more high-minded of their own supporters. Graham Wallas, for example, deplored the display of anti-Chinese posters on hoardings during the election campaign.[102] Charles Masterman rated Chinese labour 'first, undoubtedly' among the causes of the Liberals' election triumph.[103] The Conservative *Daily Telegraph* later reviled the 'Yellow Parliament . . . born in the mendacity of the Pigtail elections'.[104] All this certainly exaggerates the issue's contribution to the Liberal landslide, but it was an important element in the victory—and one for which Samuel might, had he been more inclined to self-advertisement, have claimed the lion's share of the credit. The new Prime Minister, Campbell-Bannerman, seized the opportunity at the opening meeting of his election campaign, in the Albert Hall on 21 December 1905, to give an undertaking that all recruitment and transportation of Chinese to South Africa would stop forthwith. The speech was received with rapture even though it was inaudible to much of the audience. Perhaps that was fortunate, for the pledge was not fulfilled.

[101] Balfour to HS, 22 Nov. 1905, HLRO HS A/23/29.
[102] Colin Holmes, *John Bull's Other Island: Immigration and British Society 1871–1971* (London, 1988), 79.
[103] Lucy Masterman, *C. F. G. Masterman: A Biography* (London, 1939), 64.
[104] Quoted in Neal Blewett, *The Peers, the Parties and the People: The British General Elections of 1910* (London, 1972), 309.

At a Cabinet meeting on 3 January, Asquith pointed out that it was legally impossible to withdraw the 14,700 licences that had been issued by the previous government. Recruitment ceased only in November 1906. The last shipload of labourers returned to China in 1910.[105]

Thus both the Congolese and the Chinese agitations eventually achieved a reversal of British policy. As his irritated response to Churchill's cynical remark had indicated, Samuel felt impelled to take up these causes less by political calculation than by a conviction of rectitude worthy of Gladstone himself. 'This crusade is moral', Trevelyan, speaking of the Chinese labour issue, told his constituents in 1904.[106] Samuel would certainly have agreed. At the end of his career he declared that 'looking back now at the various movements in which I have taken part during fifty years of contact with public affairs, I see none that rendered more definite service than the opposition to Chinese labour in South Africa'.[107]

Samuel's involvement in African issues ended abruptly in December 1905. Was his obsession with Darkest Africa a diversion from his fundamental concern with Darkest England? In one sense it was, for although he remained active and vocal on social reform issues, the Congo and South Africa were his chief priorities between 1903 and 1905. At one point, shortly after his important speech on Chinese labour in February 1904, he half-apologized in one of his open letters to his Cleveland constituents for not having spoken in the House in support of a motion by Keir Hardie on unemployment. He would have done so, he said, 'had it not been that I have had so recently to make a large demand upon the attention of the House. There is no more fatal mistake for a new member of the House of Commons to make than to speak too frequently—even though he spoke with the tongue of angels.'[108] Samuel himself would probably not have accepted the antithesis between the two concerns which he, like many other Liberal imperialists, saw as intertwined. In any case, he soon made ample amends for any omission as he moved, after December 1905, into the most politically fruitful and socially creative phase of his career.

[105] Richardson, *Chinese Mine Labour*, 6, 166; Randolph S. Churchill, *Winston S. Churchill*, ii (London, 1967), 117–18; Stephen Koss, *Asquith* (London, 1976), 76.
[106] Quoted in A. J. A. Morris, *C. P. Trevelyan, 1870–1958: Portrait of a Radical* (New York, 1979), 61.
[107] Samuel, *Memoirs*, 46.
[108] *North-Eastern Daily Gazette*, 20 Feb. 1904.

4

The Children's Charter

===

I prefer association to gregariousness. . . . It is a community of
purpose that constitutes society.

(Disraeli)

AT THE beginning of December 1905 Samuel was far away from the
political battleground on a walking holiday with Charles Trevelyan
on the Isle of Arran, where, six centuries earlier, Robert the Bruce had
hidden before returning to the mainland to assume power. Samuel's
parliamentary successes and organizational acumen afforded him some
ground to hope for office when Campbell-Bannerman was appointed
Prime Minister on 5 December. But he was still among the most junior of
Liberal MPs and therefore near the back of the queue of eager aspirants
jostling for preferment. If he could justly lay claim to any position, that
might have been the under-secretaryship at the Colonial Office. This plum
was awarded to Churchill, who had held aloof from both the Congo and
Chinese labour campaigns.

A few days after his return to London, however, Samuel was offered the
under-secretaryship at the Home Office by the new Home Secretary,
Herbert Gladstone. The job seems to have been offered first to Thomas
Whittaker, a prominent temperance advocate, but he told Gladstone that
'business arrangements make it impossible'.[1] Gladstone had known and
respected Samuel for many years as a result of their work together for the
Liberal party organization. He had put Samuel's name forward for the
Cleveland seat in 1902, suffering in consequence a series of tiresome
letters from Philip Stanhope, the defeated candidate for the nomination.[2]
Moreover, he was beholden to Samuel's uncle, Sir Samuel Montagu, for
at least one substantial recent contribution to the party's central budget.[3]
Some time before, Gladstone's cousin, Alfred Lyttelton, had commended
Samuel highly. Lyttelton had been the butt of Samuel's parliamentary

[1] Whittaker to Gladstone, 9 Dec. 1905, BL Add. MS 46063.
[2] Trevor Lloyd, 'The Whip as Paymaster: Herbert Gladstone and Party Organization',
English Historical Review, 99 (1974), 794.
[3] See Sir Montagu Samuel-Montagu [*sic*] to Gladstone, 4 Mar. 1905, BL Add. MS
46062/144.

attacks over the Congo and Chinese labour but he eulogized his young critic as a potential candidate for office. Gladstone, aware of what he called 'certain appalling deficiencies' in his own parliamentary capabilities, was anxious to find a subordinate whose strength as a speaker might compensate for his own weakness. He therefore had ample reason to recommend Samuel's name to the new Prime Minister.

Campbell-Bannerman, however, distrusted Samuel's imperialist proclivities. In 1903 he had written of him, 'This gentleman is a little too-too'.[4] In response to the suggestion of Samuel's name he made what Gladstone later described as 'a terrible grimace', and, reverting to his native Glaswegian dialect, recalled he had been 'fashed up' by one of Samuel's speeches on South Africa.[5] Gladstone nevertheless pressed the point. The Prime Minister relented, enabling Samuel to take up the position on 12 December.[6]

A delighted Samuel told Gladstone that of all the junior positions in the Government this was the one he would most have wished.[7] Samuel's family and the Jewish community in general took pride in the appointment, and a celebratory dinner was held in his honour by the Maccabeans, a Jewish dining club.[8] The satisfaction was not quite universal. Beatrice Webb noted sourly in her diary: 'Herbert Samuel, an old friend but a young person to whom I have taken almost a dislike—has made a surprising advance in obtaining the under-secretaryship at the H.O., leaving poor C. P. Trevelyan behind.'[9] She nevertheless invited Samuel to a party of young Liberals a few weeks later. Graham Wallas offered his congratulations but regretted that Samuel had not been appointed to the Board of Education instead.[10] Samuel's friend Walter Runciman, who at first feared that he, like Trevelyan, had been passed over, wrote furiously to Churchill:

They still keep me dangling about here, more or less restless. Up till last night and especially after I heard of some of the apptmnts yesterday morning which are out today, I was rather angry. The Home Office job is really the most unpopular thing that has been done. I wonder if you know what led to it? HJG[ladstone] actually saw Samuel & booked him without consulting anybody, & when everybody else in the Cabinet objected he claimed that it had gone too far & could not be recalled. He was

---

[4] Quoted in John Wilson, *CB: A Life of Sir Henry Campbell-Bannerman* (New York, 1974), 463.

[5] Gladstone to HS, 11 Jan. 1916, HLRO HS A/29/12.

[6] Letter of appointment, 12 Dec. 1905, PRO HO 45/14538.

[7] Samuel to Gladstone, 11 Dec. 1905, BL Add. MS 45992.

[8] *Jewish Chronicle*, 9 Mar. 1906; Maccabeans papers, Anglo-Jewish Archives, University College, London.

[9] Entry dated 15 Dec. 1905, BLPES Beatrice Webb diary, 2379.

[10] See HS to Wallas, 29 Dec. 1905, HLRO HS A/162.

thereupon (at their dinner on Saturday night) asked why he had not taken me & left Samuel alone, & he replied that Samuel had written a good deal about Factory Legislation (leaflets he meant) & was interested in Home Office subjects. Thus he disposed of one post, & CB acquiesced. Samuel had already been rejected by George Whitely for the Whips' Office.[11]

Runciman was subsequently appointed to the junior position at the Local Government Board under the Presidency of John Burns—a less desirable position than Samuel's. Samuel, who was incapable of writing such a shameless letter as Runciman's, unconsciously, or perhaps thoughtlessly, rubbed salt into his friend's wound by bantering about the comparative attractions of the two offices.[12]

In the general election that followed in January 1906, Samuel was elected unopposed in Cleveland, one of only thirty-seven unopposed returns in England, Wales, and Scotland. The failure of the Conservatives to contest the seat was a tribute to Samuel's zeal in nursing his constituents since the by-election of 1902. Among the ironstone miners he was by now a local hero. He wrote to his wife from Saltburn in January 1906: 'The people were continually prophesying that I shall be Prime Minister and almost burst into praying over me. I have several times felt greatly moved. It is a heavy charge to have the hopes of so many people centred on one's poor self.' He concluded on a smug note: 'With an uncontested election, an Under-Secretaryship at thirty-five, a considerable income, three healthy sons and a most charming wife, I count myself a fortunate man.'[13]

Relieved of any contest in his own constituency, Samuel spoke to audiences of 2,000 each in Whitby, Scarborough, and Harrogate. Meanwhile, he set to work enthusiastically at the Home Office, eager to advance the programme of social reform that he had laid out in *Liberalism*. The Liberals' massive victory, which left them with an unassailable 130-seat majority over all other parties in the House of Commons, had been achieved on no programmatic basis at all. 'This is no conclusive list; I am not here to frame or to propound any programme

[11] Walter Runciman to Churchill, 13 Dec. 1905, in Randolph S. Churchill, *Winston S. Churchill*, vol. ii, Companion part 1 (London, 1969), 414.

[12] HS to Runciman, 22 Dec. 1905, WR 11 [letter misdated 1915 in Newcastle University Library list].

[13] HS to BS, 7 Jan. 1906, HLRO HS A/157/305. Samuel was one of 16 Jews (12 Liberals, 4 Conservatives) in the House of Commons in 1906. The others included his brother Stuart and his cousin Edwin Montagu (Alderman, *Jewish Community*, 79). He was one of 31 Balliol MPs of whom 22 were Liberals. There were 4 Balliol men in the Cabinet— Asquith (Chancellor of the Exchequer), the Earl of Elgin (Colonial Secretary), Grey (Foreign Secretary), and Earl Loreburn (Lord Chancellor) (Melvin Richter, *The Politics of Conscience: T. H. Green and His Age* (Cambridge, Mass., 1964), 294 n.). Samuel was one of 8 members of the Rainbow Circle elected (the others included Ramsay MacDonald and Charles Trevelyan) (minutes of Rainbow Circle, 7 Mar. 1906, BLPES Coll. Misc. 575/2).

whatsoever', Campbell-Bannerman had declared a few months earlier.[14] Yet the Unionist rout aroused among progressives high expectations of a blissful new dawn.

The responsibilities of the Home Office, when Samuel joined it in 1905, included a patchwork of powers and duties: among these were functions related to the administration of justice, prisons and reform schools, supervision of police authorities as well as direct control of the Metropolitan Police, control of immigration and naturalization of aliens, industrial law (factory Acts, shops Acts, truck Acts, workmen's compensation Acts), intoxicating liquors, dangerous drugs, explosives, firearms, public morals (including obscene publications, betting, prostitution and licensing of plays), transport, burials, fairs, open spaces, wild birds, elections, and matters of royal prerogative such as the granting of pardons or of reprieves in capital cases. In some cases, such as the licensing of plays, the Home Office had responsibility without power: the power of theatrical censorship was vested in the Lord Chamberlain's Office. In others, such as matters of royal prerogative, the Home Office had power without responsibility. Many of its functions rubbed against the edges of other ministries such as the Local Government Board, the Lord Chancellor's Office, and the Board of Trade. The department's officials and ministers found that much of their time was taken up with day-to-day management of its miscellaneous ragbag of responsibilities and it has been suggested that civil servants in the Home Office 'may have helped to immerse Herbert Gladstone in administrative routine'.[15] Moreover, a recent historian suggests that 'the department . . . was generally more comfortable with its law and order responsibilities than with its involvement in aspects of social welfare'.[16]

The atmosphere of the Home Office exactly suited Samuel. Much of the time of the department was still taken up with arcane questions of precedence and prerogative, hangovers from the past that had remained part of its administrative bailiwick. Samuel, who had a penchant for the quaint, enjoyed handling such ancient curiosities. But it was the ministry's more important and expanding social responsibilities and the need for accurate statistical information thereby generated that excited his greatest enthusiasm. He quickly established excellent working relations with Gladstone and the senior officials of the department. During his first two years in office his private secretary was Frank Elliott, who had entered the

[14] Quoted in Samuel H. Beer, *British Politics in the Collectivist Age* (New York, 1969), 58.
[15] J. R. Hay, *The Origins of the Liberal Welfare Reforms 1906–1914* (London, 1975), 39.
[16] Jill Pellew, 'The Home Office and the Aliens Act, 1905', *Historical Journal*, 32/2 (1989), 371.

THE CHILDREN'S CHARTER 87

Home Office in 1898 and had served Samuel's Tory predecessor, Thomas Cochrane, in the same capacity. Elliott later wrote that he had made himself the power behind Cochrane's throne: 'I answered his letters for him, revised his speeches in Hansard, told him what minutes to write, prepared his speeches on H[ome] O[ffice] matters (all the good parts, including the jokes!).' He found Samuel a very different type of master: 'Whereas I led Cochrane by the hand, with you I struggled behind somewhere in the offing.'[17] Samuel never allowed civil servants to dominate him at any point in his ministerial career. He maintained his authority not, as in the case of some other ministers, by bullying or ideological bluster, but by a capacity for hard work and a mastery of detail that enabled him to compete intellectually with the best of his officials. Samuel also appointed an unpaid parliamentary private secretary, Sir Rowland Whitehead, to help with bills and other parliamentary odd jobs.[18] As a result of Gladstone's acknowledged incompetence as a front-bench performer, Samuel found that much of his time was taken up piloting bills through committees and answering parliamentary questions.

The Home Secretary's variegated responsibilities always elicited more questions than any other department except perhaps the Post Office. Among those dealt with by Samuel were queries on the Scottish fish curing industry, lunacy commissioners, the hours of work of florists' assistants, 'Pharaoh's Serpent' eggs (a poisonous compound 'made to ignite and not to eat', from which a 4-year-old child had perished), 'lunacy through religious excitement', limerick competitions, imperial heraldry, premature burial, the Great Pan-Asiatic Tea Company (a doubtful trader), suicides of insurance agents, the complaint of an imprisoned suffragette that her shoes didn't fit, and the Drury Lane Theatre performing horse.

Samuel dealt efficiently with such minutiae, but he was more interested in the larger prospect of innovative legislation. The Government as a whole came to power with only the fuzziest vision of, and no commitment to, laying the foundations of a welfare state—to use the anachronism that was later applied retrospectively to its reforms. Samuel probably came closer than any other minister to having formulated a comprehensive legislative programme for social reform with an intellectual basis in Liberal doctrine. The proposals set out in *Liberalism* did not include many of the more advanced reforms, such as national insurance, towards which the Asquith Government moved after 1909. The book nevertheless foreshadowed many of the thirty-four Acts of Parliament that Gladstone and Samuel jointly shepherded through the House of Commons between 1905 and 1909. For Samuel, if not for others among his colleagues, these

[17] Elliott to HS, 21 Dec. 1907, HLRO HS A/24/11.
[18] Whitehead diary, 6 and 9 Mar. 1906, HLRO Hist. Coll. 211, Whitehead papers 16.

were not simply isolated pieces of legislation but building blocks of a larger whole based on the conception of the state as an organic community.

The difficulty of rising above the administrative to the legislative sphere was driven home to him on his first day of office in the initial problem with which he was confronted: the Aliens Act of 1905. This measure was a product of the anti-alien agitation that had disfigured politics, particularly in the East End of London, over the previous few years. The immigration of large numbers of East European Jews to London and, to a lesser extent, to the provinces, especially Manchester, Leeds, and Glasgow, had begun after 1881. In the census of 1901 a total of 247,758 aliens were counted in Britain. A great part of these were East European Jews whose arrival had raised the estimated Jewish population of London from 47,000 in 1883 to 150,000 by 1902.[19] The immigrants were heavily concentrated in Yiddish-speaking communities in and around the Whitechapel constituency represented until 1900 by Sir Samuel Montagu and thereafter by his nephew Stuart Samuel. Genuine problems of poverty, overcrowding, and harsh working conditions in the tailoring trade fed the xenophobic demand for restriction of immigration. A Royal Commission on Alien Immigration in 1903 advocated in its majority report stricter control of aliens as well as repatriation of those considered to be 'undesirable'. Balfour's Government introduced an Aliens Bill in the spring of 1904 that included many of the Commission's recommendations. But it came under intense fire in the House of Commons and was abandoned. A new bill, incorporating some concessions to the anti-restrictionists, was submitted to the House and passed into law in August 1905.[20]

Samuel opposed both bills from the outset.[21] This, after all, was in a sense the issue that had first aroused Samuel's passionate political concern when he participated in his elder brother Stuart's election campaign in the East End in 1889. In the parliamentary opposition to the second bill he deferred to his brother who was more of a recognized spokesman on Jewish issues. But he launched a powerful attack of his own against the measure in the House of Commons in May 1905—a speech in which he provided an unwitting foretaste both of his own forthcoming ministerial embarrassment over the bill, and of a more distant historic pronouncement. Samuel defended the Jewish immigrant population against the various accusations made against them. He added an eloquent panegyric on the Jews in general, insisting they were a 'race not to be despised'—a

[19] Maurice Freedman (ed.), *A Minority in Britain: Social Studies of the Anglo-Jewish Community* (London, 1955), 139; see also Lloyd P. Gartner, *The Jewish Immigrant in England 1870–1914* (London, 1960).

[20] See Bernard Gainer, *The Alien Invasion: The Origins of the Aliens Act of 1905* (London, 1972).

[21] *North-Eastern Daily Gazette*, 30 Apr. 1904.

phrase echoed in his influential Cabinet memorandum on Palestine a decade later.[22] He admitted that some of the immigrants had faults arising largely from the oppression under which they had lived. 'But [he continued] they have a capacity for better things which soon shows itself, and if you give to these broken plants a little soil and water they will soon revive and they will not be the least useful and beautiful in your garden.'

Striking the Conservatives at a sensitive point, he then said:

I wonder what Disraeli would have thought of this Bill. On April 19th[23] you covered his statue with flowers, but the day before you introduced a Bill which might exclude from this country such families as his [ministerial cries of 'No, no!']. Indeed, if they were destitute and could not prove that they were able to earn their own living they would be excluded. A progenitor of Lord Beaconsfield was an alien, and there may have been many men who have risen to distinction whose fathers were destitute when they arrived in this country.

Turning to a member who had inquired what the Liberals would do if they were in power, Samuel was cautious but nevertheless gave a hostage to fortune in his response: 'I am not authorized to speak for anyone but myself, but I think the view widely entertained upon these benches is that we should be prepared to exclude the criminals, paupers, and diseased if possible, but even if we pass this Bill on that head we think it is impracticable. We are in favour of a measure of expulsion for dealing with these classes. . . . If this Bill is passed it will be found that its administration will be beset with innumerable difficulties and it will soon become a dead letter.'[24] During the committee stage of the bill he pointed out some of the difficulties of enforcing specific aspects of the bill.[25] On the report stage he moved an unsuccessful amendment to exempt from the definition of an 'undesirable alien' any person who could show that he would be supported by relatives.[26] Samuel also spoke against the bill outside Parliament and published an article on 'Immigration' in the *Economic Journal* of September 1905, in which he placed his opposition to the bill within a broad framework of economic, social, demographic, and racial aspects of migration.

Although the Act had received the Royal Assent in August 1905 the appointed date at which it was to take effect was delayed until 1 January 1906 in order to enable the Home Office to set up the necessary machinery of control at the ports. Samuel thus found himself in the unenviable position,

---

[22] See below, p. 209.

[23] The anniversary of Disraeli's death in 1881—commemorated for many years as 'Primrose Day'.

[24] *Parl. Deb.* 4 s., vol. 145 (2 May 1905), cols. 724–33.

[25] *Parl. Deb.* 4 s., vol. 148 (28 June 1905), cols. 351, 425; vol. 149 (10 July 1905), cols. 128–9. [26] *Parl. Deb.* 4 s., vol. 149 (17 July 1905), col. 919.

when he arrived at the Home Office in December 1905, of being obliged
to supervise the enforcement of a measure that he had opposed as
unenforceable just a few months previously. One of the first letters he
received after the announcement of his new appointment was a plea from
the *Haham*, Moses Gaster, urging amendment of the Act. Gaster added
that he had 'no doubt that the operation of the Bill will now be carried out
in a less harsh and oppressive manner than a literal interpretation of the
text would warrant'.[27] The Liberals might, of course, have sought to
amend or even repeal the Act after they secured their massive majority in
January 1906. But the Cabinet does not appear to have considered these
options seriously. Samuel, of course, as a very junior minister, was in no
position to affect the decision to maintain the Act, even had he dissented
from it. Some time later his uncle asked him privately whether there was
any chance of repeal, but he seems to have realized the hopelessness of the
question for he added, 'If not, may I state it privately as your opinion to
prevent the Jews from knocking their heads against a stone wall?'[28]
Gladstone's decision upon taking over the Home Office was that whatever
the Liberals' previous opinions, the Act was now the law of the land and
must be implemented. Home Office officials, however, complained of
the admininstrative complications of giving effect to the Act's often
exceedingly vague stipulations. At one point the Permanent Under-
Secretary, Sir Mackenzie Chalmers, wrote to Gladstone: 'I should like to
repeal this unworkable act.'[29] The new Liberal ministers thus found
themselves not only in an awkward political spot over the Act but also
facing potential friction with their civil servants.

One of the key areas of controversy during the passage of the bill had
been the question of treatment of religious and political refugees. The
opposition had succeeded in inserting a clause ensuring that the traditional
right of asylum in such cases would be preserved intact. One of the early
decisions of the new government, in which Samuel participated, was to
revise its predecessor's administrative memorandum to the immigration
boards established under the Act, in order to stress more strongly that
political or religious refugees were not to be refused admission.[30] This
section of the Act was, in the event, administered with notable leniency.[31]
Under the Government's liberal interpretation of this and other clauses of
the Act, immigration to Britain was not seriously impeded. The number of

[27] Gaster to HS, 13 Dec. 1905 (copy), Gaster papers, Mocatta Library, University
College, London.
[28] Lord Swaythling to HS, 13 Dec. 1907, HLRO HS A/24/10.
[29] Quoted in Pellew, 'Home Office', 375.
[30] Minute by Samuel, 26 Jan. 1906, PRO HO 45/10326/131787/5; circular letter to
immigration boards, 9 Mar. 1906, PRO HO 54/10326/131787/9.
[31] See Pellew, 'Home Office', 377.

arrivals declined after 1906, but until the outbreak of the First World War the country kept a more than half-open door to most comers.

On the related issue of naturalization, the Home Office came under pressure from the Board of Deputies of British Jews to reduce the fee which stood at £5.[32] Winston Churchill, never one to limit his interventions to his own area of departmental responsibility, supported the Board in pressing for a reduction in the fee. Churchill, who had taken a consistently liberal line on all aliens-related issues, wrote to Samuel arguing that 'this is another instance of that same odious principle of a poverty test which we stigmatized in the Aliens Act, which accords the truest enfranchisement to a well-to-do person however undesirable he may be, & shuts the door with a slam in the face of the poor man however honestly and high-mindedly he may have lived'.[33] Both Sir Samuel Montagu and Stuart Samuel had pressed successive governments to reduce the fee for many years.[34] But Gladstone strongly opposed any reduction in the fee, telling the Cabinet in July 1907 that if there was any case for changing the fee it should not be decreased but increased as applicants for naturalization under the existing arrangements were 'far from being all desirable citizens even now'.[35] Churchill raised the question again in 1908 but still without success. Samuel found himself placed in an uncomfortable position by his colleague when an anti-alien MP demanded to know whether the Government intended to give effect to a pledge by Churchill concerning a reduction in the fee. Samuel was compelled to evade the point entirely in his reply.[36]

Another unrewarding holdover from the previous administration was a departmental committee set up at the Colonial Office by Lyttelton in 1905 to consider a report by the writer and agricultural reformer Henry Rider Haggard on Salvation Army colonies in the USA and at Hadleigh in Essex. Samuel had been appointed to the committee and among the other members was Sidney Webb. Lyttelton instructed the committee 'to advise the Government whether any steps can usefully be taken for promoting agricultural settlements in the British Colonies of persons taken from the cities of this country'. Samuel had long been an admirer of the Salvation

[32] See minutes of Law and Parliamentary Committee, 7 Mar. 1906, Board of Deputies archives C 13/1/6.

[33] Churchill to HS, 7 Dec. 1906, in Randolph Churchill, *Winston Churchill*, vol. ii, Companion part 1, 604–5.

[34] See Eugene C. Black, *The Social Politics of Anglo-Jewry 1880–1920* (Oxford, 1988), 317 n.

[35] Cabinet memorandum by Gladstone, 29 July 1907, PRO CAB 37/89/75.

[36] *Parl. Deb.* 4s., vol. 187 (30 Apr. 1908), cols. 1398–1404. The fee remained £5 through Churchill's own tenure at the Home Office from 1910 to 1911; in 1913 it was reduced to £3. See J. M. Ross, 'Naturalisation of Jews in England', *Transactions of the Jewish Historical Society of England*, 24 (1975), 68.

Army and of the colonization schemes advanced by its founder, William Booth, in his *In Darkest England and the Way Out* (1890), as a partial solution of the problems of overcrowding and unemployment in Britain. Samuel himself had recommended in *Liberalism* the establishment of state-supported farm and forestry colonies in Britain.[37] Between 1903 and 1905 he had repeatedly pressed the Government to appoint a Royal Commission to investigate these and other possible solutions to the problem of unemployment.[38] The committee's deliberations extended across the change of government. Its report, submitted in May 1906, rejected Haggard's proposals for state support of the Salvation Army's colonies but recommended that a Treasury grant-in-aid be given to committees formed to promote emigration.

Samuel, by now a member of the Government, could not easily support proposals for state expenditure without in some measure committing the Government. While concurring with all the negative recommendations of the committee, he therefore entered a reservation concerning the proposal for state subsidy of emigration. His reasoning provides valuable insight into his thinking on unemployment at this period. In the first place, he maintained that emigration benefited individuals not the community. National funds should be used only 'to secure a national advantage'. Secondly, the proposal appeared to be to send the best rather than the worst elements overseas. There was no national advantage in that. Thirdly, he argued against the notion of sending such people overseas because they were 'economically superfluous'. 'Unemployment', he insisted, 'is almost invariably a temporary misfortune; and a temporary evil demands a temporary relief. . . . To propose emigration as a cure for temporary distress is—to use Swift's illustration—like a man cutting off his feet because he has no shoes.'[39] Another committee member entered a similar dissent. The report was shelved.

Samuel's views on the unemployed, and in particular on the distinction between the deserving and undeserving elements among them, emerge even more clearly in a minute on the report of a committee on vagrancy. This had recommended stricter police control of vagrants and suggested that 'habitual vagrants' should be sent to labour colonies to be administered by local authorities and partly subsidized by the central government.[40]

[37] *Liberalism*, 128–32.
[38] See e.g. *Parl. Deb.* 4 s., vol. 118 (19 Feb. 1903), cols. 314–18; HS to Balfour, 2 Dec. 1904 (copy), HLRO HS A/155 III/34.
[39] *Report of the Departmental Committee Appointed to Consider Mr Rider Haggard's Report on Agricultural Settlements in British Colonies*, Cd. 2978 (London, 1906); see also Harris, *Unemployment*, 124–35.
[40] *Summary of Recommendations of the Departmental Committee on Vagrancy* (London, 1906).

The establishment of such penal colonies was endorsed by the Poor Law Inspectorate and by many local boards of guardians.[41] Samuel too favoured it:

The establishment of institutions of this character has long appeared to me to be most desirable. Experience shows, it is true, that their reformative influence is likely to be small. But the plan is obviously a better way of dealing with the class in question than an alternation of casual wards and short terms of imprisonment. Above all, it will furnish a powerful deterrent to persons who are disposed to take up a vagrant life.

Samuel rejected the committee's suggestion that local authorities should be primarily responsible for such colonies, arguing instead that they should be managed and funded by the state. Revealingly he added, as if as an afterthought:

It may be suggested incidentally that some term should be chosen to denote these institutions which should not be liable to confusion with the term 'farm colony'. It is essential that, in dealing with the unemployed, every effort should be made to emphasize the distinction between the methods adopted for the relief of the deserving and those adopted for the punishment of the undeserving. 'Farm colony' is the phrase ordinarily used to describe an institution to which men temporarily out of work may voluntarily go for assistance. The idea of farm colonies in the public mind will be lowered, and their value will therefore be impaired, if the penal institutions to which habitual vagrants are committed by magistrates are called by a similar name and appear to form part of the same system.

Samuel proposed the establishment of two such penal colonies as an experiment.[42] But the entire concept of labour colonies, whether of the voluntary or the reformatory type, was roundly rejected by John Burns who, as President of the Local Government Board, exercised authority in this sphere. The scheme for penal colonies never materialized; a few voluntary colonies were established in the course of the next few years but the idea that the state should actively promote these as a solution to unemployment was never realized.[43]

More rewarding for Samuel than the frustrations arising out of such committees, the embarrassments flowing from the Aliens Act, and the trivia of departmental business was the work of drafting new legislation and piloting it through the House of Commons. During his first year in office he took charge of five minor Acts. He shared responsibility for the conduct of three others of which the most important was the Workmen's Compensation Act. This extended coverage to a large number

---

[41] See Harris, *Unemployment*, 142.

[42] Memorandum by HS, 11 June 1906, PRO HO 45/10520/138276/6.

[43] See Harris, *Unemployment*, 187–98; Kenneth D. Brown, *John Burns* (London, 1977), 120–4.

of occupational categories, among them seamen, fishermen, shop assistants, and postmen, thereby adding about six million workers to those already entitled to compensation for industrial injuries under an Act of 1897. The period of disablement that gave entitlement to compensation was reduced from a fortnight to a week. Section 8 of the Act extended its provisions to industrial diseases; this part was based on French law and emerged from lengthy examination in a departmental committee over which Samuel presided. It was the first English legislation covering industrial diseases: six diseases of major importance were scheduled and it was left open for further diseases to be brought under the Act by order.[44] In the final stages of consideration of the bill, an amendment was put forward, supported by Masterman, Lyttelton, Hardie, and Sir Charles Dilke, specifying that *all* industrial diseases, including lead poisoning and 'phossy jaw' (scourge of the matchgirls), should automatically be included in rights of compensation.[45] In his parliamentary report to the King that day Gladstone paid generous tribute to the 'speech of great lucidity' in which Samuel opposed the amendment. The bill was not, in fact, a controversial measure. On the third reading Hardie expressed sorrow that Samuel had not held out more hope of an extension of the diseases clause.[46] But a further nineteen diseases were brought under the Act within the following two years on the recommendation of a Home Office committee presided over by Samuel.[47]

While the bill was proceeding through the House, Samuel, accompanied by a Home Office official, Malcolm Delevingne, attended an international conference at Berne on night work of women in factories and on the use of dangerous phosphorus in match-making. An earlier conference of experts in 1905 had paved the way for two draft international conventions that were now debated. But the British Government had announced that it would not sign on the ground that the drafts contained inadequate enforcement provisions. The British felt no particular urgency about securing agreement since, as the British delegate in 1905 had pointed out, England had had legislation barring women's night work on the statute book for thirty years.[48] The change of government in Britain led to a more positive approach to the idea of international regulation of labour conditions. Samuel was accorded plenipotentiary powers by the Govern-

[44] See Sir Malcolm Delevingne to HS, 4 Nov. 1942, HLRO HS A/24/20; Sir Edward Troup, *The Home Office* (2nd edn., London, 1926), 176.

[45] *Parl. Deb.* 4 s., vol. 166 (5 Dec. 1906), cols. 974 ff.

[46] *Parl. Deb.* 4 s., vol. 167 (13 Dec. 1906), col. 719.

[47] Delevingne to HS, 4 Nov. 1942, HLRO HS A/24/20; *Report and Minutes of Evidence of the Departmental Committee on Compensation for Industrial Diseases*, Cd. 3495 and 3496 (London, 1907); *Second Report and Minutes*, Cd. 4386 and 4387 (London, 1908).

[48] See John W. Follows, *Antecedents of the International Labour Organization* (Oxford, 1951), 163–4.

ment and found himself speaking (in French) repeatedly at the conference 'as almost all the proposals are made by England or depend on our adhesion'.[49]

Although general agreement was reached on the convention banning women's night work, the British failed in what Samuel called 'our critical proposal—the establishment of an International Commission for the settlement of difficulties arising from the Convention with a further provision for the reference of disputes that cannot be settled by arbitration'.[50] Samuel told the conference 'that England was anxious that any agreement arrived at on the subject of the regulation of night work should be real and effective, and that unless the provisions of such conventions were fully observed it was clear that their whole purpose—the limitation of those forms of industrial competition which prevented desirable social reforms—would be missed'. The point might have impressed the Rainbow Circle, but not all delegates to the conference were persuaded. Samuel continued that 'neither diplomatic correspondence nor the cumbrous machinery of conferences' would meet the need: 'a commission was the only practicable method.'[51] This insistence on a permanent enforcement body contained the germ of the idea of the International Labour Organization, established in 1919. At the Berne conference, however, the proposed commission was strongly opposed by Germany. In his report on the conference to the Foreign Secretary, Samuel gave his view that beneath the stated objections of the Germans was 'a further and more cogent motive underlying their opposition . . . the fear that the Socialist party, possessing an international organisation might find means, through the Parliaments of various countries, to use the Commission as a weapon for the advancement of inconvenient proposals'.[52] In view of the German insistence that the British proposal, if adopted, would infringe on national sovereignty, Samuel was in the end obliged to yield. The convention, signed by all participants in the conference, contained no reference to a commission. After a marathon seven-hour concluding session the conference agreed that a *vœu*, a non-binding declaratory statement, would be issued to open the way for further diplomatic action.[53] No such action was taken, however, before the First World War. In spite of this failure to secure international enforcement, the British Government

---

[49] HS to BS, 18 Sept. 1906, HLRO HS A/157/352.
[50] Ibid.
[51] Sir Malcolm Delevingne, 'The Pre-War History of International Labor Legislation' in James T. Shotwell (ed.), *The Origins of the International Labor Organization* (New York, 1934), 44.
[52] HS and Malcolm Delevingne to Sir Edward Grey, 27 Sept. 1906, HLRO HS A/28/5.
[53] Text of convention and of *vœu* in Shotwell (ed.), *Origins*, 491–5.

introduced legislation the following year designed to adjust the law in order to comply fully with the terms of the convention.[54]

The second convention discussed at the conference closely interested Samuel. As he had discovered at the time of his investigations of Swedish match factories in 1891, the debate over conditions in the match industry was bound up with arguments about international competitiveness. Since Japan and Norway absolutely refused to sign the proposed convention prohibiting the use of white phosphorus, and since the Swedish delegate at the Berne conference made equivocal statements, the British would not endanger their own match industry by signing. By 1906 the British had in any case more or less eliminated the disease of 'phossy jaw' by means of stringent regulation of working conditions in factories where phosphorus was used. The British refusal to sign was tempered by an undertaking given by Samuel that Britain would be prepared to accede if the recalcitrants did the same. In a private letter to Grey after the conference, Samuel suggested that the Foreign Office might communicate on the subject with Japan. But he opposed any attempt to exert pressure on Japan as had been suggested to him privately by the Swiss delegate.[55] Although the Japanese position did not change, scientific advances soon afterwards enabled all match manufacturers to end the use of phosphorus. By 1913 most countries, including Britain, had either signed the convention or taken equivalent measures internally. In Britain Samuel helped produce the White Phosphorus Matches Prohibition Act of 1908, an uncontroversial measure that banned the manufacture, sale, and importation of such matches. In this manner the scourge of 'phossy jaw' that had so shocked Samuel two decades earlier was finally eliminated.

The two conventions in themselves thus had little direct effect on labour conditions in Britain. Their seminal importance lay in the fact that they were the earliest international agreements regulating conditions of labour. This was Samuel's first foray into foreign affairs. The Home Office was an unusual launching-pad for diplomatic action, and the episode, perhaps inevitably, produced some interdepartmental friction. Samuel, always a stickler for accuracy, complained about a mistake in transcription of a telegram he had sent through diplomatic channels from Berne. The Foreign Office, its dignity apparently affronted, did not bother to reply. When Samuel raised the matter again, Grey's private secretary, Louis Mallet, minuted: 'It is very impertinent of Samuel to return to the charge.'[56] The minute itself, as written by a civil servant of a minister,

[54] Employment of Women Act, 7 Edw. VII, c. 10; see *Parl. Deb.* 4 s., vol. 179 (2 Aug. 1907), cols. 1465–6.
[55] HS to Grey, 11 Oct. 1906, PRO FO 800/97/20.
[56] Undated minute, Oct./Nov. 1906, PRO FO 800/97/24.

might have been regarded by some as 'impertinent'—but Samuel had not yet acquired the personal standing in the Whitehall hierarchy that was later to be one of his most useful political assets.

The main piece of legislation that occupied Samuel in the following session was the Probation of Offenders Bill. The bill was entirely un-controversial and passed with ease. Indeed, it attracted little attention at the time, although it was later recognized as having brought about a dramatic change in the English criminal justice system. Before 1907 probation was virtually unknown in Britain. Although courts possessed the power to release prisoners on recognizances of good behaviour, they hardly ever did so, mainly because, in the absence of a probation service, there was no provision for ensuring good conduct. The closest equivalents were the unofficial social workers known as 'police court missionaries' who assisted prisoners 'bound over' to keep the peace. A probation system had been introduced in Massachusetts in 1878 and had spread to other American states. The only place in Britain where a rudimentary probation service existed before 1907 was Glasgow, where six policemen had been appointed probation officers in 1905. In 1906 Samuel presided over a Home Office committee which drafted the terms of the 1907 Act. The measure created a professional probation service and enjoined on probation officers the duty 'to advise, assist and befriend' those entrusted to their charge.[57]

Although it met general approval, the Probation Bill encountered some pockets of scepticism. When a magistrate wrote to the Home Office expressing doubts, Samuel minuted in characteristic style: 'An interesting letter. There may be some disadvantage in legislation of this character, but it does not follow that there is a *balance* of disadvantage.'[58] Samuel introduced the second reading of the bill in the House of Commons and faced little objection. Only one member, C. B. Stuart-Wortley, KC, Conservative MP for Sheffield, Hallam, seemed to grasp the innovative nature of the bill, pointing out that it 'created, by using a new word, a new *status pupillaris*' and 'a new kind of legal relationship'. The bill passed without a division.[59] Gladstone subsequently appointed Samuel chairman of a Home Office committee on the administration of the Act.[60] The committee approved the appointments of many of the old 'police court missionaries' as probation officers for adults and of women as children's

---

[57] See Troup, *Home Office*, 136–41; *Probation*, 8/6 (June 1957); *Observer*, 5 May 1957; *Times Educational Supplement*, 10 May 1957; *Glasgow Herald*, 6 May 1957.
[58] HS minute, 29 Apr. 1907, PRO HO 45/10340/139389.
[59] *Parl. Deb.* 4 s., vol. 174 (8 May 1907), cols. 294–9.
[60] Note by Gladstone, 26 Sept. 1907, PRO HO 45/10367/156623/1; *Report and Minutes of Evidence of the Departmental Committee on the Probation of Offenders Act, 1907*, Cd. 5001 and 5002 (London, 1909).

probation officers. Perhaps because it had passed with so little controversy or publicity, the Act was at first hardly used in some parts of the country and misunderstood in others. Some magistrates who disapproved of the Act were initially reluctant to make use of its provisions. In a letter to Charles Trevelyan in November 1907, Samuel asked him to use his family's influence in Northumberland to correct the mistaken notion of the county's Clerk of the Peace that the probation officers for the area should be policemen 'which is not at all what was contemplated'. 'The officers [Samuel explained] should be men or women who are keen about philanthropic work and who would be eager to help the offenders put under their supervision.'[61] In spite of these teething troubles, the system expanded rapidly. In its first year of operation 8,023 offenders were placed on probation. By 1957, when Samuel joined in celebrations of the fiftieth anniversary of the Act, the number on probation had risen to 45,000

A much more controversial and time-consuming measure for which Samuel bore a large measure of responsibility was the ill-fated Licensing Bill of 1908. Here was a problem that had gnawed at the Liberal conscience for two generations. Samuel had devoted a chapter of *Liberalism* to proposals for temperance legislation. Their central feature was 'a reduction in the number of public-houses and an extension, together with stricter enforcement, of the laws against drunkenness'. Samuel added that it seemed 'probable that when legislation is introduced it will take the form of a general reduction of the number of licences to a fixed proportion to the number of the population of each area'.[62] On the question of compensation to licence-holders whose licences were discontinued, Samuel rehearsed the arguments for and against but reached no conclusion. In 1904 the Unionists enacted a Licensing Act which provided that compensation should be paid for licences taken away on grounds other than misconduct. The money was to be paid out of funds raised from the trade, and the Home Office was made the central authority for administering the Act. Temperance enthusiasts denounced the Act as a 'brewers' Bill', but it did reduce the number of licences in England and Wales, which had stood at 101,940 in 1901, to 94,794 by 1909.

In late 1906 Samuel was entrusted with the task of preparing a new bill. His draft provided for a reduction over a period of fourteen years of 34,000 licences and for local option in the granting of new licences (general local option in Wales and Monmouthshire).[63] The draft suggested that reduction should be based on the ratio of public houses to population

---

[61] HS to Trevelyan, 8 Nov. 1907, CPT 18.   [62] *Liberalism*, 63, 66.
[63] See HS to Gladstone, 19 and 31 Dec. 1906, BL Add. MS 45992/187 ff.

with adjustments for areas of low population density.[64] Compensation would be paid for suppressed licences but on a formula that would yield much lower payments than under the 1904 Act.[65] The bill also reduced Sunday opening hours, excluded children from public houses, and increased restrictions on licensed clubs. The bill was originally announced in the King's Speech at the opening of the 1907 session, but was postponed to 1908 probably for fear of rejection by the House of Lords. It evoked some strange responses, reflective less of its actual provisions than of ancient prejudices and loyalties. J. A. Hobson complained that the bill was essentially conservative.[66] The Conservative William Joynson-Hicks, who declared himself 'fully pledged as a temperance man', said it 'embodied in naked form pure socialism'.[67]

The debate on the second reading, in April 1908, followed shortly after the resignation of Campbell-Bannerman and the succession of Asquith as Prime Minister. The bill had been introduced by Asquith, but with his elevation the main burden of its defence fell upon Samuel who acquitted himself well, blinding the opposition with financial statistics.[68] On the second reading it had a majority of 246. To counter the 980 Conservative blocking amendments the Government imposed a guillotine. The unpopularity of the bill seemed to be attested on 27 September when a monster anti-temperance demonstration attracted 200,000 merry revellers to Hyde Park.[69] In the committee stage Samuel displayed mastery of detail and such confidence that F. E. Smith, the lordly Conservative MP for Liverpool, Walton, adjured him 'to be not always so absolutely certain as he appeared to be'.[70] After weeks of discussion, Samuel concluded the debate on the third reading on 20 November by rounding on the Tories who had complained again about the closure: 'A time-limit of fourteen years would itself have been inadequate. . . . The tactics of the Opposition have been very transparent; prolonged discussions, interminable speeches. . . . We are faced today by the old issue of wealth against commonwealth. The Government believe that intemperance, next to poverty itself, is the greatest social evil afflicting our country.[71] We are

[64] 'Licensing Bill, 1907; Draft Report', 7 Jan. 1907, PRO CAB 37/86/3.

[65] 'Licensing Bill: Proposed Basis of Compensation' by L. N. Guillemard, 1 Jan. 1907, PRO CAB/37/86/2.

[66] J. A. Hobson, *The Crisis of Liberalism: New Issues of Democracy* (London, 1909), 91–2.

[67] *Parl. Deb.* 4 s., vol. 195 (4 Nov. 1908), col. 1263; Randolph Churchill, *Winston Churchill*, ii. 254.   [68] *Parl. Deb.* 4 s., vol. 187 (28 Apr. 1908), cols. 1202–24.

[69] See Peter Rowland, *The Last Liberal Governments: The Promised Land 1905–1910* (London, 1968), 160–1.

[70] *Parl. Deb.* 4 s., vol. 194 (20 Oct. 1908), cols. 1058–60.

[71] In his personal habits Samuel was abstemious though not abstentionist; in later life he was sometimes observed at formal dinners unobtrusively watering his glass of wine.

convinced that intemperance is in large degree the product of the opportunities and facilities for intemperance. We know that this Bill will
greatly lessen those facilities and opportunities.'[72]

The Government won handsomely on the third reading, but the bill was
doomed four days later when a meeting of 250 Conservative peers at
Lansdowne House decided to reject it in the Lords. They did so in the face
of an earlier private warning by the King to Lansdowne of the inadvisability
of total rejection of the bill by the Lords. The outcome was not unexpected
by Liberal tacticians and Samuel had earlier toyed with the idea of the
Government's declaring the bill a financial measure which would be
automatically precluded from veto by the Lords. But Sir Courtney Ilbert,
Clerk of the House of Commons, was doubtful, and the idea was
dropped.[73] When the Lords rejected the bill by 176 votes, Liberal fury
knew no bounds. Churchill said, 'they have started the class war, they had
better be careful.'[74] And Asquith sounded the tocsin at the National
Liberal Club: 'Is this state of affairs to continue? We say to-night that it
must be brought to an end, and I invite the Liberal Party to-night to treat
the veto of the House of Lords as the dominating issue in politics—the
dominating issue because in the long run it overshadows and absorbs
every other.'[75] The rejection of the bill was one more milestone along the
road to the constitutional crisis of 1910–11.

If the Licensing Bill was a defeat for the Liberals, for Samuel personally
it turned out to be a personal success. His spirited defence in the teeth of
the Conservative assault was widely admired. Years later, Asquith's son,
Lord Justice Cyril Asquith, recalled that his father, when asked once what
was the most outstanding parliamentary performance that he remembered
in his career, mentioned Samuel's handling of the Licensing Bill in 1908.[76]

Although the Licensing Bill took up a large part of Samuel's time for
two years after late 1906, he managed to devote attention to other, more
fruitful, pieces of legislation. Among these was the curious case of the
Deceased Wife's Sister's Marriage Act of 1907. This was originally
introduced as a private member's bill, but the Government made time
available for its passage. The bill had a hoary ancestry in Westminster
lore. Similar bills, designed to remove the barrier to such marriages in
England or the colonies, had been introduced on no fewer than thirty-two
occasions since 1850. Many of these had passed in the Commons but been
rejected in the Lords. The 1907 bill encountered opposition from a small

[72] *Parl. Deb.* 4 s., vol. 196 (20 Nov. 1908), cols. 1653–6.
[73] HS to Asquith, 10 Sept. 1908, HLRO HS A/24/15.
[74] Randolph Churchill, *Winston Churchill*, ii. 322.
[75] Quoted in Koss, *Asquith*, 106.
[76] Unsigned note (possibly c.Mar. 1949), HLRO HS A/155/XIII/71.

minority, leading to an all-night sitting on the third reading. Samuel, who felt strongly on the subject, stayed till the end, 'being not a little ashamed of the fact that it was not passed long ago, and not a little indignant with the seventeen narrow-minded, short-sighted, but long-winded bigots who kept us up all night in the attempt to stop the Bill by obstruction'.[77] The bill passed the Lords soon afterwards. A little-noted aspect of the Act, however, was its retention of wives' sisters in the class of persons with whom adultery was regarded as incestuous. This assumed legal significance in the following year as a result of the passage of the Incest Act, another back-bencher's bill for which the Government provided time. This made incest a crime in England (hitherto proceedings had been possible only in ecclesiastical courts), punishable by severe sentences. Samuel helped steer the bill through the Commons in the summer of 1907.[78]

Another private member's initiative for which Samuel helped find government time was the Advertisements Regulation Act of 1907 which authorized local authorities to make by-laws outlawing large hoardings. It was the first Act of its kind, and Samuel pressed the Commons to pass it even though it 'would not add sixpence to anyone's wealth but was simply one for suppressing ugliness'.[79] In his enthusiasm for such legislation Samuel was ahead of his time. He felt a lifelong concern for such environmental issues. When he was High Commissioner in Palestine in the 1920s one of his first ordinances was a law designed to curb what he regarded as offences against the pristine landscape of the Holy Land. On a visit to Israel in 1951 he noticed that, although his ordinance was still in force, hoardings had sprouted. He wrote to the Prime Minister, David Ben Gurion, to protest at the erosion of 'the distinction that Palestine has held for thirty years of being the only country in the world which is not vulgarized by being bespattered with commercial advertisements'.[80] The letter won some support and led the Israeli Government to take action to curb the menace.[81] In England, too, Samuel waged several doughty battles in the final phase of his life against threats to cherished features of the rural and urban environment.

As a minister Samuel was perhaps at his most effective in committee discussion of bills, where his command of detail, calm demeanour, and patience wore down the most stubborn opponents. A typical instance occurred during consideration of a controversial bill in 1907. On this

[77] HS to BS, 15 Aug. 1907, HLRO HS A/157/389.

[78] See Home Office file on Incest Bill, PRO HO 45/10357/152169.

[79] Parl. Deb. 4 s., vol. 176 (14 June 1907), cols. 16–28.

[80] HS to Ben Gurion, 16 Apr. 1951, ISA 100/29.

[81] Jerusalem Post, 24 Apr. 1951; Zeev Sharef (Israeli Government Secretary) to HS, 16 Nov. 1951, ISA 100/29.

occasion Jack Tennant, a Liberal MP and brother-in-law of Asquith, had come down from Scotland to propose a series of wrecking amendments on the committee stage. Samuel described him as being 'in a very bitter mood, and still more fuming when none of his amendments received much support, while several proposed by Ramsay MacDonald and other people were accepted and passed'.[82] Samuel's private secretary, Frank Elliott, depicted the scene in a letter to Beatrice Samuel: 'This was the sort of thing that happened again and again. Someone moved an amendment more or less hostile. The Home Secretary opposed it. Then Members rose one after another bringing in side issues and red herrings and so on and so on till the Committee was ruffled and confused & generally bad tempered. Finally up gets Mr Samuel, pointing out fallacies here, & soothing down people there, until everyone saw clearly what the point at issue was & began to purr, & the amendment was rejected. It really was as good as a play.'[83] In the business of pushing through Parliament a large volume of legislation, some of it highly contentious, Samuel's effectiveness on such occasions raised his standing considerably in the Government.

Of all the bills for which he was responsible at the Home Office, one received his special care and became closely identified with Samuel's name: the Children Act of 1908. A landmark in the evolution of state acceptance of responsibility for children, this was an omnibus bill that built on a great deal of earlier legislation. The concept of such responsibility was still fairly recent. As late as 1881 Lord Shaftesbury had declared the evils of child abuse 'enormous and indisputable' but 'of so private, internal and domestic a character as to be beyond the reach of legislation'.[84] Campaigns by moral and social reformers against cruelty to children and child prostitution, as well as pressure from bodies such as the National Society for the Prevention of Cruelty to Children, founded in 1889, had produced several Acts, not all very effective, designed to prevent the most outrageous assaults on the rights and welfare of children. Since 1906 the Government had already enacted four measures directly bearing on children: an Act, introduced by the Labour Party, that empowered local authorities to provide school meals for underfed children; another that required medical inspection of schoolchildren; an Act, introduced as a private member's bill, requiring notification of all births within thirty-six hours; and the Probation Act which brought about the appointment of probation officers for child offenders.

Samuel had long regarded children as a suitable object of state inter-

[82] HS to BS, 14 Aug. 1907, HLRO HS A/157/388.
[83] Elliott to BS, 14 Aug. 1907, HLRO HS A/155/III/51a.
[84] Quoted in George K. Behlmer, *Child Abuse and Moral Reform in England 1870–1908* (Stanford, 1982), 52.

vention. In *Liberalism* he had noted that 'the State has recognized its duty to the orphan and deserted children, and the children of grossly neglectful or cruel parents'.[85] In 1903 he had written in one of his open letters to his constituents: 'I hold very strongly the view that the system of large institutions for children is a mistake and that they should be either boarded-out with working people if they are normal children, or, if they are deficient or epileptic, be kept in very small homes where they can be given individual attention.'[86] And in 1904 he had spoken briefly in Parliament on a scheme for sending Poor Law children to Canada: he approved the idea in principle, but objected that 'it was proposed to practically establish a wing of the English workhouse on Canadian soil and to segregate the children and place them in a special home'.[87] But apart from these statements Samuel had not expressed any special interest before 1906 in problems of child welfare.

Soon after he arrived at the Home Office, he received a visit from a Scotswoman, Mrs M. R. Inglis, who urged the formation of a ministry for children. Samuel later said that this was the germ of what became the Children Bill.[88] He began in the summer of 1906 by instructing officials to flag proposed amendments to the law concerning committals to day industrial schools for inclusion in an omnibus measure.[89]

By July 1907 work on drafting what turned out to be a mammoth bill moved into top gear under Samuel's direction. The bill would consolidate the existing laws on industrial and reform schools and would cover Ireland, which had hitherto had its own laws on the subject, as well as England, Wales, and Scotland. It would also cover child cruelty and infant life protection. Legislation concerning child employment was, however, excluded from the purview of the bill. In order to produce a non-controversial bill that would not be overwhelmed with amendments, the Home Office recommended a draft of which it could 'be stated that it merely consolidates the law, with certain minor amendments which have been found desirable'.[90] By November an outline was ready, and Gladstone wrote to Campbell-Bannerman, 'Our idea is that it should be a Children's Charter.'[91] The proposed bill consolidated twenty-two Acts

---

[85] *Liberalism*, 121.

[86] 'Letter from St Stephen's', *North-Eastern Daily Gazette*, 20 June 1903.

[87] *Parl. Deb.* 4 s., vol. 135 (2 June 1904), cols. 640–1. [88] *Memoirs*, 54.

[89] Minutes by HS, 28 Aug. and 4 Oct. 1906, PRO HO 45/10346/142634. Industrial schools, which had their origin in the 'ragged schools' of the early nineteenth century, were intended chiefly for the children of vagrants and paupers, whereas reformatories were for juveniles convicted of offences. Such schools had been established under Acts dating back to 1854 and 1866 and were under the supervision of the Home Office. In 1907 there were 102 industrial schools in England and Wales and 44 reformatories.

[90] Memorandum by G. A. Aitken, 17 July 1907, PRO HO 45/1036/154821/1.

[91] Gladstone to Campbell-Bannerman, 18 Nov. 1907, BL Add. MS 45988/229–30.

and would be divided into five parts. In a memorandum prepared by Samuel at that time he explained some of the thinking behind the bill, summarized its chief features, drew attention to certain clauses that remained open pending further consultation, and showed that, in spite of the bill's 'consolidating' character, it extended existing law in several directions. The memorandum was printed for circulation to interested government departments.

As expounded in Samuel's memorandum, the first part of the bill was to deal with infant life protection. Several changes were proposed to tighten the law against 'baby-farming'. Samuel noted that dispute had arisen over the question of whether homes that took only one baby at a time in return for payment should be subject to inspection: the NSPCC was in favour; the LCC against. Samuel leant towards the NSPCC view, but given the division of opinion he proposed that the matter be referred to a Select Committee. The second part of the bill was devoted to prevention of cruelty: amendments to existing law were designed to prevent child deaths from fire and from 'overlying' (inadvertent suffocation of an infant in bed by a sleeping or drunk parent); the age-limit in the law dealing with child prostitution was raised from 14 to 16. Samuel showed the zeal of a new convert, or reformed addict, in his attention to part three, which dealt with juvenile smoking (he himself had been a moderate cigarette smoker but had given up in 1904). The draft proposed a ban on the sale of tobacco products to persons under 16, declared that it was the duty of a constable who saw a child smoking 'to confiscate the tobacco', and suggested that consideration should be given to subjecting a child found smoking 'to a penalty—a small fine, or brief detention in default'. Part four, which dealt with reformatories and industrial schools, proposed a large number of detailed amendments to existing law. It also opened for consultation the question of how such institutions were to be financed; Samuel laid down as a guiding principle: 'It neither can, nor ought, to be expected that charitable subscriptions will provide for what is properly a state charge.' The fifth part, concerning juvenile offenders, proposed that children should not, in future, be detained pending trial except in cases of 'homicide or other grave crime'. This part also proposed strengthening a law, hitherto little used, whereby parents could be punished for crimes committed by their children. Such punishment, Samuel argued, 'by penalising the parent, in proper cases, for the misconduct of the child, would strengthen the sense of parental responsibility, and conduce to a more careful and effective exercise of parental control'. This section also provided that no child under fourteen should be imprisoned, and that in the cases of 'young persons', defined as aged between fourteen and sixteen, only those certified as 'unruly' should be imprisoned. Samuel noted under this head that the establishment of juvenile courts in London and large towns was under consideration. Even from this early memorandum it was plain that what was intended was much more than a mere consolidation of existing law.[92]

In the course of the following months a number of changes were made as a result of comments from other government departments, criticism in Parliament, and representations from the large number of voluntary organizations concerned in one way or another with children. Submissions were received from the Ragged School Union, the National Vigilance Association, the Social Purity Alliance, the Association of Poor Law Unions, the Church Penitentiary Association, and many similar bodies. Samuel met representatives of the Salvation Army, the Showmen's Guild, the Wholesale Tobacconists Association, and the NSPCC, to mention only a few.[93] Many of the recommendations from voluntary bodies were contradictory and several from government departments did not find favour. For example, the Metropolitan Police Commissioner, Sir Edward Henry, considered that 'a penal sanction is no remedy for overlying'.[94] But Samuel pointed out to Parliament that 1,600 children had died in a single year in England and Wales from being smothered in this fashion. The penalty, he conceded, should be light, save where drunkenness, the most common cause, was proved. Samuel persuaded an initially reluctant Education Board to agree to a clause that sought to improve arrangements for the education of children of vagrants.[95] This was incorporated in an additional, sixth section of the bill. Following the report of the Select Committee on one-child baby homes, it was decided to bring these too within the Act. Among other additions to the bill were clauses enabling courts to be cleared when children gave evidence in a case 'where an offence against or any conduct contrary to decency or morality is charged', and clauses excluding children from public houses, prescribing a penalty for giving liquor to children, and providing for the cleansing of verminous children.

Samuel introduced the first reading on 10 February 1908. It contained 119 clauses and covered 72 pages; ultimately it grew to a total of 134 clauses. In dealing with the fifth and most innovative part of the bill, he dwelt on what he said were its three main principles. First, 'the child offender ought to be kept separate from the adult criminal'—hence the need for juvenile courts which 'should be agencies for the rescue as well as the punishment of children'. Secondly, 'the parent must be made to feel

[92] 'Children's Bill' by HS, Nov. 1907, PRO HO 45/10361/154821/22.
[93] See PRO HO 45/10361/154821 (also files 10362–4).
[94] Henry to HS, 27 Jan. 1908, PRO HO 45/10362/154821/55.
[95] HS to BS, 3 Feb. 1908, HLRO HS A/157/419.

more responsible for the wrong-doing of his child'. And thirdly, 'the commitment of children in the common gaols, no matter what the offence may be that is committed, is an unsuitable penalty to impose.'[96] Gladstone reported later to the King that 'the bill was very well received by the House and was introduced amid cheers'.[97] The Times declared that the bill met 'with universal approval' and commented: 'The friendly reception of the Bill is in the main ascribable to the belief that it promises more for the welfare of society than much more pretentious measures.'[98]

Almost the only contentious note was introduced by the former Conservative Home Secretary, Akers-Douglas, who, while generally welcoming the bill on its second reading, remarked that the clauses on juvenile smoking 'are in the nature of grandmotherly legislation and . . . would probably lead to a good many laughable scenes of constables pursuing small boys who would drop their cigarettes in running away. Such scenes would not tend to support the dignity of the law.'[99] After further discussion of juvenile smoking on the report stage, Gladstone wrote to the King that the Opposition had developed

a determined but unexpected resistance to the proposals, in which Mr Balfour took part. Mr Samuel who conducted the Bill with tact and ability agreed to give up the Clause making it an offence for boys to smoke in public places. This was under compulsion. The Opposition at this late period of the Session have it in their power to wreck the Bill, and a policy of conciliation was necessary.[100]

Josiah Wedgwood, Liberal MP for Newcastle-under-Lyme, introduced a number of amendments to strengthen the bill, one of them a clause to prevent the pawning of children's clothing. This evoked impassioned protests from pawnbrokers, whose trade newspaper called it 'a calamity'.[101] A deputation of Irish MPs and pawnbrokers visited Samuel to remonstrate.[102] Wedgwood's clause did not remain in the Act. Otherwise, the bill proved so uncontroversial that it passed through all its stages without a division on any major issue.

The Children Bill represented an extension of state responsibility to all children, not merely paupers or victims of cruelty. Akers-Douglas's complaint about grandmotherly legislation drew on the conventional vocabulary of protest against state encroachment on the private domain

[96] Parl. Deb. 4 s., vol. 183 (10 Feb. 1908), cols. 1432–8.
[97] Gladstone to King Edward VII, 10 Feb. 1907, Royal Archives, R37/86.
[98] The Times, 3 Apr. 1908.
[99] Parl. Deb. 4 s., vol. 186 (24 Mar. 1908), cols. 1266–70.
[100] Gladstone to King Edward VII, 13 Oct. 1908, Royal Archives, R37/37.
[101] The Pawnbrokers' Gazette and Trade Circular, 25 Apr. 1908; see also record of deputation of National Pawnbrokers' Association to HS, 31 Mar. 1908, PRO HO 45/10363/154821/161; and Charles James Thompson (for National Pawnbrokers' Association) to HS, 25 Apr. 1908, PRO HO 45/10363/154821/186.
[102] Record of deputation, May 1908, PRO HO 45/10363/154821/195.

in this period. In this case it was not without substance—as Gladstone admitted in one of his parliamentary letters to the King.[103] Akers-Douglas's point might indeed be made more generally: the bill as a whole reflected an uneasy mixture of philanthropic, collectivist, and moralizing impulses. Some of the clauses, among them those on smoking, particularly in their original form, also bear the personal imprint of Samuel's puritanical, not to say 'grandmotherly', approach to many social questions.

Samuel became the darling of the NSPCC as a result of the passage of what was widely hailed as a Children's Charter. Indeed, the Act was better received by contemporaries than by historians. The Webbs, in their great history of the English Poor Law, published in 1929, wrote carpingly that it 'purported to give complete protection against everything gravely harmful to child development. But all that was done was to enact that such acts of neglect or cruelty should be punishable as crimes; just as, for several centuries, Parliament sought to prevent vagrancy by punishing it as a crime! The Home Office, which took a lot of trouble to draft the statute, apparently overlooked the fact that no array of penal statutes will, in themselves, amount to a framework of Prevention.'[104]

The most recent historical analysis of the Act is no less grudging, especially in its appreciation of Samuel's role. It stresses the omnibus nature of the Act, and, emphasizing the contribution of the voluntary organizations, argues that 'Samuel's handiwork was itself largely derivative'.[105] Samuel deserves more credit than that. He pulled together the often contradictory submissions of the voluntary bodies into a coherent whole. As for the bill's consolidatory nature, this was overemphasized by contemporary propaganda for tactical parliamentary reasons. The Act passed through its final stages just as the furore over the Licensing Bill was rising to a height. Hence, as Gladstone explained to the King, the overriding need to secure consensus if the Children Bill were to pass. As we have seen, its innovations were numerous and in several instances far-reaching. Three dozen old Acts were repealed in whole or in part, and over a hundred changes to the law were made by the new Act. The cumulative effect even of the small changes was significant. One little-noticed effect of the Act, for example, was to restrict the authority of justices to order the birching of young boys. The ending of child imprisonment and the institution for the first time in England of a countrywide system of juvenile courts[106] were important reforms in themselves. The

[103] Gladstone to King Edward VII, 12 Oct. 1908, Royal Archives, R37/36.

[104] Sidney and Beatrice Webb, *English Poor Law History, Part Two: The Last Hundred Years*, (London, 1929), 614.

[105] Behlmer, *Child Abuse*, 220–3.

[106] Juvenile courts had existed since 1869 in Massachusetts and since 1884 in Canada, but could be found before 1908 in only a few English cities such as Birmingham.

Children Act in these ways gave expression to underlying shifts in social attitudes regarding children and sought to realize the 'community of purpose that constitutes society' which Samuel plucked out of Disraeli's *Sybil*.

A related measure, the Prevention of Crime Act, also passed in 1908, enacted further reforms in the treatment of young offenders. Samuel helped draft and defend the bill which expanded the hitherto experimental Borstal school into a national system of reformatory education for offenders aged between 16 and 23. A second section of the bill provided for 'preventive detention' of 'habitual criminals' for periods of between five and ten years in addition to any other sentence—a new departure in British penal doctrine. Samuel had more to do with the first than the second section of the Act, and he claimed to have originated the general application in the Act of the word 'Borstal', hitherto used only of the institution at Borstal in Kent from which the name was taken.[107] In 1938, when travelling in the Punjab, he came across a 'Borstal' and wrote that he was 'rather touched to find the name that I had invented, in default of a better, when we introduced the system thirty years ago, in use so far away'.[108]

The end of the 1908 parliamentary session also marked the end of Samuel's major legislative work at the Home Office. Remarkably, in spite of the fact that he was to hold higher office continuously for a further eight years, as well as for a year in 1931-2, he never again initiated the passage of a single memorable bill. His contribution to the Liberal Government's reform programme must therefore stand or fall almost entirely on his first crowded years in office. Gladstone showed appreciation of his subordinate's work by presenting him in 1910 with a bound volume of all the Acts which they had jointly brought to the statute book. This impressive tome includes, in addition to the Acts for which Samuel held direct responsibility, most notably the Probation and Children Acts, others such as the Coal Mines Regulation Act, popularly known as the 'Miners' Eight Hours Act', that Samuel helped defend in Parliament. Amid the gathering frustrations of his later career, when personal success was not matched by legislative achievement, Samuel would often look back to these years as a golden age of harmonious and constructive political activity.

---

[107] There seems good reason to recognize Samuel's paternity of this neologism, since in a minute dated 23 Oct. 1907 he referred to 'a Borstal reformatory', in a general sense, thus antedating the first such usage recorded in the *Supplement to the Oxford English Dictionary* (minute by HS, 23 Oct. 1907, PRO HO 45/10356/151410/10).

[108] HS diary-letter, Lahore, 6 Feb. 1938, Godfrey Samuel papers, Cardiff.

5

A Sermon in Crude Melodrama

The best Governments are always subject to be like the fairest crystals, where every icicle and grain is seen, which in a fouler stone is never perceived.

(Francis Bacon)

SAMUEL'S CAREER between 1905 and 1913 was marked by steady, unspectacular progress up the political ladder. While involved in the major political struggles of the day—the conflict over the Parliament Bill and the Irish question—he did not play a front-rank role. Much of his time in these years was taken up in relatively unrewarding administration rather than the social reform legislation in which he was most interested. Two episodes, however, diverted his attention. The first, a rumpus over theatrical censorship, was a revealing comedy of social manners. The second, the Marconi scandal, developed into a serious political drama.

By early 1909 Samuel's stock was rising rapidly and it was plain that it would be merely a matter of time before he entered the Cabinet. He had not hitherto been in a hurry to move. In early 1907 there had been some talk of a junior position at the Treasury but Runciman was appointed. Samuel told Gladstone that in any case he did not want to leave the Home Office.[1] When Asquith became Prime Minister in April 1908, Samuel speculated that he might become Financial Secretary to the Treasury, in succession to Runciman, who entered the Cabinet as President of the Board of Education, or Under-Secretary at the Colonial Office in succession to Churchill, who also attained Cabinet rank as President of the Board of Trade. But he told his mother that he was 'very comfortable with plenty of useful work in hand and plenty more in prospect' at the Home Office.[2] Asquith offered him the Financial Secretaryship to the Admiralty, but Samuel said he would prefer to stay where he was and Asquith told him that this would not prejudice his future prospect of promotion 'but the contrary'.[3] Asquith recognized Samuel's work, particularly his wasted

[1] HS to CS, 3 Feb. 1907, HLRO HS A/156/258.
[2] HS to CS, 7 Apr. 1908, HLRO HS A/156/289.
[3] Note by HS, 12 Apr. 1908, HLRO HS A/155/III/56; cf. Lord Fisher [1st Baron Fisher of Kilverstone], *Memories and Records*, i (New York, 1920), 56.

labours on the Licensing Bill, by the award of a Privy Councillorship in November 1908.

With the end of the exceptionally strenuous 1908 parliamentary session, Samuel could afford to relax. He joined a skiing party at Klosters in the Engadine. Among the participants were several young Franklins and other members of Samuel's extended family, some young Fabians, a Cambridge element that included Rupert Brooke, and the two 'semi-middle-aged daughters of Edmund Gosse'.[4] The following April he visited Liverpool where several of his relatives still lived. He cycled the 220 miles home. 'It took me two whole days and three half days riding', he reported to his eldest son.[5] He spoke to the Rainbow Circle on 'Public Responsibility for Children'—one of his rare return visits to the group after 1906. Otherwise he had little to keep him occupied apart from minor administrative details of the Children Bill and the quotidian chores of the Home Office.

The King's Speech in February 1909 foreshadowed next to no significant Home Office legislation. Samuel therefore helped the Board of Trade with its Trade Boards Bill and the Treasury with work on the budget (the 'People's Budget'). The only Home Office legislation for which he had responsibility that year was the Cinematograph Bill which he introduced on the second reading as 'a small departmental Bill . . . to safeguard the public from the danger which arises from fires at cinematograph entertainments'. No opposition had been anticipated but a Conservative MP, William Watson Rutherford, delayed the bill's passage calling it 'grandmotherly'.[6] The critic spoke truer than he knew, for by an unexpected judicial quirk the Act's provisions became the legal basis for the system of film censorship in Britain. 'We had in mind [Samuel explained long afterwards] only the question of fire and the safety of buildings; but a clause provided that local authorities might attach conditions to the presentation of films. That was interpreted by the Courts to cover the subject-matter of films. The inflammable character of them was not limited to physical fire, but also to the effect upon the passions and upon the mind in general. That was not in the least our intention.'[7] Some extra work devolved on him when Gladstone fell victim to a prolonged illness, but he still felt underemployed and restless.

In June 1909 his opportunity came: the Chancellor of the Duchy of Lancaster, Lord Fitzmaurice, resigned because of ill health. Asquith

---

[4] HS to BS, 22 and 23 Dec. 1908, HLRO HS A/157/431, 432.
[5] HS to ES, 14 Apr. 1909, ISA 100/42.
[6] HC Deb. 5 s., vol. 3 (21 Apr. 1909), cols. 1596–7.
[7] Minutes of meeting of Film Consultative Committee, Home Office, 26 Nov. 1931, PRO HO/45/15208.

offered Samuel the job, which carried with it a seat in the Cabinet, and he
happily accepted. His elevation was generally welcomed in the Liberal
press, the *Daily Chronicle* commenting that he had 'proved himself
peculiarly neat and handy in the conduct of public business'.[8] The
appointment was the first of a practising Jew to a British Cabinet[9] and
there was rejoicing in the Jewish community. In the mind of the Prime
Minister, Samuel's Jewishness seems to have been an asset rather than a
barrier to his advancement, as Jack Pease noted in his diary: 'Asquith
expressed his admiration for Jewish ability and their pertinacity and [the]
way Samuel had got on.'[10] At 38, Samuel was the third-youngest member
of the Cabinet, after Churchill and Walter Runciman who was just a few
days younger than Samuel.

At that period newly appointed Cabinet ministers had to resign their
seats and offer themselves for re-election. Samuel accordingly applied
for the Chiltern Hundreds and set off for Cleveland. He had continued, as
a junior minister, to tend the constituency conscientiously, spending
frequent weekends at the Zetland Hotel in Saltburn, a great Victorian pile
on a cliff overlooking the North Sea: 'The Zetland once more [he wrote to
his wife on one such visit]. Again in the big solitary dining-room. As usual
the wind is howling round its six windows. I have had the familiar fried
sole and tea at six o'clock, followed by a meeting—with supper in
prospect afterwards.'[11] Since 1902 Samuel had spoken at 275 meetings in
the constituency.[12] In particular, he had made a point of always speaking
at the annual miners' demonstrations that were an important seasonal
ritual in the area. The by-election served as an early test of public reaction
to the 'People's Budget'. The ground seemed favourable since the ILP
decided not to put up a candidate and a 'democratic invasion' of Middlesbrough artisans into Redcar had added nearly two thousand voters to the
register since 1902, most of them expected to be Liberals.[13] The Conservatives put up an amiable but weak candidate, Windsor Lewis, whose
chief qualification appeared to be that he was the nephew of the Bishop of
St Asaph.

Samuel's difficulties during the campaign arose not from his opponent
but from other causes. The first appeared in the alluring form of Miss
Adela Pankhurst, 'attired in green with a purple cap of the Napoleonic
type', who drew audiences of thousands to hear suffragette orations at

[8] Quoted in *North-Eastern Daily Gazette*, 26 June 1909.
[9] Disraeli, of course, had been converted to Christianity at the age of 13.
[10] Diary entry, 29 June 1909, Nuffield College, Oxford, Gainford papers 39/67.
[11] HS to BS, 6 Oct. 1906, HLRO HS A/157/362.
[12] *North-Eastern Daily Gazette*, 30 June 1909; list of meetings, HLRO HS A/7.
[13] See HS to CS, 24 Jan. 1909, HLRO HS A/156/298; *North-Eastern Daily Gazette*, 26
and 29 June 1909.

Redcar and Guisborough.[14] Later, Mrs Emmeline Pankhurst herself arrived and addressed several meetings in the constituency. Samuel protected this flank to some extent by securing his wife's presence at meetings, although she would not attend any on the sabbath.[15] The second, and for Samuel more serious, threat resulted from the terms of the Miners' Eight Hours Act that had been passed, with Samuel's help, the previous year. The Act laid down a strict rule that there must be sixteen hours between each work shift—a condition insisted upon by the coal miners, but one that proved inconvenient to the Cleveland ironstone miners who had been used to working a 'back shift' after an eight-hour rest early on Saturday mornings, an arrangement that enabled them to take a long weekend break. Samuel promised to secure an amending bill at an early date to meet the ironstone miners' complaint.

The two sources of trouble combined when Mrs Pankhurst's Women's Social and Political Union issued a pamphlet which not only attacked Samuel for keeping suffragettes in gaol but also printed a letter from his old antagonist Keir Hardie criticizing him on the miners' hours issue.[16] After urgent messages between Samuel and Gladstone, the Home Secretary gave a firm commitment to introduce an amending bill. A telegram from Gladstone announcing the pledge arrived just in time for Samuel to read it out at the annual miners' demonstration which coincided with the climax of the election campaign. The support of the local miners' leader, Joseph Toyn, further helped to defuse the issue. On election day WSPU representatives stood outside polling stations urging electors to cast their votes against a government that imprisoned women. But the miners' vote held firm for the Liberals and Samuel was returned, although with a majority reduced from 2,036 in 1902 to 971 in spite of a higher poll. Samuel attributed the decline to the influence of the liquor trade but the margin was still comfortable enough for him to return to London to resume his duties in a contented frame of mind.

The only problem was that he had no duties. Apart from purely formal oversight of the administration of the Duchy of Lancaster, the position amounted to a ministry without portfolio. He had little to do except attend meetings of Cabinet and Parliament. When he took his seat at the Cabinet table for the first time on 16 July 1909, John Burns found him 'quiet, imperturbable, almost academic'.[17] He spoke several times in Parliament on the controversial Finance Bill, and stepped in for the still indisposed Gladstone on a few occasions to submit the daily parliamentary

---

[14] *North-Eastern Daily Gazette*, 29 and 30 June 1909.
[15] BS to CS, 2 July [1909], HLRO B/3/63.
[16] *North-Eastern Daily Gazette*, 8 July 1909.
[17] Diary entry, 16 July 1909. BL Add. MS 46327, leaf 29.

report to the King, normally written by the Home Secretary.[18] But in general he found the enforced inaction of his high office frustrating.

The only significant political activity for which he was responsible in 1909 was his chairmanship of a joint Select Committee of the two Houses appointed to examine the question of theatrical censorship. The formation of the committee in July followed the rejection by the Lord Chamberlain two months earlier of an application for a licence to perform Shaw's *The Shewing-up of Blanco Posnet*. The offence alleged against the play was blasphemy.[19] Shaw subtitled the piece 'A Sermon in crude Melodrama', but the succeeding events savoured more of Shavian comedietta—or Whitehall farce.

Theatrical censorship, in the form of the licensing of particular plays for performance, had existed in England since at the latest 1549. From 1628 it had been exercised by the Lord Chamberlain whose powers were given statutory form in 1737 and 1843. The 1843 Act, which applied to England, Wales, and Scotland, but not to Ireland, conferred on the Lord Chamberlain an unfettered authority to prohibit the performance of plays where 'he shall be of opinion that it is fitting for the preservation of good manners, decorum or of the public peace so to do'. The duties of censor were in fact performed by a subordinate official, the Examiner of Plays. The holder of that office in 1909 was G. A. Redford, a former bank manager who had had a previous run-in with Shaw in 1898 over *Mrs Warren's Profession* against which he had issued 'an uncompromising Veto'. Shaw dubbed the unfortunate official the 'Malvolio of St James's Court' and waged an unrelenting battle to abolish his position.[20] Although the Lord Chamberlain's office was formally quite independent of any government department, the Home Office answered for the censor in the House of Commons[21] and the Home Secretary was occasionally consulted in advance about 'questions of principle or of law that are likely to arise.'[22] Hence the desirability of Home Office

[18] Reports on proceedings for 23, 24, 27, and 28 Sept. 1909, Royal Archives, R. 39/ 82 ff.

[19] Douglas Dawson (Lord Chamberlain's Office) to W. P. Byrne (Home Office), 20 May 1909, PRO HO 45/10549/157288.

[20] Dan H. Laurence (ed.), *Bernard Shaw: Collected Letters*, ii, *1898–1910* (New York, 1985), 13–14 ff.; Holroyd, *Shaw*, i. 334–5.

[21] As the Lord Chamberlain was a member of the royal household, paid out of the civil list, it was held that parliamentary questions in the House of Commons could not be asked directly concerning his conduct or decisions. The only way in which the matter could be raised in Parliament was by special motion as in the case of matters concerning the Lord Chancellor, the Speaker, and judges of the High Court (unsigned note by the Speaker of the House of Commons, HLRO HS A/33/9). This lack of accountability was a further aggravation to the anti-censorship lobby.

[22] Troup, *Home Office*, 200.

representation on such a committee. Given Gladstone's illness Samuel was the obvious choice.

Samuel had, as we have seen, already expressed an opinion in his *Liberalism* in favour of the continuation of theatrical censorship. This was no passing whim but a settled conviction arising from a deeply rooted sense of the requirements of public decency. His longstanding friendship with Shaw did not lead him to modify his opinion. On issues such as this Samuel's Liberalism was not unconditionally libertarian. His eldest son called him 'puritanical in the extreme' and indeed he combined prudishness with a surprising tendency to philistinism in aesthetic judgements.[23] Like the British public, Samuel was prone to periodic fits of morality. And, like the nation as a whole, he had an unfortunate tendency to make a ridiculous spectacle of himself on such occasions. This, alas, was one such occasion.

The seed of the committee had been planted in December 1907 by a public letter of protest against the censorship system that was signed by seventy-one authors and playwrights, among them Harley Granville-Barker (whose *Waste* had been banned by Redford), J. M. Barrie, Joseph Conrad, John Galsworthy, Edward Garnett (whose *The Breaking Point* had fallen under the axe), W. S. Gilbert (whose *Mikado* had been temporarily refused a licence in 1907 for fear of upsetting the Japanese government and court), Thomas Hardy, Somerset Maugham, George Meredith, Gilbert Murray, H. G. Wells, W. B. Yeats, and—the *fons et origo* of the document—Shaw. The letter was followed in early 1908 by another, signed by a further seventy-one public figures who included Sidney Ball, Max Beerbohm, H. A. L. Fisher, Bertrand Russell, and the Webbs, as well as Winston Churchill, Charles Masterman, Hilaire Belloc, and other influential politicians and publicists. In June 1908, after meeting a deputation of authors headed by Arthur Pinero, Gladstone wrote to Asquith suggesting 'a new arrangement . . . of a nature which would commend itself to the public as combining competence to deal with higher morality problems, and commonsense in regard to the ordinary questions of decency'. As to what the 'new arrangement' should be Gladstone was vague, suggesting some sort of standing advisory board. Asquith approved the idea in July 1908 and a board was appointed. Before it could meet, however, Shaw orchestrated, with crackling brilliance, a further public outcry over the ban on *Blanco Posnet*. This led to the appointment of Samuel's committee.[24]

[23] Edwin Samuel, *A Lifetime in Jerusalem: The Memoirs of the Second Viscount Samuel* (London, 1970), 7–8.
[24] File of documents on theatrical censorship, PRO HO 45/10549/157288; evidence of Comptroller of Lord Chamberlain's Department to Select Committee in *Report from the*

The committee was composed of five members from each House of Parliament. None could claim great literary or theatrical standing. They met from July to November 1909. Their mandate was 'to report on any alterations of the law or practice which may appear desirable'. They interviewed forty-nine witnesses, among them Redford, John Galsworthy, Hall Caine, G. K. Chesterton, Granville-Barker, Sir Herbert Beerbohm Tree, the Speaker of the House of Commons, the Bishop of Southwark, various dramatists, critics, theatre managers, directors of music halls, and—the star turn—Shaw. A little strangely, given the stress that was laid on the Lord Chamberlain's total discretion in censorship decisions, that great panjandrum was not himself required to attend for interrogation. Indeed, even mention of his name (Viscount Althorp) seems to have been regarded as almost taboo. In spite of this curious lacuna, the committee's proceedings led to several revealing exchanges:

SAMUEL. On what principles do you proceed in licensing the plays that come before you?

REDFORD. Simply bringing to bear an official point of view and keeping up a standard. It is really impossible to define what the principle may be. There are no principles that can be defined. I follow precedent.

SAMUEL. Generally, you read a play with a view of detecting in it, should it be there, indecency or passages that may be offensive to religious sentiment?

REDFORD. Yes.

SAMUEL. If it were proposed to perform a Greek play in public would that come under your consideration? [. . .]

REDFORD. I should say so; for an English translation certainly.

SAMUEL. Why are political allusions in pantomimes considered objectionable?

REDFORD. The stage is not a political arena, and it is not desirable that specially important political questions, perhaps involving diplomatic relations with Foreign Powers, should be touched upon. That is the practice of the Office.

SAMUEL. May it not be a healthy thing for politicians to be satirized on the stage?

REDFORD. Personally, I do not think so.

These replies in open session were hardly of a sort to raise the public estimation of the Examiner, nor perhaps to guarantee a serious reception for the committee's earnest deliberations.

Shaw's behaviour towards the committee, a masterpiece of public relations, was deliberately calculated to strike a note of levity that would make a mockery of the entire censorship system. Before his entrance on the stage of the House of Lords committee room in which witnesses were

Joint Select Committee of the House of Lords and the House of Commons on the Stage Plays (Censorship) together with the Proceedings of the Committee, Minutes of Evidence and Appendices (London, 1909).

questioned, he prepared a lengthy memorandum setting out his views. This was distributed in advance to the committee, the press, and all and sundry. But as the editor of his letters puts it: 'Being chief actor and author was not sufficient. . . . Shaw appointed himself director, stage manager, puppet master, and fencing instructor! He conferred endlessly with Herbert Samuel. . . . He prepared a series of "Model Proofs" of testimony for co-operating peers, churchmen and titled ladies, to suggest the lines that statements from each of them to the committee might follow.'[25] Nor was this all. When the appointed day for his appearance before the committee arrived, he disrupted the proceedings by demanding to be allowed to read out his immensely long written statement. After this had been refused, Samuel and Shaw engaged in a dramatic dialogue that might have been the stuff of one of Shaw's own plays.

SAMUEL. You admit that in all ages and all countries there have been representations on the stage deliberately intended to incite to sexual immorality?

SHAW. Almost all performances—that is too strong—but I should say a very large percentage of performances which take place at present on the English stage under the censorship licence have for their object the stimulation of sexual desire.

SAMUEL. You think that any outrage on religion, or attack upon religion, or ridicule of sacred personages, should be allowed on the stage?

SHAW. I think it should. I think that the public would look after that. I think that the danger of crippling thought, the danger of obstructing the formation of the public mind by specially suppressing such representations is far greater than any real danger that there is from such representations.

More followed, in which, as was only to be expected, the nimble-witted man of letters danced merrily round the questions posed by the solemn statesmen.

Indignant at what he affected to regard as the committee's affront to his professional honour, Shaw redoubled his efforts to upset the entire applecart of censorship. He wrote to Samuel privately: 'I shall fly to the last refuge of the oppressed: a letter to The Times.' With characteristic effrontery he added: 'I cannot think for the life of me why you let them spoil your blue book by cutting me out of it.'[26] The offended dramatist arranged for the blue-pencilled passages of *Blanco Posnet* to appear in print in the *Nation*—the Lord Chamberlain's prohibition, after all, extended only to performance, not publication. Most damagingly of all, he took advantage of a loophole in the law. The Lord Chamberlain's authority over theatrical performances extended only over Great Britain. Shaw therefore arranged for *Blanco Posnet* to be performed at the Abbey Theatre in his native Dublin. No legal method of preventing this could be

[25] Laurence (ed.), *Shaw's Letters*, ii. 748–9.
[26] Shaw to HS, 31 July 1909, HLRO HS A/33.

discovered by the irate Irish authorities, and the performance took place on 25 August even as Samuel's committee was still examining some of the lesser witnesses. The public display of blasphemy occurred without, so far as is known, provoking an increased incidence of atheism in Ireland or other untoward effect.[27] But Shaw had succeeded in his primary aim of demonstrating that the law was an ass, and Samuel as that animal's most immediate guardian inevitably shared in the attendant ridicule.

The committee's report, drafted by Samuel, admitted that 'with rare exceptions all the dramatists of the day ask either for the abolition of the censorship or for an appeal from its decisions to some other authority'. On the other hand, the theatre managers generally favoured the retention of a licensing system. The committee rejected the suggestion that the existing laws against indecency, blasphemy, and libel in printed publications would suffice to deal with stage productions:

Ideas or situations which, when described on a printed page may work little mischief, when presented through the human personality of actors may have a more powerful and more deleterious effect. The existence of an audience, moved by the same emotions, its members conscious of one another's presence, intensifies the influence of what is done and spoken on the stage. Moreover, scenes in a play may stimulate to vice without falling within the legal definition of indecency; they may include personalities so offensive as to be clearly improper for presentation, which yet are not punishable as libellous; they may outrage feelings of religious reverence without coming within the scope of the Blasphemy Laws; and they may give occasion for demonstrations injurious to good relations between this country and Foreign Powers without coming within the purview of any law whatsoever.

On these grounds the committee decided that some censorship system must remain. At the same time the report recognized that

a Censorship with a power of veto before production is open to grave objection. Secret in its operation, subject to no effective control by public opinion, its effect can hardly fail to be to coerce into conformity with the conventional standards of the day dramatists who may be seeking to amend them. Those standards are not absolute. It is an axiom underlying all our legislation that only through the toleration of that which one age thinks to be an error can the next age progress further in the pursuit of truth.

Having rehearsed the two sides of the question, after the style of *Liberalism*, Samuel's report proceeded to recommendations.

Rejecting Gladstone's proposed arbitration board, the committee commented: 'The question at issue is not to be regarded in the light of a dispute between two individuals, to be decided by the opinion of a third party acceptable to both. It is the question by what means the state, on behalf of the community, is to prevent the public performance of plays

[27] See Michael Holroyd, *Bernard Shaw*, ii (London, 1989), 230–1.

which are improper for such performance.' This passage, heavily marked
by Samuel in his personal copy of the report, undoubtedly reflected his
fundamental attitude to the problem. His view combined Gladstonian
moralism with an étatist interventionism based on the conception of an
organic community that he had preached in *Liberalism*. While the
upholding of censorship no doubt also accorded with his own puritanical
inclinations, Samuel should not be construed as a humbug or a Mrs
Grundy. The failing, if failing it was, may be understood less as personal
idiosyncrasy than as part of the collective mentality of elements within the
New Liberalism, arising directly out of its thought.

The committee recommended that although prior licensing of plays
after scrutiny by the Examiner should be continued, the Lord Chamberlain
should no longer retain the right to veto the production of an unlicensed
play. In cases of indecency, the performance of unlicensed plays should be
prosecuted and courts empowered to impose penalties and ban further
performances for periods of up to ten years. In cases other than indecency,
including 'offensive personalities', 'violence to the sentiment of religious
reverence', or plays 'calculated to conduce to crime or vice' or 'to impair
friendly relations with any Foreign Power', a standing committee of the
Privy Council should be created with the power to ban performance of a
play for up to ten years. The intention behind these proposals was no
doubt liberalizing, although, in practice, the spelling out for the first time
of specific grounds of potential prohibition would probably have had
anything but a liberalizing effect. In the event, the committee's recommendations were not acted upon. Theatrical censorship in Britain was not
abolished until 1968. The Select Committee's report would probably
have been quietly discarded to the parliamentary archives had it not been
for the reaction of that supreme Edwardian social irritant, George
Bernard Shaw.

Baulked of his desire to enliven the parliamentary blue book, Shaw
issued his 11,000-word statement which, he said, would rival the *Areo-
pagitica*, as the preface to the published edition of *Blanco Posnet*. One of
the most sparkling of his prefaces (Conrad called it 'somewhat imbecile—
in the classical meaning of the term'[28]), it poured scorn on the censor, on
the censorship system, on the committee, and on poor Samuel—but did
so with such typically Shavian cheerfulness, good humour, and lack of
personal rancour as to leave the victims with no ground whatsoever for
complaint and little room for rebuttal. Most damning of all was Shaw's
critique of the specific grounds for censorship proposed by the committee:
'Now it is clear that there is no play yet written, or possible to be written,

---

[28] Quoted in Holroyd, *Shaw*, ii. 234–5.

in this world, that might not be condemned under one or other of these heads. How any sane man, not being a professed enemy of public liberty, could put his hand to so monstrous a catalogue passes my understanding.'[29] No less incisive criticism of the committee's report came from Max Beerbohm who laughed it to pieces in an elegant little essay in the *Saturday Review*.[30] There the comic opera ended—save that in Herbert Samuel's biography it was succeeded after a short interlude by a morality play of a very different order of seriousness.

In February 1910 Asquith offered Samuel the position of Postmaster General. During the entr'acte of the previous months, two events, one private, the other public, had taken the spotlight off Samuel's theatrical embarrassments. The private event was Samuel's near-death from drowning in the sea off Saltburn. He survived with no ill effects and with a useful little swirl of sympathetic local publicity. The public event was the general election of January 1910, provoked by the House of Lords' rejection of the 1909 budget. This was the longest election campaign in modern British history: it lasted from 3 December to the end of January and the last day of polling was on 10 February. It was also perhaps the most intense. Feeling on both sides was raised to a high pitch, and men (and voteless women) trudged miles through biting cold to attend vast political meetings. Journalists, vying for superlatives, said that it was the most momentous campaign of their lifetimes, or since 1832, or since the Civil War.[31]

In Cleveland Samuel again faced a challenge from Windsor Lewis, and in view of his reduced majority at the recent by-election he could not afford to be complacent. He opened his campaign at Redcar, speaking under a banner that asked: 'Shall the Peers or the People Rule?' With more than usual warmth in the face of shouting in the crowd, he declared 'that he would give ten years of his life, if need were, to carry through a measure freeing this country from the domination of the peerage'.[32] In the course of three weeks he spoke at seventy-one meetings including several in neighbouring constituencies. Among the latter was a speech at a large meeting in Darlington on 22 December on behalf of the local Liberal candidate, the Hungarian-born Ignatius Trebitsch Lincoln. Samuel was later to have cause to regret his endorsement of the candidacy of this con-man and traitor.[33] Although Samuel encountered further trouble over the Miners' Eight Hours Act which had not yet been amended, Joseph Toyn

[29] Bernard Shaw, *The Shewing-up of Blanco Posnet* (London, 1927 repr.), 361.
[30] *Saturday Review*, 20 Nov. 1909.
[31] Blewett, *Peers, Parties, People*, 128–9.
[32] *Cleveland Standard*, 11 Dec. 1909.
[33] See Bernard Wasserstein, *The Secret Lives of Trebitsch Lincoln* (2nd rev. edn., London, 1989).

as usual carried the miners' vote solidly into the Liberal camp. A potential danger from a new quarter appeared in the shape of Samuel's predecessor, Sir Alfred Pease, who was reported to have announced that he would vote for the Conservative candidate, but fortunately for Samuel, Pease's personal influence in the district was now much diminished.[34] According to the *Cleveland Standard*, Samuel maintained 'a great hold on the mining centre of the constituency, who simply idolize him in some villages'.[35] The campaign ended with torchlight processions and what the Liberal press called 'six thrilling addresses' by Samuel. Excitement was said to be 'at fever heat'.[36] The result, declared on 20 January 1910, was decisive: Samuel doubled his by-election majority, a success all the more striking by comparison with the general decline in Liberal fortunes. The overall Liberal parliamentary majority of 1906 was wiped out. Liberals and Conservatives emerged almost exactly level in the House of Commons. Henceforth the Government was, as a result, dependent on the support of the 82 Irish and 40 Labour MPs.

Samuel did not immediately accept Asquith's offer after the election to move him to the Post Office. Press speculation had put him at the Home Office in succession to Gladstone or at the Local Government Board replacing the do-nothing incumbent, Burns. Both of those ministries offered scope for reformist legislation of the sort that Samuel wanted.[37] The General Post Office would afford few such opportunities. But it was at least an executive position, unlike the Duchy of Lancaster. Samuel therefore accepted, comforting himself with the reflection that he would probably not remain in the job for very long.[38] He stayed there for four years, his longest service in any department.

The General Post Office at this time was one of the largest businesses in the world. On a turnover of £24,000,000 it earned £4,000,000 profit for the Treasury each year. With a work-force of over 200,000 it was the largest single employer of labour in Britain. It was also one of the most labour-intensive. At this time there were still up to twelve deliveries a day in London! Following staff complaints, Samuel commissioned investigations that resulted in significant improvements in almost Dickensian labour conditions. In particular, he ended the system whereby the Post Office employed 14,000 boy messengers, dismissing 4,000 of them each

[34] The report may, in any case, have been false—to judge from Pease's effusive letter of congratulation to Samuel after the announcement of the result. See *North-Eastern Daily Gazette*, 12 Jan. 1910; Pease to HS, 20 Jan. 1910, HLRO HS A/155/IV.
[35] *Cleveland Standard*, 15 Jan. 1910.
[36] *North-Eastern Daily Gazette*, 15 Jan. 1910.
[37] HS to CS, 6 Feb. 1910, HLRO HS A/156/326.
[38] HS to CS, 13 Feb. 1910 [misdated], HLRO HS A/156/320; Gainford diary, 15 [Feb.] 1910, Nuffield College, Oxford, Gainford papers 38/85.

year when they reached the age of 16. He implemented a modernization programme that began the transformation of the Post Office into a technologically advanced and efficient organization run on business lines.

In November 1910 Samuel presided over the opening of the 'London Chief Office' of the GPO in the newly-built King Edward's Building in St Martin's-le-Grand. From these imposing headquarters Samuel pressed forward with the mechanization and automation of the Post Office's systems. Motorized vans, replacing horse-drawn wagons, gradually came into general use (at a maximum speed of twelve miles per hour). In 1912 the first automatic telephone exchanges were installed at Epsom and Caterham. A 6½-mile London Post Office underground railway line from Paddington to Whitechapel was planned under Samuel's direction, and an Act was passed in 1913 to enable it to be built. A feature of the plan from the outset was that the trains would be driverless. The scheme was suspended during the First World War, but the railway eventually opened in 1927.[39]

The first experimental air mail service began in September 1911. This was a privately operated service that ran with the sanction of the Postmaster General. During its seven days of operation it carried 133,000 items from Windsor to Hendon in a Blériot monoplane and a Farman biplane at a price of 1s. 1d. per letter, thirteen times the surface rate. Samuel received delivery of the world's first air letter on 9 September. Unfortunately one of the pilots was seriously injured in the course of the experiment. The scheme was not judged a success in other ways. Samuel was informed that the operation 'has given an amount of trouble not justified by its results the chief of which appears to be a great deal of cheap notoriety attained by the Contractors'.[40] After this failure, public air mail service was not resumed until after the First World War.[41]

The most important structural change under Samuel's administration was the completion of the Government's take-over of the National Telephone Company, the first nationalization (although the term was not widely used at that time) of a major industry in modern Britain. The measure gave the Post Office virtual monopoly control of the telephone

[39] Evan Evans, 'The Post Office (London) Railway: Its Equipment and Operation', printed paper, 1929, Post Office Archives.

[40] Memorandum on 1911 Aerial Post and accompanying documents, Post Office Archives, E 6060/1914; see also HLRO HS A/37; and The Times and Evening Standard, 11 Nov. 1911.

[41] During the First World War the RAF operated an aerial postal service for official correspondence between England and France. The first public international air mail service was introduced between London and Paris in Nov. 1919. The first government demonstration flight of air mail in the USA was in 1911 but regular service did not begin there until 15 May 1918.

system in Great Britain.[42] After difficult negotiations with the company and the passage of necessary legislation, the NTC system merged with that of the Post Office on 31 December 1911.

Samuel enjoyed the management of this large, innovative, and progressive organization, but the job was not without its headaches. One of the more troublesome was the tendency of many MPs, not to mention other disgruntled persons, to complain directly to the Postmaster General if their telephone calls went awry for any reason. Since the National Telephone Company, anticipating dissolution, had neglected to invest in urgently needed capital equipment for several years, the telephone lines were severely overloaded when the Government took them over, so that the number of complaints soared. Nor was the telephone service the only cause for protests. Scottish and Irish MPs grumbled about inadequate telegraph services. F. E. Smith delivered a fiery speech about the dismissal for misconduct of a telegraph boy in Liverpool. And a constant stream of grouses about undelivered letters, ill-treated postmen, Welsh-speaking postmasters, the right of postal employees to wear a shamrock on St Patrick's Day, the Andes railway route for Australian mails, and so forth cascaded into Samuel's office in St Martin's-le-Grand.

A persistent nuisance was the self-styled champion of what was termed 'postal reform', the Kentish baronet Sir John Henniker Heaton, MP. Known as the 'Father of Imperial Penny Postage', he was constantly agitating for price reductions and other schemes of varying degrees of practicability. Samuel described him privately as 'a muddle-headed man who makes the most preposterous proposals and has no more idea of finance than a cow', but he nevertheless showed endless patience and paid him due courtesies in public, even adopting some of the more harmless of his ideas.[43] As a Parthian shot, upon his retirement from the House of Commons in December 1910, Henniker Heaton submitted a list of sixty-two suggested 'reforms', one for each year of his life. It says much at least for Samuel's tact that, by the time he left the Post Office in 1914, this

---

[42] After the telephone came into use in about 1880 the Post Office, which possessed a statutory monopoly of electrical communication, granted licences, expiring in 1911, to various companies to operate telephone services. These companies amalgamated in 1889 into the National Telephone Company. In 1896 the Post Office purchased all the country's trunk wires and operated them henceforth, adding a great many more to the system. In 1902 the Post Office opened its own local telephone service in London. As a result, the Post Office system in 1911, on the eve of the take-over of the NTC, already owned 100,000 of the 600,000 telephones in the country. The 1911 nationalization was therefore both an expansion of the GPO's own network and a reassertion by the Post Office of its original monopoly. A municipal service was, however, retained after 1911 in Portsmouth and Hull.

[43] HS to CS, 12 Feb. 1911, HLRO HS A/156/368.

exacting critic 'made no secret of the fact that he considered Mr Herbert Samuel the greatest Postmaster General England has ever had'.[44]

Interference from a more august source arose as a result of the death of King Edward VII in May 1910. Since by custom all British postage stamps bore the head of the reigning monarch, the accession of a new king necessitated a new issue of stamps. As it happened, philately was King George V's main, almost his only, intellectual interest—if such it may be termed. As the owner of the world's greatest stamp collection, he held decided views on the design of the new issue. In consequence, much of Samuel's time was taken up with the commissioning of artists, inspection of sketches, and consultation on the subject with the King and his private secretary as well as with the President of the Royal Academy, the Master of the Mint, the Board of Inland Revenue, the Treasury, and Post Office experts.[45] Endless discussion of the size of the King's head, the design of the heraldic lion, the frame, the scroll, and the knot of oak and laurel leaves, not to mention the technical aspects of production, reduced the King and everybody else concerned to a state of despair. The inevitable delays, by no means entirely the fault of the meddlesome monarch, but partly arising from the Mint's preoccupation with the new George V coinage, led to criticism of the failure to produce the whole of the new issue by Coronation Day on 22 June 1911.

The repeated redesigns and compromises led to a product that satisfied nobody. The new issue was condemned in the House of Commons as an 'atrocity' and the King lamented that 'a Stamp totally unworthy of this Country has been produced'.[46] Samuel promised to introduce improvements, whereupon the round of consultation was renewed, the King once again complaining about the effigy of his head and the background (too dark).[47] At one stage the King became so annoyed that he suggested scrapping the whole series and reinstating the old Edward VII series for the time being.[48] A visit by Samuel to Balmoral in September 1912 soothed the royal disposition, but the King continued to find fault with new designs, demanding a deeper tint and a 'graduated' rather than a

[44] Mrs Adrian Porter, The Life and Letters of Sir John Henniker Heaton Bt. (London, 1916), 205.

[45] See HS correspondence with Sir Arthur Bigge, 1910–11, Royal Archives, GV 4130; and extensive documentation (including minutes by HS), 1910–11, Post Office Archives, E 22006/1911 and E 10639/1911.

[46] HC Deb. 5 s., vol. 27 (28 June 1911), cols. 420–1; F. E. G. Ponsonby to Sir M. Nathan, 28 June 1911, Royal Archives, GV 2090/1.

[47] Stamfordham to HS, 8 Nov. 1911, Royal Archives, GV 2090/6; and Ponsonby to Sir A. King, 24 May 1912, ibid., GV 2090/17.

[48] Unsigned note, 11 Nov. 1911, Royal Archives, GV 2090/8.

'solid' surround.[49] Only in 1913 did the monarch's almost obsessive attention to these details of philatelic manufacture subside.

Meanwhile, George V's accession had had the larger effect of complicating the constitutional crisis over the powers of the House of Lords. Samuel did not play a direct part in the constitutional conference of Liberals and Unionists that sat from June to November 1910 without reaching agreement. Nevertheless, he echoed Grey and Churchill in urging on Asquith in early 1910 the policy of House of Lords reform that was pressed by the Liberals in the conference.[50] The ultimate failure of the conference was due to the Conservative insistence that Irish Home Rule must be included in the category of bills which, if rejected two years running by the House of Lords, would be subject to a referendum. Cabinet members not present at the conference were not fully informed of its discussions, but after a conversation on the subject with Lloyd George Samuel wrote to him proposing that the Liberals might undertake not to introduce a Home Rule bill in the present Parliament.[51] No such agreement was reached, and in November 1910 Asquith called the second general election within a year. At the same time he demanded, and within twenty-four hours received, a pledge from the King that he would, if called upon to do so after the election, create a sufficient number of new peers to ensure passage of a Liberal Government's legislation for reform of the House of Lords. The Liberals' star performer on the hustings was Lloyd George who was in peak oratorical form, portraying the Lords as a kind of grating across a river, which let through the little fish but stopped the salmon. The people wanted salmon for dinner sometimes, said the Chancellor of the Exchequer, and they meant to remove that grating.[52] The overall result of the December 1910 election was almost identical with that of the previous January, thus opening the way for the Liberals to proceed with parliamentary reform.

Samuel, who was again opposed by Windsor Lewis, spent £1,800 on his campaign in Cleveland.[53] He could not rival the vivid imagery of Lloyd George, but in his speeches to mining audiences he gave vent to unusual passion, declaring, 'Everything I care about in politics depends upon our victory now—social reform, religious equality, and democratic self-government.'[54] The campaign was marred by an unusual amount of

---

[49] Stamfordham to HS, 12 Oct. 1912, Royal Archives, GV 2090/25; sim., 3 Feb. 1913, ibid., GV 2090/35.

[50] HS to Asquith, 3 Feb. 1910, Asquith papers, Bodleian Library, Oxford 12/105–6; see also Blewett, *Peers, Parties, People*, 149–50.

[51] HS to Lloyd George, undated [1910], HLRO Lloyd George papers C/7/9/5.

[52] *North-Eastern Daily Gazette*, 30 Nov. 1910.

[53] HS to CS, undated [c.Dec. 1910], HLRO HS A/156/361.

[54] *North-Eastern Daily Gazette*, 30 Nov. 1910.

rowdyism which literally reached Samuel's front door in the shape of a boot thrown by a suffragette. Little damage was caused, and Samuel's reaction was philosophic, but a much more serious incident about the same time caused him deep embarrassment and great annoyance. In November 1910, the 21-year-old Hugh Franklin, nephew of Samuel's wife and a militant sympathizer with the suffragettes, witnessed the so-called 'Battle of Downing Street', a scuffle in which Birrell's knee was hurt. He overheard the Home Secretary, Churchill, instruct the police to arrest a suffragette. Determined on revenge, he stalked Churchill to Bradford, heckled him at an election meeting, followed him to the train back to London, and attacked him with a whip, shouting, 'Take that you dirty cur!' Fortunately Churchill was not hurt. Samuel was furious, writing to his mother, 'Hugh Franklin's cowardly and stupid attempt to assault Churchill deserves severe punishment. I shall have no more to do with the young donkey, now or in the future.'[55] Franklin was sentenced to six weeks imprisonment. In 1913 he was arrested again for setting fire to a railway carriage as 'a form of political protest' and received a sentence of nine months. In prison he pursued what Samuel called 'the whole idiotic programme of his silly movement': he went on hunger strike and was forcibly fed.[56] The suffragette agitation had little effect in Cleveland, but almost inevitably the third election in the constituency within eighteen months led to a diminution of enthusiasm. Samuel's majority was slightly reduced to 1,527.

When Parliament resumed Samuel found himself drawn closer to the inner circle of strategic political planning. He helped Asquith with the Parliament Bill and the Irish Home Rule Bill. He also served on the Cabinet committee that dealt with Home Office bills and in this capacity turned the tables on Churchill, who had urged a more liberal aliens policy when Samuel was at the Home Office, by pressing for the elimination of a clause in the Aliens (Prevention of Crime) Bill that provided for the imprisonment of aliens who could not provide sureties.[57] In March 1911 Samuel wound up for the Government on the second reading of the Parliament Bill. The House was crowded in preparation for the critical vote and the atmosphere was electric. Samuel delivered a combative speech, writing afterwards to his mother: 'As I was not in the smallest degree nervous, I must confess that I had a very happy evening! I spoke with much more

[55] HS to CS, 4 Dec. 1910, HLRO HS A/156/354.
[56] HS to CS, 23 Feb. 1913, HLRO HS A/156/431. Randolph Churchill, *Winston Churchill*, ii. 400; *The Times*, 10 Mar. 1913; Roger Fulford, *Votes for Women* (London, 1957), 232–3.
[57] HS to Churchill, 6 Feb. 1911, Randolph Churchill, *Winston Churchill*, vol. ii, Companion part 2 (London, 1969), 1246.

freedom and vehemence than I usually do.'[58] The speech earned a number of accolades, and even Balfour sent him a message of congratulation.[59] At 10.55 p.m. on 10 August Samuel was speaking in the House of Commons on the Government resolution on payment of MPs, when news arrived of the vote in the Lords on the Parliament Bill. 'There has never been in our time so exciting a division,' wrote Samuel to his mother, 'for there has been none, touching large issues, where the result was uncertain until the last moment.'[60] Faced with the prospect of a massive creation of Liberal peers, enough Conservatives deserted the 'Diehards' to give the Government a majority of 17 in the Lords on the crucial division. This was the climax of the constitutional struggle and there was rejoicing on the Government benches. A few days later Samuel was present in the House of Lords to witness the royal assent being given to the Parliament Act, an occasion, he said, that filled him with 'violent satisfaction'.[61]

Samuel's effective parliamentary performances in 1911 and his managerial skill at the Post Office enhanced his reputation and his standing in the Government. Winston Churchill, who liked to enliven his parliamentary reports to the King with witty personal observations, described the debate on the Post Office estimates in May 1911 thus:

Mr Secretary Churchill with his humble duty to Your Majesty: the Postmaster general yesterday made a vy interesting annual statement of the works & projects of his Department. Mr Herbert Samuel is a most efficient Minister who works with mechanical regularity from morning till midnight and whose health appears quite unaffected by the most strenuous exertions. . . . There seems to be no end to the wonderful work of the immense Postal machine, which in spite of the increasing pay of its servants & their demands, yields a handsome yearly income to the state, & discharges its vast & intricate duties with marvellous precision.[62]

This was a generous tribute from a disinterested observer—unless there were a whiff of satire in the juxtaposed comparisons of the human with a machine and of the machine with a human. Unhappily for Samuel, not all were so disinterested, and many were far from generous.

Indeed, the striking, and had he but known it, alarming, fact about Samuel's reputation at this time is that in spite of his admitted efficiency and diligence, he was not greatly liked, particularly at Westminster. For example, Charles Hobhouse, a Cabinet colleague, wrote in his diary in

---

[58] HS to CS, 5 Mar. 1911, HLRO HS A/156/371.
[59] HC Deb. 5 s., vol. 22 (2 Mar. 1911), cols. 662–70; BS to CS, 3 Mar. 1911, HLRO HS A/155/IV/20; Churchill to King George V, 3 Mar. 1911, Randolph Churchill, Winston Churchill, vol. ii, Companion part 2, 1053–4.
[60] HS to CS, 13 Aug. 1911, HLRO HS A/156/384.
[61] HS to BS, 18 Aug. 1911, HLRO HS A/157/561.
[62] Randolph Churchill, Winston Churchill, vol. ii, Companion part 2, 1081.

1912: 'Samuel is industrious, a good speaker, and clear thinker. His judgement is respected and his advice accepted, but everyone thinks him absolutely self-centred and his whole horizon bounded by his own career. He would never have time to pick any unfortunate fellow creature out of the mire.'[63] The judgement was grotesquely unfair, particularly since one of Samuel's special characteristics as a minister was to offer, whenever he had any spare time, to help other ministers out with their work. But such offers were sometimes interpreted as interference rather than helpfulness, and in any case, whatever its justice, the dislike for Samuel remained. The sources of this feeling are a little obscure. No doubt, and as events were to show, anti-Semitism had something to do with it. But it is plain that the distaste was often personal rather than merely racial. 'Exactly why his fellow ministers dislike him so [wrote Charles Masterman's wife in December 1909] is a little difficult to define. It is not, or at any rate, not very considerably on account of his race. There are other Jews in the House, far more typical, for whom the House has a great affection. But his manner is unfortunate and there is universally a feeling that he plays for his own hand.'[64]

To some, Samuel seemed at times inhuman and priggish. In H. G. Wells's novel, *The New Machiavelli*, published in early 1911, Samuel appears in thin fictional disguise as 'Lewis, a brilliant representative of his race, able, industrious and invariably uninspired'. The novel was conceived primarily as a diatribe against the Webbs on account of their censorious attitude to Wells's sexual peccadilloes. Horror at what Samuel called the 'abominable incident', in which Wells had fathered a child by the daughter of a friend, had led former friends to break off relations with the errant novelist, in Samuel's case to the extent of cutting him in the street.[65] Vengefully savaging the Webbs and their set as 'prigs at play', Wells took the opportunity to poke fun at Samuel's apparently mechanical humanity. He invented the following satirical dialogue supposedly overheard at a dinner party given by the 'Baileys' (i.e. the Webbs):

'I want,' said Britten, repeating his challenge a little louder, 'to hear just exactly what you think you are doing in Parliament.'

Lewis [i.e. Samuel] laughed nervously, and thought we were 'Seeking the Good of the Community.'

'*How?*'

'Beneficent Legislation,' said Lewis.

[63] Entry dated 13 Aug. 1912, in Edward David (ed.), *Inside Asquith's Cabinet: From the Diaries of Charles Hobhouse* (London, 1977), 121.

[64] Lucy Masterman diary, 1 Dec. 1909, Birmingham University Library.

[65] Record by Frank Singleton of conversation with HS, 6 Feb. 1939, HLRO HS A/161/2.

'Beneficent in what direction?' insisted Britten. 'I want to know where you think you are going.'

'Amelioration of Social Conditions,' said Lewis.

'That's only a phrase!'

'You wouldn't have me sketch bills at dinner?'

'I'd like you to indicate directions,' said Britten, and waited.

'Upward and On,' said Lewis with conscious neatness . . .[66]

Samuel found the attack on himself 'quite mild'—reasonably enough, since, as we have seen, Samuel did, in fact, 'sketch bills at dinner'.[67] But if the shaft did not strike a nerve in its victim, it struck home in the minds of its readers.

Samuel's efficiency and accuracy jarred. On one occasion in 1913, after the Irish Nationalist MP Tim Healy launched what was described as a 'wild-cat spring' at Samuel in the House of Commons, the *Sunday Times* suggested: 'Possibly his very band-box perfection got on the nerves of Mr Healy, who is not over-particular whether he wears his hat with the front to the fore or not. At any rate, his incursion seemed to be devoid of any other motive.'[68] T. P. O'Connor, MP wrote of Samuel as a 'composed, self-confident, vigilant figure' who 'has everything stowed away in that very retentive memory of his and . . . cannot be tripped up on any statement or fact or figure'.[69] This was not hyperbole as the following exchange that took place in the House of Commons in 1912 illustrates:

AUSTEN CHAMBERLAIN. The moment the British tobacco tax is reduced the Irish additional tax exceeds the limits provided by this Bill. (Hon. Members: 'No')
HERBERT SAMUEL. That is provided against.
CHAMBERLAIN. How?
SAMUEL. It is in the Bill.
CHAMBERLAIN. Where?
SAMUEL. Page 13, line 28 [Clause 17, Subsection (3) (b).]
CHAMBERLAIN. I admit I had overlooked that provision . . .[70]

Such rejoinders might be effective, but they they were not endearing. In this instance Chamberlain expressed his annoyance privately, alluding to Samuel's 'hoity-toity and superior' manner.[71] This was the jaundiced view of an opponent. But Samuel left a similar impression even on many Liberals.

---

[66] H. G. Wells, *The New Machiavelli* (Penguin edn., Harmondsworth, 1946), 215–16.
[67] HS to CS, 12 Feb. 1911, HLRO HS A/156/368.
[68] Quoted in T. M. Healy, *Letters and Leaders of My Day* (London, 1928), 511.
[69] *Reynolds's Newspaper*, 14 Sept. 1913.
[70] *HC Deb.* 5 s., vol. 43 (7 Nov. 1912), col. 1515.
[71] Sir Austen Chamberlain, *Politics from the Inside: An Epistolary Chronicle 1906–1914* (London, 1936), 492.

The Liberal journalist A. G. Gardiner, writing in 1908, called him 'the type of efficiency':

There is no more industrious man in the Ministry. . . . It is impossible to trip him up, either in fact or in feeling. . . . He conveys no impression of enthusiasm and is as free from passion as an oyster. He will never give his leader or his party a moment's disquiet, for he will never depart a hair's-breadth from the path of strict correctitude. He says exactly the right word in exactly the right accent. . . . Mr Samuel's path is as defined and absolute as a geometrical line. He is the artificer of politics, confident of his aim, master of himself and his materials, secure in his opinion, inflexible in his purpose—a splendidly efficient instrument, but never an inspiration.[72]

Samuel thus excited little affection among the political class and consequently aroused little sympathy when he suddenly became the object of an unscrupulous and venomous campaign of personal denigration.

The Marconi scandal, of which Samuel was a central figure and an innocent victim, had its origins in a contract between the Post Office and the British Marconi Company for the construction of an imperial network of wireless telegraph stations to be used for both civil and naval communications. The accusation at the heart of the affair was that the contract was in some way illegitimate and had been granted by the Postmaster General, Herbert Samuel, for direct or indirect pecuniary advantage. Around this central core the accusers wrapped a complex and confusing wrapping-paper of subsidiary allegations, most of them vague and ill-defined but expressed in vitriolic language whose general theme was the notion of a dark web of Jewish conspiracy. A second major accusation, which surfaced later in the affair, was that several ministers in Asquith's Government had used prior knowledge ·of the impending signature of the contract with the Marconi Company to invest in its shares with a view to lining their pockets. Both accusations were subsequently shown to be without foundation, although the second had just sufficient substratum of truth in the behaviour of Lloyd George and Rufus Isaacs, though not of Samuel, to endanger the political positions of these two senior ministers.

Guglielmo Marconi had first succeeded in transmitting wireless messages over long distances between 1896 and 1899 in southern England. In the summer of 1899 the British navy began successful experiments in naval communication by means of Marconi's system. The first wireless message was transmitted across the Atlantic from Poldhu in Cornwall to St John's, Newfoundland in December 1901. The implication of Marconi's discoveries for naval warfare as well as civil communications were soon recognized, and in 1904 the Post Office signed an agreement with the

[72] A. G. Gardiner, *Prophets, Priests and Kings* (London, 1908), 242–7.

company established by Marconi in England, permitting the operation of transmitting stations. At an international conference in Berlin in 1906 a convention regulating wireless telegraphy was agreed by the powers. By 1907 Marconi had begun a regular service for sending transatlantic messages for the press and the general public as well as messages to and from ships at sea.

An early foretaste of the coming scandal was given to the Cabinet, of which Samuel was not yet a member, in July 1907. A Select Committee of the House of Commons, set up to consider whether Britain should ratify the Berlin convention, had split, with a majority favouring ratification and a minority opposed. The minority report had suggested that the question was 'primarily one of national strategic importance' and that ratification of the convention would assist the foreign competitors of the British Marconi Company.[73] In a confidential Cabinet paper the Postmaster General, Sydney Buxton, strongly recommended ratification and alleged that Arthur Lee, the Conservative MP who had drafted the minority report, had colluded with Cuthbert Hall, Managing Director of the Marconi Company, to gain 'access to confidential and secret official documents, of which they can only have had knowledge through a gross breach of faith on the part of some Official'.[74] The Cabinet eventually decided to adopt the majority recommendation and the convention was ratified in 1908.

Samuel's first expression of interest in Marconi's discoveries appeared as early as February 1903 in the form of a parliamentary question to the then Postmaster General, Austen Chamberlain, asking 'whether facilities will be given through the General Post Office for the transmission of messages by wireless telegraphy to the Continent of America and elsewhere'. In his reply Chamberlain said the matter was under consideration, and he added: 'I am also in communication with the Marconi Wireless Telegraph Company upon the subject of their relations with the Post Office.'[75] The question arose from Samuel's first meeting with Marconi which occurred about that time. On 22 February 1903 Samuel wrote to his mother: 'You may have seen my question on wireless telegraphy. I was introduced to Marconi the other day—an absurdly boyish-looking, but nevertheless strong-featured youth; he speaks English without any trace of an accent.'[76] Apart from one other parliamentary question later that year, Samuel displayed no further interest in Marconi or in wireless telegraphy before his appointment to the Post Office.

[73] Copy of draft report by Arthur Lee, 13 June 1907, PRO CAB 37/89/68.
[74] Buxton to Cabinet, 12 July 1907, PRO CAB 37/89/72.
[75] Parl. Deb. 4 s., vol. 118 (19 Feb. 1903), col. 286.
[76] HS to CS, 22 Feb. 1903, HLRO HS A/156/218.

On 25 June 1909, the day that Samuel entered the Cabinet, Marconi unveiled in *The Times* the first outline of his scheme for 'an imperial system of wireless telegraphy'. The first official proposal for such a project was submitted by the Marconi Company in March 1910, shortly after Samuel took up his position at the Post Office. By this time the British Government had purchased most of the Marconi Company's short-distance stations around the British coast, leaving the company with two stations operating under a government licence and intended primarily for transatlantic traffic. The new plan put forward by the Marconi Company was designed 'to connect the Mother Country and the principal Colonies and India *inter se* by means of stations which would for the most part be of moderately long range, say, from 1,000 to 2,000 miles'. An initial network of eighteen stations would connect Africa, India, Malaya, China, and Australia. The company did not seek financial assistance but merely licences to erect and operate the stations.[77]

The proposal was submitted to an interdepartmental body known as the Cables Landing Rights Committee. This included representatives of the Colonial, India, Foreign, and War Offices as well as the Post Office, the Admiralty, and the Treasury. Samuel was not a member. At its first meeting to consider the scheme, on 6 April 1910, the committee concluded that 'notwithstanding the desirability of providing a system of wireless communication throughout the Empire, there were manifold and serious difficulties in the way of accepting the Company's application'. It never-theless decided to refer the matter for instructions to the various departments concerned and to consider the matter further once those had been received.[78] The initial reaction in the Post Office was not favourable. On 20 April the Secretary of the Post Office (its most senior civil servant), Sir Matthew Nathan, suggested that the Government should set up its own chain of wireless telegraph stations: 'There are several reasons [Nathan wrote] why the proposed service should be provided by the State as a national undertaking rather than by a Private Company for the purposes of profit.' The chief ground of Nathan's opposition was that 'the grant of a concession to the Marconi Company would place a virtual monopoly of Imperial wireless communication in the hands of a private Company'.[79] A few days later Samuel commented: 'I approve', adding that he thought it important that any arrangement by the Government for sharing telegraphic

---

[77] Memorandum of interview between Godfrey Isaacs and F. J. Brown (Secretary of the Cables Landing Rights Committee), 7 Mar. 1910, printed copy in 'Imperial Wireless Installations: Copies of Correspondence relating to the Contract for Imperial Wireless Stations', General Post Office confidential print, 1912 [hereafter GPO confidential print], HLRO HS A/39.

[78] Minutes of meeting, 6 Apr. 1910, ibid.

[79] Minute by Nathan, 20 Apr. 1910, Post Office Archives, E 11846/1912/III.

traffic with the existing cable companies should be only for a limited period.[80] As a result, when the Cables Landing Rights Committee met again on 27 April, the Post Office representative stated that 'the Postmaster General much preferred that the proposed system, to the early provision of which he attached much importance, should from the first be in the hands of the State'. This opinion had a decisive effect, for in its report on 23 May 1910 the committee urged 'that the proposed stations should be erected and worked by the Imperial Government and the Colonial Governments concerned rather than by a private company, provided that this course would not give rise to undue delay'.[81] Far from giving undue favour to the Marconi Company's application, at least at this initial stage, Samuel was, on the contrary, instrumental in the committee's decision to recommend a state-run scheme.

During the next few months, however, interdepartmental consultations revealed technical and financial obstacles to a state-constructed network. The technical difficulties arose from the Marconi Company's jealous guardianship of the secrets of its long-distance systems. Short of expropriation, they could not be made to yield them up. In an interview in January 1911 with the recently appointed Managing Director of the company, Godfrey Isaacs (brother of the Attorney-General, Rufus Isaacs), Nathan enquired whether the company might co-operate with the Government in a joint system. The reply was negative. Isaacs pointed out that the company was in a strong position since it not only possessed the most advanced technical apparatus but had already obtained a monopoly for the erection of stations in Spain and Italy. Faced with the prospect that the Marconi Company might develop an international system elsewhere, excluding the British Empire altogether, Nathan backed away from his original opposition to an arrangement with Marconi: 'A State-owned system [he wrote in February 1911], however desirable in itself, seems out of the question, because it is most improbable that the Treasury would risk the money involved at the present stage of wireless development.' Nathan argued instead for a revised scheme involving co-operation between the Marconi Company and the Eastern Cable Company. In response Samuel simply wrote: 'I agree.'[82]

The Cables Landing Rights Committee reconsidered the matter on 8 March 1911. The chairman, Jack Tennant, said that 'personally, he would regret to see an Imperial wireless system in other than Government hands. But if the Government authorities were not ready or willing to

[80] Minute by HS, 25 Apr. 1910, ibid.
[81] Minutes of meetings on 27 Apr. and 23 May 1910, Post Office Archives, E 11846/1912/IV.
[82] Minute by Nathan, 21 Feb. 1911, Post Office Archives, E 11846/1912/VIII.

establish such a system, others would step in and set up a chain of stations which would not be "all-red." ' To the surprise of the Post Office, the Treasury was, after all, prepared to consider a state-owned system. The Admiralty and War Office representatives strongly supported a Government system, though they said that if that were impossible they would be prepared to support the original Marconi proposal.[83] The result, after further discussions, was a compromise whereby the committee recommended a scheme, drawn up by the Admiralty, for stations owned and operated by the Government, to be set up with technical assistance from the Marconi Company. The question which government department should be primarily responsible was left open for further consideration.[84] Eventually the Post Office, the Admiralty, and the Marconi Company agreed that the Post Office would be responsible for setting up and running the stations, using the Marconi Company as sub-contractors, and paying the company a royalty, based on volume of transmissions, for the use of its patents and unpatented inventions. This proposal was approved by the Committee of Imperial Defence and in June 1911 was submitted to the Imperial Conference, attended by the Prime Ministers of the self-governing Dominions. In presenting it to the conference, Samuel stressed the urgency on strategic grounds of proceeding as fast as possible. A resolution generally favouring the scheme was carried unanimously, although the Prime Minister of New Zealand uttered a warning: 'If we get to the time when the erecting of these stations is to be carried out, I think it ought to be competed for publicly, and if any particular company whose system is acceptable is the lowest, or if any competing offer is not satisfactory, then I think the work should be handed over to the Admiralty and carried out under their experts.'[85]

From the summer of 1911 Samuel began to involve himself personally in the scheme. On 2 August he met Godfrey Isaacs to discuss terms. A week later he presided at a meeting of a special interdepartmental committee that included Dominion representatives. Samuel told the committee that he thought the Post Office should try 'to get a definite and more satisfactory offer from the Marconi Company'. He pointed out 'that the alternative was to ask for competitive tenders, but that no other Company was known to have any practical experience of high-power working'. The representatives of the Admiralty, the War Office and the

[83] Memorandum of discussion, 8 Mar. 1911, GPO confidential print, HLRO HS A/39; minute by Nathan, 11 Mar. 1911, Post Office Archives, E 11846/1912/IX.

[84] Report of Cables Landing Rights Committee, 29 Mar. 1911, GPO confidential print, HLRO HS A/39; minute by Nathan, 30 Mar. 1911, Post Office Archives, E 11846/1912/XII.

[85] Minutes of discussion at Imperial Conference, 15 June 1911, Post Office Archives, E 11846/1912/XII.

India Office concurred, and the committee decided that Samuel should pursue his talks with Isaacs.[86] After difficult negotiations, in which Samuel beat down the terms and conditions demanded by the company, a tentative agreement was reached in January 1912.[87] On 7 March 1912 the Post Office formally notified the Marconi Company that its tender for the erection of the Imperial Wireless Station chain had been accepted.[88] The following day Samuel sent a handwritten memorandum to the King, explaining the proposed contract: 'It is intended that the stations shall form an additional means of communication, for commercial and other purposes, between the United Kingdom, India, Australia, New Zealand and South Africa, and it is expected that they would prove of the highest strategic value in time of war.' Five stations were to be established initially, in England, Cyprus (or Egypt), Aden, Bangalore, and Singapore. Other stations would be set up by the Governments of Australia, New Zealand, and South Africa.[89] The Post Office would pay for and operate all the stations except the one at Bangalore which would be charged to the Indian Government. 'The erection of these stations [Samuel informed the King] will place the British Empire in this regard far in advance of any other country.'[90] After a long gestation the scheme now seemed assured of a happy birth. In fact, the real trouble was about to begin.

Since the previous October the press had reported on the negotiations between the Government and the Marconi Company.[91] As a result the price of shares in the British Marconi Company and in its associated American company began to fluctuate wildly. *The Times* reported on 23 April 1912 that the speculation had 'degenerated into a dangerous gamble'. At the same time, the newspaper stated that wireless telegraphy had proved its 'humanitarian value' in facilitating the rescue of large numbers of survivors from the *Titanic* a few days earlier, and it conceded that the imperial wireless scheme had 'vast utility on Imperial and commercial grounds'. From May 1912 onwards questions, at first merely seeking information, began to be asked in the House of Commons. On 19 July the contract, or 'indenture', was signed between the Post Office and the Marconi Company. The onslaught began the next day, with the first

[86] Minutes of meeting of Interdepartmental Committee on Imperial Wireless Telegraphy Scheme, 9 Aug. 1911, Post Office Archives, E 11846/1912/XXVIII.

[87] See Post Office documents, Dec. 1911–Jan. 1912, Post Office Archives, E 11846/1912/XXXII–XXXIX.

[88] Post Office to Marconi Company, 7 Mar. 1912, Post Office Archives E 11846/1912/XLVII.

[89] The final version of the contract, laid before Parliament on 19 July 1912, provided for six stations: in England, Egypt, the East African Protectorate, South Africa, India, and Singapore.

[90] HS to King George V, 8 Mar. 1912, Royal Archives, GV 5008.

[91] *Evening Standard*, 26 Oct. 1911; *Evening News*, 31 Jan. 1912.

of several articles, all hostile to the contract, published in the magazine *Outlook* by a journalist, Wilfred Lawson. Other such articles followed in the *National Review* and in the *Eye Witness*, edited by Cecil Chesterton.

These early attacks, published in obscure organs, did not attract wide public attention. But over the next few months the controversy spread into the general press, including papers such as the *Spectator* and the *Globe*, and eventually into Parliament. The main source of the fountain of bile was the small set of reactionary writers at whose centre reposed the large two-headed pantomime beast that Shaw christened the 'Chester-belloc'. G. K. Chesterton, who had already attained great celebrity with the publication the previous year of *The Innocence of Father Brown*, had a Liberal political background but had lately grown disenchanted with the party system. He had first met Samuel in 1904 at the home of one of Samuel's Franklin cousins and encountered him again when he gave evidence to the Select Committee on Theatrical Censorship in 1909. Although they had not become friends there is nothing to suggest that there was any particular personal animus in Chesterton's participation in the campaign of vilification against Samuel over the Marconi contract. There was probably some truth in the common view that his genial, impressionable nature was led astray by the overpowering effect on him of the personality of his close friend Hilaire Belloc.

This gifted but malevolent figure, of whom it can perhaps most charitably be said that he was fundamentally out of joint with his time, had gone up to Balliol at the start of Samuel's penultimate term there in January 1893. Although both were active in university Liberal politics, they do not seem to have had anything to do with each other. Their brand of Liberalism was, in any case, quite different, as became apparent in 1897 when Belloc, with others, published *Essays in Liberalism by Six Oxford Men* which criticized the collectivist views associated with the Rainbow Circle and the *Progressive Review*. Belloc had strongly supported the movement against Chinese labour on the Rand, and on this account was regarded for a while as a radical Liberal. Of mixed Anglo-French parentage, he had been naturalized as a British subject in 1902. He was elected to Parliament as Liberal MP for Salford South in 1906, but, growing ever more violently antagonistic to what he saw as corrupt party politics, decided not to stand for re-election in December 1910. As early as 1907 he had written scurrilous verses attacking the ennoblement of Sir Samuel Montagu as Lord Swaythling. By 1912 he had fashioned a conspiratorial view of a world that he saw as dominated by sinister Jewish financiers manipulating corrupt politicians.

Although Belloc was the guiding spirit of the scandalmongers, his successor as editor of the *Eye Witness*, Cecil Chesterton, took the role of chief public prosecutor. The younger brother of G. K., Cecil was a former Fabian and Christian Socialist who had recently been baptized as a Roman Catholic. Without his brother's saving grace of *bonhomie*, and lacking Belloc's brilliant, if uneven, literary talent, Cecil purveyed the set's anti-Semitic world view in unrestrained and unabashedly libellous language.

On 7 August, when the Marconi contract was presented for the first time for debate in the House of Commons, Samuel was subjected to close questioning. The next day Chesterton's *Eye Witness* carried a fierce personal attack on him, declaring that it had been 'secretly arranged between Isaacs and Samuel that the British people shall give the Marconi Company a very large sum of money through the agency of the said Samuel, and for the benefit of the said Isaacs'. Denouncing the contract as a 'swindle, or rather theft, impudent and bare-faced' and regretting that 'we have in this country no method of punishing men who are guilty of this kind of thing', the article seemed deliberately designed to goad its victims into prosecution for libel.

Samuel picked up a copy of the paper at King's Cross Station as he left for his annual holiday in the north. Immediately on arrival in Saltburn he wrote to the Attorney-General, Rufus Isaacs, who had also been named in the attack, discussing what action might be taken against the 'gross and unrestrained libel':

One's natural inclination is, of course, at once to have application made for a writ, and I am not at all sure that that is not the right course. There can be no doubt as to the result of an action. It is hardly necessary for me to say that during the long negotiations that preceded the conclusion of the contract there was no action of mine that I would wish withdrawn from any measure of publicity whether in the courts or in Parliament.

The circumstances that deter me from at once coming to the conclusion that proceedings ought to be taken are the obvious ones,

first that this contemptible rag has a very small circulation, its pages are always full of personal abuse, its articles cannot influence any opinion which is worth hearing, and an action would give an immense publicity to the libel;

secondly, it would not be a good thing for the Jewish community for the first two Jews who have ever entered a British Cabinet to be enmeshed in an affair of this kind;[92]

and thirdly one does not wish to soil one's hands with the thing. . . .

On the other hand, it is a grave thing when Ministers are directly accused of corrupt action, by a newspaper no matter how obscure and scurrilous, for them to do nothing.

---

[92] When Samuel later read this letter out in public session to a parliamentary committee of inquiry he omitted this clause, although he showed the whole document to the committee. See Kenneth Lunn, 'The Marconi Scandal and Related Aspects of British Anti-Semitism 1911–1914', Ph.D. thesis (Sheffield, 1978), ch. 6.

Clearly in a dilemma, Samuel asked for Isaacs' legal advice and suggested also consulting the Prime Minister.[93]

Isaacs replied from Marienbad, where he was on holiday with Lloyd George, that he considered Samuel's 'reasons for not proceeding by action outweighed the first and natural impulse to issue writs at once'. He considered 'it was better to treat the rag with contempt—its malevolence and prejudice were so marked that only the most blind partisan could be led to believe the statements'. Isaacs then averred: 'I need not tell you—I am sure—that there is not one ounce of truth in the statements about myself.' But the precise terms of his denial contained an admission that proved, when it eventually became public, to be the most damaging element in the affair:

I never held a share or an interest direct or indirect in this Marconi Company or indeed in any Marconi Company until after the contract with the Government was announced—I then bought some American Marconis and hold same [?] now— & except for that Company which is entirely independent of this country and is a separate company I have not and never have had any financial interest in Marconis.

In his letter to Samuel, Isaacs did not mention that his holiday companion, Lloyd George, as well as the Government Chief Whip, the Master of Elibank, had also purchased shares in the American Marconi Company.[94]

The following week the *Eye Witness* published a crudely sarcastic 'Defence of Mr Samuel', suggesting that he owed his position to bribes paid to politicians by his uncle, Lord Swaythling.[95] Further weekly attacks followed, adorned with reference to 'the chosen—shall we say people', 'alien money-lenders', and several 'Songs of the Samuels', sour-tempered and feeble verses infused with spiteful innuendo. These efforts were supplemented in the October issue of L. J. Maxse's *National Review* by another prose piece by Lawson. In spite of the offensive nature of these articles, the Isaacs brothers and Samuel decided not to take legal action, supported in this course by the Prime Minister.[96] Charles Masterman, the Financial Secretary to the Treasury, who had himself fallen foul of the Chesterbelloc, wrote to sympathize with Samuel: 'I expect your decision is right on the matter. . . . Belloc, of course, is merely mad with jealousy of yr race: Cecil Chesterton is a malignant & pestilential little toad who makes up for absence of his brother's brains by such muck as this.'[97]

---

[93] HS to Isaacs, 8 Aug. 1912 (copy), HLRO HS A/37/3.
[94] Isaacs to HS, 14 Aug. 1912, HLRO HS A/38/I/6.
[95] *Eye Witness*, 15 Aug. 1912.
[96] Rufus Isaacs to HS, 19, 29, and 31 Aug. 1912, HLRO HS A/38/I/6, 7, 8; Godfrey Isaacs to HS, 27 Aug., 5 Sept. 1912, HLRO HS A/38/I/9 & 10.
[97] Masterman to HS, 16 [?] Aug. 1912, HLRO HS A/37/12.

By the time Parliament reconvened in October 1912 the volume of rumour was so great that the Government felt obliged to propose the formation of a Select Committee of the House of Commons 'to investigate the circumstances connected with the negotiation and completion' of the Marconi agreement. On 11 October the Commons debated the motion to form such a committee. The debate was opened by Sir Henry Norman, Liberal MP for Blackburn, who opposed the contract on scientific and commercial grounds, although he dissociated himself from the charge of corruption. Other members, however, particularly the Conservative Lord Robert Cecil and the Labour MP George Lansbury, referred to the rumours. Apart from one or two angry but insubstantial interjections, Lloyd George remained silent. Rufus Isaacs made a carefully worded statement:

Never from the beginning, when the shares were 14s., or £9, have I had one single transaction with the shares of that company. I am speaking on behalf, I know, of both my right hon. Friend, the Postmaster-General and the Chancellor of the Exchequer, who, in some way or other, in some of the articles, have been brought into this matter.

Samuel was the last speaker from the Government front bench:

I confess [he began] that, after reading for months past allegations, insinuations, attacks, accusations of maladministration and favouritism, and even worse, it is to me a profound relief to be able to stand at this Table in the light of day and give an answer to these assertions. I should like, in the first instance, to confirm, in unqualified terms, what has been said. . . . Neither I myself nor any of my colleagues have at any time held one shilling's worth of shares in this company, directly or indirectly, or have derived one penny profit from the fluctuations in their prices. It seems shameful that political feeling can carry men so far, that lying tongues can be found to speak and willing ears be found to listen to wicked and utterly baseless slanders such as these.

Samuel continued, in the face of repeated interruptions, to defend the terms of the Marconi contract. He recapitulated the history of the Government's decision to build the network, the work of the various committees and departments involved, the technical appraisals of the Marconi system and its rivals, and the urgency attached to the implementation of the scheme. It was a cogent and persuasive apologia. The Home Secretary, Reginald McKenna, in his parliamentary letter to the King reported: 'It was quite clear from the manner in which his speech was received in the House that his explanation was regarded as entirely satisfactory.'[98]

The Select Committee, composed of six Liberals, six Conservatives, two Irish Nationalists, and one Labour MP, began its hearings on 25

[98] McKenna to King George V, 11 Oct. 1912, Royal Archives; *HC Deb.* 5 s., vol. 42 (11 Oct. 1912), cols. 667–750.

October 1912. Some of the Conservatives entered the proceedings with a less than open mind. Leopold Amery recorded in his diary on 27 October his impression of the first witness, Sir Alexander King, Chief Secretary to the Post Office: 'A shifty looking fellow and pretty unscrupulous in his statements.'[99] Other witnesses included civil servants, MPs, and journalists, among them Lawson and Maxse. Later, evidence was heard from Lloyd George, Rufus Isaacs, and Samuel, as well as from Belloc, Godfrey Isaacs, and Commendatore Marconi himself. The committee quickly came to agree with the Government view as to the urgency of proceeding with some form of imperial wireless telegraphy system. But they felt unable, in the absence of independent expert advice, to form an opinion as to the competing merits of the Marconi system and its rivals. They therefore issued an interim report in January 1913 proposing the formation of a separate committee of experts to advise on the technical merits of the rival schemes.[100] Such a committee was constituted by the Government under the chairmanship of Lord Parker of Waddington. Immediately after the announcement of the Government's approval of the formation of this expert committee, Godfrey Isaacs wrote to Samuel asking that, in view of the delay in securing parliamentary ratification of the contract, the Government should agree 'to the Company's treating the Contract as no longer binding on either party'.[101] Samuel opposed releasing the company from the contract since he considered it a highly advantageous one to the Government. Consequently, a reply was sent to the Marconi Company refusing to release it from the agreement.[102] Meanwhile the Select Committee continued its investigation into the charges of governmental corruption.

All this time, as the affair dragged on through committee after committee, the press campaign continued, with an increasingly ugly overtone of anti-Semitism. After consulting Asquith, Samuel and Isaacs finally determined to prosecute.[103] Since most of the accusers in the British press had, with an eye on the law of libel, taken care to confine themselves to vague insinuations and generalized accusations of corruption rather than specific charges, it was decided to proceed against the French newspaper *Le Matin* which had printed detailed allegations in its issue of 14 February. Samuel wrote to his mother: 'Though it is unfortunate that it is

---

[99] John Barnes and David Nicholson (eds.), *The Leo Amery Diaries*, i, *1896–1929* (London, 1980), 87.

[100] Special Report from the Select Committee on Marconi's Wireless Telegraph Company, Limited, Agreement, 14 Jan. 1913, Post Office Archives, E 2682/1913.

[101] Godfrey Isaacs to HS, 15 Jan. 1913, Post Office Archives, E 25527/1913/XV.

[102] HS to CS, 26 Jan. 1913, HLRO HS A/156/427; Sir A. King to Marconi Company, 5 Feb. 1913, Post Office Archives, E 25527/1913/XV.

[103] Asquith to HS, 24 Feb. 1913, HLRO HS A/38/I/29.

a French and not an English paper which gives us the opportunity of taking the matter into court, we have to seize our opportunity where we find it.'[104] Shortly before the case was heard, he wrote to her again:

My part in the matter is absolutely plain; my statement will be complete and entirely satisfactory to the public. But Rufus Isaacs and Lloyd George a year ago bought some shares as an investment in the *American* Marconi Co. *after* my agreement with the English co. had been arranged. The fact has to be stated, and although there was nothing dishonourable in what they did it was certainly unwise and the statement which Rufus Isaacs will make in the witness-box on Wednesday will undoubtedly give rise to a great deal of hostile comment. . . . For my part I have nothing to reproach myself with in connection with this unpleasant business from first to last.[105]

To his former chief Herbert Gladstone, now Governor-General of South Africa, he wrote that he was maintaining a 'mens aequa' regarding Marconi.[106] This calm conviction of his own innocence was characteristic of Samuel and helped him endure the stress of this lengthy personal crisis.

The case was heard in the King's Bench Division Court No. IV on 19 March 1913. The drama of the proceedings was heightened by the participation, as counsel for the plaintiffs, of Sir Edward Carson and F. E. Smith, two of the most celebrated advocates of the time—who were also leading figures in the Unionist Party.[107] They were assisted by Raymond Asquith, son of the Prime Minister. Carson delivered a powerful opening statement, detailing the origins of the contract and exonerating Samuel of any wrongdoing. For the first time, however, he revealed publicly that Isaacs and Lloyd George had bought shares in the American Marconi Company. Samuel was then called to the witness-stand and questioned by Smith. Once again he went over the history of the contract and denied having bought any shares 'in any Marconi company'. He was followed by Isaacs who affirmed his innocence of corruption but stated that he had bought shares in the American company. Counsel for *Le Matin* admitted the libel and apologized, whereupon judgement was rendered in favour of the plaintiffs.[108] For Samuel the verdict was a moral vindication, but for Isaacs and for the Government as a whole it was a pyrrhic victory since the scandalmongers had now been presented with an admission that could be exploited to great political effect.

Two months later Samuel gave evidence in court again, this time in a libel action lodged by Godfrey Isaacs against Cecil Chesterton. Samuel

---

[104] HS to CS, 16 Feb. 1913, HLRO HS A/156/430.
[105] HS to CS, 16 Mar. 1913, HLRO HS A/156/434.
[106] HS to Gladstone, 27 Apr. 1913, BL Add. MS 45992/273.
[107] According to Randolph Churchill, it was his father who persuaded Carson and Smith to appear in the case (Randolph Churchill, *Winston Churchill*, ii. 555).
[108] *The Times*, 20 Mar. 1913.

had nothing to do with instituting the suit but he wrote to his mother that he was 'not sorry to give evidence'.[109] Carson and Smith appeared again, this time as counsel for Isaacs. When Samuel testified (the *Globe*, which had adopted an anti-Marconi line, noted that he 'took the oath in the Jewish fashion'), he 'spoke in calm, clear tones to the jury, and without using a note seemed to exercise a remarkable control over his memory in regard to names and dates'.[110] Given the number of occasions on which Samuel had had to traverse the same ground, his fluency was perhaps not surprising and contrasted tellingly with the lame performance of the accused. Under cross-examination by Carson, Chesterton tried to back down, asserting that he had not made any accusation of corruption against Godfrey Isaacs though he avowed that he had 'accused the Postmaster General of having given a contract which threw him open to the suspicion that he had been unduly influenced by the fact that Mr Godfrey Isaacs was the Attorney-General's brother'. When Carson asked 'What did Mr Samuel get out of it?', Chesterton replied: 'I don't think Mr Samuel got anything out of it.'

CARSON. Then he entered into this corrupt bargain for the benefit of another person while he was getting nothing out of it himself?
CHESTERTON. Surely that is a very common kind of corruption for a public official to give away advantages to private people.[111]

In summing up, the judge asked 'how . . . could the plea of justification for the charge of corruption be upheld when the defence had admitted that Mr Samuel had not been guilty of corruption?'[112] Chesterton was found guilty, fined £100, and ordered to pay all costs. Perversely the Chester-belloc clique affected to regard the outcome as a moral victory. Few shared this opinion.[113] Cecil Chesterton was generally discredited and even the sympathetic *Globe* did not spring to his support, fastening instead on the subsidiary matter of the appearance of Carson and Smith on behalf of Isaacs, which the newspaper assailed as 'mistaken chivalry'.[114]

On 13 June the Select Committee issued its report. The committee had split, but, since there could be only one report from a Select Committee, the House of Commons found itself faced with one official report, representing the pro-Government majority, and three unofficial reports. All absolved Samuel of any wrongdoing, although Amery tried to have it both ways by accusing 'the secretarial side of the Post Office' of 'a bias, degenerating at times into sheer unscrupulousness', while in the same

[109] HS to CS, 2 Mar. 1913, HLRO HS A/156/432.
[110] *Globe*, 27 May 1913.
[111] Ibid., 5 June 1913.   [112] Ibid., 7 June 1913.
[113] See Frances Donaldson, *The Marconi Scandal* (London, 1962), 185–9.
[114] *Globe*, 13 June 1913.

breath declaring, 'I am convinced that there are no grounds for even a suspicion that any improper influences were at work'. In regard to the share purchases, the official report concluded that Lloyd George and Rufus Isaacs had not committed any dishonourable act. The minority statements criticized the purchase of shares in the American Marconi Company and the subsequent reticence of the ministers in that matter as an impropriety. With this important exception, the differences were more matters of style than substance, the unofficial statements by Lord Robert Cecil and Amery being much more hostile in tone towards the ministers than the majority report.[115] A debate on the official report was set for 18 June, and was preceded by a Cabinet meeting at which Asquith asked Lloyd George and Isaacs what they intended to say. Lloyd George with 'a spark of fire in his eye' protested his innocence while Isaacs was 'less bellicose'.[116] Asquith reported afterwards to the King that the two had agreed to make statements 'which while disclaiming anything in the nature of impropriety will admit error of judgement'.[117]

The debate in the Commons took place on a motion regretting 'the transactions of certain of His Majesty's Ministers in the shares of the Marconi Company of America, and the want of frankness displayed by Ministers in their communications on the subject to the House'. An emollient Isaacs admitted his mistake, though he said: 'It never occurred to me during the whole course of these transactions that any human being could suspect me of corruption because I purchased American Marconi shares some six weeks after the announcement was made of the acceptance of the tender of the British Marconi Company by the British Government.' Lloyd George followed in more combative spirit: 'The charge [of corruption] has been exploded, but the deadly after-damp remains, and the noxious fumes of these slanders are at this very moment poisoning the blood of the people who are considering even minor charges which are brought against us.' Complaining of 'undeserved calumnies, slanders, insults', he declared himself 'conscious of having done nothing which brings a stain upon the honour of a Minister of the Crown. If you will, I acted thoughtlessly, I acted carelessly, I acted mistakenly, but I acted innocently, I acted openly, and I acted honestly.' In accordance with precedent the two accused ministers then withdrew while the debate continued. Asquith delivered a long speech defending his ministers and adding: 'There is another element in the case to which I feel bound to call attention, because, happily, it is also new in our political life. No one who has followed the history of these transactions can be blind to the fact that

[115] See Donaldson, *Marconi*, 198–204, 260–96; also *The Times*, 23 and 24 July 1913.
[116] Pease diary, 17 June 1913, Nuffield College, Oxford, Gainford papers 38/73.
[117] Asquith to King George V, 17 June 1913, PRO CAB 41/34/21.

the most disgraceful appeals were made from the beginning to racial and religious animosity.'

Samuel made a 'personal statement' rebutting the 'shameful slanders' to which he had been subjected and once again defending his handling of the Marconi contract. He concluded:

During the last year every action of mine in all these prolonged negotiations has been under the microscope. Almost every word I have spoken in interviews and elsewhere has been magnified as by a megaphone. I do not complain of that. But I claim now to the House that this inquiry, searching as it has been, has not given the smallest colour—has not provided one atom of foundation for any allegation or suggestion that any action of mine, on any occasion, in any particular, has been due to any motive except an unqualified desire to render the best service in my power to the great public interests committed to my charge.[118]

The vote at the end of the two-day debate was largely on party lines—though Carson and F. E. Smith abstained; a majority supported a resolution that accepted the statements of regret by Lloyd George and Isaacs but acquitted them of any charge of corruption or of acting in bad faith.

That marked the end of the affair as a major political event, although the Chesterton confraternity continued to engage in literary *embuscades* for several years. Samuel came out of the ordeal with clean hands. But he did not emerge politically unscathed. Indeed, it appears that his very innocence tended to increase his unpopularity among his colleagues. John Burns, commenting in his diary on the Commons debate, noted that Samuel was 'very prim and proper and precise as usual in his defence'. A few weeks later he wrote: 'H.S. clear and precise yet not satisfactory as is proved [?] by this wretched [?] bitterness long drawn out.'[119] Chatting over supper a day or two after the debate, Masterman remarked to Lloyd George that 'Herbert Samuel was not exactly a favourite with the party at this moment'. The Chancellor 'shook his head menacingly'.[120] Lloyd George cannot have relished the unfortunate light thrown on his own behaviour by the shining purity of Samuel's conduct. Sprouting from this seed of half-conscious resentment, Lloyd George's dislike for Samuel ultimately grew into a bitterly contemptuous loathing. He gave an early expression of this feeling in April 1914, after Samuel had committed what Lloyd George considered a budget leak: the Chancellor described Samuel

[118] *HC Deb.* 5 s., vol. 54 (18–19 June 1913), cols. 391 ff.
[119] Burns diary, 18 June and 16 July 1913, BL Add. MS 46335.
[120] Lucy Masterman diary, 23 June [extract refers to *c*.20 June] 1913, Birmingham University Library.

to a confidant as 'a greedy, ambitious and grasping Jew with all the worst characteristics of his race'.[121]

The anti-Semitic feeling that bubbled up during the Marconi affair dismayed the Jewish community in England. The affair demonstrated the continuing force of traditional anti-Jewish ideas that had played a role in the anti-alien agitation a decade earlier and that were to acquire new dimensions with the rise of xenophobia during the First World War and of anti-Bolshevism after 1917.[122] Several members of Samuel's family, targets for the poison darts of Chesterbelloc, suffered without redress. A prime example was Samuel's elder brother Stuart who figured in the so-called 'Little Marconi' or Indian silver scandal in 1912. This originated with purchases of silver made on behalf of the Indian Government by the firm of Samuel Montagu & Co., of which Sir Stuart Samuel was a director. According to laws dating back to 1782 and 1801, an MP might not sit and vote while in contractual relations with the Government. On technical grounds arising from these ancient statutes, Sir Stuart Samuel was compelled to resign from Parliament in 1913. In recommending vacation of the seat, the Judicial Committee of the Privy Council acknowledged that 'no suggestion has been made of improper motive'. Expressing sympathy in a leader, *The Times* agreed that 'Sir Stuart Samuel was, of course, morally innocent'.[123] In the ensuing by-election he was re-elected for Whitechapel with a reduced majority. Subsequently, following a complaint by a 'common informer', he was obliged to forfeit £25,000 in penalties and costs. Fortunately Sir Stuart Samuel could afford these large amounts, equivalent to nearly £1 million in 1991 values.[124] In launching this frivolous and vindictive legal pursuit, the Marconi muckrakers made him a scapegoat not for his brother's sins but, on the contrary, for Herbert Samuel's irreproachable and irritating unassailability.

Apart from the damage done to innocent individuals and to the Jewish community, the Marconi scandal had other effects. It distracted and weakened the Government for several months. It debased the level of political discourse at a time of deepening social unrest manifested in the violence arising from labour disputes, the Irish question, and the women's

---

[121] J. M. McEwen (ed.), *The Riddell Diaries 1908–1923* (London, 1986), 82 (entry dated 25 Apr. 1914).

[122] See Colin Holmes, *Anti-Semitism in British Society 1876–1939* (London, 1979); Lunn, 'Marconi Scandal'.

[123] *The Times*, 12 Apr. 1913.

[124] Archives of Messrs. Samuel Montagu & Co., London; *Special Committee on Vacation of Seat (Member Holding Contract)* (London, 19 Dec. 1912); sim. (London, 22 Jan. 1913). See also G. R. Searle, *Corruption in British Politics 1895–1930* (Oxford, 1987), 201–12.

suffrage issue. As Dangerfield put it, the affair showed 'to what unseemly lengths, down what bemired by-paths, politicians were capable of dragging their cause'.[125] Not the least important result was the failure to complete construction of the wireless chain before the outbreak of the First World War. In April 1913 the Parker committee of experts, while recommending some changes in the Marconi contract, endorsed the Post Office's judgement that the company was the only one capable of constructing the long-distance wireless network.[126] Hardly, therefore, had the scandal begun to subside than Samuel was entrusted with the thankless task of renegotiating the contract. Few changes were, in fact, found to be necessary. The modified agreement was the occasion for some Conservative recrimination in the House of Commons but by now most of the acrimony had evaporated.[127] After the final debate on ratification on 8 August 1913, Samuel said that 'he felt as if he had been playing a heavy salmon for two years and landed it at last'.[128] By August 1914 little progress had been made in constructing the chain of stations. Later the contract was cancelled unilaterally by the Government and a new round of disputes and litigation dragged on for more than a decade. Construction of an imperial wireless telegraphy system was finally completed by the Marconi Company in 1927.[129]

In 1922 Samuel and Belloc played a discordant coda to the affair. Belloc published his anti-Semitic work *The Jews*—'my admirable Yid book', as he called it.[130] Here he portrayed the Jews as an alien body, denounced Jewish Bolshevism and Jewish finance-capitalism, accused the Jews of secrecy, of war-profiteering, and so forth. Samuel was offended by a passage where Belloc had called him 'the spokesman of the famous declaration in the House of Commons that no politician had touched Marconi shares'. The reference was to the debate on 11 October 1912 when Samuel had denied that ministers had purchased shares in 'this company'. He wrote to Belloc to protest, pointing out that he had not made the declaration attributed to him. Once again he distinguished between the English and American companies, suggesting that Belloc was 'entitled to say, if you wish, that you do not draw the same distinction. That may be a matter for controversy. But you are not entitled to say that I

[125] George Dangerfield, *The Strange Death of Liberal England* (London, 1961), 309.
[126] HS memorandum on meeting with Parker, 5 May 1913, Post Office Archives, E 3436/1913/30; Parker to Samuel, 6 May 1913, HLRO HS A/38.
[127] HC Deb. 5 s., vol. 55 (16 July 1913), cols. 1342–92.
[128] Diary of A. C. Murray MP, entry dated 8 Aug. 1913, National Library of Scotland MS 8814.
[129] See Donaldson, *Marconi*, 243; W. P. Jolly, *Marconi* (London, 1972), 210–11.
[130] Quoted in A. N. Wilson, *Hilaire Belloc* (Penguin edn., Harmondsworth, 1986), 258.

made a statement in the House of Commons which, as a matter of fact, I did not make.' Samuel's letter concluded:

Should your book be re-printed in a second edition, I doubt whether you will correct your mis-statement; for it is plain from every chapter of it, in spite of many protestations, that you are quite incapable of fairness where members of the Jewish community are involved. Nevertheless, I send you this contradiction in order that you should at least not be able to say that your falsehood had passed without protest.

Belloc replied in the third person:

Mr Belloc will withdraw nothing of what he has said & written repeatedly in this grave matter. He is fully conscious from the circumstances that a lie was intended and conveyed and that its author is unworthy of any public office. Nor will the power unfortunately possessed through the corruption of our politics, by men of Sir Herbert's kidney intimidate him or deter him from speaking the truth.[131]

Of course, the reference to Samuel's 'kidney' was not anatomical in intention, and was typical of the allusive scurrility with which Belloc waged his campaign.

The Marconi affair was the most painful episode in Samuel's career. Even though he was vindicated in the eyes of all except Belloc, Chesterton, and their acolytes, some of the mud stuck. In her judicious analysis of the affair, published in 1962, Lady Donaldson concluded that Samuel 'throughout the whole course of the case, was free from all blame unless one attached blame to loyalty'.[132] But recent historians show less understanding for Samuel's reticence in the debate of 11 October 1912.[133] And the latest biographer of Hilaire Belloc writes with a rebarbative vulgarity reminiscent of Cecil Chesterton: 'It is hard to see why Lady Donaldson's heart bleeds for these obvious crooks. The Master of Elibank, Isaacs, Lloyd George and Samuel manifestly tried to make themselves rich by the Marconi contract. Why else had they bought shares? . . . The whole thing stinks.'[134] Samuel had to endure such careless lumping for years afterwards. The calumnies do not seem to have soured him or upset him deeply as the Indian silver affair affected his emotional cousin Edwin Montagu. But the experience undoubtedly left its mark, and the scandal's anti-Semitic colouring perhaps contributed to Samuel's deepening interest in the Jewish predicament in the modern world—an interest that was shortly to bear unexpected fruit.

---

[131] HS to Belloc, 8 Aug. 1922 (copy), and Belloc to HS, 26 Aug. 1922, HLRO HS A/38/II/65–6.

[132] Donaldson, Marconi, 58–9.

[133] Searle, Corruption, 175; Bentley Brinkerhoff Gilbert, 'David Lloyd George and the Great Marconi Scandal', Historical Research, 62, 149 (Oct. 1989), 295–317.

[134] Wilson, Belloc, 195.

6

The Infant Samuel Goes to War

=

If you would preserve peace, then prepare for peace.

(Enfantin)

THE MARCONI imbroglio apart, the years before the First World War were happy, prosperous, and fulfilling ones for Samuel. His substantial private income was supplemented by the Postmaster General's salary of £2,500, providing him with a comfortable annual surplus. Soon after his elevation to the Cabinet, Samuel took a long lease on a house in Porchester Terrace, close to the homes of various Franklin relations and other members of the 'Cousinhood'. Said to be the longest terrace in Europe, this agreeable Bayswater address was close to the New West End Synagogue and to Kensington Gardens. Samuel lived in one or another house on this street for most of the rest of his life. He would often walk across Kensington Gardens to visit his mother at the Royal Palace Hotel or traverse all four royal parks to reach Westminster. Samuel's house, grand without being ostentatious, had formerly been occupied by William Whiteley, millionaire owner of the 'universal provider' stores. The lease, improvements, and outfitting cost Samuel about £5,000. Decorated in pale grey and white, with many bare walls, the house gave an elegant but cold impression. It remained the family home until 1920. Once they had moved into the house in 1910, the Samuels' social life expanded. They entertained more often and on a larger scale. Dinner guests included the Webbs, Winston Churchill, Sir Matthew Nathan, George and Charles Trevelyan, Augustine Birrell, Sydney and Noel Buxton, J. A. Spender, Erskine Childers, Charles Masterman, John Burns, Jack Pease, Walter Runciman, the Maharaja of Baroda, and the Kabaka of Buganda (renewing the acquaintance Samuel had made in 1902), as well as a sprinkling of Franklin, Samuel, and Montagu relatives.

About the same time, Samuel purchased a convertible Delaunay-Belleville motor car from the Maharaja of Cooch-Behar. Sometimes the Samuel family would drive up to the Yorkshire moors and then over to the beach at Saltburn. Each summer they would travel up to Cleveland by train with a wagonful of trunks and portmanteaus. They would stay in some country house rented from a member of the local Quakerocracy, one of these the former home, at Hutton Rudby, of Elizabeth Fry, the prison reformer. The house was full of relics and no doubt the author of the Probation Act delighted at the thought of sojourning with her shade.[1]

In spite of the wearisome, time-consuming, and often unrewarding nature of many of his duties at the Post Office, Samuel also devoted considerable attention during these years to general policy issues on which he helped the Prime Minister directly. Apart from his work on the Parliament Act, the most important such issue was Ireland. Samuel served on the Cabinet Committee that drafted the ill-fated third Home Rule Bill. He became the recognized Cabinet expert on the financial aspects of Irish Home Rule. His views acquired heightened importance because the Irish Secretary, Birrell, was amiably idle and carried little weight in the Cabinet even in matters affecting his own department. The finance clauses were regarded as crucial, since they represented the 1912 bill's only significant departure from the second Home Rule Bill of 1893. Samuel negotiated these provisions of the proposed legislation with the Irish parliamentary leader, John Redmond.[2]

Samuel's complex proposals, presented to the Cabinet in December 1911, provided for a large annual subsidy (later reducible) to be paid from the Imperial to the Irish Exchequer. The Irish leaders particularly disliked the fact that the scheme left customs and excise largely under British control but they swallowed their doubts for the sake of the bill as a whole. Samuel's proposals allowed the Irish Government limited powers to vary the duties but a back-bench Liberal revolt led to an amendment eliminating these powers. So complicated was Samuel's scheme that few understood it.[3] He was the main Government spokesman on the finance clauses throughout the consideration of the bill in the Commons and spoke almost every day during the endless, dreary committee stage. Even the ranks of Tuscany could scarce forbear to cheer Samuel's mastery of the subject—as a report in the staunchly Unionist *Standard* illustrates:

Mr Samuel took everyone by the hand, as it were, led them up to the blackboard, and for over an hour babbled amazing statistics. Of course, it was not the Postmaster-General who ought to have done this, but the Chancellor of the Exchequer or the Chief Secretary. But Mr Birrell could not, and Mr Lloyd George was not there. However, Mr Birrell leaned forward, a fist on each knee, admiration beaming through his glasses on the statistical Samuel, and occasionally he gave a jerk of his chin and remarked 'Hear, hear,' just as though he knew all about it. . . . 'Hear, hear,' said Mr Birrell

[1] See Edwin Samuel, *Lifetime in Jerusalem*, chs. 1 and 15.
[2] Asquith to King George V, 8 and 15 Dec. 1911, PRO CAB 41/33/32, 33; HS to Redmond, 4 Apr. 1912, National Library of Ireland, Redmond papers, MS 15,224.
[3] HS draft of Irish finance proposals, 14 Nov. 1911, HLRO HS A/41/4; HS to Cabinet, 22 Oct. 1912, PRO CAB 37/112; see also Patricia Jalland, *The Liberals and Ireland: The Ulster Question in British Politics to 1914* (Brighton, 1980), 44–8, 161–9.

emphatically, and then he proceeded to polish his spectacles. All at once Mr Amery, across the way, began to pop up and interrupt. Mr Samuel kept pushing him down, and Mr Amery kept popping up again. The charge was made that the Irish Parliament could introduce Protection. 'No, sir,' said the Postmaster-General, 'for every loophole has been closed by the Government amendments.'[4]

This was Samuel at his annoyingly efficient best, and on such occasions he was an invaluable asset to the Government.

Samuel's financial plan could work only if Ulster, the richest and most developed part of the island, were included in an all-Irish Home Rule arrangement. Partly for this reason, Samuel was one of those who opposed the excision of Ulster from a Home Rule Ireland. Like Asquith, he seems at first to have underestimated the potential for violent resistance by Ulster Protestants to the imposition on them of Catholic rule from Dublin. After September 1911, when Carson made a defiant speech to 100,000 Orangemen at Craigavon, it was already clear that Ulster was girding for battle. Yet in July 1912 the Prime Minister insisted in a speech in Dublin that 'Ireland is a nation, not two nations, but one nation'.[5] Of course, Asquith had to reckon with his dependence in the House of Commons on the support or at least the abstention of the Irish Nationalists. Parliamentary tactics were thus allowed to override political reality. A fortnight after Carson's Craigavon 'review', Samuel bearded the Ulster leader in his own den by addressing a meeting in Belfast. Speaking to a friendly audience of local Liberals, Samuel laid out the case for Home Rule in a unified Ireland. Asserting that he had always been an imperialist, he declared, 'It is because I am an Imperialist that I am a Home Ruler.' His response to demands for Ulster's exclusion was: 'I can give you the most definite and unqualified assurance that the rights of Ulster Protestants in the Home Rule Bill which will be introduced will be most amply safe-guarded.' As for Carson, Samuel compared him to a rhinoceros that 'tries conclusions with the railway train on the Uganda Railway', and warned 'it is not the train that suffers. . . . He does his best to make our flesh creep; but it does not creep at all.'[6]

Samuel's emphasis in Belfast on his devotion to the empire drew on the federalist 'Home Rule all round' idea that had been popular for some years. The expectation was that Home Rule would be extended in due course to all parts of the United Kingdom. But Samuel took it further in an article in the *Nineteenth Century* in October 1912, in which he argued for an empire-wide federal system. Of course, this was to discount the degree

[4] *Standard*, 9 Jan. 1913.
[5] Quoted in Roy Jenkins, *Asquith: Portrait of a Man and an Era* (New York, 1964), 279.
[6] HS speech (printed text), 6 Oct. 1911, HLRO HS A/41/1.

of effective independence already attained by the self-governing Dominions, but the piece testifies to the enduring force of the imperialist element in Samuel's liberalism.[7] His later embrace of Zionism owed much to this.

As Ulster moved closer to open rebellion, Liberal opinion began to waver on the question of whether Ulster should be forcibly included in the all-Ireland Home Rule arrangement envisaged in the bill which had by now passed twice in the Commons and been rejected twice in the Lords. As the end of the Lords' period of delay approached, Asquith opened talks with Bonar Law in October 1913. Samuel wrote to the Prime Minister from Canada, where he was visiting as a guest of the federal government, suggesting an ingenious constitutional compromise which would preserve the unity of Ireland while affording more tangible safeguards to the Ulster Protestants:

The representatives of the four Protestant counties [Antrim, Armagh, Down, and Londonderry[8]] in the Senate and House of Commons of the Irish Parliament might be given a place in the constitution under some suitable title (Qy. the Ulster House). The Bill might provide that no measure passed by the Irish Parliament should apply to those counties unless it had the assent of the Ulster House.

The sanction of a statutory Committee of that House should also be necessary for all appointments to offices in the gift of the Government within those counties.

Such provision might be for a term of years, at the expiration of which they would be reviewed by the Imperial Parliament.

They would enable the representatives of North-East Ulster not only to veto, so far as their own district was concerned, legislation or appointments distasteful to them, but would enable them to bargain very effectively with the majority in the government of the country as a whole.[9]

Samuel argued for his proposal in Cabinet upon his return to England, but the Prime Minister reported to the King on 14 November, 'This was rejected by the Cabinet with practical unanimity; it would give satisfaction to neither party, and would create the maximum of friction.'[10]

Samuel nevertheless continued to press for some solution short of a divided Ireland. In December he circulated a memorandum to the Cabinet that elaborated on his proposal. This revised plan left open the question of the exact area to which the special 'Ulster' provisions would apply. The 'Ulster House' within the Irish Parliament would be entitled to meet, if it wished, as a distinct body in Belfast. It would be given power to amend as well as to veto legislation affecting its area. The administration of Ulster

---

[7] 'Federal Government', *Nineteenth Century*, 72 (1912), 676–86.
[8] Even the Liberal advocates of Ulster exclusion were not generally prepared at this time to concede also Tyrone and Fermanagh.
[9] HS to Asquith, 10 Oct. 1913, Bodleian Library, Oxford, Asquith papers 38/226–9.
[10] Asquith to King George V, 14 Nov. 1913, PRO CAB 4/34/34.

would remain under the control of London rather than Dublin for as long as Ulster wished. But (here was, for Samuel, the crucial point):

To give to the Ulster House a veto on the application to Ulster of the financial measures of the Irish Parliament would introduce complications of the most formidable character, constitutional as well as fiscal. Indeed, it is difficult to see how any workable financial scheme, of any kind, can be evolved, based upon a fiscal separation between Ulster and the rest of Ireland. I would suggest that the Ulster veto should not be applicable to financial legislation of the Irish Parliament, but that, so long as the dual system continues, the proceeds from Ulster of any new (or increased[11]) taxation levied over Ireland by the Irish Parliament should be ear-marked to be spent for the benefit of Ulster.[12]

But this last effort to preserve all-Ireland Home Rule in a modified form was doomed to failure.[13]

Instead, Lloyd George proposed that any county (in effect this meant the four counties) be permitted to opt out of Home Rule altogether for six years by means of plebiscite. This became the basis of the Government's new scheme presented to Parliament by Asquith on 9 March 1914. Then came the Curragh 'mutiny', when General Gough and some sixty other cavalry officers in Northern Ireland announced that they would not obey any order to initiate active military operations against Ulster. As gun-running and the growth of private armies moved Ireland to the brink of civil war, the Government was driven closer to simple exclusion of Ulster from Home Rule. Samuel accordingly found himself compelled to advise the Prime Minister on what he had earlier stated was virtually impossible: a financial scheme based on the division of Ireland between a Home Rule south and a London-ruled north.[14]

The last pre-war attempt to resolve the problem took place at the Buckingham Palace Conference of Liberals (Asquith and Lloyd George), Conservatives (Bonar Law and Lansdowne), Unionists (Carson and Craig), and Nationalists (Redmond and Dillon), from 18 to 24 July 1914. In a letter to Asquith on 23 July, Samuel suggested an arrangement whereby Tyrone would be excluded from Home Rule for three years at the end of which it would 'have the right, exceptionally, of voting itself

---

[11] Added in handwriting on Prime Minister's copy.

[12] HS memo to Cabinet on 'A Suggestion for the Solution of the Ulster Question', 18 Dec. 1913 (distributed after 20 Dec.), Bodleian Library, Oxford, Asquith papers 39/61–3; final version: PRO CAB 37/117/95.

[13] Samuel's resistance to the partition of Ireland foreshadowed his rooted opposition in the 1930s to the partition of Palestine. Similarly his proposed 'dual system' for Ireland bears comparison with the system of communal autonomy that he later inaugurated in Palestine. See below, pp. 267 and 381–3.

[14] HS to Asquith, 29 June 1914, Bodleian Library, Oxford, Asquith papers 39/277; see also Jalland, *Liberals and Ireland*, 162.

into Home Rule'—'unless in the third year the Imperial House of Commons by resolution orders an extension of the period'. Samuel conceded that 'the plan on merits is not a good one', but he pointed out that 'any plan will be a good one if it can be the basis of a settlement'.[15] The weary tone denoted virtual despair. The conference was on the verge of collapse. It was too late for ingenious compromises.

The Irish issue was, in any case, now overshadowed by larger events. As Churchill put it in a famous passage in his *World Crisis*: 'The parishes of Fermanagh and Tyrone faded back into the mists and squalls of Ireland, and a strange light began immediately, but by perceptible gradations, to fall and grow upon the map of Europe.'[16] The deepening European crisis led the Government to freeze its plans for amending legislation. The Home Rule Bill was placed on the Statute Book but a Suspensory Act postponed its entry into operation for twelve months or until the end of the war if it should last longer. Samuel was one of the two Cabinet ministers who attended with Redmond at the bar of the House of Lords when the bill received the royal assent on 18 September. He shook Redmond's hand, but the Irish leader displayed no emotion at the passage of the neutered Act.[17] Meanwhile the amending bill that had been planned to deal with Ulster (the procedural device had been Samuel's suggestion[18]) was itself indefinitely postponed. The Irish problem was thus shelved for the duration of the war—or so people thought. Two years later Samuel was to find himself suddenly responsible for dealing with the dramatic consequences of the Government's pre-war failure to grasp the nettle of Irish nationalism.

While Samuel contributed to the making of the Government's Irish policy between 1911 and 1914, it was never the centre of his attention in these years—nor, given his almost completely unconnected departmental responsibilities, was his involvement on the financial side anything except volunteer activity to assist the Prime Minister in an area where the Irish Secretary's indolence was exceeded only by his manifest incompetence. In spite of his almost Herculean labours inside and outside his department, however, Samuel was slow to receive further promotion. In October 1911, when Churchill moved from the Home Office to the Admiralty, Asquith offered Samuel the Presidency of the Board of Agriculture. In political terms this would have been a side-step rather than advancement and the post itself held no intrinsic attraction for Samuel. He turned it down, and Runciman (again his shadow) was appointed, whereupon

---

[15] HS to Asquith, 23 July 1914, Bodleian Library, Oxford, Asquith papers 39/243–4.
[16] Winston S. Churchill, *The World Crisis 1911–1918*, i (London, 1968), 114.
[17] David (ed.), *Asquith's Cabinet*, 192.
[18] See Jalland, *Liberals and Ireland*, 201.

Samuel noted gleefully: 'Everybody is chaffing Runciman about turnips and the price of bacon. I am well out of that hay-cart.'[19]

In January 1914 Asquith offered Samuel the Presidency of the Board of Trade. The post carried a salary double the £2,500 he was receiving at the Post Office and in terms of prestige represented a small step of promotion. But when Asquith told Samuel that he was also thinking of moving Burns from the Local Government Board, Samuel immediately replied that he would much prefer to go there. In a letter to his mother he explained his preference for this position, generally regarded as lower-ranking than the Board of Trade:

In the first place the work of the Liberal Party in the next four years will be largely concentrated on the land question, and the urban side of that attaches closely to the L.G.B. It is a subject in which I am very keenly interested and I should greatly like to have an active part in carrying out the reforms which are pending. Secondly, the gigantic task of re-modelling our whole system of Local Taxation will have to be undertaken before long. . . . The questions of Poor Law reform and Public Health interest me greatly and belong entirely to the L.G.B. Finally, the Board of Trade has had a succession of active and alert Presidents—Lloyd-George, Winston Churchill and Sydney Buxton, and I question whether they have left many things of importance still to do. John Burns, though his work has been admirable on the two or three questions on which he has concentrated himself, is not very receptive of new ideas, and I should probably find a wide field of activity open.'[20]

Asquith decided to move Burns to the Board of Trade and to give Samuel the Local Government Board. He confirmed the recently enhanced status of the position as equivalent to a Secretaryship of State, carrying a salary of £5,000. Recommending the new appointments to the King, Asquith wrote: 'Mr Samuel is one of the ablest of our young men, and well-fitted for the place quitted by Mr Burns.'[21]

Samuel's new ministry was situated in a modern building in Whitehall, just across Parliament Square from the House of Commons, much closer to the nerve-centre of power than St Martin's-le-Grand. Created by Gladstone in 1871, the Local Government Board was an anomaly in being a central government department designed to oversee local government. Its responsibilities ranged widely and included housing and town planning, but it was centrally concerned with poor relief and public health. A heavy drag on its effectiveness was the legacy of the nineteenth-century Poor Law with its moralistic and by this time anachronistic assumptions about the diagnosis and treatment of poverty. As Sir Arthur

[19] Asquith to HS, 10 Oct. 1911, HS to Asquith, 11 Oct. 1911 (copy), HLRO HS A/155/IV/23, 23a; HS to BS, 24 Oct. 1911, HLRO HS A/157/582.
[20] HS to CS, 11 Jan. 1914, HLRO HS A/156/452.
[21] Asquith to Lord Stamfordham, 27 Jan. 1914, Royal Archives, GV K643/1.

Newsholme, who served as the Board's Principal Medical Officer under Samuel, put it later: 'So far as Public Health is concerned, the Local Government Board was hampered throughout its forty-eight years' existence by its Poor Law duties and traditions.'[22] It might have been expected that the only 'Labour', albeit Lib–Lab, minister in the Liberal Cabinet would have turned this ministry into a power-house of social reform and innovation. But Burns had been a sad failure as a minister. He invariably followed the advice of his civil servants when they told him to do nothing. When, more rarely, they recommended action, he generally stopped it. Yet his peculiar status as the only working-man in the Cabinet made him, if not indispensable, at any rate irremovable. In 1909 the Royal Commission on the Poor Law had produced a majority report advocating major changes including replacement of the Poor Law Boards of Guardians by 'public assistance' authorities appointed by local councils and working closely with voluntary organizations. The much more radical minority report, written by the Webbs, advocated the total abolition of the old Poor Law system, the creation of a new Ministry of Labour, the organization of public works, and the transfer of health and public assistance functions to committees of local councils. Burns rejected both reports and many essentials of the system inaugurated in 1834 remained unchanged. 'Go on with . . . economising', he instructed J. S. Davy, Chief Inspector of the Poor Law Division of the Board, in 1911.

Samuel's approach promised to be more dynamic and interventionist. The Webbs' house organ, the recently founded *New Statesman*, welcomed his appointment: 'To Mr Samuel more than to any other member of the Ministry we may look for a revival of that appreciation of the value of Local Government and for a sense of the important part that it ought to play in nearly every social reform.'[23] A few weeks later the Webbs happened to meet Samuel and Lloyd George at the opera and took the opportunity to engage them in discussion. The encounter led to further meetings with Lloyd George and encouraged Beatrice Webb to believe that the Government might support her 'big scheme for maternity and infancy under the Public Health Authority'. Recording the occasion happily in her diary she commented that Samuel could be counted on 'as an ardent supporter, honestly intent on promoting a really big development of Public Health, during his term of office'. She continued: 'He has spent two evenings with us; he is sound in his proposals and very industrious. But he is said to carry little weight with the Cabinet.'[24]

[22] Sir Arthur Newsholme, *The Ministry of Health* (London, 1925), 97.
[23] *New Statesman*, 21 Feb. 1914.
[24] Entry dated 22 Apr. 1914, BLPES Beatrice Webb diary, 3289–90.

Samuel found that Burns had left 'appalling legislative arrears' at the Local Government Board.[25] He set housing and local taxation reform as his first priorities.[26] In a speech in Sheffield in May 1914 Samuel outlined his thinking on these subjects. He condemned the antiquated rating system as 'Elizabethan' and regressive, and declared that the Government planned 'relief of rates upon houses and improvements—but not of rates on land values'. The major executors of the proposed improvements in housing and town planning were to be the local authorities which were to be armed with greater powers, including 'adequate powers of compulsory purchase' of land. Samuel proposed that it should be made 'a statutory duty of the local authorities to see that the population of their districts are adequately housed and that the health laws are properly observed', and he said 'grants from the Exchequer to those localities should be conditional on those duties being efficiently performed'.[27]

The first and, as it turned out, only significant piece of legislation Samuel introduced at the Board was one regulating the supply and sale of milk and cream. The bill was designed to remedy a major problem of public health. In 1907 a Royal Commission on Tuberculosis had reported, after six years of investigation, that legislation was urgently required to prevent the sale of infected milk. Burns had contemplated a narrowly conceived milk bill in 1907, but owing to bad drafting and lack of supervision by Burns the bill had to be dropped.[28] A broader bill was prepared in 1909 but Burns had still not succeeded in securing its passage by the time he left the Board. More than 53,000 cases of tuberculosis were reported in England and Wales in 1911, and of these a quarter were of non-pulmonary tuberculosis in children under 15 (this form of the disease among children was particularly associated with infected milk).[29] Samuel introduced his bill in May 1914: the occasion was chiefly memorable for the fact that Asquith, who was due to follow on another subject, arrived at the House late: 'Happily [the Prime Minister later wrote to his intimate correspondent Venetia Stanley] the Infant Samuel was on his legs dilating on milk and a little diluting his subject to give me time.'[30] The Milk and Dairies Act, which passed with next to no opposition, gave the Local Government Board powers to register all dairies and to make orders for their inspection by local authorities. Other provisions prevented the sale

[25] HS to Herbert Gladstone, 14 Apr. 1914, BL Add. MS 45992/275.
[26] HS to CS, 21 Feb. 1914, HLRO HS A/156/458.
[27] Urban Land and Housing Reform, speech by HS at Sheffield, 14 May 1914 (London, 1914).
[28] Brown, Burns, 127–8.
[29] HC Deb. 5 s., vol. 62 (12 May 1914), cols. 945–8.
[30] Asquith to Venetia Stanley, 12 May 1914, in Michael and Eleanor Brock (eds.), H. H. Asquith: Letters to Venetia Stanley (Oxford, 1982), 72.

THE INFANT SAMUEL.

1 'The Infant Samuel' (Punch, 17 June 1914)

of infected, contaminated, or dirty milk. In particular, Medical Officers of Health were empowered to stop the supply of milk from any dairy where tubercular milk was known or suspected.[31] The Act, however, lay virtually dormant on the statute-book until 1925 and even then it proved ineffective.[32]

In other matters Samuel utilized the administrative powers of the Board much more energetically than his predecessor. In July 1914 the Board sent out a circular offering grants to local authorities for maternal and child welfare centres. The object was to make 'medical advice, and, where necessary, treatment . . . continuously and systematically available for expectant mothers and for children till they are entered on a school register'. Samuel said that he looked forward to such activity 'becoming part of the normal operations of the Public Health Service'.[33] The circular led to a rapid proliferation of maternity and child welfare centres and probably contributed to the decline in the infant mortality rate from 95 per thousand in England and Wales (high compared with other developed countries) in 1914 to 72 per thousand by 1920.[34]

A major blot on the social conscience of Edwardian England was obliterated by Samuel in another administrative action that had been long planned but not implemented by Burns: the several thousand children who were still kept in workhouses were removed under an order issued in the spring of 1914. Other reforms in Poor Law administration were also introduced. A further important administrative change was the establishment of an Intelligence Department at the Local Government Board, charged with gathering information and maintaining contact with voluntary organizations. And Samuel ordered a survey of all hospital and dispensary provision, voluntary or municipal, in each sanitary district. All these measures pointed towards the expansion of the Local Government Board into a full-fledged Ministry of Public Health, an objective that commanded support from Lloyd George and Haldane as well as leading public health officials.[35]

But this aim, like Samuel's other plans for peaceful social reform, was tossed aside by the tidal wave that engulfed the British Government at the end of July 1914. The Cabinet met repeatedly in crisis session throughout

[31] See Local Government Chronicle, 3 Oct. 1914.

[32] See Linda Bryder, Below the Magic Mountain: A Social History of Tuberculosis in Twentieth-Century Britain (Oxford, 1988), 133; F. B. Smith, The Retreat of Tuberculosis 1850–1950 (London, 1988), 183–4.

[33] County Councils Association Official Gazette, Nov. 1914.

[34] J. M. Winter, The Great War and the British People (London, 1986), 141.

[35] See diary of Sir George Newman, 25 Mar., 19 June, 8 July 1914, PRO MH 139/2; HC Deb. 5 s., vol. 63 (18 June 1914), cols. 1294–345; New Statesman, 27 June 1914; also Winter, Great War, 193–204.

that month. But the crisis they were discussing was the danger of civil war in Ireland, not the one that had begun with the shots fired at Sarajevo on 28 June. It was not until 25 July that Asquith even mentioned the threat to European peace in his Cabinet letters to the King. Even then, in his description of the Cabinet on 24 July, it took second place to the Cabinet wrestlings with Ireland. The precipitant of this final awareness was the Austrian ultimatum to Serbia on 23 July—'the most formidable document I have ever seen addressed by one State to another that was independent', as Grey termed it.[36] Unlike Asquith, Grey, Lloyd George, and Churchill, Samuel was not a major player in the events of the next eleven days, but in a decision of such historic magnitude every Cabinet member took his share. 'Each must be led by his own conscience, and none can put the responsibility on his neighbour', Samuel wrote to his mother on 30 July.[37] Samuel contributed more than might be indicated by his relatively junior Cabinet rank to the collective decision. Indeed, the special importance of Samuel's activities during these dread days was that he helped bring about a decision that was genuinely collective—one in which all save Morley and Burns joined. That decision took Britain into the war under a Liberal rather than a coalition government and preserved for a while the unity of the Liberal Party.

Before July 1914 Samuel had played next to no part in the making of British foreign policy. His chief interests and ambitions in politics lay squarely in the domestic arena. In spite of his penchant for offering help to fellow ministers this was almost always in financial or home affairs. Even his earlier involvement in imperial matters virtually disappeared after he entered government. The only significant exception to this immersion in internal British issues had been his vigorous opposition in the Cabinet to Churchill's efforts to accelerate the naval building programme. In July 1912 he had been one of four ministers (the others were McKenna, Lloyd George, and Hobhouse) to speak strongly in Cabinet against Churchill's proposals.[38]

In December 1913 he again opposed Churchill's naval estimates which called for an increase in expenditure of nearly 6 per cent over the previous year. Samuel proposed that two capital ships be laid down rather than the four requested by Churchill, and he suggested reductions in numbers of men, and in the construction of submarines and light cruisers. Churchill defended his estimates and a fierce Cabinet battle ensued. The opponents of increased naval spending included Runciman, Hobhouse, Simon, and

[36] Quoted in Zara S. Steiner, *Britain and the Origins of the First World War* (London, 1977), 221–2.
[37] HS to CS, 30 July 1914, HLRO HS A/156/467.
[38] Hobhouse diary, 10 July 1912, in David (ed.), *Asquith's Cabinet*, 117.

Jack Pease as well as Samuel. These were not very influential ministers, but at a critical Cabinet meeting on 16 December—described by John Burns as 'in some respects the most serious since 1906'[39]—Lloyd George seemed to throw his considerable political weight against Churchill. For a while there was talk of Churchill being forced out of the Cabinet.[40] Several Cabinet meetings failed to settle the dispute and a decision was postponed over the Christmas holiday.

On 1 January 1914 Lloyd George gave a press interview which made public his opposition to large increases in naval spending. The interview mobilized Liberal opinion against Churchill. A series of informal meetings followed in an atmosphere of growing crisis. On 18 January the editor of the *Manchester Guardian*, C. P. Scott, a confidant of Liberal ministers, visited Lloyd George who told him that 'he had McKenna and Samuel downstairs and they were going into the Naval estimates with some Treasury officials. . . . He and McKenna and Samuel had agreed that Churchill must go.'[41] Churchill circulated a series of Cabinet papers containing facts and figures to buttress his demands. Samuel responded on 21 January with a handwritten memorandum to the Prime Minister in which he criticized Churchill's statistics.[42] Masterman, a friend of Samuel, denounced his attitude as 'indecent' and said that he and Simon were trying 'to hound Winston out of the Cabinet'. 'This is evident from their manner and they cannot conceal it', he said.[43] Eventually, Asquith coaxed Lloyd George and Churchill into a compromise—effectively a victory for the Admiralty. Once the Chancellor of the Exchequer had abandoned the hunt, the 'beagles' were in no position to carry on the pursuit. The crisis passed.

Samuel's advocacy of naval economies did not, however, place him in the near-pacifist camp of Morley and Simon. During the July crisis, he belonged to a middle group in the Cabinet that worked to preserve Cabinet unity so far as that was feasible, to keep Britain out of the war if possible, to use the possibility of British participation as a deterrent to Germany, and to devise a formula that would fulfil Britain's treaty obligations to Belgium without, it was hoped, bringing about British involvement in war in her defence.

[39] Burns diary, 16 Dec. 1914, BL Add. MS 46335.
[40] Asquith to King George V, 11 and 20 Dec. 1913, PRO CAB 41/34/39; Riddell diary, 14 Dec. 1913, in McEwen (ed.), *Riddell Diaries*, 72; Randolph Churchill, *Winston Churchill*, ii. 654–65.
[41] Trevor Wilson (ed.), *The Political Diaries of C. P. Scott 1911–1928* (London, 1970), 75.
[42] HS memorandum, 21 Jan. 1914, Asquith papers, 25/150–4, Bodleian Library, Oxford.
[43] Riddell diary, 23 Jan. 1914, in McEwen (ed.), *Riddell Diaries*, 78–9.

Throughout the crisis Samuel wrote to his mother and his wife narrating, with unusual frankness and detail, the development of feeling in the Cabinet. In his first such letter, on 26 July, he told his mother that he feared that by the end of the week Europe might be 'engaged in, or on the brink of, the greatest war for a hundred years, and possibly the bloodiest war in its history'. At that point he did not expect Britain to fight: 'I hope that our country may not be involved. But even of that one cannot be sure. At this stage I think it will not be.'[44] The next day he wrote to his wife: 'We had a Cabinet this evening which lasted just an hour. I am still inclined to be pessimistic about the outlook, but we are doing our best to localize the conflict.'[45] And on the following day: 'The situation looks no better. The news has just come in that Austria has declared war on Servia. That was clearly inevitable. There is a strange silence from Russia.'[46] On 29 July he wrote again to his wife: 'I still think that the probabilities are that the fuse which has been fired will quickly bring a catastrophic explosion. . . . We nineteen men round the table at Downing Street may soon have to face the most momentous problem which men can face. Meantime our action is held in suspense, for if both sides do not know what we shall do, both will be less willing to run risks.'[47]

By 30 July, as the Russian mobilization slowly cranked into motion, and as the railway timetables of the other powers dictated a speedy response, Grey's efforts at mediation were seen to have failed utterly. The question before the British Cabinet was no longer whether the war could be localized, nor whether a general conflict could be contained, but rather whether some way could be found to prevent British involvement without irreparably damaging British interests. Grey, Asquith, Churchill, and Haldane believed that a German defeat of France, carrying in its wake German dominance of western Europe and German control of the Channel, would be intolerable. They were the most inclined to go to war. Burns, Morley, Simon, and Beauchamp were the most opposed. Other members of the Cabinet, among them Samuel, were at first less clear in their own minds what would constitute a *casus belli*. But Samuel was by this time growing steadily more pessimistic:

It will be the most horrible catastrophe since the abominations of the Napoleonic time, and in many respects worse even than they. . . .

Tomorrow we have a fateful Cabinet and have to decide what this country shall do. It may be that the Cabinet will split, but I don't think it will. I had half an hour's talk at

[44] HS to CS, 26 July 1914, HLRO HS A/156/466.
[45] HS to BS, 27 July 1914, HLRO HS A/157/689.
[46] HS to BS, 28 July 1914, HLRO HS A/157/689.
[47] HS to BS, 29 July 1914, HLRO HS A/157/691.

midnight last night with Grey. It is marvellous how serene, and indeed cheerful, he keeps—cheerful, that is, in his demeanour, not in his outlook.[48]

Apart from Cabinets and departmental business, Samuel spent much time during these days talking to ministers (Lloyd George, Hobhouse, and McKinnon Wood) and MPs with the aim of fashioning a policy that would prevent a break-up of the Government over the issue of war or peace. On 1 August he went to the Foreign Office in the morning and read the night's telegrams. Later that morning the Cabinet met for an inconclusive discussion. Samuel wrote to his wife: 'We may be brought in under certain eventualities. A suggestion of mine was adopted by the Cabinet which may a good deal affect the issue. I am less hopeful than yesterday of our being able to keep out of it. The Cabinet is solid as yet, but the testing time may come tomorrow.'[49]

Samuel's suggestion, which he amplified in a series of meetings the following day, was that Britain should put the onus of provoking any intervention on Germany. His intention, however, in putting forward the proposal was still at least as much to prevent British involvement as to provide a justification for war. He suggested that the two contingencies which should be seen as *casus belli* were a German naval attack on the northern coast of France and a German threat to the independence of Belgium. Although German attacks on both the French coast and Belgium were expected, neither of these conditions was as open-and-shut as it might seem, and diplomatic paths might still have been manœuvred around them to preserve British neutrality or perhaps to limit her involvement. The former condition was based on the mistaken expectation in London that a German naval attack on the French coast would take place in conjunction with the German land assault. The Anglo-French understandings of 1912 had left the French ports in the Channel virtually undefended, and it would clearly be against the British interest to see these in the hands of the Germans. Of course, British action at sea to preclude such a threat might be undertaken by means of demonstrative mobilization, without necessarily going to war. And even if Britain did go to war on this basis, hostilities might be limited to naval encounters in the Channel and North Sea. Indeed, even after Britain declared war on 4 August, there seemed at first to be no question in the minds of many ministers of dispatching the British Expeditionary Force to the continent. In the event, the Germans did not bring out their navy, so the first condition did not apply.

The second point, on the other hand, apparently involved a clear treaty

<hr>

[48] HS to BS, 30 July 1914, HLRO HS A/157/692.
[49] HS to BS, 1 Aug. 1914, HLRO HS A/157/696.

obligation. Yet here too the question became murky on close examination. Did Britain have a duty or merely a right to intervene? Should mere German passage of troops through Belgium in order to attack France be regarded as a threat to her independence and neutrality and therefore a *casus foederis* under the 1839 treaties? Samuel and others distinguished between a German attack on France through the Ardennes, which might be concentrated in the Grand Duchy of Luxemburg and encroach marginally on Belgium, and a full-frontal attack on the heart of Belgium. 'I don't see why we need come in if they go only a little way into Belgium', said Churchill. Samuel's formula was designed to limit British involvement to the latter, and, it was mistakenly thought, less likely, contingency of an attack on central Belgium.[50]

On Sunday, 2 August the Cabinet faced its moment of truth. Samuel described the day's events in a lengthy letter to his wife:

The Cabinet sat today from 11 to 1.30 and from 6.30 to 8. This morning's Cabinet almost resulted in a political crisis to be superimposed on the international and financial crisis. Grey expressed a view which was unacceptable to most of us. He is outraged by the way in which Germany and Austria have played with the most vital interests of civilisation, have put aside all attempts at accommodation made by himself and others, and while continuing to negotiate have marched steadily to war.

I expressed my own conviction that we should be justified in joining in the war either for the protection of the northern coasts of France, which we could not afford to see bombarded by the German fleet and occupied by the German army, or for the maintenance of the independence of Belgium which we were bound by treaty to protect and which again we could not afford to see subordinated to Germany. But I held that we were not entitled to carry England into the war for the sake of our goodwill for France or for the sake of maintaining the strength of France and Russia against that of Germany and Austria. This opinion is shared by the majority of the Cabinet with various degrees of emphasis on the several parts of it. We sanctioned a statement being made by Grey to the French Ambassador this afternoon, to be followed by a statement in Parliament tomorrow that we should take action if the German fleet came down the Channel to attack France (Almost the whole of the French fleet is in the Mediterranean). But Burns dissented, feeling that Germany may regard this declaration as an act of hostility and may declare war on us because of it. He is for neutrality in all circumstances. It is probable that he will resign to-night and Morley may go with him. Strong efforts are being made to persuade them not to go.

After the Cabinet Samuel lunched at Beauchamp's. There and in conversations during the afternoon with Lloyd George, Harcourt, Simon and others he found broad concurrence in his formula. He called on McKenna

---

[50] See Michael Brock, 'Britain Enters the War', in R. J. W. Evans and Harmut Pogge von Strandmann (eds.), *The Coming of the First World War* (Oxford, 1988), 145–78; also Steiner, *Britain and the Origins*.

and then visited the Prime Minister at 10 Downing Street. Asquith said to him: 'I shall stand by Grey at any event.'[51]

That afternoon Asquith wrote to Venetia Stanley: 'There is a strong party including all the "Beagles" and reinforced by Ll George Morley & Harcourt who are against any kind of intervention in any event. Grey of course will never consent to this, & I shall not separate myself from him. Crewe, McKenna, & Samuel are a moderating intermediate body.'[52] Samuel's vital role in the crisis was to turn this 'intermediate body' into the makeweight and thereby to fashion a compromise that secured general assent to his formula.[53] His contribution, and the motives that lay behind it, emerge from his further narrative to his wife:

When the Cabinet resumed at 6.30 the situation was easier, the point of contention was not pressed and with the exception of the two I have mentioned we remain solid.

Had the matter come to an issue Asquith would have stood by Grey in any event and three others would have remained. I think all the rest of us would have resigned. The consequence would have been either a Coalition Government or a Unionist Government, either of which would certainly have been a war ministry. Moreover, the division or resignation of the Government in a moment of utmost peril for the country would have been in every way lamentable.

Samuel's formula, although it provided a basis two days later for the British entry to the war, was still not seen by him as necessarily leading to British involvement:

I still have hopes that Germany will neither send her fleet down the Channel nor invade Belgium, and we shall be able to keep England at peace while rendering France the greatest of all services—the protection of her northern coasts from the sea and the protection of her 150 miles of frontier with Belgium. If we can achieve this, without firing a shot, we shall have accomplished a brilliant stroke of policy. For this object I have been working incessantly all the week. If we do not accomplish it, it will be an action of Germany's, and not of ours, which will cause the failure and my conscience will be easy in embarking on the war . . .

The next morning, 3 August, the Cabinet met at 11.00 a.m. This was an occasion of great emotion in which even the normally impassive Samuel evidently shared:

The fateful Cabinet is just over. Burns, Morley, Simon & Beauchamp have resigned [Simon and Beauchamp subsequently withdrew their resignations]. No announcement to be made yet. The rest of us stood firm as we are sure our policy is right, much as we hate the war. The Germans have invaded Belgium [This was apparently based

[51] Memorandum by Samuel, 24 June 1929, BL Add. MS 46386.
[52] Asquith to Venetia Stanley, 2 Aug. 1914, in Brocks (eds.), *Asquith Letters*, 146.
[53] See K. M. Wilson, 'The British Cabinet's Decision for War, 2 August 1914', *British Journal of International Studies*, 1 (1975), 148–59.

on false or premature reports], and the King has appealed for our help. It is said they have also invaded Holland and Switzerland—every neutral state within reach [These reports too turned out to be mistaken]. Our participation in the war is now inevitable. Those four men have no right to abandon us at this crisis—it is a failure of courage.

The Cabinet was very moving. Most of us could hardly speak at all for emotion. The Prime Minister goes on out of sheer sense of duty. As I write I hear the crowds cheering in Whitehall [The letter was written at 11 Downing Street where Samuel lunched with Lloyd George].

The world is on the verge of a great catastrophe. After all the suffering there may perhaps emerge a finer civilisation, and the bitter experience of these days may bring a greater hatred of the use of force in the next generation.[54]

After lunch Samuel drove with the Chancellor through the crowds to the House of Commons:

He [Lloyd George] was warmly cheered by the excited people, waving little Union Jacks. 'This is not my crowd', he said. 'I never want to be cheered by a war crowd.' It was a moving sight and I could not help thinking and saying that they all knew little what was meant, and that there will be a different spirit three months from now.[55]

At the House of Commons Grey made what Asquith described as 'a most remarkable speech—about an hour long—for the most part conversational in tone & with some of his usual ragged ends; but extraordinarily well reasoned & tactful & really *cogent*'.[56] Samuel wrote to his wife at 5.30 p.m.: 'Grey has made his able statement. But too much France and not enough Belgium and Channel in it to please me. However, the H. of C. is almost solid.'[57] The next day the Germans invaded Belgium. Following the German failure to respond to a British ultimatum, war was declared without any formal consultation of the Cabinet. Oppressed by the distasteful yells of the bellicose mob, a deeply pacific government turned to form the nation into marching order.

[54] HS to BS, [3] Aug. 1914, HLRO HS A/157/698.
[55] The thought was in many minds. That same day Asquith wrote to Venetia Stanley: 'You remember Sir R. Walpole's remark: Now they are ringing their bells; in a few weeks they'll be wringing their hands.' (3 Aug. 1914, in Brocks (eds.), *Asquith Letters*, 148.)
[56] Ibid.
[57] HS to BS, 3 Aug. 1914, HLRO HS A/157/699.

7

Liberalism at War

===

Nous sommes anti-militaristes guerriers.

(Anon.)

THE OUTBREAK of the war abruptly halted Samuel's plans for social
reform legislation. 'These are not days in which any minister can sketch
out an ambitious legislative programme', he lamented to a conference of
county councillors in early 1915.[1] His ideas for peacefully and gradually
extending the sphere of the state in social life seemed to have met an
immovable obstacle. In fact, war vastly extended the intervention of the
state in private life and snuffed out the vestiges of individualist liberalism
of Cobden and Bright. During the first twenty-eight months of the war
Samuel found himself obliged to collude in the erosion of those very
elements in historic liberalism to which he had earlier clung as principles
of continuity that must not be jettisoned: free trade, freedom of expression, a
free Ireland, and freedom from conscription.

These dilemmas were hardly felt in the early days of the war, as Samuel
laboured with redoubled energy. With Lloyd George and others he
worked on emergency financial measures. Banks were closed for four
days; the Stock Exchange was also closed for a period; and £1 and 10s.
banknotes were issued. He was appointed chairman of a small subcommittee that prepared secret 'instructions for the guidance of the civil
population' to be issued in the event of an invasion of Britain. All ordinary
business of the Local Government Board was put aside in order to deal
with the anticipated problems of social relief. On the day war broke out
Samuel was appointed chairman of a committee to advise on measures
necessary to deal with the distress arising from the war. He organized a network of regional and functional subcommittees on which he made a special
effort to draw in men and women of all parties including a noticeable
number of opponents of the war. Ramsay MacDonald served on the main
committee as did Burns who agreed in addition to chair the subcommittee
for London. Other members included Beatrice Webb and Henrietta

[1] HS speech to Executive Council of County Councils Association, 27 Jan. 1915,
County Councils Association Official Gazette, Feb. 1915.

Adler. Walter Long, a former Conservative President of the LGB, served as chairman of a subcommittee for agricultural districts, and another on women's employment was headed by the Marchioness of Crewe and included Lily Montagu and Margaret Bondfield.

An indication of the utter unpreparedness of the Government for the kind of war that they were to face was Samuel's statement to Parliament on 6 August that it was 'certain that, to some extent, unemployment is likely to ensue in the near future'.[2] In fact, the 'distress' turned out to be very different in origin. The committees coped with the consequences of the hand-over of many Poor Law institutions to military uses, looked after camps for enemy aliens, and organized the distribution of relief to dependants of soldiers and sailors.[3] 'We are all working like horses', Samuel wrote on 5 August from the Reform Club, where he was lodging, to his wife at Hutton Rudby.[4]

The patriotic enthusiasm accompanying the outbreak of hostilities produced an outpouring of voluntary activity that the Government decided should be directed into useful channels. Samuel was assigned the task of supervising these efforts. A National Relief Fund, headed by the Prince of Wales, collected £4,907,000 within seven months.[5] Samuel received unsolicited advice on how the fund should be administered from well-meaning dignitaries such as the Archbishop of York and the Duchess of Albany, who suggested that 'gifts of cattle & cows' should be collected 'to be fed to the populace as required'.[6] The task of reconciling sometimes divergent views from eminent quarters required considerable delicacy.[7] On 18 August Samuel wrote to his wife: 'I went to see the Queen again about her needlework and women's employment schemes and had a quarter of an hour's talk with her. She is a very practical woman.'[8] Two days later he wrote after seeing the Queen again: 'Am appointing a Committee to carry out her ideas. She wanted to appoint it herself [Queen Mary had, in fact, written at length to the Prime Minister on the subject] which would never have done!'[9]

---

[2] HC Deb. 5 s., vol. 65 (6 Aug. 1914), cols. 2130–4.

[3] Memorandum on the Steps Taken for the Prevention and Relief of Distress Due to the War, Cd. 7603 (London, 1914); Report on the Special Work of the Local Government Board Arising out of the War (up to the 31st December 1914), Cd. 7763 (London, 1915).

[4] HS to BS, 5 Aug. 1914, HLRO HS A/157/701.

[5] Report on the Administration of the National Relief Fund up to the 31st March 1915, Cd. 7756 (London, 1915).

[6] Wedgwood Benn to HS, 9 Aug. 1914 (enclosing memorandum by Duchess of Albany), PRO MH 57/183.

[7] See correspondence in PRO MH 57/183, 196, and 197.

[8] HS to BS, 18 Aug. 1914, HLRO HS A/157/721.

[9] HS to BS, 20 Aug. 1914, HLRO HS A/157/723; Queen Mary to Asquith, 19 Aug. 1914, in Brocks (eds.), Asquith Letters, 180.

Diplomatic handling of a different sort had to be applied to some of Samuel's collaborators in the relief effort. Burns, in particular, seethed with resentment of his successor: 'H. S. not as grateful as he might be for the strong support he has received nor sufficiently appreciative of the heritage of sound relief procedure we handed over to him after we left the L.G.B. H. S. is afraid of L. G. and inclined to be a fly in and [? from] the spider's Webb.' Both the imperious plural and the contemptuous reference to the author of the Minority Report of the Royal Commission on the Poor Law presaged trouble.[10]

A more serious problem, revealing of how the famous principle of 'less eligibility', enshrined in the Poor Law, immediately broke down under the impact of large-scale war, arose from the departure on active duty of large numbers of breadwinners. Many of their wives were driven to seek Poor Law relief—a demeaning recourse for respectable working-class people. Samuel recognized this as 'a shameful thing' and took action to diminish the stigma.[11] On 6 August a bill was passed in Parliament providing that receipt of poor relief by the wife or child of a soldier or sailor absent on service should not involve electoral disqualification (one of the many conditions attached to the receipt of poor relief). Seebohm Rowntree and William Beveridge were called upon to give expert advice about the establishment of a 'statistical measure of relative distress' that would serve as a basis for the distribution of relief.[12] Over the next few months the administration of the Prince of Wales Fund was disfigured by wrangling over scales of relief, with accusations that 'the indirect tho' powerful pressure of starvation' was being 'used as a means to secure enlistment'.[13]

The dispute was envenomed by personal antagonisms. In particular, John Burns, balked of the trappings of office which he had greatly relished, vented his frustration by renewing his old feud with the Webbs. Burns championed low payments against the more generous proposals of the Webbs and the Labour representatives. 'For Heaven's sake [wrote Sidney Webb to Samuel on 10 September], hold up the proposal to fix the maximum scale of relief . . . *actually below* the Poor Law standard. . . . I wonder whether those who are pushing this *uneconomic* policy of an inadequate scale realise how serious this will be. It will, of course, be laid hold of by the hostile newspapers, *where it will come just in time to*

---

[10] Burns diary, 24 Aug. 1914, BL Add. MS 46336.

[11] HS to BS, 15 Aug. 1914, HLRO HS A/157/716.

[12] Masterman to HS (enclosing memorandum by Beveridge), 7 Sept. 1914, PRO MH 57/195.

[13] See Walter Long (reporting such accusations) to HS, 29 Aug. 1914, PRO MH 57/183; see also Royden Harrison, 'The War Emergency Workers' National Committee, 1914–1920', in Asa Briggs and John Saville (eds.), *Essays in Labour History 1886–1923* (London, 1971), 235 n.

reinforce powerfully the movement which the I.L.P. is fomenting against the Labour Party for supporting the war and the Government. . . . I cannot conceive what some of your colleagues are thinking of.'[14]

Samuel sympathized with the Webbs' position. In an obvious reference to Burns's London committee, Samuel later wrote that some 'committees were inclined to regard themselves as having been established, not for the prevention and relief of distress, but for the prevention of relief of distress'.[15] Samuel's attitude enraged Burns, as may be seen from his apoplectic diary entries:

17 September: L.G.B. early for Sub-Committee . . . B[eatrice] W[ebb] sly, devilish sly, defeated last week and angry with true intriguing instinct she had subdued Samuel to her will. . . . Beat Cave at billiards and then went to L.G.B. and beat Samuel out of his Webb entrenchments. Not a soul supported him. It was the most contemptible surrender to the Pauperisers I have seen in public life.

23 September: Generally Committee agreed [with Burns] but the slippery Samuel who fears electoral clamour from the Pauperisers of the Poor led by the Webbs dodged and ducked and evaded from the chair all he could. A Sub Committee was appointed to find a way out for the 'politicians' who are not statesmen and who are enemies not friends of the honest poor. I spoke to Samuel sharply and firmly. . . . I rebuked him both for his ingratitude to us [sic] for our help and cowardice in surrendering to a [word illegible] and discourtesy in not telling us he was going to change his views. He got angry and retorted like the acidulated pug he is.[16]

The endless bickering in Burns's London sub-committee, its failure to reach a decision on the issue, and the discrepancies and inconsistencies of the policies of the regional and functional subcommittees produced a stream of complaints.[17]

The Webbs, better exponents than Burns of the art of public relations, engineered a press campaign in support of their position. With the help of the *Daily News* they eventually routed Burns. On 31 October their mouthpiece, the *New Statesman*, congratulated the committee of the Prince of Wales's Fund on abandoning 'the slow starvation policy'. Burns boasted to his diary that he had won the battle; but the scales finally adopted tell a different story. Samuel, the consummate chairman, somehow left both sides with the impression that they had won a victory. Burns continued to feel aggrieved, but Sidney Webb thanked Samuel for the

[14] Sidney Webb to HS, 10 Sept. 1914, PRO MH 57/195.
[15] Herbert Samuel, 'Government Measures on War Distress', *Nineteenth Century*, 78 (1915), 1114–23.
[16] Burns diary, BL Add. MS 46336.
[17] See e.g. Memorandum on 'Distribution in Scotland of Grants from the Prince of Wales's Fund', 1 Sept. 1914, PRO MH 57/195; Sir John Simon to HS (with enclosure), 28 Sept. 1914, PRO MH 57/183; Edgar Jones MP to HS, 5 Oct. 1914, PRO MH 57/194; W. H. Dickinson MP to HS, 16 Oct. 1914, PRO MH 57/195.

'gratifying' result, and added: 'I hope you don't think I am unappreciative of the excellent way in which you are improving on your predecessor (!)'[18]

Samuel also earned high marks from the Webbs for his readiness to allocate large sums of Government money for public works to relieve unemployment. But this openhandedness provoked a squeal of protest from the Treasury.[19] Edwin Montagu, by now Financial Secretary to the Treasury, wrote to his cousin stressing the need for economy in wartime and asking for an explanation of a newspaper advertisement that seemed to suggest that the state would furnish 'millions' to provide employment wherever necessary.[20]

In the event, the Government's well-laid plans proved superfluous. After an initial surge of unemployment in August 1914, the war quickly brought a labour shortage as hundreds of thousands volunteered for the armed forces and as war industries geared up for production. By early 1915 unemployment had been virtually eliminated and the number of paupers in receipt of Poor Law relief was the smallest for forty years. In February 1915 Samuel was able to announce to the annual Central Poor Law Conference that trade had 'rapidly recovered, and, as they were all aware, was now in a very satisfactory state, and the problem became, one not of opening up new means of employment, but rather of transferring labour from industries which were suffering from the war to others which had been stimulated by demands following the war'.

Samuel's speech made it clear that the war had not changed his fundamentally moralistic attitude towards the problems of unemployment and poverty. He dwelt again on the Poor Law's distinction between the deserving and the undeserving poor, and reminded his audience that 'it was useless to blink the fact' that in every community 'a certain proportion of people, idle, dishonest and dissolute, . . . sooner or later through their own faults of character, became dependent for their maintenance upon the assistance of others'. These Smilesian nostrums might have been enunciated by his predecessor. But Burns cannot have been delighted by the contrast pointed by an editorial in the *Local Government Chronicle*: 'Whilst he [Burns] did good work as President of the greatest of our domestic administrative departments one always realised that the permanent officials were his masters, and that he lacked just that power

---

[18] Sidney Webb to HS, 24 Oct. 1914, PRO MH 57/195; see also Brown, *Burns*, 182; and *New Statesman*, 31 Oct. 1914.

[19] *New Statesman*, 3 Oct. 1914; see also *HC Deb.* 5 s., vol. 65 (6 Aug. 1914), cols. 2130–4; also vol. 66 (14 Sept. 1914), cols. 840–5; and vol. 68 (16 Nov. 1914) col. 240; *Local Government Chronicle*, 8 and 29 Aug., 12 Sept., 17 Oct., and 21 Nov. 1914; and HS to Edwin Montagu, 1 Sept. 1914, PRO MH 57/197.

[20] Montagu to Lloyd George, 2 Oct. 1914 (enclosing copy of letter to HS), HLRO Lloyd George papers C/1/1/29.

which carries the educated and cultured classes with the speaker. Mr Herbert Samuel, on the other hand, shows that, whilst he will take advice to the fullest extent from the permanent officials, he will insist on being master of the ship and on laying the course that is to be sailed.'[21]

Samuel's most difficult administrative task arising from the war, and one for which he could look to no bureaucratic precedent, was the accommodation of the masses of Belgian refugees who flocked to Britain in the wake of the German occupation of all save a tiny part of their country. A few reached Britain in the third week of August, following the Belgian Government's abandonment of Brussels. The first organized boatload of 479 refugees arrived on 6 September. Daily sailings from Antwerp to Tilbury brought more. After the fall of Antwerp on 9 October, a panic surge developed. Nine-tenths of the population fled, mainly to Holland, and 26,000 arrived in England in a single week. No such abandonment of an entire city had occurred in Europe in living memory, and the onset of a new era of barbarism was grimly forecast. When Ostend fell on 17 October the flow was momentarily halted, but then resumed with sailings from Flushing and Calais to Folkestone. By the end of the year, 100,000 had arrived.

They were received with mixed feelings by a population that evinced the utmost abstract sympathy for 'gallant little Belgium', but xenophobic disdain at the arrival of hordes of foreigners who had to be housed, fed, and put to work without appearing to take away jobs from natives. The voluntary War Refugee Committee, of which Samuel's former chief, Gladstone, was the moving force, proved inadequate to the challenge posed by the unexpected flood. In early September the Government was compelled to intervene. The Foreign Office, the Board of Trade, and the Home Office were all reluctant to take on this major new responsibility. In the end a Prime Ministerial fiat laid down that the Local Government Board would be entrusted with it.[22] Samuel thus found himself saddled with the task of coping with the influx in co-ordination with Gladstone's committee and a nationwide network of subcommittees. When the voluntary welcoming effort in Folkestone collapsed under the weight of numbers, Samuel nominated his brother-in-law, Leonard Franklin, to take charge there as representative of the board. Various other members of his family joined in the voluntary effort, occasioning a complaint from Chesterton's *New Witness*: 'To give Jews the control of Palestine would be a noble act of high statesmanship. To give the Jews the control of

[21] *Local Government Chronicle*, 13 Feb. 1915.
[22] Peter Cahalan, *Belgian Refugee Relief in England During the Great War* (New York, 1982), 58–63.

England is at least a folly which recoils on our heads alone. To give Jews the control of our honoured Belgian guests is an outrage.'[23]

Much of the initial effort was spontaneous, haphazard, and improvised, but an efficient system for channelling the flow of newcomers was rapidly established. The Aldwych Skating Rink was taken over for the headquarters of the voluntary committee. Temporary accommodation was found for thousands at Alexandra Palace and Earl's Court. About sixty thousand Belgians were in London at the end of the year, with more dispersed throughout the country (except in 'prohibited areas' on the east or south coast). By 1916 more than a quarter of a million refugees had arrived. Thirty nationalities were represented, although 95 per cent were Belgian. Over ten thousand were Jews, including many Russian Jews, who were turned over to the Jews' Temporary Shelter and other Jewish bodies. From being regarded initially as a burden, the Belgians were soon transformed into a valuable supply of labour for war industries deprived of much of their normal workforce. By the end of the war, after which most of the Belgians were repatriated, it was reported that the Government had spent £3,202,797. 8s. 4d. on maintenance and associated expenses.[24]

The historian of the refugee relief effort suggests that the generous response of the Government and of voluntary organizations to the refugee emergency arose in part from a sense of guilt and shame at the British failure to prevent the invasion and occupation of Belgium.[25] Among Liberal politicians the feeling may have gone deeper. Churchill records his view of Belgium in the first days of August: 'I saw in Belgium a country with whom we had had many differences over the Congo and other subjects. I had not discerned in the Belgium of the late King Leopold the heroic nation of King Albert.'[26] Churchill, indeed, opposed any organized civilian exodus from Belgium: 'They ought to stay there & eat up continental food, & occupy German policy attention. . . . This is no time for charity.'[27] Samuel, who had more reason than Churchill to remember the Congolese controversy, was more hospitable in his attitude, doubtless welcoming the opportunity to demonstrate goodwill towards a country

[23] New Witness, 17 Dec. 1914.

[24] 'Treatment of Aliens in Time of War' (report of subcommittee of Committee of Imperial Defence), 17 Oct. 1914, WR 84; HS to CS, 15 Nov. 1914, HLRO HS A/156/470; First Report of the Departmental Committee . . . on Belgian Refugees in this country, Cd. 7750 (London, 1914); Report . . . of L.G.B., Cd. 7763; 'Memorandum on the Reception of Belgian Refugees. January 1915', PRO MH 8/15 (also further documents in MH 8/20); Report of the War Refugees Committee (London, 1916); G. A. Powell, compiler, Four Years in a Refugee Camp (London, 1919); 'Report on the Work Undertaken by the British Government in the Reception and Care of the Belgian Refugees', 18 Dec. 1919, HLRO HS A/47/8.

[25] Cahalan, Belgian Refugee Relief, 6.   [26] Churchill, World Crisis, i. 122.

[27] Churchill to Grey, 7 Sept. 1914, quoted in Cahalan, Belgian Refugee Relief, 69.

that was now plaintiff rather than accused in an aggressively prosecuted atrocity propaganda campaign.

Apart from the relief and refugee problems, both of which eased after the first few hectic weeks of the war, Samuel found himself underemployed at the Local Government Board. He therefore adopted his earlier practice of offering his services to other departments. He was not the only minister to step outside departmental limits in this period. The worst offender was Churchill whose quixotic lone expedition to Antwerp to organize the last-ditch defence of the city, in defiance of a Cabinet instruction to return, led the King's private secretary to conclude that he 'must be quite off his head'.[28] But whereas Churchill's Cabinet colleagues admired his bravado and rapidly forgave him, Samuel's well-intentioned overtures earned little gratitude. Following Samuel's help to the Treasury in the early days of the war, Edwin Montagu complained to Lloyd George that his cousin was spending 'his whole time in trying to bag other people's departments'.[29] When Samuel asked Lloyd George in March 1915 whether he could 'be of use in any of the new enterprises that are on hand', Montagu scribbled unkindly on the letter: 'It seems to me the Chancellor has enough sponge-holders as it is.'[30]

Lloyd George nevertheless put Samuel in charge of a committee which was considering the vexed question of revision of the liquor laws to meet the special needs of wartime when drunkenness was alleged to be interfering with vital munitions production. 'Drink is doing more damage . . . than all the German submarines put together', Lloyd George asserted in a public speech on 28 February 1915.[31] The King set an example on 1 April by taking the 'pledge' for the duration of the war. But ministers decided that compulsion would be necessary for ordinary mortals. Asquith at first disliked the idea: 'You'll never do it. The country will never stand total prohibition,' he told Lloyd George. But when the Chancellor told him 'that you would be able to get alcoholic drink if you could produce a doctor's certificate', the Prime Minister 'brightened up' and fell in with Lloyd George's plans. Churchill alone demurred and insisted he was not going to give up his liquor—thereby earning a sharp rebuke from Lloyd George in the presence of Samuel and Montagu.[32]

Samuel's expertise, acquired during the attempt to pass the abortive Licensing Bill of 1908, made him an obvious choice to chair a committee

[28] Comment by Stamfordham quoted in Martin Gilbert, Winston S. Churchill, iii (London, 1971), 120.
[29] Montagu to Lloyd George, 2 Oct. 1914, HLRO Lloyd George papers C/1/1/29.
[30] HS to Lloyd George, [Mar. 1915], HLRO Lloyd George papers C/7/9/7.
[31] Quoted in Brocks (eds.), Asquith Letters, 307.
[32] Frances Stevenson diary, 4 and 8 Apr. 1915, in A. J. P. Taylor (ed.), Lloyd George: A Diary by Frances Stevenson (New York, 1971), 39, 41.

to frame what turned out to be a highly ambitious scheme. 'We are thinking [Samuel wrote to his wife] of nationalizing the drink trade—no less—so getting complete control by the State over all the public-houses and putting the whole thing permanently on a decent footing—in addition to the immediate restrictive measures due to the war.'[33] Samuel's brief required him to report within four days with a plan for what he said would be 'the largest financial transaction ever attempted'.[34] He finished within the allotted time after sitting up until 1.45 a.m. working with Simon on the final draft. The proposals provided for state purchase of all breweries, government control of all retail liquor trade that was not purchased, temporary prohibition of retail trade in spirits, and reduction in alcoholic content (i.e. watering-down) of all beer.[35]

Lloyd George was delighted and wrote to Samuel who had retired to bed with a minor ailment: 'I am so sorry—for selfish among other reasons—that you are laid up at this moment. I need your help badly in tackling this awful problem.' In Samuel's absence the Cabinet discussed the scheme and, according to Lloyd George, even Churchill supported it.[36] But the proposals threatened powerful entrenched interests and aroused strong opposition. The Prime Minister remained dubious. The Cabinet was divided. The Irish objected to the ban on whiskey. And Horatio Bottomley, the former Liberal MP and demagogic rabble-rouser, denounced the assault on the working-man's beer. In the end, the scheme was whittled down drastically: nationalization was abandoned; control of the retail trade was set up only in areas of special importance to the war effort; a Liquor Traffic Central Control Board was established; beer was diluted and pub opening hours reduced.

Perhaps appropriately, this final botched attempt at radical temperance reform turned out to be the last legislative gasp of the last Liberal government in Britain. In May 1915 the resignation of the First Sea Lord, Admiral Fisher, following the disastrous failure of the first assault on Gallipoli, lit the fuse of a major political crisis. After several days of horse-trading with the Conservatives, Asquith formed a Coalition Government. The inclusion of Conservatives in the Cabinet necessitated the sacrifice of some Liberals. Asquith did not, at this time, rate Samuel as one of his most able ministers. In a 'class list' of his Cabinet that he sent to his intimate correspondent Venetia Stanley in February 1915, Samuel was placed eleventh out of twelve; five were bracketed at the lowest position; Edwin

[33] HS to BS, 7 Apr. 1915, HLRO HS A/157/774.
[34] HS to BS, 9 Apr. 1915, HLRO HS A/157/776.
[35] 'Liquor Trade Committee (England and Wales) Report', 14 Apr. 1915, HLRO HS A/44/7.
[36] Lloyd George to HS, 19 Apr. 1915, HLRO HS A/155/IV/40.

Montagu, a new entry, was excluded; so also was 'our dear Birrell who is in a class by himself'—he seems to have been regarded by Asquith as a sort of team mascot.[37] Asquith, who had been Samuel's chief patron, apparently regarded him as a hardworking and reliable 'beagle' rather than as a political heavyweight. His nickname for him was 'the Infant Samuel'. Occasionally he mocked Samuel's seriousness and lack of small talk, although he later came to feel that he had underestimated him. Lloyd George showed his gratitude for Samuel's late-night labours on the drink bill by telling the newspaper magnate Sir George Riddell that Samuel 'had not done well' and 'would probably have to go'.[38] Samuel had no personal political following and was still unappreciated by fellow ministers. Hobhouse noted that Samuel was 'very able, not liked or trusted by anyone, but much used, and his wits often drawn on'.[39]

In these circumstances it was hardly surprising that Samuel was one of the Liberals dropped from the Cabinet. Asquith offered him his old job at the Post Office 'with a temporary suspension of Cabinet rank'.[40] He promised Samuel that he would be brought back into the Cabinet at the first vacancy for a Liberal and he agreed to Samuel's requests that he should receive the daily print of Foreign Office dispatches and that he might also serve on Cabinet committees. In the new Cabinet, Lloyd George became Minister of Munitions, McKenna became Chancellor, Churchill was demoted to the Duchy of Lancaster, Balfour took over at the Admiralty, and Bonar Law became Colonial Secretary. Among those dropped was Hobhouse whom Samuel replaced at the GPO. Samuel wrote to him considerately: 'Of all the detestable features of this detestable business the replacements of Liberal ministers by their own colleagues are the worst. But you will believe me when I say that I have had no part in bringing about this arrangement, and have not lifted a finger to secure the retention of office.'[41] Hobhouse reacted with bitterness: 'This morning I heard from Samuel that he deeply regretted supplanting a colleague, and only did it at the insistence of the P.M. Unfortunately Jack Pease met him yesterday, and asked him how he *could* take the place of a friend and colleague, to which he had replied, "Oh well one must look after oneself".'[42] The alleged remark is so out of tune with Samuel's character that, with charity to all parties, one may suspect that the tale grew with the telling. But the incident is again revealing of Samuel's unpopularity.

[37] Asquith to Venetia Stanley, 26 Feb. 1915, in Brocks (eds.), *Asquith Letters*, 452.
[38] McEwen (ed.), *Riddell Diaries*, 114–15 (19 May 1915).
[39] David (ed.), *Asquith's Cabinet*, 229 (entry for 23 Mar. 1915).
[40] Asquith to HS, 26 May 1915, HLRO HS A/48/5.
[41] HS to Hobhouse, 26 May 1915 (copy), HLRO HS A/48/10.
[42] David (ed.), *Asquith's Cabinet*, 247 (27 May 1915).

Disappointed in being forced out of the Cabinet after six years, Samuel spoke to his Conservative successor at the Local Government Board, Walter Long, with whom he was on good terms. Long later reported to the party leader, Bonar Law: 'Samuel came to see me & told me that Asquith had told him he would very much like to bring him back into the Cabinet but felt he could not do so without your entire approval. He asked my opinion: I told him I could not express one but I would carry on his prayer to you.'[43] But Law had no reason to press Asquith on the subject. Samuel remained outside the Cabinet. He continued for a while to supervise the Belgian refugee effort but otherwise could find little to occupy him. In a letter to his old friend, Graham Wallas, in July 1915, he confessed that he was not glad to go back to the Post Office.[44] Apart from arguments about proposed increases in postal rates, the first in the 75-year history of the Post Office, and parliamentary questions from patriots concerned about threats to national security from German-speaking postmasters, he found nothing to challenge him at St Martin's-le-Grand. By November he was so bored that he went to see the Prime Minister with the curious proposal that he might exchange offices with Edwin Montagu who was still Financial Secretary to the Treasury. He said Montagu had told him at the time of his appointment that he 'did not find his post congenial'.[45] Asquith gave an evasive reply. A few days later, however, Churchill's resignation gave Samuel an opportunity to remind Asquith of his promise to restore him to the Cabinet at the first Liberal vacancy. A little sententiously, he urged the Prime Minister 'not to take these personal considerations into account' if it were 'more to the public interest to leave Churchill's place unfilled than to act upon the assurances you very kindly gave me last May'.[46] Asquith secured Bonar Law's agreement to Samuel's return to the Cabinet as both Postmaster-General and Chancellor of the Duchy of Lancaster (unpaid).

Samuel was told by the Solicitor-General that his appointment to the additional position made it legally advisable for him to resign his parliamentary seat and stand in a by-election. In view of the truce between the parties it was not expected that the election would be opposed. The *North-Eastern Daily Gazette* even announced that as it was regarded as a mere formality Samuel did not intend to issue an election address. But his role in the Liberal Government's anti-drink legislation provoked a rogue elephant candidacy sponsored by Horatio Bottomley's 'Business Government League'. Reginald Knight, a Leeds businessman and former

[43] Long to Law, 30 May 1915, HLRO Bonar Law papers 50/3/69.
[44] HS to Wallas, 8 July 1915, BLPES Wallas papers 1/53/72–5.
[45] Note by Samuel, 8 Nov. 1915, HLRO HS A/50/1.
[46] HS to Asquith, 13 Nov. 1915 (copy), HLRO HS A/50/2.

Conservative, declared that he was running to protest against the Government's curtailment of liberty: 'I like a glass of beer, so does the working-man, and the Liquor Order is nothing but treachery to the workers, who are doing so much for the country at this crisis. It is the thin end of Prohibition.'[47] Samuel had not planned even to visit the constituency, but in view of the opposition he had to do so. The campaign was unusually short—only three days—and since Samuel enjoyed the support of local Conservatives as well as Liberals and the miners' leaders, there could be no doubt of the result. Nevertheless, he had to spend £921 on electioneering. The *North-Eastern Daily Gazette* ridiculed Knight's candidature as 'an idle and mischievous adventure . . . ludicrous also'.[48] Bottomley himself turned up in Cleveland and addressed large crowds. Even the *Gazette*, which strongly supported Samuel, conceded that Bottomley had 'audacity, the gift of the gab, and faculty for utilizing the passing humours of unthinking masses'.[49] Bottomley's newspaper, *John Bull*, denounced Samuel as 'the complete embodiment of the spirit of grandmotherly, puritanical, goody-goody legislation'.[50]

The by-election was the first to be contested since the outbreak of the war and was therefore keenly observed as a barometer of the Government's standing. The result was not altogether reassuring:

SAMUEL (Coalition Liberal)	7,312
KNIGHT (Business Government League)	1,453
Majority	5,859

The less than shining victory was a warning to the Government of the unpopularity of its liquor legislation; it also served notice to Samuel that he could not take his constituency for granted.

A more serious issue than the working-man's beer now loomed: conscription. The continuing stalemate on the Western Front had produced an agitation by the military chiefs, the Conservative Party, and a section of the Liberals headed by Lloyd George for an end to reliance on voluntary recruitment. Several Liberal ministers argued against compulsion and threatened to resign, although in the end only the Home Secretary, Simon, did so. Samuel had devoted a long passage in his *Liberalism* to arguing against conscription at the time of the Boer War. He had argued that it was uneconomic, inefficient, 'a grave invasion of personal liberty', that it would 'familiarise the whole people with militarist ideas' and 'would probably lower the standard of sexual morality'.[51] All these arguments, except, perhaps, the last, were voiced in the Cabinet by

[47] *North-Eastern Daily Gazette*, 6 Dec. 1915.   [48] Ibid., 7 Dec. 1915.
[49] Ibid., 9 Dec. 1915.   [50] *John Bull*, 11 Dec. 1915.
[51] *Liberalism*, 368–76.

the opponents of conscription in December 1915—but not by Samuel. Speaking in the House of Commons on 6 January in support of the Government's first conscription bill, Samuel declared himself 'driven to support this Bill against all my predilections, against my strong bias in favour of voluntary service, by the hard, cold logic of facts'. The arguments against conscription, he said, were 'valid in normal times. They cannot be pressed to-day. . . . We must give up this much liberty in order to save the rest.'[52]

Four days later Asquith offered Samuel the Home Secretaryship in place of Simon. Samuel wrote to his mother that he feared 'the position would be an uncomfortable one, exposing one to constant criticisms and attack', but he accepted immediately.[53] Appointment to one of the five Secretaryships of State represented substantial promotion and he was delighted to return to the Home Office—'my first love among the Departments'.[54] He was succeeded as Chancellor of the Duchy of Lancaster by Edwin Montagu. The presence, once again, of two Jews in the Cabinet aroused critical comment. Tennant, the Under-Secretary at the War Office, for instance, expressed disappointment at not being promoted and groused that the Jews were still the chosen people whereas he had got the 'passover'.[55] But the Conservatives voiced no objection: F. E. Smith had written approvingly to Churchill about Samuel's speech on conscription.[56] The permanent officials at the Home Office, headed by Sir Edward Troup, warmly welcomed his return.

A few weeks after Samuel's appointment as Home Secretary, he spent a weekend in Oxford, staying at Balliol and meeting old friends. He went on a twelve-mile walk with his old tutor, A. L. Smith. Away from the pressures of Whitehall he tried to peer ahead into the mists of the post-war world. On his return to London he produced a draft Cabinet paper entitled 'After the War', in which he set out the results of these futuristic cogitations:

When the war is over and the pressure which binds this Government together is relaxed, is it to break into its component parts on the first party issue that arises and becomes acute—the bringing into operation of the Government of Ireland Act, or whatever it may be? And if so, are our politics again to consist chiefly in disputes over

[52] *HC Deb.* 5 s., vol. 77 (6 Jan. 1916), cols. 1147–57.
[53] HS to CS, 6 Jan. 1916, HLRO HS A/156/497; see also HS to CS, 10 Jan. 1916, HLRO HS A/156/499.
[54] HS to CS, 11 Jan. 1916, HLRO HS A/156/500.
[55] McEwen (ed.), *Riddell Diaries* (16 Jan. 1916), 150; see also Lady Randolph Churchill to Winston Churchill, 12 Jan. 1916, in Martin Gilbert, *Winston S. Churchill*, vol. iii, Companion part 2 (London, 1972), 1367–8; *New Witness*, 13 Jan. 1916.
[56] F. E. Smith to Churchill, 11 Jan. 1916, in Gilbert, *Churchill*, vol. iii, Companion part 2, 1366–7.

Home Rule and Ulster, the House of Lords, Plural Voting, Tariff reform, and the Land Taxes? It is a dreary prospect.

Samuel proposed two basic alternatives. The first was based on the proposition that the war had 'brought into clear relief the defects of our national organisation':

Although opinions may differ whether a tariff is the best means of promoting industry, it is certain that our old non-chalant methods with respect to production and trade ought not to continue; in planting and helping new industries at home and in capturing markets abroad, the State should play a larger part than hitherto.

Samuel urged that Britain 'ought now to embark on a great era of national organisation and active industrial and social development, such as Germany initiated for herself after the war of 1870'.

In order to achieve this, he put forward a second proposal: 'the organic union of the Empire'. This followed, in outline, the ideas that he had developed in his 1912 article on 'Federal Government'.[57] The memorandum passed virtually unnoticed and does not even seem to have been circulated officially. It remains of piquant interest, given Samuel's later views, for its stress on the benefits of extending the wartime coalition into the peace, for Samuel's continuing faith in imperialism, and for his apparent readiness to take a less purist view of free trade—but then neither he nor any other minister had objected the previous autumn when McKenna had made the first breach in that Liberal dyke, by introducing high duties on the importation of a number of luxury items.

Meanwhile Samuel returned to his quotidian duties. In April 1916 he proposed to the Cabinet the introduction, for the first time in Britain, of daylight saving time. Here too the inspiration came from the German example. In proposing the measure to Asquith, Samuel noted its recent introduction in Germany and Austria, and reported estimates that fuel savings of £3 million per annum might result from its introduction in Britain.[58] Daylight saving time had been considered by a Select Committee of the House of Commons in 1908, and bills had been introduced to Parliament in each of the last four sessions before the war, without advancing beyond the first reading. Objections from the Post Office, from farmers, from the Stock Exchange and elsewhere had previously thwarted the measure. But the war presented an opportunity for overcoming such opposition. On 8 May a motion was introduced in the House of Commons advocating the change. Lord Hugh Cecil, Conservative MP for Oxford University, who was renowned for both his oratory and his traditionalism,

[57] Proof of memorandum, 21 Mar. 1916, Austen Chamberlain papers, Birmingham University Library, AC 12/212.
[58] HS to Asquith, 14 Apr. 1916, PRO HO 45/10811/312364.

spoke against it. 'If there was a general need for getting up earlier and going to bed earlier in the summer,' he argued, 'should we not see large numbers of people doing it without any alteration of the law or any alteration of the clock?' The House nevertheless voted by 170 to 2 in favour of the resolution.[59] Summer time first came into effect when the clocks were moved forward one hour at 2.00 a.m. on Sunday, 21 May 1916. Vestiges of local timekeeping in the United Kingdom, such as the public clocks in Canterbury which were set five minutes in advance of Greenwich, finally succumbed to the standard national measure. Later in the summer, legislation was introduced to unify British with Irish time, which had been twenty-five minutes earlier. The bill carried in spite of vigorous opposition by John Dillon and Tim Healy who continued grumbling about it for several months.[60]

Irish opposition was rooted in a principled objection to English inter-ference with Dublin time—although in earlier years there had been strong sentiment in Ireland in favour of a common time. But the bitterness with which the Irish leaders spoke even on such an apparently non-contentious subject was a reminder of the chasm that yawned between the two islands as a result of the bloody events of April 1916. The Easter rising that left 450 Irish and 103 British military dead brought Samuel back briefly into Irish affairs. When Birrell resigned as Irish Secretary on 1 May, Asquith wept. He found great difficulty deciding on a replacement. He offered it to Montagu who said no. He pressed it on Lloyd George, who agreed only to try to bring the Irish Nationalists and Unionists together. It was not until three months later that a successor was appointed: H. E. Duke, 'the least distinguished holder of the office since 1880' in the judgement of Roy Jenkins.[61] During the interregnum, responsibility for Irish affairs devolved automatically on the Home Secretary.[62]

Samuel played only a secondary role in the efforts to fashion a new Irish settlement. At first Lloyd George seemed close to attaining an agreement between Carson and Redmond based on immediate Home Rule with a six-county-Ulster exclusion. As to whether this exclusion was to be temporary or permanent, Lloyd George devised an ambiguous formula while giving contradictory private assurances to each side. Samuel, with his unrivalled knowledge of the vexed problem of Irish finance, helped prepare the draft legislation for giving effect to the agreement. His involvement in no way reassured the Irish parliamentary leaders: 'If it be true [wrote Healy on 7 July] that it is Herbert Samuel who is drafting the

---

[59] *HC Deb.* 5 s., vol. 82 (8 May 1916), cols. 301 ff.
[60] *HC Deb.* 5 s., vol. 85 (1 Aug. 1916), cols. 72 ff.; also vol. 87 (21 Nov. 1916), col. 1217.
[61] Jenkins, *Asquith*, 402.   [62] See Troup, *Home Office*, 228–9.

Bill, it will be as narrow as it can be made.'[63] Nor did the bill, when drafted, satisfy the Unionists, several of whom threatened to leave the Cabinet if their demands were not met. On 21 July Carson wrote to Samuel:

The one condition on which I agreed to negociate at all was the exclusion of the Six Counties & I have never agreed or been entitled to agree that this shd be provisional nor have I any authority to do so. To leave a suggestion in the Bill that the question of the inclusion was to come up for consideration when the war is over is quite impossible. . . . I can assure [you] my position in this matter is just as difficult as Redmond's.[64]

The next day Lloyd George and Samuel met Redmond and informed him that the exclusion of Ulster must be permanent. The nationalists could not accept the permanent partition of the island. In the absence of agreement, the bill was dropped. The prospect of an Irish settlement once again receded into the mist.

While Irish affairs thus reached a dead end again at the level of high politics, Samuel remained responsible for a related issue that deeply coloured the long-term outcome of the Irish question: the treatment of Irish rebel prisoners. General Maxwell, the military commander, had sanctioned the execution of fifteen men, among them Patrick Pearse and James Connolly, in the immediate aftermath of the revolt. Asquith himself had visited Ireland from 11 to 19 May and paid a call on the Sinn Fein prisoners in Richmond Barracks. He praised their 'lovely eyes' and ordered their transfer to internment camps in England.[65] While Asquith was in Dublin he made Samuel his 'medium of communication and public statement' on Ireland.[66] In this capacity Samuel became also the butt of vehement denunciation in the House of Commons by his former friend John Dillon and other Irish members.[67]

Samuel insisted that he was 'not prepared to act as a mere mouth-piece of the people in control in Dublin' and he demanded 'that if I am to defend acts of administration I must have a voice in approving them'.[68] In early June he paid a short visit to Dublin himself in order, as he put it in a letter to the King, to 'place himself in personal touch with those who are directly

    [63] T. M. Healy to F. J. [?] Healy, 7 July 1916, in Healy, *Letters and Leaders*, 573.
    [64] Carson to HS, 21 July 1916, HLRO HS A/41/19; see also HS to Cabinet, 20 July 1916, PRO CAB 37/152/10; Walter Long to HS, 21 July 1916, Wiltshire Record Office, Long papers 947/404.
    [65] Jenkins, *Asquith*, 398.
    [66] Asquith to HS, 10 or 11 May 1916 [?], Bodleian Library, Oxford, Asquith papers 34/172–4.
    [67] HC Deb. 5 s., vol. 82 (11 May 1916), col. 947.
    [68] HS to CS, 21 May 1916, HLRO HS A/156/511.

charged with the conduct of affairs there'.[69] Samuel was shocked by the
extent of the damage, resulting from the rebellion, that he encountered in
Dublin. Whole blocks of buildings lay in ruins. Martial law was still in
force. Samuel met Redmond in the Irish capital and consulted him about
the Government's steps. But the execution of the rebel leaders had
inflamed public opinion which had previously been unsympathetic to the
rising. Redmond's was now a waning star. Samuel wrote to Rufus Isaacs
on 3 June: 'I hear on all hands that public feeling is not good. The
punishments have rather turned sentiment to the side of the rebels—but
so far as can be told there is nothing serious in the present situation.'[70]

A total of 1,867 Sinn Feiners, including five women, were interned in
England on ground of participation in the rebellion or 'strong suspicion of
complicity'. They were held under Regulation 14B of the Defence of the
Realm Act (DORA) which empowered the Home Secretary to detain
indefinitely any person regarded as having 'hostile origins or associations'.
The regulation had originally been drafted with a view to use against
enemy aliens, but it was applied to the Irishmen because Asquith thought
it would smack of *ex post facto* penal legislation' to promulgate a new
regulation.[71] The 'hostile associations' of the rebels, Samuel suggested in
a Cabinet paper, 'can be established, if questioned, by the known connection
of the Sinn Fein movement with Germany.' He pointed out that Regulation
14B had been 'attacked on the ground that it deprives British subjects of
the right of trial in a Court of law, and authorises imprisonment by Home
Secretary's order' and he warned that 'these criticisms will probably
become more widespread if the procedure is now applied to this large
body of persons, particularly since their connection with Germany is only
indirect'.[72] The Cabinet approved the application of Regulation 14B, and
the prisoners were moved from prisons to internment camps provided by
the War Office. Asquith expressed the wish that 'the process of combing
out the "innocents" shall be prosecuted with vigour'.[73] The disposition of
the five women gave rise to some difficulty, since Troup considered 'it
would be very undesirable to send the ladies . . . to Aylesbury and make
them consort with German brothel-keepers from Antwerp'. They were
eventually lodged in a wing of a women's prison.[74] The men were mainly
held at a camp at Frongoch in Wales.

[69] HS to King George V (parliamentary report), 1 June 1916, Royal Archives.
[70] HS to Isaacs, 3 June 1916, India Office Records, MS Eur. F 118/99.
[71] Sir Edward Troup to Sir Robert Chalmers, 10 May 1916, PRO HO 144/1455.
[72] Cabinet paper on 'Irish Rebels Interned in England' by HS, 15 May 1916, PRO CAB
37/147/36.
[73] War Office [copy of unsigned letter] to Brig. Gen. Byrne, Dublin, 22 May 1916, PRO
HO 144/1455.
[74] Troup to Byrne, 6 June 1916, ibid.

Samuel asked an advisory committee under Judge Sankey to hear applications for release from Irish prisoners and to advise on cases of Irish civil servants suspected of disloyalty.[75] On the committee's recommendation a majority of the prisoners were freed within a few months. By August all save 569 had been released.[76] Although Samuel handed over Irish affairs to the newly appointed Chief Secretary, Duke, in early August, he remained responsible for the administration of the internment camp for Irish prisoners. Irish MPs subjected him to a bitter barrage of complaints of maltreatment and demands for release of the prisoners. Samuel announced that the Government was prepared to free 'a considerable number' on condition that they gave 'an assurance that they will not again engage in rebellion—at all events during the period of the War'.[77] Such pledges were not forthcoming, but in December 1916 Duke announced that the remainder of the internees would be released unconditionally. Meanwhile, the breakdown of Lloyd George's attempt at mediation and the ineffective leadership of Redmond were polarizing Irish politics. The martyrologies of the fifteen executed rebel leaders accentuated the drift away from parliamentarism. And to these was added the cult of a sixteenth martyr whose execution by order of the Home Secretary resonated in history.

Sir Roger Casement (he had been knighted in 1911) had had no recorded contact with Samuel since their collaboration in the campaign against Belgian atrocities in the Congo. His arrest at Tralee on 21 April as he landed from a German submarine led to his trial on a charge of high treason. On 29 June he was found guilty of 'aiding and comforting the King's enemies without the realm' and of 'waging war against the King by setting forth on a warlike expedition'.[78] He was sentenced to death, and an appeal was rejected. Following the capital sentence, it lay with Samuel, as Home Secretary, whether to recommend to the King the exercise of the royal prerogative of granting a reprieve. This was not a decision that Samuel felt he could take alone. Such questions were rarely considered at Cabinet level, but Asquith's Cabinet discussed the case repeatedly and at great length. On 5 July, while the appeal was still pending, Grey and others urged strongly that 'it would be better (if possible) if he [Casement] were kept in confinement as a criminal lunatic than that he should be executed, without any smirch on his character, & then canonized as a martyr in Ireland & America'.[79] The idea of declaring Casement a lunatic

[75] HS to Sankey, 8 June 1916, Bodleian Library, Oxford, MS Eng. Hist. c. 548.
[76] Grey to Cabinet, 24 Aug. 1916, HLRO HS A/55/9.
[77] HC Deb. 5 s., vol. 86 (18 Oct. 1916), col. 690.
[78] Memorandum in HLRO HS A/53.
[79] Asquith to King George V, 5 July 1916, PRO CAB 41/37/25.

arose from the Government's perusal of his diary which had fallen into official hands. This notorious document revealed Casement to be a homosexual. Submitted for an opinion to an 'alienist', it was pronounced to constitute no evidence of insanity, though its author was said to be 'abnormal'.[80]

On 18 July Samuel circulated to the Cabinet memoranda by two senior Home Office officials, Troup and Sir Ernley Blackwell, the Legal Assistant Under-Secretary. Both were strongly in favour of execution. Blackwell wrote: 'It is difficult to imagine a worse case of high treason than Casement's. It is aggravated rather than mitigated by his previous career in the public service, and his private character—although it really has no relation to the actual offence with which he is charged—certainly cannot be pleaded in his favour.' Blackwell noted that his diaries 'show that he has for years been addicted to the grossest sodomitical practices', but insisted that these provided no basis for certification of lunacy. On the 'question of expediency', Blackwell wrote:

The Foreign Office from the start appear to have taken the view that in order not to alienate more Irish–American sentiment we could not safely hang Casement unless we first published the fact of his private character as disclosed in his diaries.

There are obviously grave objections to any sort of official or even inspired publication of such facts while the man is waiting trial or appeal, or even waiting execution. Perhaps I do not fully appreciate the danger which the Foreign Office sees ahead in America if the law is allowed to take its course in this country, but the attitude adopted is rather a humiliating one.

I see not the slightest objection to hanging Casement, and *afterwards* giving as much publicity as possible to the contents of his diary as decency permits, so that at any rate the public in America and elsewhere may know the sort of man they are inclined to make a martyr of.

Troup's views echoed those of Blackwell, and their circulation by Samuel affirmed a strong Home Office view in favour of execution. The case developed into an interdepartmental battle. The report of the 'alienist' left Grey and the opponents of execution little with which to counter the Home Office view, save the danger of anti-British feeling in America, which both Blackwell and Troup pooh-poohed.[81] On 19 July, therefore, the Cabinet came to what Asquith reported as a 'unanimous' decision that Casement should be hanged.[82]

On 31 July Samuel reported to the King that he could not 'find that there is any strong feeling at the present time with respect to Casement in

[80] Asquith to King George V, 14 July 1916, PRO CAB 41/37/26.
[81] Cabinet paper, 'The Casement Case', 18 July 1916, PRO CAB 37/151/35.
[82] Asquith to King George V, 19 July 1916, PRO CAB 41/37/27.

any quarter of the House of Commons'.[83] The Cabinet considered the matter for the last time on 2 August. Asquith reported to the King that urgent appeals for mercy from 'authoritative and friendly quarters in the United States' were weighed in the balance. Pleas for a reprieve had also been entered by the Archbishop of Canterbury, Bernard Shaw, G. K. Chesterton, C. P. Scott, and a large number of other writers, churchmen, and public figures. Nevertheless, the decision to hang Casement was reaffirmed. The same day, the British Ambassador in the United States warned the Foreign Office that if Casement were executed 'a most serious situation' should be anticipated in America. He strongly urged that Casement should be reprieved 'as a personal favour' to President Wilson. He added that publication of Casement's diary would 'only be looked on as an act of revenge and would only be effective if his life is spared'.[84] The cable reached the Foreign Office at 8.05 a.m. on 3 August. By the time it was deciphered, typed, and distributed, it was too late. Casement was hanged in the execution shed at Pentonville Prison just after nine o'clock that morning.

The death-knell of Casement echoed in Anglo-Irish mythology for half a century, its political reverberations accompanied by the dark background rhythm of prurient interest in his 'Black Diaries', opened to public inspection only in recent years. Samuel's role in this affair was not impressive. In an abstract discussion of the death penalty in his memoirs, in which he made no mention of the decision to hang Casement, Samuel laid emphasis on the unique burden of the Home Secretary: 'Here, and here alone, responsibility is personal and undivided. . . . The Home Secretary is under no obligation to be guided by the advice of the Office or to follow precedent. He must carry his responsibility alone.'[85] In this, the most important of the death sentences on which Samuel had the duty to advise the King, he sheltered behind the Cabinet and behind civil servants who, at least in the case of Blackwell, seemed almost as much concerned with asserting the prerogatives of the Home Office as with reaching a sensible political decision. No doubt such interdepartmental jealousies did not influence Samuel. But a letter to his wife, written on the eve of Casement's execution, discloses the presence in his mind of a no less disturbing consideration:

I have been having, as you may imagine, a time of some anxiety on account of the Casement case. Much pressure has been brought to bear from many quarters—here, in Ireland and in America—in favour of a reprieve. There has been much doubting in the Cabinet—among a few. . . . I have had no doubt all through that, as the man is

[83] HS to King George V, 31 July 1916 (parliamentary report), Royal Archives.
[84] Sir Cecil Spring-Rice to Foreign Office, 2 Aug. 1916, HLRO HS A/55/4.
[85] *Memoirs*, 220–1.

certainly not insane, there is no good ground on which he could be reprieved. Although his execution will create a (somewhat artificial) storm in America, and give rise to a certain amount of passion in Ireland, and although the Manchester Guardian and the Nation will denounce us, his reprieve would let loose a tornado of condemnation, would be bitterly resented by the great mass of the people in Great Britain and by the whole of the army, and would profoundly and permanently shake public confidence in the sincerity and the courage of the Government. In the end the Cabinet unanimously came to this conclusion. But there are moments when a Home Secretary's post is far from agreeable. Had Casement not been a man of atrocious moral character, the situation would have been even more difficult.[86]

Forgotten was Samuel's public encomium of Casement, at the time of the Congo agitation, as 'a gentleman of the highest standing and reliability'. Samuel's letter would seem to suggest that the determining consideration in favour of putting Casement to death was the howl of the mob. That, perhaps, might be argued to be only marginally less defensible than the equivalent argument on the other side—that Casement should be reprieved because of American public opinion.[87] What seems more shocking is Samuel's final reflection. Apparently the knowledge of Casement's homosexuality made Samuel's mind easier as he took the decision. The attitude was of a piece with Samuel's lifelong horror of sexual deviation. But even by the standards of the time, it must rank as one of the less creditable episodes in Samuel's career.

One side-effect of the Irish revolt that was to have a lasting impact in Britain was the imposition of restrictions on the sale of firearms. On 26 May 1916 Samuel wrote to Lloyd George:

You may be dealing with the question of disarmament in Ireland and it may be of assistance in your negotiations to suggest that any measure with that object should not be an Irish statute but should apply to the whole of the United Kingdom.

I am strongly of opinion that the present system of almost uncontrolled sale and possession of rifles, revolvers and automatic pistols should be ended in this country and that all persons who possess them should be called upon either to obtain new licences—which should be sparingly given—or to surrender them. Restrictions of a rigid character should be imposed on future sales. The Home Office quite concurs in this view. I have spoken to the P.M. and also to Walter Long—both of whom agree.

[86] HS to BS, 2 Aug. 1916, HLRO HS A/157/844.

[87] A few months earlier, in a case that raised some similar issues involving mental competence and the importance of overseas public opinion, Samuel commuted the death sentence passed on a Canadian officer who had murdered a soldier. The Home Office record of the case stated that although the culprit was 'a man of abnormal mind', it was doubtful 'whether such abnormality was sufficient in itself to justify commutation'. Samuel, however, decided on a reprieve after receiving strong representations from Canada which suggested that 'prisoner's execution would create an unfavourable impression there as it would be felt that prisoner had been more severely dealt with than he would have been in his own country' (undated memorandum, HLRO HS A/53).

Irish prejudices might be soothed if a disarmament Act applied to Great Britain equally.[88]

No such Act was passed, but regulations under the all-embracing Defence of the Realm Act enabled the Home Office to institute a system of strict controls which was continued by legislation after the war. As a result Britain avoided the excesses of civilian armament that became prevalent in the USA and parts of Europe.

This infringement of individual liberty aroused few critics, but other administrative decisions taken by Samuel under DORA offended Liberal scruples at sore points and also divided Samuel from some of his oldest political comrades. The most painful schism was with Charles Trevelyan, who had resigned his parliamentary secretaryship at the Board of Education at the outbreak of the war. Together with E. D. Morel, Ramsay Mac-Donald, and others, he was a founding member of the Union of Democratic Control, which campaigned against the war from September 1914 onwards. The activities of the UDC and its sympathizers raised questions of freedom of the press and of free speech which the Home Secretary, responsible for public order and charged under DORA with supervision of censorship, had to answer. The introduction of conscription in early 1916 raised additional questions of the rights of conscientious objectors. As Home Secretary, Samuel's actions in 1916 on such questions of civil liberties severely disappointed many of his former friends.

Immediately upon his appointment, the opposition presented itself in the debates in Parliament on the first Military Service Bill which introduced conscription for single men aged between 18 and 41. Trevelyan, who was not himself a conscientious objector, argued against the establishment of tribunals to assess the bona fides of objectors: 'The only judge of a man's conscience is the man himself', he insisted. Samuel retorted that if Trevelyan's proposal were accepted 'there would be a very considerable number of unconscientious conscientious objectors, and it might be regarded as a mere matter of form, by men of a certain class, to say "We do not want to serve, and all we have to do is call ourselves conscientious objectors."' Hence, Samuel suggested, the need for tribunals that would review cases.[89] The decisions, often inconsistent, sometimes malevolent, taken by the tribunals, gave critics of conscription further ammunition. In a Commons debate on the subject in June 1916 one MP turned Samuel's own words against him by reading out *in extenso* an extract from *Liberalism* that denounced compulsory military service and attacked the justification of war 'by elaborate and plausible sophisms'.[90]

[88] HS to Lloyd George, 26 May 1916, HLRO Lloyd George papers D/14/1/21.
[89] *HC Deb.* 5 s., vol. 78 (19 Jan. 1916), cols. 447 ff.
[90] *HC Deb.* 5 s., vol. 82 (1 June 1916), col. 2983.

Once conscription was the law of the land, Samuel faced the problem of how to handle anti-conscription meetings, particularly those organized by the Independent Labour Party and addressed by Philip and Ethel Snowden and Sylvia Pankhurst. Samuel soon faced a stream of protests from Snowden against police interference with such meetings. Charles Trevelyan, Graham Wallas, Lord Courtney, and others complained of police restriction of other anti-war activities. Samuel always ordered inquiries into serious complaints, but his answers rarely satisfied his correspondents.[91] The real source of trouble was not the administration of the law but the law itself. DORA endowed the Home Secretary with such Draconian and comprehensive authority that almost any police act could be justified. It gave little comfort to Courtney, for example, to be informed that convictions of anti-war propagandists had been legitimately secured on the ground that they had breached DORA Regulation Number 2 which prohibited attempts to 'cause disaffection among the civil population'.[92]

Samuel received another cunning and forceful reminder of old associations in April 1916 in the form of a letter from E. D. Morel. Writing to Samuel's home address, and marking the letter 'personal', Morel drew attention to attacks on the UDC in Chesterton's *New Witness* and in Parliament. These included the suggestion that Morel was a 'paid agent' of Germany. Morel denied the further allegation that the Congo Reform movement had been engineered in the interests of Germany. As for imputations based on his former connection with Casement, Morel wrote: 'Casement's defection was a sad blow to all his friends, myself among them, and his friends in this country included many men of distinction and public position. Moreover, he was a servant of His Majesty's Government, not of mine.'[93] There is no record of any reply by Samuel. In the House of Commons he stated merely that he had no information which would 'in any way substantiate the charges' against Morel. When he suggested that Morel might seek remedies in the courts, an MP unkindly pointed out that 'Mr Morel is simply following the example of certain members of the present Government in refusing to take action against the "New Witness" '.[94] In 1917 Morel was sentenced to six months in prison for sending printed literature to a foreign country. Samuel took no part in the decision to prosecute, which was taken after he

---

[91]   See, e.g., Snowden to HS, 18 May 1916, PRO HO 45/10814/312987; HS memorandum, 26 June 1916, ibid.; Trevelyan to HS, 9 Feb. 1916, PRO HO 45/10801/307402/5; HS to Trevelyan, 12 Feb. 1916, ibid.; HS to Trevelyan, 6 Mar. 1916, CPT 66; HS to Wallas, 25 Feb., 8 Mar. 1916, BLPES Wallas papers 1/56/26, 29.

[92]   HS to Lord [Leonard] Courtney, 1 Mar. 1916, BLPES Courtney papers XII/5.

[93]   Morel to HS, 3 Apr. 1916 (copy), BLPES Morel papers F8/125.

[94]   *HC Deb.* 5 s., vol. 81 (5 Apr. 1916), cols. 1186–7.

left office. Indeed, he resisted an attempt in 1916, initiated by the Attorney-General, F. E. Smith, to ban Morel's polemic *Truth and the War*, although the reason seems to have been less a matter of liberal principle than of technical legal difficulty in securing a conviction. The book sold twenty thousand copies.[95]

One book which the Home Office did seek to ban was *Revelations of an International Spy* by Ignatius Trebitsch Lincoln. This had been published in New York in January 1916 and the customs authorities were instructed to prevent its importation to Britain. Over Home Office objections the book was eventually permitted to be imported to the UK after the military authorities certified that it was harmless. Lincoln, who had volunteered his services to Germany as a spy in 1914, was on the run in the United States. Samuel pressed the Foreign Office to secure his extradition, and shortly afterwards he was captured and returned to England where he was sentenced to three years for fraud. Yet again, Samuel, who had spoken for Lincoln during his successful election campaign at Darlington in 1910, was compelled to distance himself from a former acquaintance.

In December 1916, following the arrest of Fenner Brockway for publishing an article which Samuel condemned as 'propaganda with the direct purpose of resisting the operation of the Military Service Act',[96] a statement of Home Office policy on such matters was sent to the Foreign Office:

Mr Secretary Samuel . . . has given very careful consideration to the question of the desirability and justification of instituting proceedings in respect of books, newspaper articles or speeches, which give general support to pacifist organizations, or state the German version of the facts regarding the origin of the war or ascribe responsibility for its origin or continu[ation] to our Allies. The question was specially considered in connection with Mr. Morel's books and certain articles by Mr. Philip Snowden in the 'Labour Leader' on both of which the Attorney-General was consulted. It was agreed that prosecutions in such cases would raise large political questions and would assume the proportions of a State trial. Mr Herbert Samuel is disposed to think that the points at issue are less for the courts of law to determine than for Parliament and public opinion. If any direct attempt were made to attack any of our Allies in respect of their conduct of the war or if articles were published intended to sow distrust between them and this country, the particular case would have to be specially considered; but, in general, he is of opinion that prosecutions, which would have to be numerous if a policy of repression was once decided upon, would cause more harm than good. They would in his opinion have the effect of advertising the speeches and publications which are now, for the most part, left in obscurity: they would probably not succeed in preventing the repetition of the offences: and they would be likely to give rise to an

---

[95] See Marvin Swartz, *The Union of Democratic Control in British Politics During the First World War* (Oxford, 1971), 121; see also Taylor, *Trouble Makers*, 132–66.
[96] Minute by HS, 6 Dec. 1916, PRO HO 45/10817/316469/20.

agitation damaging our cause in America and elsewhere, based upon the charge that His Majesty's Government was using the powers of the executive to prevent freedom of speech and to conceal important facts from the nation.[97]

In line with this approach, Samuel's tenure as Home Secretary was marked by relatively few official restrictions of freedom of speech.

Complaints of assaults on civil liberties did not emanate only from radicals opposed to the war. Gilbert Murray, a strong Liberal supporter of the war, wrote to Samuel to complain of the imprisonment of one of his Oxford pupils, Raymond Postgate (later a well-known writer, historian, and gastronome). Murray conceded that some of the conscientious objectors were 'as obstinate as mules' but he maintained that 'the Military authorities are like rampant griffins' and that there was 'a good deal of unnecessary friction and suffering'.[98] Sir George Riddell, chairman of the *News of the World*, visited Samuel to complain about the press censorship regulations which, he said, were 'causing much dissatisfaction'.[99] W. W. Ashley, Conservative MP for Blackpool, drew attention in Parliament to DORA Regulation 14B which permitted indefinite detention without trial of any persons, whether of British or other nationality, who were judged by the Home Secretary, acting on the advice of the military authorities or of specified civilian committees, to be a danger to the public safety or the security of the realm. British, but not enemy, citizens were permitted to appeal to an advisory committee, but otherwise had no recourse. Ashley, whose ancestor the 1st Earl of Shaftesbury had been chiefly responsible for the passage of the 1679 Habeas Corpus Act, called the advisory committee 'pure "eyewash"': 'The Home Secretary is the absolute judge as to who is to be interned. He can release or shut up anybody he likes, and we have here frankly, nakedly and openly, the system of the Bastille, of *lettres de cachet*, and of the Star Chamber.' Samuel pointed out that the measure had been used sparingly in cases other than enemy citizens. Leaving aside the more than thirty thousand enemy citizens who had been detained, plus a handful of naturalized Germans and Austrians and a few others of German origin, there were only eight 'British subjects of British origin' interned (this was before the mass internment of Irish rebels later that spring). He justified the regulation—which had been framed by his purist Liberal predecessor, Simon—as necessary in conditions of war. It was an able apology for the

---

[97] Blackwell (Home Office) to Under-Secretary, Foreign Office, 7 Dec. 1916, PRO HO 45/10786/297549.
[98] Murray to HS, 19 Apr. 1916 (copy), Bodleian Library, Oxford, Murray papers 375/11.
[99] *Lord Riddell's War Diary 1914–1918* (London, 1933), 179.

Government's position, but Samuel none the less found himself, for a Liberal, in a highly uncomfortable position.[100]

Anti-war radicals were not the only ones who suffered restriction under DORA. A case in point was the fiercely pro-war Christabel Pankhurst—a militant suffragette like her sister; but whereas Sylvia had moved to the anti-war left, Christabel moved to the patriotic right. Christabel's newspaper *Britannia* was raided by the police and closed down. *Britannia* had published violent attacks on the Foreign Office and impugned the loyalty of one of its senior officials, Sir Eyre Crowe, who was German-born but strongly hostile to Germany. Samuel defended the suppression on the ground that the paper had printed statements which were 'absolutely untrue' and 'calculated to prejudice our relations with our Allies'.[101] When *Britannia* resumed publication from a secret address Samuel gave instructions that its printing press should again be seized. As before, the action was taken by executive decree, since Samuel noted 'the Attorney-General agrees with me that it is not advisable to prosecute'.[102] After a second press seizure failed to silence *Britannia*, Samuel arranged with the Post Office for issues to be stopped in the mail.[103]

Nor were all complainants troubled by the over-heavy hand of authority. Some criticized the Home Office for not being severe enough. Sir Courtenay Warner, Liberal MP for Lichfield, wrote to Samuel asserting that the ministry was 'too lax' in using DORA against anti-war agitations and aliens.[104] No less a person than King George V expressed concern when *The Times* printed a report of a court-martial containing allegations by the accused, Private C. H. Norman, a socialist conscientious objector of highly belligerent disposition who enjoyed a character testimonial from Bernard Shaw. Norman stated that he had been severely maltreated, kept in a strait-jacket, put on a bread-and-water diet, forcibly fed, abused and insulted. The burden of the King's complaint was that the report should have been suppressed. In his reply Samuel wrote that he sympathized with the King's view that harm might be done by the exaggerated propaganda of conscientious objectors against the military authorities. But he felt bound to add that in this case 'the Commandant appears to have exceeded his duty in some directions, and he has been removed'.[105]

By far the most troublesome civil liberties case with which Samuel had

---

[100] *HC Deb.* 5 s., vol. 80 (2 Mar. 1916), cols. 1236 ff.

[101] Ibid. (15 Mar. 1916), col. 2081.

[102] HS to Troup, 30 Mar. 1916 (copy), PRO HO 45/10796/303883/11.

[103] See Home Office minutes, May 1916, PRO HO 45/10796/303883/13.

[104] Sir Courtenay Warner to HS, 5 June 1916, PRO HO 45/10801/307402/63.

[105] Stamfordham to S. W. Harris (Home Office), 2 July 1916 (with cutting from *The Times* of 1 July concerning case of Private C. H. Norman), PRO HO 45/11170/311336/5. Draft of Home Office reply to Stamfordham (approved by Samuel on 4 July 1916), ibid.

to deal was that of Bertrand Russell. One of the founders of the UDC, Russell had taken leave of absence from his Cambridge lectureship in order to concentrate on anti-war propaganda. His activities on behalf of the militant No-Conscription Fellowship soon brought him into conflict with the authorities. In April 1916 Russell wrote a leaflet for the Fellowship, protesting against what he alleged was the wrongful treatment of a conscientious objector. After five others had been arrested for distributing the pamphlet, Russell wrote to *The Times* on 17 May 1916, announcing that he was the author and taking primary responsibility. Foolishly, the authorities responded to this provocation by issuing a summons under DORA.

Rex v. *Bertrand Russell* was heard before the Lord Mayor of London in the Justice Room at the Mansion House on 5 June. Russell was found guilty of contravening Regulation 27 of DORA by 'making statements likely to prejudice the recruiting and discipline of His Majesty's forces'. He was found guilty and fined £100. The accused succeeded brilliantly, however, in turning the hearing into a *cause célèbre* by delivering a speech in which he rounded on his accusers, and in particular on the Home Secretary. Dissecting Samuel's parliamentary pronouncements on conscientious objection, Russell pretended to show that 'Mr Herbert Samuel infringed his own regulation'. This was knockabout stuff. More impressive was the use to which Russell put the occasion to expound the creed of the No-Conscription Fellowship and to locate the anti-conscription struggle within the tradition of English libertarian dissent. He concluded by expressing 'a great debt of gratitude to the Government for this persecution' and avowing that he and his fellow-pacifists were 'grateful for the opportunity of performing a service—namely, the endurance of persecution which is open to us'.[106] Russell did not offer evidence in his defence, no doubt in the hope of ensuring a conviction. He then appealed against the conviction in the equal expectation of winning further propaganda points. The appeal was rejected. Since he refused to pay the fine, £100-worth of his belongings were seized from his rooms at Trinity College, Cambridge. Among the items taken was the Butler Gold Medal awarded to him in 1915 by Columbia University.[107] Two weeks later, in the most disgraceful act in its history, the Council of Trinity College voted unanimously to remove its most illustrious member from his lectureship.

If the affair had stopped at that point, it might have passed as a

[106] *Rex* v. *Bertrand Russell: Report of the Proceedings* . . . (pamphlet issued by the No-Conscription Fellowship, London, 1916).
[107] See Ronald W. Clark, *The Life of Bertrand Russell* (New York, 1975), 286; for a full discussion of Russell's wartime political activities, see Jo Vellacott, *Bertrand Russell and the Pacifists in the First World War* (New York, 1980).

laughable example of a heavy-handed Government losing a propaganda battle on ground of its own choosing. Instead, the Government compounded its error by granting Russell his dearest wish—continued persecution. The original prosecution of Russell, whatever its political merits, had at least been technically justifiable in law. The Government's next move was politically even more questionable and legally more doubtful. A few days before the Mansion House trial, the Foreign Secretary was informed by the British Ambassador in Washington that Russell planned to visit the United States to deliver a series of lectures at Harvard. Informed that Russell had confessed to authorship of an anti-conscription pamphlet, and before he had even been convicted for the offence against DORA, Grey informed Samuel that he intended to withhold from Russell the passports that would be necessary if he were to undertake the journey.[108]

Samuel, who was invited by Grey to comment 'as to the true facts of the case', replied not only with the facts of Russell's trial and conviction, but also with the opinion that no passport should be issued to him.[109] Samuel also approved the interception by MI5 of a letter Russell had written to Professor James H. Woods of the Harvard Philosophy Department.[110] The letter, which Russell was later to publish in his memoirs,[111] contained some exaggerated anti-conscription rhetoric but nothing that might endanger national security. Russell had by now succeeded in goading the Government into actions that were both illiberal and stupid.

On 25 August Troup wrote to the Director of Public Prosecutions asking him to advise the Home Secretary whether Russell should be prosecuted under DORA for a speech he had made in Cardiff. Enclosing a transcript of the speech which Samuel had specially requested from the Chief Constable of Cardiff, Troup made it clear that he favoured prosecution:

The whole speech is, and is intended to be, mischievous and, if any one regarded it, is 'likely to cause disaffection'. But I think the statements which most definitely contravene regulation 27—as being likely to prejudice our relations with a foreign power—are those about Russia on page 8. [This referred to a passage where Russell had asserted that the main cause of the continuation of the war was 'the Russian desire to possess Constantinople'.]

We cannot dismiss Bertrand Russell's remarks as insignificant. He writes and speaks with a good deal of misguided cleverness—he is anxious to go on an Anti-

[108] Lord Newton (Under-Secretary, Foreign Office) to Under-Secretary, Home Office, 1 June 1916, PRO HO 45/11012/314670.

[109] Home Office to Foreign Office, 9 June 1916 (copy), ibid.

[110] General Cockerill (MI5) to Home Office, 13 Aug. 1916, PRO HO 45/11012/ 314670; attached minute by Troup, 14 Aug. 1916, initialled by Samuel to indicate approval; also Home Office to Cockerill, 15 Aug. 1916 (copy), ibid.

[111] The Autobiography of Bertrand Russell, ii (Boston, 1968), 83–4.

British mission to the U.S.A. and a letter stopped by the Censor (Boyd, my private Secretary, could find it, I think) shows how deliberately hostile he is.

Still it is a difficult question whether we should do more harm than good by prosecuting—He would make a clever defence, and would publish it as a pamphlet.[112]

The DPP replied deprecating a prosecution on the sensible ground that this would merely attract greater publicity to Russell's views than they would otherwise receive. Instead he advised that the Home Office should instruct the press censor to ensure that no meeting addressed by Russell should be mentioned in the press and should instruct the police that any pamphlet or leaflet by Russell should be seized.[113]

In the light of this legal advice, Samuel agreed that a prosecution would not be advisable. But Russell possessed an unsurpassed capacity for getting under official skin. Hardly had one silly proposal been disposed of than another, no less misconceived, was placed before Samuel. On 31 August Troup reported that Russell intended to go to Haverhill in Suffolk to address a meeting of fifty conscientious objectors who were working there. Even Colonel Vernon Kell of MI5 expressed doubts about whether DORA could properly be applied to prevent Russell going to Haverhill, which was inside a 'prohibited area'—prohibited, that is, to enemy aliens and other persons whose loyalty was suspect. Since Samuel was on holiday in Cleveland, Troup and Blackwell decided to authorize the prohibition themselves. Troup noted that Samuel, who was on the point of returning to London, could easily withdraw the order if he saw an objection to excluding Russell from all prohibited areas. But plainly determined somehow to bag his prey, Troup added: 'I think it would then be necessary to exclude him from certain areas such as South Wales and any places where our conscientious objectors are at work.'[114]

Immediately on his return to London Samuel countermanded the order, commenting: 'I think it would be difficult to defend an order excluding him from all prohibited areas, as they cover about a third of the country. There is no suspicion, of course, that he is an enemy agent.' At the same time Samuel approved a more narrowly framed order along the lines suggested by Troup.[115] Unfortunately, by the time Samuel's instruction was issued, Russell had already been served with the order barring him from all prohibited areas. The comic opera aspect of the affair was accentuated by the fact that the order was signed by Lieutenant-Colonel the Hon. A. F. V. Russell, a cousin of Bertrand Russell. The philosopher Russell was predictably indignant, protesting that he had 'not the faintest

[112] Troup to Sir Charles Mathews, 25 Aug. 1916, PRO HO 45/11012/314670.
[113] Mathews to Sir E. Blackwell, 28 Aug. 1916, ibid.
[114] Troup minute, 31 Aug. 1916, ibid.
[115] Minute by Samuel, 1 Sept. 1916, ibid.

interest in getting military information'.[116] Once the order had been issued, however, the authorities were disinclined to look foolish by immediately withdrawing it. They therefore scrambled to find reasons to justify it. Forgetting his earlier doubts about the order, Kell now insisted it should be maintained and even extended. He consulted his War Office colleagues and then wrote to Blackwell:

We all agreed that it would be most undesirable to withdraw or modify the order as matters stand at present. I think the opening sentence of Mr Russell's speech at Cardiff on 6th July is sufficient to condemn the whole: 'I do not believe there is now any good and valid reason why this war should continue to be prosecuted.'

A man who goes about preaching such a doctrine as this, at the present moment, is a danger to the State; and as such is not a suitable person to be allowed into prohibited areas, where he would have special opportunities of airing his vicious tenets amongst dockers, miners and transport workers. If Mr Russell should still persist in making speeches similar to his Cardiff one in un-prohibited areas, then the next step will be to confine his movements to a particular area.[117]

Two days later Samuel discussed the case with Kell and agreed to the order remaining in force on condition that Lloyd George, who was away, should be consulted.[118]

The order meanwhile gave Russell exactly the opportunity he sought to engage liberal sympathy for his unjustified treatment as virtually an enemy agent. He was not without influential friends. Runciman wrote to Lloyd George suggesting that unless the War Office had reason to suspect him of treachery the order should be withdrawn.[119] Gilbert Murray took up the case directly with Samuel who replied that the order 'was made by the War Office and I was not consulted about it'. He added that if Russell were to give an undertaking to refrain from 'harmful propaganda', the order would be withdrawn and he would be given a passport to America.[120] The controversy became so inflamed that the Prime Minister asked to be told 'who was responsible for the steps taken against Mr Bertrand Russell and what are the reasons which led to them'.[121] Whereas Samuel had told Murray that he had not been consulted about the order, the War Office told the Prime Minister that Samuel had approved the action. Both statements were, of course true—up to a point. The Home Office, which had pressed so strongly for the order, could hardly shuffle off responsibility, and Troup prepared a memorandum that sought to justify the decision.[122]

[116] *Morning Post*, 2 Sept. 1916.
[117] Kell to Blackwell, 3 Sept. 1916, PRO HO 45/11012/314670.
[118] Minute by Troup, 7 Sept. 1916, ibid.
[119] Runciman to Lloyd George, 7 Sept. 1916 (copy), WR 126.
[120] HS to Murray, 10 Sept. 1916, Bodleian Library, Oxford, Murray papers 375/105–6.
[121] David Davies (10 Downing Street) to S. W. Harris (Home Office), 15 Sept. 1916, PRO HO 45/11012/314670.   [122] Memorandum by Troup, 18 Sept. 1916, ibid.

Russell had now succeeded not only in causing maximum confusion in the bureaucracy but also in securing support from all parts of the political spectrum. On 21 September the guardian of the High Tory conscience, Lord Hugh Cecil, wrote to Samuel urging that Russell be allowed to go to America:

The powers which the Government exercise under the Defence of the Realm Act are exceedingly oppressive ones if they are not exercised with the most scrupulous care; and it certainly appears to go beyond the need of defending the realm to stop a man like Mr Russell from giving any lectures he likes in America. The Americans are not so silly as to be seriously influenced by his lectures, one way or the other. And there is no real ground that I know of for suspecting Mr Russell of anything worse than unreasonable pacifist opinions. It seems open to the gravest objection that powers really intended to protect the country against treason, sedition, or other grave crime, should be employed to harass a man who holds unpopular views.[123]

But Samuel was now too deeply entrenched to withdraw. He replied to Cecil reiterating all the arguments in favour of the order and insisting: 'I do not think it can reasonably be maintained that in time of war a person who has been found guilty of gross misrepresentation and of attempts to create disaffection in his own country should be allowed to proceed to a neutral country in order to conduct a similar campaign of misrepresentation there.'[124]

This became Samuel's standard line of defence as an avalanche of protests descended upon him. If it did not convince Cecil (and he wrote to Samuel to say so[125]), its failure to carry conviction to Samuel's fellow-Liberals may be readily imagined. Coming after successive invocations of DORA by the Home Office, the Russell case seriously dented Samuel's reputation as an exponent of liberal principles. What must have been, for Samuel, the most disturbing criticism came from his old friend and ideological mentor Graham Wallas who wrote comparing the regulations issued under DORA to the Pitt Acts of 1795 and the Six Acts of 1817. Complaining that the Coalition Cabinet leant 'wholly on the right', Wallas suggested: 'An ordinary intelligent Radical working man would find it extraordinarily difficult to point out anything said or done by the Government on war-policy, on fiscal policy, on Irish policy, during the last year and a half which shows that liberal ideas and feelings have had any weight with them. One knows the difficulties but they do not prevent causes having their effects.' And he added the postscript: 'Why on earth the Government won't let Bertie Russell go and work, as he will have to work, hard at philosophy at Harvard I can't conceive. I suppose there is

[123] Cecil to HS, 21 Sept. 1916, ibid.   [124] HS to Cecil, 28 Sept. 1916, ibid.
[125] Cecil to HS, 30 Sept. 1916, ibid.

some personal quarrel in the background.'[126] Samuel desired the good opinion of Wallas more than that of any other human, and this comprehensive indictment, expressed in a letter that was personally very friendly, must have stung. His reply to Wallas was notably lame. He briefly reiterated the old arguments against Russell, and on the larger question he wrote: 'There is little room for the characteristic activities of Liberalism during a war. But it is to be seen a good deal in the things that have not been done!'[127]

Samuel tried to justify his action, at least to Trevelyan and Wallas, by sending them privately transcripts of Russell's offending speech in Cardiff. Neither was mollified. Wallas, indeed, wrote back in a much less friendly tone than he usually adopted towards Samuel, fiercely criticizing the Government's conduct in the Russell case, and bitterly protesting: 'To me the present military control of world discussion is a horrible tragedy. The best breeding stock of Europe is being steadily exterminated, and, to an extent which has never happened in any war before, the military authorities have prevented non-official discussion of the situation.'[128]

The emotional tone of this communication points to another difference between Samuel and his old radical friends. Unlike Trevelyan, Morel, and Wallas, Samuel does not seem to have been personally touched by the slaughter of a generation in Flanders and on the Somme. The normal, even tenor of his official and personal life continued after August 1914 as it had before. His correspondence seldom referred to the war at least until 1918. It was almost as if, at the emotional level, the war passed him by. In the Russell case Wallas was quite wrong if he thought there was any personal quarrel between Samuel and Russell.[129] Kell, Blackwell, and Troup evidently got hot under the collar on the subject, but Samuel dealt with this, as with so much else, *sine ira ac studio*. This was his strength as an administrator, but his weakness as a politician.

Samuel was not entirely alone in Asquith's Cabinet in giving the impression of lack of affect. So, too often, did the Prime Minister himself—and it helped bring him down in December 1916. Samuel deliberately avoided and rather despised the self-advertising impetuosity of Churchill and the Celtic extravagance of Lloyd George. Both seemed to him too close to demagogy. His model was rather the 'last of the Romans' who was asked by a lady visitor 'Mr Asquith, do you take an interest in the War?', and whose biographer comments that he was 'too fastidious to

---

[126] Wallas to HS, 8 Oct. 1916, HLRO HS A/155/IV/54.
[127] HS to Wallas, 10 Oct. 1916, BLPES Wallas papers 1/56/82.
[128] Wallas to HS, 27 Oct. 1916, BLPES Wallas papers 1/76/103.
[129] Russell, for his part, bore Samuel no personal ill will for his treatment in 1916. In later years the two were quite friendly. See below, pp. 394 and 398.

pretend to an enthusiasm which he did not feel'.[130] Yet beneath Asquith's calm public demeanour, his private correspondence with Venetia Stanley revealed the ebb and flow of strong tides of emotion. When Venetia agreed to marry Edwin Montagu in 1915, the Prime Minister was distraught beyond bounds. Samuel did not attend his cousin's wedding, and he too probably discountenanced the marriage—but for a different reason: he shared, although in less dogmatic form, the disapproval of Jewish–Christian intermarriage that had led his late uncle, Lord Swaythling (Sir Samuel Montagu), before his death in 1911, to attach a condition to his will that his children must marry within the faith. Unlike the Prime Minister, Samuel did not form flirtatious liaisons with young society girls. He wrote no billets-doux. He struck visitors as cold and inscrutable, 'rather like an Oriental statue'.[131] Yet he, too, behind an impassive façade concealed a passionate secret commitment, albeit political not personal, that amazed even his closest colleagues.

[130] Jenkins, *Asquith*, 348.   [131] Riddell, *War Diary*, 179.

8

Eastern Melodies

===

For in the background figures vague and vast
Of patriarchs and prophets rose sublime;
And all the great traditions of the past
They saw reflected in the coming time.

(Longfellow's epitaph on the earliest Jewish
settlers in New England)

IN DECEMBER 1914 Chaim Weizmann, a Reader in Biochemistry at Manchester University, met Herbert Samuel for the first time. He went to see him armed with an introduction from C. P. Scott, editor of the *Manchester Guardian*, in order to discuss the aims of the Zionist Organization of which he was an influential, although not yet a leading, member. In his autobiography, *Trial and Error*, Weizmann recounts that shortly after his first encounter with Scott, the well-connected newspaperman had offered to put him in touch with Lloyd George and had then said: 'You know, you have a Jew in the Government, Mr Herbert Samuel.' Whereupon Weizmann responded: 'For God's sake, Mr Scott, let's have nothing to do with this man.' Explaining this sharp reaction, Weizmann writes: 'I thought, on general grounds, that Herbert Samuel was the type of Jew who by his very nature was opposed to us.'[1]

When Weizmann met Samuel he received a pleasant surprise. In a report to the Zionist Organization Executive a few weeks later, he described the occasion in detail. Weizmann had begun by speaking of the acute distress in Eastern European Jewry and explaining the Zionist interpretation of the moral and political dilemma of Jewry. 'If the Jews', he said, 'had at present a place where they formed the important part of the population, and led a life of their own, however small this place might be, something like Monaco, with a University instead of a gambling hall, nobody would doubt the existence of the Jewish nation, all the fatal misunderstandings would disappear.'

[1] Chaim Weizmann, *Trial and Error* (London, 1949), 190–1.

Samuel listened to Weizmann's 'short exposé' and then responded:

He remarked that he was not a stranger to Zionist ideas; he had been following them up a little of late years, and although he had never publicly mentioned it, he took a considerable interest in the question. Since Turkey had entered the war, he had given the problem much thought and consideration, and he thought that a realization of the Zionist dreams was possible. He believed that my demands were too modest, that big things would have to be done in Palestine; he himself would move and would expect Jewry to move immediately the military situation was cleared up. He was convinced that it would be cleared up favourably. The Jews have to bring sacrifices, and he was prepared to do so. At this point I ventured to ask in which way the plans of Mr Samuel were more ambitious than mine. Mr Samuel preferred not to enter a discussion of his plans, as he would like to keep them '*liquid*', but he suggested that the Jews would have to build Railways, harbours, a University, a network of Schools, etc. The University seems to make a special appeal to him. He hopes that great things may be forthcoming from a seat of learning, where the Jews can work freely on a free soil of their own. He also thinks that perhaps the Temple may be rebuilt, as a symbol of Jewish unity, of course, in a modernised form.[2]

Weizmann was astounded by Samuel's attitude. Immediately after the meeting he sent his wife a telegram, and later the same day he wrote to her: 'Messianic times have really come. It turns out that he knows a great deal about Zionism, even about Ahad Ha'amism,[3] and taking Ahad Ha'amism's point of view awaits the liberation of Jewry from the spiritual yoke.'[4] In an exultant spirit, Weizmann reported to Scott that he had found Samuel's views 'quite a revelation'. Samuel was so well-informed about Zionism that Weizmann 'could clearly tell him nothing new'. Full of gratitude to Scott for effecting the introduction, Weizmann added: 'You can easily imagine, Sir, how delighted I was to hear all that from Mr Samuel, whom I certainly did not expect to express such views.'[5]

Weizmann's astonishment was natural. Samuel was not, on the face of things, a likely recruit to Zionism in the period before 1914. The Anglo-Jewish banking patricians were generally hostile to the idea of Jewish nationalism which they tended to regard as incompatible with their status as British citizens and as a threat to the position of civil equality that had been won, after a long struggle, with the admission of Jews to Parliament in 1858. Zionism was not, at this time, the great force within the Jewish community that it later became. In 1916 the total of contributions to Zionist funds from English Jews was only about £500. Even in 1917 the

[2] Report by Weizmann to Zionist Executive, 7 Jan. 1915, WA.
[3] Ahad Ha'am (Asher Ginzberg) was the exponent of 'spiritual' or 'cultural' Zionism; later this was identified with 'non-political' Zionism that questioned the desirability of a Jewish state. But Weizmann was not using the term in that sense here.
[4] Weizmann to Vera Weizmann, 10 Dec. 1914, WA.
[5] Weizmann to Scott, 13 Dec. 1914, WA.

various Zionist groups in England together had only about 4,000 members. In truth, Zionism in England during the two decades before 1917 was the preserve of a minority of quarrelsome enthusiasts led by a handful of equally quarrelsome visionaries, many of these, such as Weizmann, immigrants, and none of them of any substantial weight in English political life.[6] For an ambitious Anglo-Jewish politician such as Samuel to embrace Zionism not only ran against the ideological grain of his class; it would also have seemed, before 1914, evidence of lack of political seriousness. Samuel was nothing if not politically serious. Why, then, did he take up Zionism with such uncharacteristic fervour?

The answer would seem to lie partly in Samuel's upbringing and partly in his character. Although members of the 'Cousinhood', the Samuel family in the late nineteenth century exhibited some special characteristics. Their Judaism was not attenuated and their connections to the Jewish community had not dwindled into mere matters of form. No other Anglo-Jewish family could boast a figure such as Moses Samuel, the Liverpool Hebrew littérateur. As communal overlords only the Rothschilds could compare with Samuel Montagu, but they allowed their daughters, though not their sons, to marry non-Jews, preferably aristocrats such as Lord Rosebery, whereas Montagu sought even beyond his dying day to compel his children to marry within the fold. Given the early death of his father, the formative influences on Samuel were his mother and his uncle. His mother's strictness on matters of *kashrut* and her interest in marrying him off to the Chief Rabbi's daughter have already been noted. His uncle adhered unyieldingly to an orthodoxy which, while it did not compel his nephew's respect, undoubtedly left an enduring mark. The effect on Montagu's children of his dictatorial efforts to instil orthodoxy was predictably to incite rebellion. His daughter Lily, much to his distress, became a founder of the Liberal Jewish Synagogue. His son Edwin once said that he had been striving all his life to escape from the ghetto.[7] Herbert Samuel's relationship with his uncle had been difficult and he too had rebelled. But unlike his cousin Edwin, he was only half-successful, and perhaps only half-hearted, in his revolt. With his marriage to Beatrice Franklin he had settled down to a social pattern of outwardly conventional orthodoxy only a little more relaxed than that of the previous generation.

Samuel's Zionism, far from being inconsistent with his background, is more properly understood as a logical progression from it. It may be seen as an attempt to come to terms on a secular plane with the spiritual disorientation that he plainly felt in 1897 (the year of his marriage, also

---

[6] See Stuart A. Cohen, *English Zionists and British Jews: The Communal Politics of Anglo-Jewry, 1895–1920* (Princeton, 1982).
[7] Stein, *Balfour Declaration*, 498.

the year of the first Zionist Congress) in being compelled to do what he had earlier sworn he would never do—make a show of adherence to Judaism while having inwardly lost faith. Zionism helped him reconcile the conflict between belief and action that had troubled him so deeply. Not for nothing was he later to entitle what he regarded as his most important work of philosophy *Belief and Action*.[8]

Far from constituting a revolt against the conventional political wisdoms on which he was brought up, his attraction to Jewish nationalism emerged naturally from the *idées reçues* of his youth, just as his supposed rebellion against a Conservative family background dissolves in the Liberalism of his Liberal father, elder brother, grandfather, uncle, and great-uncle. The Samuels did not share the common horror of the Anglo-Jewish élite at the notion of Zionism. The key figure here is Samuel Montagu who has generally been marked down in Zionist historiography as an enemy of the cause. The reality was different. It would be more correct to define him as one of the earliest English enthusiasts for Zionism. He went to the unusual length of visiting Palestine in 1875 and again in 1905. He bought land in Palestine. He took the chair in 1891 at a meeting of the British group of *Hovevei Zion* (Lovers of Zion). He praised Zionism for championing the revival of Hebrew as against Yiddish. He lobbied the British Government in 1891 for support for Jewish settlement in Palestine. When he met Theodor Herzl, founder of political Zionism, in 1895, he told him that he thought of settling in Palestine with his entire family. When Herzl published his manifesto, *Der Judenstaat*, Montagu sent a copy to his political hero, Gladstone. In a newspaper interview in 1896 Montagu spoke of two million Jews settling in Palestine.[9]

The reason for the common attribution of anti-Zionist views to Montagu emerges from some further remarks in the same interview:

Supposing somebody were to come to me with the statement, 'The scheme can be carried through', why, then I should offer all the support I could. That is the point—how is it practicable? . . . Necessarily the [Jewish] state would have to come into existence under the sanction and guarantee of the Great Powers and the utmost goodwill would be needed in the whole matter.[10]

These words might have been uttered twenty years later by his nephew Herbert. It is true that Montagu later concluded that political Zionism was not practicable so long as the Turks ruled Palestine. But Samuel

---

[8] London, 1937.
[9] See *Theodor Herzls Tagebücher 1895–1904* (Berlin, 1922), i. 322 and *passim*; also *Jewish World*, 1 May 1885, 14 Feb. 1901, 24 Mar. 1905; *The Times*, 25 and 29 May, 11 June 1891; *Jewish Chronicle*, 4 Mar. 1892, 29 May 1896, 30 Nov. 1900; *Daily Mail*, 2 Nov. 1898; *Leeds Mercury*, 1 Oct. 1900.
[10] *Daily Chronicle*, 25 Feb. 1896.

Montagu's later depreciation of Zionism was not on ground of principle but rather on the point of whether it was practical politics. In 1905, with other Anglo-Jewish notables, he signed a letter to *The Times* declaring that after the death of the 'noble-hearted Herzl' Zionism had 'faded into a vision of the distant future'.[11] This was the vision that his nephew was destined to help realize.

Samuel Montagu's intense interest in Palestine was not an idiosyncratic quirk. Other members of the Samuel family followed his lead in this direction. Herbert Samuel's cousin Sydney Samuel, a director of the *Jewish Chronicle*, visited Palestine in 1875 and later wrote a book about the Jewish communities of the East. Herbert's brother Dennis visited Palestine in 1898. Palestine, for the Samuels, was not some faraway Ottoman province of which they knew or cared little, as it was for most upper-class English Jews, but a topic of considerable fascination and frequent debate.

What was Herbert Samuel's own attitude to Zionism before 1914? The evidence is sparse but suggestive. According to his own account, in an interview in 1949, he began to take an interest in the subject after reading Herzl's *Jewish State*.[12] Unfortunately he did not say when that was, and since it was a pamphlet rather than a book it does not figure in his list of 'books read'. But with his uncle pressing it upon Gladstone immediately upon publication, we may surmise that Samuel read it not,long afterwards. His interest thus kindled was further stoked by conversations that he had with the husband of his wife's close friend Lucy Gaster. Moses Gaster, *Haham* (Chief Rabbi) of the Sephardi Jewish congregations in England, was a passionate early Zionist and a formidable figure in the Jewish community. Samuel was not close to him. But their wives' friendship brought them together from time to time and Samuel later told the historian Leonard Stein that when conducting his early enquiries into Zionism he had turned for enlightenment to Gaster.[13] It was Gaster who, in 1910, interceded successfully with Samuel to help accelerate the naturalization of Chaim Weizmann.[14]

Among the fragmentary indications of Samuel's early interest in Zionism one curiosity stands out. This is a letter written to Samuel in July 1900 by an acquaintance of his, an 88-year-old English lady resident in Florence, Lucie Alexander. Mrs Alexander congratulated Samuel's baby son, Edwin, on signing his first letter, and said that she would bequeath it to his family so that 'when he is an old man he will enjoy showing it to his grand-

---

[11] *The Times*, 8 Dec. 1905.   [12] See *Jerusalem Post*, 9 Nov. 1970.
[13] Stein, *Balfour Declaration*, 106.
[14] Weizmann to Gaster, 6, 10, 20, and 22 Nov. 1910, WA; HS to Gaster, 11 Nov. 1910, CZA A203/188.

children'. Then she added: 'Perhaps before that time he may have been Governor of the Holy Land, for I believe in the prophecies as much as you do that the country shall be restored to its owners.'[15] Twenty years later, Herbert Samuel himself was ruler of Palestine and his son Edwin was destined to serve as an official in the Government of Palestine for almost the entire period of the British mandate. Was this extraordinary prophecy merely an old lady's flight of fancy? Or was it, as may be suggested by the phrase 'as you do', an allusion to some conversation with Samuel on one of his several visits to Florence?

A second more tangible piece of evidence resulted from Samuel's trip, already described, to East Africa, when he travelled up-country on the newly built Uganda railway. The following year, the so-called 'Uganda project' became the subject of serious discussion between the British Government and the Zionist Organization. Samuel played no direct part in these discussions between the Zionists, represented by Herzl and Leopold Greenberg, editor of the *Jewish Chronicle*, and the Colonial Secretary, Joseph Chamberlain, who is said to have been the initiator of the idea of an autonomous Jewish settlement on the Uasin Gishu plateau in East Africa—an area that he had glimpsed from the Uganda railway on his own visit to the region in 1902.[16] But in September 1903 Samuel gave a newspaper interviewer his views on the possibilities of Jewish settlement in East Africa. Characteristically, and in a manner reminiscent of his uncle Montagu's attitude to Zionism, he discussed the Uganda project not in terms of the passionate clash of principle between the Zionists proper and the 'territorialists' that rent the Zionist movement asunder, but rather in purely practical terms. Was the climate suitable? Was land available? What were the economic possibilities? He concluded:

The success of any scheme of colonisation depends upon two factors—the suitability of the country which is chosen and the suitability of the people who colonize. The central regions of British East Africa are admirably adapted for a new settlement, and the prosperity of the enterprise may be held to be conditioned only by the character and qualifications of the would-be settlers.[17]

During the following decade Samuel had occasional contacts with the Jewish Territorialist Organisation, the breakaway group from Zionism, led by the writer Israel Zangwill, but he did not commit himself to their cause—nor, for that matter, to the Zionists'.

Between 1905 and 1914, while serving in the Government, Samuel said

[15] Lucie Alexander to HS, 13 July 1900, HLRO HS B/8/40a.
[16] See Robert G. Weisbord, *African Zion* (Philadelphia, 1968); Julian Amery, *The Life of Joseph Chamberlain*, iv (London, 1951), 256–70.
[17] *Jewish World*, 4 Sept. 1903.

and did little about Jewish affairs. He left that to his brother Stuart who had succeeded Samuel Montagu as Liberal MP for Whitechapel and as an acknowledged spokesman in the House of Commons for Jewish interests. But although Herbert Samuel seems studiously to have avoided too public an identification with what were regarded as Jewish causes, two political controversies in these years thrust him willy-nilly into situations where, as a Jew, he was bound to feel specially sensitive. The first was the argument over the Aliens Act. One of Samuel's first tasks at the Home Office had been to implement this legislation which he had earlier declared impossible to implement and which many regarded as a product of anti-Jewish sentiment. The other was the Marconi affair in which Samuel, together with other members of his family, had been the butt of a campaign of anti-Semitic attacks of a scurrility quite new to British politics. Yet while these events no doubt served as reminders of the limitations of Jewish acceptance in English society, it would be mistaken to see Samuel's Zionism primarily as a reaction to such manifestations of anti-Semitism.

Samuel's reading in the period before 1914 included very few books on Jewish religion or politics. In June 1904 he read C. G. Montefiore's *Liberal Judaism*, but he was never sufficiently attracted to its doctrines to abandon the orthodox New West End Synagogue of which he remained a member all his life. In January 1905 he read various books on the aliens question, then near the centre of political controversy. He also read at this time Disraeli's novel *Tancred*, an exotic pastiche about Near Eastern politics of which the fundamental theme is Zionism—or a strange kind of Zionism *avant la lettre* as refracted through the fantastic imagination of Disraeli. The book evidently made an impact on Samuel, for it is one of the few to appear more than once in his reading list. He read it again in August 1920 shortly after taking up office in Palestine as High Commissioner under the British mandate. Discussing Disraeli's motives in producing this curious work, Sir Isaiah Berlin has written: 'The Eastern melodies were called into being in response to the need to construct a *persona*, an inner image of himself with which he could establish for himself a place in the world, and play a part in history and society.'[18]

These words might also be applied to Samuel for whom Zionism was the one political passion of a singularly passionless career. Zionism offered, for the President of the Local Government Board in 1914, not an outlet for personal ambition but something grander: an opportunity to leave his mark not only in the sphere of local taxation reform and social welfare but at the level of nation and empire in the era of nationalism and

[18] Isaiah Berlin, 'Benjamin Disraeli, Karl Marx, and the Search for Identity' (presidential address to the Jewish Historical Society of England, 15 Nov. 1967), *Transactions of the Jewish Historical Society of England*, 22 (1970), 11.

imperialism. More than that, Zionism might help restore the inner equilibrium, the *mens aequa* that Samuel valued more than most men, that had been severely disturbed in the early 1890s, and only partly and superficially restored after his marriage. Thus his search for a national resolution of the problem of the Jewish people in the modern world was at the same time at the personal level a quest for mental tranquillity, an exercise in re-identification in a non-religious form with a Jewish background whose spiritual components he found intellectually unacceptable. In Zionism Samuel consummated the marriage of belief and action.

At the end of October 1914 the Ottoman Empire entered the war on the side of the Central Powers. The moment that Samuel Montagu had spoken of a decade earlier had suddenly arrived. The dissolution of the Turkish dominions was no longer a distant mirage but was quite possibly imminent. Consequently Zionism was transformed, at any rate in Herbert Samuel's mind, from a far-fetched vision to a practical proposition. Montagu was by now dead. But his nephew felt, as he later put it, a 'special obligation' as the first Jew, or (as he more precisely recalled, thinking of Disraeli's withdrawal from the community by his father) the first member of the Jewish community, in a British Cabinet, to take the initiative on behalf of Zionism.[19] The speed with which he acted, uncharacteristic of a politician who liked to ponder and enquire rather than take precipitate action, suggests that the seed which now germinated had been planted long before. Within days of the Turkish declaration of war, and a month before his first meeting with Weizmann, Samuel launched the political enterprise in Whitehall and Westminster that was to lead three years later to the Balfour Declaration.

On 2 November 1914 Grey reported to the Cabinet on the situation arising out of the Turkish declaration of war. According to Asquith's report to the King, 'the Cabinet were of opinion that after what had happened we ought to take a vigorous offensive ... Henceforward, Great Britain must finally abandon the formula of "Ottoman integrity" whether in Europe or in Asia.'[20] A week later Asquith delivered a major speech at

[19] Herbert Samuel, *Great Britain and Palestine* (Lucien Wolf Lecture to Jewish Historical Society of England, London, 1935), 12; see also HS to ES, 27 Jan. 1918, ISA 100/44.
[20] Asquith to King George V, 3 Nov. 1914, PRO CAB 41/35/56 (misdated 8 Nov. in PRO). About this time Asquith recounted to Venetia Stanley a strange nightmare: 'My dreams continue. . . . There was another . . . in which (with the concurrence of all my colleagues) I was supplanted by Herbert Samuel—as Prince Hal says "a Jew, an Ebrew Jew". Do you think that is going to be my fate? I wonder. I take refuge in the Beatitude: "The meek shall inherit the earth"—and no Jew was ever meek!' (Asquith to Venetia Stanley, 3 Nov. 1914, in Brocks (eds.), *Asquith Letters*, 306). The editors of Asquith's letters point out a minor slip: the quoted remark is spoken by Falstaff not Prince Henry. Is it perhaps too far-fetched to suggest another slip, Freudian in nature? Did Asquith fear being 'supplanted' by Samuel, or was his subconscious concerned about a rival of a different

the Lord Mayor's Banquet in the Guildhall in which he declared: 'It is the Ottoman Government, and not we who have rung the death-knell of Ottoman dominion not only in Europe but in Asia.'[21]

Samuel saw this as his cue. On the day of Asquith's Guildhall speech he had a long talk with Grey:

I said that I myself had never been a Zionist, because the prospects of any practical outcome had seemed so remote that I had not been willing to take part in the movement. But now conditions are profoundly altered. If a Jewish State were established in Palestine it might become the centre of a new culture. . . . I thought that British influence ought to play a considerable part in the formation of such a state, because the geographical situation of Palestine, and especially its proximity to Egypt, would render its goodwill to England a matter of importance to the British empire. . . . Grey said that the idea had always had a strong sentimental attraction for him. The historical appeal was very strong. He was quite favourable to the proposal and would be prepared to work for it if the opportunity arose. If any proposals were put forward by France or any other Power with regard to Syria, it would be important not to acquiesce in any plan which would be inconsistent with the creation of a Jewish state in Palestine.[22]

Samuel also had a brief talk with Lloyd George who had referred in Cabinet that day to 'the ultimate destiny of Palestine' and who told Samuel that he was 'very keen to see a Jewish state established there'.[23] Shortly afterwards Lloyd George told C. P. Scott that he had had 'a "whole hearted" i.e. "heart to heart" conversation with Samuel and had been astonished to find how that cold and dry person suddenly kindled and they had sympathized on the common ground of a small nationality'.[24]

Thus by the time Samuel met Weizmann on 10 December 1914 he had already quite independently initiated discussion of Zionism at the highest levels of the Government. Nor did he exaggerate in terming his own plans 'more ambitious' than Weizmann's. For the Zionist spokesman referred only to a 'Monaco' whereas Samuel had talked of a fully-fledged Jewish State. The meeting with Weizmann was something of a revelation not only to Weizmann but also to Samuel. Probably for the first time he came into direct contact with a Zionist who was his intellectual equal and who possessed political antennae of the utmost sensitivity (Gaster was a considerable scholar of Romanian and Hebrew literature, but he had little

sort—Samuel's cousin? Edwin Montagu had proposed to Venetia Stanley in 1912 but she had refused him. Within two months of Asquith's dream, however, he was once again pressing his suit.

[21] Quoted in Stein, *Balfour Declaration*, 103.
[22] Memorandum by HS, 9 Nov. 1914, ISA 100/0.
[23] Ibid.   [24] Wilson (ed.), *Diaries of C. P. Scott*, 113.

political sense). Although Samuel left no contemporary record of his first impressions of Weizmann, his actions and his later recollections show that he regarded him with considerable respect. In 1918, for example, he wrote to his son Edwin: 'I never see him [Weizmann] without being more and more impressed by his breadth of view and sound judgment, and by—a rare combination—his union of those qualities with a passionate fervour and enthusiasm. The Zionist cause is wonderfully fortunate in having such a leader.'[25] For several years after their first meeting the two men worked closely together with a common objective. For Samuel's scheme to meet with serious consideration from his Cabinet colleagues it was essential for him to be able to present a Zionist leader who could inspire confidence as a serious politician, devoted to British interests, capable of dragooning the argumentative ranks of British Zionists, strong enough to overcome resistance to Zionism within the Anglo-Jewish community, commanding influence among the masses of Russian Jews, and possessing the necessary qualities of discretion, clarity of exposition, and firmness of purpose. Weizmann not only fulfilled this prescription, he also possessed a personal magnetism that could win over interlocutors such as Balfour and Lloyd George and persuade them, in defiance of reality, that behind him stood a great force, 'world Jewry', which could help sway the political balance in Russia and America decisively in Britain's favour.

In the course of the next few weeks, Samuel took up the Zionist cause with his usual systematic efficiency and with an unwonted intensity. On 25 December Weizmann visited his home with Gaster. They agreed that 'what appeared to us most desirable was the establishment of a British Protectorate over Palestine'.[26] Samuel also sought information about conditions in Palestine from the British and American consuls in Jerusalem who were in London, as well as from two other former residents in Jerusalem, and he talked about Zionism with Sir Philip Magnus, MP for London University and a Vice-President of the Anglo-Jewish Association. He met two of the leading Russian Zionists, Nahum Sokolow and Yehiel Tschlenow, both recent arrivals in London. And he arranged for Weizmann to go with him to meet Lloyd George at breakfast in the Chancellor's official residence at 11 Downing Street. He saw Weizmann on at least two further occasions in the next few days, discussed Zionism with Lord Reading (Rufus Isaacs), and went to Tring to confer with Lord Rothschild and C. G. Montefiore, leading Anglo-Jewish notables. Meanwhile he read works on the ancient and modern history of Palestine and the Jews,

[25] HS to ES, 8 Oct. 1918, ISA 100/44.
[26] Weizmann to Zionist Executive, 7 Jan. 1915, WA.

among them *The Jews of Today* by the Zionist and sociologist Arthur Ruppin.

The result of all this activity was a draft Cabinet memorandum entitled 'The Future of Palestine'. In this remarkable document, utterly different in tone from all his previous Cabinet papers on such mundane subjects as postage rates and Irish finance, Samuel spoke of 'a stirring among the twelve million Jews scattered throughout the countries of the world':

A feeling is spreading with great rapidity that now, at last, some advance may be made, in some way, towards the fulfilment of the hope and desire, held with unshakable tenacity for eighteen hundred years, for the restoration of the Jews to the land to which they are attached by ties as ancient as history itself.

Withdrawing a little from his earlier advocacy, in his conversation with Grey, of a Jewish State in Palestine, he pointed out that the Jews were still only a small minority of the population of the country. On that ground, he wrote, 'it is felt that the time is not ripe for the establishment there of an independent, autonomous Jewish State'. In a passage remarkable for its prescience Samuel argued:

If the attempt were made to place the 400,000 or 500,000 Mahommedans of Arab race under a Government which rested upon the support of 90,000 or 100,000 Jewish inhabitants, there can be no assurance that such a Government, even if established by the authority of the Powers, would be able to command obedience. The dream of a Jewish State, prosperous, progressive, and the home of a brilliant civilisation, might vanish in a series of squalid conflicts with the Arab population. And even if a State so constituted did succeed in avoiding or repressing internal disorder, it is doubtful whether it would be strong enough to protect itself from external aggression from the turbulent elements around it. To attempt to realise the aspiration of a Jewish State one century too soon might throw back its actual realisation for many centuries more.

The solution to the problem of Jewish minority status and weakness in Palestine, he suggested, was 'the annexation of the country to the British Empire'. Under the imperial umbrella the Zionists would be enabled to purchase and colonize land. 'Jewish immigration, carefully regulated, would be given preference so that in the course of time the Jewish people, grown into a majority and settled in the land, may be conceded such degree of self-government as the conditions of that day may justify.'

Samuel drew particular attention to the advantages to British strategic interests in Egypt of the annexation of Palestine. But he dwelt also on more idealistic motives: the traditional Protestant sympathy with the idea of a Jewish restoration, the 'redemption' of the Christian holy places from the 'vulgarisation' to which they had been subject, the parallels with earlier British support for the national struggles of Greece and Italy. In a

1 *Louis Samuel (1794–1859),*
paternal grandfather of
Herbert Samuel

2 *Edwin Samuel (1825–77),*
father of Herbert Samuel

3 *Clara Samuel (1837–1920),*
mother of Herbert Samuel

4 *Samuel Montagu (born Montagu*
Samuel), 1st Baron Swaythling
(1832–1911)

5 Herbert Samuel, aged 16, at fancy dress ball given by Samuel Montagu, 1887

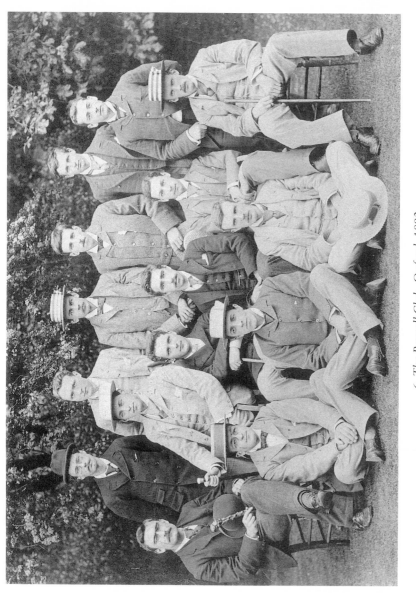

6 *The Russell Club, Oxford, 1892*

7 *Benjamin Jowett, Master of Balliol College, Oxford*

8 *Graham Wallas, 1893*

9 *Charles Trevelyan, 1895*

10 *Election scene in South Oxfordshire, 1895*

11 Beatrice Samuel (1871–1959)

Mr. Herbert Samuel, thanking his supporters after his victory at Redcar.

A. Gallant Photo, Redcar.

12 *Samuel at Redcar after an election victory in his Cleveland constituency*

13 Samuel with Winston Churchill and Joseph Walton at Liberal demonstration, Saltburn, 1909

14 Herbert and Beatrice Samuel outside the Zetland Hotel, Saltburn, 1910, in their Delaunay-Belleville landaulette, purchased the previous year from the Maharaja of Cooch-Behar

15 31 Porchester Terrace, Bayswater, Samuel's London home from 1910 to 1920

16 Samuel lands at Jaffa to take up office as High Commissioner of Palestine, 30 June 1920

17 *Samuel in High Commissioner's uniform, at the door of Government House, Jerusalem*

18 *Samuel addresses sheikhs at es-Salt, Transjordan, August 1920*

19 Samuel family group in garden of 35 Porchester Terrace, Bayswater, late 1920s

20 *Samuel with Eduard Beneš and Norman Davis at Geneva Disarmament Conference, 1932*

21 *Samuel lecturing at the Hebrew University of Jerusalem, December 1940*

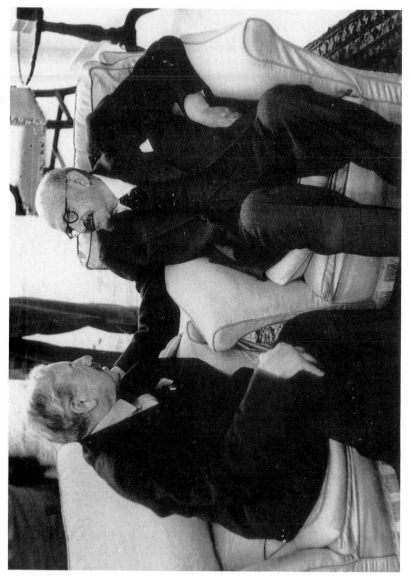

22 *Samuel with President Chaim Weizmann in Israel*

further passage that showed political foresight, he discussed the problem in relation to post-war Anglo-German relations:

Although Great Britain did not enter the conflict with any purpose of territorial expansion, being in it and having made immense sacrifices, there would be profound disappointment in the country if the outcome were to be the securing of great advantages by our allies, and none by ourselves. But to strip Germany of her colonies for the benefit of England would leave a permanent feeling of such intense bitterness among the German people as to render such a course impolitic. We have to live in the same world with some 70,000,000 Germans, and we should take care to give as little justification as we can for the hatching in ten, twenty, or thirty years hence, of a German war of revenge. Certain of the German colonies must no doubt be retained for strategic reasons. But if Great Britain can obtain the compensations, which public opinion will demand, in Mesopotamia and Palestine, and not in German East Africa and West Africa, there is more likelihood of a lasting peace.

Surveying the alternatives to British rule in Palestine, Samuel opposed annexation by France, arguing that France should be satisfied with the recovery of Alsace and Lorraine, and with obtaining 'the greater part of Syria, including Beirut and Damascus'. He rejected internationalization of Palestine which 'would lay the country under a dead hand' and would create 'a theatre of intrigue'. Annexation to the British Empire by the 'indirect method' of incorporation in Egypt had the disadvantage that 'in the eyes of the Jews, it would offer a much less strong appeal than would the possibility of the growth of a Jewish State under the direct suzerainty of Great Britain'. As for leaving the country under Turkish rule 'with guarantees for improved government and greater facilities for Jewish colonisation', such guarantees were, he argued, in the light of Turkish history unlikely to prove effective.

Samuel conceded that Palestine alone could not solve the Jewish question in Europe. But he suggested 'it could probably hold in time 3,000,000 or 4,000,000, and some relief would be given to the pressure in Russia and elsewhere'. He concluded with rare eloquence:

Let a Jewish centre be established in Palestine; let it achieve, as I believe it would achieve, a spiritual and intellectual greatness; and insensibly, but inevitably, the character of the individual Jew, wherever he might be, would be ennobled. The sordid associations which have attached to the Jewish name would be sloughed off, and the value of the Jews as an element in the civilisation of the European peoples would be enhanced.

The Jewish brain is a physiological product not to be despised. For fifteen centuries the race produced in Palestine a constant succession of great men—statesmen and prophets, judges and soldiers. If a body can again be given in which its soul can lodge, it may again enrich the world. Till full scope is granted, as Macaulay said in the House of Commons, 'let us not presume to say that there is no genius among the countrymen of Isaiah, no heroism among the descendants of the Maccabees.'[27]

Samuel did not circulate the draft to the Cabinet immediately, but showed it first to Grey and Asquith to secure their approval.[28]

To ministers accustomed to receiving memoranda that dealt with pressing diurnal issues, this paper, conceived on the plane of millennia and formulated in orotund periods, evoked universal amazement. Asquith wrote to Venetia Stanley: 'It reads almost like a new edition of *Tancred* brought up to date. I confess I am not attracted by this proposed addition to our responsibilities. But it is a curious illustration of Dizzy's favourite maxim that "race is everything" to find this almost lyrical outburst proceeding from the well-ordered and methodical brain of H.S.'[29] Grey was dubious about Samuel's proposal for a British protectorate which he felt might raise difficulties with the French. He suggested as an alternative the neutralization of the country under international guarantee. The Christian holy places should be placed under a commission of the Christian powers. And he proposed 'to vest the government of the country in some kind of Council to be established by the Jews'. Samuel nevertheless continued to urge the advantages of a British protectorate and told Grey that the Zionists were 'anxious to know what they could do to help'. Grey said the most useful action they could take would be to seek support for their proposals from the Governments of 'France, Russia, the United States and other countries'.[30] Samuel also showed his memorandum to Haldane, who responded with cautious sympathy, and, with Grey's approval, to Lord Rothschild.[31] In the light of these reactions, Samuel joined with Weizmann in seeking to stimulate a unified approach by the Jewish community to the British Government along the lines advocated in the memorandum. He encountered a surprising degree of support even among elements hitherto hostile towards Zionism.

In early March 1915 Samuel circulated a revised version of his memorandum to the whole Cabinet. This was similar to the original, except that it gave greater prominence to the strategic and *realpolitik* considerations in favour of a British protectorate and omitted some of the more 'lyrical' passages.[32] On 9 March the Cabinet considered the future of the Ottoman territories. According to Jack Pease, 'Samuel made a caveat in Jewish interest that holy places should not go to the French. Damascus he was

[27] HS Cabinet paper, [21] Jan. 1915, PRO CAB 37/123/43.
[28] See HS to Grey, 22 Jan. 1915, PRO FO 800/100.
[29] Asquith to Venetia Stanley, 28 Jan. 1915, in Brocks (eds.), *Asquith Letters*, 406.
[30] Memorandum by HS, 7 Feb. 1915 (on talk with Grey on 5 Feb.), ISA 100/1.
[31] Haldane to Samuel, 12 Feb. 1915, ibid.; note by HS, 14 Feb. 1915, ibid.
[32] HS Cabinet memorandum [11 ?] Mar. 1915, PRO CAB 37/126/1.

willing, but not Jerusalem.'[33] Asquith made no recorded comment in Cabinet, but in private he wrote to Venetia Stanley:

I think I told you that H Samuel had written an almost dithyrambic memorandum urging that in the carving up of the Turks' Asiatic dominions, we should take Palestine, into which the scattered Jews cd. in time swarm back from all quarters of the globe, and in due course obtain Home Rule. (What an attractive community!) Curiously enough, the only other partisan of this proposal is Lloyd George, who, I need not say, does not care a damn for the Jews or their past or their future, but who thinks it would be an outrage to let the Christian Holy Places . . . pass into the possession or under the protectorate of 'Agnostic Atheistic France'! Isn't it singular that the same conclusion shd. be capable of being come to by such different roads?[34]

Samuel's memorandum had no immediate result. Nor did Samuel intend or expect that it would. All concerned understood that any effective decision must await the advance of British troops from Egypt into Palestine. Grey had also made it clear that if the Zionists hoped for British support they must demonstrate that they enjoyed substantial support from Jews in Britain and elsewhere, and they must also persuade other governments to endorse their claims. Only thus could Britain avoid the accusation of using Zionism as a stalking-horse for its own imperial ambitions in the Levant. Both the military and political conditions took nearly three years to realize. In the meantime a committee of officials under Sir Maurice de Bunsen worked on a statement of British 'desiderata' in anticipation of the break-up of the Ottoman Empire. The committee's report, however, submitted to the Government in June 1915, did not even mention Zionism.[35] The disastrous British defeat at the hands of the Turks at Gallipoli served as a warning that the 'sick man' still retained qualities of recuperation and resilience. Partly in the hope of securing military aid to inflict a death-blow on the Turks, Britain in the course of 1915 and 1916 embarked on the labyrinthine negotiations with the Arabs of the Hejaz and with the French Government that led (in the first case) to the Hussein–McMahon Correspondence and (in the second) to the Sykes–Picot Agreement—primary exhibits for the post-war prosecution in the case of the 'twice-promised land'. Samuel played only a peripheral role in these discussions and this much excavated turf need not be further disturbed here.[36]

[33] Diary entry, 9 Mar. 1915, Nuffield College, Oxford, Gainford papers 40/7.
[34] Asquith to Venetia Stanley, 13 Mar. 1915 (ii), in Brocks (eds.), *Asquith Letters*, 477.
[35] See Isaiah Friedman, *The Question of Palestine, 1914–1918* (London, 1973), 19–21; also David Vital, *Zionism: The Crucial Phase* (Oxford, 1987), 98–102.
[36] The most authoritative recent investigation is Elie Kedourie, *In the Anglo-Arab Labyrinth* (Cambridge, 1976). George Antonius, *The Arab Awakening* (London, 1938) is the classic statement of the view that Britain entered into conflicting undertakings.

After his initial flurry of Zionist activity in late 1914 and early 1915, Samuel refrained from trying to push the Cabinet towards a speedy decision that might well have been negative. He had achieved the crucial first step of placing the subject on the agenda of serious political discussion at the highest level. Over the next two years he continued to educate himself about Zionism and to give Weizmann quiet encouragement, advice, and (within the limits imposed by Cabinet secrecy) information that the Zionists needed in order to advance their cause in influential quarters so as to be ready for the day of decision whenever that might come. Weizmann who, like Samuel, understood the virtue of patience, maintained his Messianic optimism: 'We look to you [he wrote to Samuel on 21 March 1915] and to your historical role which you are playing and will play in the Redemption of Israel.'[37]

Samuel's elimination from the Coalition Cabinet in May 1915 disappointed Weizmann, but they remained in contact, and Samuel's access to Foreign Office dispatches enabled him to monitor events in the Near East on which he occasionally sent Grey unsolicited letters of advice. After Samuel's resumption of Cabinet rank towards the end of the year, Weizmann wrote to him, concerned over news, which he had picked up in Paris, of the opening of the secret talks between British and French representatives that eventually led to the Sykes–Picot Agreement partitioning the Levant between British and French zones. Weizmann said that he had heard that the British Ambassador in Paris, Sir Francis Bertie, had declared that 'as far as he knows, England would view with dissatisfaction any predominance of another great power in Palestine, although may not be inclined to take it for herself'. Weizmann commented: 'I think one can dismiss the rumours about a settlement or agreement concerning Palestine as without foundation.'[38] Samuel responded vaguely: 'I think the conclusion at which you have arrived is probably correct.'[39]

Shortly afterwards, however, he took steps to safeguard the Zionists' position in any Anglo-French arrangement. He discussed the problem with the chief British negotiator, Sir Mark Sykes, and sent him a copy of his Cabinet memorandum. This was Sykes's first introduction to Zionism of which he was to become an enthusiastic proponent. The Sykes–Picot Agreement of May 1916 provided for an international regime, whose nature was undefined, in the greater part of Palestine west of the River Jordan. The area north of a line from Acre to Tiberias was placed in the French zone, and the southern part of the country as far north as Gaza and Hebron was assigned to Britain, as was Transjordan. Sykes wrote to

[37] Weizmann to HS, 21 Mar. 1915, WA.
[38] Weizmann to HS, 19 Dec. 1915, WA.
[39] HS to Weizmann, 20 Dec. 1915, WA.

Samuel suggesting that this scheme, under which Zionism was apparently to be limited to the 'internationalised' central area of the country, should satisfy the Zionists:

I think on the whole that the boundaries as marked are more favourable to the realisation of Zionist aims than if they were wider—By excluding Hebron and the East of the Jordan there is less to discuss with the Moslems, as the Mosque of Omar then becomes the only matter of vital importance to discuss with them, and further does away with any contact with the Bedawi [bedouin], who never cross the river except on business.

I imagine that the principal object of Zionism is the realisation of the ideal of an existing centre of nationality rather than boundaries or extent of territory.[40]

Whatever the merits of the agreement, however, it remained in the realm of diplomatic limbo so long as General Murray's Egyptian Expeditionary Force remained stuck in Sinai.

Although Samuel's position as Home Secretary between January and December 1916 gave him no formal *locus standi* to involve himself in negotiations over the future of the Near East, he continued to keep a close eye on diplomatic developments. At the same time he was drawn, rather unwillingly, into direct responsibility for an unforeseen problem that had a significant bearing on Zionism: the question of recruitment of Russian Jews in England into the Russian army. Partly because of the high fees charged for naturalization,[41] many thousands of Russian immigrants in England, most of whom were Jews, had neglected to apply for British citizenship before the outbreak of the war. Recent arrivals were in any case ineligible. Many immigrants were therefore liable for call-up to the Russian army. Since one of the predominant motives for departure from Russia had been fear of military service, and since the immigrants, many of whom were socialists, were unanimous in their loathing of the Tsarist regime, few could be found who would voluntarily return to Russia to join the colours.

So long as Britain herself did not resort to conscription there was no public pressure for its infliction on Entente nationals in Britain. But sentiment changed after the enactment of compulsory limited service for British citizens in early 1916, and its enforcement on broad sections of the population. The white feather that had been thrust on British non-volunteers and the obloquy that accompanied conscientious objection seemed all the more applicable to a group that had benefited from the advantages of British asylum but now refused to fight either for their country of birth, now Britain's ally, or for their country of refuge in its hour of direst need. The issue blew up into a nasty public row by mid-

---

[40] Sykes to HS, 26 Feb. 1916, ISA 100/2.   [41] See above, p. 91.

1916. In the East End of London tempers flared and relations between Jews and non-Jews were endangered. Within the Jewish community acrimonious arguments broke out over the correct policy to be adopted, and in particular over whether Russian Jews should be recruited to the British army as individuals, or as a distinctive Jewish unit as urged by the Zionists. As minister responsible for aliens, as a Jew, and as one who had championed the notion that Jewish nationalism could be realized in a form that would benefit British strategic interests, Samuel found himself confronted with a potentially embarrassing controversy.

At first, Samuel sought to resolve the issue by supporting a scheme for the voluntary recruitment of Russians in England into the British army. But the immigrants proved singularly reluctant to come forward. In the hope of stimulating more recruits, Samuel announced in Parliament on 29 June that 'it should be intimated' to Russians of military age that 'they will be expected either to offer their services to the British Army or to return to Russia to fulfil their military obligations'. This seemed to raise the spectre of mass deportations to Russia. But when he was asked whether those who refused to enlist would be deported, he replied: 'I do not put it quite so crudely as that.'[42] Samuel's announcement aroused a storm of protest among immigrant groups, particularly those on the left. The Committee of Delegates of the Russian Socialist Groups in London issued a bitter protest: 'We came here counting upon safety—and now it is proposed to carry us forcibly back to Russia from which we escaped, unless we submit to the act of brutality demanding from us that we should enter the British Army.'[43] Samuel nevertheless announced on 11 July that Russians would be required either to serve in the British Army or to return to Russia for military service there. He added that tribunals would be set up which would 'grant exemptions on principles similar to those which apply to British subjects'. When an MP enquired what would be the position of political refugees, he replied: 'I see no reason why they should not serve in our Army.'[44]

Further protests followed Samuel's policy statement. Emile Durkheim, the eminent French-Jewish sociologist, who had persuaded the French Government to refrain from coercive measures against Russian Jews who would not serve in the French Army, prepared a long memorandum which was forwarded to Samuel by Lucien Wolf.[45] Durkheim pointed to

[42] HC Deb. 5 s., vol. 83 (29 June 1916), col. 1084.
[43] 'To the Emigrants from Russia', July 1916, copy in YIVO Institute, New York, Lucien Wolf papers 203.
[44] HC Deb. 5 s., vol. 84 (11 July 1916), cols. 178–9.
[45] A prominent journalist and historian, Wolf had before the war edited the bulletin Darkest Russia which published details of Tsarist oppression. During the war he became a

the discrepancy between British and French policy as well as the damage that coercion might cause to the Allies in American public opinion.[46] The socialist *Herald*, edited by George Lansbury, published a long editorial opposing compulsion and appealing to Samuel 'not to hand over any living soul to Russia, and not to betray a fellow Jew'.[47] The *Manchester Guardian* accused the Government of 'tearing up by the roots the proud British tradition of offering an asylum to the oppressed and the political or religious refugee'.[48]

Joseph King, the radical Liberal MP for Somerset North, attacked the policy in Parliament, and pleaded that Samuel 'not press his idea of deporting them until that threat is made wholly and absolutely necessary'. Samuel undertook to look into proposals for facilitating the naturalization of Russian recruits to the British Army. He voiced doubts about the idea that had been put forward of a separate Jewish unit but nevertheless did not rule it out. And he declared, 'There is no question at the present time of deportation', adding that he was willing to allow an interim period for a further voluntary recruiting campaign before resorting to compulsion.[49]

Further parliamentary protests followed from Charles Trevelyan and from Philip Morrell, who delivered a powerful onslaught pointing out that conscription was not applied to Irishmen or Indians. Morrell's concluding remarks struck Samuel close to the bone:

I have claimed in the past close personal friendship with the right hon. Gentleman. I am under obligations to him. I followed in his footsteps in South Oxfordshire. I do not say one word in any way personally against him. I admire the Jewish race, and I think the right hon. Gentleman has a right to be proud of his race. Therefore I do suggest to him, and I ask him to pause before pursuing a policy which, if he carries it out, will, I think, bring infamy on his name.

Here, then, was yet another civil liberties issue that drove Samuel apart from former colleagues.

Samuel refused to bend. He insisted that while he was 'proud to belong to the Jewish race', he viewed the problem 'with complete impartiality, seeking to do merely my duty as a member of the British Government'.[50] The response disturbed the *Manchester Guardian*: 'Mr Samuel seems to have thought it somehow incumbent on him to display austerity towards

leading spokesman for anti-Zionist elements in the Anglo-Jewish community and in this capacity maintained frequent contact with Samuel. Something of a communal busybody, Wolf strongly favoured the compulsory conscription of the Russian immigrants.

[46] Durkheim memorandum, 14 July 1916, YIVO Institute, New York, Lucien Wolf papers 51 (8)/5461–9.

[47] *Herald*, 15 July 1916.   [48] *Manchester Guardian*, 28 July 1916.

[49] *HC Deb.* 5 s., vol. 84 (24 July 1916), cols. 1413–25.

[50] *HC Deb.* 5 s., vol. 85 (1 Aug. 1916), cols. 168–78.

the Jewish immigrant.'[51] The paper also enquired why, if Russian Jews were forbidden to serve in the navy (which accepted only sons of British-born citizens), they should be forced into the army.[52] On the other hand the *East London Observer* congratulated Samuel on his firmness towards the Russian Jews whom it called 'parasites' and 'uninvited "guests" who have long outstayed their welcome'. The paper warned of the danger of disturbances: 'The misbehaviour of any offensive foreign bounder, or the impertinence of a Whitechapel Jew boy, may light the smouldering fires of native feeling.'[53] The newspaper was generally hostile to Jews, to Liberals, and to the MP for Whitechapel, Sir Stuart Samuel. This was not exactly a quarter from which Herbert Samuel craved praise. To one who still thought of himself as an advanced Liberal and a Zionist it must have been both distasteful and even troubling.

On 14 August Samuel met a deputation of Russian trade unionists who protested that 'in the East End the question of deportation touched them most'. They declared that 'so long as the threat hangs over them they could not consider the question of serving in the British Army'. Samuel told his visitors, 'I have no desire—I never had—to deport anybody to Russia', but he continued:

The only question I have had in mind was, how to meet the growing bitter feeling in the East End of London and elsewhere. . . . The attitude I should like to have seen was the recruiting offices crowded with Russian Jews, who would say, we realize our duty, we know we have been well treated. I should like to have seen the Jews eager to do their duty in the cause of justice and humanity in this war. Nothing of the kind occurred. The Jews stayed at home, and paid not the slightest attention. A small number came, under 700 all told out of 25,000 of military age. Speaking here within these four walls (this is not for general publication), speaking myself as a member of the Jewish race to other members of the Jewish race, you can see what the effect upon public opinion here and throughout the world must necessarily be if this were allowed to go on. The Russian Jew in the East End of London would be regarded . . . as a shirker.[54]

Nevertheless, perhaps affected by the wave of criticism and by a series of meetings with Weizmann and other Jewish leaders, Samuel drew back slightly. He agreed to allow a further period of a few weeks during which an intensive voluntary recruiting campaign would be conducted in the areas of immigrant concentration. In the meantime there would be no official mention of the possibility of deportation. A committee of influential Russian Jews, headed by a banker, Gregory Benenson, undertook to co-operate in the effort. In response to the demand for separate Jewish units,

[51] *Manchester Guardian*, 8 Aug. 1916.   [52] Ibid., 14 Aug. 1916.
[53] *East London Observer*, 5 Aug. 1916.
[54] Record of meeting, 14 Aug. 1916, PRO HO 45/10818/318095/54.

however, Samuel stated that there were 'considerable military difficulties in the way' although he said that 'so far as practicable, arrangements will be made for men wishing to serve together to do so'.[55] In early September the Home Office issued public notices announcing that voluntary enlistment would remain open until 30 September (later extended to 25 October). A liberalized naturalization policy without fee would be enforced for Russians who enlisted in the British Army. The notices, issued in both Yiddish and English, made no reference to the threat of deportation.[56]

The new policy did not yield impressive results. The Benenson committee was slow in launching its pro-recruitment campaign and in the meantime the Russian socialist groups carried on their energetic propaganda against all forms of military service. On 5 September Samuel wrote to Gaster expressing his distress at the 'failure of the Russo-Jewish committee to get started with its propaganda'.[57] Five days later he wrote again to warn: 'If the voluntary recruiting campaign fails, the question of deportation must necessarily arise in a very acute form.'[58] On 21 September Benenson and Weizmann appeared at the Home Office, in response to a summons from Samuel, to explain why they had still not launched their campaign. They said that opposition to recruitment in the East End was so strong that they did not even dare hold meetings or start propaganda 'because they were convinced that, in present circumstances, it would be a failure and would merely result in the destruction of their own influence'. They reported that the only hope of a large number of people coming forward appeared to be a 'compromise' whereby recruits might serve in labour units rather than as combatants.[59] Although Samuel turned down the suggestion of a 'compromise', he indicated, in a Home Office memorandum a few days later, that if a large number of volunteers declared their willingness to serve in non-combatant units, 'it might ultimately be found better to accept them than to proceed with deportations'.[60]

Samuel also received the Russian Zionist Vladimir Jabotinsky, whose efforts to create a 'Jewish Legion' on the side of the Allies had resulted in the formation of the Zion Mule Corps, a Jewish auxiliary unit within

---

[55] HS to Lucien Wolf, 15 Aug. 1916, YIVO Institute, New York, Lucien Wolf papers 39; undated memorandum by Wolf, 'Russian Jews and Military Service', ibid. 51 (8)/5450–9; HS to Wolf, 17 and 22 Aug. 1916, Archive of Board of Deputies of British Jews C/11/2/9; Wolf to HS, 21 Aug. 1916, ibid.; HC Deb. 5 s., vol. 85 (22 Aug. 1916), cols. 2458–9.

[56] Copies in YIVO Institute, New York, Lucien Wolf papers 87/11177–8; and ibid. 203.

[57] HS to Gaster, 5 Sept. 1916, University College, London, Gaster papers.

[58] HS to Gaster, 10 Sept. 1916, ibid.

[59] Minute by HS, 21 Sept. 1916, PRO HO 45/10819/318095/109.

[60] Memorandum by HS, 30 Sept. 1916, PRO HO 45/10819/318096; see also Weizmann to HS, 29 Sept. 1916, ibid.; Weizmann to HS, 3 Oct. 1916, WA.

the British army at Gallipoli. Following the disbandment of that unit, Jabotinsky had renewed pressure on the military authorities to agree to the formation of a Jewish force that would fight with the British, preferably on the Palestine front. Jabotinsky told Samuel that he opposed the idea of labour units 'as derogatory to the Jewish people'. He claimed that 'although there were undoubtedly a number of shirkers among the Russian Jews, there were also a very large number who would be prepared to fight' in a Jewish legion. If such a unit were formed he was 'quite convinced that he could secure the men'. Samuel replied that if a large number of volunteers offered to serve in such a legion 'the offer could no doubt be considered by the Government', but in the meantime what was needed was that Russian Jews should volunteer to serve in ordinary units of the British Army.[61]

Although Benenson, Weizmann, and Jabotinsky did finally embark on a recruitment campaign, the results were embarrassingly meagre. On 26 October Jabotinsky, who had started a daily Yiddish newspaper to further the cause, confessed to Samuel that he had not met 'with any adequate success'.[62] As the Government's self-imposed deadline approached, Samuel began to search for some solution other than deportation to Russia. On 11 October he asked Troup: 'Is it quite clear that deportation orders cannot be made against these men requiring them to proceed to some country other than their own?' Samuel also asked for an official expression of view from the Foreign Office as to the standing in international law of legislation to compel aliens in Britain to serve in the British Army—'not that I favour its adoption [he added], but it will probably be necessary to make a definite statement as to the impracticability of this proposal when the matter comes to be debated in Parliament'.[63] The Foreign Office replied that, although there was no exact precedent, 'if two Allied belligerent States choose to come to an arrangement of the nature proposed with regard to their respective subjects or citizens only, there would be nothing contrary to International Law in such a proceeding'.[64]

In these circumstances a Cabinet Committee was called upon to make recommendations for further action. The committee's conclusions, drafted by Samuel, were circulated to the Cabinet on 3 November. A total of only 700 Russians had voluntarily enlisted or attested their willingness to serve. The committee rejected deportation 'partly because of the objection on grounds of sentiment to sending back a large number of men who came

[61] HS minute, 21 Sept. 1916, ibid.
[62] Jabotinsky to HS, 26 Oct. 1916, PRO HO 45/10819/318095.
[63] HS minutes, 11 Oct. 1916, ibid.
[64] Foreign Office to Home Office, 24 Oct. 1916, PRO HO 45/10819/318095/143.

here as refugees . . . partly on account of the physical difficulties of transport'. The alternative of deportation to a neutral country was rejected since it would contravene international agreements. The committee therefore recommended 'legislation to bring these men within the sphere of the Military Service Acts'. They stated, however, that they were 'inclined to recommend' that those who wished to leave for some other country, such as America, before the legislation came into force should be permitted to do so.[65] On 7 November Asquith reported to the King that this proposal had been approved by the Cabinet the previous day, though he added that he himself had dissented.[66]

A last, ineffectual gasp of the Liberal spirit, Asquith's token gesture was also one of his last actions as Prime Minister. A month later he was out of office, to be replaced as head of a new Coalition Cabinet by Lloyd George. Samuel played no part in the intrigues surrounding the formation of the new government. Whether Asquith fell as a result of a 'palace revolution' (Jenkins's phrase[67]) or because of the 'disillusion of [his] friends' (as suggested by Dr Hazelhurst[68]), Samuel donned neither the cloak of revolution nor the mask of disillusion. It has been suggested that in his *Memoirs* Samuel 'reshaped his chronicle of events in a manner more flattering to himself but less useful to the historian'.[69] But the supposed evidence in support of this allegation collapses on close examination. (See appendix at end of chapter.) Samuel, in fact, remained loyal to Asquith until the end.

On the evening of 7 December, Lloyd George kissed hands on his appointment as Asquith's successor. He gave the King a list of appointments to various offices, but he did not include the Home Office or the Ministry of Munitions, explaining that 'he still hoped he might induce Mr

[65] HS to Cabinet, [3] Nov. 1916, PRO CAB 37/159/8.

[66] Asquith to King George V, 7 Nov. 1916, PRO CAB 41/37/39. Following diplomatic exchanges with Russia, the Military Service (Conventions with Allies) Act was passed in July 1917. Samuel spoke from the opposition front bench in support of the measure (*HC Deb.* 5 s., vol. 92 (15 May 1917), cols. 1559–63). The Act gave Russians of military age in Britain a choice between service in the British Army and return to Russia. The threat of violence arising from the issue was realized in the summer and autumn of 1917 when disturbances broke out in the East End of London and in the Jewish quarter of Leeds (Holmes, *Anti-Semitism in British Society*, 130–6). A few hundred men did return to Russia as a result of the measure. A similar number of Russian Jews in England joined the 38th battalion of the Royal Fusiliers that, together with two other Jewish battalions mainly from Palestine and America, saw active service in 1918 on the Palestine front.

[67] Jenkins, *Asquith*, 421.

[68] Cameron Hazelhurst, 'Asquith as Prime Minister, 1908–1916', *English Historical Review*, 85 (1970), 529.

[69] J. M. McEwen, 'The Struggle for Mastery in Britain: Lloyd George Versus Asquith, December 1916', *Journal of British Studies*, 18/1 (Fall 1978), 131.

Samuel and Mr Montagu to join his Administration'.[70] Samuel was called
to the War Office that same evening and invited by the new Prime
Minister to continue as Home Secretary. Samuel refused the offer, giving
as his reasons that he did not feel confidence in the new administration,
that he felt there should be 'an alternative government if things went
wrong', and that he 'greatly disliked the way the change had come about'.
Samuel's account of the conversation, written immediately afterwards,
concludes: 'We parted on friendly terms.'[71] The next day Samuel went to
see Asquith, told him that his refusal to serve under Lloyd George was
'definite', but added that if Asquith wished him to carry on in office he
would do so. Asquith, according to Samuel's account, said he could not
advise Samuel one way or the other, whereupon Samuel said that in that
case his decision stood.[72] For the next two years, therefore, Samuel sat
with Asquith on the Opposition front bench.

In spite of the rumours current at the time to the effect that Samuel was
anxious somehow to find some way to remain in office, there is no real
evidence that he had any desire to serve under Lloyd George or that he felt
great distress at leaving the Government at this juncture. Beatrice Webb
recalled an encounter with him walking with his children in Hyde Park
immediately after the fall of Asquith. She found him 'quite cheerful about
the situation although the quarrel was bitter'. He told her that 'he had
weighed the two points of view, and decided that Asquith was right, and
that he must stick to him'.[73] Samuel's disdain for what he regarded as the
underhand and ungentlemanly methods by which Lloyd George had
ousted Asquith undoubtedly played a large part in his decision. At the end
of December Samuel went to Brighton for what he described as 'the first
complete holiday I have had for years'. In a letter to his son Godfrey he
wrote : 'I enjoy immensely having no pouches to deal with every day.'[74]
He had held office continuously for eleven years, he was still only 46, and
in the normal course of political events he might look forward to high
office in the future. (In the event, in the whole of his remaining career he
was to hold ministerial office again for little more than a year.) He seems,
indeed, to have welcomed the prospect of a spell in opposition as an
opportunity to read and reflect, to restore his frayed connections with
radical Liberalism, and to prepare a constructive programme of post-war
social reforms.

---

[70] Note by King's private secretary, 7 Dec. 1916, 7.30 p.m., Royal Archives, GV
K1048A/1.
[71] Note by Samuel, 7 Dec. 1916, HLRO HS A/56/8.
[72] Note by Samuel, 8 Dec. 1916, ibid.
[73] Note by F. Singleton of talk with Beatrice Webb, 6 Feb. 1939, HLRO HS A/161.
[74] HS to Godfrey Samuel, 29 Dec. 1916, Godfrey Samuel papers, Cardiff.

Probably with all these objectives in mind, he and Montagu dispatched Wallas to the editor of the *New Statesman* to enquire (according to Beatrice Webb's account) whether the paper would 'become the organ of H.M. opposition'. The Webbs insisted on maintaining the independence of their organ but they agreed to 'consultations' with the Liberal opposition and to the publication of 'communications'. This haughty attitude did not bode well; nor did it lead to a renewal of old intimacies. Later Beatrice commented: 'The only result of this rapprochement was a series of dull articles by Herbert Samuel on Liberal policy. We saw something of [our] old acquaintance during the following spring. But with the rise of the Labour Party to independent life the connection ceased.'[75] Samuel did revive his friendship with Wallas, whose book *The Great Society* he read with admiration.[76] He even attended a meeting, addressed by Wallas, of the Rainbow Circle, with which his links over the previous decade had dwindled almost to zero. But the schism between Samuel and the new radicalism produced by the war was too wide to be papered over. When Samuel rose from the opposition benches in April 1917 to protest against a Home Office ban on the export of the *Nation*, insisting that if such a proposal had been put to him at the Home Office he would 'not have dreamt' of approving it, Ramsay MacDonald interjected: 'Oh, yes, you would!'[77]

Samuel's articles for the *New Statesman* in May and June 1917 reflected the controversies that had surrounded his tenure of the Home Office the previous year. Published as a series entitled 'The War and Liberty', the essays wrestled with the problem of how to reconcile the demands of modern war with the principle of individual liberty. Samuel took the opportunity to defend once again his handling of such matters as press censorship, internment under Regulation 14B, and conscientious objection. But even he seems to have found the exercise tiresome, concluding one of the pieces with a sigh by looking forward to the end of the war and the disappearance of DORA 'into the limbo of forgotten things, to the profound relief of a long-suffering nation'.[78] The articles were later published as a small book, but it received next to no attention. The greater freedom of opposition thus did not enable Samuel to restore his radical credentials. The Asquithians in any case muted their criticisms of the Government for fear of harming the war effort. The chief result of such self-censorship was to make the opposition look feeble and ineffectual.

[75] Entry dated 3 June 1917 and note dated Apr. 1918, BLPES Beatrice Webb diary, 3495.
[76] HS to Wallas, 31 Jan. 1917, BLPES Wallas papers 1/57/7.
[77] *HC Deb.* 5 s., vol. 92 (17 Apr. 1917), cols. 1624–6.
[78] *New Statesman*, 16 June 1917; the other articles appeared on 26 May, 2, 9, 23 and 30 June 1917.

But liberation from official responsibilities had a more significant consequence for Samuel: it led to his deeper immersion in Zionism. On 7 February 1917 he participated in an important meeting at Gaster's home at which Sir Mark Sykes, MP, who had been introduced to Gaster by Samuel the previous year, met Lord Rothschild, Weizmann, and several leading Zionists. The purpose of the meeting was to seek some understanding on the future of Palestine between the Zionists and Sykes, who had emerged as a key figure in the Government's policymaking in the Near East. Sykes insisted that he was attending 'in his private capacity' rather than in his formal position as member of the War Cabinet Secretariat and adviser to the Foreign Office on Middle East affairs.

Gaster and Rothschild opened the discussion by urging the creation of what Rothschild defined as 'a Jewish state in Palestine under the British crown'. Samuel followed. Unlike the other participants (except Sykes) he was aware of the contents of the Sykes–Picot Agreement of the previous year, with its provision for the vaguely defined internationalization of central Palestine, with much of the north of the country assigned to the area of French influence. No doubt with this agreement in mind, he stressed the impracticality of schemes for condominium or internationalization. He also referred to the question of Jewish immigration, suggesting (according to the minutes—which do not purport to be a verbatim record):

What was asked for was full liberty for the Jews of the world to immigrate. It might not be possible to give this unrestricted right until proper arrangements had been made for their reception, otherwise the experiment might break down. The best plan was for the Suzerain government to grant the full right of immigration to all Jews but for the Chartered Company[79] or some other Jewish authority to exercise a right of regulation.

Weizmann emphasized two points: first, 'that the Jews who went to Palestine would go to constitute a Jewish nation and be 100% Jews, not to become Arabs or Druses or Englishmen'; secondly, 'that the Suzerain authority should not put any restriction on Jewish immigration'.

In the course of the discussion Sykes tried to steer the Zionists towards an arrangement that would be compatible with the agreement he had negotiated with Picot. He suggested 'that the Zionists should approach M. Picot . . . and convince the French'. But Samuel and others argued that it was 'the business of the British Government to deal with the French and dispose of their pretensions'. When Sykes turned the conversation towards a consideration of the proposed frontiers of Palestine and suggested

---

[79] The Zionist proposals, which Samuel had helped draft, called for the creation of a Jewish non-profit-making Chartered Company that would develop the country.

boundaries similar to those defined in his secret agreement, the Zionists objected to the exclusion of Galilee, Jerusalem, and other areas from the territory that 'should be put under the authority of the Company'. According to the record Samuel 'was particularly emphatic' in driving home these objections. Towards the end Samuel 'once again emphasized the strategic arguments for a British Palestine'. When the question was raised directly 'whether any pledge had been given about Palestine', Sykes invited Samuel to say 'what had taken place'. Samuel replied 'that he could not reveal what had been done by the Cabinet'. Whereupon Sykes stated that 'with great difficulty the British Government had managed to keep the question of Palestine open'.[80]

In spite of Samuel's reticence and Sykes's half-truth it nevertheless emerged clearly that, if the Zionists were to hope for success, they must secure some form of endorsement of their ambitions from the French. Sokolow was accordingly dispatched to Paris to meet Picot and other French officials and ministers. Samuel kept in close touch with Weizmann over these discussions and also participated in efforts to secure American support for Zionism.[81] After prolonged talks in Paris and a side-visit to Rome to meet Italian and Vatican officials, Sokolow obtained a formal letter from the French Foreign Ministry giving an assurance of French sympathy for Zionism.[82]

While these diplomatic *pourparlers* proceeded, the military position on the Palestine front began to change. In June 1917 Allenby succeeded Murray as commander of the Egyptian Expeditionary Force. The hitherto sluggish offensive against the Turks was now infused with new energy. By 3 November Allenby's army had captured Beersheba. Three days later British forces moved into Gaza. The road to Jerusalem and the heart of Syria now seemed open and Allenby moved swiftly to capitalize on his breakthrough.

Two of the three conditions for a British Cabinet decision in favour of Zionism now seemed close to fulfilment. Formal French acquiescence had been obtained and a British entry to Jerusalem appeared imminent. Only the third condition, unified Jewish backing for Zionism, remained in doubt. By June 1917 the Zionists had built up their support within the Board of Deputies of British Jews sufficiently to stage what amounted to a 'communal revolution'.[83] In a show of strength on 17 June they demonstrated that they could command a majority over their opponents.

[80] Memorandum on meeting, 7 Feb. 1917, ISA 100/99.
[81] See Weizmann to Justice Louis D. Brandeis, 8 Apr. 1917, WA; also HS to Weizmann, 9 and 23 Apr. 1917, ibid.; and Weizmann to C. P. Scott, 26 Apr. 1917, ibid. See also Stein, *Balfour Declaration*, ch. 27.
[82] Jules Cambon to Sokolow, 4 June 1917, in Stein, *Balfour Declaration*, 416–17.
[83] See Cohen, *English Zionists*, 275.

The next day Samuel wrote to Gaster declining a proposal that he should serve as President of the Board.[84] In his place the Board elected his brother Stuart who shared, albeit less emphatically, his sympathy for Zionism.

The support of the recognized representative body of Anglo-Jewry, as well as that of Chief Rabbi J. H. Hertz, Lord Rothschild, and the Samuels, gave Zionism a powerful impetus. But the anti-Zionists in Anglo-Jewry still included many of the old élite. Of these the one closest to the centre of power at this time was Edwin Montagu. Unlike his cousin, Montagu was fundamentally estranged from Judaism and as passionate an enemy of Zionism as Samuel was its advocate. In August 1916 he had written to Grey's Private Secretary, Eric Drummond:

It seems to me that Jews have got to consider whether they regard themselves as members of a religion or of a race. . . . For myself, I have long made the choice. I view with horror the aspiration for national entity. . . . I regard with perfect equanimity whatever treatment the Jews receive in Russia. I am convinced that the treatment meted out to Jews in Russia will be no worse or no better than the Russian degree of general civilization . . . Could anything be more disastrous than for Jewish Englishmen and Jewish Americans to be bracketed with the Jewish Russians, sharing the same verdict for their part in this war? . . . Jewish Nationalism . . . is to my mind horrible and unpatriotic. . . . I implore the Foreign Office . . . to discountenance this pro-German anti-civilization national tendency on the part of the Jews.[85]

In December 1916 Montagu, like Samuel, had refused office under Lloyd George, but the following summer he succumbed to temptation and agreed to serve as Secretary of State for India. Asquith had been a virtual father-figure for Montagu and the betrayal of his former leader caused him no less anguish than his rebellion against his father. Soon after his acceptance of office Montagu wrote Samuel an awkwardly phrased letter attempting to justify his conduct.[86] The cousins had never been close. Although there was no decisive estrangement, their political paths, which had run along parallel lines for the previous decade, now diverged.

Against this background, Montagu, in August 1917, circulated a Cabinet paper which, by its very title, must have astounded its recipients as much as had Samuel's pro-Zionist memorandum of March 1915. Under the headline 'The Anti-Semitism of the Present Government', Montagu erupted into a furious denunciation of Zionism which he denounced as 'a mischievous political creed untenable by any patriotic citizen of the United Kingdom'. He insisted 'that there is not a Jewish nation', asserted that British Government support for Zionism would make 'aliens and foreigners by implication, if not at once by law, of all

[84] HS to Gaster, 18 June 1917, University College, London, Gaster papers.
[85] Montagu to Drummond, 3 Aug. 1916, PRO FO 800/99.
[86] Montagu to HS, 27 July 1917, HLRO HS A/155/V/3.

their Jewish fellow-citizens', and denied 'that Palestine is to-day associated with the Jews or properly to be regarded as a fit place for them to live in'.

This angry philippic by the only Jew in the Cabinet did not halt the movement towards British support for Zionism. The Foreign Office felt that a pro-Zionist declaration might help sway Jewish opinion in Russia and America towards Britain and in favour of the war effort. At the back of politicians' and officials' minds was also the thought that, once Allenby's forces entered Palestine, a British-promoted Zionism might be an effective barrier against French ambitions. In view of Montagu's bitter protest, it was decided to invite a number of 'representative Jewish leaders' to present their views to the Cabinet. Apart from Montagu nine were polled: six (the Chief Rabbi, Lord Rothschild, Herbert and Stuart Samuel, Weizmann, and Sokolow) submitted pro-Zionist replies, while three (Sir Philip Magnus, MP, C. G. Montefiore, and Leonard Cohen) wrote in an anti-Zionist sense. The exercise was less a genuine attempt to gauge opinion than a formality designed to assuage Montagu. The positions of most, if not all, the respondents were known before they were asked, and the inquiry was in a sense rigged in order to secure the desired result. This is plain from the inclusion in the list of Sokolow who was not even a British citizen. The replies were printed and circulated as a Cabinet memorandum on 17 October. Samuel's appeared first—appropriately in view of his role in initiating Cabinet-level consideration of Zionism. His statement was a brief endorsement of the draft declaration that had already been prepared in the Cabinet. Weizmann concerted his reply with Samuel.[87]

Two weeks later the Cabinet approved the terms of the single-sentence declaration, embodied by Balfour in a letter to Lord Rothschild dated 2 November 1917:

His Majesty's Government view with favour the establishment in Palestine of a national home for the Jewish people, and will use their best endeavours to facilitate the achievement of this object, it being clearly understood that nothing shall be done which may prejudice the civil and religious rights of existing non-Jewish communities in Palestine, or the rights and political status enjoyed by Jews in any other country.[88]

Every word and nuance of this sentence was to be quoted, misquoted, chopped, and chewed by rival nationalist politicians and their champions over the next three decades. Issued primarily as a diplomatic expedient at the height of the war, it came to be regarded by some as 'one of the greatest mistakes in our imperial history', at any rate when 'measured by

[87] Weizmann to HS, 10 Oct. 1917, WA; Cabinet memorandum, 'The Zionist Movement', 17 Oct. 1917, PRO CAB 21/58.
[88] Facsimile, frontispiece to Stein, *Balfour Declaration*; original in BL Add. MS 41178.

British interests alone'.[89] Samuel, who, after Weizmann, probably had the greatest share in its paternity, would never have agreed with that judgement. He was to spend five of the next seven years as the person primarily responsible for attempting to reconcile the declaration with British interests.

The immediate reaction to the publication of the Balfour Declaration on 9 November was an immense outpouring of joy among Jews and a wave of gratitude towards the British Government. The Zionists organized a 'great thanksgiving meeting' at the London Opera House. The theatre was packed and an overflow crowd had to be accommodated in the Kingsway Theatre. Witnesses concurred that Samuel's was the most remarkable utterance among the many speeches. The *Jewish Chronicle* declared that 'those who have heard him on other occasions were astonished at the warmth and the energy, the eloquence and the fire, which he put into his speech'. What rendered its reception the more impressive was that Samuel did not disguise the difficulties that confronted the Zionists. He stressed three conditions for success in Palestine. First, 'there must be full, just recognition of the rights of the Arabs who constitute a majority of the population of that country.' Secondly, 'there must be a reverent respect for the Christian and Mohammedan Holy Places which in all eventualities should always remain in the control and charge of representatives of those faiths.' Thirdly, there should be no attempt to establish any political control over Jews in the Diaspora.

Samuel concluded with an emotional, almost visionary expression of what he saw as the fundamental purpose and justification of the Government's pronouncement:

I see in my mind's eye those millions in eastern Europe, all through the centuries, crowded, cramped, proscribed, bent with oppression, suffering all the miseries of active minds, denied scope, of talent not allowed to speak, of genius that cannot act. I see them enduring, suffering everything, sacrificing everything in order to keep alight the flame of which they knew themselves to be the lamp, to keep alive the idea of which they knew themselves to be the body; their eyes always set upon one distant point, always believing that somehow, some day, the ancient greatness would be restored; always saying when they met their families on the Passover night, 'Next Year in Jerusalem'. Year after year, generation after generation, century succeeding century, till the time that has elapsed is counted in thousands of years, still they said, 'Next Year in Jerusalem'. If that cherished vision is at last to be realized, if on the Hills of Zion a Jewish civilisation is restored with something of its old intellectual and moral force, then among those left in other countries of the world I can see growing a new confidence and a new greatness. There will be a fresh light in those eyes, those bent

[89] Elizabeth Monroe, *Britain's Moment in the Middle East 1914–1956* (London, 1965), 43.

backs will at last stand erect, there will be greater dignity in the Jew throughout the world. (Cheers) That is why we meet today to thank the British Government, our own Government (Cheers), that has made all this possible, that we shall be able to say, not as a pious and distant wish but as a near and confident hope, 'Next Year in Jerusalem'. (Loud and prolonged cheers)[90]

Samuel spoke the final words in the original Hebrew. His wife, in a letter to their eldest son, Edwin, who was on his way to Egypt to join Allenby's army as a junior officer, described the effect of the final words as 'wonderful'. Samuel, who did not normally blow his own trumpet, wrote to his son: 'An inspiring meeting to speak to, and they say I made the best speech of my life—which, however, is not much praise of it.'[91]

Beatrice Samuel joked that the Hebrew words might not pass the military censor. She need not have worried. Two days later, from his camp in southern Palestine, Allenby wrote to Samuel promising to look out for Edwin, and adding: 'At present, I have somewhat overrun the limits of Transport & supply, but I hope soon to get going again. My right is 2,800 ft. up in the mountains, close to Jerusalem. My left is on the sea shore, N. of Jaffa.'[92] Within the next week the Turkish garrison in Jerusalem fled and Allenby entered the city in triumph, inaugurating British rule in Palestine. The news reached London on the first day of the Jewish festival of Hanukkah. Samuel telephoned his wife from the House of Commons to tell her, and spoke of going to synagogue 'in honour of the historic event'.[93] On 16 December Samuel wrote to his son, by then in Egypt: 'The fall—or rather the liberation—of Jerusalem has caused much emotion in this country. I have received dithyrambs from all sorts of people, mostly strangers.'[94] The presence of his son on the intelligence staff of the conquering army imbued the event with a special significance for Samuel, whose personal fate was soon to become closely interwoven with that of the holy city.

APPENDIX

J. M. McEwen has questioned the contemporaneity of notes written by Samuel during the crisis of December 1916. He argues: 'From internal evidence it seems clear that Samuel's diary entries for 4 and 5 Dec. 1916 were written after those of 6, 7, and 8 Dec. This hides the fact that early in the crisis Samuel was keen to continue in office

[90] *Jewish Chronicle*, 7 Dec. 1917.
[91] BS to ES, 1[?] Dec. 1917, ISA 103/11 (671/5); HS to ES, 9 Dec. 1917, ISA 100/43; see also Weizmann to J. Kann, 6 Dec. 1917, WA.
[92] Allenby to HS, 4 Dec. 1917, ISA 100/3.
[93] BS to ES, 11 Dec. 1917, ISA 103/11 (617/5).
[94] HS to ES, 16 Dec. 1917, ISA 100/43.

under Lloyd George but could not sever himself from Asquith and the other Liberal ministers.'[95] Five items of evidence are offered to buttress this hypothesis:[96] (1) An alleged 'difference in style between his [Samuel's] diary entries for 4 and 5 December . . . and the entries for the 6th and 7th'. Samuel did not, in fact, keep a 'diary' at this period; he did, however, often keep notes on important events, and the style of those for 4 and 5 December 1916 is no different from that of the notes for 6 and 7 December—nor, indeed, from that of the many other such notes preserved among his papers. (2) McEwen points out that in the published version (on p. 121 of Samuel's *Memoirs*) of one of these notes, Samuel appears to write that Carson brought a letter to Liberal ministers gathered at Downing Street, whereas in fact the postman was Curzon. Such an error, McEwen maintains, would be unlikely in a contemporary note. But in reality the error was one of transcription; the original handwritten note (evidently not consulted by McEwen) refers correctly to Curzon.[97] (3) McEwen points out a discrepancy between Samuel's account of the meeting of Liberal ministers on 6 December and that of Crewe; but this might place in doubt Crewe's accuracy rather than Samuel's; indeed, Crewe's account has been questioned on quite separate grounds;[98] moreover, the discrepancy between the two accounts in any case refers only to the attitude of Montagu and not to that of Samuel himself. McEwen adds under this head that Josiah Wedgwood did not include Samuel among ministers believed to be loyal to Asquith in a memorandum he wrote at the time. But Wedgwood was not a first-hand participant in these events; he was at most on the outer margin. His opinion is useful at best as evidence of rumours that were flying around at the time. (4) Various newspapers suggested that Samuel and Montagu would break ranks and serve under Lloyd George. But this is not in itself conclusive or even persuasive evidence of Samuel's attitude; disinformation was rife, and Northcliffe and Max Aitken in particular were planting stories in the Lloyd George interest. The newspaper stories were indignantly denied by Samuel directly to Asquith on 6 December. Of course, he may have been lying. But if he were somehow trying to wriggle out of his union with Asquith, the emphatic denial would have been a dangerous and pointless manœuvre. (5) Cecil Harmsworth is reported by McEwen to have written in his diary that when Northcliffe visited Lloyd George at the War Office on 2 December 'he saw the two clever Hebrews—Samuel and Montagu, both of whom owe their political fortunes to Asquith—already there staking out claims'.·But if he wrote this, Harmsworth must have misunderstood Northcliffe: Montagu was indeed at the War Office on that day; but the other 'Hebrew' there was not Samuel but Reading (who also owed his political fortune to Asquith).[99] Finally, if Samuel was so keen to exaggerate his loyalty to Asquith, why did he refuse the strong entreaty of Margot Asquith in 1945 that he include in his *Memoirs* her recollection that during the crisis her husband had said: 'Herbert Samuel is a loyal fellow, & a true friend. He never makes a bad speech,

---

[95] McEwen, 'Struggle for Mastery', 131.

[96] Professor McEwen has kindly amplified on the matter in a letter to the author dated 9 May 1989 in which he presents the five items of evidence in support of his view.

[97] Compare the original note, 5 Dec. 1916, HLRO HS A/56/1, with the erroneous transcription in Samuel, *Memoirs*, 121.

[98] See A. J. P. Taylor, *Beaverbrook* (Harmondsworth, 1974), 165.

[99] See Jenkins, *Asquith*, 432–4.

& tho' he enjoys his present position as Home Secretary, & Lloyd George is certain to make a personal appeal to him to remain in an office where he is doing fine work, he will refuse to change his allegiance. He will stick to me.'?[100] True, Margot herself was not above improving the shining hour. But if Samuel were so anxious to demonstrate his constancy surely he would not have demurred at her desire that he publish the statement.

[100] Margot Asquith to HS, 19 Nov. 1942, HLRO HS A/56/4a; note by HS, 18 Feb. 1945, HLRO HS A/56/5.

9

High Commissioner

===

Ah, yes, we're all brothers now—all Cains and Abels.
(Douglas Jerrold)

RUMOURS THAT Samuel might be appointed Governor of a British-ruled Palestine began to circulate within a few weeks of the Balfour Declaration. On 8 February 1918 the French-Jewish anti-Zionist Sylvain Lévi submitted a memorandum to the French Foreign Ministry complaining that the 'ambitious' Samuel was being tempted by the Zionists with the prospect of becoming 'His Britannic Majesty's first proconsul in the Zionist State'.[1] Samuel himself wrote to his son Edwin in June: 'I see how great a privilege it would be to help to build up again the old Palestine.' But he evidently felt torn between the attraction of Zionism and the possibility that he might return to office in Britain: 'Should I be justified in withdrawing such experience and judgment as I may possess from the sphere of British political action in order to devote myself to sharing in the re-creation of Palestine? I don't know. It depends upon the conditions here and the conditions there at the end of the war, and upon the part which I may be asked to play in the one or the other.'[2] Circumstances ultimately resolved the dilemma for Samuel as, in the course of 1918 and 1919, he was squeezed out of an effective role in British politics.

Samuel's first year on the Opposition front bench had perhaps advanced his standing within the disoriented ranks of Asquith's supporters, but he remained without a personal following in parliament or in the country. His parliamentary activity had been devoted mainly to the time-consuming chairmanship of a Select Committee on National Expenditure. He spoke in Parliament frequently, but his selection of causes was perhaps misjudged. At a time when the nation was in the final agonies of a life-and-death struggle, Samuel's espousal of a bill that called for raising of the age of consent to 17 did not win him many admirers as the man of the hour. In November 1917 there was some discussion in senior Conservative circles of the appointment of Samuel or Runciman as Air Minister—'supposing

[1] Lévi memorandum, 8 Feb. 1918, quoted in Vital, *Zionism: The Crucial Phase*, 347.
[2] HS to ES, 9 June 1918, ISA 100/44.

they could be detached from Asquith'.[3] The idea won little favour, saving both men from a potentially embarrassing choice. In January 1918 Samuel heard a rumour that he might be asked to take over again as Home Secretary. Unlike Montagu the previous summer, he was not anxious to return to office. But he no longer ruled it out a priori. While expressing doubt about the authenticity of the rumour, he wrote to his wife that if it were true 'the situation would be rather awkward—more difficult than it was a year ago. I don't know what Asquith's attitude would be now on such a point. It might be made, perhaps, the occasion for reconciliation all round.'[4] (The previous May Asquith himself had momentarily considered, but then rejected, the possibility of accepting the Lord Chancellorship.) Again, however, Samuel's loyalty to Asquith was not subjected to the test of an offer from Lloyd George.

In the spring of 1918 the Opposition acquired a little more bite as it moved to a more aggressive stance in Parliament. Asquith appointed Samuel chairman of a committee of ex-ministers and MPs charged with drawing up a Liberal social and economic programme for the post-war period. The plans were drawn up with an eye on the forthcoming election, expected in the autumn, and on the more radical proposals being advanced by the Labour Party. The task seemed to revive Samuel's early radical instincts:

The one thing most worth doing in politics [he wrote to his son Edwin in October] is to try to raise the standards of life of the mass of people at the bottom of our social system, in other words Social Reform. The more I consider things the more I am ashamed of the wretched condition in which the majority of the people have to live in the circumstances imposed upon them by our civilization—save the mark! There are many other things of importance—but that is, in normal times, the most urgent; and statesmen and political systems ought to be judged primarily in relation to that.[5]

In Parliament Samuel delivered a number of effective speeches that established his position as Asquith's most effective lieutenant in the Commons. Bernard Shaw wrote to Charles Trevelyan in February 1918:

I told Samuel last November that he would be Prime Minister; and as you see, he is very sensibly taking on the work of criticism and questioning and so forth that means 'You say that there is no one in the world but Lloyd George and Asquith: if one goes out the other must come in. Well, what do you think of ME?' There you see the practical and really modest Jew as distinguished from the proud and unpractical Englishman who, conscious of his merits, expects the world to recognize it without prompting. . . . If you feel equal to a deliberate assumption of responsibility it is clear

[3] John Baird to Bonar Law, 18 Nov. 1917; Baird to Curzon, [18?] Nov. 1917, HLRO Bonar Law papers 82/6/8.
[4] HS to BS, 9 Jan. 1918, HLRO HS A/157/904.
[5] HS to ES, 8 Oct. 1918, ISA 100/44.

to me that you and Samuel can very soon become the alternative nucleus to the George gang and the Asquith ruin.[6]

But Shaw's erratic political judgement did not reflect general political opinion which tended to view Samuel as an energetic and reliable work-horse rather than as a captain of men.

Samuel did succeed in repairing his relations with two groups from whom he had become estranged. The first was the Irish nationalists who had attacked him so bitterly after the Easter Rising. In the spring of 1918 the Government secured the passage of a bill (never implemented) enabling it to conscript Irishmen. Samuel joined the Irish MPs in opposing the measure. As a result he was reconciled with Dillon and Healy. 'You remember the bitterness of Healy's attacks on me?' he wrote to his wife: 'We are now bosom friends.'[7] The second group with whom he mended his fences was the suffragette movement from which in earlier days he had suffered much abuse. Like many Liberals, including many radicals, he had resisted women's suffrage before 1914 on the ground that the time was not ripe. The part played by women in the war effort changed many opinions including Samuel's. The change was enacted, with only a small rearguard opposition, in June 1918. Some distinctions between men and women remained, however, among them the exclusion of women from Parliament. In October 1918 Samuel introduced a resolution in the Commons urging that women should be made eligible to serve as MPs.[8] The vote on the motion was 274 in favour and only 25 opposed. A bill was introduced almost immediately and passed through all its stages easily. It received the Royal Assent on 21 November 1918—in time for women to stand for the first time as candidates in a general election the following month.

The general election of December 1918, the first for eight years, took place in the exhausted euphoria of victory. The Liberals were split between the followers of Asquith and the Coalition supporters of Lloyd George who were issued with the famous 'coupon' (a letter of support signed by Lloyd George and Bonar Law). Samuel was not favoured with a 'coupon'. Although some Unionists in Cleveland protested, the local party put up a candidate, duly 'couponed', against Samuel. The 'Squiffite' Liberals had held exploratory conversations with the Labour Party in October with a view to some electoral arrangement. The Liberal Chief Whip, J. W. Gulland, met Arthur Henderson to try to secure the with-

[6] Shaw to Trevelyan, 28 Feb. 1918, in Dan H. Laurence (ed.), *Bernard Shaw: Collected Letters*, iii, 1911–1925 (New York, 1985), 529–31.

[7] HS to BS, 4 Apr. 1918, HLRO HS A/157/911; see also HS to BS, 30 July 1918, HLRO HS A/157/934.

[8] *HC Deb.* 5 s., vol. 110 (23 Oct. 1918), cols. 813–22.

drawal of Labour candidates standing against former Liberal ministers such as Samuel and Runciman.[9] But at a conference in November Labour resolved on complete independence of both wings of its former Liberal ally. As a result, Samuel found himself confronted, for the first time in Cleveland, with a three-cornered contest.

The Coalition Conservative candidate, Sir Park Goff, a barrister, was a stranger to the constituency, though he enjoyed the support of Sir Alfred Pease whose influence was diminished but whose name still counted for something in the district. Horatio Bottomley's *John Bull* once again campaigned against Samuel, backing the Conservative candidate. Goff also enjoyed the support of Brigadier-General Henry Page Croft's nationalist and anti-Semitic National Party. The Labour candidate, Harry Dack, an ironstone miner and Primitive Methodist, had succeeded Samuel's old ally Joseph Toyn as President of the Cleveland Miners' and Quarrymen's Association in 1911. Toyn's support had been crucial in the past in securing the miners' vote for the Liberals. Now that their own President was standing, their former loyalty to Samuel was strained beyond its limits. On the other hand, Samuel had carefully tended the constituency throughout the war, and he retained a strong personal following as well as the backing of the *North-Eastern Daily Gazette*.

The election took place on a transformed register and in constituencies whose boundaries had been redrawn. As a result of the enfranchisement of women and of virtually universal manhood suffrage as well as of redistribution, the Cleveland electorate had grown from about 14,000 to nearly 37,000, of whom a third were women. Earlier in the year Samuel had been quite sanguine about his chances since, on the face of things, the redistribution seemed likely to favour the Liberals in Cleveland. The constituency had been shorn of the agricultural areas around Stokesley, Ayton, and Yarm, while other areas had been added, most notably the South Bank and Grangetown districts of Middlesbrough, densely populated industrial neighbourhoods with about 9,000 working-class voters.[10] But this favourable prognosis failed to reckon with the impact of a Labour candidate. By the end of October he was less optimistic: 'A three-cornered fight, in these conditions, will be exhilarating [he wrote to Edwin Samuel]. I like being put on my mettle. But the consequence may be, of course, that I shall lose my seat, which might set me free, at all events for a time, for other things.'[11]

[9] Memorandum by Gulland, 9 Oct. 1918, HLRO HS A/63/5.
[10] See HS to BS, 10 Jan. 1918, HLRO HS A/157/905; see also HS to CS, 4 Aug. 1918, HLRO HS A/156/558.
[11] HS to ES, 27/9 Oct. 1918, ISA 100/44.

The contest in Cleveland developed almost into a competition as to who would offer greater support to Lloyd George. Samuel adopted the slightly curious position of announcing at least qualified support for the Coalition:

The present Government [he declared] is a combination of parties. Mr Lloyd George, who is its head, wishes to continue for the settlement following the war the union of parties which happily prevailed during the war. He wishes to use that union in order to pass, by common agreement, a number of bills for the benefit of the people. In this I think he is right. If I am returned to Parliament I should support him in that policy.[12]

Samuel's equivocal attitude was no doubt dictated by considerations of electoral prudence. But it had a genuine basis of admiration for Lloyd George's programme of social reform. 'It is what I have been eager for all my life', he wrote to his eldest son.[13] The Labour candidate announced that 'he had always voted in favour of retaining Labour in the Cabinet and he would have continued to do so as long as the Coalition Government remained in office, and no general election was declared'.[14] Meanwhile Goff eschewed any party label, referring to himself as 'Official Coalition Candidate', and avowing himself 'a strong and loyal supporter of Mr Lloyd George and the Coalition Government'. He pronounced the Prime Minister 'the greatest leader in the world'.[15]

The general level of political discourse in the 1918 election was, by common consent, not high, but in Cleveland it descended to a nadir of demagogy. Goff fed the appetite for revenge by denouncing the ex-Kaiser as 'beyond the pale of human civilisation' and the 'Huns' as 'a distrusted, despised, dishonoured and detested race'.[16] Whereas the keynote of Goff's campaign was 'Make Germany pay', Samuel's main theme was social reform. Yet even Samuel, who despised the cynicism with which anti-German hysteria was being whipped up and exploited, felt compelled to agree that the deposed Emperor should be brought to justice.[17] The redrawing of the constituency boundary had brought in a significant Irish vote and, in the hope of capturing this, Samuel appealed to Dillon for a message of support.[18] But in spite of their reconciliation, no such message seems to have arrived. The influence of the Irish parliamentary party had in any case sadly declined, as the results of the election in Ireland itself

[12] Quoted in Trevor Wilson, *The Downfall of the Liberal Party 1914–1935* (London, 1968), 181; see also *The Times*, 25 Nov. 1918.
[13] HS to ES, 24 Nov. 1918, ISA 100/44.
[14] *North-Eastern Daily Gazette*, 23 Nov. 1918.
[15] Election leaflet, HLRO HS A/64; *North-Eastern Daily Gazette*, 2 Dec. 1918.
[16] *North-Eastern Daily Gazette*, 26 Nov. 1918.
[17] Ibid., 27 Nov. 1918.
[18] HS to Dillon, 4 Dec. 1918, Trinity College, Dublin, MS 6792/655.

were to demonstrate. A campaign of whispers against Samuel obliged him to issue a series of denials of rumours on the Irish and other issues: that he had not backed Home Rule wholeheartedly, that he had financial interests in Germany, that he had opposed the stationing of anti-aircraft guns in the constituency, that he was an Austrian, that he had said working-men were not much use after 40, and that he had given a pledge never to run against a Labour candidate.[19] In countering such absurd accusations he was hampered by the great influenza epidemic which led the medical authorities to ban public meetings over much of the constituency for the greater part of the campaign. Polling took place on 14 December, but the count was delayed for a fortnight to allow for the arrival of soldiers' ballots.

The result was a crushing defeat for the Asquithian Liberals, none of whose former ministers was elected. Only 28 independent Liberals were returned as against 136 Coalition Liberals, 339 Coalition Unionists, and 63 Labour members. Asquith himself was humiliatingly defeated in East Fife by a Conservative who did not even hold the 'coupon'. Samuel too was a victim of this catastrophic Liberal rout:

GOFF (Coalition Unionist)	8,701
DACK (Labour)	8,610
SAMUEL (Liberal)	7,081
Majority	91

Before the result was declared Samuel reckoned that he had won a majority in the old Cleveland division where he could still count on his old personal following. He did not feel the same confidence about the newly added districts. A majority of the new Cleveland voters, both those in the additional areas detached from Middlesbrough and the formerly voteless males added to the register by the 1918 Act, probably voted Labour. Cleveland thus fits into a larger pattern of Liberal electoral failure that has been viewed as a consequence of the 'fourth Reform Act' of 1918, which, in addition to enfranchising most women over 30, enlarged the male electorate by one third. Samuel had, of course, been an exponent of manhood suffrage and of working-class representation, although the historians who point to the 'franchise factor' as the murderer of the Liberal Party note that even Samuel, in his *Liberalism*, had suggested the possibility of 'raising the age of citizenship at the same time that the other qualifications are lowered' as a way of reducing the 'dangerous' influence of 'immature' voters.[20] In Parliament in 1917 Samuel opposed reduction

---

[19] *North-Eastern Daily Gazette*, 5, 9, 10, and 11 Dec. 1918.
[20] Matthew, McKibbin, and Kay, 'Franchise Factor', 723–52. These authors are mistaken, however, in implying that Samuel's suggestion was motivated by nervousness of youthful working-class voters alone. On the contrary, he insisted that if the voting age were

of the voting age to 19. On the other hand, he advocated abolition of the Poor Law disqualification, abolition of university seats, and enfranchisement of women in university seats if these were retained. He also joined the High Tory Lord Hugh Cecil and others in opposing a successful amendment to disenfranchise conscientious objectors.[21] In 1927 Samuel again took up with Lloyd George his proposal for raising the voting age.[22]

Even with the franchise reform there can be no doubt that Samuel would have won handsomely had it not been for the intervention of the Labour candidate. The breakdown of the old progressive alliance must therefore be coupled with the advent of the new working-class electorate as the cause of the Conservative victory in Cleveland. Given a Labour candidate, Samuel might reasonably have hoped to win if the 1918 Act had included provision for some form of proportional representation or for the alternative vote. Samuel had, in fact, been one of the leading advocates of the alternative vote in the debates on the bill—he suggested it would help Labour most.[23] In the version of the bill passed by the House of Commons such a provision had been included. But it was knocked out by the House of Lords, reinstated, and finally deleted again by the Commons.[24]

Suddenly, in December 1918, Samuel found himself not only without a seat, but without a leader, and almost without a party, since the Liberal Party in Parliament was on the verge of disintegration and could barely summon the courage to elect a new leader. Eventually Sir Donald Maclean donned the threadbare mantle. Characteristically philosophical in defeat, Samuel wrote to his friend Runciman:

Viewing the matter dispassionately, and making all allowances for defects and blunders, there is no doubt that L.G. has rendered, on balance, very great services to the country. . . . If the present Government does carry out a large policy of social reconstruction, it would be factious to oppose it. . . . But I feel pretty sure of one thing.

raised, the sons of the rich as well as of the poor should be disqualified. See Samuel, *Liberalism*, 242–3.

[21] *HC Deb.* 5 s., vol. 95 (25 and 26 June 1917), cols. 68–9, 287–9; vol. 99 (15 and 21 Nov. 1917), cols. 687–8, 1269 ff.

[22] HS to Lloyd George, 4 Apr. 1927, HLRO Lloyd George papers G/17/9/5.

[23] Under the alternative vote, electors rank-order candidates. If no candidate wins an absolute majority, the bottom candidate is eliminated and his votes redistributed according to the expressed preference—and so on until one candidate achieves an absolute majority. Samuel would not, therefore, have won in Cleveland in 1918 under the alternative vote.

[24] *HC Deb.* 5 s., vol. 92 (23 May 1917), cols. 2341–50; vol. 97 (9 Aug. 1917), cols. 645–50; vol. 99 (22 and 28 Nov. 1917), cols. 1506–14, 2140 ff.; vol. 100 (4 Dec. 1917), cols. 309 ff.; vol. 101 (31 Jan., 5 and 6 Feb. 1918), cols. 1805–11, 2194 ff., 2277 ff. See also D. E. Butler, *The Electoral System in Britain 1918–1951* (Oxford, 1953), 10–11, 38–9.

It is possible that there may be room in our politics, when they return to the normal, for three parties. It is not possible that there will be room for four.[25]

The logical inference was that the Liberals must reunite, and Samuel's kindly remarks about Lloyd George suggest that his mind had now opened to preparedness to serve in the Coalition Government.

Before the result of the election had become known, Churchill had written privately to Lloyd George talking of the possibility that Samuel might be recalled to the Home Office—though Churchill warned that, if Samuel were to be appointed in addition to Montagu and Reading, 'three Jews among only seven Liberal Cabinet ministers might I fear give rise to comment'.[26] But Lloyd George made no such proposal. In a conversation with the Minister of Munitions, Lord Inverforth, a few weeks later, Samuel said he might be interested in some executive post in the ministry. The response was an offer of the post of Controller of Disposal of Surplus Stores (Huts and Hutting Material Section). Inverforth assured Samuel that this was 'a very important Section', but to a man who had been spoken of not so long before as a potential Prime Minister, such an invitation must have seemed like an insult.[27] He also declined an invitation to serve as chairman of a Royal Commission on the functioning of the Workmen's Compensation Act.[28]

He did, however, accept a temporary position as British Special Commissioner in Belgium. In 1917 he had been one of the founders of the Anglo-Belgian Union and, building on his role in the reception of Belgian refugees in 1914 and 1915, had cultivated close relations with Belgian politicians in exile. He had visited Belgium in February 1919 and on his return had written a series of articles for The Times describing the devastation wrought there during the war.[29] As Special Commissioner, Samuel's job was to supervise British aid for relief and industrial reconstruction. The work occupied him from April to July 1919 and he was able to secure the release of credits to help restore the Belgian currency, reduce barriers to Anglo-Belgian trade, and provide British assistance for the rebuilding of Belgian harbours, bridges, and canals.[30] In an atmosphere of renewed Anglo-Belgian amity, his efforts earned him the highest Belgian decoration from King Albert, brother and successor of King Leopold, bête noire of the Congo agitation.

---

[25] HS to Runciman, 9 Jan. 1919, in Samuel, Memoirs, 132–3.
[26] Churchill to Lloyd George, 26 Dec. 1918, HLRO Lloyd George papers F/8/2/49.
[27] Inverforth to HS, 7 Feb. 1919, HLRO HS A/155/V/18.
[28] Edward Shortt to HS, 11 Mar. 1919, HLRO HS A/155/V/19.
[29] The Times, 12, 13, and 14 Mar. 1919.
[30] Report of British Special Commission to Belgium, 31 July 1919, HLRO HS A/62/6.

Upon his return to England in June the question of his employment arose again. Bonar Law proposed his appointment as chairman of a Royal Commission on agriculture—possibly seeing this as a device for neutralizing him politically.[31] But Lloyd George paid no more attention to this than he had to an earlier suggestion from Haldane that Samuel might become President of the Board of Trade.[32] Meanwhile Samuel declined further offers which, if not quite at the level of Controller of Huts, were hardly more dazzling opportunities. These included a request that he serve as chairman of an advisory committee on the Royal Ordinance Factories and an invitation to direct the Government's housing bonds campaign. Samuel's reasons for rejecting these offers were not based on their lowly status. So long as he was kept busy at work that interested him, Samuel cared little about status. Another consideration, however, had come to dominate Samuel's thoughts: Palestine.

Even before his electoral defeat, Samuel had mused on the prospect of moving to Palestine in some governmental capacity. 'There is just a possiblility [he wrote to Edwin Samuel in December 1918]—though not yet a probability—that my destiny may be cast, for some years at least, in Palestine. . . . The more I reflect over Palestinian affairs, the nobler seems to me the task of helping to lay the foundations of the future Common-wealth.'[33] Ever since the Balfour Declaration he had maintained close contact with the Zionists, particularly Weizmann. Frequently when the Zionists encountered official obstacles they turned to Samuel to intercede on their behalf. His connection with Zionism was strengthened by the attachment of Edwin Samuel as liaison officer to the Zionist Commission, headed by Weizmann, that was dispatched to Palestine with Government approval in the spring of 1918. In October Samuel agreed to serve as chairman of a committee to prepare Zionist desiderata for presentation to the Government in advance of the expected Peace Conference. The members included Weizmann and other Zionists as well as non-Zionist Jews and Lord Bryce, a former Cabinet minister and ambassador in Washington. At its first meeting Samuel urged 'that the Chartered Company idea should be given up' and replaced by a 'Jewish Council for Palestine in which the Zionist Organization and the Palestinians themselves should both be represented; its seat to be partly in London and partly there'.[34] The change was adopted and incorporated into the Zionists' proposals.[35]

[31] Bonar Law to Lloyd George, 18 June 1919, HLRO Bonar Law papers 97/4/17; see also Lord Ernle to Lloyd George, 18 June 1919, HLRO Lloyd George papers F/15/8/61.
[32] Thomas Jones to Lloyd George, 11 Apr. 1919, HLRO Lloyd George papers F/23/4/52.
[33] HS to ES, 18 Dec. 1918, ISA 100/44.
[34] HS to ES, 2 Nov. 1918, ISA 100/44.
[35] See HS to ES, 16 Nov. 1918, ISA 100/44.

In January 1919 Samuel crossed to Paris with Weizmann and Israel Sieff to represent the Zionists at the Peace Conference. The ambitious scope of the Zionist programme alarmed the Foreign Office, and as a result Samuel revised the proposals, eliminating the demands for a Jewish governor and for a Jewish majority on the Executive and Legislative Councils.[36] 'Our proposals', he wrote, 'were very well received by the American and the British delegations.'[37] Following the formal appearance of Weizmann with other Jewish representatives before the Supreme Allied Council, Samuel held a celebratory dinner party in his honour in London. When the Peace Conference shortly afterwards decided on the dispatch of a commission of inquiry to the Middle East, Samuel wrote to the Foreign Secretary, Balfour, to convey the anxiety of the Zionists at the consequent delay in settling the future government of Palestine which was still under a British military administration. 'An appearance of indecision at Paris', Samuel warned, 'is likely to create an increasingly unfavourable atmosphere in Palestine.' He suggested that the fate of Palestine should be separated from that of other territories in the region and dealt with immediately.[38] Balfour replied promising to try to exclude Palestine from the purview of the proposed commission.[39] He added:

May I take this opportunity of stating frankly that the position in Palestine is giving me considerable anxiety. Reports are reaching me from unbiassed sources that the Zionists are behaving in a way which is alienating the sympathies of all the other elements of the population. The repercussion is felt here and the effect is a distinct setback to Zionism.[40]

Balfour asked Samuel to warn the Zionist leaders 'to avoid any unauthorised interference in the administration of the country'. Samuel did as requested but he wrote back to Balfour suggesting that there was 'another side to the case'. The Jews of Palestine, he stated, 'feel a sense of grievance that the military administration there usually proceed as though the Declaration of November 1917 had never been made, and think that even an equality of rights as between Jews and Arabs is often withheld'.[41] Samuel saw it as his role to prevent the deteriorating relations between British officials and Jews in Palestine from upsetting the diplomatic negotiations in London

---

[36] Memorandum by Sir Louis Mallett, 30 Jan. 1919, PRO FO 608/98/247; 'Memorandum of the Zionist Organization relating to the Reconstruction of Palestine as the Jewish National Home', Jan. 1919, WA.

[37] HS to ES, 16 Feb. 1919, ISA 100/45.

[38] HS to Balfour, 27 Jan. 1919, PRO FO 800/215.

[39] In view of British and French objections to the proposed inquiry, a purely American body, the King–Crane Commission, was sent to the Middle East, including Palestine. Its report was hostile to Zionism but little attention was paid to its recommendations.

[40] Balfour to HS, 31 Mar. 1919, ISA 100/5.

[41] HS to Balfour, 7 Apr. 1919, PRO FO 800/216.

and Paris. Throughout this period his overriding aim was to cement the Anglo-Zionist alliance and to ensure that Britain would be the sole ruling power in Palestine.

At a meeting of the Palestine Advisory Committee on 10 May 1919, attended by officials from the Foreign and War Offices as well as Weizmann and other Zionists, Samuel sought to reassure both the Zionists and the Government representatives. Referring to the enthusiasm aroused among Jews by the Balfour Declaration, he warned: 'If there were any withdrawal from the position taken in that Declaration it would be regarded by the Jews throughout the world and also by a large number of nations in the Anglo-Saxon countries with profound disappointment and indignation.' At the same time he deprecated 'one or two unauthorised and powerful public statements' that had been made by Zionists, among them a suggestion that the Arabs of Palestine should be removed to Syria to make way for the Jews:

It may be possible that with complete agreement and goodwill a certain proportion of the Arabs may desire to remove to equally good or better land, possibly with some kind of financial inducement. If so, well and good, but any movement of that kind must be absolutely voluntary and conducted without any form of pressure.... There will be the most equitable and sympathetic treatment of the Arab populations of the country. If we were to go to Palestine to oppress other people it would be an unspeakable disgrace.[42]

Meanwhile the political atmosphere in Palestine continued to deteriorate as the British military administration, impressed by the volume of Arab opposition to Zionism, urged the British Government to reverse its pro-Zionist policy.[43] On 31 May the Foreign Office informed Samuel of a report received from the Chief Political Officer of the military administration, Gilbert Clayton, to the effect that the Arabs of Palestine would resist Zionism 'by every means in their power, not excluding armed resistance'. Samuel's proposals were invited 'as to how the present hostility to Zionism in Palestine can be allayed by the administrative authorities on the spot'.[44]

After consulting with Weizmann and Balfour, Samuel sent a lengthy reply suggesting that the primary responsibility for the tension in Palestine lay with the military administration itself:

The attitude of the administrative authorities in Palestine does not appear to be fully in harmony with that of His Majesty's Government. It is now a year and a half since Mr Balfour's Declaration was made. No public pronouncement on the subject of Palestine

[42] Draft minutes of meeting, 10 May 1919, CZA Z4/16009.
[43] Clayton to Foreign Office, 2 May 1919, PRO FO 371/4180.
[44] W. Tyrrell (Foreign Office) to HS, 31 May 1919, ISA 100/5.

has yet been issued, and from the reports which reach us from various quarters, it would seem that the British Administrators in Palestine do not always conduct their relations with the Arabs on the basis that the declaration of November 2nd 1917 embodies the settled lines of policy.

Samuel proposed that the military authorities be informed that the forthcoming League of Nations mandate for Palestine would embody the substance of the Balfour Declaration, that the Arabs would not be despoiled of their land or forced to leave, that there would be no rule of the majority by the minority, that religious liberty would be preserved, and that the French and United States Governments were pledged to Zionism. The population should be told that 'the matter is a *chose jugée*, and that continued agitation could only be to the detriment of the country and would certainly be without result'. In conversations at the Foreign Office he complained that officials such as the Military Governor of Jerusalem, Colonel Ronald Storrs, 'took every opportunity of injuring Zionist interests'. He 'earnestly hoped' for the appointment of officers 'with a better understanding of the intentions of His Majesty's Government', suggesting in particular General Wyndham Deedes, Allenby's former head of intelligence under whom Edwin Samuel had served.[45] Samuel also stressed the importance, in the negotiations with the other powers, of ensuring suitable boundaries for Palestine, and he urged that Transjordan should be included in Palestine.[46]

Samuel's representations aroused controversy in official circles. Curzon, who had never been friendly to Zionism, and who was to take over from Balfour as Foreign Secretary in October 1919, commented, 'To a large extent the Zionists are reaping the harvest which they themselves sowed.'[47] Balfour, on the other hand, advocated compliance with the Zionists' demands.[48] In the end a telegram was dispatched to Palestine along the lines suggested by Samuel, emphasizing that Zionism was a *chose jugée*.[49] About the same time some of the reputedly anti-Zionist senior officials in the military administration were replaced. Storrs, however, was retained in Jerusalem, and Deedes, who was serving as military attaché in Constantinople, remained there at the insistence of Curzon.

Samuel meanwhile agreed to chair another advisory committee dealing with the economic development of Palestine, and of a subcommittee on financial affairs. Among those attending the first meeting of the

[45] Sir Ronald Graham to Curzon, 2 July 1919, PRO FO 371/4181/344.
[46] HS to Foreign Office, 5 June 1919, PRO FO 371/4181/38; see also Weizmann to HS, 2 June 1919 (copy), CZA Z4/15445.
[47] Curzon minute, 3 July 1919, PRO FO 371/4181/347.
[48] Balfour to Curzon, 1 July 1919, PRO FO 371/4181/294; Balfour to Curzon, 1 Aug. 1919, PRO FO 608/99.
[49] Foreign Office to Colonel French, 4 Aug. 1919, PRO FO 371/4181/296.

subcommittee in November 1919 were James de Rothschild and J. M. Keynes.[50] In a report completed in January 1920, the committee recommended that the Anglo-Palestine Bank, the main Zionist financial organ, should be transformed with a view 'to securing in Palestine the position of a central bank . . . which would commend itself to the Government of Palestine as the most suitable repository of funds'. It proposed the creation of 'another set of institutions . . . to make advances to co-operative groups of workmen, in order to enable them to undertake public or private works'. A distinctive Palestinian currency, linked to the Egyptian pound, should be issued by the Government. The currency unit should have 'a Palestinian name' and the subsidiary units 'should also have Palestinian names, historical Hebrew terms being used where practicable'. Finally, the committee urged that 'the decimal system should be adopted as far as possible'.[51]

These discussions led to an invitation to Samuel to visit Palestine in a semi-official capacity to advise on financial affairs. By now it was commonly understood that Samuel would become the first head of a civil administration as soon as the military occupation regime was ended. Before his departure Samuel even wrote to Curzon approving the designation of the post as 'High Commissioner' rather than 'Governor', thus differentiating Palestine, a mandated territory, from a British Crown Colony.[52] In anticipation of his appointment Samuel and his wife were learning Hebrew, and Weizmann sent him a Hebrew Bible by way of encouragement.[53]

Although his mission was formally restricted to financial affairs, Samuel's primary preoccupation throughout the visit, his first to Palestine, was with Arab opposition to Zionism. His concern was heightened by the tense intercommunal relations that he found in Palestine. The problem was not new to him. He had, as we have seen, been one of the first to appreciate that it might develop into the most formidable challenge

[50] Minutes of meeting, 20 Nov. 1919, ISA 100/25b.

[51] Report of committee, 6 Jan. 1920, HLRO HS B/13. Samuel Montagu (Lord Swaythling) had been a lifelong advocate of the decimal system; Herbert Samuel too consistently favoured decimalization of the currency.

[52] HS to Curzon, 7 Jan. 1920, BL India Office Records, MS Eur. F 112/218. Curzon later tried to reduce the title to 'Commissioner' on the ground that 'Palestine is much smaller than Egypt and there is a High Commissioner for Egypt'. But Samuel retorted that Palestine 'looms very large in the eyes of the world'. Lloyd George supported Samuel, and Curzon gave way after discovering that the little free city of Danzig had been allocated a High Commissioner by the League of Nations (Philip Kerr to Lloyd George, 26 May 1920, HLRO Lloyd George papers F/90/1/10; Curzon to HS, 4 June 1920, ISA 100/6). The Arabic title, taken from Mesopotamia, was 'al-mandub al-sami' (see BL India Office Records L/P&S/11/181); the Hebrew version was 'ha-natsiv ha'elyon' (the word 'natsiv' appears in 1 Kgs. 4: 19 and 2 Sam. 8: 6 in the sense of 'officer' or 'political resident').

[53] See HS to BS, 13 Jan. 1920, Dan Samuel papers.

confronting the Zionists. Shortly before his departure for Palestine he received a letter from the Emir Faisal, son of the ruler of the Hejaz, and himself head of the military administration of Syria, in which the Arab potentate repeated his 'firm conviction' that the mutual confidence that had led to a 'perfect understanding' with Weizmann would help prevent any misunderstandings.[54] But Samuel, unlike Weizmann, understood the limited value of such pronouncements; he did not fall into the common Zionist error of believing that agreements with Arab leaders outside Palestine would permanently damp down Arab anti-Zionism within the country.

Samuel was so impressed by the depth of opposition to Zionism which he found in the course of his visit that he even reconsidered his own position. From Jerusalem he wrote to Edwin Samuel, who was now an undergraduate at Balliol College, Oxford:

The more I see of conditions here the more I am confirmed in my original opinion that it would be inadvisable for any Jew to be the first Governor. It would render more difficult, I am inclined to think, and not more easy, the fulfilment of the Zionist programme. Arab Nationalist and Anti-Zionist feeling is a very real thing, and although it is probable that it will die down, perhaps in a comparatively short time, it is strong enough for the time being to cause much embarrassment. With a Jew as Governor, many measures would be viewed with suspicion and would provoke antagonism which would be accepted without much question at the hands of a non-Jewish British Governor. I shall not come to any final conclusion in my own mind until I have had an opportunity of talking the matter over with Dr Weizmann.[55]

Samuel did not hide his concern over Arab–Zionist relations from the Palestinian Jews who immediately reported back to Weizmann, himself en route to Palestine. 'Nothing but bad news all along the line,' Weizmann wrote to his wife from Cairo. 'Samuel—so they assure me—weak, frightened and trembling. The Jews are very disappointed in him. Of course, I can't yet judge for myself, but there is obviously a great deterioration.'[56] Nor was Weizmann much reassured when he met Samuel in Jerusalem a few days later: 'Samuel has achieved something, but very little, very, very little. He is altogether too cautious; he's under the influence of these people [officials of the British military administration], and will need a big shaking up before he understands the real situation.'[57] That the first meeting between Weizmann and Samuel on Palestinian soil should have bred such sour comments was an unpropitious sign of greater disillusionments to come.

[54] Faisal to HS, 10 Dec. 1919, ISA 100/5.
[55] HS to ES, 22 Feb. 1920, ISA 100/46.
[56] Weizmann to Vera Weizmann, 21 Mar. 1920, WA.
[57] Weizmann to Vera Weizmann, 29 Mar. 1920, WA.

In a report to Curzon at the end of his two-month visit to Palestine, Samuel analysed the Arab nationalist movement but nevertheless concluded that it was 'not deep-seated'. He argued that there was 'no evidence of anything in the nature of a widespread and formidable national movement against Zionism'.[58] One reason, perhaps, for the difference between the emphasis of this letter and that of his conversations with Zionists in the Middle East was that he was conscious that the Foreign Secretary was an opponent of Zionism who might turn such a report, if incautiously worded, against the Zionist cause.

Hardly had Samuel left Palestine than a series of Arab anti-Jewish riots broke out in Jerusalem on 4 April 1920 that left 9 dead (5 of them Jews) and 244 wounded (211 Jews). The disturbances led to bitter Zionist accusations that the British authorities in Palestine had condoned or even encouraged the 'pogroms' and had done little to protect the Jews while interfering with their attempts to protect themselves. The question of the future of Palestine, bogged down in Anglo-French disagreement since the armistice, now came to a head. In London pro-Zionists, among them James de Rothschild and C. P. Scott, spoke to Lloyd George, and secured an undertaking that 'the whole matter would be discussed and settled' at the inter-allied conference that was about to convene at San Remo. The Prime Minister also told Scott that Samuel should go to San Remo 'to present the Zionist case'.[59]

Accordingly Samuel, who had stopped in Florence for a holiday on his way home from Palestine, received an urgent summons to join Lloyd George at San Remo. Curzon and Balfour were also present, and Weizmann and Sokolow turned up to lobby on behalf of the Zionists. Lloyd George now took the bit between his teeth and fulfilled his promise to Scott. The French grumbled but were compelled, both by their weakness on the ground in Palestine and by their need for British support elsewhere, to recognize Britain as ruler of Palestine. The conference took this decision in spite of the fact that the League of Nations, under the auspices of which the mandate would be administered, and from which body it theoretically derived authority, was still in an embryonic condition. Moreover, the disposition of occupied enemy territory prior to a peace treaty might be held to be invalid in international law. A treaty with the ghost of the Ottoman regime was signed at Sèvres in August 1920, but the revolution of Mustafa Kemal (Atatürk) prevented its ratification. The Council of the League of Nations finally approved the terms of the mandate only in July 1922, and it did not formally take effect until September 1923. But in the godlike mood of diplomatic creativity *ex*

[58] HS to Curzon, 2 Apr. 1920 (copy), ISA 100/6.
[59] Wilson (ed.), *Diaries of C. P. Scott*, 384–5.

nihilo that inspired the peacemakers, such legal niceties were swept aside. Not only was the mandate assigned to Britain, but the British Government decided that the time had come to dismiss the military administration in Palestine, whose credit had collapsed as a result of the Jerusalem riots. It decided to establish a civilian administration immediately, and Samuel was invited by Lloyd George to assume the supreme authority in the new government. Although he mentioned to Lloyd George his own doubts about the wisdom of appointing a Jew, he had little real hesitation in accepting. Nor did he waver in his decision when Allenby, echoed by Curzon, later urged him to withdraw in favour of a non-Jew.[60]

In spite of his recent differences with Samuel, Weizmann was elated at the news of his appointment: 'A new era is now approaching and much will now depend on ourselves. It is all still like a dream. . . . One chapter has ended in a most dramatic way, and now the construction of the New Palestine begins! Samuel is greatly delighted and has already wired Deedes, offering him the post of Chief of Staff.'[61] Samuel's offer of the second position in the administration, the Civil Secretaryship, to Deedes was one of his first acts after hearing the news.[62] He also offered positions in the government to several English Jews nominated by the Zionist Organization. Some officers of the military administration remained, among them the Senior Judicial Officer, Norman Bentwich, who was connected to Samuel by his marriage to a Franklin. To the chagrin of some Zionists Ronald Storrs was retained as District Commissioner of Jerusalem. In order to curtail the period of uncertainty Samuel was to proceed to Palestine as soon as possible. He was appointed for a period of four years, with the possibility of extension for a fifth, at a salary of £4,000. At his own suggestion he was awarded a knighthood. Storrs had suggested a barony—arguing that 'the survival of the patriarchal-feudal sentiment' in the East rendered a title necessary for a ruler. Samuel said he disapproved of hereditary titles but he asked the Government for a GCB since he had been 'advised by everybody that it is important among orientals that he should have some kind of handle'. He was awarded only a GBE, the lowest-ranking order of knighthood.[63]

Before leaving London Samuel held a series of discussions with Zionist representatives on the policies that he intended to pursue in Palestine. He

[60] HS memorandum on talk with Curzon, 12 May 1920, ISA 100/6; HS to Curzon, 14 May 1920 (two letters of this date), BL India Office Records, MS Eur. F 112/218.

[61] Weizmann to Vera Weizmann, 26 Apr. 1920, WA.

[62] See Bernard Wasserstein, *Wyndham Deedes in Palestine* (Anglo-Israel Association pamphlet, London, 1973), 12–13.

[63] Storrs to HS, 7 May 1920, ISA 100/7; Philip Kerr to Lloyd George, 26 May 1920, HLRO Lloyd George papers F/90/1/10.

agreed that the military administration's prohibition of Jewish immigration and land purchase would be lifted. The Zionist Organization would be given authority to 'frank' immigrants for whom it would take financial responsibility for a period of, say, a year. He accepted Zionist proposals designed to facilitate land transfers and the lease for development by the Zionists of 'public domain and other unoccupied land'. He stressed that such leases could be granted only 'subject to the interests of the present tenants', and he pointed out 'the difficulty of dealing with those interests which would in many cases be based not on legal title but on customary rights'.[64] In addition, Samuel discussed proposals for a large development loan to be raised by the Government from 'the leaders of Jewish finance', the composition of the projected Advisory Council in Palestine, and the functions of the 'Jewish Agency', the representative Jewish body recognized in the draft mandate.[65]

Before leaving England he spent a weekend in Bournemouth with his mother, took her for walks in her bath-chair, and played some rounds of bezique. She agreed that it was his duty to go to Palestine.[66] Clara Samuel died the following November aged 83. Herbert was particularly grieved to find himself overseas at the time of her death. The cynosure of her affections, he had remained close to her throughout the years, never faltering in the regularity of his weekly correspondence; whenever he had moved to a new job, his first act had always been to write her a letter on his new official notepaper. She had taken immense pride in his progress, forecasting that he would one day become Prime Minister. After her death some of the edge seemed to disappear from his ambition—almost as if he felt that it would hardly be worth attaining the premiership if he could no longer look forward to addressing his mother a letter on 10 Downing Street notepaper. She left £38,273, a considerable sum in 1920 values, of which the bulk was shared between her sons Herbert and Gilbert. Apart from a number of small legacies, she also left £300 'for assisting in settlement of Jews in Palestine'.[67] Herbert received her satinwood furniture, which, however, he judged unsuitable for Government House in Jerusalem, and a little Victorian stool-cum-music-box which would begin to play when an unsuspecting person sat on it. This toy had delighted him as a child and continued to afford him amusement into old age.

Samuel travelled to Palestine via Paris and Rome where he called on French, Italian, and Vatican officials and ministers, as well as the Pope,

---

[64] Minutes of meeting, 4 June 1920, WA.
[65] Minutes of meeting of HS and Deedes with Zionist representatives, 16 June 1920, CZA Z4/25078; HS to Weizmann, 20 June 1920, CZA Z4/25016.
[66] HS to BS, 7 and 9 May 1920, HLRO HS A/157/1018, 1019.
[67] Will and probate of Clara Samuel, Somerset House, London.

upon all of whom he impressed his intention to respect the rights of all religions. He arrived off Jaffa on 30 June aboard a British warship, to be greeted by a welcome of royal proportions. As he was rowed to the landing-stage, aeroplanes performed a ceremonial fly-past and naval guns and a shore battery roared alternate salvoes in salute. He stepped ashore in the plumes and white uniform of a British proconsul, wearing a sword. Max Nurock, an Irish-born Zionist who was to be Samuel's private secretary in Palestine, recalled that for the waiting Jewish crowd the episode 'took on a messianic and a vice-regal character'.[68] A symptom of the problems that awaited him was manifest in the form of the ceremony: the Mayor of Jaffa greeted him in English, but the Mayor of the neigh-bouring all-Jewish city of Tel Aviv, Meir Dizengoff, did so in Hebrew in spite of a previous agreement that English would be used throughout 'so as not to raise the delicate question of language'.[69] In view of warnings that Arab nationalists might attempt to assassinate him, he was driven from Jaffa by armoured car to Lydda, and from there by special train to Jerusalem. He was accompanied by Storrs who, unknown to Samuel, carried a Browning automatic 'cocked and ready in case of emergency'.[70]

On his arrival at Jerusalem railway station he heard another address of welcome from the mayor, Ragheb Bey Nashashibi. He then drove to his official residence, the former Kaiserin Augusta Victoria Hospice on the Mount of Olives, to the east of the city. There he was received by the outgoing Chief Administrator, General Sir Louis Bols. The transfer of authority was immediate, but Bols jokingly demanded that Samuel sign a receipt and handed him a ready-made form: 'Received from Major General Sir Louis Bols, one Palestine, complete'. Samuel signed, adding the common commercial escape clause, 'E. & O.E.' ('errors and omissions excepted').[71] During the next few days Samuel entered a round of formal and informal meetings with Muslim, Jewish, and Christian notables, religious dignitaries, and Bedouin chiefs, as well as British officials. The high point came on 7 July with a large assembly in his official residence to which special trains brought dignitaries from all over southern Palestine. Amid much imperial pomp and oriental circumstance, Samuel read out a message from the King.

[68] Undated note by Nurock, ISA 100/7; see also Max Nurock, 'With Samuel on the Mount of Olives', *Jerusalem Post*, 4 Nov. 1960; Y. Yaari-Polenskin, *Sir Herbert Samuel* [Hebrew] (Tel Aviv, 1926), 43–4; Elizabeth L. McQueen, 'A Historic Event in Palestine', *New York Times Current History Magazine*, 14 (July 1921), 583–6.

[69] HS to BS, 3 July 1920, ISA 100/41.

[70] Remarks by Storrs, in Samuel, *Great Britain and Palestine*, 26; see also Sir Ronald Storrs, *Orientations* ('Definitive edition', London, 1943), 336–7.

[71] The document was sold at auction in New York in 1960 for $5,500 (*New York Times*, 11 Feb. 1960; Justin G. Turner to HS, 9 Mar. 1960, ISA 100/35 aleph).

In a speech following the King's message Samuel laid out the main lines of the policy that he intended to pursue. He stressed that there would be equal justice for all religions and persons, that taxation would be made equitable, and that corruption would be suppressed. On the burning questions arising from Zionism he declared that land sales would be resumed subject to restrictions to prevent speculation and to ensure that 'no injustice is suffered by existing cultivators, graziers and owners'. The ports would be opened 'to a limited immigration, its numbers proportioned to the employment and the housing accommodation available in the country'. At the same time he announced an amnesty for most of those who had been imprisoned following the riots of the previous April, and for all political prisoners.[72]

Samuel's installation as High Commissioner aroused immense enthusiasm among Zionists and among many Jews hitherto lukewarm to Zionism who saw in Samuel a Nehemiah leading his people home from exile.[73] Hebrew 'Hymns of redemption' were composed in honour of the first Jewish ruler in the Holy Land since Agrippa II:

Samuel, O Herbert Samuel! With standards and shields the British sent thee to us, Governor of Palestine. To thy brethren thou didst proclaim a royal decree, Appointing our lord and master from the seed of the faithful.
All eyes dwell upon Jerusalem: the sun of Zionism glows with greater splendour And over our brows our banners wave, shielding and sheltering us everywhere.
From Zion shall go forth the Law, from within a nation pure, To kindle the lamp in the House of God.[74]

Carpets were woven bearing Samuel's image. Ingenious designs in which his head was delineated by Hebrew blessings were inscribed in gold ink by expert calligraphers. His picture hung on the walls of Jewish homes, often next to that of Herzl. Expectations raised to almost Messianic heights could not but lead to disenchantment.

Samuel retained in Palestine his reputation for aloofness and *froideur*. One of his senior officials, in a diary entry, presents a chilling portrait of his almost mechanical efficiency whether at work or at play:

Sir Herbert could be extremely frigid as well as extremely human. At his office table and in discussion he was often icily cold and almost repelled those in front of him by the isolation of his manner. . . . The hidden warmth of his character came out when he

---

[72] Text of speech, ISA 100/104.
[73] See Neil Caplan, *Palestine Jewry and the Arab Question* (London, 1978), 66–72.
[74] This hymn was composed by a young Damascene Jew, Nissim Farrah. It was one of several intoned in the Menashe Synagogue, one of the largest in Damascus, when Sir Stuart Samuel visited the city in 1921 and was royally received in the Jewish quarter as brother of the 'Governor of Israel'. The English rendering is by Isaac Abbady and Max Nurock. See memorandum, 'Echoes of Redemption', by Professor Joseph Joel Rivlin, ISA 100/38.

was playing with children. . . . Official dinner parties were rather formal, as His Excellency afforded with meticulous care exactly five minutes to each guest after dinner in the extraordinary, bizarre drawing-room. . . .[75]

A significant instrument of control kept by Sir Herbert was the 'little black book' carried in his waistcoat pocket. An entry was made therein for every important matter on which he wanted an answer, whether it was about a new ordinance being drafted by the Attorney-General, or a promise from the Postmaster-General to connect a settlement to the telephone system or a report from the Director of Health about a measles epidemic in a village. At each interview the famous little black book was brought out and entries were not erased until the High Commissioner had got what he wanted. It was both a bugbear and a delight.[76]

Yet for all his apparent lack of personal warmth, Samuel succeeded in building up, at the outset of his tenure of office in Palestine, a large store of goodwill in all communities in the country.

For the early months of Samuel's administration, his policies seemed blessed by good fortune. A recurrent preoccupation in this period was with the definition of the northern and eastern borders of Palestine which had not yet been fixed. In the north he was immediately presented with a delicate diplomatic problem when the French army, in late July 1920, ruthlessly deposed the Emir Faisal whose enthusiastic but ineffectual supporters had declared him 'King of Syria' the previous March. On 1 August the dethroned monarch sought refuge in Palestine together with his brother Zaid, an entourage of notables, a bodyguard of 17 with rifles, 72 followers with 25 women, 5 motor cars, 1 carriage, and 25 horses. A harried governor of Haifa complained that the retainers were 'round the place and in and out like a swarm of bees, and one never knows how many meals are required for lunch or dinner. . . . *They cannot stay on here indefinitely.*'[77] Samuel received Faisal personally with full honours and, on instructions from London, conveyed a message that the British hoped to be able to reward him in the future.[78] But he did not encourage the uninvited guest to stay for an extended visit. Shortly afterwards Faisal left for Europe.

Faisal's deposition and the assumption of power in Damascus by the French left a power vacuum in Transjordan, previously under the vague

[75] Almost identical scenes left a different impression on a more sympathetic observer. Helen Bentwich, in a letter to her aunt Beatrice Samuel describing the High Commissioner's first large reception in Jerusalem, wrote: 'I was amazed at his readiness in making apt remarks to each in turn, & the fresh way in which he greeted even the very last. Jerusalem was enchanted, one & all' (Helen Bentwich to BS, HLRO HS B/13/11).
[76] Unpublished memoirs of Edward Keith-Roach, Private Papers Collection, Middle East Centre, St Antony's College, Oxford.
[77] Quoted in Storrs, *Orientations*, 431.
[78] See Mary C. Wilson, *King Abdullah, Britain and the Making of Transjordan* (Cambridge, 1987), 43.

authority of Faisal. Under the Anglo-French wartime agreements, Trans-jordan had been assigned to the British sphere of influence, and Samuel was anxious lest the French step into the void created there by the collapse of Faisal's authority. On 7 August he therefore sent a 'personal and private' telegram, marked 'very urgent', to Curzon:

Forgive my addressing personal message to you and Prime Minister. Am deeply convinced that we shall be making grave error of policy if we do not now include Trans-Jordania in Palestine. It will certainly result in anarchy or French control across the border. Either would be disastrous and involve larger garrison here and greater expense. I should never advise Government to embark on military adventure. This is not such. Will Government authorise occupation if there is spontaneous formal and public demand from heads of all tribes and districts concerned?[79]

Samuel's sense of urgency was increased by what appeared to be French encroachments from the north on the zone assigned to the British by the Sykes–Picot agreement.

Curzon raised the issue in a meeting with French ministers the next day. He protested that the French had summoned sheikhs from as far south as Kerak to go to Damascus. He declared that 'if that were the case he must say at once that the British Government were bound to protest and they might have to send up their troops into the threatened districts'. Philippe Berthelot, Secretary-General of the French Foreign Ministry, responded that he 'was quite certain that there was a mistake'. He granted that 'local French officials on the spot might have been guilty of a certain amount of excess of zeal', but he assured Curzon that the French intended to adhere to their wartime agreements.[80] Armed with this French assurance, Curzon instructed Samuel that there must be no immediate inclusion of Trans-jordan in Palestine and that no more than a few political officers, without military escorts, might be sent to Transjordan to prevent the territory's 'relapse into a state of anarchy'.[81]

Samuel, nevertheless, showed many signs of wishing to go beyond these very limited instructions with a view to extending British protection over the disputed area. On 13 August he wrote to his wife, who was still in England: 'A great many sheikhs from across Jordan have come in to see me to urge British occupation as the only means of saving their country from anarchy—picturesque men, many of them in Bedouin dress, bearded and swarthy, clomping across my tiled floor with iron-shod boots. They

[79] HS to Curzon, 7 Aug. 1920, R. Butler and J. P. T. Bury (eds.), *Documents on British Foreign Policy 1919–1939*, 1st ser. xiii (London, 1963), 334.

[80] R. Butler and J. P. T. Bury (eds.), *Documents on British Foreign Policy*, 1st ser. viii (London, 1958), 716 ff.

[81] Curzon to HS, 11 Aug. 1920, in Butler and Bury (eds.), *Documents*, 1st ser. xiii. 337.

are an amiable and courteous people. I love them all!'[82] On 20 August he left Jerusalem with a handful of officers in four cars and crossed over into Transjordan. 'It is an entirely irregular proceeding [he confessed to his wife], my going outside my own jurisdiction into a country which was Faisal's, and is still being administered by the Damascus Government, now under French influence. But it is equally irregular for a government under French influence to be exercising functions in territory which is agreed to be within the British sphere; and of the two irregularities, I prefer mine.' Joined by a small cavalry escort, Samuel proceeded on horseback to es-Salt to which he made a processional entry with the cavalry, a small detachment of Palestine mounted police, a few political officers, and a number of Bedouin and camp-followers. The assembled notables of the area greeted him warmly and unanimously asked for British protection. The following day, Samuel, in full dress uniform, delivered an address, translated sentence by sentence into Arabic, to a crowd of about 600 gathered in the courtyard of a Catholic church. Again he was presented with demands for British administration, except from 'one unknown person who asked for an Emir from the Hedjaz'. 'It was all quite spontaneous', he wrote later.[83] 'I think it will be regarded as rather a striking tribute to the confidence of the people in the British, that I have been able to take over this vast stretch of wild country—roughly 250 miles by 50—by myself with 50 soldiers and 12 policemen.' On the way back to Jerusalem he was serenaded by Bedouin singing anthems celebrating the virtues of the 'Viceroy' of the country.[84]

Without authorization from London, indeed contrary to his instructions from the Foreign Office, Samuel had thus, in what amounted to little more than a weekend picnic trip, quadrupled the area of territory under his administration. Curzon cabled what amounted to a reprimand on 26 August: 'His Majesty's Government have no desire to extend their responsibilities in Arab districts and must insist on strict adherence to the very limited assistance which we can offer to a native administration in Trans-Jordan. . . . There must be no question of setting up any British administration in that area and all that may be done at present is to send a

---

[82] HS to BS, 13 Aug. 1920, ISA 100/41.

[83] Perhaps there was an element of self-delusion in this remark. But there is no reason to doubt the basic accuracy of Samuel's account of the episode. Mary Wilson, the recent historian of these events, although relying on Samuel as her source, refrains altogether from mentioning the Arab requests for British rule. She writes: 'In the confusion and disarray which followed Faysal's expulsion, no one among the inhabitants or the political refugees had sufficient stature or local backing to defy what Samuel had so mildly proposed' (Wilson, *Abdullah*, 47). That is, no doubt, a plausible apologia for the un-nationalist conduct of the inhabitants. But while their speeches may need to be excused, at least before the court of Arab nationalism, it seems over-protective thus to censor them altogether.

[84] HS to BS, 20 Aug. 1920, ISA 100/41.

maximum of four or five political officers with instructions on the lines laid down.'[85] This amounted to an official repudiation of Samuel's attempt to enlarge the British Empire almost single-handed. But he remained convinced that the River Jordan was, as he put it to Curzon, a 'very bad frontier strategically, economically and politically', and he awaited a convenient moment to give effect to this view notwithstanding the Foreign Office's initial rebuff.[86] In the meantime, the area remained in a limbo, with only six British political officers stationed there exercising a strange form of local benevolent dictatorship.[87]

Samuel's opportunity came a few months later. In the autumn of 1920 Faisal's brother Abdullah moved north from the Hejaz with armed men, apparently intending to attack the French in the hope of regaining Syria for the Arabs. Abdullah's activities further soured Anglo-French relations in the Levant and appeared to Samuel to indicate the need for a definitive settlement concerning Transjordan. In early 1921 control of Palestine policy was shifted from the Foreign Office to the Colonial Office, headed by Churchill, who shared not only Samuel's enthusiasm for Zionism but also his imperial zeal. In March 1921 Churchill presided over a conference of British officials in Cairo at which an attempt was made to reach decisions on a number of pressing issues. It was agreed that Faisal would be installed as King of Iraq and Abdullah as ruler of Transjordan. Samuel and Deedes expressed reservations about Abdullah as did T. E. Lawrence, but in the end agreed to the proposal.[88]

The Transjordan settlement had certain strings attached. First, Abdullah, who was to be 'Emir' rather than 'King', was given clearly to understand that he must abjure any attack on the French that might embroil the British in an undesired conflict with their erstwhile allies. Secondly, Transjordan was to be included formally within the area of the League of Nations mandate for Palestine, but with a separate administration subject to the overall supervision of the High Commissioner. Thirdly, the clauses of the mandate that gave effect to the establishment of the Jewish National Home in Palestine were to apply, as hitherto, only to the area west of the Jordan. Following the conference Churchill visited Palestine and stayed with Samuel at Government House. Abdullah was escorted to Jerusalem by Lawrence and inducted into the details of the proposed arrangement which was sweetened by Churchill's promise of a 'stipend' of £5,000.[89] The arrangement, initially contracted for a period of only six

[85] Curzon to HS, 26 Aug. 1920, Butler and Bury (eds.), *Documents*, 1st ser. xiii. 344.

[86] HS to Curzon, 7 Aug. 1920, Butler and Bury (eds.), *Documents*, 1st ser. xiii. 333; see also HS to Lloyd George, 28 Oct. 1920, HLRO Lloyd George papers F/44/8/3.

[87] See Sir Alec Seath Kirkbride, *A Crackle of Thorns: Experiences in the Middle East* (London, 1956), 18–28.

[88] Wilson, *Abdullah*, 48–50.   [89] Ibid. 53.

months, laid the foundation for one of Britain's most enduring Middle East alliances. Abdullah proved a cheerful and compliant client. He abandoned his threats, though not his long-term designs, against Syria. He co-operated with the British Resident who directed the policy of his little emirate. And he proved amenable to friendly approaches and cash gifts from the Zionists. From time to time he volunteered his services as King of Palestine, but such pretensions were discouraged by the British at any rate until 1948. Samuel's expansionist aim was thus achieved but at the price of the exclusion of Transjordan from the Jewish National Home.[90]

The settlement of Palestine's northern borders took a little longer. The main area of difference between the British and the French was in the north-east corner of the country where the British sought to include the headwaters of the Jordan and the Litani in Palestine. The Zionists pressed strongly for such borders on the ground that they were necessary for the success of the ambitious hydroelectric scheme proposed by the Russian Zionist Pinhas Rutenberg whose Palestine Electric Corporation became one of the largest enterprises in Palestine. The Rutenberg scheme was seen as an essential foundation for the economic development of the Jewish National Home. At a meeting with Rutenberg on 24 November 1920 Samuel undertook to do what he could to procure a favourable settlement of the boundary dispute.[91] The result was only a partial success. An Anglo-French Convention, signed in December, excluded the Litani headwaters from Palestine. On the other hand, the agreement provided for a joint commission to delimit the frontier in consultation with 'Zionist engineers' so as to include the source of the Jordan in Palestine. The border, as finally agreed in 1923, incorporated all the Jewish colonies in the area in Palestine. The whole of Lake Huleh and the Sea of Galilee also fell within Palestine.[92] The boundary settlement enabled Rutenberg to proceed with his project. It also ended the period of acute tension between Britain and France over the Near Eastern mandates.

While Samuel's external policy met with substantial results, his efforts

---

[90] This price, regarded as too high by many Zionists, gave rise to the myth that Palestine was 'partitioned' in 1921. In fact, what occurred was a huge addition to the territory of Palestine, not any subtraction. Zionist disappointment at the loss of what they had never been promised and never possessed led to the idea that they had been somehow cheated out of part of their birthright. The legend persists. See e.g. Yitzhak Gil-Har, 'The Separation of Trans-Jordan from Palestine', in Lee I. Levine (ed.), *The Jerusalem Cathedra*, i (Jerusalem, 1981), 284–313; and *Jerusalem Post*, 28 and 30 June 1983. For an authoritative analysis of the question, see A. P. Alsberg, 'The Delimitation of the Eastern Border of Palestine', *Zionism*, 3 (1973), 229–46.

[91] Record of meeting, 24 Nov. 1920, CZA Z4/16010.

[92] Texts of the agreements in Cmd. 1195 (1920) and Cmd. 1910 (1923).

to reduce internal tension in Palestine between Jews and Arabs were less successful.

For the first few months of his administration it seemed as if he had indeed succeeded in his aim of reconciling the Arab majority of the population to the steady development of the Jewish National Home through Jewish immigration and land purchase. The main obstacle during the winter of 1920–1 appeared to be not Arab opposition but Jewish reluctance to provide the Zionists with the financial resources they needed to make a reality of the Jewish National Home. The great development loan that Samuel had envisaged was repeatedly delayed for legal and technical reasons.[93] When those were finally overcome, the awful truth was revealed: the Zionists had been guilty of what amounted almost to a confidence trick in which they had deceived themselves as well as others. The 'leaders of Jewish finance', it turned out, were not at all eager to perform the role assigned to them by Samuel and Weizmann.[94] In July 1920 a Zionist Conference proclaimed the establishment of a 'Palestine Foundation Fund' (Keren Hayesod) of £25,000,000. But when Weizmann visited North America in 1921 and 1923 to raise these funds, he found that contributions amounted to only a small fraction of what had been anticipated. The fund-raising failure had a direct impact on the Zionist enterprise in Palestine. Shortly after his arrival in Palestine Samuel had authorized an immigration schedule of 16,500 for the first year. With immigrants' dependants that would have brought in up to 70,000 immigrants by mid-1921. Yet as early as October 1920 the Zionists' cash resources were so inadequate that they asked for a reduction from 16,500 to a mere 1,000 certificates.[95] Samuel consented, although he expressed disappointment to Weizmann: 'It would be a mistake to attempt to limit the number of Jewish immigrants in the near future to so small a figure as 1,000. There will be a very considerable demand for labour here.'[96]

In early October Samuel convened an Advisory Council consisting of eleven British officials and ten Palestinians (four Muslims, three Christians, three Jews), all nominated by the High Commissioner rather than elected.

---

[93] See the correspondence in PRO FO 371/5139 and 5286; also CO 733/36.

[94] Signs of this had been apparent even earlier. In Oct. 1920 Sir Alfred Mond told Sir Eyre Crowe of the Foreign Office that 'appeals for financial support from Jewish capitalists were meeting with a cold reception because, whilst most of the capitalists are opposed to Zionism, all the advantages are to go to the Zionists in Palestine' (minute by Crowe, 23 Oct. 1920, PRO FO 371/5286/104 (verso)). When the Government of Palestine, following Samuel's departure, finally issued a loan of £4,475,000 in 1927, it did so not by appeal to Jewish financiers but as a normal commercial proposition. Samuel himself bought £400 worth of the issue (HS to ES, 27 Dec. 1927, ISA 100/52).

[95] Moshe Mossek, Palestine Immigration Policy under Sir Herbert Samuel: British, Zionist and Arab Attitudes (London, 1978), 12.

[96] HS to Weizmann, 29 Nov. 1920, CZA Z4/15445.

He told the first meeting that it was 'to be regarded only as a first step in the development of self-governing institutions' and he welcomed the 'greater spirit of harmony among all sections and creeds'.[97] At the end of October Samuel sent the Prime Minister a long private letter inviting him to visit Palestine and reporting on the first three months of his regime:

I find not the slightest difficulty in getting all the different sections to work together. There is a small group of Arab anti-Zionists, whose policy at the moment is to ask for an elected assembly, in the hope that an Arab majority upon it would succeed in preventing the execution of the Zionist provisions in the Mandate, when it comes. But I am convinced that the mass of the population are quite contented.[98]

But not everybody shared Samuel's sunny confidence, and the unexpected concord of his honeymoon period was already beginning to dissipate. 'The truth is', wrote Harry Sacher, an English Zionist resident in Palestine, 'that Samuel has sacrificed much in the hope of getting quiet and cultivating confidence.'[99]

In December 1920 an Arab nationalist congress met at Haifa and issued anti-Zionist resolutions that were dispatched to London and to the League of Nations. Samuel dismissed the meeting's political significance: 'It was attended by about 25 persons. The Societies which they represent are a mere handful and need not be taken seriously in themselves, although undoubtedly they stand for a considerable body of opinion latent in the country, which might at any time be stirred into activity by an aggressive or unsympath[et]ic policy on the part of the Government.'[100] But a certain underlying nervousness was evident in Samuel's reluctance to agree immediately to War Office proposals for a further slimming of the British military garrison in Palestine below the level of 7,200 men to which it had been reduced from 25,000 six months earlier.[101] Churchill's visit to Palestine in March 1921 gave Samuel an opportunity to show the Colonial Secretary the first fruits of his policy of cautious promotion of Zionism and conciliation of the Arabs. Churchill was greatly impressed by what he saw of the Jewish agricultural colonies, but he struck a very different note from Samuel in an encounter with a delegation of Arab nationalists who came to complain about Zionism. Refusing point-blank to consider any change in the Balfour Declaration policy, Churchill declared that it was 'manifestly right'. Moreover, he insisted that Britain

[97] Text of speech, 6 Oct. 1920, CZA Z4/1188.
[98] HS to Lloyd George, HLRO Lloyd George papers F/44/8/3.
[99] 'Extract from letter from Mr H. Sacher', 1 Nov. 1920, CZA Z4/25038.
[100] HS to Curzon, 19 Dec. 1920, BL India Office Records, MS Eur F 112/218; see also resolutions of Third Palestine Arab Congress, Dec. 1920, and 'Political Report for December' by HS, PRO FO 371/6374.
[101] HS to Foreign Office, 27 Dec. 1920, PRO WO 106/204.

had the right to decide the destiny of Palestine because British forces had liberated the country at the cost of 2,000 lives. At the same time he expressed the hope that Zionism would be established by consent, and he promised that Arabs would not be dispossessed.[102]

A month later an explosion of intercommunal violence shattered Samuel's illusions about Arab–Jewish harmony and provoked a painful re-examination of his attitude towards the Jewish National Home, and a consequent shift in British policy in Palestine. The anti-Jewish riots began at Jaffa on 1 May 1921 and spread to neighbouring towns and villages. The disturbances lasted a week and left 47 Jews and 48 Arabs dead, as well as 146 Jews and 73 Arabs wounded. Martial law was declared on 3 May, and British forces used all means at their disposal, including aeroplanes, to quell the outburst. Samuel's instinctive response, however, was to attempt conciliation rather than repression. On 14 May the town crier in Jaffa announced that the Government had decided on a temporary ban on Jewish immigration. The news was acclaimed as a victory by Arabs. Jews reacted with deep indignation to what appeared to them weakness in the face of violence.[103] Although immigration was permitted to resume at a low rate after a few weeks, the episode soured the attitude of Palestinian Jews to Samuel for a long time. Weizmann, who was in New York, counselled restraint to his fellow-Zionists but he too was disturbed and pleaded for a reversal of the decision.[104] Churchill gave Samuel public support but privately he considered the High Commissioner's handling of the crisis weak. *The Times* criticized Samuel's policy in a leader on 14 May: 'The stoppage of Jewish immigration into Palestine after the Jaffa riots is doubtless a temporary measure, but its wisdom is open to serious doubt, and it will need to be supplemented by a stronger assertion than we have yet had of the will and policy of the Palestine Government.' Thus in a matter of days Samuel's apparently glittering success had vanished to be replaced by Arab quasi-revolt, Zionist protests, Colonial Office disapproval, and press criticism.

Samuel was not, in fact, a politician who changed tack with the wind. He tended, once he had made up his mind on an issue, to stick to his opinion stubbornly. In the face of this renewed evidence of fierce Arab antagonism to the Jewish National Home, he did not now abandon his long-standing commitment to Zionism. But if he could be obstinate he was also a realist. He had already come under pressure from the War

[102] Memorandum on meeting, 28 Mar. 1921, PRO AIR 8/37/150.
[103] *Palestine: Disturbances in May 1921: Reports of the Commission of Inquiry with Correspondence Relating Thereto*, Cmd. 1540 (London, 1921); see also Wasserstein, *British in Palestine*, 100 ff.
[104] Weizmann to Zionist Executive, 13 May 1921, WA; Weizmann to Balfour, 15 May 1921, ibid.

Office to reduce the expensive Palestine garrison. He knew that neither the British Government nor public opinion would countenance long-term deployment of large forces in Palestine in order to prop up Zionism. In the budget-cutting mood in Britain at the time, there was strong pressure for a reduction in such commitments. Nor could the Jews in Palestine, barely 10 per cent of the population, effectively defend themselves, even if the British were prepared to arm them and disarm the Arabs. Zionism, therefore, could not be established by force of arms. The condition for its success, at least in the short term, appeared to be, if not Arab consent, at least Arab acquiescence. Samuel's self-delusion of the previous ten months as to the readiness of the Arabs to accept Zionism in return for the benefits of an honest, efficient, uncorrupt, and fair-minded *pax Britannica* now gave way to a much more realistic and pessimistic view of the likely Arab reaction.

On the basis of this sort of analysis, Samuel reformulated his policy. In his first major public pronouncement after the riots, a speech on the King's Birthday on 3 June 1921, he contended that there had been an 'unhappy misunderstanding' of the meaning of the Balfour Declaration. In redefining it, he sought to reassure the Arab majority that their interests would be safeguarded. If any measures were needed to convince the Muslim and Christian population that their rights were 'really safe', such measures would be taken. 'For the British Government [he declared], the trustee under the Mandate for the happiness of the people of Palestine, would never impose on them a policy which that people had reason to think was contrary to their religious, their political, and their economic interests.'[105] A torrent of Zionist outrage burst forth in response to the speech, which was seen as a further concession to violence. Weizmann deprecated the public criticism of the High Commissioner by Zionists and sent him a telegram saying 'Deeply appreciate your position. Please rely on my co-operation.'[106] But when it became clear to him that Samuel's speech foreshadowed an important shift in policy he too protested vigorously—although in private.[107] In letters to Lloyd George and Churchill, Weizmann called Samuel's speech 'timid and apologetic'.[108] Weizmann even considered attempting to secure the replacement of Samuel by General Sir George Macdonogh, a former Director of Military Intelligence and a warm pro-Zionist, but he did not pursue this idea, probably fearful

[105] Text of speech in *Palestine Weekly* (special supplement), 3 June 1921.
[106] Weizmann to HS, 12 June 1921, CZA Z4/305/9.
[107] See Weizmann to HS, 19 July 1921, WA.
[108] Weizmann to Lloyd George, 21 July 1921, HLRO Lloyd George papers F/86/8/2; 'The Situation in Palestine' (memorandum by Weizmann submitted to Churchill), 21 July 1921, PRO CO 733/16/254–76.

of the consequences of any attempt to unseat the Jewish High Commissioner.[109]

Samuel remained convinced, as he told Weizmann, that 'a policy of coercion would be doomed to failure'. He reminded the Zionist leader that 'this failure would not only be due to the moral and physical difficulty of applying it in Palestine, but also to the serious political reaction which it would undoubtedly cause in Great Britain'. He pressed Weizmann to 'enter into relations' with a delegation of Arab nationalists, headed by Musa Kazem Pasha al-Husseini, who travelled to London in July 1921. Samuel, who only a few months earlier had dismissed the importance of the nationalists, now suggested that 'they do undoubtedly represent a large body of opinion in Palestine'. Over-optimistically he opined: 'I think the members of that Delegation desire to arrive at a settlement, and they understand clearly that such a settlement can only be on the basis of the maintenance of the Balfour Declaration.'[110] As Samuel and the British Government were soon to discover, the Delegation understood no such thing. They conceived the primary purpose of their mission as to seek the abrogation of the Balfour Declaration and the nullification of the Jewish National Home.

In a long private letter to Weizmann on 10 August Samuel tried to persuade him of the significance of Arab opposition to Zionism. Recalling his stress on this at the time of his first visit to Palestine in early 1920, he said that, after a year of administration there, his conviction on the point had been greatly strengthened. 'Unless there is careful steering [he continued] it is upon the Arab rock that the Zionist ship may be wrecked.' Rejecting Zionist contentions that the root of the problem was the lack of sympathy of certain British officials in Palestine or that the problem might be solved by taking harsh repressive measures against particular nationalist leaders, Samuel insisted:

It is essential to face the facts of the case. Those facts in my opinion are that a very large number of Arabs, including a large number of the educated classes, have come to believe that Zionism means the overwhelming of themselves and their people by immigrant Jews, with the consequence that in the course of time they will lose not only their political predominance but also their lands and their Holy Places. . . . Now these people will not accept the fate which they think is in store for them without a fight. . . . The Zionist policy is not based upon such stable foundations in Great Britain that it can afford to see those foundations shaken. . . . I am convinced that if on your own

---

[109] See Macdonogh to Weizmann, 4 Aug. 1921, CZA Z4/16055; and record of conversation between Weizmann and Sir John Shuckburgh (Colonial Office), 10 Jan. 1922, CZA Z4/16145.

[110] HS to Weizmann, 1 July 1921, CZA Z4/16035.

shoulders were placed the responsibility of governing Palestine you would come to exactly the same conclusion.[111]

The Colonial Office's discussions with the Arab Delegation continued for several months and were joined on one occasion by Weizmann. Throughout the exchanges the Delegation stuck to its rejection of any accommodation based on the Balfour Declaration policy. By the end of the year the talks had reached an impasse. Samuel therefore moved towards the view that the solution lay not in an agreed compromise but in a settlement imposed from above that would preserve the Government's commitment to the Jewish National Home while giving the Arabs a framework in which to protect their interests. By early 1922 he had worked out with the Colonial Office the outline of a constitution for Palestine. The essential element in this scheme was a legislative council that would include both elected members and unelected officials. The composition of the proposed council was artfully devised to ensure that Arab nationalists would be unable by themselves to command a majority. It was laid down, moreover, that the council could not pass any ordinance which was repugnant to the mandate. Samuel believed, mistakenly, that such constitutional carpentry would provide sufficient safeguards to reconcile the Arab nationalists.

In May 1922 Samuel returned to England for leave after nearly two years' absence. Shortly after his arrival he spoke on Palestine to members of both Houses in a committee room at the House of Commons. Afterwards Edwin Montagu, who had been in the audience, wrote to congratulate him:

You compressed accuracy, skill, knowledge and confidence into a very short space of time. The chorus of approval was universal. As you know, I regarded the Balfour declaration with strong opposition and disapproval, and even today would give anything that it should not have been made in the interests of the British Empire and of our race. But it seems to me that conflict of opinion on the basis of the policy must have ended when the declaration was announced and endorsed and any view held as to its advisability is only of historic interest. It is almost a platitude to say that Great Britain's promises in regard to the East particularly, and indeed elsewhere, ought to be kept and honoured without hesitation, and made as successful as human effort can make them. For these reasons I rejoice in your success yesterday and in your story of progress.[112]

In the course of his visit Samuel also met the Palestine Arab Delegation, Zionist leaders, and other groups interested in Palestine. But he devoted his primary attention to putting the final touches to a policy statement that had been in preparation for several months.

[111] HS to Weizmann, 10 Aug. 1921, CZA Z4/16151.
[112] Montagu to HS, 24 May 1922, ISA 100/9.

The Palestine White Paper of June 1922, though sometimes called the 'Churchill White Paper', was in fact formulated by Samuel, although it was partly based on a Colonial Office draft of the previous November. The document was carefully designed to mollify the Arab nationalists while adhering to the essence of the Balfour Declaration policy. In a passage intended for Arab eyes it explained that the Government had never 'at any time contemplated, as appears to be feared by the Arab Delegation, the disappearance or the subordination of the Arab population, language or culture in Palestine'. On the other hand, the Jews were informed that the Government's understanding of the meaning of the Balfour Declaration and of the Jewish National Home was that they were 'in Palestine as of right and not on sufferance'. On the key issue of Jewish immigration, the White Paper laid down that arrivals must not exceed the economic absorptive capacity of the country. The statement was ambiguous on one central point: the question of whether the mandate might lead to Jewish sovereignty. A proposal some months earlier by Samuel and Deedes that the Zionists should explicitly renounce such an ambition had been vehemently rejected by Weizmann.[113] The White Paper left the question open. It neither prescribed nor precluded the eventual establishment of a Jewish State in Palestine.

On the issue of immigration the White Paper merely provided a formula, 'economic absorptive capacity', for what was already reality even before the May 1921 riots. It had been the Zionists, not Samuel, who had initiated that policy under pressing financial constraints. In January 1922 Samuel wrote to Weizmann reminding him of this, and pointing out that if he had not restricted immigration during the previous few months, the Zionist Organization would once again have had to do so—'and borne the odium itself'. Samuel could not forbear from adding: 'I hope you will appreciate my friendly service.'[114]

Both the Zionists and the Arab Delegation were invited to signify their acceptance of the policy statement. The Zionists did so, albeit à contre-cœur. Weizmann realized that Samuel was the Zionists' last, if not their best, hope: 'he is meek and mild and timid. Still he is, with all that, the best we can have in the circumstances.'[115] The Arab Delegation refused to give its endorsement and a Palestine Arab Congress in Nablus in August 1922 rejected the White Paper outright. Samuel was not alarmed by the rejection, remarking that the congress had 'breathed fire, but not slaughter'.[116]

[113] See Wasserstein, *British in Palestine*, 115.
[114] HS to Weizmann, 20 Jan. 1922, CZA Z4/16146.
[115] Weizmann to David Eder, 3 June 1922, WA.
[116] HS to Godfrey Samuel, 3 Sept. 1922, Godfrey Samuel papers, Cardiff.

Samuel returned to Palestine via Geneva where he visited the head-quarters of the League of Nations and met officials responsible for the mandates. The Palestine mandate itself finally received approval from the League Council in July 1922, thus enabling the Government to proceed with the implementation of the constitutional plans that had been worked out earlier in the year. The Arab nationalists, however, organized a boycott of elections to the legislative council in February 1923. Only 18 per cent of qualified Muslims and 5.5 per cent of Christians voted, as against a turnout of 50 per cent among Jewish voters. After the election six of the elected Arabs withdrew, evoking a preposterous statement from the Government that 'no right of withdrawal after election is admitted'.[117] The boycott proved so effective that the attempt to convene the council had to be abandoned.[118] After this humiliating setback Samuel tried to reconvene a nominated Advisory Council but with a revised membership. Samuel hoped to draw in the leaders of the Arab nationalist movement and other prominent notables, but the nominees either refused to serve or withdrew their acceptances one by one. By the late summer of 1923 the Advisory Council too had collapsed.

In the wake of these successive political fiascos, Samuel's own position began to appear precarious. The resignation of Lloyd George the previous October and the assumption of office by a purely Conservative Government opened the possibility of a change in Palestine policy. Opposition to Zionism in Parliament over the previous two years had come mainly from Conservatives, particularly in the House of Lords. Sections of the Conservative press were calling for Britain to get out 'bag and baggage' from all the Near Eastern mandates. The Zionists were therefore worried.

In April 1923 the well-informed Zionist office in London picked up rumours that Samuel might be 'politely recalled' and replaced as High Commissioner. Leonard Stein, the Political Secretary of the Zionist Organization, commented:

I was one of the few who were from the beginning anything but enthusiastic about H[is] E[xcellency]'s appointment. I always felt that, just because he was a Jew, his very high-mindedness and scrupulous sense of propriety would, from our point of view, weaken his hands in carrying out the policy of the Mandate. He could not, or was bound to feel that he could not, do what a non-Jewish High Commissioner could. Consequently, from first to last, his regime has inevitably been a series of apologies and explanations. All this is part of the price we have to pay for a Jewish High Commissioner, in whom so many Zionists saw an invaluable asset. At the same time, the appointment having been made, and H.E. having held office nearly three years, we

---

[117] *Palestine: Papers Relating to the Elections for the Palestine Legislative Council 1923*, Cmd. 1889 (London, June 1923).
[118] See Wasserstein, *British in Palestine*, 120–4.

have to consider what would be the effects of his resignation at the present stage. . . . Whatever his weaknesses may have been, and however severely he may have been criticised in many parts of the Jewish world, I am sure that H.E.'s presence in Palestine is still a great moral asset in the eyes of the entire Zionist public, and that the loss of that asset would produce serious depression in the Zionist ranks. When all is said and done, H.E.'s presence in Palestine has become a symbol.[119]

This less than enthusiastic endorsement of Samuel reflected the general depression in Zionist ranks at this time.

British officials too were beginning to despair of ever finding a workable basis for the government of Palestine. In a private conversation in April 1923, Sir John Shuckburgh, head of the Middle East Department of the Colonial Office, said that 'he could see no end, no solution to the problem'. He expressed a 'sense of personal degradation'. British policy in Palestine, he felt, had been built upon an ambiguity. 'He could not go on, they could not go on, feeling this sense of equivocation.' The elections had been 'a farce and a failure'. The present policy of attempting to reconcile the Arabs to Zionism had no prospect of success. Consequently, the Government ought to decide 'either to proceed to carry out our policy by force if need be or to modify the fundamental basis of the offer which is of course the building of the National Home'. Shuckburgh went on to argue that 'we cannot contemplate the use of force. . . . The electorate in England would never tolerate it.' The logical conclusion was, therefore, 'our final[ly] disembarrassing ourselves of these promises'.[120]

These were not merely the after-hours musings of a frustrated civil servant. In the summer of 1923 the new Government set up a Cabinet Committee, presided over by Lord Curzon, to examine Palestine policy afresh and to advise the full Cabinet whether Britain should remain in Palestine and whether, if she remained, the pro-Zionist policy should be continued.

In spite of the darkening political scene around him, Samuel was buoyantly optimistic. In June 1923 he visited London again and gave evidence to the Cabinet Committee. He did so in a cheerful mood, writing to his son Edwin before his appearance: 'The attitude of the Government with respect to Palestine is all that could be wished.'[121] Samuel's two meetings with the Cabinet Committee justified his confidence. In the first he explained meeting his policy of conciliation, arguing that Arab opposition to Zionism was based, to a large extent, on a misunderstanding of its

[119] Stein to F. H. Kisch (Chairman of Palestine Zionist Executive), 10 Apr. 1923 (two letters), CZA S25/10275.
[120] Conversation of Shuckburgh with Sydney Moody, 13 Apr. 1923, transcript in Evyatar Friesel, 'British Officials on the Situation in Palestine, 1923', *Middle Eastern Studies*, 23/2 (Apr. 1987), 194–210.
[121] HS to ES, 1 July 1923, ISA 100/48.

goals. The Arabs were opposed to a Jewish state, to a flood of Jewish immigration, and to their lands being confiscated. But 'none of these things', Samuel maintained, was 'included in the programme of the Government', and 'none of them are now contemplated by responsible Zionist leaders'. The country was now quiet and being governed with a light hand. There was no corruption, no censorship, no coercion. He still hoped that the Advisory Council scheme could be realized, and that the Arab members would not withdraw.

After his statement the committee interrogated him on some of the chief problems facing the Palestine Government:

CURZON. Will you tell us what restrictions you put on immigration?

SAMUEL. They are very severe. If we were to open the doors they would come in at the rate of 5 or 6,000 a month. . . .

AMERY. Does the Zionist Organization acquiesce cheerfully?

SAMUEL. It acquiesces but not cheerfully. It is always pressing for more people to come in. . . .

[The discussion turned to the Palestine Gendarmerie, headed by a former commander of the 'Black and Tans' in the Irish troubles.]

CURZON. Is our old friend Tudor in command?

SAMUEL. Yes.

CURZON. Is he reproducing his Hibernian methods?

SAMUEL. No. The British Gendarmerie works there very well and are extremely successful. . . .[122] If I may suggest it, the whole direction of our policy should be aimed at this—to give sufficient encouragement to the Jews in the way of developing the National Home, and so forth, to induce them to maintain their enthusiasm and interest in Palestine, but not to go so far as to lead the Arabs to think that they are being oppressed and put under Jewish domination. That is the middle course that I have been trying to steer.[123]

Samuel's studied reasonableness seemed to win over some of the doubters on the committee. The Colonial Secretary, the Duke of Devonshire, remarked after the meeting to Shuckburgh, 'This has settled everything.'[124]

A few days later Samuel met the committee again and dealt with questions from Curzon on the central issue of Arab opposition to Zionism. Curzon expressed concern about the preferential treatment accorded to the Zionist Organization which had been granted a special role under the

---

[122] The Palestine garrison had been reduced to 2,800 by Dec. 1922. Samuel had planned to make up the shortfall by recruiting a mixed defence force of Jews and Arabs, but this proposal was dropped after the 1921 riots. Instead, two paramilitary forces were recruited: a British Gendarmerie, composed mainly of former 'Black and Tans', and a Palestinian one drawn from the local population. As a result Samuel was able to reduce defence expenditures considerably.

[123] Minutes of meeting, 5 July 1923, PRO CAB 27/222/7 ff.

[124] See Devonshire to HS, 18 Feb. 1924, ISA 100/11.

mandate as the recognized 'Jewish Agency'. He suggested the creation of a corresponding Arab Agency with members nominated by the Government. After some discussion general agreement was reached on this proposal which was incorporated as the main element in the final report of the committee, drafted by Curzon.[125] Samuel also met a subcommittee of the Committee of Imperial Defence where the strategic value of Palestine was discussed. Service ministers and chiefs who were present generally doubted that there was any positive strategic advantage to Britain in occupying Palestine, except as a means of keeping others out. Samuel insisted on the necessity, from the point of internal security, of finality: 'Any idea that the British occupation was a temporary measure would produce instability.' In the end the committee agreed unanimously that, as Lord Derby, the Secretary of State for War, put it, 'though Palestine was not of real strategic value, it was desirable to remain in possession of it'.[126]

The Conservative Government therefore decided to remain in Palestine, to maintain the essentials of the Balfour Declaration policy, and to continue to support Samuel's policy of Zionist development conditioned by conciliation of Arab opposition.[127] This was a crucial decision that owed much to Samuel's persuasiveness in committee. When a Labour Government came to power in January 1924 it did not interfere with what was now established as a non-partisan national commitment. Only in the late 1930s, under the pressure of overwhelming international events, did a British Government shift decisively away from that policy. The two decades of breathing space accorded to Zionism after the Balfour Declaration were crucial in enabling it to create a viable semi-autonomous economy, an underground army, and the embryonic institutions of a national state. The weakness of the Zionists in 1923 both in Palestine and in British politics was such that a British decision to abandon the Jewish National Home might have aborted the Zionist enterprise. That the Cabinet decided otherwise was not the least of the services rendered by Samuel to Zionism—although it was little recognized by Zionists then or since.

The Arab Agency scheme met with no more success than Samuel's earlier constitutional proposals. Samuel presented the proposal to what he called 'a fully representative meeting of Arab notables' in Jerusalem on 11 October 1923. The meeting had been preceded by strenuous Govern-

---

[125] Minutes of meeting, 9 July 1923, PRO CAB 27/222/17; draft report of Cabinet Committee, July 1923, PRO CO 733/54/455 ff.; report as circulated, 27 July 1923, PRO CAB 23/46.
[126] Minutes of meeting, 12 July 1923, PRO CO 537/869.
[127] Cabinet minutes, 31 July 1923, PRO CAB 23/46/188 ff.

ment efforts to induce some of the less fervently nationalistic notables to co-operate. But the notables, headed by Musa Kazem Pasha al-Husseini, announced that their reply was a unanimous negative.[128] The Zionists resented the proposal for an Arab Agency and were relieved at the Arab rejection.[129] The Arab leaders had now rejected a legislative council, an advisory council, and an Arab Agency. The Colonial Office decided that they had had enough and would countenance no further constitutional proposals. Even Samuel now began to realize that conciliation by such means would not suffice. For the rest of his term, indeed for the rest of the mandate, Palestine was governed as a virtual dictatorship by the High Commissioner.

The failure to construct a constitution led to a decisive change of direction in the politics of Palestine. Throughout his first three years in office Samuel's overriding aim had been to devise a unitary and unifying political framework that would draw all communities in Palestine together. When that failed, he resorted, very much against his own personal inclination, to the only feasible alternative: an attempt to deal with each community separately on the basis not of national but of communal institutions. The Palestine Zionist Executive, recognized as the Jewish Agency, became the main Jewish communal institution. The Supreme Muslim Council developed into the closest analogue in Arab Palestine. The Council had not existed under Ottoman rule. A British creation, it was set up in December 1921. Although theoretically representative only of Islamic religious interests, it became the main institutional organ of the Arabs of Palestine. The establishment of this body by the Palestine Government has been termed by the Council's most recent historian 'an act of appeasement towards the Palestinian Muslims'.[130] The Government undoubtedly intended to reassure the Muslims that they would control their own religious affairs. Hence the wide powers accorded to the Council, the lack of supervision by the Government, and the subsidization from public funds of a body which in addition derived substantial revenues from the *awqaf* (religious trusts) and other sources. But the most important element of 'appeasement' in the formation of this body lay in the choice of its first head. Haj Amin al-Husseini, who had been elected mufti (styled 'Grand Mufti') of Jerusalem in April 1921, became the first President (*Ra'is al-'Ulama'*) in January 1922. His election to both posts

[128] *Palestine: Proposed Formation of an Arab Agency*, Cmd. 1989 (London, Nov. 1923), see also Wasserstein, *British in Palestine*, 128–9.

[129] See Weizmann to Kisch, 14–16 Nov. 1923, CZA S25/745; and Weizmann to Colonial Office, 15 Nov. 1923, PRO CO 733/36/341 ff.

[130] Uri M. Kupferschmidt, *The Supreme Muslim Council: Islam under the British Mandate for Palestine* (Leiden, 1987), 17.

was stage-managed by government officials with the knowledge and blessing of Samuel.[131]

No decision taken by Samuel during his period of office in Palestine aroused greater retrospective condemnation by Zionists than his installation in dual positions of power of a man who had been convicted of incitement to riot after the April 1920 Jerusalem disturbances and had fled to Transjordan where he had been pardoned by Samuel on the occasion of his visit to es-Salt in August 1920. Samuel could not, of course, foresee the Mufti's later role as the leader of the Palestine Arab revolt between 1936 to 1939, as organizer of an anti-British coup in Iraq in 1941, as broadcaster for the Nazis from Berlin, and as a Pied Piper who led his people into defeat, exile, and misery. Samuel recognized the young nationalist's gifts: his commanding presence, his eloquence, his capacity to charm. In his endowment of Husseini with these high offices and their accompanying powers, Samuel hoped to satisfy Muslim demands for religious autonomy and to create a legitimate Arab authority that would co-operate with the Government at least to the extent of helping maintain law and order. In his evidence to the Cabinet Committee in 1923, Samuel maintained that 'the Mufti and his personal friends are always active in times of political crisis—and we have them every month or two—in preventing people getting too excited and too violent'.[132] Samuel never intended that the Mufti should become the single most powerful figure in Arab Palestine. That aggrandizement occurred gradually, and the plenitude of the Mufti's power became visible only after Samuel's departure from Palestine. Nevertheless, Husseini's earlier record in the 1920 riots might have given Samuel pause for thought. Samuel's offhand comment to the Cabinet Committee that 'after all he did not do much more than anybody else' suggests a defensive blindness to the Mufti's real character. Samuel failed to perceive the Mufti's love of intrigue, his intransigent and uncompromising hostility not only to Zionism but also to British imperialism, his readiness to resort to any lengths of brutality against his own people as much as against the Jews and the British, and his bloated ambition to become leader of the entire Muslim world. No man was, in fact, less suited by personality for the collaborative role that Samuel conceived in investing him with such authority. Like Neville Chamberlain's (and, as we shall see, Samuel's) misplaced trust in Hitler, Samuel's faith in the Mufti was a profound error of personal and political judgement.

Samuel's abandonment of the attempt to build a unified political community in Palestine and his recourse instead to a system in which the Government of Palestine presided like an umpire over what were to

[131] See Wasserstein, British in Palestine, 98–100, 131–2.
[132] Minutes of meeting, 9 July 1923, PRO CAB 27/222.

develop into two rival quasi-governments prepared the way for the ultimate collapse of the mandatory regime. In a sense, what Samuel created was a form of internal, or institutional partition of Palestine on a communal basis, a decade before the country's territorial partition began to be seriously discussed. Samuel always opposed partition and would have been horrified at the thought that his administration had helped bring it about. Yet this was the main long-term legacy of the structure that he bequeathed to Palestine when he left office in mid-1925. At that time, it seemed as if his policies had achieved some success. In spite of the collapse of all Samuel's constitutional efforts, there had been no serious disturbances after 1921. The size of the British garrison had been steadily reduced. Arab nationalist activity died down after 1923. Jewish immigration had resumed and reached the unprecedented number of 33,135 in 1925.

In April 1925 Samuel welcomed Balfour and other dignitaries at the formal opening of the Hebrew University of Jerusalem. The ceremony took place in an amphitheatre on Mount Scopus commanding a majestic view of the country to the east. Samuel was one of several speakers to the audience of seven thousand that included his son Edwin and his 2-year-old grandson David (who also attended the sixtieth anniversary convocation of the university in the same spot in 1985). He quoted the Book of Proverbs: 'Wisdom hath builded her house, she hath hewn out her seven pillars ... she crieth upon the highest places of the city.' And in words that echoed his enthusiastic Zionism of a decade earlier he spoke of the Hebrew University as one of the noblest parts of the nascent Jewish National Home. Ahad Ha'am, who was present at the ceremony, was one of many who were deeply moved by Samuel's speech which he pronounced the most Zionist in spirit of all the speeches that day. He declared that if Samuel had done nothing more for Zionism save deliver that speech his name would have a place in its history.[133]

At the end of June 1925 Samuel's term of office as High Commissioner ended. He travelled to various parts of the country, part of the way on horseback, to say goodbye. The Zionists and some Arabs fêted him on the eve of his departure. The Arab nationalist press displayed a division of opinion: al-Karmil condemned Arabs who had attended the valedictory festivities; on the other hand Filastin, while reasserting its opposition to his policy, bade him a cordial enough farewell.[134] Although the Zionists were warmer in their public expressions, they too evinced mixed feelings.[135]

The English Zionist Harry Sacher, in an article reviewing Samuel's

[133] Ha-'Olam, 2 Sept. 1930; see also Arthur Ruppin, diary entry, 1 Apr. 1925, in Pirkei Hayyai, iii (Tel Aviv, 1968), 95.
[134] al-Karmil, 6 July 1925; Filastin, 7 July 1925.
[135] See Wasserstein, British in Palestine, 149–50.

period in Palestine, expressed the common Zionist criticism with brutal candour: 'Although Sir Herbert Samuel has been in public life for a generation, he lacks some of the qualities of a man of the world. One has constantly the feeling that he is too much of a puritan and too much of a recluse to see the badness that may be hidden behind a fair exterior, or to distinguish the solid worth which may accompany a Rabelaisian manner.' Sacher recalled that in the early days Samuel had shared with the Zionists the visionary desire 'to create a new heaven and a new earth in Palestine', but he argued that Samuel had bent too much with the wind of Arab anti-Zionism: 'One may guess that his somewhat old-fashioned Liberalism is peculiarly sensitive to the appeal of a majority. There has probably always been within him something of a conflict between the Jew desirous to help in the creation of the National Home and the Liberal haunted by the phrase "self-determination".'[136] While there were grains of truth in this analysis of Samuel's character, the conclusion was a superficial inter-pretation that became a conventional wisdom among Zionists only because it was a convenient way of avoiding deeper realities—both about Samuel and, more importantly, about the nature of the Arab-Jewish conflict in Palestine.

In a long report on his quinquennium of government in Palestine, Samuel summed up what he saw as the achievements. The country had been pacified: 'The spirit of lawlessness has ceased; the atmosphere is no longer electric.' The exaggerated hopes of the Jews and fears of the Arabs had both given way to more realistic expectations as a result of the definition of policy in the 1922 White Paper. Samuel dwelt, in particular, on the progress made in Jewish agricultural settlement. At the same time he argued that the Government had been 'as active in promoting the welfare of the Arabs as if there had been no Zionist complication and no [Arab] refusal to co-operate'. He admitted that the Arabs complained that the Government favoured the Jews unduly, and the Jews that they had been left to build the National Home unaided by the Government:

So far as there is any truth in these criticisms it is the latter that has most substance.... But the consequence has been that the Jewish movement has been self-dependent. If it has had the moral encouragement of the Balfour Declaration and of the official recognition of the Hebrew language, if it has been able to rely on the Government of Palestine to maintain order and to impose no unnecessary obstacles, for all the rest it has had to rely on its own sacrifices, its own men. What the future will bring it would be foolish to try to forecast. . . . But this one factor, at least, is propitious: that the building of the National Home has not been the work of any Government; it is not an

---

[136] Harry Sacher, 'Sir Herbert Samuel as High Commissioner', *New Judea*, 3 July 1925.

artificial construction of laws and official fostering. It is the outcome of the energy and enterprise of the Jewish people themselves.'[137]

This passage goes to the heart of what he saw as his role in Palestine. In spite of the acute soul-searching that he underwent following the May 1921 riots, his view of Zionism in 1925 had changed little since 1915. He had never conceived of a Jewish State being born overnight. He had always recognized that Arab opposition was a reality that must condition the pace of Zionist development. But he continued, like Ahad Ha'am, to regard the essence of Zionism as self-emancipation and self-realization.

As Professor Evyatar Friesel has remarked, Samuel's Zionism was bound up with his attitude to his own Jewishness. Friesel goes on, however, to argue that Samuel's experience in Palestine, particularly in May 1921, led to a redefinition of his personal and political position: 'He could be brought to recognize Arab political nationalism, but he simply did not know how to cope with *Jewish* political nationalism. There was no place for any political dimension in his Jewish self-definition.'[138] This seems overstated. Zionism for Samuel was more than a philanthropic or recreational exercise. It was not the political element that he disliked, but the prospect of its imposition by force and of the 'series of squalid conflicts with the Arab population' of which he had warned in January 1915. His Liberalism did not lead him to jettison political Zionism in the face of Arab nationalism, any more than Ulster opposition led him to reject Irish Home Rule. In both cases an understanding of the force of the opposition led him to the view that coercion was neither morally acceptable nor politically feasible—*a fortiori* in Palestine where the Jews were, as yet, a small minority. The success of Zionism must, therefore, he believed, be conditioned by the degree of its acceptance by the existing Arab majority.

As for his self-definition, Samuel never accepted the view expressed by Edwin Montagu that a Jewish State would give rise to accusations of divided loyalty against Jews outside Palestine. He demonstrated the depth of his personal commitment to Zionism at the end of his term of office by

[137] *Palestine: Report of the High Commissioner on the Administration of Palestine 1920–1925* (London, 1925). In the first of a series of articles in the *Sunday Times* on Samuel's administration of Palestine, Sir Hall Caine called the report 'the most distinguished public document of the kind since Lord Cromer's report before leaving Egypt.... Without a flamboyant passage, the Report reads like a Romance.... The severity of its style cannot always suppress the sense of marvel which comes on reading it.... I think the work that has been done in Palestine during the past five years is more than worthy of the highest traditions of British colonial rule. And it places Sir Herbert Samuel once for all in the front rank of British administrators' (*Sunday Times*, 21 June 1925).
[138] Evyatar Friesel, 'Herbert Samuel's Reassessment of Zionism in 1921', *Studies in Zionism*, 5/2 (Autumn 1984), 213–37.

proposing to live in a house on Mount Carmel and to devote the rest of his life to writing philosophy there. He abandoned the scheme under protest when his successor, Lord Plumer, insisted that the continued presence in the country of a former High Commissioner would be 'a source of very grave embarrassment'.[139] Samuel appealed to the Colonial Secretary, Amery, but to his intense chagrin, Plumer's ruling was upheld. 'It is a great blow', Beatrice Samuel wrote to their son Edwin.[140] Samuel would not have left Britain to govern any other part of the British Empire, except, perhaps, for the great political prize of the viceroyalty of India. He went to Palestine and wished to remain there only because Zionism was, for him, a form of self-realization. Writing of the original impulse for Samuel's Zionism, Norman Bentwich wrote many years later that he 'would probably have disclaimed a religious inspiration'. Nevertheless, Bentwich continued, 'his philosophy of free-will and determinism . . . would accept the influence of generations of ancestors on his mind and on his fitness to be the instrument of a religious dream and belief of his people.'[141]

[139] Plumer to HS, 28 May 1925, ISA 100/12.
[140] BS to ES, 21 July 1925, ISA 103/11 (671/5).
[141] Norman Bentwich, *Herbert Samuel's Religious Beliefs* (London, 1966), 6–7.

10

Pacifier

===

The Strength of Britain lies in her coal-beds. . . . The Lord
Chancellor now sits upon a bag of wool; but wool has long ceased
to be emblematical of the staple industry of England. He ought to
sit upon a bag of coals, though it might not prove quite so
comfortable a seat.

(Disraeli)

'AS SOON as we left the coast of Palestine we got into calmer waters!'
Samuel wrote aboard ship in the Mediterranean in early July 1925.[1]
Samuel's intention after leaving Palestine was to tour the Mediterranean
coastline, spend some time in Europe writing his projected book on
philosophy, and then visit India in the autumn. There seemed little to
draw him back immediately to England. He had no house there. He had
no job there, nor any immediate prospect of one even had he desired it.
When Samuel had left England five years earlier, the Liberal Party had
been split, but a Liberal Prime Minister held office and Liberalism still
seemed a force to be reckoned with. By 1925 the party was uneasily
reunited but further away than ever from power. Only 40 Liberals had
been returned in the election of October 1924. Asquith was again
defeated and moved to the Lords. Runciman summed up the sorry
débâcle in a letter to Samuel after the election: 'The disasters to the Liberal
Party are so overwhelming that they have shaken up the whole machine,
local as well as central.'[2] Even had Samuel wished to return to England at
this juncture, therefore, the political scene was uninviting.

In August 1925, however, he received an urgent request from the
Conservative Prime Minister, Baldwin, to undertake the chairmanship of
a Royal Commission on the coal industry. Samuel was at first reluctant to
accept, but he agreed to travel to Aix-les-Bains, where Baldwin was
spending his summer holiday, in order to discuss the proposal. Baldwin
described the encounter in a letter to the Chancellor of the Exchequer,
Churchill, who also favoured Samuel's appointment:

[1] HS to Norman Bentwich, 6 July 1925, CZA A/255/82.
[2] Runciman to HS, 19 Nov. 1924, HLRO HS A/155/V/33.

The infant Samuel duly arrived as the clock was striking six on Monday evening. Cool, competent and precise as when he was first lent to this temporary world by an inscrutable providence, it was the work of a moment for him to grasp our problem in all its manifold implications. But he would have none of it and for 'worthy reasons'. ... Very strong private reasons with which I sympathise. Would we do our utmost to find a substitute? Until we could assure him we had done so, he couldn't look at it. Hence the fevered telegrams which passed and now all is well. I think he is quite the best man we could have. The brief talk we had convinced me.[3]

Samuel's appointment was announced at the end of August and he returned to London shortly afterwards.

The British coal industry in mid-1925 had reached a point of acute crisis. Since the end of the war its chronic difficulties had taxed the patience of successive governments. Coal was one of several of the older heavy industries that entered a long decline after 1918. But its size (it was the largest industry, apart from agriculture, in Britain, employing over a million men), its complexity, its unique relationship to other industries, and its traditions of labour militancy rendered its intractable problems a national concern that became something close to a national trauma.

During the later part of the war the industry had been placed under government control. Between 1917 and 1921 the Government pumped £40,000,000 into the industry. But there was little capital investment or mechanization since the primary objective was production for the war effort. During this period the industry lost ground in many of its traditional overseas markets. Although still the world's largest coal exporter in the early 1920s, the British coal industry, like the British Empire, seemed overstretched, undercapitalized, and vulnerable to new and dynamic competitors. Following labour unrest in 1919, a Royal Commission under Sir John Sankey had recommended the nationalization. But the Sankey Commission had been divided: only the chairman's casting vote gave a majority for public ownership of the mines, although there was unanimous approval of nationalization of mineral royalties. For this reason among others, Lloyd George's Government had found it convenient more or less to ignore the Commission's proposals. That precedent was to have a significant bearing on the course of events in 1925–6. Lloyd George did take one important step in 1919: his Government enacted a seven-hour miners' working day, exclusive of 'winding-time'—a victory which, once gained, they proved loath to surrender. And in 1921 the industry was 'decontrolled', that is, the Government sought to disengage itself from direct involvement in setting prices or wages.

The crises of the industry in 1921 and 1925–6 arose from the glut of

---

[3] Baldwin to Churchill, in Martin Gilbert, *Winston S. Churchill*, vol. v, Companion part I (London, 1979), 530–1; see also Baldwin to HS, 19 Aug. 1925, HLRO HS A/159/1.

coal on the world market in those years and from the inability of the British industry to compete in price with coal produced in Germany, Poland, and the United States. Conflicting interpretations were offered of this competitive failure. The miners alleged inefficiency in management, argued that the number of small mining companies was excessive, and urged reorganization under public ownership.[4] The mine-owners attributed their problems to high labour costs and saw the solution primarily in terms of lower wages and longer hours. Less interested observers suggested other causes such as the effects of German reparations, the slower pace of mechanization in Britain, substitution of alternative energy sources (oil, hydroelectricity, lignite), and the return to the gold standard. The industry had enjoyed a brief and illusory return to relative prosperity from 1922 to 1924, but this was due to short-term causes, notably the United States coal strike of 1922 and the French occupation of the Ruhr. As a result of this short-lived boom the miners succeeded in 1924 in negotiating a favourable wage rise.

By late 1924 the French and Belgian withdrawal from the Ruhr and the resumption of large-scale German production produced a reversal. The return of sterling to the gold standard in April 1925, while not in itself the cause of the market collapse, dealt a body blow to an already ailing industry.[5] In May 1925 60 per cent of all coal mined in Britain was being produced at a loss.[6] Exports shrank from 79.5 million tons in 1923 to 50.8 million in 1925. Unemployment in the industry grew to 16 per cent. But since labour costs in the industry averaged 65 to 75 per cent of the total costs of production, and since the cost of closing and reopening a

---

[4] By 1926 adverse market conditions had reduced the number of collieries to about 2,500 and the number of business undertakings to about 1,400 (*Report of the Royal Commission on the Coal Industry*, Cmd. 2600 (London, 1926), i. 45).

[5] The Samuel Commission, while conceding that the return to gold had produced 'a temporary ill-effect upon all branches of our export trade', suggested that 'this effect has now spent itself' and that with the general stabilization of currencies 'this factor has now ceased to be of primary importance' (*Royal Commission Report*, i. 9). By contrast, Keynes, in his famous polemic *The Economic Consequences of Mr Churchill*, written in 1925 but published only in 1931, declared: 'I should pick out coal as being above all others a victim of our monetary policy. On the other hand, it is certainly true that the reason why the coal industry presents so dismal a picture to the eye is because it has other troubles which have weakened its power of resistance and have left it no margin of strength with which to support a new misfortune' (repr. in Sidney Pollard (ed.), *The Gold Standard and Employment Policies between the Wars* (London, 1970), 37). When Samuel came to work with Keynes on the Liberal Industrial Inquiry in 1928 he did not change his mind on this issue. Samuel wrote the chapter on 'Coal' in the so-called 'Liberal Yellow Book': his analysis there of the problems of the industry did not allude at all to the return to gold (*Britain's Industrial Future: being the Report of the Liberal Industrial Inquiry of 1928* (London, 1928), ch. 25).

[6] Barry Supple, *The History of the British Coal Industry* (Oxford, 1987), 223.

mine was high, owners tended to press for lower wages rather than close loss-making mines and lose their entire investment.[7]

On 30 June 1925 the owners announced that the existing agreement would terminate on 31 July. They offered a new agreement of which the central feature, and the most offensive to the miners, was a reduction in wages. The miners' union refused to accept what they saw as a diktat and threatened a strike which, it appeared, would be joined in sympathy by the railway, transport, and seamen's unions. On 13 July the Government set up a court of inquiry under H. P. Macmillan, a KC who had served as Lord Advocate in the first Labour Government. Although the miners boycotted its proceedings, the inquiry reported on 28 July largely in their favour. But neither side accepted its recommendations and the Government was compelled to intervene directly to try to avert a stoppage at the end of the month that seemed likely to develop into a general strike.

A few hours before the deadline on 31 July the Government announced an interim solution. For a fixed period of nine months a subsidy would be paid to the owners that would prevent any necessity for wage reductions.[8] During that period a Royal Commission would investigate the industry and make recommendations for a permanent solution to its problems. Samuel had not, in fact, been the Government's first choice to head the Commission. The chairmanship had earlier been offered to Viscount Grey[9] but he declined citing 'physical disability'.[10] 'I don't suppose any sane man likes to take on the job under the circumstances,' Frances Stevenson wrote to Lloyd George.[11] Samuel was under no illusion as to the thanklessness of the task that faced the Commission. 'If it fails [he wrote to Edwin Samuel] there will be a tremendous strike, in which not only the miners, but probably the dockers and railwaymen will engage, and everyone will abuse the Commission. If it succeeds, its work will be forgotten in a month. But some-one has to undertake it, and since the

[7] W. M. Kirby, The British Coalmining Industry, 1870–1946: A Political and Economic History (London, 1977), 12–13, 67.

[8] Some saw this a subsidy to the miners since their wages were maintained. A. J. P. Taylor suggests that it was just as much a subsidy to the owners since it propped up profits (English History 1914–1945 (Oxford, 1965), 241). M. W. Kirby argues that the beneficiaries were overseas buyers, since the subsidy was used to finance competitive price reductions by exporters (Coalmining Industry, 78). No doubt all shared in the hand-out. The subsidy was originally expected to cost £10,000,000; its eventual cost was £23,000,000.

[9] Viscount Grey of Falloden, formerly Sir Edward Grey (1862–1933); not, as stated by Professor Supple in his British Coal Industry, 225, Earl Grey (1879–1963).

[10] Kirby, Coalmining Industry, 235.

[11] Frances Stevenson to Lloyd George, 19 Aug. 1925, in A. J. P. Taylor (ed.), My Darling Pussy: The Letters of Lloyd George and Frances Stevenson 1913–41 (London, 1975), 92.

Cabinet, Baldwin told me, were unanimously of opinion that I was the [man?] for chairman, I cannot escape the obligation.'[12]

Unlike the Sankey Commission, which had been composed, except for the chairman, of known partisans of each side, the Government deliberately appointed to the Samuel Commission members who had little or no previous involvement with the coal industry. The three other members were Sir William Beveridge, Director of the London School of Economics, Kenneth Lee, a Manchester cotton manufacturer, and General Sir Herbert Lawrence, a banker. The one who carried the most weight with his colleagues and who worked most closely with Samuel was Beveridge.[13] Three of the four (Samuel, Beveridge, and Lee) were Liberals and the harmony with which the Commission worked as well as the unanimity of their report undoubtedly owed much to this shared political outlook.[14]

Although Samuel had had no direct involvement with the coal industry, he was familiar with many of the problems of mining as a result of his connection with the Cleveland ironstone miners between 1902 and 1918. His work on the definition of industrial diseases under the Workmen's Compensation Act had educated him on that aspect of coal mining. In 1908 he had played a part in the enactment of the Miners' Eight Hours Act. In 1916, as Home Secretary, he had been responsible for the Coal Mining Organization Committee that supervised the production of coal prior to the full government take-over of the industry. In 1919 he had supported the Sankey Commission's recommendation that minerals be nationalized and he had appeared to favour some larger degree of public control: 'Even if it be not found practicable, at the present stage, to conduct through a State Department the direct management of this vast industry . . . still it is certain that the State, as owner of the minerals, would have at least to impose conditions upon their working.'[15] This pronouncement apart, he had said little in public about coal since the war. His absence from England for the previous five years had precluded any involvement in the disputes in the industry and this negative qualification as well as his known capacities as a committee man and conciliator made him an obvious choice to head the Commission.

The Commission's terms of reference required it 'to inquire into and report upon the economic position of the Coal Industry and the conditions

[12] HS to ES, 25 Aug. 1925, ISA 100/48.

[13] See José Harris, *William Beveridge: A Biography* (Oxford, 1977), 334–41.

[14] A memorandum prepared for Lloyd George in 1929 itemized the points of similarity between the Samuel Commission's report and the report of a Liberal committee on the coal industry, entitled 'Coal and Power', completed in 1924 and approved by the Liberal Party (memorandum by Malcolm Thomson, 29 Nov. 1929, HLRO Lloyd George papers G/29/1/8).

[15] *Daily News*, 1 Nov. 1919.

affecting it and to make any recommendations for the improvement thereof'.[16] The chief immediate issues that divided miners from owners and that the Commission would have to resolve were four. First, wage rates: the owners insisted on reductions; the miners refused that absolutely. Second, the question whether a new agreement should be negotiated nationally, as favoured by the miners, or district by district, which was the owners' preference. Third, hours: the owners demanded and the miners resisted repeal of the Seven Hours Act. And finally the question of ownership and organization of the industry: the owners fought to retain the status quo; the miners again urged public ownership. Behind these pressing areas of controversy lay the larger question of economic policy rather than industrial relations, how the industry might become once again sufficiently competitive to regain the lost export markets crucial to its prosperity.

At the outset of the Commission's work Beveridge pressed unsuccessfully for evidence to be taken in private session, arguing that publicity would provoke 'recriminations, heated cross-examinations, dangerous admissions and the like'.[17] The Commission examined 76 witnesses in 33 public sittings in a large committee room off Westminster Hall. As Beveridge noted, the 'proceedings often became a dog-fight—particularly when prominent mine-owners and miners . . . were under mutual cross-examination'.[18]

On the first day of public proceedings, on 15 October 1925, a wrangle developed following Samuel's opening statement, when the miners' leader, Herbert Smith, complained about the Commissioners' previous visits to certain collieries: 'We are not satisfied about your visits to the pits, because we think there must have been some pre-arrangement with somebody in regard to those visits, and we have not been consulted.' Samuel explained that the pits had been selected for inspection 'by the Mine Inspectors who are wholly impartial persons'. These early visits, he said, 'were not of a formal character, but were more in the nature of what the miners will appreciate when I say it was in order to enable us "to get ou[r] eyesight" '. He promised that the Commission would welcome suggestions from both miners and owners as to which pits should be examined in future, more formal visits. In the course of their investigations the Commission visited twenty-five collieries and on several occasions insisted on going down the pits to the coal face.

A further row followed Samuel's announcement that, in accordance with assurances given by the Prime Minister, representatives of the

[16] *Royal Commission Report*, i. p. ix.
[17] Beveridge to HS, 15 Sept. 1925, BLPES Beveridge papers VIII/3.
[18] Undated fragment of note by Beveridge, ibid.

Miners' Federation (workers) and of the Mining Association (owners) would be given an opportunity of cross-examining witnesses to the Commission. Spokesmen for the Mineral Owners' Association, representing landowners whose land sat on coal, and for the National Federation of Colliery Enginemen, Boilermen, and Mechanics protested that they too should be given similar facilities. Samuel said that the Commission had considered the question and decided to reject such requests since if these applications were granted other interested parties too would have to be granted such rights. They would, however, be able to give evidence in the normal manner. The mineral owners' representative retorted that it was a 'monstrous injustice' that they should not be able to defend their rights against those who were attacking them. Samuel replied: 'I think the Royalty Owners will find their interests will be quite safely guarded'—a promise that was not altogether honoured, at least in the eyes of the royalty owners. Asked by the enginemen's representative on the basis of what principle 'this difference is made between the two parties and other bodies that are interested and have representation in the mining industry', Samuel replied: 'I suppose, the small yielding place to the large.' Samuel's response did not mollify the aggrieved applicants. The proceedings thus began on a sour note.[19]

The bitterness of the conflict between the owners and the miners and their utter mutual incomprehension emerged with dramatic intensity in the course of the public sessions. The miners' chief representatives were Herbert Smith, a tenacious Yorkshireman who had been born in a workhouse and had gone down the pit at the age of 10, and A. J. Cook, a fiery orator who spoke of a strike as if it were an Armageddon that would usher in the New Jerusalem. No man in England at that time was more hated by the possessing classes than Cook. Smith and Cook clashed repeatedly with the leading employers' representative, Evan Williams, whose rejoinders were no less combative and unconciliatory. The miners played to the press gallery by enquiring innocently of mine-owning witnesses how much they made each year. The reply that this was none of the questioner's business invariably gave rise to intemperate and unproductive altercations. Evidence was given by senior civil servants, technical experts, and representatives of the royalty owners and other interested groups. Among witnesses sympathetic to the miners were Ernest Bevin (on behalf of the Transport and General Workers' Union), Emanuel Shinwell (former Secretary for Mines), and R. H. Tawney who presented the Miners' Federation scheme for public ownership. Eleanor Rathbone, appearing for the Family Endowment Society, urged a scheme

[19] *Report of the Royal Commission on the Coal Industry*, vol. ii, part A: *Minutes of Evidence* (London, 1926), 1–3.

for family allowances in the industry.[20] The Duke of Northumberland, the proprietor of huge mineral-rich lands inherited from a remote ancestor, defended the royalty owners' case in the face of angry cross-examination by Cook. C. P. Markham, a colliery-owner with a reputation as a moderate, showed little moderation in his responses to needling questions from the miners. Most of the owners seemed, from their evidence, to see themselves as engaged in a Manichaean struggle against socialistic revolutionaries out to destroy the industry as a prelude to nationalization.

Not all the owners took such a belligerent line. David Davies, a Welsh Liberal MP who was also a coal-owner, wrote to Samuel after the Commission had finished taking evidence confessing that his fellow-owners' attitude filled him with dismay: 'Personally, I sincerely regret that the Mining Association should have made so feeble an attempt to assist the Commission in solving this difficult problem.' Davies particularly criticized the owners' rigid attitude on the question of hours. While he recognized that the British producers were facing 'unfair competition' from French and German mines working long hours, he argued that 'the only way of arriving at a standard working day of so many working hours is by some process of common agreement'. He suggested that such an agreement might be reached through the medium of the International Labour Office. Secondly, he proposed the establishment of 'some permanent independent Tribunal to arbitrate on all disputes in the Coal Trade'.[21] Although the Commission did not make specific recommendations on these two points, it indicated tentative agreement with both in its report.[22]

On the crucial issue of wages, the other Commissioners were much influenced by an analysis conducted by Beveridge which contested the miners' claims as to the depreciation of their real wages. Beveridge argued that 'so far from having lower rates of real wages now than before the War, the miners have appreciably higher rates'. His contention rested partly on technical adjustments of cost-of-living estimates, but also on other evidence such as the different post-war balance of the labour force as between skilled and unskilled workers. He also argued that the reduced family responsibilities of miners as a result of the falling birth-rate should

---

[20] Beveridge had persuaded Miss Rathbone to give evidence. His support for the proposal brought about its inclusion among the Commission's recommendations. The Government did not implement it. The episode was, however, important in the development of Beveridge's thinking on the subject. See Harris, *Beveridge*, 341–6.

[21] Davies to HS, 20 Jan. 1926, National Library of Wales, papers of Lord Davies of Llandinam F/3/1; see also Davies to Thomas Jones, 21 Jan. 1926, in Keith Middlemas (ed.), *Thomas Jones: Whitehall Diary*, ii (London, 1969), 3.

[22] *Royal Commission Report*, i. 153, 178.

be factored into the calculation.[23] Beveridge's analysis was subjected to withering criticism by an expert in the Ministry of Labour who condemned it as 'very biased'.[24] It nevertheless helped persuade the other members of the Commission that wage reductions were economically necessary and also not unjust.[25]

The hearings continued until early January 1926, but by 22 December Samuel had already drawn up 'the skeleton of the Report, which meets with favour'.[26] Samuel wrote about a third of the report himself and drafted a further third.[27] Samuel called the Coal Commission 'quite the hardest piece of work I have ever done', but whereas Beveridge sat up till three in the morning, working on his sections, Samuel functioned with his usual mechanical regularity. He wrote on four days a week from 9.00 a.m. to 11.00 p.m., held meetings on two days, and took Saturdays off.[28] With their differing regimens, the Commissioners succeeded in completing their work within six months.

The Commission's report stressed the need for large structural changes in the industry. It rejected wholesale nationalization as offering no 'clear social gain' while carrying the risk of 'grave economic dangers'. The Commission did, however, favour nationalization of mineral royalties: 'The error which was made in times past, in allowing the ownership of the coal to fall into private hands, should be retrieved. The mineral should be acquired by the State.' The report urged the amalgamation of small units of production, to be encouraged by a carrot rather than a stick: 'This may often be effected from within, but in many cases it will only take place if outside assistance is given. Any general measure of compulsory amalgamation, on arbitrary lines, would be mischievous; the action to be taken should be elastic.'[29] On distribution, the Commission recommended

[23] Memorandum by Beveridge, 'Miners' Wages and the Cost of Living', c.4 Jan. 1926, PRO LAB 41/202.

[24] Minute by John Hilton, 13 Jan. 1926, ibid.

[25] See Royal Commission Report, i. 154–8, 280–8; see also Harris, Beveridge, 337–8.

[26] HS to ES, 22 Dec. 1925, ISA 100/50.

[27] He dealt with what he called 'the more general' chapters, among which were: 3 'Utilisation of Coal', 5 'Structure of the Industry', 6 'Nationalisation of Mines'—though Beveridge contributed to this, 7 'Royalties', 10 'Employers and Employed: General Observations', and 16 'Safety and Health'. Beveridge wrote four chapters that were 'more strictly economic'; 11 'Output', 12 'Wages', 13 'Hours', and 20 'Profits', as well as parts of others, and he directed the statistical work. Lee wrote chapter 4, 'Research'. Chapter 1, 'General Statement', was largely the work of Ernest Gowers, Permanent Under-Secretary of the Mines Department in the Board of Trade and a master of mandarin style.

[28] HS to ES, 7 Jan. and 13 Feb. 1926, ISA 100/51; HS to Norman Bentwich, 11 Mar. 1926, CZA A/255/82; Beveridge to HS, 29 Jan. 1926, BLPES Beveridge papers VIII/3; Lord Beveridge, Power and Influence (London, 1953), 219–20.

[29] The Commission's belief that substantial further economies of scale could be achieved by greater concentration in the industry has been questioned; see Neil K. Buxton, 'Entrepreneurial Efficiency in the British Coal Industry between the Wars', Economic

that local authorities be empowered to engage in retail marketing of coal. The report proposed a number of reforms in miners' conditions: a family allowance system; profit-sharing schemes; general establishment of pit-head baths; and 'annual holidays with pay'—to be introduced 'when prosperity returns to the industry'.

All these recommendations might address some of the industry's long-term problems, but would not resolve the immediate dispute. The 'dominant fact', in the eyes of the Commission, was that the industry was running at a loss. They declared continuance of the subsidy 'indefensible' and insisted that it must 'stop at the end of its authorised term, and should never be repeated'. They based this conclusion on grounds of principle and the danger of setting a bad precedent. Asserting that it was wrong for taxpayers' money to support ailing industries, they warned: 'If recourse is had to this means in one crisis in one trade—unless it is definitely ruled now to be inadmissible as a policy—there will inevitably be pressure to resort to it in another crisis or in another trade. The result would be destructive to the national finances.'[30] The Commission rejected the owners' demand for an increase in hours. They also supported the miners in favouring national rather than district wage agreements. On the other hand, they accepted that if the existing hours were to be retained, some reduction in wages would be necessary: 'A disaster is impending over the industry, and the immediate reduction of working costs that can be effected in this way, and in this way alone, is essential to save it.' The Commissioners recognized that, even given wage reductions, many collieries would have to go out of business, thereby giving rise to what they delicately called 'the necessity for a transfer of labour on a considerable scale'. They recommended that the Government prepare plans and allocate funds to deal with such unemployment.[31]

The Commission sought to establish a link between its long-term and short-term proposals by declaring: 'Before any sacrifices are asked from those engaged in the industry, it shall be definitely agreed between them that all practicable means for improving its organisation and increasing its efficiency should be adopted, as speedily as the circumstances in each case allow.'[32] This passage provided a basis for the miners' subsequent refusal to consider wage cuts in the absence of an agreement on the structural reorganization of the industry. Here was the missing link that might bring both parties to the negotiating table. But the Commission

History Review, 2nd ser., 23 (1970), 476–97. The recent exhaustive analysis by Professor Supple goes some way towards rehabilitating the Commission's view (*Coal Industry*, 230–1, 341–58, 386–410).

[30] *Royal Commission Report*, i. 223.
[31] Ibid. 232–7.   [32] Ibid. 229.

could not—and the Government, it turned out, would not—enforce that linkage.

The Commission's report was signed on 6 March 1926 and published a few days later. At 3d. a copy, it became a record best-seller: by 1943 it had sold 105,000 copies. Of comparable state papers issued during Samuel's lifetime only the Beveridge Report sold more.[33] Beatrice Webb wrote to Samuel welcoming the report: 'Sidney tells me the Report is very good from a scientific point of view, though of course he would have liked the recommendations to be rather more advanced. However, short steps are sometimes the best way to a given goal. I hope it may lead to the peaceful evolution towards national control in one form or another.'[34]

On the other hand, the reception of the report by those most directly involved was much less enthusiastic. Herbert Smith denounced the Commission as 'a combination of prosperous individuals who had considerable experience in capitalist government with prosperous individuals whose financial and commercial interests were a guarantee that they would not betray the capitalist class'.[35] Sir Adam Nimmo, a leading coal-owner, later complained: 'There is not a suggestion of expansion. There is no note of adventure. The industry is not told to go and fight it out with competitors, wherever found, in the spirit of courage and daring. The outstanding note is—cut it down.'[36] The Government's reaction was guarded. The Secretary for Mines, G. R. Lane-Fox, urged the Government to give its full support to the report, but he carried little weight and his advice was rejected. A Cabinet Committee examined the Commission's proposals and concluded that 'the policy of the Government at the outset of the negotiations should be to express their readiness to accept the proposals of the Commission so far as the State is implicated, and their willingness to give effect to them provided the Mining Association and the Miners' Federation carry out the obligations severally imposed on them and the two parties reach agreement where agreement is required'. While the committee felt that nationalization of royalties 'should not, at any rate at this stage, be resisted', they advised that it might be postponed for three or four years. The Commission's proposal for municipal trading in coal was rejected. On the other hand, the committee suggested that the compulsory provision of pit-head baths 'should receive the cordial support of the Government'.[37] In spite of his private reservations about some

[33] HM Stationery Office to HS, 3 Mar. 1943, HLRO HS A/66/26.
[34] Beatrice Webb to HS, 27 Mar. 1926, HLRO HS A/159/4.
[35] Quoted in Kirby, Coalmining Industry, 76.
[36] Quoted in Robert Skidelsky, Politicians and the Slump: The Labour Government of 1929–1931 (Harmondsworth, 1970), 24.
[37] Report (by Baldwin) of Cabinet Committee on Report of Royal Commission on the Coal Industry, 20 Mar. 1926, PRO CAB 27/316.

aspects of the report, Baldwin announced on 24 March that the Government would follow the recommendations of the Commission provided that both sides of the industry would accept the report as a package without any quibbles.[38] But owners and miners alike stuck mulishly to their original positions.

Immediately he had finished work on the report, Samuel left for San Vigilio on Lake Garda in order to continue work on his projected philosophy book. Before his departure he was invited by the Government to become the first chairman of the Central Electricity Board at a salary of £5,000, but he 'had no hesitation in refusing'.[39] Although Samuel's primary reason for going abroad was to seek peace and quiet for his writing, he admitted to Runciman the secondary motive of wishing to avoid any involvement in the inevitable controversy following publication of the Commission's report.[40] Disturbing news from England soon interrupted his stay in Italy.

During the last two weeks of April, as the end of the nine-month subsidy approached, the Government entered actively into negotiations with both sides of the coal industry. These took place under the shadow of an announcement by the Mining Association that the 1924 agreement would end on 30 April. In the absence of a new agreement, which they insisted must be on a district basis, they threatened a lock-out. In spite of pressure from the Government, including an offer to continue the subsidy 'for a very limited period', the miners stuck rigidly to their refusal to consider any increase in hours or reduction in wages in advance of agreement on reorganization of the industry. The miners were stiffened in their attitude by the promise of support from the Trades Union Congress in the event of a strike. But the TUC also indicated that it supported the Samuel Commission's proposals. This imperceptible crack in their solidarity was later to prove fatal to the miners' cause.

On the evening of 30 April the owners posted notices at their pits stating the terms on which miners would henceforth be employed. These included an eight-hour day and reduction of wages to approximately 1921 levels. Beveridge and Lawrence notified Baldwin that they considered these proposals 'astonishing' and 'wholly unreasonable'.[41] Even the Prime Minister was shocked, calling the owners' action 'not an offer but an ultimatum'.[42] A lock-out was now inevitable and the Government moved forward with implementation of its contingency plans for the expected general strike in sympathy with the miners.

[38] See Supple, *Coal Industry*, 240.
[39] HS to ES, 9 Mar. 1926, ISA 100/51.
[40] HS to Runciman, 10 Mar. 1926, WR 203.
[41] Supple, *Coal Industry*, 241.   [42] Kirby, *Coalmining Industry*, 86.

Unlike his two fellow-commissioners, Samuel remained completely aloof from the controversy until 2 May, when he drafted a letter to Baldwin offering to return to London to try to help in securing a settlement.[43] After sleeping on it, however, he decided not to dispatch the letter and instead cabled to the Prime Minister: 'If no settlement desire return in case could assist renewed negotiations. Kindly telegraph prospects local press obscure.'[44] Privately Samuel expressed irritation at the owners' stance: 'The Report has been criticised in some newspapers for not being specific enough on the subject of national and district negotiations. But we had to allow a certain latitude to the parties who were presumably not children. We indicated clearly what we thought would be the "reasonable course". Certainly nothing that we said justified the owners in trying to force the men to engage in district negotiations before general principles had been settled nationally.'[45] But he was careful to make no public statement of any sort, keeping open the possibility of playing some mediating role. Wallas wrote to him on 3 May: 'A Liberal who was trusted might give a lead to the whole country now.'[46] Others saw Samuel less as a potential saviour than as the villain of the piece. At 4.00 a.m. on the night of 3–4 May a sleepless Beatrice Webb wrote in her diary: 'It is that mean wriggling of the Baldwin Cabinet, to some extent justified by the wriggles of the Liberal Commission of Herbert Samuel and Beveridge— typical Liberals—that has brought about the General Strike of tonight.'[47]

Baldwin's reply to Samuel's offer is lost, but the Prime Minister gave Samuel no encouragement to return to England. On 4 May, as the work stoppage began, Samuel, still in San Vigilio, wrote to his wife who was visiting Palestine: 'Late this morning I got this telegram from Baldwin. Of course, he cannot ask me to come unless he sees some way of making use of me, but I am quite clear that I ought to go on with my own initiative.'[48] The decision to attempt mediation was therefore one that he took alone, without the approval of the Government and without consultation with anyone. Even Wallas's letter arrived after his departure for London.

Samuel travelled back via Paris, lunching with Weizmann whom he met on the train. On arrival at Dover on the afternoon of 6 May he found young Cambridge men 'in their old clothes and no hats' acting as volunteer porters. He had telegraphed ahead to arrange for a car to meet him. The driver turned out to be Major Segrave, a famous racing motorist, who transported him to London at high speed. Once lodged at

[43] HS to BS, 2 May 1926, HLRO HS A/157/1071.
[44] HS to Baldwin, 3 May 1926, CUL Baldwin papers 21/163.
[45] HS to ES, 3 May 1926, ISA 100/51.
[46] Wallas to HS, 3 May 1926, HLRO HS A/159/6.
[47] Entry dated 3/4 May 1926, BLPES Beatrice Webb diary, 4288.
[48] HS to BS, 4 May 1926, HLRO HS A/157/1072.

the Reform Club, he got in touch first with J. H. Thomas with whom he had established good relations in 1924 when Thomas had been responsible for Palestine as Colonial Secretary in the Labour Government. Thomas, a former trade union leader, served as Samuel's main link with the TUC over the next few days. He also had a talk with Beveridge whom he met repeatedly in the course of the crisis. Beveridge prepared a draft memorandum with suggestions for a settlement of the underlying coal dispute. Samuel used this as a basis for his own proposals.[49] On 8 May he met Baldwin as well as Arthur Steel-Maitland, the Minister of Labour, and Sir Horace Wilson, Secretary to the Ministry. He also held 'long conferences of about three hours each' with TUC leaders and with Evan Williams. In the latter discussions he was accompanied by Beveridge and Lawrence. In order to avoid publicity most of these meetings took place at a secret location, the home in Bryanston Square of Sir Abe Bailey, a South African mining magnate and politician who was a friend of Thomas.

In his meeting with the Prime Minister, Samuel produced a draft letter that he proposed to send to the TUC as the basis for a settlement. The letter urged an immediate end to the General Strike, agreement on reorganization of the coal industry, an assurance from the TUC that the coal dispute would be settled 'generally on the lines of the report as a whole', continuation of the subsidy until the end of May, and reopening of the mines on the terms prevalent before 30 April. After Samuel had left, Baldwin discussed Samuel's intervention with Neville Chamberlain, Lord Birkenhead (F. E. Smith), and Steel-Maitland. They agreed that the Government should not give any tincture of official support to Samuel's negotiations.[50] Later that day Steel-Maitland wrote to Samuel stressing the point: 'I am sure that the Government will take the view that while they are bound most carefully and most sympathetically to consider the terms of any arrangement which a public man of your responsibility and experience may propose, it is imperative to make it plain that any discussion which you think proper to initiate is not clothed in even a vestige of official character.'[51] Samuel gave an assurance that in all his conversations he was emphasizing that he held no authority from the Government.[52]

Samuel described the progress of his negotiations in two long letters to his wife. In the first, on the morning of Sunday, 9 May, he recounted his activities during the first two days of his intervention:

[49] Beveridge memorandum, 6 May 1926, HLRO HS A/66/5.
[50] See diary of Thomas Jones, 8 May 1926, in Middlemas (ed.), *Jones Diary*, 42.
[51] Steel-Maitland to HS, 8 May 1926, HLRO HS A/66/11.
[52] HS to Steel-Maitland, 9 May 1926, HLRO HS A/66/11a.

The situation I found to be this:-

1. The Government say that they cannot discuss anything, so long as the General Strike continues. They were quite sympathetic to anything I might attempt in order to bring about a resumption of negotiations, but they could take no part in it.

2. The Labour people are well aware that the strike must be beaten, but they cannot call it off until they are assured that the stoppage of the mines will be ended so that the negotiations should be resumed in a free atmosphere.

3. The mine-owners say that they cannot re-open the mines on the previous conditions of employment without the renewal of the subsidy.

4. The Government say that they cannot renew the subsidy unless there is a prospect of success in the negotiations, and that there is none so long as the miners will not accept the wage proposals in the Commission's report.

5. The TUC Committee, which is now acting on behalf of the miners, say that wage reductions ought to be conditional on reconstruction of the industry and that there has been no sufficient assurance that that will be effected.

My object has been to get the Labour people to agree

(a) to withdraw the strike notices
(b) to compel the miners to accept the wage recommendations.

If that were done all the rest would follow automatically—the Government would renew the subsidy for a few weeks, the mines would restart, and the negotiations would resume. In order to facilitate (b) I have made two or three proposals relating to recommendations in the Report, which should ease matters a good deal.

After my second conference with the T.U. leaders—who all entirely approve my suggestions, and say that if they had been made during the negotiations there would have been no breach (but that may be true—or not) I wrote out yesterday evening, at their request, all my suggestions and my proposals of procedure. I wrote hard for about 2½ hours, and got the thing done at the time arranged, for them to discuss with their General Committee. Apparently they have failed to get agreement, for Thomas telephoned me an hour ago to say that 'things looked very black'. He added that it was not because there was anything wrong in my ideas, but because of some question of procedure that had been adopted by the Govt. in relation to the strike. He could not, of course, say very much on the telephone, but I am to meet him later in the day to learn what happened last night. There the matter stands at the moment.

The strike is intensely unpopular and was a most foolish undertaking on the part of the Labour leaders. They know that it must necessarily fail, and are grateful to me for trying to find a way out for them. I am still hopeful that something may come of it.[53]

Later that Sunday Samuel held further meetings with Thomas, Beveridge, Lawrence and with leaders of employers' organizations.

The next day, Monday, 10 May, he lunched with Lane-Fox, the genial but ineffectual Secretary for Mines. In a comment that was typical of his straightforwardness, but also perhaps of an innocence that verged on

[53] HS to BS, 9 May 1926, HLRO HS A/157/1077.

naïvety, Samuel wrote to his wife that he had 'had to be very careful not to tell him of my negotiations as the Govt. must be kept out of the matter absolutely'. He had spent two hours that morning with the TUC leaders. Nevertheless, at his lunch with the responsible minister he told him nothing of the morning's transactions. In the afternoon he met the TUC negotiators for three further hours

and that was the crucial meeting, as the miners were present for the first time— Herbert Smith, A. J. Cook and [W. P.] Richardson. We discussed the thing through and through with energy but without heat. Indeed with the greatest of good humour. Cook took little part. . . . I have a liking and respect for the other H.S. . . .

The Trade Union Committee were hugely pleased with our afternoon's talk. But in the evening they had another conference with the miners, then separate meetings, then a final conference which lasted till 1.30 in the morning, and ended in the miners' definite refusal of my suggestions.

Thomas rang me up this morning [11 May], very depressed, to say so. At 10 o'clock the ex-Commissioners came to see me, including Lee who had motored up from Manchester. At 11 I went over to the Labour Dept. and dictated to a typist a long report to the Prime Minister on all I had done.[54]

At lunchtime on 11 May it appeared, therefore, that Samuel's mediation effort had collapsed.

In his letter to Baldwin, Samuel gave an account of his negotiations over the previous four days. He confirmed that he had not purported to speak on behalf of the Government. In his analysis of the causes of the deadlock, Samuel placed the blame squarely on the obduracy of the miners. The 'real crux of the situation', he suggested, was 'the impossibility of reopening negotiations on the coal question so long as the miners' veto on any form of wage reduction remains.' The TUC, it appeared, were 'not in a position to end the [general] strike without the miners' concurrence'. On the relationship between the miners and the TUC Samuel commented: 'So far as the Miners' Federation is concerned it is Herbert Smith, and not Cook, who is the dominating influence and his position up to the present is quite immovable. The T.U.C. were deceiving themselves when they informed me that there was no longer an absolute veto upon any kind of reduction in any circumstances. My clear view is that the veto remains exactly the same now as it was throughout the negotiations.'[55]

Samuel did not, however, dispatch the letter to Baldwin. Shortly after dictating it, he met the TUC leaders again and discovered that a decisive

[54] HS to BS, 11 May 1926, HLRO HS A/157/1078. It was perhaps an indication of the Government's real attitude (of wishing to encourage Samuel's mediation without appearing to do so) that he was afforded such facilities for his 'private' effort as the car at Dover and the official typist in Whitehall.
[55] HS to Baldwin, 11 May 1926 (draft), HLRO HS A/159/12.

breach had taken place between the TUC and the miners. The miners' 'veto' was no longer recognized as binding by the TUC:

It was fortunate [that it was not sent] because on meeting the trade unionists [at 3.00 p.m. that afternoon] I found that they had finally decided (so they said) to settle the matter, and if the miners did not agree, to require them to do so. The basis was to be a letter from me conveying a memorandum of the points we had agreed in our conversations. They wanted a few points added, mostly in order to make things easier for the miners. I was able to accept all but one, in the form they proposed, or an amended form. They did not improve the memorandum, but there was no harm in them, and it was necessary. The one I rejected was a paragraph about no victimisation after the strike was over. I said that was not my business. They agreed and did not press it. I came back here [Stuart Samuel's house in Mayfair, to which he had moved from the Reform Club] to write out the documents afresh in final form, and sent for my ex-colleagues again, for although they do not come on in this Act, I was anxious to be sure that there was nothing in the memorandum they would definitely oppose if it came to be negotiated upon. They were very lukewarm, and indeed timid, about the whole undertaking, but made one or two important suggestions as to form.[56]

After minor amendments had been agreed with the TUC, the documents were typed out by Thomas's secretary. They took the form of an exchange of letters between Samuel and Arthur Pugh, Chairman of the TUC General Council, Samuel's letter being accompanied by the agreed memorandum. Meanwhile the miners' representatives were conferring privately in a room next door to the TUC leaders. According to A. J. Cook, the miners were assured by their TUC brethren that 'the General Council had guarantees that satisfied them that the Government would accept these proposals, and that on the strike being withdrawn the lock-out notices also would be withdrawn'.[57] But the miners were justifiably sceptical as to the solidity of the alleged 'guarantees'. Smith asked whether Samuel's memorandum was open to amendment. Pugh replied, 'No, you must take it or leave it.' When the miners still manifested dissatisfaction, Thomas tried a different approach: 'You may not trust my word. But will you not take the word of a British gentleman who has been Governor of Palestine?'[58] Even this argument failed to persuade the suspicious miners that they were being promised anything.

Samuel waited at his brother's house for confirmation that the document had been accepted as a basis for calling off the strike. No message arrived. He waited until 1.00 a.m. and then telephoned Thomas who told

[56] HS to BS, 11 May 1926, HLRO HS A/157/1078.
[57] Lansbury's Labour Weekly, 19 June 1926.
[58] Patrick Renshaw, Nine Days that Shook Britain: The 1926 General Strike (Garden City, NY, 1976), 233–4; see also Geoffrey McDonald, 'The Defeat of the General Strike', in Gillian Peele and Chris Cook (eds.), The Politics of Reappraisal 1918–1939 (London, 1975), 64–87.

him that the TUC had definitely decided to call off the General Strike and
to publish the correspondence with Samuel, but that the TUC leaders
were still arguing with the miners. The miners in the end refused to accept
Samuel's memorandum as an acceptable basis for a return to work. The
TUC decided to call off the General Strike anyway. The letters between
Samuel and Pugh were exchanged at 10.00 a.m. the next morning, 12
May, and released to the press at noon. At 11.00 a.m. Samuel met
Baldwin and Steel-Maitland and gave them copies of the documents.
Baldwin expressed his thanks. Samuel's account concluded: 'Afterwards
Thomas came to see me exhausted with fatigue and almost weeping
because the Govt. had not given a definite promise about the withdrawal
of the lock-out notices. They could not do so at this stage, until the miners
have declared their final attitude. The miners are still recalcitrant.'[59]

Samuel's memorandum called for resumption of negotiations in the
coal industry and, contrary to what he had urged in the Royal Commission
report two months earlier, for a renewal of the Government subsidy 'for
such reasonable period as may be required for that purpose'. In order to
facilitate agreement, he proposed the establishment of a National Wages
Board with representatives of employers and workers as well as 'a neutral
element and an independent Chairman'.[60] On the crucial issue of linkage
between wages and reorganization, he wrote: 'There should be no
revision of the previous wage rates unless there are sufficient assurances
that the measures of reorganisation proposed by the Commission will be
effectively adopted.' Samuel also laid down principles on which a wage
agreement might be based, including provision for a minimum wage. In
his accompanying letter to Pugh, Samuel again declared that he had been
'acting entirely on my own initiative, have received no authority from the
Government, and can give no assurances on their behalf'. Nevertheless he
undertook to recommend the proposals to the Government strongly
'when the negotiations are renewed'.[61]

Thus ended the General Strike—which was not, in fact, general. The
number of workers who participated, not counting the locked-out miners,
was estimated as 1,580,000 and about 15,000,000 work-days were lost
in the course of the nine-day strike.[62]

[59] HS to BS, 11 May 1926, HLRO HS A/157/1078.
[60] The Royal Commission had proposed such a Board but only in a tentative way (*Royal
Commission Report*, i. 153). See above, p. 278. Beveridge had resurrected the idea more
emphatically in a memorandum for Samuel on 6 May 1926, HLRO HS A/66/5. See also
two unsigned undated memoranda apparently drafted by Beveridge in early May 1926,
BLPES Beveridge papers VIII/2 and VIII/3.
[61] Manuscript draft of the memorandum, 11 May 1926, HLRO HS A/159/9.
[62] *Ministry of Labour Gazette*, 34/7 (July 1926), 242.

Samuel's negotiation of an end to the General Strike won him many plaudits. Thomas, who wrote that he was 'nearly knocked out', declared that Samuel had helped avert what 'might easily have developed into a revolution'.[63] Walter Runciman wrote that Samuel's intervention was 'the best achievement of your life'.[64] Margot Asquith gushed: 'It's rather cheek of me but I *must* write to tell you how splendid I think you have been, *so* self-sacrificing, *so* kind, & *so* clever. . . . I long to have a talk with you.'[65] The *Manchester Guardian* joined in the general acclaim, but it also pointed unconsciously to the weakness of the whole arrangement when it patted the TUC on the head for its 'confidence in Sir Herbert Samuel's capacity to induce the Government to accept his suggestions.'[66]

In reality, the Samuel memorandum, having served as a figleaf to hide the nakedness of the TUC's surrender, was immediately disowned and rejected by all other parties concerned. The morning after the strike ended, Baldwin told the Deputy Cabinet Secretary that it was necessary 'to repudiate Samuel at once by publishing the letters exchanged between him and Arthur Steel-Maitland because the T.U.C. were trying to suggest to the public that the Samuel document was in some way a condition of their calling off of the General Strike—which of course it was not'.[67] At a meeting of senior ministers with the miners' leaders later the same day, Herbert Smith told Baldwin, 'I have finished with Samuel as far as I am concerned. I want to make that perfectly clear.'[68] The next day Evan Williams led a delegation of mine-owners to 10 Downing Street and echoed Smith's words in the same room the previous day:

We feel that Sir Herbert Samuel has done very great disservice both to the Government and to the owners in butting in, if I may use the phrase, as he did in negotiating with the T.U.C., consulting with the Miners' Federation and producing this formula without discussing the matter in any sort of way at all with the owners. I think I have told you before he did come to see me one evening. I refused to discuss anything with him in the nature of terms for negotiation while the general strike was on. He indicated one or two things he had in his mind in order to get my opinion on them, but I do not think he put them all forward because he considered I was an impossible fellow who did not understand my business or that I was stupid and obstinate, but he has put this forward to the T.U.C. and to the Miners' Federation. . . . Our position is we are not prepared to discuss a settlement upon the basis of the Samuel formula.

Baldwin, in his reply, again swept Samuel's memorandum aside: 'I agree with all you have said about the Samuel formula.' He added, revealingly,

[63] Thomas to HS, 18 May 1926, ISA 100/13.
[64] Runciman to HS, 15 May 1926, HLRO HS A/66/16.
[65] Lady Oxford to HS, 13 May 1926, HLRO HS A/159/15.
[66] *Manchester Guardian*, 13 May 1926.
[67] Thomas Jones diary entry, 13 May 1926, in Middlemas (ed.), *Jones Diary*, 54.
[68] Stenographic notes of meeting, 13 May 1926, PRO CAB 27/318.

that he had been 'rather alarmed' when he had first read Samuel's memorandum and that he remained 'a little anxious . . . lest the miners' delegates should adopt that formula and want to negotiate on it because I feel from our point of view there are several modifications we should want to make in it'.[69]

Given such unanimity of Government, mine-owners, and miners' leaders in condemning Samuel's memorandum, it is hardly surprising that it achieved nothing beyond opening a convenient escape hatch from the general strike for the TUC. On 16 May Samuel sent Baldwin a formal letter detailing his proposals for a settlement of the coal dispute along the lines laid out in his memorandum.[70] But in the ensuing negotiations Samuel's memorandum did not become the basis for a package deal. Baldwin adopted some of Samuel's proposals, including a National Wages Board, in a scheme he put forward a few days later, but this was rejected by both sides. The Government then decided on legislative action. A Coal Mines Act which became law on 8 July restored the eight-hour day. It was followed on 4 August by the Mining Industry Act which placed on the statute book some of the Samuel Commission's recommendations, notably the provision of pit-head baths to be financed by a 5 per cent levy on coal royalties. The Act included limited provisions designed to encourage amalgamations in the industry. But the major long-term recommendations of the Commission relating to amalgamations, nationalization of royalties, municipal trading in coal, and so forth were ignored, although a departmental committee was appointed to inquire into co-operative marketing of coal. By late September 1926, as miners were drifting back to work in some districts, the Miners' Federation at last accepted the Royal Commission Report. But their acceptance came too late. The owners scented total victory and would now be satisfied with nothing less. The lock-out ended only in November as the last of the miners were starved into submission.

Samuel played no direct role in the tragic final act. The TUC leaders, anxious to cover the tracks of what was denounced by the miners and by the far left as an ignominious betrayal, pretended that they had been somehow misled. Pugh, for example, wrote to Samuel on 18 May maintaining that he and his colleagues had acted on the understanding that 'the proposals contained in the [Samuel] Memorandum "could be got"—as I believe were the words you used during one of our visits'.[71] Samuel commented to his wife on the 'sad letter from Pugh . . . lamenting

[69] Stenographic notes of meeting, 14 May 1926, ibid.
[70] HS to Baldwin, 16 May 1926, HLRO HS A/66/18.
[71] Pugh to HS, 18 May 1926, HLRO HS A/66/19.

the fact that the Govt. had not adopted my memorandum'.[72] Samuel made one last effort with Baldwin but this was a pro forma exercise. He knew that, as *The Times* put it on 15 May, the Government's 'hands were, and are, completely free'. The Government's recognition of Samuel's efforts to bring about industrial peace was limited to the award of a KGCB (a higher rank of knighthood than the one he already held) and a silver inkstand bearing the royal arms. Otherwise they felt they were quit of any responsibility to take his proposals seriously. Samuel himself appreciated that his usefulness in this sphere had now come to an end. He therefore turned down suggestions from Thomas, at the end of May, and MacDonald, in September, that he intervene once again.[73]

In some ways Samuel's role in seeking to pacify British industrial strife in 1926 bears comparison with his attempts at political pacification in Palestine between 1920 and 1925. In each case he persisted against all odds in seeking a solution by agreement not coercion. In each he distinguished between short-term palliatives and longer-term remedies, while failing sufficiently to provide effective mechanisms to link temporary expedients to structural change. In each he sought to position himself as an Olympian above the fray, only to be denounced as a partisan. In each, it might be argued, he placed too much reliance on solutions of a traditional Liberal sort—constitutions, frameworks, formulas—that would paper over conflicts without resolving them. Above all, in each case he displayed a faith in the ultimate reasonableness of men that in the last resort took insufficient account of the savagery of collective hatreds in the era of mass politics.

In this last lay perhaps the fundamental weakness of his Liberalism as a functional ideology in the post-liberal age. By 1926 many of Samuel's former colleagues in the Liberal Party had moved to one side or other of the barricade. Churchill had joined the Conservatives; Trevelyan had joined Labour. In October 1926, while attending the Labour Party's annual conference at Margate, Beatrice Webb mused: 'There is today no reason why Keynes, E. D. Simon and Herbert Samuel should not be among the leaders of the Labour Party—they are certainly more advanced than J. R. M[acDonald] and J. H. T[homas] in their constructive proposals.'[74] But Samuel would have none of it. He remained convinced of the distinctive value of Liberalism and, far from abandoning what appeared to be a sinking ship, he now resolved to re-enter British politics as a Liberal leader.

[72] HS to BS, 20 May 1926, HLRO HS A/157/1087.
[73] HS to BS, 27 May 1926, HLRO HS A/157/1092; HS to MacDonald, 4 Oct. 1926, PRO PRO 30/69/1171.
[74] Entry dated 12 Oct. 1926, BLPES Beatrice Webb diary, 4408.

11

Organizer

=

I'm liberal. You, you aristocrat
Won't know exactly what I mean by that.
I mean so altruistically moral
I never take my own side in a quarrel.

(Robert Frost)

IN JUNE 1926 Samuel spent a weekend with his old friends the Webbs.
Beatrice left in her diary a characteristically acidulous portrait of him
at the age of 55, on the eve of his return to British politics:

He has changed little, either in appearance and manner or in outlook from the rich
young man conscientiously and energetically entering public life whom we first knew
nearly forty years ago. He is just a trifle stouter and more debonair; he is even *more*
economical in personal expenditure, circumspect in behaviour and discreet in speech;
these are tendencies which have grown on him. He is less conceited—indeed he is not
conceited at all. Considering his marked success as a Cabinet Minister, Parliamentarian
and Pro-Consul—he is in fact singularly modest. The exercise of power has not
hardened his heart, and industry and experience have extended and matured his
facilities. He is an estimable citizen, an able public servant, a devoted husband and
father. He is not exciting; his words leave no pictures either of events or persons; his
arguments are restricted in scope and his conclusions though sensible are common-
place. His sense of humour takes the irritating form of tactless irony at the expense of
the person he is talking to. All the same I thoroughly appreciated an eight mile walk
with him and twenty-four hours talk about the past, present and future.

Beatrice's clearsightedness often got in the way of her affectionate impulses. She was, in fact, happy to see him again: 'Our long standing
relations with Herbert Samuel, like the man himself, ha[ve] worn well.
Three pedestrian minds enjoyed a week end together and we parted with
the kindliest feelings of mutual respect and friendship.'[1]

---

[1] Samuel reciprocated the Webbs' renewed amiability. When Beatrice celebrated her
seventieth birthday in Jan. 1928, he wrote her a long and cordial, though hardly intimate,
letter ('Dear Mrs Webb'—thus to a close friend of 35 years' standing!) in which he avowed:
'Your long friendship, its kindness and its helpfulness, are among the things in my life that
I value most.' (20 Jan. 1928, BLPES Passfield papers II.4.i.22.)

Beatrice expressed some puzzlement at Samuel's political stance. On the one hand, he would not cross over to Labour: 'He does not believe in the supersession of Capitalism though he is ready to accept some degree of public control by public administration.' On the other, he seemed disengaged from organized Liberalism: 'He did not criticise Lloyd George; but his gesture implied moral contempt for his old colleague. When one comes to think about it, he said no good word for any of his Liberal ex-colleagues. He did not run them down—he hardly mentioned them—one would gather that with no one of them was he on intimate terms and that their attitude to him would be equally neutral.'[2]

Samuel's eight years out of Parliament and five out of England had distanced him from the squalid quarrels and petty recriminations that characterized Liberalism in that period. His reputation had grown as a result of his apparent successes in Palestine and in the General Strike. His temporary withdrawal from British politics had left him almost the only senior Liberal not closely identified with either the Lloyd George or the Asquith wings of the broken butterfly that was the Liberal Party. But in spite of his earlier resolution to turn to philosophy, his experience with the Coal Commission renewed his taste for politics, and from February 1926 he spoke confidentially of returning to political activity in England.[3] The tug of Palestine remained, but he wrote to his eldest son: 'I feel sure that I can be much more useful in British politics than in anything else.... I am not really qualified to do the sort of work that Weiżmann is doing or to influence for long the people who are his constituents.'[4]

Samuel never for a moment considered following Trevelyan and other friends into the Labour Party. 'Nothing has happened [he wrote to Runciman in March 1926] during the six years that I have been out of politics to lead me to change my opinions on the main issues in any way. When the present Government begins to get unpopular, as some day it must, many people will begin to regret that the only alternative is Socialism; and unless the Labour Party discards that, the conditions will be there for a revival of Liberalism.'[5] He wanted first to finish his book on philosophy and only then to return to what he called 'my poor water-logged party'.[6]

When the General Strike ended, Samuel had planned to return to Italy to resume writing. But he was detained in England by the death, on the day after the strike ended, of his brother Stuart at whose house he had been staying. The two had never been intimates. Stuart did not share

[2] Entry dated 28 June 1926, BLPES Beatrice Webb diary, 4327–30.
[3] HS to ES, 13 Feb. 1926, ISA 100/51.   [4] HS to ES, 9 Mar. 1926, ibid.
[5] HS to Runciman, 10 Mar. 1926, WR 203.
[6] HS to Wallas, 26 Apr. 1926, BLPES Wallas papers 1/66.

Herbert's puritanism. He lived on a more lavish scale and indulged in high life, champagne, and the company of women. Herbert was shocked, many years later, on a visit to New York, to discover a grown-up nephew, the illegitimate son of Stuart, of whose very existence he had hitherto been ignorant.

A week after the end of the strike he lunched with Runciman and discussed the latest party brawl between Lloyd George and Asquith (now Earl of Oxford). Runciman pressed Samuel to re-enter politics.[7] Samuel's sympathies were wholly with Asquith but he did not yet feel ready 'to take a hand again'.[8] In July 1926 he returned to the Continent, planning to resume work on his book. The following October the crisis in the Liberal Party came to a head. The 74-year-old Asquith, in a state of exasperation with Lloyd George, finally concluded that 'Liberal reunion' was 'a fiction, if not a farce' and resigned the party leadership.[9] The press speculated that Samuel might succeed him.[10] But Samuel wrote to Asquith that he intended to return to the Continent to finish his book and only then return to England and consult him 'as to the best course to pursue on re-entering British politics after an interval of nearly a decade'.[11] To Edwin Samuel, meanwhile, he confessed that he found it 'gratifying that some people are thinking of me as a possible leader'.[12]

Samuel's plans were again disturbed by a family death. His last surviving brother, Gilbert, died in late October, leaving a tangled state of personal affairs. Samuel returned to England for the funeral and found himself drawn back inextricably into the maelstrom of Liberal politics. The resignation of Asquith had left the party in a state of chaos and general disgruntlement. In spite of the nominal 'reunion' in November 1923, the party still maintained two rival organizations, the 'official' machine under the control of the Asquithians and the personal organization of Lloyd George. This latter enjoyed the benefit of the 'Lloyd George fund', allegedly derived from the proceeds of the sale of honours during Lloyd George's premiership. More than anything else, the fund poisoned relationships within the party. Lloyd George sought to maintain personal control over the fund while using it as a device for fastening his grip over the entire party. The Asquithians denounced the fund as an affront to political decency. At the same time, given their own impoverished organization, they were unable to resist the temptation constantly dangled

[7] HS to BS, 20 May 1926, HLRO HS A/157/1087.
[8] HS to BS, 2 June 1926, HLRO HS A/157/1094.
[9] Memorandum by Asquith, 6 Oct. 1926, quoted in Wilson, *Downfall of Liberal Party*, 354–5.
[10] See e.g. *Daily Herald*, 15 Oct. 1926.
[11] HS to Lord Oxford, 18 Oct. 1926, HLRO HS A/155/VI/24.
[12] HS to ES, 22 Oct. 1926, ISA 100/51.

before them by Lloyd George that it might be used to replenish the coffers of a genuinely reunited party. The animosity between the two factions was so intense that neither Lloyd George nor any conceivable Asquithian candidate could hope to command the united allegiance of the party.

Samuel, who had pondered from afar the depressing condition of the party, now decided to intervene. He indicated the definitive character of his return by arranging to take a seven-year lease on 35 Porchester Terrace, the old Franklin family home in which his wife had grown up, just two doors away from the house he had occupied until 1920. On 26 October he began a round of discussions with Asquith, Lloyd George, and other Liberal leaders to whom he presented a plan for restoring party unity. The scheme, as he presented it to Lloyd George, involved leaving the question of party leadership 'in abeyance' and summoning a Liberal conference under a neutral chairman. That conference should 'make suitable declarations' on party policy and appoint an executive committee of seven or eight to run the party. 'Let L.G. make a proper disposition with regard to his fund; then carry on a vigorous programme in the country in which I should take an active part.' Lloyd George expressed general approval, and Samuel wrote to his wife: 'Asquith's resignation makes a great change, and I am clear that the time for action is now.'[13]

Samuel was heartened by the response he encountered from other leading Liberals of both factions. And in spite of his personal revulsion from Lloyd George, he was attracted by the radicalism of Lloyd George's policies, particularly the land programme which had been the centrepiece of Lloyd George's efforts over the previous year. 'The Land Policy, as finally formulated, is a very fine one—on the lines I have always worked for, but going further and much more fully elaborated. The doubtful features of the earlier drafts have been eliminated. I shall be able to advocate it wholeheartedly.'[14] In November 1926 he received an offer to stand for Parliament in a by-election at Hull Central, where the Liberal MP had joined the Labour Party, but he refused, saying that he did not wish, at that stage, to return to the House of Commons.[15] In the following weeks he turned down further approaches, including one from his old constituency of South Oxfordshire.[16] The initial promise of party unity meanwhile faded, as renewed squabbles erupted over 'the wretched question of Ll.G.'s fund'. Samuel privately shared the aversion of Grey and other Asquithians from Lloyd George's character and methods: 'You

[13] HS to BS, 27 Oct. 1926, HLRO HS A/157/1115.
[14] HS to BS, 29 Oct. 1926, HLRO HS A/157/1118.
[15] V. Phillips to HS, 5 Nov. 1926, HLRO HS A/155/VI/25; HS to ES, 15 Nov. 1926, ISA 100/51.
[16] John Murray to HS, 18 Dec. 1926, HLRO HS A/155/VI/28; R. C. Williams (Swansea West) corr. with HS, Dec. 1926–Jan. 1927, HLRO HS A/155/VI/29–35.

are quite right [he wrote to Edwin Samuel in December] in thinking that his personality is the difficulty. It is indeed the only one.'[17] Grey and his adherents formed themselves into a body of Asquithian irreconcilables known as the Liberal Council whose members included Walter Runciman, Donald Maclean, Herbert Gladstone, H. G. Gardiner, Gilbert Murray and Violet Bonham-Carter (Asquith's daughter). But Samuel recognized that the elemental force of Lloyd George must be effectively harnessed if the Liberal Party were to have any hope of returning to power. He therefore swallowed his personal distaste and decided to work with him.

An important step forward was taken on 19 January 1927, when agreement was reached on the disposition of the Lloyd George Fund. The Liberal Party Administrative Committee accepted an offer by Lloyd George of £300,000 to be used for the Liberal campaign in the next election plus £35,000 per annum for party administrative expenses over the next three years.[18] But the dissension continued, and Samuel tired of the endless argument. In February 1927 he wrote to Norman Bentwich: 'The quarrelings in the Liberal Party are lamentable. I will take no part in them and propose to walk steadily along my own path. So far as I can judge the great mass of Liberals are only anxious to get on with the reconstruction of the party, and are more annoyed by these disputes than interested in them.'[19] Shortly afterwards he nevertheless acceded to a unanimous request from the party's Administrative Committee to take over as head of the Liberal Party Organization. He consented on condition that he would be answerable only to the committee—not, therefore, to Lloyd George.[20] Samuel's refusal to stand for Parliament left Lloyd George as Chairman of the parliamentary party, a position which he succeeded in transmuting into that of *de facto* party leader in the country. Characteristically, Samuel did not complain of this. He was content to throw himself into the task of revivifying the arthritic party organization and to seek to overcome past differences by uniting the party on a new and radical programme.

On 28 February Samuel marked his return to public life by a speech to the Eighty Club at the Hotel Cecil. He declared that he had come 'to make to you a profession of my political faith'. At the top of his agenda he still placed 'what Carlyle used to call "the Condition of the People Question" ', to which he advocated non-socialist but radical solutions. He outlined the work of policy formulation that had begun on Lloyd George's initiative

[17] HS to ES, 17 Dec. 1926, ISA 100/51.
[18] Wilson, *Downfall of Liberal Party*, 364–5.
[19] HS to Bentwich, 30 Jan./1 Feb. 1927, CZA A/255/607.
[20] HS to Lloyd George, 9 Feb. 1927, HLRO Lloyd George papers G/17/9/4; Wilson, *Downfall of Liberal Party*, 367.

under the aegis of the Liberal Industrial Inquiry. He raised an uneasy laugh by remarking: 'Mr Lloyd George is taking the humble role of Chairman of one of these sub-committees—an example of that meekness which is well-known to be one of his distinguishing characteristics.' In the final part of his speech he made a fervent and surprisingly candid call for party unity:

What are we to think of the quarrels and controversies that have helped of late to reduce Liberalism to impotence . . ? Let us have done with them once and for all! . . . Our divisions are about persons, or one may rather say about a person. One point of principle has indeed been brought into mention, and it is of fundamental importance. It is that no party ought to be influenced in the policy it adopts by the source of the funds which it receives. As to that there can be no two opinions. It would be intolerable that policy should be deflected this way or that by a magnet of gold.[21]

The speech was well received by all sections of the party. Colonel T. F. Tweed, Lloyd George's chief organizer (or 'hench man' as Margot Asquith termed him) reported: 'Lloyd George is delighted with your speech last night. He was full of praise this morning for what he termed your "courage and directness".'[22]

Samuel's decision to take the helm was widely welcomed in the party. Augustine Birrell, an Asquithian of purest vintage, wrote to him: 'I have declined to join the Liberal Council as I do not care about new Organisations, but my views in regard to a certain gentleman are just as strong as they were before. . . . You are really the one person who is in the position to pull the Liberal Party together.'[23] Birrell's reservation showed how superficial was the unity that had been attained. Nevertheless, Samuel set to work with his customary efficiency and energy. He published a string of articles in the popular press and addressed fifty-three meetings in the course of the next five months.[24]

At the end of March he delivered his first important speech in the north at a large meeting in the Free Trade Hall in Manchester. The audience was sympathetic and had been 'warmed up' by mass singing of Liberal songs. Samuel was accorded an enthusiastic welcome in this great sanctum of Liberal oratory. The *Manchester Guardian* took his speech as 'one token among many of new heart and a new purpose in the Liberal party'. The paper opined further, 'There will be no difference of purpose or of

---

[21] *Full Steam Ahead* (text of speech by HS on 28 Feb. 1927, published by Liberal Publication Department, London, 1927).
[22] Tweed to HS, 1 Mar. 1927, HLRO HS A/155/VI/47.
[23] Birrell to HS, 24 Feb. 1927, HLRO HS A/155/VI/43.
[24] See *Reynold's Weekly*, 13 Mar. 1927; *Daily News*, 13 Mar. 1927; *John Bull*, 23 Apr. 1927; *Evening News*, 19 May 1927; *Daily Mirror*, 17 June 1927.

urgency between him and Mr Lloyd George'. At the same time the Liberal organ noted the special quality of Samuel's public performances:

There was in his speech last night, for all its weight and quiet ardour, a curious element of detachment which reminds one of Mr Baldwin in his more reflective mood. He weighed Conservatism, he weighed the Labour party, with scrupulous fairness, in the balance, giving to each such credit as it might fairly claim, and a good deal more than some ardent spirits might be inclined to allow. Yet this was but the preliminary to a dissection of their shortcomings the more effective and ruthless because of its judicial calm. The method has its drawbacks as an appeal to the political partisan in us all, but it has the advantage of being pretty solidly based on the truth, or at least on conviction, and it has a singular attraction for the doubtful and the unpledged, who represent today probably a far larger proportion of the electorate than ever before in our history.[25]

Samuel's public persona evoked similar responses throughout his career.[26] He not only lacked the native crowd-pleasing ability of Lloyd George but seemed to despise the cultivation of such devices. In the great age of the political mass meeting his 'air of cold realism', as a sympathetic commentator termed it, was a disadvantage in a party leader.[27]

But Samuel, like Baldwin, succeeded in turning a defect in one medium into a virtue in another. The quiet, understated reasonableness that would fail to stir great crowds worked a different, but politically just as effective, magic on much larger audiences of atomized individuals listening to their wireless sets. Samuel had given his first broadcast talk (on Palestine) over the BBC in November 1925. By the early 1930s he had developed into a skilled radio speaker with resonant, old-fashioned locutions, slow delivery, clear enunciation, varied intonation, and a pleasant baritone voice. His mastery of this new means of political propaganda was a significant element in his emergence as a major national politician in this period.

Although Samuel's primary focus between 1927 and 1929 was on organization, he also played an important role in the formulation of a new party policy. The impressive central feature of new Liberal thinking was the Liberal 'Yellow Book' entitled *Britain's Industrial Future*. This was the product of the Liberal Industrial Inquiry, conducted by a formidable group of politicians, businessmen, and thinkers, who included J. M. Keynes, E. D. Simon, Charles Masterman, Seebohm Rowntree, and L. T. Hobhouse as well as Lloyd George and Samuel.[28] The programme of

---

[25] *Manchester Guardian*, 24 Mar. 1927.   [26] See above, p. 68.

[27] James Corbett, 'Sir Herbert Samuel and the Liberal Party', *Fortnightly Review*, 128 (July 1927), 71–83; see also Wilson, *Downfall of Liberal Party*, 370.

[28] The spelling of 'Enquiry' was altered to 'Inquiry' for fear that the acronym formed from the initial letters might 'provoke rude scoffing' (note on front of folder on L.I.I. among papers of Waldo McGillycuddy Eagar, Reform Club MS Eagar 12).

industrial reconstruction and interventionist state action laid out in the
'Yellow Book' was heavily influenced by Keynes who drafted the section
dealing with 'National Finance'. Samuel contributed a chapter on 'Coal'
that followed the lines of his Royal Commission Report of 1926. The
'Yellow Book', published in March 1928, became the basis for Liberal
propaganda in the 1929 general election. It paved the way for the
Liberals' manifesto, *We Can Conquer Unemployment*, published in
1929. Samuel wrote a number of newspaper and periodical articles
highlighting the proposals for 'ownership-sharing' in industry and public
works programmes designed to act as 'buffer-employments'.[29]

Many of the ideas in the 'Yellow Book' had been thrashed out in
discussions among Liberal intellectuals at the annual Liberal Summer
Schools from 1921 onwards. Samuel attended his first Summer School in
Cambridge in 1927 and thereafter became a regular participant. In his
inaugural address to the 1927 meeting, Samuel discussed the relationship
between Liberals and the Labour movement. While ritually slaughtering
Marxian socialism, he dwelt on the points of identity between Labour and
'social Liberalism'. He concluded tantalizingly: 'I entertain an expectation,
although I feel no certainty, that this course will lead, some day and
somehow, to a restoration of the old alliance between Liberalism and the
Labour movement, to the lasting benefit of both.'[30]

The Liberals received a fillip in mid-Parliament by a string of by-
election victories. In late March 1927 they scored successes at Leith and at
Southwark North, the latter a gain from Labour. At the end of May they
won the Leicestershire seat of Bosworth from the Conservatives. But in
June they narrowly failed to regain Westbury in Wiltshire, a seat with an
old Liberal tradition. After some less impressive results the following
winter, they gained Lancaster in February 1928 and St Ives in March.
They were encouraged—perhaps too much encouraged—by these victories.[31] Samuel thought he scented a general election triumph. In May
1927 he wrote to Edwin Samuel from the National Liberal Federation
conference at Margate: 'After years of defeat and depression, there is now
a feeling of buoyant optimism. . . . Although we have only about 40
members in the present Parliament, out of 615, there is a growing feeling
in the country that we shall dominate the next one.'[32]

[29] Herbert Samuel, 'The Liberal Industrial Report', *Contemporary Review*, 133 (Mar.
1928), 277–84; see also *John Bull*, 3 Mar. 1928; *Spectator*, 3 Mar. and 26 May 1928.
[30] Herbert Samuel, 'Liberals and the Labour Movement', *Contemporary Review*, 132
(Oct. 1927), 409–21.
[31] Cf. Chris Cook and John Ramsden (eds.), *By-Elections in British Politics* (New York,
1973), 73–4; M. W. Hart, 'The Decline of the Liberal Party in Parliament and in the
Constituencies 1914–1931', D.Phil. thesis (Oxford, 1982), 346; Michael Bentley, *The
Liberal Mind 1914–1929* (Cambridge, 1977), 111–12.
[32] HS to ES, 29 May 1927, ISA 100/52.

Samuel's hope that the prospect of victory might serve to unify the party was only partially realized. In February 1928, just as the 'Yellow Book' was published to a disappointing reception, a renewed imbroglio broke out over money.[33] The controversy coincided with a renewal of factional strife arising from the St Ives by-election campaign, where the Liberal candidate, Hilda Runciman, wife of Walter, issued a policy statement which, Samuel wrote to Sir John Simon, was 'quite counter to the proposals on land policy' that had been adopted by the party.[34] Her action was regarded and intended as a calculated snub to Lloyd George. Samuel felt obliged to accede to urgent requests to go to St Ives to speak on her behalf. He explained to Lloyd George: 'If I were to keep aloof in this critical election it would mean that I was cutting myself off definitely from the whole of the section which comprises, or sympathises with the Liberal Council. . . . At the same time I shall make it clear in my speech that I stand for the whole forward policy of Liberalism, and when the by-election is over I shall endeavour to meet the Council section and arrive at a clear understanding whether they do or do not accept that policy.'[35] Lloyd George returned a raging blast in which he denounced the 'state of indiscipline' in the party, complained that Samuel's intervention at St Ives would 'shatter our effort', and accused Samuel of going back on an engagement regarding the disposition of money from the Lloyd George fund.[36]

The two groups continued to stab each other in the back for months, and Samuel found it difficult to maintain a middle position. Asquith had died in February 1928, but his eccentric widow kept the eternal flame of factional hatred alive for years by firing off vituperative private notes in all directions, attacking Lloyd George and all his works. Immediately after Hilda Runciman's by-election victory, Samuel tried to clear the air by meeting members of the Liberal Council.[37] But the encounter did little to dissipate the profound mistrust of Lloyd George among the dwindling remnant of the Asquithian faithful.

The record of a meeting of the party's Organization Committee in July 1928 affords a revealing glimpse of the distempers that flew out of the Pandora's box of the Lloyd George fund. At the meeting Samuel was asked about the financial position of the party.

[33] See Lord St Davids to HS, 9 Feb. 1928, HLRO HS A/71/3; H. F. Oldman to HS, 10 Feb. 1928, A/71/4; T. F. Tweed to Oldman, 10 Feb. 1928, A/71/4a; HS to St Davids, 17 Feb. 1928, A/71/6; St Davids to HS, 20 Feb. 1928, A/71/5; memorandum by HS, 23 Feb. 1928, A/71/7.
[34] HS to Sir John Simon, 23 Feb. 1928, Bodleian Library, Oxford, MS Simon 61/149–51.
[35] HS to Lloyd George, 26 Feb. 1928, HLRO HS A/71/8.
[36] Lloyd George to HS, 28 Feb. 1928, HLRO HS A/71/9.
[37] HS to Walter Runciman, 9 Mar. 1928, WR 216.

He replied that he was unable at present to make a statement. Pressed with regard to this, he said that they had received £100,000 [apparently from the Lloyd George fund] which was almost entirely expended. No further payment had as yet been made, but an application had been put forward and he had no doubt that a further like sum would be forthcoming.

Asked to name the amount which he had received on account of the £300,000 promised [from the Lloyd George fund] for the General Election, he said that he was not in a position to make any statement as to this. Further pressed, he said that Major [H. L.] Nathan, a member of committee present, who, he understood, was Solicitor to Mr Ll. G. for the purposes of the Fund, should be asked if he had anything to say. Major Nathan replied that the position between himself and his Clients was of a confidential character, and he could not make any statement without authority, but he could say that certain legal difficulties still stood in the way, but it was hoped that they would be cleared up in a short time.

A note attached to this record suggests that £150,000 was paid over from the fund to the party machine on 6 July, and Samuel said that he expected to receive the remaining £150,000 'very soon'.[38] The episode demonstrated the morass into which a great political party had sunk. Samuel, who despised Lloyd George's financial methods, no doubt felt keenly the humiliation of having to hold out the party's cap for Lloyd George's doles. What made matters worse was that as head of the party organization he became the butt of vehement attacks by critics of Lloyd George. He suffered his unenviable lot with characteristic phlegm.

In October Hilda Runciman wrote to Samuel 'with the confidential frankness of an old friend', accusing him of having thrown in his lot 'with those who had accepted the financial domination of Mr Lloyd George', who, she declared, was 'a political crook'. 'I have always thought it your influence [she continued] more than that of any man that induced many bewildered and reluctant people to accept the humiliation of the Party's dependence on a Personal Fund under Mr Lloyd George.'[39] Samuel repudiated the suggestion of financial dependence, but agreed 'that it would have been very preferable if Lloyd George had transferred the whole of his fund at once. The fact that he has not done so is not, in my opinion, a reason for breaking off relations. As to the question of Lloyd George's leadership, I am unwilling to let myself be obsessed by that to the exclusion of the much more important things which are at stake.'[40] But

[38] Handwritten note by Sir Donald Maclean attached to memorandum, [7] July 1928, Bodleian Library, Oxford, Dep. c. 468.
[39] Hilda Runciman to HS, 17 Oct. 1928, HLRO HS A/71/10.
[40] HS to Hilda Runciman, 22 Oct. 1928, HLRO HS A/71/11.

what Samuel called 'these miserable disputes' dragged on interminably and weakened the party's appeal to undecided voters.[41]

Signs of a waning of the Liberal revival were evident in by-election results in the later part of 1928. At Carmarthen, where the sitting Liberal MP had crossed to the Conservatives, the Liberals won back the seat by the barest of margins. At Ashton-under-Lyne, where they had hoped for victory, Labour gained the seat from the Conservatives, leaving the Liberal at the foot of the poll. In nine further by-elections before the general election of May 1929, the Liberals scored two gains, but one of these was in a straight fight with the Conservatives. The Liberal came bottom of the poll in five of the remaining seven contests. By October 1928, J. L. Garvin of the *Observer* was already predicting that the Liberal resurgence had run out of steam.[42]

The Liberals nevertheless approached the general election with a confident mien, announcing that they would field more than 500 candidates. Samuel rashly declared: 'We shall do so, not in the least with the purpose or the desire of holding the balance in the next House of Commons. That does not interest us at all. Our purpose is to secure a definite and independent majority in the House of Commons—in the next Parliament, if possible; if not, in the one after.'[43] Yet even the imminence of a general election did not put an end to the Liberals' bickering. In particular, Grey and his adherents made difficulties about appearing on the same platform as Lloyd George.

Most contemporary observers gave Samuel high marks for restoring some measure of outward unity and inner efficiency to the party's central apparatus. Historians have largely concurred, although a recent study suggests that the new vigour at the centre was not transmitted to the party's grass-roots organization in the constituencies which remained very weak.[44] Lloyd George, far from appreciating Samuel's efforts, evinced irritation at the respect Samuel had earned: 'Samuel's inordinate vanity which bids him want always to pose as leader has landed him in trouble. If his courage and capacity were equal to his conceit I should resign in his favour.'[45] This was a churlish return for Samuel's self-effacing activity over the previous two years.

In February 1929 Lloyd George discussed with Maclean an appeal that Samuel had made to Conservatives to support the Liberals. The two

[41] See Walter Runciman to HS, 22 Nov. 1928, WR 221; HS to Walter Runciman, 25 Nov. 1928, ibid.; see also V. Phillips to HS, 19 Dec. 1928, HLRO HS A/157/VII/29.
[42] *Observer*, 14 and 21 Oct. 1928.
[43] Letter to the editor, *Observer*, 21 Oct. 1928.
[44] See Hart, 'Decline of Liberal Party', 357.
[45] Lloyd George to Frances Donaldson, 5 Feb. 1929, in Taylor (ed.), *My Darling Pussy*, 126.

agreed that Samuel's move was 'inapt' since such appeals alienated the Liberal left wing 'and further would evoke no response other than contempt from the Tories'.[46] Yet within a fortnight of that conversation Lloyd George himself discussed with Churchill the conditions under which the Liberals might support a Conservative government after the next election.[47] Evidently what was 'inapt' as a public appeal was legitimate as a secret manœuvre. Meanwhile, in a conversation with Samuel in the same week, Lloyd George 'said that if any attempt were made in the next Parlt. to induce the Lib. Party to support a Socialist Govt. the Party would be split from top to bottom'.[48] Lloyd George's contortions did not remain secret, and attracted criticism. A commentator in the *Evening Standard*, for example, deplored the Liberals' 'sad declension' from 'the old Liberalism with its fine tradition, to that of bargaining and trafficking between Conservatives and Socialists'.[49]

The general election of May 1929 was the Liberals' last serious push for power and they waged the campaign with a renewed zeal that for a while cast into the shade the internecine hatreds and mud-slinging of the previous few years. In order to concentrate on campaigning, Samuel gave up day-to-day direction of the Liberal machine. He had accepted the Liberal nomination for Darwen, a working-class Lancashire seat dominated by the cotton industry, and he devoted much of his time to the constituency. Buoyed up by a favourable press for the Liberals' rallying call of 'We Can Conquer Unemployment', he entered the campaign in optimistic spirit. In April he traversed the country from Cornwall to Aberdeenshire, addressing eighty-four meetings, many attended by enthusiastic audiences of several thousand. Several of his speeches were relayed simultaneously to Liberal meetings in other towns. Such devices were a novelty and attracted publicity. His daughter Nancy spoke for him at Darwen—the 'flapper' vote of women aged between 21 and 30 was a new factor in this election—and she took the chair at a Liberal rally in the Albert Hall. Samuel's party political broadcast on the BBC further excited Liberal enthusiasm.

Samuel spent most of May in Darwen where he faced the sitting Conservative MP, Sir Frank Sanderson, as well as a Labour candidate. Although a Liberal had won the seat in 1923, Conservatives had held it at nearly every election since 1895. They had even won it narrowly in 1906. Samuel thus faced an uphill battle, particularly given the Labour candidacy.

[46] Memorandum by Maclean on talk with Lloyd George, 8 Feb. 1929, Bodleian Library, Oxford, Dep. c. 468.
[47] See Bentley, *Liberal Mind*, 114.
[48] Note by HS, 13 Feb. 1929, HLRO HS A/72/1.
[49] *Evening Standard*, 11 Feb. 1929.

The central theme of his speeches and campaign literature was the Liberal claim to offer a solution to the problem of unemployment—the dominant issue in a declining mill town such as Darwen. Ten thousand turned out in the Market Square to hear a debate on unemployment between Samuel and his Labour opponent. The Liberal emphasis on unemployment was denounced by Churchill, who was temporarily amnesiac about his own radical speeches on the subject in olden days: 'I think it is one of the meanest things that has ever been done to exploit unemployment for party purposes. The only object of the people who are running it is to get employment for themselves.'[50] But Samuel's campaign struck fire in Darwen. As in Cleveland, he won the hearts of working-class voters to a degree that would have surprised London high society. 'Who is Sir Herbert Samuel?' a Liberal councillor asked at one of his meetings. Back came the reply from the audience in the local dialect: 'He's a gradely man.'[51] Lloyd George came to speak on his behalf to an audience of ten thousand at the Anchor football ground. The former Prime Minister delivered a panegyric of praise for Samuel and continued with a characteristically rousing speech, not at all disconcerted by a heckler who called out, 'What about homes for heroes?'[52] The turnout at Darwen was 93.6 per cent, reflecting the efficient organization of both Conservatives and Liberals. Samuel won, but only by a majority of 462 over the Conservative on a poll of more than 38,000.

Notwithstanding Samuel's local triumph, the results in the rest of the country came as a bitter disillusionment to the Liberals. Although they won 5.3 million votes as against more than 8 million each for Conservatives and Labour, they increased their number of seats to only 59. In the new House the Liberals held the balance between the Conservatives (261 seats) and Labour (287). Samuel's reaction to the 'miserable outcome' was philosophical, although he expressed outrage at the action of his Liberal neighbour in the Preston constituency, W. A. Jowitt, who, a week after the election, joined the Labour Party and became Attorney-General in the Labour Government formed by Ramsay MacDonald.[53] Other former Liberals who joined the Government included Noel Buxton, Wedgwood Benn, Christopher Addison, and Charles Trevelyan.

Baldwin resigned almost immediately to make way for Labour, but it was the Liberals who found themselves obliged to pay the political price of helping to prop up the new Government. Immediately after the formation of the new administration, Samuel wrote to his old friend

[50] Speech by Churchill, 13 May 1929, in Robert Rhodes James (ed.), *Winston S. Churchill, His Complete Speeches* (London, 1974), iv. 4621–2.
[51] *Darwen News*, 18 May 1929.   [52] Ibid., 29 May 1929.
[53] HS to ES, 10/11 June 1929, ISA 100/53.

Sidney Webb, newly appointed Colonial Secretary, in the hope of establishing a basis for co-operation. Webb responded cordially: 'Of course, there is an almost endless succession of things on which we ought to be able to join forces. But I wonder what you meant by the phrase in your last speech as to applications of Socialist theory being outside the sphere of possible agreement. I should have thought that you (and I) had been supporting "applications of the Socialist theory" for the past twenty years.' Webb instanced municipal housing, the BBC, the electric grid, factory Acts, social welfare schemes, and 'Collective Taxation deliberately for the purpose of equalizing, *pro tanto*, wealth distribution (e.g. progressive death duties, Supertax etc.)'.[54] Samuel replied: 'None of the social activities that you mention disturb me in the slightest. I am wholeheartedly in favour of all of them. . . . The "socialist theory" to which I am opposed is that which favours a general, or at least a widespread, socialisation of production and distribution.' He warned that he would feel compelled to 'diverge' if Labour tried to enact such socialist measures.[55]

In his first speech after re-election to the House of Commons, in the debate on the King's Speech, Samuel tried to set the tone and the terms of Liberal co-operation with the Government. Not surprisingly, given the results of the election, he reminded the House of the Liberals' longstanding advocacy of electoral reform and asked for 'some definite and formal assurance' from the Government of expeditious action on the subject. He declared that 'the problems of unemployment must have priority over all else'.[56] In his parliamentary report to the King, MacDonald wrote that Samuel 'was quietly and unostentatiously effective'.[57] The *Sunday Times* judged his speech 'the best performance of the week', and other papers echoed that view.[58] The speech reinforced Samuel's position as second only to Lloyd George among Liberals—first for the many Liberals who detested the party leader. C. P. Scott wrote to Samuel a few days later in a strange state of wishful thinking:

It is quite true, as you say, that Liberalism has conquered the country as, in spite of certain evil incidents, one has faith that it may conquer the world, and emphatically true that the Liberal party has been denied the usual rewards of its conquest. None the less I feel sure that we are the controlling power in the country, not merely as holding the balance in Parliament, but because we represent the real will and purpose of the nation. We acclaim you therefore as the real Prime Minister, whatever the ostensible

---

[54] Sidney Webb to HS, 12 June 1929, HLRO HS A/155/VII/43.
[55] HS to Sidney Webb, 17 June 1929, HLRO HS A/155/VII/43a.
[56] *HC Deb.* 5 s., vol. 229 (4 July 1929), cols. 299–314.
[57] MacDonald to King George V, 4 July 1929, Royal Archives.
[58] *Sunday Times*, 7 July 1929.

occupant of the chair of State may think or say. Forgive me if this is too exuberant a view.[59]

Samuel's view was less exuberant. While he considered the Government 'quite sincere' about setting up a three-party conference on electoral reform, he noted that continuing divisions within his own party had led to his being 'looked upon as a kind of supplementary or deputy leader'.[60]

The Liberals in the Parliament of 1929 to 1931 presented a sorry spectacle of division and confusion. The internal recriminations had resumed immediately after the election. In the van was Margot Asquith, who bombarded Samuel with notes attacking Lloyd George as an 'untrustworthy liar' and much else.[61] The Lloyd George fund continued to exercise its baneful influence on intra-party relations. Moreover, Grey informed Herbert Gladstone that 'even if L.G. parted with all his fund, the Liberal Council would not dissolve, as we had no confidence in L.G. as leader'. Samuel loyally defended Lloyd George in conversation with Grey, doubting that the party would have fared better at the election without him, and arguing that 'anyhow, he was a Fact that could not be ignored'. But Grey retorted that 'he must be the most prominent person in any party to which he attached himself, but that he was a disintegrating force and fatal to Liberal success'.[62] Meanwhile, as the heirs of the dying party argued over the inheritance, several members of the Liberal family, out of disgust, disappointment, or ambition, crept away from the corpse and joined Labour or the Conservatives.

The real problem facing the Liberals was that their supposed parliamentary power was based on a threadbare bluff. Their position in the country, not to mention their demoralized internal condition, was such that they dared not take the ultimate step of precipitating another general election. Nor, given their internal divisions, could there be any prospect of their transferring support *en bloc* to the Conservatives. Their marriage of convenience with the Labour Government thus rested on a constantly maintained but utterly unreal threat of imminent divorce. The Government reacted to an implausible threat with an insincere offer: electoral reform. But the all-party inquiry into this, vaguely anticipated in the debate on the King's Speech, was delayed for six months.

Meanwhile, the Liberals' disunity and the limitations of their parliamentary position were displayed publicly in the parliamentary debates in

[59] C. P. Scott to HS, 10 July 1929, *Manchester Guardian* Archives, John Rylands University Library, Manchester, 135/438.
[60] HS to ES, 14 July 1929, ISA 100/54.
[61] Lady Oxford to HS, 8 June 1929, HLRO HS A/155/VII/38.
[62] Grey to Gladstone, 3 Aug. 1929, BL Add. MS 46478/161–3; see also Ramsay Muir to Lloyd George, 1 Dec. 1929, HLRO Lloyd George papers G/15/6/16.

the winter of 1929–30 on the Government's Coal Mines Bill. This measure proposed to create 'a central coordinating scheme for the whole of Great Britain' for the regulation of the production, supply, and sale of coal. In many ways it represented an extraordinary attempt by a Labour Government to appease the coal-owners. In the hope of satisfying them, the Government discarded its pre-election pledge to the miners of a seven-hour day, and instead sought a reduction from eight to seven and a half hours. The bill made no mention of nationalization of mineral royalties, a 'socialist' measure that Samuel would have supported.[63] Nor did it make provision for the compulsory amalgamations that since 1926 had come to be seen by Samuel as something approaching a panacea for the mining industry's ills.

Samuel supported the reduction in working hours as well as other features of the bill, but remarkably for a Liberal addressing a Labour Government, he complained of the postponement of nationalization of royalties. He particularly disapproved of the bill's failure to promote concentration of units of production. He pointed out that the bill departed from Labour's own declared policy, which had been similar to the Liberals': 'They cannot justly complain if, having put aside their own policy, we do not do so also.'[64] In the vote on the second reading two days later, the Government's majority was reduced to 8. Forty-four Liberals followed Lloyd George and Samuel into the opposition lobby; 2 voted with the Government; and 6 abstained. This three-way division was to become an embarrassingly common characteristic of parliamentary Liberalism over the next few years, one which diminished the party's reputation and effectiveness. Lloyd George, restlessly, cynically man-œuvring, glimpsed in all this an opening for party advantage which he exploited with gusto. Samuel, by contrast, took the high ground of seeking to improve the bill and build Lib–Lab co-operation.[65] Hugh Dalton, Under-Secretary at the Foreign Office, commented: 'Though Lloyd George desired to bring us down, Samuel had been seeking for days to find a bridge, and I think we were at fault for not responding better before things finally grew critical.'[66] Nevertheless, the Liberals had given the Government a severe jolt and they sought to take advantage of their position to secure their dearest desire: electoral reform.

A three-party conference on electoral reform was set up in early December under the chairmanship of a former Speaker, Lord Ullswater.

[63] Nationalization of mineral royalties was postponed to a later bill—which was killed in Oct. 1930 by the newly appointed Minister of Mines, Emanuel Shinwell.

[64] HC Deb. 5 s., vol. 233 (17 Dec. 1929), cols. 1297 ff.

[65] See HS to ES, 24 Dec. 1929, ISA 100/54.

[66] Dalton diary, 19 Dec. 1929, in Ben Pimlott (ed.), The Political Diary of Hugh Dalton 1918–40, 1945–60 (London, 1986), 82–3.

Samuel was the leading Liberal representative. Lloyd George did not serve on the committee, but his daughter Megan, MP for Anglesey, kept a watching brief. The Liberals encountered some sympathy in other parties for electoral reform. Churchill, for example, told Samuel 'that it really was necessary to find some electoral device which would enable the Liberal party to be represented'. On the other hand, Churchill's fellow-Conservative Leopold Amery disagreed: 'I said I did not see why. I believed in the two-party system and Liberals could dribble off to the other two parties until finally only Samuel was left and he could then toss up.'[67] The Liberals now recognized that their only hope of survival as a major political force lay in somehow inducing the Labour Party to acquiesce in a change in the electoral system.[68] But when the issue finally came to a head in the Ullswater committee, it was Labour rather than the Conservatives who opposed Samuel's proposals.[69] According to Samuel's account, the Conservatives were unenthusiastic about any change, but held that if a change were made it should be to proportional representation rather than the alternative vote,[70] to which they strongly objected. Labour, on the other hand, saw the alternative vote as a lesser evil than PR. The Liberals favoured PR but, failing that, would back the alternative vote.[71] By July Ullswater wrote to Samuel that the conferees were merely 'beating the air & wasting time'.[72] Shortly afterwards the conference collapsed.

The Government's position was consistent with Labour's long-term policy since the early 1920s of seeking to supplant the Liberals rather than to co-operate with them. They gave way to the Liberals on the coal bill and incorporated amendments to encourage amalgamations. But they dodged and dallied on electoral reform. In April 1930 Lloyd George and Samuel held secret discussions with Arthur Henderson and Philip Snowden.[73] These paved the way for an arrangement in June whereby the Liberals were invited by MacDonald to confer regularly with a committee of ministers.[74] The Liberals used these meetings to press for government action to reduce unemployment by the methods advocated in the 'Yellow Book', notably large public works programmes. The Labour leaders

[67] Diary entry, 7 Nov. 1929, in John Barnes and David Nicholson (eds.), *The Empire at Bay: The Leo Amery Diaries 1929–1945* (London, 1988), 51–2.
[68] See memorandum by Ramsay Muir, 8 May 1930, HLRO HS A/73/10.
[69] John Ramsden (ed.), *Real Old Tory Politics: The Political Diaries of Sir Robert Sanders, Lord Bayford, 1910–35* (London, 1984), 245.
[70] See above, p. 236.
[71] Herbert Samuel, 'Electoral Reform', *Nineteenth Century*, 109 (Jan. 1931), 4–13.
[72] Ullswater to HS, 4 July 1930, HLRO HS A/73/6.
[73] See Henderson to HS, 18 Apr. 1930, HLRO HS A/73/5.
[74] David Marquand, *Ramsay MacDonald* (London, 1977), 546–7; Skidelsky, *Politicians and the Slump*, 226–7.

listened but did not follow the advice. In September MacDonald met Lloyd George and Samuel who demanded electoral reform as the price of their continued support. Samuel said that he 'thought the Government ought to be kept in office for two years longer, and that this might be arranged on terms'. The Cabinet discussed the Liberal demands and agreed on 'the inopportuneness of a general election' (by-election results had not been running in Labour's favour). According to the record kept by the Cabinet Secretary, 'it was pointed out that an understanding with the Liberal party, based on some plan of electoral reform, would extend the life of the Government for two years, since a scheme of electoral reform would take two years to complete and carry.[75] The Government would be able to pursue its parliamentary programme and the situation might improve.' On this Micawberish basis, the Cabinet agreed to tell the Liberals that they were 'prepared to go further into the question of the alternative vote'. The decision was taken with little enthusiasm. Mac-Donald, in particular, had been a longstanding opponent of such measures. The Government's stratagem was palpably designed to string the Liberals along for as long as possible.[76]

In January 1931 the Home Secretary, Clynes, held talks with the Liberals in which agreement was reached on the terms of the proposed electoral reform bill.[77] The draft included provision not only for the alternative vote but also for the abolition of university seats and other remaining vestiges of plural voting. Samuel was closely involved in these discussions. He called the bill 'largely my own offspring'.[78] But he had few illusions about the likelihood of success: 'As the House of Lords is unlikely to pass it, there will probably be no results from it at the next election, but its introduction and its passage through the H. of C. will facilitate Lib. & Lab. co-operation.'[79] 'Incredulous laughter' greeted Samuel's claim that the Liberals did not support proportional representation out of self-interest. *The Times* considered the merriment 'excusable'.[80] The general expectation, supported by subsequent independent estimates, was that the Liberals would have benefited most from the alternative vote.[81]

[75] The Conservative majority in the House of Lords was bound to oppose any measure for electoral reform. Therefore the only hope of passage lay in application of the provisions of the 1911 Parliament Act for overcoming a Lords veto. The Act effectively limited the Lords' delaying power to two years from the date of the second reading in the House of Commons. But application of these cumbersome procedures would require a governmental resolve to see the thing through. No such determination was there. The Liberals were chasing a will-o'-the-wisp.

[76] Memorandum by Cabinet Secretary, 25 Sept. 1930, PRO CAB 23/90 B.

[77] Cabinet minutes, 6 Jan. 1931 (first of three Cabinets that day), PRO CAB 23/66/2 ff.

[78] HS to ES, 30 Jan. 1931, ISA 100/56.   [79] HS to ES, 11 Jan. 1931, ibid.

[80] *The Times*, 4 Feb. 1931; *HC Deb.* 5 s., vol. 247 (2 Feb. 1931), cols. 1493–508.

[81] Butler, *Electoral System*, 189–91.

Yet private calculations by the Liberal Organization in November 1930 had suggested that Labour would profit at least as much as the Liberals from the introduction of the alternative vote.[82] Even on this bill, on which the Liberals might have been expected to display unity, they exhibited divisions. In a debate in March on the clause abolishing university representation, Samuel spoke for abolition and was joined in the lobby by Lloyd George and Isaac Foot; but Maclean, Simon, and Runciman supported retention.[83]

Meanwhile the Government deepened its consultations with the Liberals. By April 1931 four Labour leaders (MacDonald, Snowden, Henderson, and Thomas) and four Liberals (Lloyd George, Samuel, Lothian, and Sinclair) were meeting weekly.[84] In May the Cabinet agreed that copies of certain Cabinet memoranda and other confidential documents would be sent to Samuel 'who, as a Privy Councillor, would be careful to treat them with full regard to the obligations of his Oath as a Privy Councillor'.[85] The press even suggested that Samuel was about to enter the Government.[86] He denied rumours of a Lib–Lab pact and in a formal sense he was correct.[87] But the alignment of the Liberal leadership with the Labour Government was close enough by June 1931 to lead Sir John Simon, who had already, the previous November, declared his opposition to co-operation with the Government, to resign the party whip. The defection of Simon, one of Samuel's oldest political friends, was a blow. He was followed by two other Liberal MPs who formed the nucleus of what became the 'Simonite' Liberal faction.

In June it seemed momentarily as if the Government might fall as a result of strained Liberal–Labour relations over the land tax clauses in the Finance Act. But Lloyd George, who initiated the crisis ('with his usual impulsiveness' said Samuel[88]), and MacDonald drew back from the political precipice. By-elections continued to promise serious setbacks for both Liberals and Labour in the event of a general election.[89] This crisis was merely a passing squall. By late July Lloyd George was musing on a possible Lib–Lab coalition and he appears to have gone so far as to distribute hypothetical offices in such a government, whose formation would prevent any immediate election.[90]

---

[82] 'Forecast of the Next Election', 6 Nov. 1930, HLRO HS A/73/11.
[83] *HC Deb.* 5 s., vol. 249 (16 Mar. 1931), cols. 1788–94.
[84] Entry for 28 Apr. 1931, in Pimlott (ed.), *Dalton Diary.*
[85] Cabinet minutes, 6 May 1931, PRO CAB 23/67/29 ff.
[86] *Manchester Guardian*, 25 May 1931.
[87] Herbert Samuel, 'Lib–Lab Pact: The Truth', *John Bull*, 16 May 1931.
[88] HS to ES, 22 June 1931, ISA 100/56.
[89] See memorandum by HS, 1 July 1931, HLRO HS A/76/1; also Marquand, *MacDonald*, 598–601.
[90] See Taylor (ed.), *My Darling Pussy*, 144–5; and Marquand, *MacDonald*, 602.

It is tempting to see a connection between this Lib–Lab *rapprochement* and the formation of the National Government later that summer. By mid-1931 the Liberal leaders were attuned to the idea of coalition. The cardinal point for Lloyd George, the master tactician, was that such an alliance would help avoid a general election in which his party seemed bound to lose ground. Samuel too was conscious of this consideration. But he was moved by more highminded (others might call them innocent) principles to favour a resurrection of the 'progressive alliance'. When the Liberals did enter the National Government, without Lloyd George and without the bulk of the Labour Party, a month later, they did so without preserving electoral reform and without securing a cast-iron commitment that there would be no early election. The new Government, when it came, turned out to be neither 'progressive' nor a cohesive alliance.

There was an unconscious appositeness in a little-noticed event on 1 July 1931, when several of the surviving senior members of the Rainbow Circle, not including MacDonald or Samuel, held an informal meeting at the Reform Club and resolved to discontinue the little society that had, in its heyday, created and embodied so much of the thought and spirit of the new radicalism of the 1890s.[91] Samuel had not been an active member for years. But he had continued to pay a subscription as if by that token to signal that he remained a man of the left. His symbolic membership of the party of progress thus lapsed almost simultaneously with his choice, in the political crisis of July–August 1931, of the opposite side of the barricades.

[91] P. Alden to S. S. Wilson, 1 July 1931, BLPES Coll. Misc. 575/6.

12

Decemvir

===

When you live on the banks of the River Pudma, you must make
friends with the crocodile.

(S. Lall)

SAMUEL'S ACTIONS during the financial crisis of the summer of 1931 can
be understood only against the background of his half-concealed
position during the gathering economic storm of the previous two years.
Half-concealed, because although he had paid lip-service to the ideas of
the Liberal 'Yellow Book' his economic thinking remained fundamentally
unaffected by Keynes. Lloyd George no more believed in Keynesianism *on
principle* than the Celt in him believed in leprechauns. But his eclectic,
unorthodox, opportunist mind, like Roosevelt's, eagerly plucked any new
idea, particularly one involving energetic action rather than supine passivity.
Samuel, by contrast, did believe *in principle* that the age of *laissez-faire*
was dead, but this scion of a merchant banking dynasty was constricted
by an almost Gladstonian financial orthodoxy that dictated his actions in
1931.[1] Although he had read Keynes's *The End of Laissez-Faire* in 1926,

---

[1] When *Britain's Industrial Future* was published in Mar. 1928, Samuel's brother-in-
law, Arthur Franklin, a retired banker, wrote to him criticizing the section on finance:
'From remarks made in other parts it would appear that the writer of this portion of the
book [Keynes was the anonymous author] does not get much support of his opinions from
his colleagues, and it appears to me to be rather the work of a theorist with no practical
experience and a great fondness for paradox, rather than a practical investigator. . . . The
author seems to have got a wrong-headed idea of the position of currency as regards
prices. . . . Of course, the true and only course is to endeavour to make the measure, that is
to say the currency, in all places equal so that it may form a fair criterion of international
values. The best means hitherto discovered by man is to employ a precious metal, and one
precious metal only. Once silver did the work, but for the last century or more it has been
found that only gold can do it. To complain of the action of deflation is like complaining of
the pain caused by recovery from an illness. Inflation which, in almost every case which
I can recall, was caused by the very thing which this writer recommends, the interference of
the State in the value of currency, caused an unfair balance between buyer and seller, and
because the seller is more vocal the process of curing the disease met with resistance.'
(A. E. Franklin to HS, 14 Mar. 1928, HLRO HS A/158/33). Samuel sent only a routine
reply. But there can be little doubt that he shared many of these critical views. In an article
summarizing the proposals of the Liberal Industrial Inquiry, he virtually ignored Keynes's
section on finance (*Contemporary Review*, 133 (Mar. 1928), 277–84).

had worked with Keynes on the Liberal Industrial Inquiry, and had urged him in 1929 to accept the Liberal nomination for the Cambridge University parliamentary seat,[2] there is little evidence that Samuel's basic economic outlook was affected by the association.

Samuel's discussion of unemployment in this period showed little development from his pre-war analysis of the problem. An article in the *Spectator* in May 1928 found him still pursuing his ancient argument with the Salvation Army over the efficacy of emigration as a cure.[3] True, he happily invoked Keynes before the 1929 election in an article that tried to explain how the Liberals' unemployment schemes could be paid for. But its main thrust was to assure readers of the *Daily Mail* that the matter could be managed without unduly disturbing 'the economic balance-sheet of the nation'.[4] He repeatedly stressed that the Liberals advocated 'no increase in expenditure for the purposes of the unemployed'; the public works schemes, such as the road programme, would, he suggested 'bring in their own revenue through the increasing income of the Road Fund'.[5]

As the unemployment figures ballooned in the course of 1930, the Liberals, while continuing to propose public works schemes, felt compelled to give assurances that they too favoured economies in public expenditure. Professor Skidelsky argues that they saw retrenchment as '*psychologically* necessary to give confidence in government policy . . . as a small part of a *package deal*'.[6] While this was no doubt the view of the more advanced economic thinkers, Samuel, very much a Chancellor of the Exchequer *manqué*,[7] genuinely sympathized with the Treasury approach in which balanced budgets were a real, not merely a psychological, necessity. Moreover, unlike Keynes, who was moving towards a readiness to contemplate tariffs, free trade for Samuel was the ultimate shibboleth. When E. D. Simon proposed to the 1930 Liberal Summer School that the party should consider a 10 per cent 'revenue tax' on all imports, including food but excluding raw materials, Keynes wrote in support, but Samuel was one of the many who condemned this attack on the holiest of Liberal sacred cows.[8] In an article on Mosley's economic programme in December

[2] Roy Harrod, *The Life of John Maynard Keynes* (Harmondsworth, 1972), 465.

[3] *Spectator*, 26 May 1928.

[4] *Daily Mail*, 17 May 1929; see also Herbert Samuel, 'How to deal with Unemployment', *Spectator*, 3 Mar. 1928.

[5] *HC Deb.* 5 s., vol. 239 (20 May 1930), cols. 250–66.

[6] Skidelsky, *Politicians and the Slump*, 255.

[7] In 1927 Samuel wrote a memorandum of record in favour of decimal currency—'an idea, the practicality of which I should closely consider if ever I were Chancellor of the Exchequer' (9 July 1927, HLRO HS A/77/3).

[8] See Mary Stocks, *Ernest Simon of Manchester* (Manchester, 1963), 93–4; Michael Freeden, *Liberalism Divided: A Study in British Political Thought 1914–1939* (Oxford, 1986), 121–4.

1930, Samuel concentrated on Mosley's protectionism, but he added a revealing side-swipe: 'It is not enough to declare, "We need a fresh start, a new orientation; Sir Oswald proclaims it; let us welcome his proposals." It would be a strange logic to say, "It is right that we should do something; this is something; therefore this is right" (although it is a logic that seems to have some attraction for Mr Keynes).'[9]

By July 1931, when unemployment reached an unprecedented 2.8 million, and the first intimations of a currency crisis reached senior politicians, Samuel's response was to support a combination of drastic economies and increased indirect taxation in order to balance the budget and thereby prop up the pound. Samuel's involvement began at the end of July. Lloyd George being unavailable owing to illness, Samuel was called in by the Chancellor of the Exchequer, Snowden, and given advance copies of the report of the May Committee which had been established by the Government in March, on a Liberal motion in the Commons, to recommend cuts in government spending. Snowden said that the drastic economies, amounting to £97,000,000, proposed by the May Committee could not be carried without the support of the whole House. After consulting senior Liberals, Samuel wrote to Snowden promising Liberal support for 'any practicable measures of economy'.[10] Snowden's reply on 5 August thanked Samuel for his 'helpful letter' and suggested separate Government consultations with the Conservatives and the Liberals. He indicated that there was 'no great urgency' as the Government would not make tentative decisions 'before September'.[11]

The next day, however, the Government was informed by the Joint Committee of the British Bankers' Association and the Accepting Houses Committee that a serious crisis was impending. The bankers warned that 'the progressive deterioration in our own economic and financial strength, both in respect of the budgetary position and the balance of payments' had reached a point that was 'threatening the depreciation of the currency with all its consequent evils'. They urged that 'every effort should immediately be made to restore confidence both at home and abroad', and they prescribed restriction of government expenditure, balancing of

[9] Herbert Samuel, 'The Mosley Programme', *Nation & Athenaeum*, 20 Dec. 1930. The parenthesis was the more wicked in that Samuel's article appeared in the *Nation*, of which Keynes was part-owner. But Samuel was reacting to an article by Keynes himself in which he had lumped Samuel with Snowden as typifying the sort of liberalism with which he no longer identified, preferring the more energetic variety allegedly exemplified by Lloyd George, MacDonald, Bevin, and Mosley. See *Nation*, 13 Dec. 1930; also Freeden, *Liberalism Divided*, 164; Peter Clarke, *The Keynesian Revolution in the Making 1924–1936* (Oxford, 1988), 220–1.

[10] Memorandum by HS, 13 Aug. 1931, with copy of HS to Snowden, 29 July 1931, HLRO HS A/78/3.

[11] Snowden to HS, 5 Aug. 1931, HLRO HS A/78/1.

the budget, and measures to improve the balance of trade.[12] On 11
August Samuel, who was staying in the country, received a telegram
asking him to go as soon as possible to the Bank of England. He was met
there by the Deputy Governor who outlined the 'strain on the sterling
exchange' and explained that 'the Bank thought it absolutely essential
that measures should be taken immediately to convince the world that the
British Budget would be balanced and that the economies which were
essential would in fact be made'. He was warned that 'it was a question of
days, and might at any time become a question of hours'. Two days later
Samuel saw MacDonald who told him that 'the Government were
working on a comprehensive plan to put the national finances on a sound
footing, involving very large economies'. The Budget would be balanced
and the Unemployment Fund would be put 'on a self-supporting basis—
or very nearly so'. Samuel promised Liberal support and suggested that
the Government recall Parliament.[13] He informed Lloyd George, who
was recovering slowly from a prostate operation, of these developments,
and awaited the Government's proposals.[14]

Over the next week the Cabinet wrestled with the recommendations of
the May Committee. Some economies were accepted, but the sticking
point for a majority of the Labour leaders was the recommendation for a
20 per cent cut in the unemployment benefit. On 20 August MacDonald
and Snowden met Neville Chamberlain and Sir Samuel Hoare (for the
Conservatives) and Samuel and Maclean (for the Liberals). The Liberals
supported the Conservatives' insistence on 'more drastic action in regard
to unemployment insurance'.[15] According to Samuel's contemporary
record, MacDonald and Snowden said that they intended to propose
economies of £78,500,000 to the Cabinet. These would not include a
reduction in unemployment allowances 'because of the strength of the
opposition within the Labour Party'. Samuel stressed the need for a
balanced budget and suggested recourse to indirect taxation on tea, beer,
and tobacco. The Liberals emphasized that 'it was indispensable that
some reduction be made in the scale of unemployment allowances, in
view of the increases made in recent years and the fall in the cost of living.
We felt [Samuel's account continued] that the other classes who were to
be called upon for heavy sacrifices would be indignant if no change was
made there.'[16] But when the Cabinet met TUC leaders later that day they

[12] Joint Committee of British Bankers' Association and Accepting Houses Committee
to Prime Minister and Chancellor of the Exchequer, 6 Aug. 1931 (copy), HLRO HS
A/78/2.
[13] HS memorandum, 13 Aug. 1931, HLRO HS A/78/3.
[14] HS to Lloyd George, 13 Aug. 1931, HLRO Lloyd George papers G/17/9/14.
[15] Cabinet minutes, 20 Aug. 1931, PRO CAB 23/67/317 ff.
[16] Memorandum by HS, 23 Aug. 1931, HLRO HS A/78/7.

encountered stiff resistance to the proposed economies, particularly the reduction in the dole.

The next day Samuel sent MacDonald a draft of a proposed Government announcement. He suggested that 'grave and perhaps irreparable damage might be done if any announcement of too detailed a character' were made of new taxation proposals. The draft therefore indicated only the barest outlines of a policy of which the main features were a balanced budget, no further borrowing for the Unemployment Fund, economies of 'more than £70,000,000', and 'fresh taxation, both direct and indirect'.[17] Although no action was taken on this draft, the scheme it outlined, representing the minimum programme regarded by bankers as acceptable to the currency markets, was the one ultimately adopted by the National Government.

The crisis worsened on 21 August when the Bank of England informed MacDonald that 'assistance of a substantial character must be obtained from New York and Paris'. The Government, under strong pressure from the TUC and from several Cabinet members to resist the bankers' demands, had at this stage agreed to economies of £56,000,000 which the Bank's representatives declared amounted to only £42,000,000 of 'real savings'. This amount, they warned, 'would not only not produce the required effect, but would probably worsen the position by further diminishing confidence'. Later that day the Conservative and Liberal leaders met MacDonald and Snowden again and 'made it quite clear that the proposals were wholly unsatisfactory' and would lead to the defeat of the Government 'directly the House of Commons met'. At a subsequent meeting with the Liberals that evening MacDonald was told that the Government's latest total of proposed economies, £56,000,000, would still not suffice and that 'it was impossible for the Liberal Party to support the Government in this matter'.[18] Maclean warned MacDonald, 'You cannot divide the Conservatives and Liberals now.'[19] Samuel insisted that a decision could no longer be delayed. He told MacDonald that the Liberals 'regarded it as his duty either to present more adequate proposals or to place his resignation in the King's hands'.[20] Samuel added that the Liberals, like the Conservatives, would be prepared to serve under MacDonald if he decided to form a new Government without the dissidents in the Labour Cabinet. According to MacDonald, the Liberals 'said Ll. G. associates himself with what they said & thinks I should ask King to see leaders of other Parties'.[21]

[17] HS to MacDonald (with accompanying draft), 21 Aug. 1931, HLRO HS A/78/10.
[18] Cabinet minutes, 22 Aug. 1931, PRO CAB 23/67/341 ff.
[19] Quoted in Skidelsky, Politicians and the Slump, 415.
[20] Memorandum by HS, 23 Aug. 1931, HLRO HS A/78/7.
[21] MacDonald diary, quoted in Marquand, MacDonald, 627. Samuel saw Lloyd

MacDonald spent the weekend of 22–3 August in a last-ditch effort to save the Government by securing Cabinet agreement to larger economies. In a further round of three-party discussions on Saturday, 22 August MacDonald said he 'thought it just possible' he might carry by a majority in the Cabinet an economy package of £68,000,000, including a 10 per cent cut in the dole. He asked the Opposition leaders what their attitude would be to that. According to Samuel's record, both Liberals and Conservatives said that the question whether this was adequate should be decided by the Government's financial advisers and that 'we must necessarily accept whatever decision might be arrived at by the financial authorities'.[22]

Meanwhile the prospect of a change of Government brought the King from Balmoral to London. At 10.30 a.m. on Sunday, 23 August, MacDonald saw George V and informed him that the collapse of the Government was now likely. MacDonald left with the impression that the King favoured his continuation in office as head of a National Government which would include Conservatives and Liberals.[23] The proposal was given more precision when the King saw Samuel at 12.30 p.m. According to a record kept by the King's Private Secretary, Samuel said:

that the financial situation of the country must be saved at all costs, and that this can only be effected by economies, and not by increased taxation. The views of his Party as to the future government of the Country are as follows:—The best government to introduce these unpalatable economies would be a Labour Government; this, however, seems to be an impossibility. Failing this they would favour a National Government with Mr MacDonald as Prime Minister. They would be prepared to support a Conservative Government which carried out the necessary economies, but felt that in the interests of the country a Labour or National Government would be preferable, as being more likely to carry the working classes with them.

When the King's Private Secretary enquired whether the Liberals 'would support a Conservative Government which introduced a revenue tariff', Samuel replied that that had 'never been mooted at any of their joint meetings with the Prime Minister', but that 'he did not think that they

George that day and, according to Samuel's account, he 'entirely concurred in the course we had taken and proposed to take'. On 23 Aug. Samuel saw Lloyd George again, this time with Reading, and according to Samuel, Lloyd George again expressed 'full agreement' (memorandum by HS, 23 Aug. 1931, HLRO HS A/78/7). But Lloyd George's secretary, A. J. Sylvester, noted on the same date: 'Frances [Stevenson] told me on the phone that LG had taken the line that he was ill & could not take an active part. The reason, really, is that he does not agree with Samuel & Donald Maclean. They are in agreement with the May Report; LG is not.' (Colin Cross (ed.), *Life with Lloyd George: The Diary of A. J. Sylvester 1931–1945* (New York, 1975), 37.)

[22] HS memorandum, 23 Aug. 1931, HLRO HS A/78/7.
[23] See Marquand, *MacDonald*, 630–1.

could do so'. The King said he 'thought that Sir Herbert Samuel had given a very clear exposition of the situation, and explained the necessity for a National Government'.[24] Samuel's own account of the meeting with the King added: 'I expressed the view that, in any event, a general election was greatly to be deprecated. It would not assist the solution of the financial problem, but would do much to precipitate a crisis.'[25] Later the same day the King saw Baldwin who said he would be prepared to serve under MacDonald.

Samuel's interview with the King marked a crucial point, perhaps even a turning-point in the crisis. Without the Liberals it would have been very difficult to form a National Government. MacDonald needed Liberal participation as a cloak for his alliance with the Conservatives. The King, who played an unusually active, even activist, role, was particularly affected by Samuel's clear-cut preference for a National Government over any possible alternative. The King's Private Secretary, Sir Clive Wigram, later noted:

Some time after the crisis, in discussing it with the King, I was impressed by the fact that His Majesty found Sir Herbert Samuel the clearest minded of the three (the Prime Minister, Mr Baldwin and Sir Herbert Samuel), and said that he put the case for a National Government much clearer than either of the others. It was after the King's interview with Sir Herbert Samuel that His Majesty became convinced of the necessity for a National Government.[26]

The National Government was, of course, a coalition by another name. But neither MacDonald nor Samuel had any wish to call to mind the last Coalition in which the Conservatives had submerged and eventually destroyed their partners: hence the patriotic euphemism.

At a Cabinet meeting that evening MacDonald confessed that the proposals for further economies, including a reduction of 10 per cent in unemployment benefit, 'represented the negation of everything that the Labour Party stood for, and yet he was absolutely satisfied that it was necessary in the national interests to implement them if the country was to be secured'. He added that if there were 'any important resignations, the Government as a whole must resign'. No agreement was reached and MacDonald accordingly went to the palace and informed the King 'that it was impossible for them to continue in office as a united Cabinet'.

At MacDonald's suggestion the King summoned the three party leaders to a meeting at the palace the following morning.[27] When the leaders

[24] Memorandum by King's Private Secretary, 23 Aug. 1931, Royal Archives, GV K2330 (2)1.
[25] Memorandum by HS, 23 Aug. 1931, HLRO HS A/78/7.
[26] Memorandum by Wigram, 25 Sept. 1931, Royal Archives, GV K2330 (2)1.
[27] Cabinet minutes, 23 Aug. 1931, PRO CAB 23/67/355 ff.

convened, the King set out what he already knew was the agreed position of the conferees: 'He trusted there was no question of the Prime Minister's resignation: the leaders of the three Parties must get together and come to some arrangement.' According to the King's Private Secretary, Baldwin and Samuel agreed to help

carry on the Government as a National Emergency Government until an emergency bill or bills had been passed by Parliament, which would restore once more British credit and the confidence of foreigners. After that they would expect His Majesty to grant a dissolution. To this course the King agreed. During the Election the National Government would remain in being, though of course each party would fight the Election on its own lines.[28]

A memorandum by Samuel written during the conference noted that it had been agreed that the National Government would 'not be a Coalition in the ordinary sense of the term but a co-operation of individuals'. In order to deal with the financial crisis a total of £70,000,000 in economies would be made, including a 10 per cent cut in unemployment benefit; the remainder of the deficit, now estimated at £170,000,000, would be met by increased taxation, both direct and indirect.[29]

The Liberals were fortunate in securing representation in the National Government out of proportion to their parliamentary standing. They were allowed two seats in the ten-member Cabinet: Samuel became Home Secretary and Reading Foreign Secretary. Crewe, Lothian, Maclean, and Sinclair were among those who obtained lesser positions. Lloyd George, still recuperating at his country home at Churt, was not well enough to serve, but his son Gwilym was given junior office. The Simonites remained outside the Government. On 28 August Samuel addressed a meeting of some 250 Liberals at the National Liberal Club. He dismissed as 'stuff and nonsense' the suggestion that the Labour Government had been overthrown by a 'bankers' manœuvre': 'To blame the bankers would be just as wise as to blame the thermometer for the fact that August has been cold.' He declared that the Government was 'not intended to be any long continuing combination, still less a permanent Coalition'. And he added: 'For my own part I am not a Conservative and never will be. The Liberal Party has maintained and well maintained its independence.'[30] Lloyd George's chief political organizer, Colonel Tweed, sent a highly coloured account of the meeting to Frances Stevenson:

[28] Memorandum by King's Private Secretary, 24 Aug. 1931, Royal Archives, GV K2330 (2)1.
[29] Memorandum by HS, 24 Aug. 1931, HLRO HS A/78/11.
[30] Shorthand notes of speeches at meeting, 28 Aug. 1931, HLRO Lloyd George papers G/20/2/43.

In this atmosphere of no one standing for Party because all were for Sterling I attended the Party meeting hoping for enlightenment. I gazed with awe upon the platform with its five representatives of the National Government of Great Britain and Palestine, and I felt the cold shiver I always feel when entering the mummy room of the British Museum. Preternaturally grave, men of destiny, humourless, with glassy eyes fixed on some dim distant horizon where an 18 carat golden sun tinges the roof tops of Lombard Street with its refulgent rays. The mummies were slowly divested of their cerements (one particularly ripe specimen, Lord Crewe, looked as if he might crumble to pieces at any moment) and by some ventriloqual trick were then made to speak. Reading very much the elder statesman . . . Samuel, dull and prosy, overwhelmed with his sense of responsibility, but with one remarkable interlude: 'There is one man who in these days has played a noble part—', gulp, tears in his eyes, handkerchief, glass of water, more gulps, and then faintly whispered 'Mr Ramsay MacDonald'. Followed by the shrill piping of Donald Maclean saying precisely nothing and saying it supremely badly. Grey (a badly preserved specimen lent from some private collection and not to be confused with the National Exhibits) spoke quite shortly but on the whole made the most effective comments. . . . Archie [Sinclair] did not speak but sat looking as if someone had just informed him of Flodden field. . . . When I surveyed our team on the platform at today's meeting I remembered and sorrowed that the ancients before they embalmed their mummies first of all removed their entrails. If the Chief had joined the Government they would at least have possessed one man of guts, vigour and real statesmanship.[31]

This unflattering group portrait by a member of Lloyd George's entourage spelt trouble ahead for Samuel.

Although Lloyd George had given formal support to the establishment of the National Government, he was privately fuming at the misfortune that had put him out of action just when he might have had a chance of returning to office. In reply to an oleaginous note from the Prime Minister, he sent a letter in which flattery ('The attitude you have taken is truly a heroic one') was combined with ill-concealed hunger for office ('. . . if the promise of the Doctors is redeemed I may be of some use later on').[32] For the rest, he held his peace. But from now on his already low opinion of Samuel developed into fierce jealousy of a lieutenant who had supplanted him. This attitude of bitter personal contempt, one that bordered on loathing, was soon to be translated also into a renewed political separation between the Liberal Party and its most popular, most gifted, most erratic leader.

Lloyd George and Simon were not the only leading Liberals to be passed over. Samuel's old friend and competitor, Walter Runciman, was another. Samuel wrote him an awkward letter in which he explained that

[31] Tweed to Frances Stevenson, 29 Aug. 1931, HLRO Lloyd George papers G/28/2/2.
[32] Lloyd George to MacDonald, 30 Aug. 1931 (copy), HLRO Lloyd George papers G/13/2/16.

since there was room in the Cabinet for only two Liberals 'it would not have been possible in any case to suggest a Cabinet Office in the present circumstances'. Samuel explained that he had secured the agreement of MacDonald and Baldwin to an offer to Runciman of the War Office 'should you be prepared to take it, although we all of us realized that that was very improbable'. But there had been difficulty getting hold of Runciman 'and the Prime Minister was pressing that the matter should be settled', whereupon Samuel had offered the job to Crewe.[33] Runciman replied sarcastically and curtly. 'So far as I am concerned,' he wrote in a private letter, 'it is clear that the Jews had no place in the Cabinet for a Gentile.'[34] Samuel tried to justify his actions by showing that messages had, in fact, chased Runciman from the Post Office at Dunvegan, where he had been staying at the time. But the damage was done.[35] Thus from the very outset of the National Government the fault lines were visible along which what remained of the Liberal Party was soon to fragment.

The first task of the new administration was to present a budget incorporating economy measures that would, it was hoped, impress the currency markets sufficiently to maintain sterling's link to gold. On 26 August, at Samuel's first Cabinet meeting for fifteen years, he was appointed to the Cabinet Financial Committee charged with making recommendations for new taxation.[36] It decided to raise both direct and indirect taxes. Income tax went up to 5s. in the £. On 9 September the Government issued a White Paper in which it unveiled a package of economy measures totalling £70,000,000. These included reductions in ministerial, civil service, armed forces', police, and teachers' pay as well as a 10 per cent cut in unemployment benefit.[37] These long-awaited measures did little to calm the exchange market. As early as 10 September Reading sent an urgent message to MacDonald warning of large-scale movements of capital out of sterling. Reading added: 'considerable doubt prevails in financial circles regarding the possibility of our maintenance of the gold standard'.[38]

On 14 September, as the standard-bearers at the Bank of England prepared their last redoubts, Samuel spoke in Parliament in defence of the Government's economic policy. He admitted that the Liberals' 'policy of national development on which our hearts were set [was] necessarily subjected to some check' and that the effect of the budget 'must be to some

[33] HS to Runciman, 29 Aug. 1931, WR 215.
[34] Runciman to Sir Godfrey Collins (draft), 1 Sept. 1931, WR 245.
[35] HS to Runciman, 3 Sept. 1931, WR 215.
[36] Cabinet minutes, 26 Aug. 1931, PRO CAB 23/67/1 ff.
[37] *Memorandum on the Measures Proposed by His Majesty's Government to Secure Reductions in National Expenditure*, Cmd. 3952 (London, 1931).
[38] Reading to MacDonald, 10 Sept. 1931, PRO PREM 1/97.

extent to add to existing unemployment'. But 'the hard compulsion of financial and economic circumstances' left no choice. He added a curious warning (and prophecy):

Long ago a Cabinet of 10 was set up in order to save the Roman State. We are told by historians that the Decemvirs of that day discharged the duties of their office with diligence and dispensed justice with impartiality. They made the great mistake of continuing too long, and in their second year they came too much under the influence of the Patricians; they aroused the anger of the Plebs, and they disappeared amid universal disapproval.[39] I hope that the Decemvirs of to-day will not make that mistake.[40]

The next day the 'anger of the Plebs' erupted in the unexpected form of a mutiny at Invergordon of naval ratings protesting against pay cuts. The Government immediately promised to investigate, and if appropriate redress, the protesters' grievances. This apparent concession to force aroused fears in international markets that the Government would be compelled to trim its economy programme.

Meanwhile rumours spread that the Government was preparing for a general election.[41] The election fever was fuelled by Geoffrey Dawson, editor of *The Times*. In private discussions with MacDonald, Baldwin, and others, as well as in the editorial columns of his paper, he called for an immediate appeal to the country by the National Government.[42] The possibility of an election was discussed in the Cabinet on 17 September.[43] The Governor of the Bank of England, Montagu Norman, had suffered a nervous breakdown and had left the country on a 'rest cruise'. His deputy, Sir Ernest Harvey, told a meeting of the Cabinet Committee on the Financial Situation (MacDonald, Snowden, Reading, Chamberlain, and senior Bank and Treasury officials) 'that for the £ sterling to crash in the middle of an election would be disastrous. Much would turn on whether the Election resulted from an appeal by the National Government to the country.' Later in the same discussion, 'in reply to Mr Chamberlain, he expressed the view that from the point of view of raising further credits abroad it would be fatal for the three parties to enter an Election independently on the old lines.'[44] In the atmosphere of fear and uncertainty, financial confidence collapsed. A rapid and massive flight from sterling

[39] The reference is to the events of 451 BC and after, described in Livy's *History*, Book III, chs. 33–54. 'The Board of Ten [Livy writes], after a flourishing start, soon proved itself a barren tree—all wood and no fruit.'
[40] *HC Deb.* 5 s., vol. 256 (14 Sept. 1931), cols. 537–54.
[41] Sylvester diary, 17 and 18 Sept. 1931, in Cross (ed.), *Life with Lloyd George*, 38–9.
[42] *The Times*, 16 Sept. 1931.
[43] Cabinet minutes, 17 Sept. 1931, PRO CAB 23/68/209 ff.
[44] Minutes of meeting of Cabinet Committee on Financial Situation, 17 Sept. 1931, PRO CAB 27/462.

confronted the Government with a renewed political and financial crisis. Greatly alarmed at the prospect of an election in which they could expect further losses, the Liberals protested to the Prime Minister, who wrote to Samuel that the renewed sterling crisis had reinforced his opposition to an election: 'Obviously there is not even a theoretical justification for an Election now.'[45] Having thus set aside, for the moment, the political threat, MacDonald turned to the financial one.

After some desultory efforts to raise new loans, the Prime Minister surrendered without much of a fight. Samuel was not a member of the Cabinet Committee that supervised the last-ditch efforts to save the pound. But he participated in several of the meetings of senior ministers and officials between 17 and 20 September in the course of which the Bank of England took the position that the gold standard was no longer defensible. On the morning of Saturday, 19 September Samuel was at Downing Street when the historic decision was taken. Together with Baldwin he was called into a conference at which officials from the Bank of England, the Treasury, and the Foreign Office were briefing the Prime Minister. Harvey broke the news that there was now no alternative but to 'suspend the sale of gold'. E. R. Peacock, a Director of the Bank, said that 'a sudden blizzard had struck the world'. A telegram from the French Prime Minister, Pierre Laval, in answer to a final British request for assistance, was read out. Laval agreed with the British Treasury view that it was too late to save sterling. He mentioned the disturbing effect produced by the belief that a general election was imminent. Samuel asked Harvey whether the Bank's information confirmed that view. Harvey replied that it did and that they had 'heard the same thing from all over'. There was next to no discussion of the principle of devaluation, now recognized as inevitable. But Samuel subjected the Bank and Treasury experts to close questioning on proposed legislation giving the Government reserve powers to control foreign exchange operations. Samuel suggested that such legislation might lead to 'an immediate panic and a rush to get out of sterling at any cost'. But Sir Warren Fisher, Permanent Secretary to the Treasury, pointed out that 'Parliament might be dissolved, and if no powers existed there might be grave difficulties'. This revelation that an election remained likely cannot have been pleasing to Samuel. He retorted 'that to threaten without taking action was dangerous'.[46] At a meeting of experts at the Treasury immediately afterwards, Keynes pressed the case for the immediate imposition of exchange controls. But

[45] MacDonald to Samuel, 20 Sept. 1931, HLRO HS A/81/2.
[46] Minutes of conference at Downing Street, 19 Sept. 1931, PRO CAB 27/462; memorandum by HS, 24 Sept. 1931, HLRO HS A/81/4a; see also Diane B. Kunz, The Battle for Britain's Gold Standard in 1931 (London, 1987), 138.

he failed to persuade senior officials. Consequently the authority to impose such controls was included in the Government's draft legislation only in the form of a reserve power to be used in an emergency.[47] Meanwhile final preparations were completed for the abandonment of gold.

The Cabinet which had been formed with the central objective of preventing this very event was not even consulted. When it met on the afternoon of Sunday, 20 September, MacDonald explained that 'it had been necessary for him to take action expeditiously and with the utmost secrecy, and there had not been time to summon a meeting of the full Cabinet'. The ministers present, all of whom had believed with perfect faith until virtually that moment that the gold standard was all that stood between Britain and economic disaster, now with equal unanimity and without a peep of protest meekly agreed to what the Prime Minister and the inner group of ministers had decided 'on their behalf'.[48] The next day a bill severing sterling from gold was rushed through all its stages. The pound lost a quarter of its value against the dollar but then stabilized at the lower level. Sidney Webb's famous remark, 'Nobody told us we could do this', undoubtedly expressed the half-conscious thought of many ministers. The general expectation was that going off gold would set off an economic earthquake. Even such a relatively well-informed person as Lord Lothian, the Liberal Chancellor of the Duchy of Lancaster, had written to Samuel on 7 September urging him 'to point out that devaluation of the pound to say 10/-, if you could stop it there, would mean a reduction of working class savings by 50%'.[49] Samuel did not follow this well-intentioned advice, but there is no evidence that he differed from the conventional wisdom.[50]

The Government, having thus lost their *raison d'être*, faced the question of what to do next. Should they jettison the economy programme and resort instead to the 'national development' schemes formerly advocated by the Liberals? Samuel's adherence to the doctrines of the 'Yellow Book' was now exposed as no stronger than that of many Anglican clergymen to the Thirty-nine Articles. In fact, he hardly paid even lip-service any more to its ideas. Having embarked on a course of moral economizing under the sign of gold, the 'Decemvirs' clung to the economy programme even when it had become a crown of thorns.

[47] See Robert W. D. Boyce, *British Capitalism at the Crossroads 1919–1932: A Study in Politics, Economics, and International Relations* (Cambridge, 1987), 365.
[48] Cabinet minutes, 20 Sept. 1931, PRO CAB 23/68/215 ff.
[49] Lothian to HS, 7 Sept. 1931, SRO Lothian papers GD 40/17/143.
[50] Apart from Keynes, almost the only important advocates of devaluation before the event had been Ernest Bevin and Lord Beaverbrook.

Samuel and his colleagues faced a political as well as an economic
dilemma. Should they acknowledge their own failure and go to the
country? If so, should they do so as a united Government, which they had
sworn they would not do, or as distinct parties? Samuel set out his views
on these issues in a long Cabinet memorandum on 24 September. Perversely, given the Government's strong parliamentary majority and the
Labour Opposition's demoralized condition and strictly constitutional
behaviour, Samuel attributed the collapse of the currency in large measure to
the 'strong Opposition, which has given the impression that it is against
the whole policy of this Government'. Without impugning the Conservatives by name, he also assailed their agitation for an election as an
unsettling factor that had contributed to the devaluation. He insisted that
the stable door be kept shut even though the horse had bolted. After all, it
might bolt further:

The £ is heavily depreciated, but there is no reason in the nature of things why the
depreciation should not become heavier still. . . . The announcement of an immediate
general election, made under the same conditions as before, would produce the same
results as before. There is the gravest risk of a slide in the value of currency, and we
have not been informed of the existence of any resources which, once it started, would
be adequate to stop it.

Uncharacteristically, Samuel sounded an alarmist note suggesting that the
impending reductions in unemployment benefit and other cost-cutting
measures might lead 'even to rioting with loss of life' during an election
campaign. On the issue of tariffs Samuel displayed surprising flexibility,
verging on agnosticism:

I suggest that the Cabinet should engage in a close and continuous examination of
these questions, and should not put them aside on the grounds that the only solution
worth considering is the establishment of a general system of tariffs, and that we need
not spend time on considering that because the Liberal members of the Government
would in any case refuse their assent to it, on grounds of principle, even if it were
shown to be the indispensable means of redressing our adverse balance of trade.
Neither of these assumptions is correct. The Liberal representatives have taken up no
such attitude.

Although expressed in the language of national interest, Samuel's opposition
to an election coincided with the interest of his own party. A hostile reader
of the Cabinet memorandum (and eight of the nine ministerial readers
would be hostile) might be forgiven for interpreting his professed open-
mindedness on the subject of tariffs as indicating a readiness to abandon
even the most cherished Liberal principle in order to avoid facing the
electorate. A parenthetical aside by Samuel in which he remarked that his

views were shared by 'every school of thought' in the Liberal Party would not have disabused such captious critics.[51]

In spite of his assurance to Samuel just a few days earlier that he too opposed an election, MacDonald wobbled on the issue as he came under intense pressure from the Conservatives. In what was, even for him, an exceptionally woolly Cabinet memorandum on 26 September, MacDonald replied to Samuel's arguments, indicating that he leant towards an election in which 'a national appeal' would be made 'by those who have formed the National Government'. The appeal should be for a free hand to deal with the economic crisis. The Government, he argued, 'must have power to deal with problems as they arise'. And he specified: 'amongst those powers must be that of using a Tariff should the financial and industrial conditions require it.'[52] The next day Samuel wrote to his son Edwin: 'A struggle is proceeding for the soul of Ramsay MacDonald.'[53] As MacDonald weakened, Samuel took the unusual course of appealing to a higher quarter. He sent a copy of his anti-election Cabinet memorandum to the King's Private Secretary. Although the King in any case received all such papers, Samuel sent this further copy 'as I promised, in case it should be of use'. He took the opportunity to add that the paper had 'the entire concurrence of Mr Lloyd George'.[54]

By the end of the month the question had become not so much whether an election would take place as on what basis it would be fought. MacDonald's Cabinet paper became the opening shot in a battle over the formulation of a common programme on which the disparate segments of the National Government might wage an electoral campaign. Samuel's failure to avert an election and his readiness to participate in the search for such a common formula greatly angered Lloyd George, whose temporary political impotence sharpened the edge of his criticism of Samuel: 'One day he is as firm as Mount Zion; the next he is floating about like the ark', the invalid at Churt muttered.[55] Lloyd George circulated to leading Liberals a violently phrased memorandum denouncing an election as 'an incredible act of reckless and criminal folly'. 'Let there be no mistake', he warned, 'to fight an Election upon agreed formulas which are an acceptance of Tariffs, without the case ever having been investigated and without any of the details having been worked out, is to sign the death warrant of the Liberal Party as a separate Party.' MacDonald and the Conservatives, he suggested, 'seem to have very cleverly contrived almost

[51] Memorandum by HS, 24 Sept. 1931, HLRO HS A/81/4a..

[52] Memorandum by MacDonald, 26 Sept. 1931, HLRO HS A/81/5; see also Marquand, MacDonald, 660–3.

[53] HS to ES, 27 Sept. 1931, ISA 100/56.

[54] HS to Wigram, 28 Sept. 1931, Royal Archives, GV K2330 (2)/123.

[55] Sylvester diary, 30 Sept. 1931, in Cross (ed.), Life with Lloyd George, 39–40.

to manœuvre our Party leaders into a booby trap'. Resorting to language
that revealed his contemptuous view of his own party colleagues, he
added: 'Liberal Members may save their skins, but they will be completely
stripped of their feathers and after the Election you may have Ministers
who are nominally Liberal in the so-called National Government, but
they will only be a miserable row of plucked boobies.'[56] Lloyd George
was not alone in this view. Other prominent Liberals, including Ramsay
Muir, H. L. Nathan, and Seebohm Rowntree, informed Samuel that any
election would be 'a dog-fight' and that the proposed 'free hand' formula
was unacceptable to many Liberals since it would 'in fact leave the
Conservatives free and in a position to put through Protection and to
carry out a Tory policy under the guise of an emergency measure'.[57]

Samuel did not, of course, wield sufficient power to veto an election. He
might have followed Lloyd George's advice and resigned immediately
from the Government. But he was deterred from this course by the
divisions within his own party. As he pointed out later, his Cabinet
colleague Reading was 'lukewarm' in his support of Samuel's position
and might not have resigned with Samuel in protest against an election.
Grey too would probably have opposed such a resignation. The most
likely result of resignation would have been the virtual annihilation of the
free-trade Liberals at the polls.[58] When Liberal ministers met on 1
October to consider the issue, Lloyd George's view was rejected. He was
incensed by the news and declared that 'as a consequence of his advice not
being followed there would be financial help only for certain candidates'.[59]
But Lloyd George was woefully deluded if he really thought that he could
still deploy what remained of his notorious 'fund' as a weapon to whip his
colleagues into line. Few Liberals now regarded financial connection with
Lloyd George as anything other than a political liability.

A Cabinet meeting that evening agreed on a provisional formula which
met the Conservatives' demand for a free hand to apply tariffs if necessary.
Samuel and Reading pleaded for more time to consult their colleagues,
most particularly, Lloyd George. Some Conservatives hoped that they
might be able to use the tariff issue as a lever to force the Liberals out of
the Government. Spurred on from behind, Baldwin insisted on the urgent
need for a decision.[60] When the Cabinet broke up at midnight, the two
Liberals were given a deadline of 2.30 p.m. the following afternoon to

[56] Memorandum by Lloyd George, 30 Sept. 1931, HLRO HS A/81/11.
[57] E. H. Gilpin and ten others to HS, 30 Sept. 1931, HLRO HS A/81/13.
[58] Memorandum by HS, Dec. 1932, HLRO HS A/81/34.
[59] Sylvester diary, 1 Oct. 1931, in Cross (ed.), *Life with Lloyd George*, 40; see also
rough notes by Samuel on meeting, 1 Oct. 1931, HLRO HS A/81/15.
[60] See Keith Middlemas and John Barnes, *Baldwin: A Biography* (London, 1969),
646–7.

give their reply, failing which, the minutes stated bluntly, 'it should be assumed that their answer is in the negative'.[61] The Liberal Cabinet ministers used the brief interval to consult party leaders and also to make a final effort to persuade the King not to grant a dissolution. The following morning, 2 October, Reading told Wigram that Lloyd George 'had been very rampageous'; nevertheless, Reading 'was prepared to stick to the Prime Minister even if Sir Herbert Samuel ran out'.[62]

Samuel met the King later in the morning. Wigram recorded that the monarch found Samuel 'most obstructive and unhelpful':

He said that the National Government has not yet finished its work; now that the £ had gone there was no hurry for an election. He had been a Free Trader all his life and was not going to change or agree to a formula in a National appeal which advocated Tariffs. He might be prepared to agree to a proposal that in an emergency Tariffs might be considered but a careful enquiry would have to be made. . . .

His Majesty appealed to him as a Statesman and as one who had been a Minister of the Crown to place before everything the present dangerous situation of the country. Sir Herbert replied that he and his party were just as patriotic as the Conservatives. . . . He would be a traitor to his cause if he sold the pass now. . . . In short [Wigram editorialized], his attitude was to oppose any National Appeal and to be mischievous.[63]

The King himself wrote in his diary that Samuel had been 'quite impossible'.[64] Any lingering hope Samuel might have entertained that the palace would refuse a dissolution could be dismissed after this unhappy audience.

When the Cabinet met again later that day, the Liberal ministers reported that they had encountered strong party objections to the proposed formula, which was regarded as practically binding the Liberals to go to the country on a tariff platform.[65] A series of alternative formulas was considered and rejected.[66] The argument raged on for several days. A compromise was finally reached late on the evening of 5 October at the end of a Cabinet which, Samuel later reported to his son Edwin, 'as nearly as possible resulted in the resignation of the Government'.[67] In the end, the Cabinet agreed that 27 October would be the election date. The Prime Minister would issue an individual manifesto, to be approved by Baldwin and Samuel, 'setting forth the general policy of the National Government' and asking for 'a free hand, nothing excluded'. The attempt to devise an agreed formula on tariffs was abandoned. Each of the three parties

[61] Cabinet minutes, 1 Oct. 1931, PRO CAB 23/68.
[62] Memorandum by Wigram, 2 Oct. 1931, Royal Archives, GV K2331 (1)/24.
[63] Ibid.
[64] Quoted in Kenneth Rose, *King George V* (London, 1983), 381.
[65] Cabinet minutes, 2 Oct. 1931, PRO CAB 23/68/330 ff.
[66] Various drafts, 2 Oct. 1931, HLRO HS A/81/19–23.
[67] HS to ES, 5 Oct./1 Nov. 1931, ISA 100/56.

constituting the National Government would be free to deal with this issue in its own way in its own manifesto.[68]

The decision was reached against the background of renewed nervousness about sterling and continued pressure from the Bank of England for a unified appeal by the National Government. On the morning of 6 October Samuel joined MacDonald, Snowden, and Chamberlain in a meeting with Harvey and Peacock. The bankers stressed the importance for sterling of 'real co-operation on a national basis to secure a strong and permanent administration'. Samuel warned that 'a dissentient note might be struck in a certain quarter' (he was undoubtedly thinking of Lloyd George), but said Liberal ministers were unanimously in support of the proposed national appeal, and the National Liberal Federation 'practically unanimous'. Peacock commented that 'these declarations were very important, as naturally the Bankers had felt there was great danger in the Government going to the Country as a National Government, when in fact it was not a National Government'.[69]

Thus a Government that had come to office just six weeks earlier abjuring a 'coupon election' now sought a 'doctor's mandate'. Samuel's first act was to write in conciliatory vein to Lloyd George, referring to the fight he had put up against tariffs, and seeking endorsement of the party's election manifesto—which he promised to send to Churt as soon as it was ready.[70] The letter, with its implication that Lloyd George would have no say in drafting the Liberals' appeal, was singularly ill-judged and provoked a predictable explosion. When Lloyd George was shown the manifesto two days later, he criticized its apparent rightward tendency and the 'feebly and haltingly presented' case for free-trade. He did not reply directly to Samuel's plea for support, but made sure that Samuel was told that he had said, 'As I cannot be there to discuss the Manifesto with them, on the whole they had better issue their own manifesto under their own names.'[71] Samuel tried to persuade him to change his mind but without success.[72] Lloyd George remained furious and even gave the impression that he might throw his support to Labour.[73]

The election that followed was one of the most bitter in modern British history. The campaign took place against the backdrop of deep economic depression, mass unemployment, and heightened class antagonisms.

[68] Cabinet minutes, 5 Oct. 1931, PRO CAB 23/68/340 ff.; HS to Lloyd George, 6 Oct. 1931, HLRO HS A/81/29.

[69] Minutes of conference, 6 Oct. 1931, PRO CAB 27/462/36 ff.

[70] HS to Lloyd George, 6 Oct. 1931 (copy), HLRO HS A/81/29.

[71] Goronwy Owen to HS, 8 Oct. 1931, HLRO HS A/81/31.

[72] HS to Lloyd George, 9 Oct. 1931, HLRO Lloyd George papers G/17/9/17; see also Sinclair to HS, 9 Oct. 1931, HLRO HS A/81/33.

[73] See entry dated 10 Oct. 1931, BLPES Beatrice Webb diary, 5198.

Labour's onslaught against the National Government resounded with accusations of betrayal against MacDonald and the hapless rump of 21 National Labour candidates who followed him. The Conservatives fought on an explicit platform of protection and displayed open contempt for the free-trade scruples of their allies. The Liberals presented a sorry spectacle of organizational weakness and ideological confusion which contrasted with their impressive performance in the election campaign just two years earlier. Then they had fielded 513 candidates and had been, at least to outward appearance, unified around the expansionist, pump-priming policy of the 'Yellow Book'. Now they were divided into three factions. On the right stood 41 Simonite candidates, including Runciman,[74] known as 'Liberal Nationals', more ultramontane than the Pope in that they supported the National Government, to the extent of favouring tariffs, even though they were not admitted to its ranks. In the centre were 112 Samuelite Liberals who campaigned as free trade supporters of the National Government. Finally, there were 7 'independent Liberal' opponents of the National Government, mainly members of Lloyd George's 'family party'.[75] These last were seen as standing on the left, if only because Lloyd George, in the course of the campaign, advised Liberals to vote Labour where there was no Liberal candidate.

The Samuelite Liberals' difficulties were compounded by the ambiguity of the pre-election agreement. This implied that 'National' candidates of one party would not be opposed by candidates of another 'National' party but it did not prohibit such contests explicitly. The Conservatives took maximum advantage of this loophole to field protectionist candidates against free-trade Liberals. Only 4 Simonites were opposed by Conservatives, but 26 Samuelites faced Conservative challenges. Five of the eleven Liberal ministers were thus opposed by their own allies. Among these was Samuel himself, whose campaign in Darwen developed into a test of the cohesion of the National coalition.

Samuel had certainly expected to have a free run against Labour at Darwen. Even on that basis he could not anticipate an automatic victory, for Darwen had suffered severely from the slump. In the cotton industry, the mainstay of the area, unemployment had reached 70 per cent.[76]

[74] Runciman, although moving rapidly towards protectionism, still hovered somewhere between the Simonite and Samuelite wings of the party. In a letter to Samuel during the campaign he declared: 'No-one has any right to commit me one syllable beyond the Prime Minister's Manifesto, which I accepted as my election address' (Runciman to HS, 23 Oct. 1931, HLRO HS A/82/6).

[75] The list of Liberal candidates produced by the (Samuelite) National Liberal Federation excluded Simon but was padded by the inclusion of the followers of Lloyd George, as well as Runciman and some other candidates who leant towards the Simonites (The Times, 17 Oct. 1931).

[76] Darwen News, 14 Oct. 1931.

Samuel's re-election prospects dimmed when a protectionist Conservative candidate, Captain Alan Graham, was nominated for the seat by the local Conservative association. Samuel was indignant. He induced Baldwin to 'appeal' to the Darwen Conservatives to withdraw Graham's candidacy. But in a letter to Baldwin on 11 October Samuel wrote:

I am afraid that that appeal has not yet had its effect, as they are proceeding with their campaign on the lines that the next Parliament should adopt, without delay, a full Protectionist Tariff.... None the less, I am doing my best, of course, to keep things on the right lines, and I hope that there has been nothing in my speeches at Bradford and at Darwen to which you need take exception.[77]

Such self-abasement came ill from a Liberal leader who boasted that he had preserved the proud independence of his party. Graham's refusal to withdraw left Samuel in the humiliating predicament of contesting what was in effect another 'coupon' election—but with an unstamped coupon.

Even by the low standard of 1931 the campaign in Darwen was exceptionally abrasive. Graham's campaign was discountenanced, but not exactly disowned, by Baldwin.[78] Among those who came to speak on Graham's behalf was Page-Croft, who denounced Samuel as 'Slippery Sam' and as 'the chief architect of the present chaos and ruin'.[79] Beaverbrook, who was running a one-man crusade for 'imperial free trade' (i.e. tariffs), also spoke for Graham and urged voters to 'remember the Empire!'[80] Another speaker for Graham, referring to the Liberals' support of the Labour Government, declared: 'We began to look upon him [Samuel] in the light of a traitor who had betrayed our best interests. Mind you, I was told last night in Bolton that he betrayed the best interests of the Jews in Palestine.'[81]

The Labour candidate's attack on Samuel focused particularly on the 'means test' applied to 'transitional benefit' payments to the long-term unemployed. This handicapping of the thrifty, redolent of the Poor Law, was the most deeply unpopular feature of the National Government's economy measures and cost Samuel working-class votes. Samuel tried to avoid the subject, but he was repeatedly questioned about it and found some difficulty in framing effective replies.[82] MacDonald wrote sympathetically to Samuel, recalling that he had 'urged on the Cabinet that the sentimental feeling about the Poor Law would figure more in our treatment of the unemployed than the cuts themselves'. He suggested that Samuel might say 'that the Government had no intention of making the

[77] HS to Baldwin, 11 Oct. 1931, CUL Baldwin papers 45/30.
[78] See Middlemas and Barnes, Baldwin, 649–50.
[79] Darwen News, 10 Oct. 1931.
[80] Ibid., 21 Oct. 1931; see also Taylor, Beaverbrook, 419.
[81] Darwen News, 24 Oct. 1931.   [82] Ibid., 21 and 24 Oct. 1931.

transitional benefit people Poor Law subjects and that when the regulations are issued every care will be taken to safeguard them against that'.[83]

But the dominant issue of the campaign was tariffs. Samuel, who at times gave the impression that he regarded politics as altogether an unsuitable area of debate in this general election, initially tried to avoid that subject too, announcing in his manifesto, 'I will not be drawn in this Election into a discussion of the party questions that would divide us. The people are not called upon now to decide for or against a general and permanent system of Tariffs. That is not the issue at this election. That is not included in the Prime Minister's appeal.'[84] But the shrill attacks of his Conservative opponent compelled him to stake out his position. He invoked Keynes in support of the argument that devaluation, which was likely to help right the balance of trade, rendered protection less necessary.[85] In a letter to *The Times* on 29 September, Keynes had, in the light of 'the events of the last week', recanted for the nonce his support for tariffs. Graham, nevertheless, continued to cite Keynes as a Liberal advocate of tariffs.[86] Samuel declared that he kept 'an open mind' on the imposition of tariffs as a temporary measure to deal with an emergency, but he insisted that the election must not be regarded as a referendum that would give a mandate for permanent protection. Complaints to Baldwin about the tenor of Conservative propaganda cut little ice. In the later stages of the campaign Samuel therefore took up a more aggressive posture in defence of free trade while continuing to avow his readiness to re-examine the question 'on its merits'.[87]

The Conservatives' scant regard for the susceptibilities of their allies eventually aroused Samuel's foreboding. In a prescient letter to Mac-Donald on 16 October he complained:

The continuous Tariff propaganda which is being carried on from the Conservative Headquarters, with the dissemination of millions of purely Protectionist leaflets, is not improving matters. I have reason to think that great numbers of the Liberal rank-and-file, although they would put their trust in a Government composed like the present, genuinely fear that you yourself may be overthrown by a strong Conservative majority in the House of Commons, that the present Liberal representatives in the Government might be superseded, and that the new Parliament will, in fact, be used as an engine for establishing a purely Protectionist regime.[88]

Looking at the question from the other end of the telescope, Lord Brentford (William Joynson-Hicks), a former Conservative Home Sec-

[83] MacDonald to HS (copy), 14 Oct. 1931, PRO PRO 30/69 1176.
[84] Election address, Oct. 1931, CUL Baldwin papers 45/88.
[85] *Manchester Guardian*, 9 Oct. 1931; *Darwen News*, 10 Oct. 1931.
[86] *Darwen News*, 21 Oct. 1931.   [87] Ibid., 24 Oct. 1931.
[88] HS to MacDonald, 16 Oct. 1931, PRO PRO 30/69/1176.

retary, wrote in support of Graham that if Samuel were elected he would be 'an enemy within the gates'.[89]

The election not only strained relations between the component elements in the National Government; it also exacerbated the internecine conflicts within the Liberal Party. Samuel tried to minimize his differences with Lloyd George, expressing his sorrow 'that our views at this election to some degree diverge'.[90] On the other hand, he stigmatized Simon's 'tortuous leadership' and characterized him as 'indistinguishable from any pledged Conservative'.[91] But he himself left an opening for attack (utilized by Leslie Hore-Belisha for the Simonites[92]) on the ground of tortuousness, when he commended Runciman's allegedly openminded attitude on tariffs.[93] Runciman's apparent alignment with Simon a few days later left electors scratching their heads. *The Times* complained with malicious glee of the 'bewildering and contradictory advice' that was being offered to the Liberal voter.[94]

The result of the election in Darwen was a personal victory for Samuel. He succeeded in multiplying his 1929 majority nearly tenfold:

SAMUEL (National Liberal)	18,923
GRAHAM (National Conservative)	14,636
ROTHWELL (Labour)	5,184
Majority	4,287

The turn-out in Darwen was once again extremely high (92.2 per cent) and Samuel's achievement in winning 48.8 per cent of the vote was impressive. But the results elsewhere were depressing for the Liberals. Only 33 Samuelite Liberals were elected, as against 35 Simonites and 4 members of the Lloyd George clan. The total of 72 Liberal MPs superficially suggested an improvement from the 59 elected in 1929. But the Liberal vote declined by more than half and the average percentage poll gained by Liberal candidates declined even though they contested far fewer seats. Moreover, of the 72 Liberals elected, 62 owed their seats largely to the fact that they had not faced Conservative candidates.[95] In spite of all the Liberal complaints about their treatment by their partners, the awkward truth was now apparent: the party had degenerated into little more than an electoral appendage of the Conservatives, whose programme of tariffs and economies seemed best to accord with the mood of the electorate.

'There is a danger', Samuel wrote to his son Edwin shortly after the results were declared, 'that Ramsay MacDonald may become "the prisoner

[89] *Darwen News*, 24 Oct. 1931.
[90] *The Times*, 17 Oct. 1931.
[91] *Darwen News*, 14 Oct. 1931.
[92] Ibid., 14 Oct. 1931.
[93] Ibid., 10 Oct. 1931.
[94] *The Times*, 23 Oct. 1931.
[95] See Wilson, *Downfall of Liberal Party*, 401–2; Chris Cook, *A Short History of the Liberal Party 1900–1976* (London, 1976), 117.

of his allies" but I do not think he will.'[96] Allowing his good sense to be
overwhelmed by his goodwill, Samuel thus followed the Prime Minister
into the prison of a Cabinet dominated by their Conservative gaolers.

[96] HS to ES, 31 Oct. 1931, ISA 100/56.

13

Liberal Leader

===

He that is head of a party is but a boat on a wave, that raises not
itself but is moved upward by the billows which it floats upon.

(Sir Walter Scott)

SAMUEL'S LEADERSHIP of the Liberal Party, which had emerged almost
by accident as a result of Lloyd George's incapacitation in August
1931, was formalized after the election, when Lloyd George rejected a
conciliatory overture from Samuel. On 3 November he wrote to Samuel
refusing to attend 'a meeting of what I am informed will in fact be a
section only of the Liberal Members elected to this Parliament'.[1] Pro-
nouncing himself 'completely at variance with the disastrous course into
which the Party has recently been guided', Lloyd George stated that he
was 'not a Candidate for Election to any office in the Group'.[2] The letter
was issued to the press on 4 November, the day that Samuel was formally
elected leader of the parliamentary Liberal Party. While he hardly bothered
to observe the customary courtesies in public, Lloyd George privately
railed against the leaders of his former party. He told his inner circle of
confidants that 'he might be only half a man, but he was a bloody sight
better than two Jews'.[3] Throughout the next decade Lloyd George vented

[1] The Simonites were invited to attend but had refused (Simon to HS, 2 Nov. 1931,
Bodleian Library, Oxford, MS Simon 69/50).
[2] Lloyd George to HS, 3 Nov. 1931, HLRO HS A/84/6.
[3] Sylvester diary, 2 Nov. 1931, in Cross (ed.), *Life with Lloyd George*, 47. Simon was
widely, though wrongly, believed to be Jewish. Was Lloyd George's hostility to Samuel
fuelled by anti-Semitism? He denied it in a private letter to Lord Mottistone in Oct. 1939—
but in the following terms: 'I am glad you snubbed Samuel. I do not dislike Jews. I have had
many friends amongst them. I know their hatred of hogflesh: that ought to induce them to
disown Samuel as their spokesman, for I know him well, and I tell you he is, always has
been, and ever will be, until he gets to the bosom of Abraham, a swine of the swiniest. Then
Abraham will hate him as he would putrid pork.' Some lingering sense of shame led Lloyd
George to add '(Private and Confidential)' after this outburst (Lloyd George to Mottistone,
9 Oct. 1939 (copy), HLRO Lloyd George papers G/15/4/4). Notwithstanding such
utterances, anti-Semitism was probably little more than a rhetorical flourish on Lloyd
George's loathing of Samuel. Although they had been friendly in earlier years when Samuel
and his wife had occasionally accompanied the Lloyd Georges to the opera, their personalities were utterly different. Lloyd George had always regarded Samuel as essentially a

his frustration by means of savage private denunciations of his unworthy successor. Samuel, to his credit, reacted to Lloyd George's backstabbing with a steady temper. But his refusal to be provoked served only further to infuriate the Old Pretender in his exile at Churt.

In the aftermath of the election MacDonald reshuffled his Government in the light of the new, and to him not very palatable, realities. He told the King on 3 November that he was having great difficulty in forming his Cabinet because of Conservative demands for key positions.

Then [according to a record by Wigram] the King told the Prime Minister that he ought to make sure that if Snowden and Samuel came into the Cabinet they would not break it up when the question of tariffs was raised. The Prime Minister said he thought of leaving Samuel at the Home Office, and not asking for any undertaking beforehand about tariffs; if later on there was any kicking the Prime Minister would say, 'All right, go'. If the Prime Minister tried to secure guarantees now, Samuel might go off with his 35 supporters,[4] whereas later on he would probably not have so many followers.[5]

The Conservatives, who now commanded an independent parliamentary majority, held the whip hand within the new Government. The non-Conservative ministers, from MacDonald down, held their places by grace and favour of the Conservatives. They knew it, and for the most part adjusted their behaviour accordingly. The Samuelites proved to be the only awkwardly independent members of the Government. In the new Cabinet, enlarged to twenty members, the Conservatives demanded and received a majority of seats. They were given eleven places: Baldwin became Lord President and Neville Chamberlain Chancellor of the Exchequer. The 'National Labour' group, a parliamentary fiction rather than a party, received four. The Simonites were given two: Simon succeeded Reading at the Foreign Office; Runciman became President of the Board of Trade on the recommendation of Snowden who called him a Free-Trader of 'unshakeable tenacity'.[6] Although not needed for a Government majority, the Simonites were useful to the Conservatives as a counterweight to the Samuelite Liberals. In these unfavourable circumstances, Samuel's group was lucky to increase its representation to three: Samuel remained at the Home Office; Sinclair and Maclean, previously outside the Cabinet, were brought in as Scottish Secretary and President of the Board of Education respectively.

politician of the second rank. What rankled most with Lloyd George was his own reduction to political impotence. He would have hated *any* successor, and he readily deployed against Samuel any weapon that came to hand.

[4] Estimates of the exact numbers of Samuelites and Simonites varied, since some Liberals wobbled between the two 'National' groups.
[5] Memorandum by Wigram, 3 Nov. 1931, Royal Archives, GV K2331 (1)/49.
[6] Quoted in Middlemas and Barnes, *Baldwin*, 654.

The protectionist majority lost no time in asserting its predominance. Immediately after the election Churchill, who was not offered a ministerial position, proclaimed that the results constituted a mandate for a shift to protection.[7] At the first full meeting of the newly constituted Cabinet on 10 November, the subject of 'dumping' was raised.[8] The next day the Cabinet agreed to ask Parliament to arm ministers to deal with 'abnormal importation as and when it occurs'. A duty of up to 100 per cent would be imposed on goods imported in 'abnormal quantities'. The proposed measures would be temporary and would expire automatically after twelve months.[9] After another Cabinet the expiry date was advanced to six months.[10] The chief architects of this legislation were Chamberlain and Runciman, whose abandonment of free trade now became manifest. Samuel put up no resistance to the anti-dumping bill, presumably on the principle that it did not represent the 'general system of tariffs' he had sworn to oppose. But no pretence was made of any 'enquiry' of the sort that Samuel had insisted must precede any Liberal acquiescence to even limited protection. As if to accentuate his humiliation, the Cabinet decided to rush the bill through all its stages within a few days.[11] Frances Stevenson commented in a letter to Lloyd George, who had left on a recuperative cruise to Ceylon: 'There is no news today, except that Samuel did not vote on *any* of the readings of the Dumping Bill. I believe the Tories are furious with him. He is not a very popular person, is he?'[12]

Immediately after the anti-dumping bill had been passed, the Conservative Minister of Agriculture, Sir John Gilmour, put forward a proposal for a wheat quota. The Cabinet minutes recorded: 'While the policy of a British Wheat Quota was felt by some members of the Cabinet to be open to criticism from a political point of view, on a review of the difficulties of the international and national position, as well as of the Parliamentary situation, they did not press their objections to the point of rejection.' The proposal was approved, subject to some inessential provisos. At the same meeting, on 25 November 1931, Gilmour proposed tariffs on some 'non-essential foodstuffs'. The declared enemies of 'food taxes' gave way on this too, but asked that at least their disagreement be recorded in the minutes. The request was refused. The minutes stated: 'the Cabinet accepted the view of the Prime Minister that the recording of notes of dissent or reservation was contrary to the general principle of Cabinet

---

[7] *Daily Mail*, 31 Oct. 1931.
[8] Cabinet minutes, 10 Nov. 1931, PRO CAB 23/69/21 ff.
[9] Cabinet minutes, 12 Nov. 1931, PRO CAB 23/69/52 ff.
[10] Cabinet minutes, 13 Nov. 1931, PRO CAB 23/69/57 ff.
[11] Cabinet minutes, 16 Nov. 1931, PRO CAB 23/69/68 ff.
[12] Frances Stevenson to Lloyd George, 20 Nov. 1931, in Taylor (ed.), *My Darling Pussy*, 154.

unity.'[13] On these tariff proposals the Samuelites were not merely defeated; they were ignored. When the next stage was reached, the Fruit and Vegetables and Agricultural Products (Emergency Customs Duties) Bill, it was introduced in the House of Commons without even a courtesy reference to the Cabinet Committee on Home Affairs.[14]

Lloyd George ranted furiously when news reached him of the Samuelites' apparent pusillanimity. Cruising through the Red Sea, he passed animadversions on the traditional Jewish account of the Israelites' passage across that waterway, and talked of Samuel with 'fire in his eyes'. He promised that 'he would rub his nose in it when the time came'.[15] And he wrote to Frances Stevenson: 'If Samuel & his rabbits stand this then they will stand anything.'[16] Mixing metaphors with abandon a few days later, he inveighed against Samuel and Sinclair as 'mangy rabbits' and 'cracked swords', and anathematized them as of no 'further use to the progressive cause. . . . Let them rest where they are—despised by everybody.'[17]

The Conservatives continued to push hard for a general tariff and looked towards the forthcoming imperial economic conference, due to be held in Ottawa in the summer of 1932, as their opportunity. The Conservative plan was to introduce a protective regime and then to follow that with a system of imperial preference. The protectionists went so far as to permit a gesture towards the Samuelite demand for an 'enquiry' in the form of a Cabinet Committee on Fiscal Policy, established on 11 December 1931.[18] Samuel and Snowden were members, but the chairman was Chamberlain, and there was a clear majority of protectionists so that the result was a foregone conclusion. Even as the committee went through the motions of its 'enquiry', the Cabinet was invited, by way of preparation for Ottawa, to approve 'the general principle that tariff concessions to the Dominions may in certain cases take the form not of free entry for a commodity into the United Kingdom, but of a rate of duty on that commodity more favourable than the rate charged to any foreign country'. Once again Liberal objections were swept aside, although on this occasion the Cabinet minutes came close to infringing the rule, established only a fortnight earlier, that prohibited expressions of dissent: Cabinet approval was stated to have been given 'on the clear understanding that no Minister was committed in principle or in detail to a tax on foodstuffs of any kind, and that any decision on this subject was reserved until information was

[13] Cabinet minutes, 25 Nov. 1931, PRO CAB 23/69/111 ff.
[14] Cabinet minutes, 2 Dec. 1931, PRO CAB 23/69/158 ff.
[15] Sylvester diary, 26 Nov. 1931, in Cross (ed.), *Life with Lloyd George*, 57.
[16] Lloyd George to Frances Stevenson, 26 Nov. 1931, in Taylor (ed.), *My Darling Pussy*, 155.
[17] Lloyd George to Frances Stevenson, 29 Nov. 1931, ibid. 159.
[18] Cabinet minutes, 11 Dec. 1931, PRO CAB 23/69/224 ff.

before the Cabinet as to what advantages to British trade the Dominions were prepared to offer'.[19]

Thus the Government, with the aid of the Cabinet Secretary, managed simultaneously to approve and refuse to approve a 'general principle', and to record and refuse to record a note of dissent. Such word-twisting might satisfy Liberal scruples for a while, but it was rapidly becoming clear that the Conservatives would brook no opposition on this issue and that they welcomed rather than feared the prospect of Liberal withdrawal from the Government.

Through all this Samuel remained silent in public, save for a speech to the Eighty Club in which he spoke at length about the Wheat Quota proposal—but in terms that must have left his hearers at sea as to whether he was for it or against it.[20] Apart from dealing with questions, Samuel, hitherto a frequent parliamentary speaker, said nothing at all in the House of Commons for the first three months of the new session. One reason for his reticence was that Liberal opinion on the question of the moment stretched from the ardent free-traders to those who were looking for the first convenient opportunity to bolt for protection. In between, almost every Liberal MP seemed to have his own stopping point beyond which he would not go. The protectionists' salami-slice strategy was thus peculiarly well adapted to cause maximum dissension within Liberal ranks about when and where the party should draw the line and stand on its free-trade principles.

Throughout this period Samuel was constrained by the fear that, if he resigned, his already small band of Liberal faithful might dwindle further, since he could not be sure how many would follow him into opposition. In January 1932 he discussed the possibility of resignation with Sinclair, who followed Samuel faithfully on policy issues and could take sensitive readings of Liberal opinion in Parliament and the country. Samuel suggested that, at a suitable moment, the Liberals might withdraw from the Government but nevertheless continue to offer it general support except on tariffs. Sinclair disagreed. In a long letter to Samuel, he outlined the Liberals' dilemma. On the one hand, he agreed with Samuel 'that we could not possibly support the policy of a so-called revenue tariff if it involved staple articles and also the whole range of small luxuries of working class diet'. On the other, he believed the Liberals 'should exert every effort to arrive at a workable and satisfactory compromise in order to avoid the break-up of the Government.' He condemned the 'zealots' who, as the Liberal journalist J. A. Spender had put it, 'started crying

---

[19] Cabinet minutes, 16 Dec. 1931, PRO CAB 23/69/266 ff.
[20] *The Duty of a Liberal Party in Support of a National Government* (Speeches by Grey and Samuel, 7 Dec. 1931, published by Liberal Publication Department, London, [1931]).

before they were hurt, and have gone on crying at every deviation from
the purist Free Trade doctrine'. He pointed out that 'the Tories, or at any
rate the real Protectionist Tories, want us to go—you, Donald [Maclean]
and me. So long as we remain we are undoubtedly a drag upon the
Protectionist wheel.' Sinclair argued that resignation 'would be ascribed
by public opinion either to cowardice, levity or bigotry. . . . The only way
to obtain any sympathy from public opinion, to rally the Liberal Party
and to put heart into Free traders would be to move at once into open
opposition and to denounce the policy of the Government as a breach of
its election pledges.' Sinclair argued that resignation was 'impossible
except on a big issue'.[21] The imposition of temporary customs duties on
flowers and vegetables hardly fell into that category. A more substantial
challenge would have to be awaited.

It was presented almost immediately. In mid-January the Cabinet
Committee on the Balance of Trade completed its 'enquiry' and at its final
meeting, on 18 January, approved Chamberlain's proposals for a general
tariff. The only dissentients were Snowden and Samuel. Before the
meeting, Snowden, knowing what was about to occur, talked of resignation, and Samuel told him that he, as well as Maclean and Sinclair, would
also 'resign rather than concur'.[22] On the same day, in a letter to his eldest
son, Samuel approved Edwin's proposed definition of the word 'difficulty':
' "difficulty" is what my father remains in the Cabinet with'.[23]

On 19 January Samuel circulated a long dissenting memorandum to the
Cabinet rejecting the majority report of the Cabinet Committee. He
indicated some readiness for compromise, for example on extension of
the duties imposed under the Abnormal Importations Act. But on the
committee majority's central recommendation of a 10 per cent general
tariff he argued strenuously that it would increase raw materials costs to
British industry, would 'have a very serious effect on our entrepôt trade',
would increase the cost to the consumer of basic foodstuffs, would do
nothing to promote rationalization, would not significantly affect the
balance of trade, and would hinder rather than help the Government's
bargaining position in international trade negotiations. He found it
'unfortunate that the Committee declined to bring into consultation at
this stage the expert economists and financiers who have previously been
advising the Government'. He had accordingly solicited advice himself
from Sir Walter Layton, Sir Josiah Stamp, and Keynes. Layton had argued
'against a restriction by tariffs for reasons of balance of trade'. Stamp
favoured 'an all-round tariff but mainly with the object of "redistributing

[21] Sinclair to HS, 18 Jan. 1932, Churchill College, Cambridge, Thurso papers III/32/1.
[22] Memorandum by HS, 25 Jan. 1932, HLRO HS A/87/7.
[23] HS to ES, 18 Jan. 1932, ISA 100/57.

incomes" '. As for Keynes, Samuel quoted him as 'not now worrying about the balance of trade': 'In his opinion the Government need take no special action with regard to it. He had been in favour of an all-round tariff [i.e. before devaluation], but the currency depreciation is doing what he wanted to do by that means, and better.'[24]

Samuel's memorandum, as well as one by Snowden, reached members of the Cabinet together with Chamberlain's majority report. When the Cabinet met the next day the subject was not raised. But the underlying issue reared its head in a discussion of the proposed 'home wheat quota', in the course of which doubts were expressed, almost certainly by the Liberals or Snowden, 'as to whether it was not wider in scope than the Cabinet had anticipated, and as to whether it would not involve a more perceptible increase of cost to the consumer'.[25] This was a foretaste of the drama that was to follow.

Battle was joined on 21 January in two marathon meetings of the Cabinet. The arguments pro and con were rehearsed once again. 'At the request of certain members of the Cabinet', it was agreed that a full set of minutes would be circulated, recording *in extenso* the views expressed.[26] This departure from what had become the norm was an important signal that the Liberals, even though they might not quite realize it themselves, were not prepared to leave the Government. They were talking as much for the record as for any real effect their words might have on their interlocutors. The full set of minutes shows that the brunt of defence of the protectionist case was borne not by the Conservatives but by Samuel's fellow Liberals (or ex-Liberals—though they would have denied the prefix), Simon, Runciman, and Hilton Young. The Conservatives were no doubt privately delighted to set the two Liberal camps against each other.

The meeting began with statements from those Cabinet ministers who had not been members of the committee. Sinclair indicated in his opening remarks that he was looking for some foxhole into which he might escape from the need to resign: he 'deprecated reference to the dilemma between immediate action on the lines of the Report and resignation'. After other non-committee-members had spoken, Chamberlain presented a lengthy rebuttal of Snowden's arguments against protection. Referring to Samuel's

[24] Cabinet memorandum by HS, 19 Jan. 1932, HLRO HS A/87/1. Keynes, however, was about to change his position again. In a lecture on 4 Feb. 1932, he stated that he was not prepared to oppose a general tariff 'with any heat of conviction'. In the course of the following year he settled into the opinion that, in current circumstances, protection remained desirable. He returned to a free trade position only towards the end of his life. See Clarke, *Keynesian Revolution*, 283–4; Harrod, *Keynes*, 526, 554.
[25] Cabinet minutes, 20 Jan. 1932, PRO CAB 23/70/55 ff.
[26] Cabinet minutes, 21 Jan. 1932, PRO CAB 23/70/117 ff.

suggestion that economists should have been consulted, 'he pointed out that the result of the Home Secretary's enquiries seemed to be that they did not agree among themselves'. Samuel addressed the Cabinet at length, disputing the majority report's figures and arguing that devaluation alone would bring as much of an improvement in the trade balance as it was maintained would result from the proposed tariff. Runciman spoke gloomily about the possibility of a renewed run on the pound. Further discussion of the statistical basis of the majority report led Chamberlain to explain 'that the report did not depend on the exact accuracy of the figures'. When Simon challenged the free-traders to suggest some 'alternative proposals for immediate action', Samuel drew attention to his readiness to accede to an extension of the Abnormal Importations Act, but he did not elicit noticeable gratitude from the protectionists for his proposed 'compromise'. Towards the end of the meeting Baldwin offered 'a few observations as Leader of the largest political party in the House of Commons': he reminded his hearers, not too subtly, of the reality of the protectionist majority in Parliament. MacDonald declared that he 'was prepared in these exceptional circumstances to face a tariff'. In the end Samuel reiterated that he could not support the majority proposal. He was supported by Snowden, Maclean, and Sinclair. Whereupon the Prime Minister closed the meeting with the remark that 'all present would have to face what would be the result of a break-up of the National Government'.[27] At all events, that was what the minutes recorded. Samuel, in a memorandum written a few days later, had the Prime Minister saying: 'But you are not going to be allowed to withdraw from the National Government like that.'[28]

MacDonald met the four recalcitrants at Snowden's flat later that evening and pleaded with them to remain in office. According to Samuel, the Prime Minister 'threw out the suggestion that we should remain in the Govt. and abstain from voting when the particular proposals to which we took exception came before the House of Commons'. This was agreed by all to be impracticable. MacDonald found them unyielding: 'They admitted everything but would not budge. Maclean & Sinclair simple political minds; Samuel pettifogging on some doubtful figures of no real importance: Snowden just as stiff necked & unaccommodating as ever he has been. What a situation.'[29] Later still that night, Samuel wrote to Lothian, who was abroad, to apprise him of the reasons for what seemed at that point the Liberals' imminent resignation. In the same letter, however, he said that they would 'welcome any eleventh hour occurrence which would

[27] Cabinet minutes, 21 Jan. 1932, PRO CAB 23/70/81 ff.
[28] Memorandum by HS, 25 Jan. 1932, HLRO HS A/87/7.
[29] MacDonald diary, 22 Jan. 1932, quoted in Marquand, *MacDonald*, 713.

save us from the obligation [to resign]'.[30] An eleventh-hour deliverance in fact occurred and this letter became out of date before it was dispatched the following day.

When the Cabinet met again the next morning the Conservative Secretary of State for War, Lord Hailsham, made a proposal that opened the escape-hatch the Liberals had been groping for. He suggested 'that in the exceptional circumstances of the day some relaxation might be made of the ordinary Cabinet rule of collective responsibility':

His proposal was that those who did not find it possible to reconcile their lifelong convictions with the recommendations contained in the Report of the majority of the Committee on the Balance of Trade should be free to state that they did not agree in the policy of the Government in this particular matter and even to vote against it in Parliament.

The proposal was supported by Simon and by other ministers. Samuel then asked for an adjournment so that the four dissenters might consult among themselves. Their eagerness to avoid resignation was shown by the fact that the interval lasted no more than a quarter of an hour. When the meeting resumed, the Liberals and Snowden announced their agreement. A public announcement, embodying Hailsham's suggestion, was drafted and issued immediately afterwards.[31]

Why did the Conservatives, who had evidently concerted their action beforehand with the Simonites, offer the Liberals this *pis aller*? And why did the Liberals and Snowden accept it with such alacrity? Baldwin's biographers imply that the Conservatives had not expected the Liberals to agree.[32] Professor Marquand may be closer to the mark in suggesting that the Conservatives, or at any rate the Conservative members of the Cabinet, were looking forward to a merger with the Liberals and feared that a Samuelite withdrawal would make that impossible.[33] The arrangement was attacked fiercely by the right wing of the Conservative Party. Amery's 'first impression was that the whole world would rock with laughter at the fatuity of the proposal' and Beaverbrook agreed that it was 'crazy'.[34] The Conservative ministers, in fact, lost nothing by the arrangement which gave them everything they wanted by way of legislation while reducing the impact of the free-traders' opposition. Indeed, from most Conservatives' point of view it was preferable to retain the Liberals within the Government rather than permit them to cross the floor and attack the Government with abandon. A Liberal withdrawal, accompanied

---

[30] HS to Lothian, 21 Jan. 1932, SRO Lothian papers GD 40/17/159.
[31] Cabinet minutes, 22 Jan. 1932, PRO CAB 23/70/123 ff.
[32] Middlemas and Barnes, *Baldwin*, 662.   [33] Marquand, *MacDonald*, 713.
[34] Amery diary, 22 Jan. 1932, in Barnes and Nicholson (eds.), *Amery Diaries 1929– 1945*, 227.

by Snowden, at such an early stage in the life of the Government, would, moreover, have left MacDonald dangerously exposed as the non-Conservative head of a largely Conservative administration. Rather than risk the collapse of the entire National edifice, therefore, it seems that the Conservative leaders preferred the constitutionally unusual but otherwise purely formulaic 'agreement to differ'.

The compromise was even less popular among Liberals than among Conservatives. Although it was approved by the ancient guardians of Asquithian rectitude, Grey and Crewe, the Union of University Liberal Societies and the League of Young Liberals as well as the Scottish and Welsh Liberal Federations called for the Liberal ministers' resignation.[35] Samuel may be acquitted of caring for office for its own sake. But a resignation at this stage would have constituted a tacit admission that his entire political strategy since the previous August had been based on illusions. It would have involved an acknowledgement that Lloyd George had been right all along in his wounding admonitions. Like canaries, permitted to sing their own tune but not to fly away, the Samuelites therefore preferred to remain in the cage of the National Government.

On 4 February 1932 Samuel broke his long parliamentary silence and spoke from the Treasury bench against the import duties which had been proposed to the House of Commons that day by Neville Chamberlain.[36] Austen Chamberlain, sitting next to Amery, 'got angrier and angrier' as Samuel spoke, and 'said he felt bound to denounce the whole thing as a scandal but he was not quick enough in getting up from his seat when Samuel sat down'.[37] Samuel's ritual defence of free trade was overwhelmed by the crush of Conservatives queuing to denounce him. Four days later it was the turn of the Labour Party to join the chorus of critics, in a debate on Cabinet responsibility initiated by Lansbury who termed the National Government 'a national humbug'. F. S. Cocks, Labour MP for Broxtowe, mocked the Liberals' 'unfortunate position' with an apposite quotation from Burke: 'They are delivered up into the hands of those who feel neither respect for their persons nor gratitude for their favours . . . thus living in a state of continual uneasiness and ferment. . . . They are unhappy in their situation yet find it impossible to resign.' Conservatives joined happily in the bipartisan pastime of sticking pins in the Samuelites.[38] When the debate on import duties resumed the following day, Charles Peat, Conservative MP for Darlington, called Samuel 'a political Rip Van

[35] Crewe to HS, 25 Jan. 1932, HLRO HS A/87/3; Grey to HS, 27 Jan. 1932 (copy), HLRO HS A/87/4; Tom Stannage, *Baldwin Thwarts the Opposition: The British General Election of 1935* (London, 1980), 87; Wilson, *Downfall of Liberal Party*, 404.
[36] *HC Deb.* 5 s., vol. 261 (4 Feb. 1932), cols. 316–35.
[37] Amery diary, 4 Feb. 1932, in Barnes and Nicholson (eds.), *Amery Diaries 1929–1945*, 229.　　　　[38] *HC Deb.* 5 s., vol. 261 (8 Feb. 1932), cols. 515 ff.

Winkle who had gone to sleep in the heyday of Cobden'. 'Some of us', he added unkindly, 'wish that he was still asleep.'[39] When the not very edifying debate ended, the free traders could muster only 76 votes (Labour, the Samuelites and three Lloyd George Liberals—the head of the family had returned but was still resting at Churt) against the government motion calling for a 10 per cent *ad valorem* duty on most imports.

Samuel's response to this parliamentary battering was cheerful, even confident: 'I have lost 4 lbs. weight physically, but have gained a considerable amount politically', he wrote.[40] The opportunity to assert the distinctiveness of Liberal doctrine after months of enforced trimming seemed to hearten him. When the House of Commons debated proposed tariff increases in early May, Samuel used the privilege of the 'agreement to differ' to oppose the measure from the Government front bench. Runciman spoke for the opposite view, provoking a vehement condemnation by Churchill of the 'indecent, even scandalous, spectacle of Ministers wrangling upon the Treasury Bench'.[41] Afterwards, Samuel wrote to Runciman, regretting the altercation but at the same time reproving his old friend: 'Let me add that the position within the Government, already very difficult, will be made much harder if we make debating speeches in the House of Commons against each other's positions.'[42] Runciman replied unrepentantly: 'You have enjoyed a good deal of latitude in attacking those of us who support the Government's policy and in applauding our opponents in the House, and you are not entitled to be exempt from criticism when, no matter what may be the reason, you expose joints in your armour.'[43] The incident demonstrated the strains inevitably produced within the Government by the anomalous arrangement in January. As anti-Government feeling within the Liberal Party was fanned by Lloyd George, who returned to political activity in late May, Samuel and his colleagues began to think again about resignation.

While the Liberal ministers waited for a suitable opportunity to make their move, Samuel occupied himself with the ministerial duties of the Home Office which had been overshadowed by the dramatic events of the previous few months. As in his earlier incarnation as Home Secretary, the political environment in which he found himself was not conducive to radical reforming legislation of the type he had fostered as a junior minister at the Home Office between 1905 and 1909. But he evinced less ideological embarrassment than he had occasionally displayed during the

[39] Ibid. (9 Feb. 1932), col. 764.   [40] HS to ES, 13 Feb. 1932, ISA 100/57.
[41] *HC Deb.* 5 s., vol. 265 (4 May 1932), col. 1173.
[42] HS to Runciman, 6 May 1932 (copy), HLRO HS A/46/10.
[43] Runciman to HS, 9 May 1932 (copy), WR 215.

First World War at having to pursue *attentiste* and anti-libertarian policies. The social reformer in him now seemed dormant, and his second tenure of the Home Office produced little significant 'constructive' legislation.

On two issues that came to the fore he gave further evidence of the puritanism that had been so consistent a strand in his make-up. The first was the question of cinema censorship—which had originated in an unanticipated manner from Samuel's Cinematograph Act in 1909.[44] Local authorities had acquired censorship powers under the Act, and in 1916 the cinema owners with the approval of the Home Office, headed by Samuel, had established the British Board of Film Censors which issued certificates for the public exhibition of films and censored out scenes regarded as irreverent, cruel, or immoral. This quasi-official system of film censorship remained in force when Samuel returned to the Home Office in 1931. In the interim the rise of the 'talkies' had heightened controversy over the influence of the cinema on the young, and demands were made, on the one hand for a more stringent censorship, and on the other for greater leniency.

Samuel distinguished between political censorship and censorship on grounds of public morals. In regard to the former he displayed a liberal approach when in November 1931 he sought to facilitate the showing of 'certain Russian propagandist films' that had been refused certificates by the British Board of Film Censors. Samuel told a Home Office conference that 'he personally thought such films could not have any deleterious influence on the mind of anyone, and they were often so admirable as specimens of the art of the film that it was highly desirable that people should be afforded an opportunity of seeing them'.[45] In the same month, in fulfilment of a pledge given, but not carried out, by his Labour predecessor, J. R. Clynes, he constituted a Film Consultative Committee composed of representatives of local authorities and of the Board of Film Censors. He told the committee at its first meeting:

We do not want this country to close its eyes to things that are going on in the world and we do not want intelligent people to be refused the right of seeing films which are good in themselves merely because they may have some contentious elements in them of which most of us would disapprove.... On the other hand, we do not want to have films exhibited which may give rise to great controversy and perhaps to breaches of the peace, and which would be distasteful to a great many people; so you have to steer a very careful line.[46]

[44] See above, p. 110.
[45] Note of Home Office conference, 17 Nov. 1931, PRO HO 45/15206.
[46] Minutes of first meeting of Film Consultative Committee, 26 Nov. 1931, PRO HO 45/15208.

Samuel's ambivalence on the subject arose from his longstanding convictions on the issues of censorship and public morality, but they also reflected the pressures upon him of conflicting currents of public opinion.

In March 1932 Samuel received a deputation headed by Ellen Wilkinson, former Labour MP for Middlesbrough, who criticized inconsistent and troublesome decisions of the censors and licensing authorities. Miss Wilkinson complained of the Board of Film Censors: 'I think it still holds good that the Chairman who has to censor talkie films regrets that he is completely deaf; the Secretary, Mr Wilkinson, is so blind that he has to be led about the streets by an attendant; and the other gentleman concerned recently died at the age of 81.'[47] A second deputation, more restrictionist in sentiment, visited Samuel soon afterwards. One of its members, Dr Costley White, headmaster of Westminster School, condemned the deleterious moral influence of many films on children: 'If films with their present great freedom are allowed to go on in their present character, I fear, for one, that we are in danger of producing not physically but on the mental and spiritual side something like a C3 population when we want an A1 population.' In his reply Samuel echoed some of the deputation's concerns:

The greater liberty of expression that prevails nowadays compared with Victorian standards has been taken advantage of beyond wholesome limits. Undoubtedly the sex element in life has been over-stressed. Whether on the stage, or in fiction, or in the cinema, I think there is a general feeling now that this has been overdone, and there are signs that there is beginning a wholesome reaction in public opinion against this.

While he agreed that the Board of Film Censors was a 'wholly anomalous institution', Samuel's only substantial proposal for reform was the institution of a third category of certificate in addition to 'A' and 'U'. He also suggested that censorship might be extended to apply to posters as well as films 'because many of the posters are exceedingly objectionable and endeavour to bring the more salacious-minded among the public to see films which as a matter of fact are the pink of propriety by representing that they are of a very lurid character'.[48]

In a speech in Parliament shortly afterwards Samuel expressed his concern that in advanced civilizations 'there may occur a measure of foulness at the base of society and of dissoluteness at the top of society, and, if that spreads, nations become corrupt and in the long run decadent'. At the same time he declared that the Home Secretary was not a *Censor Morum* and maintained that it rested with public opinion 'to help remove

---

[47] Minutes of meeting, 17 Mar. 1932 PRO HO 45/15206.
[48] Note of meeting with deputation from Birmingham Conference on Film Censorship, 6 Apr. 1932, ibid.

whatever is unwholesome and ignoble in our drama, in our cinema or in our literature'.[49] No appreciable changes in the system of film censorship in Britain flowed from these deliberations.

A second issue on which Samuel's moralistic instincts were aroused was that of gambling, from which he had a lifelong aversion. His eldest son records that 'even the most innocent sweepstake was taboo, being a method of getting something for nothing'.[50] When his brother Stuart had installed a roulette wheel in his house for the entertainment of his guests, Herbert and his wife, shocked by what they regarded as a frivolous and immoral indulgence, refused to have anything to do with it.[51] This was not, therefore, a subject which he approached with an open mind. Public lotteries were prohibited in Britain, but the legalization of sweepstakes in the Irish Free State, which led an estimated £2,000,000 per annum to flow out of Britain in illicit purchases of Irish Hospitals' sweepstake tickets, compelled the British Government to address the issue in early 1932.[52] Samuel urged the Cabinet to take action, emphasizing 'that the Home Office objected rather strongly to having to try to administer a law which could not be enforced'. But his colleagues, while expressing 'great sympathy with the Home Secretary', would not sanction any preventive measures.[53] The matter was ultimately referred to a Royal Commission on the Betting Laws, whose appointment was announced by Samuel in May 1932.

Samuel found a more productive outlet for his 'grandmotherly' tendencies (as they had been termed by an earlier generation) in a new Children and Young Persons' Bill which amended his own Children Act of 1908. Samuel himself did not take the initiative for such a bill which had been under consideration in the Home Office since 1927.[54] The bill had already passed through ten drafts before Samuel returned to the department in August 1931.[55] As redrafted in late 1931, it contained two principal elements: the first concerned the treatment of juvenile offenders; the second juvenile employment. Under the first rubric the bill incorporated various minor reforms that had been proposed by an interdepartmental committee, such as the raising of the age of criminal responsibility from 7 to 8. Samuel blocked a proposal by the committee to extend the power of courts to order the whipping of young offenders; he told a Home Office conference 'that he would prefer to restrict rather than enlarge the power

[49] HC Deb. 5 s., vol. 264 (15 Apr. 1932), cols. 1135–56.
[50] Edwin Samuel, Lifetime in Jerusalem, 8.
[51] See BS to Godfrey Samuel, 16 Oct. 192[3?], Godfrey Samuel corr., Cardiff.
[52] HS to Cabinet, 24 Feb. 1932, PRO CAB 24/228/92–6.
[53] Cabinet minutes, 2 Mar. 1932, PRO CAB 23/70/335 ff.
[54] See PRO HO 45/14714/516360/1, 1a, and 1b.
[55] See PRO HO 45/14715.

to whip'. As a result, the bill proposed abolition of the power of courts of summary jurisdiction to order the whipping of children under 14.[56] On this and other points, however, the bill was whittled down during its passage through Parliament. As for juvenile employment, Samuel resisted pressure to tighten restrictions. He told a Home Office conference that 'he was very much opposed to anything which might be regarded as harassing the poor'.[57]

Samuel took a personal interest in the bill and pleasure in advancing further along the road of the 1908 Children Act. He delegated parliamentary responsibility for the bill to his junior minister, Oliver Stanley, a Conservative, with whom he established cordial working relations. Like its predecessor, the 1932 Act took the form primarily of a lengthy consolidating measure. But unlike the earlier Act it did little more than tinker with the existing law. The absence of any other attempt at, or even preparation for, reformist legislation during Samuel's third and final period at the Home Office indicates the fizzling-out of his youthful radicalism. From his pre-war role as a progressive thoroughbred he seemed to have aged into a reliable but blinkered ministerial workhorse. To be sure, he was constricted by his membership of what was, in all but name, a Conservative government. But he gave little evidence of chafing at the Tory bit. Almost as much as for MacDonald, it was an incongruous end to the ministerial career of a former member of the Rainbow Circle.

In June 1932 Samuel's attention was suddenly diverted from Sunday cinema opening and juvenile employment to larger international questions. Simultaneous conferences at Geneva on disarmament and at Lausanne on reparations and intergovernmental debts were placing heavy demands on the Prime Minister and Foreign Secretary. Samuel was summoned to Switzerland to join the British delegation, first at Lausanne, later also at Geneva. The role was an unusual one for a Home Secretary, but Samuel's reputation as a financial expert rendered him a suitable choice for the reparations conference. Samuel had also participated in the Cabinet's disarmament committee and shared the Prime Minister's faith in the possibility and desirability of securing large-scale disarmament by international agreement.

The main business of the Lausanne Conference was once and for all to lay the ghost of the reparations that been imposed on Germany in the Versailles Treaty but that Germany claimed she could not pay. The collapse of the German economy and the resignation of the Brüning Government at the end of May suggested to most people, with the notable exceptions of the French and American Governments, that any further

---

[56] Note of Home Office conference, 7 Dec. 1931, PRO HO 45/14716.
[57] Note of Home Office conference, 17 Nov. 1931, PRO HO 45/15206.

effort to secure reparations payments from Germany was doomed to failure. When the conference opened on 16 June, Samuel found himself seated next to the new German Chancellor, Franz von Papen, who, he wrote, made 'an excellent impression' and was 'evidently anxious for a Franco-German understanding'.[58] The British delegation, headed by MacDonald, pressed for total cancellation of reparations, but this was resisted by the French Prime Minister, Edouard Herriot, who maintained that the French people would never assent to total cancellation. The British were irritated by the French attitude, and Chamberlain reported to the Cabinet that 'neither of the French ministers appeared to have any market sense at all'. 'A most reliable source', however, disclosed to the British that Herriot had been given a virtually free hand by the French Cabinet to agree to cancellation provided that the Germans made a final lump sum payment 'for the reconstruction of Europe'.[59] Agreement was finally reached on this basis on 9 July.

Meanwhile Samuel moved along the shore of the Lake of Geneva in order to help Simon represent Britain at the Disarmament Conference. Here he played a more active role than at Lausanne. Samuel's views on foreign and defence issues between the wars were based on strong support for the concept of arbitration of international disputes and aversion from rearmament.[60] When the Labour Government sought parliamentary approval in March 1931 for its signature of the General Act of Arbitration, Conciliation, and Judicial Settlement, Samuel supported the action whole-heartedly, differing from his Liberal colleague Lothian, who privately denounced the Act as 'a pretentious and dangerous fake'.[61]

Like many on the left, Samuel believed that the Versailles Treaty had inflicted unduly harsh burdens on Germany, and he favoured revisions of its clauses limiting German armaments. Influenced by his friend Professor Gilbert Murray, Chairman of the League of Nations Union, he strongly supported the League and collective security. He shared the general desire of the left for large-scale disarmament, though unlike many socialists and

---

[58] HS to Baldwin, 20 June 1932, CUL Baldwin papers 119/18.

[59] Cabinet minutes, 30 June 1932, PRO CAB 23/72/2 ff.

[60] As a youth Samuel had been an admirer of Randal Cremer, carpenter, socialist, radical MP for Haggerston, and Nobel peace laureate (1903). One of Samuel's earliest visits to the House of Commons had been to hear Cremer propose a motion advocating a general treaty of arbitration with the United States (Samuel, *Memoirs*, 12). On a visit to Geneva in June 1922, Samuel had visited the room in the Hôtel de Ville in which the *Alabama* arbitration had been agreed in 1872. With uncharacteristic hyperbole he wrote to his wife: 'I regard that as one of the greatest events in the modern history of the world—the first important instance of super-national justice and the precursor of the League of Nations and all it implies' (HS to BS, 27 June 1922, HLRO HS A/157/1027).

[61] *HC Deb.* 5 s., vol. 249 (9 Mar. 1931), cols. 845–56; HS to Lothian, 9 Mar. 1931, SRO Lothian papers GD 40/17/253; Lothian to HS, 18 Mar. 1931, ibid.

Liberals he displayed sympathy for French security concerns and for the strategic requirements of Britain's imperial role. His thinking on the subject, like that of many of his generation, was conditioned by his memories of the period before the First World War. Speaking in Parliament in June 1931, he had recalled the naval race of those years and the failure to secure Anglo-German agreement on a 'naval holiday'. The menace of the German fleet, he reminded the House, was 'at the bottom of Scapa Flow'. With equal assurance he continued: 'there is no comparable menace anywhere in the world. There ought to be a great reduction in our naval Estimates ... owing to the fact that the one risk which our Navy was intended to meet has disappeared.' At the same time he opposed those, such as the Labour MP and veteran anti-armaments campaigner Sir Norman Angell, who advocated unilateral disarmament: 'There may be all kinds of risks which we cannot at present foresee, and if these risks were to be realised and we were in advance, trusting that all would be well, to lay down our arms whilst other nations were armed it might lead our country into the most appalling catastrophe, for which none of us would wish to bear the responsibility in the eyes of history.'[62]

In the final months of the Labour Government in 1931 Samuel had served as a Liberal representative on a three-party subcommittee of the Committee of Imperial Defence charged with preparing for the Disarmament Conference. In the early meetings Lloyd George had done most of the talking. Samuel by contrast restricted himself to gathering factual information. One of his few substantial contributions came in the fourth meeting on 14 May 1931, when he stressed France's need for a large air force since she had three fronts: 'Germany, Italy and ourselves'.[63] Hugh Dalton, who attended the meeting as a Government representative, found the discussion 'wretchedly inconsequent: They all say whatever comes into their heads, and no one except Samuel wants to disarm.'[64]

In the councils of the National Government Samuel's position was close to that of MacDonald. He genuinely favoured multilateral disarmament but like most of his colleagues was not prepared to countenance any commitment that might open the door to British military involvement on the Continent. He did not share MacDonald's view that French diplomacy was 'an ever active influence for evil in Europe'.[65] Recognizing the force of French security anxieties, Samuel tried hard to find a formula that would reconcile these with what he saw as the overriding need to avoid an arms race.

[62] HC Deb. 5 s., vol. 253 (29 June 1931), 927–32.
[63] Minutes of meeting on 14 May 1931, PRO CAB 16/102.
[64] Entry for 14 May 1931 in Pimlott (ed.), Dalton Diary, 145.
[65] Quoted in Marquand, MacDonald, 717.

The Disarmament Conference had opened in February 1932, but had soon bogged down in Franco-German recriminations. Germany demanded equality of armaments and a formal end to the Versailles limitations, which she had already secretly exceeded. France insisted on security and would not disarm further without cast-iron guarantees. The British would not give such guarantees and would not support French demands for the creation of an effective League of Nations police force. They nevertheless expressed impatience with the attitude of the French. Samuel played no part in the first phase of the conference in the spring of 1932, but he sat on the Disarmament Committee of the Cabinet and thus observed the progress of the conference closely.[66] In a letter to Simon in late March he expressed support for the idea of disarmament by means of agreed budgetary limitations—i.e. reductions in defence spending as a proportion of total government expenditure by particular countries. One argument in favour of such an approach, he suggested, was that the American attitude to the question of war debts was affected by European armaments expenditure: 'one of the governing considerations in the United States is that the average tax-payer does not see why he should forgo monies due to him—especially when his own Treasury is faced by an enormous deficit—if the debtor Governments are to be free to spend the money they have saved upon a renewal of the race of armaments.'[67] By the time Samuel arrived in Geneva in mid-June the conference had become, as he put it, 'almost derelict'. On 21 June Simon moved to Lausanne and Samuel was left at the head of the British delegation. He co-operated with surprising ease with Simon ('whom I now call John') and sought, in collaboration with the chief American delegate, Norman Davis, 'to save the Conference from futility'.[68]

In an effort to break the deadlock in the conference, the British, French, and Americans held a series of 'private conversations'. On 21 June Samuel reported some progress towards agreement on restriction of aerial bombing. He noted: 'It was made clear that the restriction of bombarding was not to apply to measures taken for the prevention or stopping of raids or other disturbances in Imperial or Colonial possessions or Mandated Territories. Both the French and American Delegations fully recognised the necessity for this exception which the British delegation had urged.'[69] Provisional

---

[66] Although Samuel was not formally appointed a member of the Disarmament Committee until 24 June 1932, he had participated in the earlier discussions on the subject (MacDonald to HS, 24 June 1932, HLRO HS A/155/VIII/53).

[67] HS to Simon, 2[9?] Mar. 1932, PRO FO 800/286/465–7.

[68] HS to BS, 18, 19, and 21 June 1932, HLRO HS A/157/1216–18.

[69] Aerial bombardment had been used by the British in Palestine in order to put down the riots of May 1921 and by the French in Syria to suppress a Druse revolt in the mid-

agreement was also reached on a three-ton restriction on the size of bombers. Less progress was made, however, on the subjects of artillery and tanks.[70] The next day Samuel wrote confidently to his wife: 'Our conversations have gone really well. There is a real desire to reach the maximum measure of disarmament. (We have made a *most* important provisional agreement to stop the possibility of the bombing of civil populations in time of war—if war should recur . . .).'[71] And on 25 June he wrote: 'We are all determined to get *decisions* before the summer holidays.'[72]

Towards the end of June Samuel returned to London for consultations at the Foreign Office. These took place under the shadow of a sudden 'manifesto' issued by President Hoover that called for across-the-board reductions of battleships (by one-third) and cruisers and aircraft-carriers (by a quarter). Hoover also called for the total abolition of tanks, large mobile guns, and most military aircraft. The French and British Governments were furious at this 'bombshell'.[73] Samuel felt that the British should make some effort to meet Hoover's proposals with something other than a blank negative. In the discussions in London he complained that Admiralty proposals 'could not take effect until 1937'. He challenged service representatives to be more forthcoming with proposals for substantial early reductions but evoked little enthusiasm for his plea for agreement on 'a smaller fleet at once'.[74] In Cabinet on 27 June he pressed his proposal that budgetary limitation rather than categories of weapons be used as the basis for disarmament. But he was strongly opposed by the service ministers, and the Cabinet reaffirmed an earlier decision against budgetary limitations. The Cabinet also decided that it was 'much too optimistic' to hope for 'definite decisions' by the end of July.[75]

Samuel thus returned to Geneva empty-handed, with little more to do than conduct a diplomatic holding operation. Although he remained in Geneva until the last week of July, nothing substantial was achieved.

I think the results at Geneva were as good as could be expected at this stage [Samuel reported to MacDonald on his return to London], in view of the very obdurate facts

1920s—precedents that were no doubt to the fore in the minds of both Samuel and one of the French delegates, Bertrand de Jouvenel, a former High Commissioner in Syria.

[70] Memorandum initialled by Simon and Samuel (but drawn up by Samuel), 21 June 1932, PRO FO 800/287/151–8; see also E. L. Woodward and Rohan Butler (eds.), *Documents on British Foreign Policy 1919–1939*, 2nd ser. iii (London, 1948), 526–58.
[71] HS to BS, 22 June 1932, HLRO HS A/157/1219.
[72] HS to BS, 25 June 1932, HLRO HS A/157/1220.
[73] See Edward W. Bennet, *German Rearmament and the West, 1932–1933* (Princeton, 1979), 64–6.
[74] 'Note of a conversation held at the Foreign Office', 26 June 1932, PRO FO 800/287/222–37.
[75] Cabinet minutes, 27 June 1932, PRO CAB 23/71.

with which we had to deal. Our refusal to agree to the Hoover proposal for immediate battleship reduction is not understood, and naturally has met with a considerable measure of disapproval both at home and abroad, and it is difficult to counter this by giving the Admiralty reasons.[76]

The temporary withdrawal of Germany from the Disarmament Conference in September spelt its doom, although the proceedings continued until 1934 when they were adjourned *sine die*.

A minor by-product of the conference was a meeting in the Channel Islands in late August 1932 between Samuel and Herriot. Samuel, who had Home Office business to transact on the islands, had discovered that Herriot was planning to holiday there and they arranged to meet. The presence of other French ministers, among them the Minister of the Interior, Camille Chautemps, and several officials indicated that on the French side the meeting was regarded as more than a coincidental encounter. Samuel's discussions on the island of Guernsey with Herriot and his colleagues were conducted in French in a cordial atmosphere. Afterwards Samuel wrote to Simon: 'It may interest you to know that Herriot told me in course of conversation that he had proposed to his Government and had obtained their approval for the acceptance in principle of the German claim to equality of status in matters of disarmament.' But Herriot had also said, 'We have to take account of the fact that we have a hundred enemies at our door!'[77] Samuel found Herriot 'très sympathique', but the conversations did not lead to any breakthrough in the disarmament deadlock.[78]

By the late summer of 1932 the Liberals' days in the Government were clearly numbered. In June one of their three Cabinet ministers, Sir Donald Maclean, died suddenly. Samuel pressed for the appointment of another Liberal to succeed him at the Board of Education. MacDonald supported the Liberals, but it was a sign of where the real locus of power now lay that

[76] HS to MacDonald, 26 July 1932, PRO PRO 30/69/678. Later that summer, as a result of correspondence with Gilbert Murray, Samuel arranged a private meeting with two 'League of Nations Admirals', S. R. Drury-Lowe and Sir Herbert Richmond, to discuss the battleship question. Richmond had been compulsorily retired from the navy in 1931 after he had written unauthorized articles in *The Times* on naval disarmament. He was the brother of Ernest Richmond, who had served under Samuel as an official in the Palestine Government (HS to Murray, 9 Aug. 1932, Bodleian Library, Oxford, Murray papers 214/37). Perhaps as a result of these contacts, Samuel proposed in September that the Government lay up some battleships in order to go part of the way to meet Hoover's naval disarmament proposals. The idea was roundly rejected by the Admiralty. See B. Eyres Monsell (First Lord of the Admiralty) to HS, 29 Sept. 1932 (copy), PRO FO 371/16432 (W 10960/10/98); HS to Eyres Monsell, 30 Sept. 1932 (copy) ibid.; and Eyres Monsell to HS, 5 Oct. 1932 (copy), ibid.

[77] HS to Simon, 31 Aug. 1932 (copy), PRO PRO 30/69/504.

[78] HS to BS, 30 Aug. 1932, HLRO HS A/157/1243; see also Bennett, *German Rearmament*, 199, 220.

both MacDonald and Samuel wrote to Baldwin to persuade him to acquiesce.[79] Baldwin, however, succeeded in imposing the appointment of a Conservative, Lord Irwin. Samuel accepted the decision without a fuss. Sinclair even considered it an 'admirable' strengthening of the 'left' in the National Government.[80] Samuel, who had admired Irwin's liberal policies as Viceroy of India, welcomed his Cabinet appointment as 'excellent', and asked MacDonald to issue a public statement undertaking that the next Cabinet vacancy would be filled by a Liberal.[81] But the Prime Minister refused on the ground that 'it would certainly give rise to some resentment on the part of others'. He added ominously: 'We happen, at the moment, to have struck a rather troublesome time regarding Party arrangements within the National group.' In the absence of 'some sort of understanding', he warned, 'National combination is doomed.'[82]

The *coup de grâce*, so far as the Liberals were concerned, was the Imperial Economic Conference which met at Ottawa from 21 July to 20 August. In the preparatory Cabinet discussions before the conference, the Liberals had insisted on inserting into the Cabinet minutes a statement objecting 'on Constitutional grounds' to 'any arrangement with the Dominions which was for a period of years, and which would place Parliament under any obligation to maintain particular rates of duty for a particular time'.[83] Two by-election victories, at Montrose Burghs on 28 June and North Cornwall on 22 July, left the Liberals in better heart than for a long time.[84] Sinclair, who had feared a bad result in Cornwall, was exultant and called the result a vindication of Samuel's leadership.[85] These results emboldened the Liberals to take the leap into the dark.

As soon as news arrived of the signature of the Ottawa agreements, inaugurating a system of imperial preference, Samuel began a round of consultations with leading Liberals and with Snowden, who was acting in concert with the Liberals at this period. Snowden wrote to Samuel on 23 August: 'My own feeling at present is that I cannot be dragged any further along this road without a loss of all honour and self-respect. We have now the last opportunity to withdraw, and we can do that now with a very

---

[79] HS to Baldwin, 20 June 1932, CUL Baldwin papers 119/18; HS to MacDonald, 9 July 1932, PRO PRO 30/69/678; Marquand, *MacDonald*, 724.

[80] Sinclair to HS, 16 July 1932, Churchill College, Cambridge, Thurso papers II/32/1.

[81] HS to MacDonald, 17 July 1932, PRO PRO 30/69/678.

[82] MacDonald to HS, 21 July 1932, ibid.

[83] Cabinet minutes, 12 July 1932, PRO CAB 23/72/76 ff.

[84] In percentage terms, the Liberal achievement was not impressive. At Montrose their vote declined from 77 per cent at the general election to 46.9 per cent. In North Cornwall Sir Francis Dyke Acland increased Liberal share of the vote slightly, but only thanks to the withdrawal of the Labour candidate.

[85] Sinclair to HS, c.24 July 1932, HLRO HS A/155/VIII/56.

good case.'[86] Samuel, who was staying with Sinclair in Caithness, wrote to his wife that he doubted that the Liberals could remain in the Government.[87] He was anxious, however, to ensure that all the 'Samuelite' Liberals should resign *en bloc*. Uncertainty on this point necessitated protracted party discussions before the final decision was taken. At the first Cabinet meeting after Ottawa, on 27 August, Samuel 'entered a *caveat* that this discussion was of a preliminary character, full details of the settlement not being available, there not having been time for consultation, and, therefore, pending a fuller opportunity for consideration of the question he had to make reserves for his friends and himself on the whole policy put before the Cabinet'.[88]

Meanwhile Samuel prepared a long memorandum which he distributed to his Liberal ministerial colleagues. He opened with the *obiter dictum*: 'The whole policy of bargains on Tariffs between the different parts of the Empire is dangerous.' He had been reinforced in that view by what he called 'the sordid struggles at Ottawa, the bargaining of sacrifices imposed upon interests here against sacrifices imposed upon interests in the Dominions'. A detailed analysis of the defects of the Ottawa agreements followed, in which he pointed out, among other objections, that 'any advantages which the Dominions are to give to British goods are for the most part conditional, speculative and a matter for the future', whereas the Dominions either had already been given or were shortly to receive advantages in the British market. Unemployment in Britain was unlikely to be reduced significantly by the agreements. 'Our delegates at Ottawa', he wrote, 'no doubt did their best to secure a favourable bargain, but the conditions for a good bargain did not exist. That is why the policy *ab initio* is wrong.'

Turning to party political considerations, Samuel began by declaring: 'No-one will doubt for a moment that this is the view that would have been taken by the leaders of the Party in recent years, by Campbell-Bannerman, and by Asquith.' He now admitted that the 'agreement to differ' was 'highly anomalous': 'It has involved all sorts of difficulties. It is felt by the Liberal organisations in the constituencies to be most irksome. . . . It gives easy opportunity for derisory attack. . . . All this can be faced with equanimity if there is a definite national purpose to be served.' But the emergency had been overcome. 'The national peril is past.' Above all—and this seems to have been the deciding factor in his mind:

We all of us hold the strong conviction that the continued existence of an independent Liberal Party, as powerful as the electorate will allow it to be made, is necessary in the

[86] Snowden to HS, 23 Aug. 1932, HLRO HS A/89/1.
[87] HS to BS, 24 Aug. 1932, HLRO HS A/157/1237.
[88] Cabinet minutes, 27 Aug. 1932, PRO CAB 23/72/147 ff.

national interest. . . . The Liberal workers in the country see the danger of a repetition of the experiences of forty years ago, and of the absorption of another generation of Liberal Unionists by the Conservative party. They will not suffer it in silence, and they will be right.

Resignation, he argued, 'would be a sign of independence, of vigour, and, I may perhaps be allowed to add, of a readiness for self-sacrifice, which would be likely to inspire fresh confidence in British Liberalism as a living force'.[89]

Samuel was thus clear in his own mind and gave a definite lead to his party. But it took him several weeks to persuade his fellow-Liberals. On his way south from Caithness, Samuel called on Grey who told him 'his gorge' rose at the Ottawa agreements, though he said he would favour the Liberals remaining in the Government 'if there were a real prospect that the Govt. would set to work to get world tariffs reduced'. Grey added that he would want to hear Runciman's view—Runciman still being mistakenly regarded by the Asquithian rump as a free trader at heart.[90] Earl (Sydney) Buxton, another grand old man of the party, wrote to Samuel that he would 'greatly deplore resignation at the present moment', but that as a non-minister he 'would be prepared to acquiesce' in whatever action was decided by the Liberal members of the Government.[91] Sinclair, who functioned as Samuel's deputy in the Commons, favoured resignation, although he reported that Lothian, Under-Secretary for India, had not yet made up his mind and might respond to 'strenuous appeals' from Mac-Donald and Baldwin to remain in office on grounds of national interest.[92]

On 8 September Samuel invited most of the Liberal ministers to a meeting at his home at which a consensus was reached in favour of resignation with the proviso that the party would not cross the floor but would continue to give general support to the Government on issues other than tariffs.[93] Samuel saw MacDonald the next day and warned him of the imminent resignations. An alarmed MacDonald replied by hand, pleading with the Liberals not to abandon him: 'Whatever use I may have rests on the fact that I represent a combination. If you go, I am no longer the head of a combination. . . . I should be regarded as a limpet in office.'[94]

[89] Memorandum by HS, 28 Aug. 1932, HLRO HS A/89/5.
[90] HS to BS, 26 Aug. 1932, HLRO HS A/157/1239; see also note by HS, 26 Aug. 1932, HLRO HS A/89/3; and Grey to HS, 26 Aug. 1932, HLRO HS A/89/4.
[91] Sydney Buxton to HS, 6 Sept. 1932, HLRO HS A/89/18.
[92] Sinclair to HS, 2 Sept. 1932, HLRO HS A/89/8. After lunching with MacDonald on 25 Sept., Lothian wrote to Samuel suggesting that 'the very dangerous situation in the next few weeks over German re-armament' might warrant a reconsideration of the Liberals' decision to leave the Government (Lothian to HS, 25 Sept., 1932, SRO GD 40/17/269).
[93] HS to Walter Rea, 9 Sept. 1932, HLRO HS A/89/9a.
[94] MacDonald to HS, 10 Sept. 1932, HLRO HS A/89/26.

He expressed the same concern for his personal position in a letter to the King, suggesting that his role as 'a Prime Minister who does not belong to the party in power' would become 'more and more degrading'.[95] The King sympathized with MacDonald, replying that he found the Liberals' attitude 'inexplicable, especially at a time when it is obvious that solidarity is essential both for the sake of this country and the world'. He added: 'I cannot understand why these Liberal members did not propose to resign before Ottawa, as they must have realized that the discussions at the Conference would revolve round Tariffs.'[96] On 14 September the King received Runciman at Balmoral and discussed the threatened resignations. Runciman intimated that he and Simon would remain in office. At the King's request, Runciman agreed to visit Grey on his way south to give him a personal message 'that the King hoped that Lord Grey would do everything possible to help to keep the National Government united'.[97] Grey seemed reluctant to play the appointed role. When Runciman delivered his message on 18 September, Grey declared his support for the National Government. But he refused to support the Ottawa agreements and he would not separate himself from Samuel.[98]

In the event, the Samuelites' decision was not swayed by the monarch's intervention; nor by the doubts of some of the Liberal elder statesmen; nor by the ambition for office of some of the wavering Liberal MPs; nor by the plaintive entreaties of MacDonald. On 16 September Samuel wrote to MacDonald setting out the Liberals' objections to the Government's policy and making a final pro forma request 'that further progress with the Ottawa agreements should be suspended until after the World Economic Conference [planned for 1933] has been held'.[99] On the same day he wrote to the King's Private Secretary outlining the Liberals' views and emphasizing that all the Liberal ministers as well as Grey, Crewe, Reading, and H. A. L. Fisher concurred that the resignations were necessary unless the Government's policy were changed.[100] Desperate somehow to avoid the Liberals' resignations, MacDonald, on the pretext that ministers were abroad, delayed the final Cabinet meeting at which the Liberals' proposal for 'suspending' Ottawa agreements would be discussed. The intervention of the monarch having failed, MacDonald took the extraordinary step on 21 September of involving a foreign power. He wrote to Samuel that the

[95] MacDonald to King George V, 11 Sept. 1932, Royal Archives, GV K2357/1.
[96] King George V to MacDonald, 12 Sept. 1932 (copy), Royal Archives, GV K2357/2.
[97] Memorandum by Wigram, 15 Sept. 1932, Royal Archives, GV K2357/3.
[98] Runciman to Wigram, 18 Sept. 1932 (copy), WR 254; see also Grey to HS, 17 Sept. 1932, HLRO HS A/89/49a.
[99] HS to MacDonald, 16 Sept. 1932 (copy), Bodleian Library Oxford, MS Eng. Hist. c. 509 fos. 122–5.
[100] HS to Wigram, 16 Sept. 1932, Royal Archives, GV K2357/4.

French Ambassador had called at the Foreign Office and had said that 'speaking frankly' the resignations would weaken Britain in Europe. The Ambassador had urged a delay of at least a few months. MacDonald commented: 'It is rather an unusual proceeding and only shows the great anxiety which is already beginning to show itself in responsible quarters.'[101] Samuel remained impervious even to this odd diplomatic *démarche*.[102]

The 'quarter' that felt the greatest anxiety was, of course, the Prime Minister himself. The resignations of the Liberals and Snowden would reduce the 'National' quality of the Government to little more than a flag of convenience. In those circumstances, MacDonald might well find himself displaced by Baldwin or reduced to a decorative figurehead. MacDonald tried to put on a brave face to the outside world. On 23 September he told Geoffrey Dawson, editor of *The Times*, that 'he regarded the secession of the Samuelites as settled, didn't regret Samuel as an administrator', and was considering 'doing a bit of re-shuffling'.[103] Baldwin's first reaction to the news of the Liberals' intention to resign had been: 'The dirty dogs. They always behave like this when rough weather approaches.'[104] But he had assured MacDonald when the National Government was formed that he would not try 'to hound him out unfairly' and he felt some compunction about taking advantage of the Liberal secession to extrude MacDonald from the premiership. While he shed few tears for the Liberals, therefore, Baldwin maintained his support for MacDonald. Any threat that the resignations might produce a major governmental crisis was thus precluded.[105]

The long-awaited Cabinet meeting, the last that Samuel attended, took place on 28 September. Samuel demanded suspension of the Ottawa agreements; all except Snowden and Sinclair opposed him. The discussion had a ritualistic quality, since all concerned knew the inevitable outcome. The only interesting statement was made by MacDonald, who delivered a long and maudlin speech. 'He had friends', he announced defiantly, 'and he would stand by them to the end.' Then he switched suddenly from empty bluster to breathtaking candour: 'Some people said he was imprisoned to the Conservative Party. He admitted that he was imprisoned— not to the Conservative Party but to national circumstances.' Towards the end of the meeting, Samuel mentioned two other issues on which the Liberals felt uneasy. The first was the 'means test'. The Liberals, he said,

---

[101] MacDonald to HS, 21 Sept. 1932, HLRO HS A/89/61.

[102] HS to MacDonald, 22 Sept. 1932, HLRO HS A/89/64.

[103] Dawson diary, 23 Sept. 1932, in J. E. Wrench, *Geoffrey Dawson and Our Times* (London, 1955), 302.

[104] Thomas Jones diary, 14 Sept. 1932, in Thomas Jones, *A Diary with Letters 1931–1950* (London, 1954), 55.

[105] Middlemas and Barnes, *Baldwin*, 686–8.

did not oppose the essence of the policy but merely 'comparatively minor points of administration'. The other issue was disarmament. Here he stood by his proposal for budgetary limitation 'on which his action at Geneva had been criticised'.[106] Later that day Samuel and Sinclair, as well as eight Liberal ministers outside the Cabinet including Lothian and Isaac Foot, resigned.[107]

The vacillations and second thoughts of some of Samuel's followers provided rich fodder for Lloyd George's invective and wit. He felt vindicated in his opposition to the National Government, his initial support for which had faded from memory. He now seized the golden opportunity to poke fun at Samuel. While the Liberal ministers deliberated, Lloyd George affected to believe that they were clinging to the fruits of office. He rang up the editor of the *News Chronicle* to assure him that he 'need have no doubt about Samuel. He was not going to resign. He would stick in office with the National Government on some pretext of necessity for him to do so because of international affairs.'[108] In a speech at Aberystwyth on 21 September, Lloyd George demonstrated his capacity for arresting figures of speech to wickedly brilliant effect in a mock-sympathetic comment on the Liberal ministers: 'They have their perplexities. It is what I have seen many times when a cat has pushed its head into a cream jug and cannot get it out without either breaking the jug or having someone pull it out by the tail. It is the latter process that is going on at the moment, and I hope it will succeed.'[109] That was Lloyd George in public at his best. In a private letter to Frances Stevenson on 23 September he revealed a nastier side of his character:

You need not worry abt Samuel offering to resign the leadership in my favour.
    1. He is a Jew. They surrender nothing out of their clutches.
    2. He is going to play the role of a supporter of the NG on all counts. I am out & out opposition. The two roles are incompatible.[110]

When the news arrived that the Liberal ministers had resigned, Lloyd George's response was: 'So the Jews have left the land of Gosen for the wilderness. May their bones rot there.'[111]

Simon added his own private catcall from the other end of the Liberal spectrum: 'Samuel has chosen an amazing moment to go, for the whole world is now rocking and in the middle of an earthquake it will not be

[106] Cabinet minutes, 28 Sept. 1932, PRO CAB 23/72/183 ff.
[107] HS *et al.* to MacDonald, 28 Sept. 1932 (copy), HLRO HS A/89/84.
[108] Clarke diary, 8 Sept. 1932, in Tom Clarke, *My Lloyd George Diary* (London, 1939), 163.
[109] Taylor (ed.), *My Darling Pussy*, 186–7.
[110] Lloyd George to Frances Stevenson, 23 Sept. 1932, ibid. 189.
[111] Lloyd George to Frances Stevenson, 28 Sept. 1932, ibid. 191.

much good to howl "Ottawa".'[112] At their last Cabinet together Simon had passed Samuel a friendly personal note.[113] But in truth the Simonites relished the exclusion of their chief rivals for the true Liberal label. They had now turned tables completely on the Samuelites who had been the sole Liberal representatives in the National Government a year earlier. For the remainder of the decade, as the pretensions to independence of the 'National Liberals' were gradually crushed by the Conservative bear-hug, Simon and his small cohort of followers disputed the Samuelites' claim to the 'apostolic succession'.[114]

Upon his resignation Samuel retained the support of thirty-two Liberal MPs. He also controlled what was left of the Liberal Party organization, which gave him an edge over the Simonites. Lloyd George had resurrected his separate party office, but save in Wales this presented no serious challenge to the Samuelites' grip on the party. Samuel's central purpose in choosing Ottawa as the issue on which to resign was to find a rallying-point for the party. Free trade was for Liberals a sacred turf on which they could make their last stand. Samuel thus found that most Liberals in the country approved their leaders' resignation. The same could not be said for their decision to remain on the Government side of the House. The main problem confronting Samuel for the next year was first whether, then when, to move to the Opposition benches. Once again he found it necessary to hasten slowly. As before, the main reason was dissension in his own parliamentary ranks. The Liberal Party had already split into three fragments. He had no desire to lose even more MPs by crossing the floor before he had assembled a consensus in the parliamentary party in favour of such a move.

Lloyd George took every opportunity to increase Samuel's discomfiture. When Samuel spoke against an opposition censure motion on the Government in October 1932, Lloyd George launched a violent onslaught directed less at the Government than at the Samuelites. Samuel for once flung an effective dart against his former colleague by remarking, 'My right hon. friend has attacked everyone in turn and often three or four together. . . . There will soon be no one left to attack unless Lloyd attacks George and George attacks Lloyd.' Resorting to the vivid, if mixed, metaphors of which he was a master, Lloyd George, who was on peak oratorical form in this Parliament, poured scorn on the Samuelites' position:

---

[112] Simon to Lady Hilton Young, 6 Oct. 1932, CUL MS Kennet 146/3.

[113] Simon to HS, 28 Sept. 1932, HLRO HS A/89/81.

[114] Malcolm Baines, 'The Samuelites and the National Government: A Study in Liberal Survival, August 1931–November 1933', MA thesis (Lancaster, 1986), 21 and *passim*.

I tell them that a horse that is hobbled does not make much progress, especially if he has only one leg left free, and that is the position in which the right hon. Gentleman is left. He has gone over the top; he expected a real charge forward, but he has fallen flat in No Man's land, firing at the moon. He is caught in the barbed wire which he himself helped to set up.[115]

The parliamentary exchange of compliments was a prelude to further public displays of Liberal disunity.

In a speech in January 1933 Lloyd George denounced the 'flaccid, oleaginous Whiggery of Samuel'.[116] Samuel, as ever turning the other cheek, tried to effect a reconciliation. He sent his critic a friendly note and invited him to a party luncheon.[117] But far from being mollified, Lloyd George was outraged: 'It is an insult. But it is characteristic. Samuel has no bigness about him—no understanding. . . . I am certainly not going to accept. I am summoned to a luncheon—to a social affair, to sit and hear Samuel deliver this great pronouncement of future Liberal policy—I, an ex-Leader of the party and an ex-Prime Minister. Don't you think it is disgraceful?'[118] Although Lloyd George did not attend, he sent a spy, his secretary A. J. Sylvester, who secreted himself behind a curtain and took down a summary of Samuel's speech for his master.[119] A few weeks later, advance copies of the first volume of Lloyd George's *War Memoirs* became available. This scrap-book of personal vendettas masquerading as history included a particularly ungenerous and slighting reference to Samuel.[120] As Thomas Jones, Lloyd George's former Deputy Cabinet Secretary, put it: 'he gives Samuel a good claw.'[121]

On another occasion Lloyd George wrote Samuel a ferocious letter complaining that Samuel had stolen his idea for a luncheon for Liberal intellectuals. He called Samuel's action 'underhanded and grasping' and denounced 'this kind of sneaking and snatching'.[122] Some residual sense of decorum prevented him from dispatching the letter, but years afterwards Lloyd George still 'flared up' at the thought of what he called 'the meanest thing he [Samuel] had ever done' and described his erstwhile

[115] *HC Deb.* 5 s., vol. 269 (25 Oct. 1932), cols. 861–83.
[116] Quoted in Stannage, *Baldwin Thwarts the Opposition*, 92.
[117] HS to Lloyd George, 28 Jan. 1933, HLRO Lloyd George papers G/17/9/19.
[118] Clarke diary, 27 Jan. 1933, in Clarke, *Lloyd George Diary*, 184.
[119] Sylvester diary, 6 Feb. 1933, in Cross (ed.), *Life with Lloyd George*, 91.
[120] David Lloyd George, *War Memoirs* ('new edition', London, 1938), i. 640.
[121] Jones diary, 20 Apr. 1933, in Jones, *Diary with Letters 1931–1950*, 105. Lloyd George later boasted in conversation that 'the best thing he had ever said about Samuel had, on the advice of his friends, been cut out of his manuscript. He had written: "I planted Samuel on Mount Sinai as the lineal descendant of Pontius Pilate."' Neither biblical geography nor Jewish genealogy were Lloyd George's strong points (Sylvester diary, 2 Aug. 1934, in Cross (ed.), *Life with Lloyd George*, 110–11).
[122] 'Draft of letter which was not sent', n.d., HLRO Lloyd George papers G/17/9/29.

colleague as 'the politician he hated most'.[123] Samuel reacted to Lloyd George's hostility with an almost superhuman forbearance, but Lloyd George's public gibes and taunts made any true reconciliation virtually impossible.

Humility, however necessary in other walks of life, is not always a desirable quality in a political leader. In Samuel's case, his failure to respond in kind to Lloyd George's attacks testified to his old-fashioned conception of gentlemanliness in politics—but also pointed to a fundamental weakness in his style of leadership, particularly leadership of a radical party, and most particularly of a party down on its luck. Samuel did not warm naturally to the role. A Liberal journalist found him 'aloof, without boldness or the common touch'.[124] Although his parliamentary performances earned him admiring reviews, he never built up much of a personal following beyond Westminster. Harold Laski, in a 'pen portrait' of him in the Daily Herald in February 1933, called him 'blandly aloof' and compared his cool efficiency unfavourably with the 'personal magnetism' of Lloyd George. 'I should not accuse him [wrote Laski] of any tendency to spontaneity. He has never been guilty of that heedless and instinctive generosity which refuses to count the cost.'[125] The judgement, however unfair, was shared by many, even among his followers.[126] Even loyal colleagues murmured that Samuel's leadership seemed insufficiently energetic. James de Rothschild, Liberal MP for the Isle of Ely, and a family friend, wrote to Beatrice Samuel in February 1933 suggesting that her husband should 'shed some of his natural modesty' and take a more assertive public stand that would 'best answer Mr Lloyd George and those he is inciting'. Rothschild went on to warn: 'His self-effacing modesty cannot fail to attract his friends and colleagues, but they would all be the more distressed if it became a factor to weaken his own influence in the Party.'[127]

By mid-1933 pressure built up within the party in favour of a move to Opposition. 'Our support of the Government is becoming more and more nominal', wrote Sinclair to Samuel in July. He argued that the most

[123] Sylvester diary, 21 Nov. 1938, in Cross (ed.), Life with Lloyd George, 222.
[124] Clarke diary, 27 Jan. 1933, in Clarke, Lloyd George Diary, 183.
[125] Daily Herald, 4 Feb. 1933.
[126] It is striking how few felt comfortable on first-name terms with him: among his fellow-Liberals in this period only Reading, Sydney Buxton, Sinclair, Isaac Foot, and Francis Acland seem to have called him 'Herbert'. His old friends Runciman and Simon veered from 'Herbert' to 'Samuel' depending on the vagaries of their political relations with him. Among the handful of other politicians who addressed him by his first name in the period before 1935 were Charles Masterman, Winston Churchill, and Charles Trevelyan. Only towards the end of his life did he seem to invite such intimacy from a wider circle. To Lloyd George he was always 'Samuel'.
[127] James de Rothschild to BS, 3 Feb. 1933, HLRO HS A/155/VIII/66.

November 17th, 1933.

THE TRANSFER

Stan Baldwin: "That's funny, I didn't notice he was playing for us."

Mac.: "He didn't."

(*The Samuelites will "Cross the Floor" when the new session of Parliament opens.*)

2 'The Transfer' by Strube (Daily Express, 17 November 1933).

opportune moment to cross the floor would be after Parliament reconvened the following November.[128] In late October, when he returned from a visit to the USA, Samuel found a further letter from Sinclair awaiting him. Sinclair had faced the awkward task of defending the parliamentary party's pro-Government stance at the annual conference of the Scottish Liberal Federation which passed a resolution urging a move to the Opposition benches. 'Quite frankly,' Sinclair wrote, 'the situation of the Party is bad. . . . The longer we remain in our present position the more inglorious, embarrassing and insignificant it becomes. . . . We must soon exchange a position in which our support of the Government is nominal and our nagging criticism both infuriating and ineffective for one of open and declared though not obstructive or irresponsible opposition.'[129] Samuel, who had been turning the problem over in his mind during his trip, agreed wholeheartedly: 'It is impossible for us to remain in our present political position. The Party would fade away. The most serious consequence would be that the Labour party would gain all the prestige, and consequent strength which would accrue to it, from its being regarded as the only possible alternative to the present Government.' Samuel proposed that he should lead the party across the floor at the start of the new parliamentary session. Of those he had already consulted, only Reading had not approved the proposed action.[130]

In an off-the-record interview a few days later with W. P. Crozier, editor of the *Manchester Guardian*, Samuel outlined with unusual candour the tactical considerations that influenced his decision:

He [Samuel] insisted that with regard to the position of the Liberal Party in the House he had all along realised fully the disadvantages of remaining on the Government side. It was, however, essential that when he moved he should take with him the great bulk of the Party. If he had gone over when the Liberal Ministers resigned on Ottawa the group would have been seriously split and all the enemies of the Liberal Party would have declared that he was leading it to final destruction. Now he could hope to take over the whole, or almost the whole of his followers—he hoped the lot.[131]

Samuel succeeded in carrying thirty Liberals with him to Opposition. Four former Samuelites, Robert Bernays, Joseph Leckie, William McKeag, and J. P. Maclay, remained on the Government benches. One former Simonite, A. C. Curry, joined Samuel in Opposition. One ex-Samuelite,

[128] Sinclair to HS, 18 July 1933, HLRO HS A/95/1.
[129] Sinclair to HS, 14 Oct. 1933, HLRO HS A/95/2.
[130] HS to Sinclair, 30 Oct. 1933, Churchill College, Cambridge, Thurso papers II 1934/37.
[131] Memorandum by Crozier, 4 Nov. 1933, John Rylands University Library, Manchester, *Manchester Guardian* Archive.

H. L. Nathan, who had already crossed the floor, maintained an independent position but joined the Labour Party a few months later. On
the same day that he delivered his first speech from the Opposition
benches, Samuel wrote to Lloyd George suggesting that they meet 'to talk
over the position'.[132] Some distant collaboration was inaugurated, but a
gulf of suspicion remained. Lloyd George's continuing not-so-private
contempt for Samuel is indicated by the presence among his papers of
three typed copies of satirical verses by 'Hamadryad' published in the
Saturday Review under the title 'The Slippery Slope':

> Slippery Sam has crossed the floor,
> He won't help the Government any more;
> He's sitting now on the opposite benches,
> But nobody worries and no one blenches,
> Or cares—to be brutal—a tinker's dam,
> What has become of Slippery Sam.[133]

And more in similar vein. The verses which apparently so delighted Lloyd
George reflected the general indifference of public opinion to the Samuelites'
action. In the first four by-elections held after the move to Opposition, the
average Liberal vote was reduced to a dismal 10.6 per cent. By mid-1934
Lloyd George had drifted away again. When Sinclair suggested a renewed
effort to draw him in, the Liberal whip Harcourt Johnstone expressed
doubts, although he added: 'I think we ought always to bear in mind the
possibility of abating as far as possible LG's nuisance value within the
Party.'[134]

Samuel's two years on the Opposition benches were frustrating and
unrewarding. Far from welcoming the Liberals as allies, Labour MPs,
particularly those on the left, tended to jeer at them as belated converts.
Lloyd George toyed with the idea of some form of alliance between the
Liberals and Labour, but the Labour Party displayed little interest, and
few Liberals liked the proposed strategy. In a speech at the Liberal
Summer School at Oxford in 1934, Samuel made it clear that he saw no
prospect of such a revival of the 'progressive alliance'.[135] Lloyd George
commented privately: 'They are still living in the full and blessed hope of
being redeemed at the Great Day by Tory votes!' He called the Liberals'
draft policy proposals 'poor slop' and denounced their agricultural ideas
as 'the vomit of a sick dog—soured, devitalised, bits of undigested Green,
Brown and Yellow Book'. 'The dog', he prophesied, 'is going to die—

---

[132] HS to Lloyd George, 21 Nov. 1933, HLRO Lloyd George papers G/17/9/20.
[133] HLRO Lloyd George papers G/17/9/31; *Saturday Review*, 2 Dec. 1933.
[134] Johnstone to HS, 26 July 1934, HLRO HS A/155/VIII/85.
[135] Text of speech: Herbert Samuel, 'Liberty, Liberalism and Labour', *Contemporary Review*, 146 (Sept. 1934), 257–67.

November 24th, 1933.

THE GENTLEMAN: "Who is that person, my dear?"

THE LADY: "Oh, she used to be my daily help; now she works opposite."

(Sir Herbert Samuel has lost no time in attacking the Government since he "crossed over.")

3 'Used to be my daily help' by Strube (Daily Express, 24 November 1933).

with such "vets" nothing can save him.'[136] Meanwhile, the Liberals' awkward parliamentary position and Lloyd George's dalliance with Labour enabled *The Times* to sneer at 'the unnatural equitation of the Liberal Lady on the back of the Socialist Tiger'.[137]

In October 1934 Samuel suddenly fell ill and had to have his appendix removed. A prolonged convalescence prevented his return to full political activity for some months. Churchill, with whom Samuel had recently engaged in acrimonious parliamentary debate on rearmament, but who shared Samuel's generosity towards opponents, wrote Samuel a kindly personal note advising him not to work too hard during his convalescence.[138] Lloyd George, for whom such saving grace cannot be claimed, did not write. While Samuel was out of action, Lloyd George seized the initiative and in January 1935 launched a 'New Deal' campaign in which he claimed to offer a cure for unemployment. Samuel welcomed Lloyd George's proposals, though he said that they were 'identical with those which the Liberal Party has advocated during recent years'.[139] The following summer Samuel attended the inaugural meeting at Central Hall, Westminster of Lloyd George's allegedly non-party 'Council of Action for Peace and Reconstruction'—chiefly a vehicle for Lloyd George's oratorical peregrinations round the country. Samuel did not take the campaign very seriously. He told W. P. Crozier that he had no great expectations from it and 'that there was a whole lot of Liberal opinion knocking about which found no point of focus at the present time and he thought that the Councils of Action would bring together a certain amount of voting strength in the right direction'.[140] At the Liberal Summer School at Cambridge in August 1935, Samuel spoke more warmly than a year earlier about the prospect of 'a powerful concentration of all forces of what would be called on the Continent the Left Centre and the Left'. But he offered no suggestion as to how that might be achieved.[141] Lloyd George, whatever his defects, at least seemed to be giving a lead; Samuel, whatever his virtues, appeared to follow uncertainly in his wake.

The replacement of the ailing MacDonald by Baldwin as Prime Minister in June 1935 marked a further stage in the evolution of the National

---

[136] Lloyd George to Sir Walter Layton, 29 Aug. 1934, HLRO Lloyd George papers G/141/26/1.

[137] *The Times*, 14 Aug. 1934.

[138] Churchill to HS, 3 Dec. 1934, HLRO HS A/155/VIII/90.

[139] Typescript of article by Samuel for 'Co-operation' press syndication agency, 18 Jan. 1935, HLRO HS A/91/20.

[140] Memorandum by Crozier, 19 July 1935, John Rylands University Library, Manchester, *Manchester Guardian* Archive.

[141] Text of address: Herbert Samuel, 'The Present Situation', *Contemporary Review*, 148 (Sept. 1935), 257–67.

Government into a purely Conservative administration. The change fanned rumours of an imminent general election—eventually announced for 14 November. The 1935 election lacked the drama of its predecessor, and the shape of party alignments corresponded more closely to what seemed like normality. The Liberals entered the campaign in a debilitated state. Lloyd George's speechifying of the past year had produced large audiences and enthusiastic cheers but little else. Samuel's leadership was admired in Parliament but could hardly be said to have lit a fire in the country. In 1933 Samuel had spoken of fielding at least 400 candidates at the next election and offering the electorate the possibility of returning a Liberal Government, but this was whistling in the dark. The Liberals (Samuelites and Lloyd George followers) were able to muster only 159 candidates. Almost their only significant supporters in the press were the *News Chronicle*, which leant more towards Lloyd George than Samuel, and the *Manchester Guardian*, highly respected but still only a regional paper. The party organization remained weak at the centre and had virtually collapsed at the constituency level in many parts of the country. The campaign was under-financed and lacked the dynamic mobilizing theme of the Liberals' last great push in 1929. It also lacked the Liberals' most popular leader. Lloyd George held aloof from the official Liberal leadership. He distributed 'Council of Action' questionnaires to candidates and gave his support (a devalued 'coupon') to those who turned in satisfactory replies. But the only Liberal candidates for whom he spoke were his son and daughter.

Lloyd George was invited by Samuel to deliver one of the Liberals' three wireless addresses. But both he and Snowden, who, at Samuel's invitation, delivered the second, concentrated on attacking the National Government, rather than making a positive recommendation to vote Liberal.[142] Samuel was thus the only member of the Parliamentary Liberal Party to deliver a broadcast on its behalf and the only one of the three 'Liberal' broadcasters to urge listeners unequivocally to vote Liberal. His quiet reasonableness, better adapted to radio than to rowdy public meetings, was highly effective. He attacked the Government's trade record and its administration of the 'means test'. He also became the first of a melancholy line of Liberal leaders who found it necessary to rebut the argument that a Liberal vote was a wasted vote. With so few candidates in the field there could be no brave talk of a Liberal Government. Samuel was reduced to the modest claim: 'If all Liberals would only vote solidly for Liberal candidates we would achieve some surprising results.' His advice to the majority of his listeners who would have no opportunity to vote for a

---

[142] Stannage, *Baldwin Thwarts the Opposition*, 181–2.

Liberal candidate was vague: the views of other candidates on peace and employment should be the prime considerations. But lest this be regarded as a hint to vote Labour, he added that the next parliament should exclude diehard Tories and extreme socialists alike.[143]

Samuel's campaign in Darwen took place in the shadow of an unemployment rate in the town that still stood at 30 per cent. His election address laid stress on foreign affairs and emphasized his support for the League of Nations.[144] He earned an endorsement from his friend Gilbert Murray, who declared that 'if there were half a dozen Herbert Samuels in different States of Europe the nations would be free of wars and rumours of war'.[145] But the unemployed Lancashire cotton-workers paid little attention to the pronouncements of the great classical scholar.

In 1931 Samuel had been able to draw on some limited Conservative support in spite of the presence of a Conservative candidate. Samuel estimated this might have been worth 600 votes.[146] This time there could be no such expectation. The National Conservative candidate, Stuart Russell, a Surrey stockbroker with no previous parliamentary experience, announced that he would not be led 'into any bickerings with Sir Herbert Samuel'.[147] The Earl of Dudley, who spoke on Russell's behalf, stirred some protest when he called Samuel 'a wandering Jew'. Another Conservative speaker termed Samuel 'an old speckled hen who has ceased to lay'.[148] But apart from these extravagances the campaign in Darwen was conducted at a higher level of civility than in 1931.

The key issue in the campaign was the hated 'household means test', under which the income of all members of a household was accounted in calculating eligibility for 'public assistance'. Extraordinarily, the Conservative candidate sought to use the issue as a stick to beat Samuel: 'the present means test, supported by Sir Herbert Samuel', he said, 'was working unduly harshly.'[149] Samuel who had approved the principle of the means test while he served in Government, although he had protested against some of its acerbities, could not disavow the essence of the policy. He admitted 'that there must be some kind of Means Test in order to avoid public money being spent indiscriminately'. But he objected to the inclusion of children's earnings in the calculation and pointed out that the Liberals had opposed the legislation the previous year that had brought

---

[143] HS election broadcast, 6 Nov. 1935, gramophone record, BBC Sound Archives, T 799.
[144] Election address, 4 Nov. 1935, ISA 100/112 aleph.
[145] Statement by Murray, 5 Nov. 1935 (copy), Bodleian Library, Oxford, Murray papers 74/17.
[146] HS to ES, 17 Nov. 1935, ISA 100/60.
[147] *Darwen News*, 2 Nov. 1935.   [148] Ibid., 9 Nov. 1935.
[149] Ibid.

the latest form of the test into being.[150] Samuel's careful distinctions probably did not satisfy the many working-class voters who regarded the test as a humiliation as well as a penalty for thrift. The straightforward demand of the Labour candidate for the abolition of the means test rang truer to their ears.

The *Darwen News* as well as Samuel himself attributed the result to resentment of the means test more than any other issue:

RUSSELL (National Conservative)	15,292
SAMUEL (Liberal)	14,135
KERBY (Labour)	7,778
Majority	1,157

The results in the country as a whole were no less disastrous for the Liberals. They won only 19 seats of which 4 were held by the Lloyd George family. Isaac Foot, Harcourt Johnstone, and Walter Rea were among the prominent Liberals who were defeated. The Liberals' share of the national vote declined to 6.4 per cent. The average vote obtained by Liberal candidates was a bare 13 per cent.[151]

In a letter to his son Edwin, shortly afterwards, Samuel avowed a 'blessed feeling of relief at not being in this House of Commons':

It will not be a bad thing for some-one else to try his hand at the redemption of Liberalism. The line I was on, supported by the great body of Liberals in the country and by all the party organisations, has not led anywhere, and seems unlikely to do so. Perhaps Archie Sinclair, if he is elected to the chairmanship of the Parliamentary Party, will be able to find a different line, and perhaps the Labour Party may be in a more chastened mood, and less resolved than it has been to reject any and every suggestion for an accommodation between them and us. We have mooted it repeatedly, in public and in private, but with no response at all.[152]

This was the eleventh and last election that Samuel contested. It marked the end of his career as a front-rank politician. But over the next quarter of a century he, like his party, displayed a stubborn capacity to survive and to make a fruitful contribution to British public life that belied the Liberals' shrivelled parliamentary state.

[150] Ibid., 13 Nov. 1935.
[151] Stannage, *Baldwin Thwarts the Opposition*, 232–7.
[152] HS to ES, 17 Nov. 1935, ISA 100/60.

14

Viva Voce

=======

You know my old theory that the last years of life ought to be the
best and most distinguished and the most useful.

(Benjamin Jowett)

ALTHOUGH SAMUEL'S involvement in public life did not end with his
electoral defeat he redirected the focus of his attention after 1935
from politics to philosophy. Ever since the end of his term of office in
Palestine, he had looked forward to retiring to write on philosophy. Since
1925 he had devoted most of his free time to this avocation. In spite of his
return to politics he had maintained his interest in the subject and from
1927 onwards began publishing articles on philosophical subjects.[1]
These publications led in 1931 to his election as President of the British
(later Royal) Institute of Philosophy. He took the responsibilities of this
position very seriously and expended great efforts each year on the
preparation of the annual presidential address. He also accepted an
invitation from Gilbert Murray, who served as one of the editors of the
'Home University Library', to contribute a volume entitled *Practical
Ethics* to the series. The book, which appeared in 1935, displayed
Samuel's customary virtues of clarity and organization. The reviewer for
Philosophy, J. L. Stocks, a fellow of St John's College, Oxford, took
Samuel to task for not discussing the ethics of gambling and the 'class-
ethics of Marxism', but otherwise praised the book as 'a workmanlike
performance of a difficult task'.[2] The anonymous reviewer in the *Times
Literary Supplement* commended it more enthusiastically: 'It is good to
find the English or common-sense school of philosophy so sturdily
vindicating its right to a hearing.'[3]

Samuel was sufficiently encouraged by the reception of the book to
embark on a more elaborate statement of his philosophical position.

---

[1] 'Liberty', *Contemporary Review*, 131 (May 1927), 566–75; 'The Relativity of Free
Will', *Journal of Philosophical Studies*, 4 (1929), 325–31; 'The Dual Basis of Conduct',
loc. cit., 5 (1930), 408–21.
[2] *Philosophy*, 10 (Oct. 1935), 481–2.
[3] *Times Literary Supplement*, 21 Mar. 1935, 166.

Published in 1937 as *Belief and Action*, it carried the subtitle 'An Everyday Philosophy', indicative of Samuel's hope that it would introduce philosophy to a wide popular audience. The book discussed the problem of knowledge from an empiricist position, and of morality from a vaguely deist one. The latter theme reflected Samuel's growing preoccupation in his later years with what he saw as the need for a spiritual basis for ethics. Although he maintained formal adherence to Judaism, his thought turned more towards the possibility of some unifying universalist religion. The Dean of St Paul's, reviewing the book in the *Sunday Times*, lauded it for 'stimulating the reader of average intelligence to reflection on the problems of the nature of reality and the meaning of good'.[4] The *Times Literary Supplement* reviewer suggested that there was 'more of the mystic in him [Samuel] than he allows his readers to see, perhaps more than he sees himself'.[5] Samuel was particularly pleased by a comment by Albert Einstein, a friend since Einstein's visit to Palestine in 1923 to deliver the opening lecture of the Hebrew University of Jerusalem: 'Dieser Mann spricht wie ein Seelenarzt.'[6] *Belief and Action* was the most popular of Samuel's books. Reprinted in two paperback editions, it eventually sold nearly a hundred thousand copies.[7]

The intellectual self-confidence that enabled Samuel to produce these and later philosophical works also led him to stake out idiosyncratic positions on two controversial scientific controversies. The first was the 'uncertainty' or 'indeterminacy' principle of Heisenberg which Samuel discussed in a series of extraordinarily vehement articles throughout the 1930s. He particularly disliked the attempt by Sir Arthur Eddington and others to extend the principle from the realm of theoretical physics to a more general plane. He regarded such an extension as 'deliberate unreason'.[8] Strangely, this politician, noted for his restraint in debate and reluctance to employ immoderate language, abandoned all decorum in his vendetta against Eddington and his supporters whom he denounced as 'intellectual bandits who, after stupefying their victims with mathematical formulae, try to rob them of their most valuable beliefs'.[9] Conducting his

---

[4] *Sunday Times*, 31 Oct. 1937.   [5] *Times Literary Supplement*, 16 Oct. 1937.

[6] Einstein to HS, 4 Oct. 1937, Jewish National and Hebrew University Library, Jerusalem, Einstein papers Arc. 4° 1576.

[7] *The Times*, 5 Nov. 1960. Samuel's earnings from the book were small. Penguin Books paid an advance of £100 for the Pelican edition, published in 1939. But this was based on a royalty rate of only £1 per 1,000 copies sold. Penguin therefore made no further payment. In 1962 Samuel refused permission for a reprint, thereby registering his disgust at the firm's publication of D. H. Lawrence's *Lady Chatterley's Lover*.

[8] Herbert Samuel, 'The New Doctrine of Eddington and Jeans', *Contemporary Review*, 139 (Jan. 1931), 8–13.

[9] Herbert Samuel, 'Cause, Effect, and Professor Eddington', *Nineteenth Century*, 113 (Apr. 1933), 469–78.

argument almost as if he were running a political campaign, Samuel
assembled the highest scientific authorities, Planck, Rutherford, and
Einstein, in support of his view. Eddington replied in conciliatory vein: he
did not withdraw from his position, while he denied that 'the substitution
of high probability for certainty in the political and economic sphere'
would be as disastrous as Samuel maintained. He added teasingly: 'I have
on occasion supported Sir Herbert Samuel and voted for his political
efforts for amelioration. My decision was on probability; I could not
expect complete certainty that his policy would achieve its end.'[10] Samuel
returned to the charge in an address to the International Congress of
Philosophy in Paris in August 1937, in his presidential address to the
British Institute of Philosophy in November that year, and in other
lectures and articles.[11]

The respectful attention accorded his view of this problem encouraged
Samuel to make a bolder foray into the problems of theoretical physics.
From the late 1930s he began propagating the idea of an 'ether' as the
'physical basis of the universe . . . consisting of energy in one or other of
two states—active or quiescent'.[12] The suggestion attracted considerable
publicity when he presented it at the annual meeting of the British
Association in 1951.[13] But when a recording of Samuel's address was
offered for broadcasting to the BBC, an official minuted, 'No thank you.
Kinder to Samuel not to, I think.'[14] A later note by Dr Archibald Clow
reported that Samuel's paper had 'caused considerable embarrassment to
the Section of the British Association to which it was submitted'. After
further discussions the BBC decided, after all, to accept a talk on the
subject from Samuel 'on the ground that', as Ronald Lewin[15] commented,
'it would be difficult to frame reasons for turning it down'.[16] Samuel
delivered his talk on 'The Ether Controversy' on the Third Programme in
March 1952. He published a full exposition of his theory in *An Essay in
Physics*, published by Blackwell in 1951. The book appeared with a long
letter from Einstein as a postscript. Although Einstein did not explicitly

[10] Sir Arthur Eddington, *New Pathways in Science* (Cambridge, 1935), 303.
[11] 'Analyse de l'indéterminisme', *Travaux du IXe Congrès International de Philosophie
(Congrès Descartes) (Paris 1–6 août 1937)*, vii. 21–7; Herbert Samuel, 'Civilization'
(presidential address to British Institute of Philosophy, 16 Nov. 1937), *Philosophy*, 13
(Jan. 1938), 3–18; 'The Scientist and the Philosopher' (lecture to Royal Institution of
Great Britain, 2 Dec. 1938), *Proc. Roy. Inst.*, 30, part iii, 1–23.
[12] HS to Einstein, 17 Nov. 1950, Jewish National and Hebrew University Library,
Jerusalem, Einstein papers, Arc. 4° 1576.
[13] *News Chronicle*, 11 Aug. 1951.
[14] BBC minutes, Aug. 1951, BBC Written Archives Centre HS 2B.
[15] At that time a producer in the BBC Home Talks Department, later a distinguished
military historian.
[16] Notes by Clow and Lewin, 5 and 7 Feb. 1952, BBC Written Archives Centre HS 2B.

endorse Samuel's concept of the 'ether', he treated the work with respect. On the other hand, L. L. Whyte, who reviewed the book anonymously in the *Times Literary Supplement*, paid it a backhanded compliment: 'The combined modesty and daring revealed in this essay evoke admiration, even if the author's lack of sympathy with current tendencies in physics may suggest a failure in understanding.'[17]

Samuel's attack on Eddington and his concept of the ether did not enhance his philosophical reputation. His effort to draw together religion, philosophy, and politics into a new synthesis evoked more favourable responses. This line of thought led to his most attractive work, *An Unknown Land*, published in 1942. A Utopian novel inspired by Francis Bacon's *New Atlantis*, the book provided a happy framework for the presentation of Samuel's ethical and social ideas. The latter were surprisingly communistic. He described an imaginary country, 'Bensalem', based on a non-money economy; living arrangements resembled those of kibbutzim, with communal kitchens and laundries. The system of government was by nominated boards under a constitutional monarchy. 'The country was run more like a Pall Mall club than anything else.'[18] Much of the book gently lampooned Samuel's political *bêtes noires* such as Marxism and tariffs. The religion of 'Bensalem' was Christianity of a tolerant sort, but Samuel's imaginary traveller noted the existence of a Jewish community whose 'simplified' religion was 'unaffected by the centuries of rabbinical influence'. Their practice, although based on the Mosaic laws and prophetic teachings, was 'spiritual rather than legalistic, ethical rather than theological; not mainly retrospective but forward-looking, and not tribal but universal'. Nevertheless, the ritual followed 'the old traditions, including the use of Hebrew', and the sabbath was observed. With the advance of knowledge and science, Christianity and Judaism in Bensalem were said to be 'approximating more and more to a single fundamental faith'.[19] The book was well received by reviewers and might have sold well had it not been for the wartime paper shortage.

Although philosophy became the central interest of Samuel's life after 1935, he continued to play an active role in politics. In the mid-1930s he found himself drawn into renewed involvement in Jewish affairs. The related causes were the growth of Nazi anti-Semitic persecution after 1933 and the crisis in Palestine between 1936 and 1939. Samuel's efforts to help German Jewry began almost immediately after the Nazi capture of power, when the Nazis announced their first major anti-Jewish measure, an anti-Jewish economic boycott called for 1 April 1933. In response,

---

[17] *Times Literary Suplement*, 23 Mar. 1951.
[18] Herbert Samuel, *An Unknown Land* (London, 1942), 71.
[19] Ibid. 126.

Jewish organizations, particularly in the USA, called for a counter-boycott of German goods. Shortly before the Nazi boycott was due to go into effect, the British Ambassador in Berlin reported that the German Foreign Minister, Neurath, had claimed 'that after a hard struggle in the cabinet that morning he had persuaded Hitler and his wilder colleagues to agree to cancel the boycott if he could produce declarations by prominent members of the Jewish race in England and the United States which might be endorsed by the respective governments to the effect that they were satisfied that the reports of excesses against the Jews had been exaggerated and that there was no intention of boycotting German goods'.[20] Samuel and Reading discussed the alleged offer with the German Ambassador and with the Foreign Office and agreed to issue a declaration deprecating 'exaggerated reports of occurrences' in Germany and opposing a boycott of German goods.[21] The Government undertook to 'endorse' this declaration, but specified that it would not wish to imply that it was satisfied that the reports of 'excesses' had been exaggerated.[22] The anti-Jewish boycott in Germany took place with much accompanying brutality, although it lasted only one day and was not resumed as had earlier been threatened. Samuel and Reading therefore did not issue their declaration. The episode was an early sign both of Samuel's concern for German Jewry and of his readiness to appease the German Government in the hope of securing better behaviour. Samuel joined others in Parliament in condemning Nazi anti-Jewish actions. But in the same speech in the House of Commons in April 1933 he called for a 'friendly hand' to be stretched out to Germany, pleaded the necessity for revision of the Treaty of Versailles, and argued that Germany could not be kept 'permanently on a lower international status than other countries'.[23]

The promulgation of the anti-Semitic Nuremberg laws in Germany in September 1935 produced increased Jewish emigration from Germany and pressure, especially on Britain, Palestine, and the United States, to accept German-Jewish refugees. The British Government had pursued a relatively liberal policy towards Jewish refugee immigration since 1933. Its readiness to accept refugees was based on an assurance that had been given by leaders of Anglo-Jewry to the Home Secretary in April 1933 that the Jewish community would bear the full cost of maintaining refugees until they became self-supporting.[24] When the Jewish leaders gave that

[20] Sir H. Rumbold (Berlin) to Foreign Office, 1 Apr. 1933, PRO FO 371/16720 (C 2998/319/18).
[21] Foreign Office minutes, 1 Apr. 1933, ibid.
[22] Foreign Office to Rumbold, 1 Apr. 1933, ibid.
[23] HC Deb. 5 s., vol. 276 (13 Apr. 1933), cols. 2800–7.
[24] See A. J. Sherman, Island Refuge: Britain and Refugees from the Third Reich 1933–1939 (London, 1973), 30.

assurance, their most pessimistic forecasts were that 'as many as 3,000 to 4,000' refugees might arrive in Britain. By late 1935 it became clear that much larger numbers could be expected. The Jewish community accordingly sought to enlarge the scope of its fund-raising and refugee absorption activities.

In December 1935 Samuel agreed to serve as chairman of the Council for German Jewry, formed by leading British Jews, including Lords Rothschild and Bearsted and Simon Marks, to organize a mass evacuation of Jews from Germany. The intention, Samuel wrote, was 'to get about half of them out of the country over the next few years'.[25] The following month he travelled to the United States with Bearsted and Marks to raise funds and co-ordinate the effort with leaders of American Jewry. Delicate negotiations were required in order to overcome differences between Zionists and non-Zionists and between those who favoured an economic boycott of German goods and those who saw economic incentives rather than disincentives as a more promising tactic in dealing with the Nazis. In private discussions and in public statements in America Samuel dealt with these issues. On the one hand he gave no encouragement to the boycott movement which had yielded no effective results. On the other, he denied allegations that he was 'prepared to act as a commercial champion of German trade'. He declared 'that in no circumstances would I personally endorse any project which aimed at transferring German Jewish properties through the exportation of German goods'.[26] Samuel also stated that he believed that Palestine could absorb large numbers of Jews (according to one report he said as many as two or three million) 'without displacement of the Arabs, without injury to their interests'. In the short term, he suggested that Palestine might take in 50,000 German refugees and that another 50,000 might go elsewhere.[27] In private discussions with heads of American Jewish organizations, Samuel and his colleagues secured tentative agreement on a plan that envisaged an emigration of 20,000 to 25,000 Jews from Germany annually for the next four years. A fund of £3,000,000 would be required, of which one third would be raised in Europe, and the rest mainly in the USA.[28]

Upon his return to England Samuel secured agreement on co-operation

---

[25] HS to ES, 16 Dec. 1935, ISA 100/60.

[26] *American Hebrew*, 31 Jan. 1936. This was a reference to the 'Haavarah' ('transfer') agreement negotiated in Aug. 1933 between the Jewish Agency for Palestine and the German Government. The scheme provided that part of the value of the property left behind by Jewish emigrants to Palestine could be obtained by a currency arrangement that facilitated German exports to Palestine. See Sherman, *Island Refuge*, 45–6.

[27] *New Palestine*, 7 Feb. 1936.

[28] 'Tentative heads of proposals suggested for dealing with the problem of German Jews: final drafts', 5 Feb. 1936, HLRO HS B/19/5; HS to ES, 10 Feb. 1936, ISA 100/61.

between the Zionist and non-Zionist elements in the community.[29] The
Zionists were given large representation on the Council for German
Jewry and were reassured that the fund-raising campaign would complement rather than hinder their own efforts. Weizmann was pleased with
the arrangement and wrote to the American Zionist leader Rabbi Stephen
Wise: 'Samuel is loyal and his Palestinian sympathies are beyond doubt.'[30]
Samuel spoke at a series of meetings to launch the campaign in London
and the provinces in March and April 1936. He also took the unusual step
of speaking from the pulpit of the New West End Synagogue on the first
day of Passover to appeal for contributions. Among the two Directors
appointed to supervise the work of the Council were Sir Wyndham
Deedes and Norman Bentwich, both of whom had served as senior
officials under Samuel in the Government of Palestine. In spite of a certain
amount of 'unhappy friction' between Zionists and non-Zionists in
America, Samuel was encouraged by the general readiness to unite for the
common goal: 'My team is four-in-hand—British Jewry, American Jewry,
German Jewry and the [Jewish] Agency for Palestine, and I am very
satisfied with the way in which, on the whole, it is pulling together, in spite
of an occasional "shying" now and then.'[31] By September 1936 £700,000
had been raised. By 1939 a total of more than £3,000,0000 had been
spent by the Anglo-Jewish community on the reception of refugees from
Germany, Austria, and Czechoslovakia.

   The outbreak in April 1936 of an Arab general strike in Palestine,
which broadened into a three-year-long countrywide revolt, greatly
complicated the work of the Council for German Jewry. Arab nationalist
demands for a suspension of Jewish immigration were rejected by the
British Government. From the autumn of 1936 the High Commissioner
was nevertheless instructed to take 'a definitely conservative view of the
economic absorptive capacity of Palestine'. As a result, the Palestine
administration began to limit Jewish immigration. Since his departure
from Palestine in 1925 Samuel had avoided interference in its politics. But
he had been kept closely informed by his son Edwin who was still an
official in the Palestine Government. After his election defeat he had
succeeded Reading as chairman of the Palestine Electric Corporation,
which had been founded by Pinhas Rutenberg during Samuel's period of
office as High Commissioner and had grown into the largest public utility
in the country.[32] In September 1936 he cautiously intervened behind the

   [29] Weizmann to HS, 11 Mar. 1936, WA.
   [30] Weizmann to Wise, 23 Mar. 1936, WA; see also Weizmann to Felix Warburg, 18
June 1936, WA.
   [31] HS to ES, 25 Mar. 1936, ISA 100/61; BS to ES, 9 Apr. 1936, ISA 103/11 (671/5).
   [32] Samuel's investment income had fallen since 1931 as a result of the economic
depression. In 1934 he moved from his large house in Porchester Terrace (17 bedrooms,

scenes to try to effect an end to the disturbances and to promote Arab–Jewish agreement on constitutional changes. In collaboration with Earl Winterton, Conservative MP for Horsham and Worthing,[33] who had contacts with Arab leaders, Samuel drew up a plan for an Arab–Jewish settlement that was presented to Nuri Pasha al-Sa'id, Foreign Minister and former Prime Minister of Iraq, who had previously been involved in an abortive attempt to mediate between the Palestinian Arabs and the Zionists.[34]

The scheme proposed an Arab–Jewish agreement 'covering the period to the end of 1950'. During that period Jewish immigration would be limited voluntarily so that the Jewish proportion of the population should not exceed 40 per cent. Jewish land purchases would be limited in specified areas of the country. Transjordan would be opened to settlement by both Jews and Palestinian Arabs, although the National Home provisions of the mandate would not be extended to include Transjordan. A legislative council would be established consisting of one-third Jewish, one-third Arab, and one-third Government-nominated members. Other elements in the draft included substantial expenditure on Arab agriculture and education, reaffirmation of the rights of Muslims in their holy places, and the creation of a customs union for the whole of the fertile crescent including Palestine.[35]

Samuel appears to have envisaged his intervention as a reprise, in a different context, of his performance in ending the British General Strike in 1926. As on that occasion he co-ordinated his activity closely with the British Government while insisting that he was operating as a private individual.[36] This time, however, the Government was less interested in Samuel's endeavours. A Royal Commission under Earl Peel had recently been appointed to examine the Palestine question, and the Government did not want its inquiry to be pre-empted by any arrangement between Samuel and Nuri. In 1926 Samuel could plausibly present himself as an independent and neutral figure. Now his credentials were less acceptable to all parties. On the one hand, the Government feared that Samuel, as a

---

8 servants) to a smaller one in the same street. Both houses were leased. Samuel never owned his home. With the end of his parliamentary salary, his only other earned income after 1935 came from literary royalties, occasional journalism, and broadcasts. The £2,500 salary from the PEC chairmanship covered Samuel's investment losses and therefore re-established his finances on a sound footing.

[33] As an Irish peer, Winterton could sit in the House of Commons.

[34] See Yehoshua Porath, *The Palestinian Arab National Movement: From Riots to Rebellion, 1929–1939* (London, 1977), 204–11.

[35] See text of proposals in Neil Caplan, *Futile Diplomacy*, ii, *Arab–Zionist Negotiations and the End of the Mandate* (London, 1986), 224–5.

[36] See HS to Winterton, 10 and 11 Sept. 1936 (copies), ISA 100/18.

former High Commissioner, might be regarded as in some sense an
official representative. On the other, in spite of his studious impartiality as
Governor of Palestine, he was regarded 'as a Jewish leader in the eyes of
many', as the Colonial Secretary, William Ormsby-Gore, pointed out in a
letter to Samuel.[37] In discussions at the Colonial Office Samuel agreed
that his discussions with Nuri should be tentative in nature. In spite of the
unofficial character of his intervention, he undertook to conform to the
'instructions' of the Colonial Secretary. He added that he had no doubt
that he would meet with 'great opposition' from the Zionists, 'but that
would not deter him from putting his proposals forward as, taking the
Jewish community as a whole, he knew that in many directions he would
get strong support'.[38]

Samuel had already informed Weizmann confidentially of his proposals
and received an unenthusiastic response. The Zionist leader warned
Samuel that the Palestinian Jews would 'feel bitterly aggrieved' if they
were presented with 'anything which looks like a *fait accompli*'.[39] Samuel
sought to reassure Weizmann that he 'certainly had no thought of
endeavouring to come to an agreement with the Arabs, and then presenting
such an agreement to the Zionists to be accepted or rejected'. He
explained that he intended that 'both sides should be approached simultaneously and on an equal footing'. But the first requisite was to ascertain
'whether Nuri Pasha will concur in such proposals as those for which
Lord Winterton and I have agreed to take responsibility, and be willing to
act as intermediary with the Arab leaders in Palestine'.[40] After further
discussions with Weizmann and with the Colonial Office, Samuel amended
his draft, deleting the reference to 1950 and to a 40 per cent ceiling on the
Jewish population.[41] At the same time Samuel gave an undertaking to
the Government that he would act only as a private individual. He told
the Colonial Office that the Zionists 'had approached his proposals in a
very reasonable spirit'.[42]

Armed with these equivocal responses from the Government and the
Zionists, Samuel proceeded to Paris, where he and Winterton held two
meetings with Nuri al-Sa'id on 19 September 1936. Nuri immediately
made it clear that he did not believe the draft scheme 'would be acceptable
to the Arabs of Palestine'. The proposal for a legislative council in which
Jewish and Arab delegates were equal in numbers 'would be quite
unacceptable'. The projected colonization of Transjordan 'would be

[37] Ormsby-Gore to HS, 15 Sept. 1936, ISA 100/18.
[38] Minute by Sir John Maffey, 16 Sept. 1936, PRO CO 967/92.
[39] Weizmann to HS, 14 Sept. 1936 (copy), WA.
[40] HS to Weizmann, 15 Sept. 1936, WA.
[41] 'Third and final draft of proposals', [Sept. 1936], ISA 100/18.
[42] Minute by Sir John Maffey, 18 Sept. 1936, PRO CO 967/92.

considered likely to work out very much in favour of the Jews, who would prove the real beneficiaries'. A customs union was all very well, but if Palestine were included 'again the chief beneficiaries would be the Jewish industrialists there'.[43] Samuel was not greatly impressed by Nuri. He commented later, in a private letter to the High Commissioner for Palestine, Sir Arthur Wauchope: 'The impression left upon my mind by our conversation with Nuri was that he was more concerned to promote a political union between Palestine, Trans-Jordan and Iraq, than to act as an impartial friend trying merely to help to find a way out of a difficult situation.'[44] Perhaps Samuel was naïve to expect that the Iraqi Foreign Minister could possibly be 'an impartial friend'. In any event, the failure of the meeting in Paris brought Samuel's intervention to an abrupt halt.

Although the episode had no practical result, it opened a fissure between Samuel and the Zionists. After the failure of Samuel's talks with Nuri, Weizmann told Ormsby-Gore that Samuel was 'not *of it* as we are' and 'might even prove harmful'.[45] The breach widened after the publication in June 1937 of the report of the Peel Commission, which recommended termination of the mandate and partition of Palestine into sovereign Jewish and Arab States (the latter to be joined to Transjordan), with a residual British mandatory enclave. Samuel got wind of the partition proposals in the spring of 1937 and voiced his reservations at the Colonial Office. He told his son Edwin: 'I do not like the partition project, but would not refuse consideration of any proposal if it were likely to create a good situation for the future. I should prefer the other plan, of a limitation of Jewish immigration during a period of years, the opening of T[rans]-J[ordan] to Arab and Jewish settlement, and an active phil-Arab administrative policy in Palestine.'[46]

In June 1937, before the Peel Report was published, Samuel wrote to Ormsby-Gore, warning that if, as was 'widely believed', the report recommended partition, the proposal would probably 'be received with the most vehement opposition from both sides'. He urged the Government not to commit itself to partition irrevocably without providing an opportunity for further public debate. He made it clear that he opposed partition 'on merits':

If Governments on both sides of the long and intricate frontier were agreed in making the system work, it is just possible that it might prove practicable administratively. But if the Arabs, having opposed partition now, were to make difficulties for the Jewish

[43] Memorandum by Samuel, 20 Sept. 1936, PRO CO 967/92; see also Nuri al-Sa'id's version of the conversation in Caplan, *Futile Diplomacy*, ii. 224–9.
[44] HS to Wauchope, 23 Aug. 1936 (copy), HLRO HS B/13/186.
[45] Minute by Maffey, 30 Sept. 1936, PRO CO 967/92.
[46] HS to ES, 9 Apr. 1937, ISA 100/62.

State, how could law and order be enforced? When any political terrorist, or any ordinary criminal, who committed an offence in one territory, could immediately move across the frontier in a motor along a high-road or on a donkey along a mountain path, into the jurisdiction of another police authority, who might be indifferent and unhelpful, how could Palestine be prevented from becoming a worse— and a far worse—scene of crime than now?[47]

Samuel's ability to influence policy was enhanced by his elevation to a viscountcy in the 1937 coronation honours. Samuel had rejected two previous offers of a peerage: in 1916 from Asquith and in 1926 from Baldwin. He was on record as opposing hereditary peerages and therefore felt some reluctance to accept the honour. But he wrote to his son Edwin that the prospect of spending the remainder of his life writing his memoirs did not appeal to him. The debilitation of the Liberal Party was by now so advanced that there was 'hardly a single seat in Great Britain in which a Liberal nowadays can feel any confidence of being elected'. He still wished to contribute to public life and the House of Lords would afford him a useful platform. On these grounds, he persuaded himself, like many before and since, to put aside his principled objection.[48] In a letter published in the *Manchester Guardian*, he assured the President of the Darwen Liberal Association: 'I have in no degree changed the view, which I have declared throughout my political life, that the hereditary principle is utterly wrong as the method of choosing the members of any legislative assembly. I should always use my vote in Parliament in favour of its abolition.'[49] After lengthy family deliberations on the problem of nomenclature, he took the style 'Viscount Samuel of Mount Carmel and Toxteth', the latter after the district of Liverpool in which he had been born.

Samuel hastened the decision about his new style in order that he might be introduced into the House of Lords in time to participate in the debate there on the Peel Report which was published in July 1937. His speech against partition on 20 July 1937 was regarded as one of the most formidable of his political life and significantly influenced parliamentary and official opinion. Samuel agreed with the Commission's conclusion that a deadlock had been reached in Palestine and that a new policy was required. But he rejected an imposed solution: 'I can see no reason why a British Government should engage in a policy of repression and coercion. It seems to me a monstrous thing that we should be required to lock up a whole division of our small Army in Palestine, with the possibility that in any world crisis we might have to lock up even two or three divisions.' He warned against the 'delusion . . . that all that is necessary is to remove the

[47] HS to Ormsby-Gore, 15 June 1937 (copy), ISA 100/19.
[48] HS to ES, 26 Mar. 1937, ISA 100/62.
[49] HS to Alderman Frederick Hindle, *Manchester Guardian*, 14 May 1937.

Mufti and that then all will be well'. He compared that with the calls to 'Arrest Gandhi' and 'Deport Zaghlul' which had failed to dispose of nationalism in India and Egypt.

Ruthlessly dissecting the Peel Commission's central proposal, Samuel drew attention to the serious obstacles to partition: the fact that under the Commission's proposed boundaries one-third of the Jews of Palestine, including those of Jerusalem, would find themselves outside the Jewish State; the fact that the proposed Jewish State, within the boundaries set by the Commission, would contain 225,000 Arabs as against 258,000 Jews; the fact that the Jewish State, however the boundaries might be drawn, would inevitably contain a large Arab minority. He condemned the Commission's suggestion that these problems might be resolved by 'a removal of population, or what is called, strangely enough, an exchange of population'. He pointed out that the so-called 'exchange of population' between Greece and Turkey had taken place in the wake of a savagely fought war and had been far from voluntary. As for the Commission's indication that, in the last resort, it might be necessary to remove Arabs by compulsion, Samuel put his finger on a logical contradiction: 'Yet in another part of the Report there is reference to the need of guarantees for the protection of minorities in each State. Protection of minorities! Will not these be minorities, and is the form protection is to take that they should be compulsorily uprooted and put elsewhere?' He poured scorn on the specific division of Palestine outlined in the report: 'The Commission seem to have gone to the Versailles Treaty and picked out all the most difficult and awkward provisions it contained. They have put a Saar, a Polish Corridor and half a dozen Danzigs and Memels into a country the size of Wales.' But his criticism went beyond any particular scheme and to the heart of the question: 'The noble Earl, Lord Peel, said that at all events this plan would free the Jews from the watchful hostility of neighbouring Arab States. Will not these Arab States be watching day by day what is happening to their *irredenta*, the Arabs living in the Jewish State, making grievances of every small point?'

In the final and most controversial section of his speech Samuel put forward his own alternative recommendations:

It appears to me that the Jews must be ready to make a sacrifice. They must reassure the Arabs. We cannot go on without it. Therefore they must consent to a limitation of immigration other than on the principle of economic absorptive capacity. They must accept the principle proposed by the Commission that political considerations must be brought in. I see no reason why the figure of 12,000 should be the one adopted.[50] ...

[50] Although the Peel Commission had gone beyond its terms of reference by suggesting that the mandate be terminated, it had also recommended that if the mandate were

The Jews might well be asked to consent to an agreement covering a period of years—it might well be a substantial period—and during that period the Jewish population of Palestine should not exceed a given percentage of the population, perhaps 40 percent or whatever might be agreed upon, but that is the figure I have in mind.

Secondly, the Jews who, he said, had 'never been sufficiently aware or sufficiently understanding' of the underlying loyalty of the Arabs of Palestine to the Arabism that was once again in the ascendant, would have to 'recognise the reality of Arab national aspirations'. That required the creation, with British assistance, and 'with the assent of France and the full cooperation of the Zionist movement' of an 'Arab Confederation' that might eventually include all the countries of the Fertile Crescent. Samuel's third and fourth proposals followed the lines of the scheme he had presented to Nuri al-Sa'id the previous year: development of Transjordan on the basis of settlement by both Jews and Arabs; and guarantees for the Muslim holy places. His proposals for the government of the country varied from his earlier suggestion for a Legislative Council. He now urged 'that within Palestine there ought to be two communal organisations, Jewish and Arab. The Jewish one already exists and an Arab one should be created. Those organisations should have large powers, should be representative bodies.' Significant administrative functions should be delegated to these communal authorities and they should draw on public revenues. In addition, there should be a non-elected Federal Council composed of Jews, Arabs, and British officials to advise the mandatory government.[51]

Samuel's prescription was notable for the continuity of view that it disclosed not merely with his proposals of a year earlier but with his policies of the early 1920s. Then as now his first reaction to serious Arab opposition had been to attempt to limit Jewish immigration. His idea of a Palestine that would fit naturally into a large regional confederation had first been set forth in a letter to the then Foreign Secretary, Curzon, after his first visit to Palestine in the spring of 1920.[52] He renewed the suggestion in December 1922. On each occasion it was rejected by Curzon.[53] On the face of things, Samuel's proposal for a framework of communal self-government in Palestine was new. In essence, however, it indicated a recognition by Samuel of the system of functional partition that he himself had inaugurated in Palestine. He had not wanted it. He

continued a 'political high level' for Jewish immigration should be set by the mandatory government. The suggested upper limit was 12,000 per annum for at least the next five years.

[51] HL Deb. 5 s., vol. 106 (20 July 1937), cols. 629–45.
[52] Samuel to Curzon, 2 Apr. 1920 (copy), ISA 100/6.
[53] See Wasserstein, British in Palestine, 62, 80, 157–8.

struggled against it. But his repeated efforts to create a unified political community in Palestine had utterly failed. That was why he could approve the Peel Commission's diagnosis that the mandatory government had lost all legitimacy, while contesting its prescription of drastic surgery.

Samuel's speech was greatly admired in Whitehall and Westminster. But it earned Samuel bitter criticism from most Zionists whose anger was aroused particularly by the suggestion of a ceiling on Jewish immigration. No matter that the ceiling would be only temporary. No matter that his proposal would have permitted a much larger volume of immigration than the Peel Report's 'political high level' of 12,000. No matter that the opening of Transjordan to Jewish immigration, which he called 'an essential part of the plan'[54] would have permitted further immigration beyond the limit proposed for western Palestine. *Any* limitation other than on economic grounds was seen by the Zionists as unacceptable, particularly in the light of the huge pressure for emigration from Central and Eastern Europe. In any case, Jewish Agency economists repeatedly argued that no valid economic ground for limitation existed. The *Vaad Leumi* (National Council) of Palestinian Jewry sent Samuel a telegram of protest and this was echoed by most, though not all, of the Jewish press in Palestine and elsewhere.[55] Samuel, who only a year earlier had won the plaudits of the Zionists for his deft management of the Council for German Jewry, now found that the wrath of Judah descended on his head—a strange fate for the man who had first proposed the creation of a Jewish State to a British Cabinet. But the origins of this schism could be traced back to his King's Birthday speech of June 1921, perhaps even to his eerily prophetic warning in 1915 of the danger of 'a series of squalid conflicts with the Arab population'.[56]

Samuel's separation from the mainstream Zionists, hitherto tacit, now explicit, was widely noted, and reduced whatever capacity he might have retained to play some mediatory role in the Palestine conflict. Sir Cosmo Parkinson, the Permanent Under-Secretary at the Colonial Office, commented in a private letter to Wauchope: 'I thought, reading the debate, that Lord Samuel's criticism of the Commission's proposals was very well done, but, naturally, when he came to put forward a constructive alternative, he himself becomes open to a good deal of criticism. Anyway, I doubt, from what I hear, whether there is any Jew more disliked by Jews as a whole at the moment than Lord Samuel.'[57] Weizmann wrote to Sinclair a little later: 'I am extremely sorry that Lord Samuel should have

[54] HS to Dr Maximilian Landau (Berlin), 14 Sept. 1937 (copy), ISA 100/19.
[55] *Vaad Leumi* to HS, 28 July 1937, ISA 100/19.
[56] See above, pp. 208 and 257.
[57] Parkinson to Wauchope, 6 Aug. 1937, PRO CO 967/93.

taken the line he did. I have not yet met one important Jew or Jewish group who share his view, and I am sure he is quite wrong.'[58] Samuel nevertheless persisted in his opposition to partition which he voiced again in an article in *Foreign Affairs* in October 1937.[59] One notable source of support was Churchill, who wrote to him ('Dear Herbert') in October 1937: 'The more I think of this Partition Scheme, the more sure I am it is folly.'[60]

In early March 1938, on his homeward journey from a trip to India,[61] Samuel paid a short visit to Palestine, where he discussed alternatives to partition with Ragheb Nashashibi, Ahmed Sameh al-Khalidi, and other Arab and Jewish leaders. In Egypt he met Auni Abd al-Hadi, a prominent Palestinian Arab nationalist and discussed with him the 40:10 formula: a 40 per cent Jewish population limit over the next ten years. On his return to London he wrote to Ormsby-Gore reporting his impressions. He conceded that 'a large part of the Jewish population of Palestine, especially among the younger generation, would prefer Partition'. He stressed that 'in no circumstances would any section of the Jews accept a formula which limited the Jewish population of Palestine to a minority for all time'. Abd al-Hadi had told Samuel 'without hesitation that the Arabs would accept the forty percent proposal, if it was not for a period of years but as a final settlement'. Samuel replied 'that it would be quite impossible to obtain Jewish acceptance of that. . . . Both sides must make some sacrifice if there is to be any agreement at all; the Jews have to accept a limitation on immigration other than economic, which will be a bitter pill for them to swallow; the Arabs must realize that immigration cannot be stopped, and accept a review after an interval of years.' Samuel estimated that his proposal would allow for an average Jewish immigration of 30,000 per annum over a ten year period—'apart from the results of the

---

[58] Weizmann to Sinclair, 19 Oct. 1937 (copy), WA.

[59] Herbert Samuel, 'Alternatives to Partition', *Foreign Affairs*, 16 (Oct. 1937), 143–55.

[60] Churchill to HS, 3 Oct. 1937, ISA 100/19; see also HS to Churchill, 6 Oct. 1937, in Martin Gilbert (ed.), *Winston S. Churchill*, vol. v, Companion part 3, *The Coming of War 1936–1939* (London, 1982), 780–1.

[61] Samuel had long harboured a private ambition, admitted only to his family circle, to be appointed Viceroy of India. In a letter to Chamberlain in May 1937 he had mentioned his interest in India and the Far East, and his readiness to undertake 'anything that needed doing in that part of the world, or in India, for which I might have qualifications' (HS to Chamberlain, 31 May 1937, HLRO HS A/102/3a). His trip to India lasted nearly three months during which he travelled throughout the sub-continent. He conducted scores of interviews with British officials, Indian princes and politicians, including Gandhi, Nehru, Rajagopalachari, and Bose, and he tried to make a thorough study of the workings of the new Indian constitution. Samuel's interest in India was of long standing. In 1931, at the time of the Round Table Conference in London, Gandhi had stayed at his house, breakfasting on fresh goat's milk and salted grapefruit.

proposed opening of Trans-Jordan'.[62] The result would have been a doubling of the Jewish population to 800,000 within a decade. Samuel's '40:10 formula' was broached to the Zionists later that year by Ormsby-Gore's successor at the Colonial Office, Malcolm MacDonald, but Weizmann replied that it 'would meet with determined opposition from the Jews'.[63]

Partition was rejected by the Arabs and accepted only with reservations and only as a basis for negotiation by the Zionists. But the British Government, which had initially accepted the idea in principle, gradually withdrew from it. It was persuaded to do so more by the worsening international situation in late 1938 than by the arguments of Samuel, Churchill, and others—although these, no doubt, afforded the Government a convenient cover for its reversal. With the looming possibility of war in Europe, the Government determined that it could not afford any policy in Palestine that would require a heavy commitment of British troops. There was no prospect of the implementation of partition by agreement with all parties. Partition would clearly require a large commitment of British forces if it were to be imposed. It was therefore ruled out by the end of 1938. Instead the Government moved towards a new policy which went much further than Samuel had proposed towards appeasing Arab nationalism.

A further speech by Samuel in December 1938, in which he returned to his 40:10 formula, aroused renewed protest from Zionists. Their antagonism was inflamed especially by a passage in which Samuel lectured them on their attitude to the Arabs. He dismissed the widespread Zionist notions that Arab opposition to Zionism 'was really due to a small group of wealthy landowners', or was stirred up by agents of European powers, or was the work of the Mufti, or was due to the weakness or pro-Arab sympathies of British officials. 'There is possibly some fraction of truth in all these allegations, but they leave out the factor which is more important than any of them—namely, that the Arab national movement exists, that it is a reality and not an artificial creation fostered by British timidity and foreign intervention. To think that is a mere delusion.'[64] The indignation among Jews in Palestine led to the removal from walls of popular tapestries depicting him in his High Commissioner's uniform and to the defacing of a street sign in Tel Aviv bearing his name.[65] Samuel responded with an open letter to 'a correspondent in Palestine' (Edwin Samuel) in

[62] HS to Ormsby-Gore, 7 Apr. 1938, ISA 100/20; see also Caplan, *Futile Diplomacy*, ii. 89–92.

[63] Weizmann to MacDonald, 12 July 1938, WA.

[64] *HL Deb.* 5 s., vol. 111 (8 Dec. 1938), cols. 420–31.

[65] Fifty years later his name was defaced in a different manner when 'Herbie Sam's' discothèque opened on the same beach-front promenade in Tel Aviv.

which he again defended his appointment of the Mufti in 1921 while denying that he had 'engaged in a defence of the Mufti'. He asserted that he remained deeply concerned to promote the cause that he had first advocated to the Cabinet in 1915, but he added: 'I feel distressed at the failure shown in many quarters to recognize the gravity of the present situation or to appreciate its realities.'[66]

As the position of Jews in Germany and elsewhere in Europe deteriorated, Samuel felt growing despair at the impasse in Palestine and fear lest the 'whole foundation of the J[ewish] N[ational] H[ome]' collapse.[67] He attributed much of the blame to the Zionists, writing to his son Edwin in January 1939 that Zionist policy 'in recent years seems to me to be heading for certain and irreparable disaster; possibly even to a fate for the Jews in the Middle East such as has fallen upon the Armenians. I feel bound to do what little I can to avert such a catastrophe. What I have said publicly is but a small part of what I feel.'[68] In May 1939 the full extent of the Government's tergiversation was revealed when it issued a White Paper on Palestine that rejected partition and placed a limit on Jewish immigration of 75,000 over the next five years after which the inflow would cease altogether unless the Arabs of Palestine permitted it to continue—a remote contingency. The Zionists were outraged and appealed to Samuel to intercede with the Government.[69] Samuel visited MacDonald and argued strongly that the White Paper policy 'was wrong and was inconsistent with the purpose of the mandate and the Balfour Declaration'.[70] He expressed his opposition in the press and in Parliament where he complained that the policy would 'strangle the Jewish National Home'.[71] But whereas Samuel's and Churchill's criticism of partition had been useful to the Government in its retreat from the Peel Report, their condemnation of the White Paper was ignored. The White Paper remained Government policy throughout the next six years. Thousands of Jewish refugees managed to evade British naval patrols to reach Palestine as illegal immigrants during 1939 and 1940. Many more were prevented from leaving Europe as a result of the zealous implementation of the policy by the British Government. Samuel's wartime attempts to persuade the Government to mitigate the stringency of its restrictions on Jewish refugee immigration to both Palestine and Britain were similarly unavailing.[72]

[66] Statement by HS, [24] Dec. 1938, ISA 100/63.
[67] HS to ES, 17 Dec. 1938, ISA 100/63.   [68] HS to ES, 15 Jan. 1939, ISA 100/64.
[69] 2nd Lord Reading to HS, 9 May 1939, HLRO HS B/13/240.
[70] Memorandum by HS, 15 May 1939, ISA 100/21.
[71] Sunday Times, 21 May 1939; Contemporary Review, 156 (July 1939), 8–17; HL Deb. 5 s., vol. 113 (23 May 1939), cols. 97–110.
[72] See Bernard Wasserstein, Britain and the Jews of Europe 1939–1945 (London,

Samuel's falling-out with the Zionists in the late 1930s was paralleled by a rift in the same period between Samuel and the majority of his fellow-Liberals. The issue in this case was also a consequence of the rise of Nazism: appeasement. Here too Samuel's attitude grew logically out of a long-held view: that the Versailles Treaty was unjust to Germany and should be revised. Treaty revision and general disarmament were his main prescriptions for international concord until 1935. He opposed economic sanctions against Japan after it defied the League of Nations by persisting in its occupation of Manchuria. He explained to Gilbert Murray: 'On general grounds, I think that the introduction of commercial embargoes or restrictions as a means of achieving political results is much to be deprecated.'[73] Even Murray found Samuel's *non possumus* passivity disturbing: 'This is very near to telling Japan that we are her friend and we both can snap our fingers at the League.'[74]

Throughout 1934 Samuel was among the most vociferous opponents in the House of Commons of Churchill's calls for rearmament in the face of German militarism.[75] In July 1934 when the Government announced plans for increased spending on the air force, Samuel spoke forcefully against the Government and took the opportunity also to characterize Churchill as 'a Malay running amok'.[76] The alternative that Samuel proposed was collective security, although like many adherents of that concept he was at first reluctant to carry it to its ultimate conclusion of international military sanctions against an aggressor. The Covenant of the League, Samuel pointed out in March 1935, committed signatories 'not to arm but to disarm'.[77]

Shortly afterwards, when Italy threatened to invade Abyssinia, his attitude began to evolve. From May 1935 onwards the Liberals, unlike the Labour Party, supported Government proposals for rearmament.[78] In August 1935 Samuel declared: 'If collective security is not to be a sham... then surely we cannot agree with those who would wish this country to wash her hands of the whole of this question.'[79] But his only specific proposal for British action at that stage was that the Government should

1979), 176, 204; see also Bernard Wasserstein, 'Patterns of Jewish Leadership in Great Britain during the Nazi Era', in Randolph Braham (ed.), *Jewish Leadership During the Nazi Era: Patterns of Behavior in the Free World* (New York, 1985), 40.

[73] HS to Murray, 30 May 1933, Bodleian Library, Oxford, Murray papers 64/100–1.
[74] Murray to HS, 31 May 1933, Bodleian Library, Oxford, Murray papers 64/102.
[75] HC Deb. 5 s., vol. 287 (14 Mar. 1934), cols. 419–28; vol. 296 (30 July 1934), cols. 2351–63.
[76] HC Deb. 5 s., vol. 296 (13 July 1934), cols. 671–83.
[77] HC Deb. 5 s., vol. 299 (11 Mar. 1935), cols. 59–71.
[78] See HS to Francis Boyd, 28 July 1960, and HS to Philip Unwin, 5 Sept. 1960, HLRO HS A/155/XIII/387.
[79] HC Deb. 5 s., vol. 304 (1 Aug. 1935), cols. 2898–908.

offer *Italy* a guarantee against *Abyssinian* attack against Italian Somali-
land—an idea which was adopted by the Government.[80] Nevertheless,
after Italy invaded Abyssinia, Samuel, when challenged on the point,
agreed that in the last resort force, exercised through the League of
Nations, might have to be used to preserve 'the collective system'.[81]

Although he supported rearmament after 1935, Samuel pressed the
Government to satisfy what he regarded as legitimate German claims,
including her claim for colonies. The latter reflected a consistent strain in
his thinking that he had expressed as early as 1915.[82] Indeed, he argued so
frequently and so strongly in this vein that in November 1937 he felt
compelled to explain to the House of Lords that he was 'not pro-German',
merely 'pro-peace'.[83] When the Foreign Secretary, Lord Halifax, returned
from a visit to Berlin that month, he told Samuel that his speech in the
House of Lords had been well received in the German press. Halifax
added that 'he had the impression that there was no imminent danger of
any adventure on the part of Germany if only for the reason that they had
so much to do at home'. Samuel's note on his conversation with Halifax
continued:

I said that I regarded Hitler as a man with a conscience—a conscience that sometimes
led him to do things that were very bad; but he was not a man who would do what he
knew to be a crime, as Napoleon would have done. The danger was, that being a
mystic and impetuous, he might easily be swept away at some moment of crisis. He
[Halifax] said he thought that was so. He added that there was no prospect whatsoever of
German troops suddenly marching into Austria or Czecho-Slovakia, and that there
was no reason whatever for Europe to think that it was on the edge of imminent
disaster. (He repeated that, of course, this might only be throwing dust . . .).[84]

As this conversation of myopics reveals, Samuel's appeasement was not of
the type that saw concessions as a distasteful but necessary expedient
while Britain rebuilt her military strength. He was among those who
genuinely believed in the notion that Hitler was a traditional German
statesman who would, if treated reasonably, respond in like manner.

In one of the dozens of articles he wrote in this period setting out the
case for appeasement, he declared (June 1938): 'The right course now is
not to line up the nations for a conflict that is thought bound to come, but
to take steps to obviate conflict.' One step that he opposed was British
guarantees to countries such as Czechoslovakia threatened by German
aggression. Instead he urged 'a friendly arrangement in the colonial and

---

[80] Samuel Hoare to HS, 6 Aug. 1935, HLRO HS A/155/IX/27.
[81] *HC Deb.* 5 s. vol. 305 (22 Oct. 1935), cols. 47–58.   [82] See above, p. 209.
[83] *HL Deb.* 5 s., vol. 107 (17 Nov. 1937), cols. 139–51.
[84] Note by HS on conversation with Halifax, 23 Nov. 1937, HLRO HS A/105.

economic sphere' with the Fascist powers. He admitted that 'for many reasons, political and personal, it would have been far easier to write in a different strain', but 'to be Liberal only towards Liberal States', he insisted 'is not Liberalism at all'.[85] In an address to the Liberal Summer School at Oxford on 30 July 1938, he argued vociferously along these lines, attacking Churchill's anti-appeasement campaign as 'misconceived'.[86] The speech evoked what Samuel called 'some perturbation' in his audience. The *Evening Standard* reported that Samuel had 'put the cat among the Liberal pigeons'.[87] Harold Nicolson commented acidly that Samuel had left 'the groves of orthodox Liberalism and walk[ed] with brisk bright footsteps to the very portals of the Carlton Club. . . . The Liberal Summer School were aghast at hearing such realism from their former leader. Mr Ramsay Muir devoted his whole speech to a refutation of the painful things which Lord Samuel had said. And in Berlin there will be much rejoicing at the thought that it is not only the Aryan Areopagus of Cliveden that is on their side.'[88]

Samuel's attitude towards Munich was predictably one of enthusiastic approval. At an early stage in the crisis, on 14 September, he met the Czechoslovak ambassador in London, Jan Masaryk, who predicted gloomily: 'Now that the orange has been completely squeezed it seems likely that we are going to be thrown on the muck heap.'[89] Samuel was curiously unmoved by the plight of the Czechs. His reaction to Munich undoubtedly reflected the opinion of the majority of the country but his words ill became a political descendant of Gladstone and Asquith. Explaining Germany's actions since 1933 as a 'recoil' against the 'blunders' of the victors of 1918, he admitted that Hitler's behaviour towards the Czechs was 'indefensible' but maintained that support for the Czech position in the Sudetenland could not justify a European war:

Hard though it be to say it, we are driven to the conclusion that it would be better for the Czechs to suffer those wrongs than for them, and all the great nations as well, to endure that calamity.'[90]

---

[85] Herbert Samuel, 'The Choice Before us', *Nineteenth Century and After*, 123 (June 1938), 641–55.

[86] Herbert Samuel, 'The European Situation and Collective Security', *Contemporary Review*, 154 (Sept. 1938), 257–67.

[87] HS to ES, 12 Aug. 1938, ISA 100/27c; *Evening Standard*, 1 Aug. 1938; see also *Manchester Guardian* and *Daily Express*, 2 Aug. 1938.

[88] *News-Letter*, 13 Aug. 1938.

[89] Memorandum by HS, 16 Sept. 1938, HLRO HS A/110/1.

[90] Herbert Samuel, 'British Policy in the Crisis: Why I do not Condemn it', *World Review*, Nov. 1938. In a public statement after Munich Jan Masaryk said: 'If it *is* for peace that my country has been butchered up in this unprecedented manner then I am glad of it. If it isn't, may God have mercy on our souls.'

Whereas the Liberal leader, Sinclair, boldly defied public opinion and condemned Britain's 'humiliating rout', Samuel found himself in the unusual position of dissent from the official Liberal line. 'My colleagues seem to me to contemplate a war much too lightly'. he wrote.[91] In late October the Master of Balliol, A. D. Lindsay, stood in the Oxford by-election on an anti-Munich platform as an 'Independent Progressive', supported by Labour, Liberals, and Communists, as well as Churchill, Eden, Harold Macmillan, and Edward Heath. Samuel refused a request for support, and allowed his name to be used in the campaign propaganda issued by Lindsay's Conservative pro-Munich opponent, Quintin Hogg.[92] Samuel was one of the thousands who wrote to Chamberlain after the Munich agreement to commend his action: 'Any fool may go to war, but it often needs the highest qualities of statesmanship to keep the peace.'[93]

Chamberlain was delighted with Samuel's support and went so far as to invite him to Downing Street on 25 October to offer him a Cabinet position as Lord Privy Seal. Samuel considered the proposal but turned it down, giving as his reasons dissatisfaction with the Government's policy on Spain and on tariffs, as well as his desire not to separate himself from opinion in the Liberal Party.[94] Perhaps Samuel was disappointed with the position he was offered. He had never enjoyed being a minister without portfolio. The position that he wanted more than any other, that of Viceroy of India, remained beyond reach, in spite of his hint to Chamberlain the previous year.

Samuel was 67 when he refused this last offer of Cabinet office. He remained in vigorous health—that summer he had enjoyed a 65-mile walking holiday in the Scottish Highlands. Throughout the winter of 1938–9 he remained confident that war would not come, but for him, as for many others, the German occupation of Prague at last brought a recognition that appeasement would not bring permanent peace. In a speech at Saltburn, his first there for twenty years, he supported the Government's pledge to Poland. Former constituents gave him a great welcome, but the local newspaper noted sadly that 'the people present were mainly those old enough to remember Liberalism in its heyday in the years before the War'.[95] Yet in May 1939 he spoke in the House of Lords against the reintroduction of conscription, though he reluctantly voted for the measure.[96]

[91] HS to ES, 21 Oct. 1938, ISA 100/63.
[92] HS to W. S. Belcher, 24 Oct. 1938, HLRO HS A/110/25b.
[93] Manchester Guardian, 22 Sept. 1938; HS to Chamberlain, 30 Sept. 1938 (copy), HLRO HS A/110/12.
[94] Memorandum by HS, 26 Oct. 1938, HLRO HS A/111/1.
[95] North-Eastern Daily Gazette, 1 Apr. 1939.
[96] HL Deb. 5 s., vol. 113 (22 May 1939), cols. 41–8.

When war broke out, Chamberlain invited the Liberals to join the Government, but as they were not offered a seat in the War Cabinet they refused to consider the proposal.[97] When Chamberlain had completed his reshuffle of the Government, Samuel went to see him and offered his services 'in any capacity that might be thought suitable'.[98] But no Government work was forthcoming. Throughout the war Samuel continued, rather wistfully, to hope for some position that might enable him to contribute to the national effort. When Churchill's Coalition Government was formed in May 1940, Sinclair became Secretary of State for Air outside the War Cabinet. Samuel was again disappointed. He wrote to his son Edwin: 'Winston was very sorry that I should have been crowded out of the major posts and he felt that he could not offer me a secondary one, but that he hoped to offer me some important position outside the Govt. before long.'[99] But no job of any kind materialized. When Churchill conducted a minor reshuffle in February 1942, Samuel's name was proposed for the Ministry of Works. Churchill welcomed the proposal but asked how old Samuel was. A copy of *Who's Who* was sent for, and it was ascertained that Samuel was 71, whereupon Churchill said that he thought Samuel was too old. After the war Lord Selborne told him the story. Samuel commented that 'it was the Dept. of all others I should have liked to have had'—an astonishing statement for a senior political figure, but it was characteristic of Samuel that he should have hankered after such an unglamorous but demanding position.[100]

'In default of any definite war job', he settled in Oxford where he and his wife lived for most of the war in a succession of lodging houses.[101] He continued his prolific output of articles on politics and philosophy, and began work on his memoirs. He travelled up to London regularly to attend the House of Lords. And he enjoyed walks with his eldest grandson, David Samuel, an undergraduate at Balliol, as well as with Lionel Curtis, Arnold Toynbee, and Salvador de Madariaga.

During the war Samuel encountered new celebrity as a broadcaster. He had given occasional talks on the BBC in the 1930s, but it was his wartime membership of the Brains' Trust that established him as one of the foremost wireless performers of his generation. His first appearance on the Brains' Trust was on 23 August 1942, when he joined C. E. M. Joad and Julian Huxley in what was then a recorded half-hour programme on the BBC's overseas service. Samuel called the question-and-answer format

---

[97] HS to Lothian, 13 Sept. 1939, SRO GD 40/17/404.
[98] HS to ES, 3 Sept. 1939, ISA 100/64.
[99] HS to ES, 13 May 1940, ISA 100/65.
[100] Note by HS, 7 May 1946, HLRO HS A/155/XII/22.
[101] HS to Lothian, 16 Oct. 1940 (copy), HLRO HS A/114/5.

'rather like a *viva voce* examination in a nightmare, where one doesn't even know in what subjects one is going to be examined'. After he had heard the recording, he commented that what he had said seemed all right but he did not like the way he had said it—'too precise and high-brow! I did not know I had such an Oxford manner.'[102] Typical questions were 'Why do people smoke?', 'Is gambling essentially dishonest?', 'What is the most important scientific contribution of this century?', and 'Why can a new cricket ball with a highly polished surface be made to swing or swerve in its flight, yet when the surface becomes rough the swerve is impossible to attain?' Samuel's broad knowledge, derived from voracious reading, and his common-sense, if Oxonian, manner won him approval from listeners and he became a frequent participant in the programme after 1944, when the audience attained a peak of 8.94 million—29.8 per cent of the adult population. The BBC did not, however, relate its fees to the size of its audiences: Samuel was paid 15 guineas plus a rail voucher for each appearance. The immense popularity of the Brains' Trust derived from the burning wartime hunger for educational self-improvement. From 1946 the programme was broadcast live, but the audience gradually declined. Samuel continued to appear on the radio version until 1949. When the programme moved to television he appeared there too, but with less success.

Samuel's many other radio appearances brought him in old age a broad public affection that had eluded him during his political career. In 1947 the BBC Third Programme broadcast an hour-long version of his Romanes Lecture at Oxford entitled 'Creative Man'. Less philosophy than a sort of secular sermon, this talk attested to Samuel's capacity, striking in one who had so often in earlier life been criticized as uninspired and pedestrian, to reach towards a spiritual dimension. The *Observer* considered the lecture 'luminous' and the *BBC Yearbook*, listing him among the six best broadcasters of 1947, called it 'the finest talk of the year'.[103] He also participated in several unscripted discussions with Bertrand Russell on philosophical subjects. Harold Nicolson, Alan Bullock, and Lord Hailsham acted successively as chairman. One of these conversations achieved the curious distinction for a programme of this type of being broadcast on the Light Programme. Russell and Samuel chatted happily about philosophy, their bitter differences during the First World War long forgiven. The double act evoked mixed responses within the BBC. The Corporation's Canadian representative wrote that he thought the broadcasts were not 'anything to be proud of' and suggested: 'Don't you think it is about time

---

[102] HS to ES, 23 Aug. 1942, ISA 100/66.
[103] *Observer*, 7 Sept. 1947; *BBC Yearbook 1948* (London, 1948), 7.

that the comedy team of Samuel and Russell was given a rest?'[104] On the other hand, the radio reviewer of the *Manchester Evening News* wrote, after listening to their dialogue on the Light Programme: 'one felt proud that England made them.'[105] In 1949 the BBC Listener Research Department reported: 'Only three talks in the past three years have had Appreciation Indices in the 80s and they were all by Lord Samuel.'[106]

Samuel's move to Oxford during the war brought him into close contact with his old university and college. In 1942 he helped negotiate the arrangement whereby Wytham Abbey near Oxford as well as its estate were acquired by the university. In 1946 his old college, in exercise of the 'singular privilege' of electing its own ceremonial head, invited him to become Visitor, an honour he cherished deeply and retained until 1957.[107]

In late 1944 Samuel succeeded the infirm Crewe as Liberal leader in the House of Lords. He took the responsibilities of the position seriously in spite of the sadly diminished Liberal following in the Lords as in the Commons. The Lords met at this time only twice a week, in Church House, Westminster (their own chamber was occupied by the Commons who had been evicted from their normal premises by German bombs). Samuel assumed the role of elder statesman more gracefully than Lloyd George. He maintained happy relations with Sinclair and, after 1945, with his successor, Clement Davies. In the 1945 election he delivered a much-admired Liberal party broadcast that was heard by 46.9 per cent of the adult population. He spoke at seventeen meetings during this, the first election campaign since 1892 that he had witnessed in Britain without being a candidate himself.

Samuel's *Memoirs*, which appeared that summer, were well received by critics and public. The first printing of 8,500 sold out in ten days. Robert Lynd in the *News Chronicle* wrote that they 'breathe[d] serenity and tolerance'. J. M. Thompson in the *Oxford Magazine* called the book 'the swan-song of Liberalism', but added, 'And what a fine song it is!' A rare sour note was struck by a younger Balliol man, Graham Greene, who called it 'a kind of official White Paper on the life of a Liberal leader' and complained, in terms that distressed Samuel, of his account of the Marconi affair.[108]

[104] Tom Sloan to H. Rooney Pelletier, 22 Apr. 1952, BBC Written Archives Centre HS 2B. [105] *Manchester Evening News*, 15 May 1952.
[106] *BBC Listener Research Department Newsletter*, no. 111 (Apr. 1949).
[107] The Samuel connection with Balliol extended over four generations: Herbert Samuel (matriculated 1889), his sons Edwin (1919) and Godfrey (1922), his nephew Wilfred (1909), his grandsons David (1939) and Dan (1943), his great-nephew Dennis (1956), and his great-granddaughter Maia (1982) all studied at Balliol.
[108] *News Chronicle*, 7 Aug. 1945; *Oxford Magazine*, Nov. 1945; *Evening Standard*, 27 July 1945.

After the war Samuel moved back to Porchester Terrace and resumed political and literary activities at a pace that hardly faltered until the late 1950s. Although he no longer exercised political influence beyond his own little party, he commanded, thanks to his reputation as a broadcaster, a national audience for his speeches, articles, and books. Within the Liberal Party he resisted attempts by Lady Violet Bonham-Carter and others to move the Liberals into some form of alliance with the Conservatives.[109] He campaigned vigorously in the 1950 and 1951 elections. On 15 October 1951 he became the first British politician to deliver a party political broadcast on television. The Liberal decline to only 9 seats in 1950 and 6 in 1951 depressed the party's morale and seemed to spell its extinction. But Samuel, with great tact, managed to stem the flow of defecting Liberal peers and to stiffen Clement Davies's resolve to resist Churchill's attempted seduction of the Liberals into the Tory camp. In May 1950 Davies wrote to Gilbert Murray that 'the one person standing out above all others' who realized the continuing need for Liberal independence was Samuel 'to whom I turn for guidance on all matters. . . . I do not believe I could carry on if I had not him, not merely by my side, but providing a sort of sanctuary to which I can turn for some little comfort.'[110]

In March 1948 he intervened once again in the Palestine problem as it moved towards its dénouement. Samuel had followed developments in Palestine closely since 1939 and had visited the country in 1940 and 1942. In the spring of 1948 he still opposed partition and submitted a memorandum to the Prime Minister, the United Nations Secretary-General, Trygve Lie, and to Weizmann, proposing an alternative policy reminiscent of his proposals of 1937: communal autonomy, limited Jewish immigration (150,000 in the first two years, 60,000 thereafter), and the transfer of mandatory authority to the UN Trusteeship Council.[111] But events in Palestine had now spun far beyond his or any outsiders' control. After the State of Israel was established, he recognized that, as he put it in the House of Lords in September 1948: 'Events have marched beyond the kind of bi-national State that I had been hoping for ever since I was myself High Commissioner in that country.' In the same speech he urged the Government to grant Israel recognition, which Britain, unlike the USA and the

---

[109] See corr. between HS and Lady Violet Bonham-Carter, Feb.–Mar. 1948, Jan. and May 1950, HLRO HS A/155/XIII, A/129, and A/130.
[110] Davies to Murray, 11 May 1950, National Library of Wales, Aberystwyth, Clement Davies papers J/3/26ii.
[111] Memorandum by HS, Apr. 1948, WA; HS to Clement Attlee, 15 Mar. 1948 (copy), ISA 100/26; HS to Trygve Lie, 15 Mar. 1948 (copy), ibid.; HS to Weizmann, 15 Mar. 1948 (copy), ibid.

USSR, had withheld.[112] When the Israeli Legation in London opened in November 1948, Samuel signalled his support by being the first to sign the Visitor's Book. He visited Israel in April 1949 and was present with the Israeli commander, Yigal Allon, at a Bedouin feast in the northern Negev to celebrate the withdrawal of Egyptian troops from the area.[113] The Israeli Foreign Ministry made special arrangements for him to cross the lines to visit his old friend Abdullah at his palace at Shuneh.[114] Samuel was impressed by what he saw in Israel. His old differences with the Zionists now faded into the background.

Although he hardly mentioned it in print or in public, Samuel was greatly shaken by the revelation at the end of the war of the Nazi mass murder of the Jews in Europe. This was an event which could find no place within the framework of his optimistic, 'meliorist' philosophy. In later years he told his eldest grandson David that as soon as he learned about the destruction of European Jewry he realized that there was no alternative to an independent Jewish State and he added that he believed that 'a superior culture had every right to displace an inferior [Arab] one'.[115] Both his eldest son and his eldest grandson settled permanently in Israel, and Samuel himself warmly supported Israeli causes, notably the Hebrew University with which he had been associated since its inception. A chair in political science, currently occupied by Professor Shlomo Avineri, was named there in his honour.

He continued to speak on a wide variety of subjects in the House of Lords but attracted public attention and widespread support on a rather surprising issue—homosexuality, which he denounced in fiery language in 1953: 'We find to our dismay that the vices of Sodom and Gomorrah, of the cities of the Plain, appear to be rife among us.'[116] In the ensuing public uproar, the Bishop of Liverpool supported Samuel's 'grim but timely warning', and the *Daily Mirror* acclaimed Samuel's speech: 'It puts to shame all the Mrs Grundys and ostriches who tried to bury their heads in the sand.'[117] Shortly afterwards E. M. Forster sent Samuel an article he had written advocating at least 'less social stigma' for homosexuals. Samuel replied that he was 'far from quarrelling' with that, but added, with an innocence that precludes any possibility that he intended to hurt Forster: 'If homosexuality between adults is legalised, is it not likely that it may become very widespread, possibly catered for by brothels of a special

[112] *HL Deb.* 5 s., vol. 158 (24 Sept. 1948), cols. 249–57.
[113] *New York Times*, 4 May 1949.
[114] Walter Eytan (Israeli Foreign Ministry, 15 Apr. 1949) to HS, ISA 100/27; *Palestine Post*, 21 Apr. 1949.
[115] Letter to author from 3rd Viscount Samuel, 10 Feb. 1990.
[116] *HL Deb.* 5 s., vol. 184 (4 Nov. 1953), cols. 50–7.
[117] *Liverpool Evening Express*, 5 Nov. 1953; *Daily Mirror*, 6 Nov. 1953.

type? Incomprehensible and utterly disgusting as it appears to all normal people, it seems to have the capacity to form a habit as potent as alcohol or drugs.'[118]

By the mid-1950s Samuel had attained the status of a Liberal icon and a national monument. The Jewish community regarded him as its head, and when he attended the High Holy Day services at the New West End Synagogue the congregation would stand in his honour. When he celebrated his eighty-fifth birthday in November 1955, the synagogue held a special service (at which the bar mitzvah of the 'child prodigy musician' Daniel Barenboim was also celebrated). In December 1956 he was able to make posthumous peace with a former tormentor when he spoke at the presentation of a bust of Keir Hardie to the House of Commons. In one of his last public appearances, at a Liberal 'revival rally' in the Royal Albert Hall in November 1958, the audience of 7,000 gave him the 'most tremendous cheer of the night'.[119] Samuel thus lived long enough to witness the beginning of the Liberals' resurgence, or false dawn, under the leadership of Jo Grimond. He was in the Peers' Gallery of the House of Commons in March 1962 to witness Eric Lubbock, the victor of the Orpington by-election, take his seat in the House of Commons.

Samuel's final years were clouded by the death of his wife in 1959 after a long illness, as well as by his own gathering frailty and deafness. The latter led to occasional crotchetiness, but he retained a mental agility that belied his years. He enjoyed the company of small children, among them his many descendants. He delighted in observing the birds that visited the coconut he had hanging outside the window near his desk. His last book, A Threefold Cord, a philosophical dialogue with Professor Herbert Dingle, was published in 1961 to respectful reviews. In November 1958, on the fiftieth anniversary of his admission to the Privy Council, the Queen surprised him by inviting him to remain behind after the Council meeting and awarding him the Order of Merit.[120] Samuel delivered his last important political utterance in the House of Lords in June 1961 when he was aged 90. It was an eloquent, detailed, and cogently argued speech attacking the maniacal proposal to build a motorway across Christ Church Meadow in Oxford.[121] Bertrand Russell wrote to congratulate him on defending the beauty of Oxford from 'being destroyed by the worship of Mammon'.[122] Samuel's was one of the most effective of

[118] HS to Forster, 29 Nov. 1953, quoted in P. N. Furbank, E. M. Forster: A Life, ii (New York, 1981), 334–5.
[119] Daily Express and Manchester Guardian, 11 Nov. 1958.
[120] HS to ES, 26 Nov. 1958, ISA 100/73.
[121] HL Deb. 5 s., vol. 232 (26 June 1961), cols. 865–74.
[122] Russell to HS, 27 June 1961 (copy), McMaster University, Hamilton, Ontario, Bertrand Russell Archives.

the many protests against this monstrous scheme. It was eventually abandoned.

In November 1962 Samuel fell ill. Eye trouble by this time made reading difficult. The last book he read was a large-print version of *Martin Chuzzlewit*. In his last letter to his son Edwin, written with great difficulty, he said that the effort to read and answer all the letters and cards he received for his ninety-second birthday had reduced him to despair. 'Also the shock of the America–Cuba–Russia crisis I found terrible—having been through three wars in my lifetime, and in positions of some political responsibility, the S. African war, the first German war and then the Second, to say nothing of the Irish Easter Rebellion; and now there seemed to be yet another war, fought with nuclear bombs—far more barbarous and disastrous than all the others put together.'[123] Samuel survived just long enough to learn that the missile crisis had been resolved and that his 'meliorist' faith in human rationality had not been altogether misplaced. He died on 5 February 1963.

[123] HS to ES, 18 Nov. 1962, ISA 100/73A.

Envoi

THE MEMORIAL service for Herbert Samuel at the New West End Synagogue, attended by representatives of the Queen and the Government, was the occasion of an unfortunate but significant contretemps. On the ground that the synagogue permitted mixed seating and a mixed choir, the Chief Rabbi, Israel Brodie, refused to attend, and he was joined in his boycott by the entire corps of *dayanim* (judges) of the London *Beth Din* (religious court).[1] The incident gave early warning of the communal rupture the following year in which most of the old Anglo-Jewish families defied the Chief Rabbi and seceded from the synagogue of which Samuel's father had been one of the founders. Ostensibly the issue was theological, a protest against the fundamentalist orthodoxy of the Chief Rabbi. But behind the schism was a social revolution. The children of the post-1881 immigrants from Eastern Europe had at last ended the dominance in Anglo-Jewry of the 'Cousinhood' of which Samuel had been the most venerable and impressive ornament.

The change was partly a matter of new money overtaking old. Although many members of the long-established Jewish families, including branches of the Montagu/Samuel clan, retained great wealth, others had allowed time to eat away accumulated capital. Herbert Samuel left £28,919, a respectable sum but hardly a fortune. It represented only a tiny fraction of his father's worth. Since 1931 Samuel had drawn down his capital, and several of his investments had become worthless as a result of the depression and the Second World War. During the war he had felt the pinch of high taxation and had lived in reduced circumstances. A great reviser of wills, Samuel objected on principle to taking steps to avoid death duties. In the event, his estate had to pay only £4,281. He belonged to a generation that believed it was vulgar to talk about money and he disapproved of people who did so. He was not mean, but he insisted on repayment of debts.

The old-fashioned rectitude that he observed for himself, and that he enjoined on his family in matters of personal finance, found its reflection in his moralistic approach to some of the major economic issues with which he was confronted—for example, in his distinction between the

[1] *Jewish Chronicle*, 22 Feb. 1963.

deserving and undeserving poor, in his enthusiasm for labour colonies for the unemployed, and perhaps most especially in his failure to come to terms with Keynesian economics. In spite of his relatively sophisticated grasp of economic theory, of which he had a stronger understanding than most politicians of his time, he ultimately fell back on the conventional wisdom that national finances were merely private finances writ large. His initial embrace of the 'Yellow Book' proposals almost inevitably gave way under pressure to orthodox verities. In this sense, in spite of his genuinely progressive instincts on social issues, he remained an economic Gladstonian—more so, indeed, than many of the business-oriented elements in the Liberal Party represented by men such as Runciman who were prepared to jettison free trade, to which Samuel clung as the last life-saving and grace-saving reed that differentiated Liberalism.

His strict financial rectitude, like his horror of gambling, was of a piece with his strait-laced, at times prudish, attitudes on matters of personal and social hygiene. His attitude to temperance, unlike that of the Non-conformist streak in Liberalism, did not derive from religion: Judaism has no such taboo. Samuel himself liked a glass of Graves after dinner. But he despised immoderate alcoholic consumption in the individual as a surrender to indulgence (he was shocked that Ernest Hemingway listed 'drinking' as one of his recreations) and on the collective level as a socially destructive force that stimulated crime and accentuated poverty. To some extent his non-libertarian views on sexual matters, his outrage at the libertinism of H. G. Wells, his disapproval of his brothers' mistresses, and his 'Sodom and Gomorrah' tirade against homosexuality arose from a fundamental innocence: witness his unconsciously offensive exchange with E. M. Forster. These views, unlike those of another prudish Home Secretary of the period, Joynson-Hicks, did not have their roots in religion but rather in a strong sense that individual and social morality were indivisible. This was the root of the mutual contempt between him and Lloyd George. He could not abide Lloyd George's breezy amorality in the financial and sexual spheres. Lloyd George reciprocated by despising his hyper-punctiliousness: 'Doubtless Samuel was honest in the sense that he would account for every stamp used in his office, but . . .'[2] Here too private attitudes helped shape public policy—for example in the cases of theatrical and film censorship.

In aesthetic outlook, Samuel's prudery combined with a certain philistinism to heighten the censorious tendency. For a man who was in many respects highly cultivated, Samuel's tastes were narrow: in art, in spite of a friendship late in life with Barbara Hepworth, he struggled without

---

[2] Sylvester diary, 13 Jan. 1937, in Cross (ed.), *Life With Lloyd George*, 168–9.

success to come to terms with the notion of non-representational sculpture or painting; in literature he provoked Stephen Spender to walk out of a Foyle's literary luncheon by an attack on modern poetry (T. S. Eliot's secretary stated: 'Mr Eliot can make no comment. He is a friend of Lord Samuel's'[3]). A voracious reader, he remained, in literary preferences, a late Victorian—his favourite novelist was George Meredith. His own writing was characterized by coherence of organization and a down-to-earth clarity of style, but even his best work, such as *An Unknown Land*, was sometimes marred by an irritating predilection for platitudes. Samuel recognized the tendency but did not regard it as a fault: he would not sacrifice a sound argument for a brilliant turn of phrase.

Samuel was born with, or perhaps acquired at Balliol, a supreme intellectual self-confidence that, when combined with unflagging industry and great patience, enabled him to outdistance nimbler minds in long-distance events. Occasionally this led him astray, as in his unprofitable ventures into theoretical physics, but it enabled him to endure the sneers of those, such as his cousin Edwin Montagu, who might be more quick-witted but who could not emulate his unfailing high seriousness. In politics his ability to grapple with the mysteries of Irish finance and the intricacies of licensing legislation won him a reputation for dull industry. In later life his philosophical excursions and his pontifications on the Brains' Trust led many to regard him as a sage. The truth was probably somewhere in between. In private moments of self-esteem Samuel liked to think of himself as a modern version of Francis Bacon. But Samuel was not really a polymath: his analytical intelligence was constrained by a middlebrow aesthetic and by an imagination that, while it could attain moments of spiritual insight, seldom rose beyond the pedestrian. As a result, none of his voluminous outpouring of literary works, which included a play that he tried to persuade Korda to turn into a film, outlived him.

Samuel's irenic temperament, his slowness to anger, his apparent lack of enthusiasm led contemporaries to regard him as a cold fish. 'His nature is a temperate zone in which there are no extremes of ice or fire. He is not moved, nor does he attempt to move others, by the impetus of passion.'[4] These were essential qualities in a conciliator, as in the General Strike, but they served him ill as a political leader. He lacked Lloyd George's ability to warm the hearts of vast crowds. He disdained the devices of the demagogue. As a speaker Samuel was at his best in Parliament and on the wireless rather than on public platforms. His colleague Isaac Foot said: 'His speech is an address to the jury, and if he is speaking to a crowd of ten

---

[3] *News Chronicle*, 16 Apr. 1953.   [4] *Sunday Times*, 19 Nov. 1950.

thousand it is still only a larger jury.'[5] In his later years he seemed to become less stiff and formal in his oratory. While his speeches still contained rolling periods, he allowed himself more room for whimsy and for flights of unstrained eloquence. Among his finest speeches were some of his last, delivered in the House of Lords in extreme old age like those of Lords Shinwell and Stockton in the next generation. Samuel's speeches in the Upper House were still recalled by a lobby correspondent two decades later as among the finest examples of the lost art of parliamentary rhetoric.[6]

Samuel was never a truly popular politician on the national level. He managed, by dint of lengthy cultivation, to win a genuine personal following among the farm labourers of South Oxfordshire and the ironstone miners of Cleveland. But these were declining groups of deferential workers untypical of the industrial working class among whom he never captured much broader support. Samuel genuinely believed in the 'progressive alliance', and in the early part of his career he was an earnest advocate of working-class parliamentary candidacies. Yet the parliamentary Liberal Party that he eventually came to lead was a largely middle-class body. After the early radicalism of his energetic period at the Home Office between 1905 and 1909, his performance as a senior minister disappointed left-wing friends and mentors such as Graham Wallas and Beatrice Webb. Nevertheless, the former member of the Rainbow Circle remained a man of the left, notwithstanding pronouncements in the 1950s that suggested that he viewed the Conservatives as a lesser evil than Labour. He told his children that he had much rather they turned towards Labour than towards the Conservatives: his daughter and his eldest son both joined the Labour Party.

Samuel may be credited with preserving the existence of the Liberal Party but he took charge of its destinies too late to have any hope of arresting its decline. By 1931 it was already condemned to fringe status not merely by the electoral system but by its very disinterestedness—its failure to represent any particular social group. In the 1930s the Liberals comforted themselves that they were still the party of ideas even if not of the masses. But the 1929 election had shown that ideas, even when accompanied by money, were not enough. And the Liberals' ideas in any case proved vulnerable to the pressures of an illiberal world—their economic ideas in 1931, their ideas of a new international order after 1935. Samuel's uncomfortable sojourn in the National Government and his collapse into appeasement suggest that not only as a party but also as a political ideology Liberalism could no longer cope.

[5] *Listener*, 14 Dec. 1950.   [6] *The Times*, 11 Feb. 1980.

Samuel's marriage was conventionally happy but uneventful. The woman who perhaps understood him best, and who observed him closely throughout his life, was not his wife but Beatrice Webb. In 1939 she talked about him with Frank Singleton, a would-be biographer; after the conversation she wrote, with her customary mixture of astringency and insight:

His somewhat cynical account of HS's autobiographical material—elaborate notes of interviews and correspondence with Graham Wallas and other intellectuals—was entertaining—HS always striving after *correctitude* in expression and behaviour: a carefully planned existence, a sustained and deliberate combination of integrity of thought and action, on the one hand, and personal security and advancement on the other—which corresponds with our experience of him. I have always liked and respected HS—but I have never been interested in him—*good but mediocre*, devoid of distinction, except perhaps in industry, kindliness and sanity.[7]

From Beatrice Webb this was a more favourable comment than it might appear. But in at least one respect it was unfair. Samuel's sense of public service precluded the crude self-advancement that she, in company with many others, attributed to him. Isaac Foot hit the mark more precisely: 'He was free from vanity or egotism, those worst pests of public life. He never nursed resentment and was never mindful of personal injuries.'[8] No man could have endured what Samuel had to bear at the hands of Lloyd George without those qualities.

Yet it was his very coolness and apparent lack of passion that alienated many. Lady Violet Bonham-Carter recalled an incident when her father was Prime Minister:

'Did you have fun with Herbert Samuel?' my father asked me teasingly, after a dinner during which he had observed our mutual reactions. 'Well—not exactly *fun*.' 'What is it that you miss in him?' 'Perhaps—a touch of recklessness!' My father laughed, assuring me that if *that* was what I wanted I must look elsewhere.[9]

Asquith, his wife, and his daughter all learned eventually and in different ways to appreciate better Samuel's underlying humanity, his loyalty to Asquithian Liberalism, and the depth of commitment to causes that he concealed beneath a frosty exterior.

Nothing surprised them more than his espousal of such a hopelessly romantic ideal as Zionism. It seemed laughably out of character. Here Samuel was thoroughly misjudged. Zionism, for Samuel, was no aberration. It struck a deep chord within him. Whereas Disraeli's flirtations with orientalism were perhaps an exotic cloak for political ambition, Samuel's Zionism was deeply felt. Late in life he recalled that the most moving

---

[7] Entry dated 3 Feb. 1939, BLPES Beatrice Webb diary, 6617–18.
[8] *Listener*, 14 Dec. 1950. [9] *Observer*, 10 Feb. 1963.

ceremony he had ever attended was his visit to a synagogue in Jerusalem on his first sabbath as High Commissioner in 1920: 'When there I read the opening words of Isaiah appointed for that day, "Comfort ye, comfort ye my people, saith your God. Speak ye comfortably to Jerusalem, and cry unto her, that her warfare is accomplished, that her iniquity is pardoned"— the emotion that I could not but feel seemed to spread throughout the vast congregation. Many wept. One could almost hear the sigh of generations.'[10] Zionism represented for Samuel a perfect synthesis of his Englishness and his Jewishness, his Liberalism and his imperialism, his political practicality and his religious sensibility—and the sentimental side of his nature that lay deeply buried behind his impassive public face.

The eclipse of the Liberal Party and the collapse of liberal values in the age of Auschwitz and Hiroshima, the vulgar materialism of the acquisitive society, the coarsening of standards of public and private conduct—all this saddened him. But Samuel remained to the end a 'meliorist'—a Liberal in the sense that Michael Brock has identified with the outlook of the first generation of Liberals whose attitudes, he suggests, 'may perhaps be held to enshrine the enduring essence of Liberalism'. Like the Liberals of the 1820s, Herbert Samuel was 'hopeful rather than fearful . . . valued freedom supremely and hated coercion . . . and believed moderation and reason to be the prime requirements in the ordering of human affairs'.[11]

---

[10] Memoirs, 176.
[11] Michael Brock, 'The Liberal Tradition', in Vernon Bogdanor (ed.), Liberal Party Politics (Oxford, 1983), 16.

Sources

1. Samuel Papers

Edwin Herbert Samuel [2nd Viscount Samuel] (Israel State Archives, Jerusalem; a few other papers in the possession of 3rd Viscount Samuel)

Edwin Louis Samuel (Letter book of family bank in possession of Mr Donald Samuel; *ketubah* (Hebrew marriage contract) of Edwin and Clara Samuel in possession of Mrs Gillian Sinclair-Hogg)

Godfrey Samuel (family letters in the possession of Dr W. Salaman)

Herbert Samuel (political, family and literary papers: House of Lords Record Office, London)

Herbert Samuel (personal and Palestine papers: Israel State Archives, Jerusalem)

Herbert Samuel (reading lists; Lady Samuel's dinner books; a few other papers in the possession of the Hon. Dan Samuel)

Sir Stuart Samuel (a few letters and an annotated copy of the family genealogy in the possession of Mrs Gillian Sinclair-Hogg; newspaper cutting book in House of Lords Record Office, London)

2. Other collections of private papers

Names given are in the form by which the person was most commonly known. Locations given relate only to Samuel-connected materials: in certain cases the main collection of papers may be lodged elsewhere.

Acland, Sir Francis (certain papers in possession of Sir Richard Acland)

Amulree, 1st Baron (Bodleian Library, Oxford)

Asquith, H. H. (Bodleian Library, Oxford)

Baldwin, Stanley (Cambridge University Library)

Bentwich, Norman (Central Zionist Archives, Jerusalem)

Beveridge, Sir William (British Library of Political and Economic Science, London)

Browning, Oscar (Eastbourne Central Library)

Brunner, Sir John (Liverpool University Library)

Buchan, John (Queen's University Archives, Kingston, Ontario)

Burns, John (British Library, London)

Buxton, Noel (McGill University Library, Montreal)

Carrington, 1st Earl (1st Marquis of Lincolnshire) (Papers in possession of Brigadier A. W. A. Llewellen Palmer)

Catlin, Sir George (McMaster University, Hamilton, Ontario)

Chamberlain, Austen (Birmingham University Library)

Cherry, Richard Robert (Public Record Office of Northern Ireland)

Childers, Erskine (Trinity College, Dublin)

Churchill, Winston (Transcript of interview of Randolph Churchill with Herbert Samuel, Churchill College Archives, Cambridge)

Clifford, John (one letter to Herbert Samuel in Houghton Library, Harvard University, Cambridge, Massachusetts)

Cotton, H. E. A. (India Office Library and Records, London)

Courtney, Leonard (British Library of Political and Economic Science, London)

Crewe, 1st Marquis of (Cambridge University Library)

Crook, W. M. (Bodleian Library, Oxford)

Crozier, W. P. (John Rylands University Library, Manchester)

Curtis, Lionel (Bodleian Library, Oxford)

Curzon, 1st Marquis (India Office Library and Records, London; other papers in Public Record Office, Kew)

Davies, Clement (National Library of Wales, Aberystwyth)

Davies, David (National Library of Wales, Aberystwyth)

Dawson, Geoffrey (Letter from Herbert Samuel to) (Bodleian Library, Oxford)

Dillon, John (Trinity College, Dublin)

Eagar, W. McG. (Reform Club, London)

Einstein, Albert (Jewish National and University Library, Jerusalem)

Elibank, Master of (A. W. C. O. Murray) (National Library of Scotland, Edinburgh)

Elibank, 3rd Viscount (A. C. Murray) (National Library of Scotland, Edinburgh)

Ellis, Thomas Edward (National Library of Wales, Aberystwyth)

Emmott, Alfred (Nuffield College, Oxford)

Exchange Bank of Liverpool records (Barclays Bank Archives, London)

Fitzmaurice, Lord Edmond (Bowood Estates, Calne, Worcestershire)

Garvin, J. L. (Humanities Research Center, University of Texas, Austin)

Gaster, Moses (University College, London)

Geddes, Arthur (National Library of Scotland, Edinburgh)

Gladstone, Herbert (British Library, London)

Gladstone, W. E. (British Library, London)

Gooch, G. P. (Papers owned by Mr Bernard Gooch)

Granet, Sir Guy (Modern Records Centre, Warwick University)

Granville-Barker, H. (Humanities Research Center, University of Texas, Austin)

Grey, Sir Edward (Public Record Office, Kew)

Haggard, Sir Henry Rider (Huntington Library, San Marino, California)

Haldane, R. B. (National Library of Scotland, Edinburgh)

Halifax, 1st Earl of (Edward Wood, Baron Irwin) (India Office Library and Records, London)

Hammond, J. L. (Bodleian Library, Oxford)

Hardinge of Penshurst, 1st Baron (Cambridge University Library)

Hewins, W. A. S. (Sheffield University Library)

Hoare, Sir Samuel (Cambridge University Library)

Holt, Sir Richard Durning (Liverpool Record Office)

Isaacs, Rufus (1st Marquis of Reading) (India Office Library and Records, London)

Jones, Thomas (National Library of Wales, Aberystwyth)

Keith, A. Berriedale (Edinburgh University Library)

Kerr, Philip (11th Marquis of Lothian) (Scottish Record Office, Edinburgh)

Laver, James (Glasgow University Library)
Law, A. Bonar (House of Lords Record Office, London)
Lloyd George, David (House of Lords Record Office, London; additional papers in
    National Library of Wales, Aberystwyth)
Long, Walter (Wiltshire County Record Office)
MacDonald, James Ramsay (Public Record Office, London)
Mackenzie, Sir Compton (Humanities Research Center, University of Texas, Austin)
Mallet, Sir Louis (papers in the possession of Mr Philip Mallet)
Manchester Guardian archives (John Rylands University Library, Manchester)
Marsh, Edward (New York Public Library)
Masterman, Lucy (Birmingham University Library)
Milner, 1st Viscount (Bodleian Library, Oxford)
Monckton, R. F. P. (Middle East Centre, St Antony's College, Oxford)
Montagu, Edwin (Trinity College, Cambridge)
Montagu, Samuel (newspaper cutting books in Anglo-Jewish Archives, University
    College, London)
Morel, E. D. (British Library of Political and Economic Science, London)
Morris-Jones, Sir John Henry (Clwyd County Record Office)
Murray, Gilbert (Bodleian Library, Oxford)
Pease, J. A. (1st Baron Gainford) (Nuffield College, Oxford)
Pethick-Lawrence, F. W. (Trinity College, Cambridge)
Priestley, J. B. (Humanities Research Center, University of Texas, Austin)
Primrose, Sir Henry (Duke University Library, Durham, North Carolina)
Rathbone, Eleanor (Liverpool University Library)
Redmond, John (National Library of Ireland, Dublin)
Riddell, 1st Baron (British Library, London)
Ripon, 1st Marquis of (Duke University Library, Durham, North Carolina)
Rosebery, 5th Earl of (National Library of Scotland, Edinburgh)
Roth, Cecil (Anglo-Jewish Archives, University College, London)
Runciman, Walter (1st Viscount Runciman) (Newcastle University Library)
Russell, Bertrand (McMaster University, Hamilton, Ontario)
Rutherford, Sir Ernest (Cambridge University Library)
Sankey, 1st Viscount (Bodleian Library, Oxford)
Scott, Alexander McCallum (Glasgow University Library)
Scott, C. P. (British Library)
Scott, John McCallum (University of Buckingham Library).
Seely, J. E. B. (1st Baron Mottistone) (Nuffield College, Oxford)
Shaw, George Bernard (British Library, London; also some correspondence at
    Humanities Research Center, University of Texas, Austin)
Sidey, Sir Thomas (Dunedin Public Library)
Simon, Sir Ernest (Manchester Central Library)
Simon, Sir John (Bodleian Library, Oxford; other papers in Public Record Office,
    Kew; one letter to Herbert Samuel in Houghton Library, Harvard University,
    Cambridge, Massachusetts)
Sinclair, Sir Archibald (Churchill College, Cambridge)
Smuts, Jan (Transvaal Archives Depot, Pretoria)

Storrs, Sir Ronald (Pembroke College, Cambridge)
Stuart, Alberta D. (typescript monograph on the Cleveland iron industry in Middlesbrough Public Library)
Tillett, Ben (one letter from Herbert Samuel in Modern Records Centre, Warwick University)
Trevelyan, Sir Charles (Newcastle University Library)
Wallas, Graham (British Library of Political and Economic Science, London)
Webb, Beatrice (British Library of Political and Economic Science, London)
Webb, Sidney (British Library of Political and Economic Science, London)
Weizmann, Chaim (Weizmann Archives, Rehovot)
Whitehead, Sir Rowland (House of Lords Record Office, London)
Wise, Stephen (American Jewish Historical Society, Waltham, Massachusetts)
Wolf, Lucien (YIVO Institute, New York)
Woolton, 1st Earl of (Bodleian Library, Oxford)
Young, Sir Edward Hilton (Cambridge University Library)

3. Official records

Post Office Archives (London)
Principal Probate Registry (London)
Public Record Office (Kew)
    Cabinet papers (CAB)
    Colonial Office papers (CO)
    Foreign Office papers (FO)
    Home Office papers (HO)
    Local Government Board Papers (HLG, MH, HO)
    Ministry of Labour papers (LAB)
    War Office papers (WO)
Royal Archives (Windsor)
    George V papers
    House of Commons reports

4. Other unpublished materials

Bahá'í archives (Haifa)
Balliol College archives (Oxford)
BBC Sound Archives (London)
BBC Written Archives (Caversham)
Board of Deputies of British Jews archive (London)
Fabian Society records (Nuffield College, Oxford)
Fabian Tracts: unpublished list of authors (prepared by Edward Pease) (in the possession of Professor Chimen Abramsky)
International PEN Club papers (Humanities Research Center, University of Texas, Austin)
Labour Party Archives (London)
Liverpool Jewish records (Liverpool Record Office)
Rainbow Circle records (British Library of Political and Economic Science, London)

Royal Institute of International Affairs (Chatham House, London) Transcripts of
    meetings
Samuel Montagu & Co. archives (London)
Zionist Organization (Central Zionist Archives, Jerusalem)

5. Unpublished theses

Baines, Malcolm Ian, 'The Samuelites and the National Government: A Study in
    Liberal Survival, August 1931–November 1933', MA thesis (Lancaster, 1986).
Ellins, R. E., 'Aspects of the New Liberalism 1895–1914', Ph.D. thesis (Sheffield,
    1980).
Hart, M. W., 'The Decline of the Liberal Party in Parliament and in the Constituencies
    1914–1931', D.Phil. thesis (Oxford, 1982).
Lunn, Kenneth, 'The Marconi Scandal and Related Aspects of British Anti-Semitism
    1911–1914', Ph.D. thesis (Sheffield, 1978).

6. Interviews

The late Professor Alexander Altmann; the late Professor Norman Bentwich; Lady
(Vera Brunel) Cohen; Rt. Hon. Michael Foot MP; Mr William Frankel; Mr Walter
D'Arcy Hart; Professor George Mosse; the late Mr Max Nurock; Rabbi Chaim Pearl;
the Hon. Nancy Salaman; Dr William Salaman; the Hon. Dan Samuel; 3rd Viscount
Samuel; Mr Donald Samuel; the late Hon. Godfrey Samuel; the Hon. Philip Samuel;
Mrs Helen Schwab; Mrs Gillian Sinclair-Hogg.

7. Books by Herbert Samuel

*Liberalism: An Attempt to State the Principles and Proposals of Contemporary
    Liberalism in England* (London, 1902).
The War and Liberty (London, 1917).
Practical Ethics (London, 1935).
Belief and Action: An Everyday Philosophy (London, 1937).
An Unknown Land (London, 1942).
Memoirs (London, 1945).
Viscount Samuel's Book of Quotations (London, 1947).
Creative Man and other Addresses (London, 1949).
Essay in Physics (Oxford, 1951).
In Search of Reality (Oxford, 1957).
(with Herbert Dingle) *A Threefold Cord* (London, 1961).

Index